Basic Keyboard Shortcuts for Editing Documents

 S0-DQV-930

PRESS THIS	TO DO THIS
Ctrl+E	Toggle between Edit mode and Read-only mode
Ctrl+Z	Undo last action (Edit ➤ Undo)
Esc or Ctrl+W	Close the current document
Ctrl+S	Save without closing

Moving the Insertion Point

PRESS THIS	TO DO THIS
Enter	Begin a new paragraph
Ctrl+Home	Go to first editable field
Ctrl+End	Go to last editable field
Tab (Rich Text)	Go to next tab *stop*
Tab/Shift-Tab	Go to next/previous field (plain text)
Ctrl+→	Go to beginning of next word to right
Ctrl+←	Go to beginning of next word to left

Selecting Data

PRESS THIS	TO DO THIS
Shift+→	Extend selection one character to right
Shift+←	Extend selection one character to left
Ctrl+Shift+→	Extend selection by one word to right
Ctrl+Shift+←	Extend selection by one word to left
Shift+End	Extend selection to end of the line
Shift+Home	Extend selection to beginning of line

FOR EVERY COMPUTER QUESTION, THERE IS A SYBEX BOOK THAT HAS THE ANSWER

Each computer user learns in a different way. Some need thorough, methodical explanations, while others are too busy for details. At Sybex we bring nearly 20 years of experience to developing the book that's right for you. Whatever your needs, we can help you get the most from your software and hardware, at a pace that's comfortable for you.

We start beginners out right. You will learn by seeing and doing with our **Quick & Easy** series: friendly, colorful guidebooks with screen-by-screen illustrations. For hardware novices, the **Your First** series offers valuable purchasing advice and installation support.

Often recognized for excellence in national book reviews, our **Mastering** titles are designed for the intermediate to advanced user, without leaving the beginner behind. A **Mastering** book provides the most detailed reference available. Add our pocket-sized **Instant Reference** titles for a complete guidance system. Programmers will find that the new **Developer's Handbook** series provides a more advanced perspective on developing innovative and original code.

With the breathtaking advances common in computing today comes an ever increasing demand to remain technologically up-to-date. In many of our books, we provide the added value of software, on disks or CDs. Sybex remains your source for information on software development, operating systems, networking, and every kind of desktop application. We even have books for kids. Sybex can help smooth your travels on the **Internet** and provide **Strategies and Secrets** to your favorite computer games.

As you read this book, take note of its quality. Sybex publishes books written by experts—authors chosen for their extensive topical knowledge. In fact, many are professionals working in the computer software field. In addition, each manuscript is thoroughly reviewed by our technical, editorial, and production personnel for accuracy and ease-of-use before you ever see it—our guarantee that you'll buy a quality Sybex book every time.

To manage your hardware headaches and optimize your software potential, ask for a Sybex book.

FOR MORE INFORMATION, PLEASE CONTACT:

Sybex Inc.
2021 Challenger Drive
Alameda, CA 94501
Tel: (510) 523-8233 • (800) 227-2346
Fax: (510) 523-2373

Let us hear from you.

 Talk to SYBEX authors, editors and fellow forum members.

 Get tips, hints and advice online.

 Download magazine articles, book art, and shareware.

Join the SYBEX Forum on 🖳 **CompuServe**®

If you're already a CompuServe user, just type `GO SYBEX` to join the SYBEX Forum. If not, try CompuServe for free by calling 1-800-848-8199 and ask for Representative 560. You'll get one free month of basic service and a $15 credit for CompuServe extended services—a $23.95 value. Your personal ID number and password will be activated when you sign up.

Join us online today. Type `GO SYBEX` on CompuServe.

If you're not a CompuServe member, call Representative 560 at `1-800-848-8199`.

SYBEX

(outside U.S./Canada call 614-457-0802)

Mastering Lotus®
Notes®

Kevin Brown

Kenyon Brown

Kyle Brown

San Francisco ▲ Paris ▼ Düsseldorf ▲ Soest

SYBEX®

ACQUISITIONS EDITOR: Dianne King

PRODUCT MANAGER: Richard Mills

DEVELOPMENTAL EDITOR: David Peal

EDITOR: Brendan Fletcher

PROJECT EDITOR: Michelle Khazai

TECHNICAL EDITOR: Francois Koutchouk

BOOK DESIGNER: Helen Bruno

TECHNICAL ART: Cuong Le

DESKTOP PUBLISHER: Dina F Quan

PRODUCTION COORDINATOR: Janet K. Boone

INDEXER: Nancy Guenther

COVER DESIGNER: Joanna Kim Gladden

Library of Congress Card Number: 94-68439

ISBN: 0-7821-1302-8

Manufactured in the United States of America

10 9 8 7 6 5 4

▶ *Warranty*

SYBEX warrants the enclosed disk to be free of physical defects for a period of ninety (90) days after purchase. If you discover a defect in the disk during this warranty period, you can obtain a replacement disk at no charge by sending the defective disk, postage prepaid, with proof of purchase to:

> SYBEX Inc.
> Customer Service Department
> 2021 Challenger Drive
> Alameda, CA 94501
> (800)227-2346
> Fax: (510) 523-2373

After the 90-day period, you can obtain a replacement disk by sending us the defective disk, proof of purchase, and a check or money order for $10, payable to SYBEX.

▶ *Disclaimer*

SYBEX makes no warranty or representation, either express or implied, with respect to this software, its quality, performance, merchantability, or fitness for a particular purpose. In no event will SYBEX, its distributors, or dealers be liable for direct, indirect, special, incidental, or consequential damages arising out of the use of or inability to use the software even if advised of the possibility of such damage.

The exclusion of implied warranties is not permitted by some states. Therefore, the above exclusion may not apply to you. This warranty provides you with specific legal rights; there may be other rights that you may have that vary from state to state.

▶ *Copy Protection*

None of the programs on the disk is copy-protected. However, in all cases, reselling or making copies of these programs without authorization is expressly forbidden.

To our parents, Wayne and Virginia

▶▶ *Acknowledgments*

We would like to thank the following people for the time and effort they put into making this book.

David Peal, former Developmental Editor and Product Manager at Sybex, for going the distance with us as this book evolved from an idea that we discussed over dinner during COMDEX '92 in Las Vegas to its publication.

Brendan Fletcher, Editor, for bringing his outstanding editorial skills, insight, and sense of humor to the book. Francois Koutchouk, Technical Editor, for bringing his thorough technical knowledge, expertise, and understanding of Notes to the book.

Michelle Khazai, Project Editor, for organizing our irregular manuscript submissions while trying to keep the book on schedule as it made its crazy trek through editing and production.

Kristine Plachy, Acquisitions Manager, for keeping us informed of new versions of Notes and third-party product releases during the writing of this book. Richard Mills, Developmental Editor and Product Manager, for coming to our rescue during the final stages of writing the book.

Finally, many thanks to the production team at Sybex, especially Desktop Publisher Dina Quan and Production Coordinator Janet Boone, for their hard work and perseverance.

Contents at a Glance

Table of Contents

▶▶ *Foreword*

What is Lotus Notes? That's the question that everyone has been asking since the product was first introduced five years ago.

Like so many ground-breaking products before it, it took some time for the market to grasp fully the potential of Lotus Notes. With more than 900,000 users and 5000 business partners developing Notes-based solutions, it appears that time is now. Today, Lotus Notes is the industry-standard client/server platform for developing and deploying groupware applications. Lotus Notes has become a proven solution for organizations that need to develop high-value business process applications, such as those used for customer service, sales/account management, or product development.

Clearly the groupware market—fueled by Lotus Notes—is taking off. The business opportunity facing companies that can implement groupware successfully is seemingly boundless. How do you get there? The best advice I can give you is to find a guide who can show you the way, and *Mastering Lotus Notes* may be just the guide you need.

Mastering Lotus Notes provides a comprehensive look at Lotus Notes and how it should be used. The book is helpful to both end-users who need a basic understanding of Notes and those who will be responsible for creating the applications. For managers still trying to decide whether Notes or even groupware is right for them, this book provides excellent insights into how to implement Notes applications and the benefits one can expect.

Mastering Lotus Notes presents this revolutionary product in an easy-to-learn step-by-step manner, moving logically from explaining exactly what Notes is, to using it, to creating applications. The text is replete with examples, including a walk-through of the Notes application templates provided on disk with the book. These templates, which show how actual businesses have used Notes to improve productivity and maximize the efficiency of their employees, can be customized and used in your business. A real bonus!

More than ever, organizations are looking to maximize productivity and reap the greatest return possible on their technology investments. Groupware, and specifically Lotus Notes, is becoming the means to achieving these goals. By clearly explaining what Lotus Notes is and how to use it, this book can help you and your organization achieve these goals as well.

John Landry
Executive Vice President and Chief Technology Officer
Lotus Development Corporation

▶▶ *Introduction*

Mastering Lotus Notes is a comprehensive tutorial and reference guide that both users and application developers will find invaluable. The book covers Lotus Notes releases 3.0, 3.1, and 3.1.5, and the new releases 3.2 (for the server) and Notes Express. No matter what version of Notes you're running, this book can help you use Notes to do your work and communicate with people in your company. The book also helps users become effective database designers as they take on the job of developing applications.

Notes is a flexible workflow automation tool that can help any organization, large or small, take control of virtually any kind of information. For example, Notes can help your organization:

- Service customers and requests
- Organize financial information
- Manage sales accounts
- Track product development

▶▶ *What Is Workflow Automation?*

Everybody has, at some time or another, probably been a participant in the ever-popular game of "paper chase"—filling out forms, sending documents (and then trying to find if they got to where they're supposed to), receiving and forwarding documents, filing documents (and then throwing them away when it comes time to clean up your files).

Notes endeavors, first and foremost, to *literally* replace paper documents with electronic documents; Notes is not a word processor with which you'll wind up producing paper anyway. To fully replace a paper document with an electronic version requires not only the means to create the document but to *move* the document, electronically, through a business environment in the same way a paper document would. This is what Notes workflow automation is all about. By recreating and improving on the circuit a document travels, workflow automation brings all of us closer to a paperless environment.

▶▶ *What Is Notes?*

Lotus Development Corporation, the makers of Notes, refers to Notes as a *document database*, but don't let this terminology lead you to think that Notes is just a version of a traditional database. It's more useful to think of Notes as a way of organizing documents and making them accessible to groups of people than as a kind of database in the traditional sense of the word.

Unlike a traditional database, which requires that you break information into discrete *data* fragments (such as a middle initial or social security number), a *document* is the fundamental unit of information in Lotus Notes. As you know if you've worked with databases, a document has meaning; a piece of data doesn't, at least outside of the context of the rest of the database.

A document can be as long, as complex, and as unstructured as any paper document you already use. A Notes document is something like a paper document, except, of course, that you view it on screen. Like a word-processed document, a Notes document can contain complex formatting, even images. In fact, anything that can be digitized (a fax, an image, a newsfeed, you name it) can be stored in Notes as a document. Unlike a word-processing document, a Notes document can be read, revised, and responded to by many people. It won't be tossed away accidentally or lost in a file cabinet.

▶▶ *The Benefits of Notes*

Notes' unique database structure lets you keep track of complex, relatively unstructured information, and to make that information available to groups of users on a network. As a result of this structure, Notes offers you these benefits: It keeps your information current, it keeps your information secure, and its applications accommodate the complex flows of information and divisions of responsibility within your group or even your entire organization.

But the most important benefit that Notes promotes is the efficient flow of information in a group. Notes pioneered a new type of application called *groupware*—software that enables a group of people in an organization to use the same information but in different ways, depending on specific needs.

▶▶ *What Is New in Lotus Notes Release 3.2?*

Lotus Notes 3.2 is an upgrade to the Notes server software, and is required to run Notes Express. This server version features administrative tools for designating Notes and Notes Express users from the same directory. Administrators load the 3.2 upgrade on only one server, so they don't have to upgrade all Notes servers. In an organization that might be running several servers, upgrading is quicker and easier.

Notes 3.2 also incorporates a number of bug fixes for problems encountered in previous versions. For example, in the NLM (NetWare Loadable Module) version, modems do not initialize or reinitialize properly, causing sudden disconnections. Release 3.2 remedies this problem.

Although release 3.2 is used mainly in conjunction with running the new Notes Express version, previous versions of Notes can also run on release 3.2. However, upgrading to release 3.2 isn't required if an organization is running versions 3.0 and 3.1.5 client versions of Notes.

▶▶ *What Is New in Lotus Notes Express?*

Lotus Notes Express is a new slimmed down, or "light," version of Notes 3.1.5. Lotus Notes release 3.2, the new server version, is required to run Notes Express. Notes Express is much lower in price than the full-featured client versions, and it doesn't offer as many features.

Although this version doesn't include database design capabilities included in the full-featured version, such as the ability to create forms and views, it lets users share, view, read, and compose Notes documents. However, this version doesn't allow users to access databases created in the full-featured version. Users can only access the basic applications that come with this version.

Notes Express contains five basic design templates, including discussion, news, and reference databases, Notes Mail, and Phone Book. Users can use the templates for their own needs, in particular the Notes Mail forms to compose mail messages. Notes Express can also run Lotus' cc:Mail, its e-mail software. For companies that eventually want to migrate from Notes Express to the full Notes client, this version includes an upgrade option.

▶▶ *How This Book Is Organized*

This book is organized in three parts, which makes it easy for you to find the information you need quickly.

▶ *Part One: Getting Started with Lotus Notes*

This part includes Chapters 1–10. These chapters guide the user through using (and getting the most out of) all the features found in Notes databases, including Notes Mail and using the Notes dial-up feature. The chapters are:

Chapter 1: Using Notes This chapter shows you the basic architecture of Notes, so you can begin to envision how you can use Notes in your own organization. We explain what Notes is and isn't, and we describe in general terms the benefits of using Notes. We also profile several companies that have adopted Notes, illustrating what workflow is, working in a group, the client-server relationship, and developing Notes applications.

Chapter 2: Understanding Notes Basics This chapter builds on the description of what Notes is in Chapter 1 on a practical level. We discuss viewing documents, designing forms, composing documents, and replicating databases.

Chapter 3: Working in the Notes Environment You'll learn the basics you need to find your way around in Notes. Specifically, you'll learn how to start Notes, organize the Notes workspace, use the Status Bar, work with Notes windows, and use, customize, and create new SmartIcons.

Chapter 4: Accessing Notes Databases This chapter explains the basics of using a Notes database. All databases, regardless of their uniqueness, have several features in common. The chapter identifies these features, and discusses access privileges, using the sample databases and templates, Workspace pages, opening a database, and database icons.

Chapter 5: Viewing the Contents of a Database This chapter discusses what a view is, using a view, displaying a view, what the elements of a view are, and selecting documents in a view.

Chapter 6: Creating a Document This chapter shows you how to create a document that's based on a form. We discuss composing a new document, editing a document, formatting a document, and using Notes default text attributes.

Chapter 7: Printing Views and Documents You'll learn all the ins and outs of printing with Notes, including selecting what you want to print, printing documents, printing views, choosing settings for your printer, and choosing page setup options.

Chapter 8: Importing and Exporting Data This chapter shows you how to import and export information, and discusses importing different file formats into documents and views, exporting documents and views to different file formats, and using Rich Text Format.

Chapter 9: Communicating with Notes Mail This chapter explains everything you need to know to use Notes Mail. You'll learn how to create mail messages, send mail, create address books for frequent correspondents, and reply to and forward mail.

Chapter 10: Dial-Up Notes You'll learn how to set up a remote Notes connection so you can get all the benefits of working off-site. Specifically, you'll learn how to set up your modem for Notes, use Notes scripts, call your server, and use database replicas.

▶ *Part Two: Building a Notes Application*

This part includes Chapters 11–22. These chapters guide the developer through the steps of designing a database, including forms and views, and writing formulas and macros.

Chapter 11: Learning the Notes Building Blocks This chapter familiarizes you with the building blocks of a Notes database. We discuss types of forms you can create, types of fields you can use, static text, and buttons and popup annotations.

Chapter 12: Basing a Database on a Design Template This chapter suggests a process you might follow as you analyze a database's requirements and the needs of the people who will use the database.

Chapter 13: Using Notes Templates and Databases This chapter describes the application templates and example databases that are included with Notes. You can look over the ones that interest you and make your own decisions on whether they're appropriate for your needs.

Chapter 14: Designing a Form This chapter takes you through the steps of designing the forms for the Corporate Directory database. The chapter covers form design considerations, a form's basic components, defining a form's attributes, identifying the form's type, adding fields, designating field types, and formatting a form.

Chapter 15: Creating a View This chapter takes you through the steps of creating a view. We discuss defining view attributes, using column formulas, organizing a view by categories, and writing a selection formula.

Chapter 16: Writing Formulas and Macros This chapter shows you how to use formulas in a database, and discusses defining formulas for different field types, using @functions, using variables, constants, and operators, and creating macros.

Chapter 17: Applying Workflow to a Database You'll learn about applying workflow to a Notes application. We show you how to incorporate workflow automation features into the structure of the Corporate Directory database, modifying its access control, and changing the design of the Change Request form. We discuss establishing a mail-in database document, changing a form's access control, adding routing buttons to the Change Request form, and creating macros in the Corporate Directory database.

Chapter 18: Building Security into Notes Databases This chapter shows you how you can build security into your Notes databases. We discuss changing your User ID, setting a password, logging off, and using encryption keys.

Chapter 19: Replicating Databases This chapter discusses replication by explaining how to create a new database replica, update a replica, perform selective replications, track replication events, and handle replication conflicts.

Chapter 20: Indexing a Notes Database This chapter explains the differences between using the two methods Notes provides for finding text in databases: *plain text search* and *full text search*. We discuss creating a full text index, reindexing, using the Search Bar, and using Find and Replace.

Chapter 21: Linking and Embedding Objects in Notes This chapter discusses several topics related to linking and embedding objects, including the differences between linking and embedding, inserting objects in documents, and editing embedded or linked objects.

Chapter 22: Managing Databases This chapter discusses the tasks involved in managing a database and explains getting information about databases and documents, displaying user activity, summarizing the field contents of a database, and compacting a database.

▶ *Part Three: Real-World Notes Applications*

This part includes Chapters 23–26. These chapters show you how four databases have been created by providing step-by-step walk-throughs. These same databases are included on the Companion Disk that accompanies the book. The templates are provided for you to customize to suit your own needs.

Chapter 23: Group Scheduling This chapter shows you how to create a unique 1994 calendar and appointment schedule application, which you can easily modify to suit your own needs. You can use this calendar to keep the daily schedule of any person, place, or thing. A manager can keep his or her schedule in the calendar. Then other users with Reader access can check the schedule at any time, while those with Editor access (such as an assistant) can make changes. You can do the same for scheduling the use of conference rooms, equipment, etc.

Chapter 24: Investment Profiles This chapter shows you how to create an Investment Profiles database that's based on a financial research database we located on CompuServe. We modified it extensively in order to help people in a workgroup to gather background information on companies to use as a basis for making investment decisions. This chapter takes you through the steps of designing the forms and views for the Investment Profiles database. We cover defining each form's attributes, adding fields, formatting the forms, creating the views, and writing the selection formulas.

Chapter 25: Training Facilities This chapter shows you how to create a Training Facilities database that's based on an evaluation tracking database that we located on CompuServe. We modified the application to make it useful for evaluating multiple work sites.

Chapter 26: Consultant Assignments This chapter shows you how to create a Consultant Assignments database, which is a *server-based* personnel directory application that we located on CompuServe. We've modified it extensively to help an organization to track independent contractors (known as "consultants") and retain them to provide certain services, such as designing training seminars, writing technical documentation, conducting usability testing, and so on at various sites around the country.

Appendix The appendix describes important third-party products and services that you might find beneficial.

Glossary The glossary defines all the important Notes terms that you'll need to understand and use frequently as a database designer.

▶▶ *What's Next?*

As Notes continues to evolve as *the* workflow automation platform in the world of client-server systems, we can probably expect significant developments. Recent magazine articles have speculated on what you can expect to find in Lotus Notes 4.0, which is tentatively scheduled for release in the middle of 1995. One of the more interesting new features might be the inclusion of Lotus' cc:Mail as the Notes e-mail system. Using Notes as a communication tool is obviously an integral part of distributing and tracking information in a company. As Notes provides new features and enhancements, all of us will benefit from Lotus' efforts to help us work together more efficiently.

Getting Started with
Lotus Notes

PART ONE

▶ ▶ **P**art One gets you up and running with Notes by guiding you through all of its features. Chapter 1, "Using Notes," introduces you to Notes and describes its benefits. This chapter tells you what workflow is, illustrates how Notes can help your group work better, and explains client-server applications. Chapter 2, "Understanding Notes Basics," discusses viewing documents, designing forms, composing documents, and replicating databases. Chapter 3, "Working in the Notes Environment," teaches you how to find your way around in Notes. You learn how to start Notes, organize the Notes Workspace, use the Status Bar, and work with SmartIcons.

Chapter 4, "Accessing Notes Databases," explains the basics of using a Notes database. All databases, regardless of their uniqueness, have several features in common. Chapter 5, "Viewing the Contents of a Database," discusses what a view is, using a view, and selecting documents in a view. Without a view, you wouldn't be able to access the information in the database. Chapter 6, "Creating a Document," shows you how to compose a document that's based on a form.

Chapter 7, "Printing Views and Documents," explains all the ins and outs of printing with Notes, including selecting what you want to print, and printing documents, printing views, choosing settings for your printer, and choosing page setup options. Chapter 8, "Importing and Exporting Data," discusses importing different file formats into Notes documents and views, and exporting Notes data to other Windows applications.

Chapter 9, "Communicating with Notes Mail," teaches you how to use Notes Mail. Finally, Chapter 10, "Dial-Up Notes," shows you how to set up a remote Notes connection using a modem, so you can get all the benefits of working off-site.

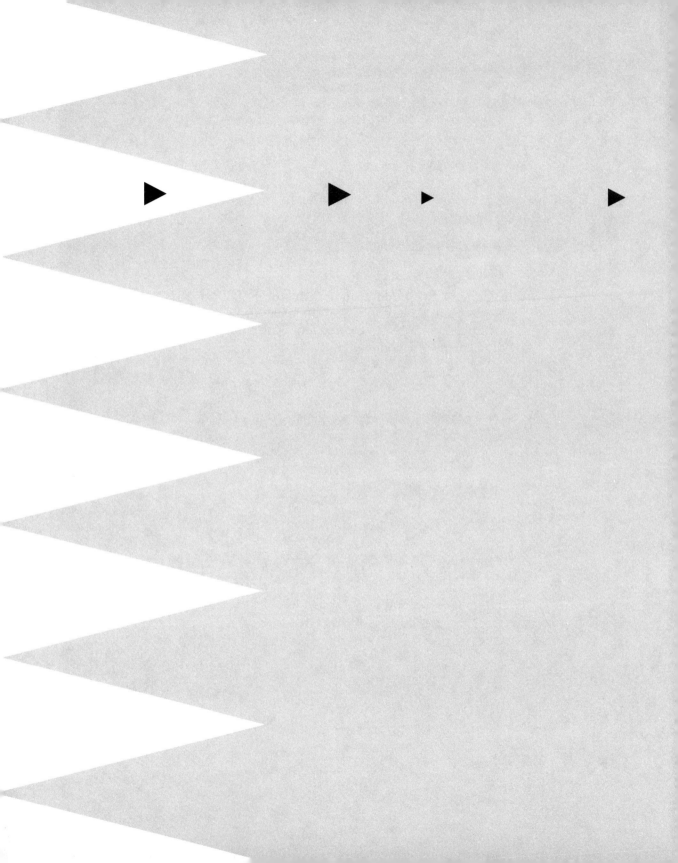

Using Notes

▶▶ *F*AST *T*RACK

▶ **Lotus Notes is**

a *document* database program. Notes organizes informations in documents that look like paper documents, not in records as in a traditional database. Notes was designed specifically to be used by groups of coworkers who share information on a regular basis over a network. You use Notes as part of a team, department, or organization; you don't use it as you would stand-alone software, such as a word processor or spreadsheet.

▶ **A document is**

the fundamental unit of information in Notes. A document can be as long, complex, and unstructured as any paper document you use. Like a word-processed document, a Notes document can contain complex formatting, different fonts, tables, or even images. In fact, anything that can be digitized can be stored in Notes as a document.

▶ **Groupware is**   **13**

> a new category of applications. As the name implies, groupware allows a group of people to work on the same information simultaneously, and use it in different ways to fit their own specific needs.

▶ **Workflow is**   **15**

> the way Notes fosters communication and the "flow" of information from one group to another, thus encouraging people to work together more effectively. Notes can structure information in a variety of ways that enhance group productivity, from managing group transactions to tracking the flow of group discussions. By using Notes to organize, access, and share information, an organization can ensure that information flows to and from each individual in the most efficient way.

▶▶ **L**otus Notes is a flexible tool that can help any organization, large or small, take control of virtually any kind of information. Notes can help your organization track product development, organize financial information, or manage sales accounts. You can use Notes to service customers and requests, manage personnel information and employee profiles, and organize schedules and group calendars. The possibilities are virtually limitless.

In this chapter, we'll show you the basic architecture of Notes, so you can begin to envision how you can use Notes in your own organization. We'll explain what Notes is and isn't, and we'll describe in general terms the benefits of using Notes. In order to more vividly illustrate the how Notes can help your organization manage and exchange information and share it, we'll profile several companies that have adopted Notes. Finally, we'll cover these topics:

- What is workflow?
- Working in a group
- The client-server relationship
- Developing Notes applications

▶▶ *What Is Lotus Notes?*

Lotus Notes is a distributed client-server database application that enables groups of people to organize, track, access, and share information over a network. You might say to yourself, "Big deal. A lot of database applications allow me to do the same thing. Why should I use Notes?" First of all, Notes' architecture—the way data is structured, managed, and disseminated—differs from other distributed database applications in the way it links people together.

The typical client-server application provides ways for people who are connected by a network to access the same data that's stored on a central server. However, in most cases these people can only access the data in a one-size-fits-all way; information is structured in the same way for each individual user, regardless of her or his needs. By contrast, Notes creates a working environment in which people can access the same database at the same time and then use the information to suit their individual needs. It offers more flexibility than the typical database.

Notes also allows you to share information with coworkers by communicating with them through its e-mail system. Like any e-mail system, Notes lets you send mail messages, as well as file attachments, to other people over a network. However, the information you can send to people through Notes mail is different from the information contained in a standard mail memo.

For example, this information can be taken directly from a database that can be accessed by different people at the same time. Because different people can use and exchange the information contained in a Notes database simultaneously, they can manage, update, and communicate information more effectively and efficiently. When properly implemented, Notes can help any organization increase productivity.

As you can already see, Notes is a multifaceted product. Accordingly, the next few sections discuss Notes from several perspectives: Notes as groupware, Notes as e-mail, and Notes as a document database. However, because the client-server relationship stands at the center of all aspects of Notes, first we'll turn to it.

▶ *The Client-Server Relationship*

If you work as part of a group in an organization (and most of us do), you are probably already sharing access to documents and files with your colleagues over a network. A network helps users share access to software and files that are used throughout an organization. It usually stores master copies of these in a central location, manages each user's access, and keeps track of modifications to shared files. It can also store printer drivers and other shared resources. This central repository of files on a network is known as a *network file server*, or just as a *server*. The server runs the network's operating system that manages all network activity.

The network file server differs from the *Notes server*. An organization's Notes server is connected to its network file server. The Notes server is the main storage area for Notes databases that are shared within an organization. It provides communication services to workstations and other Notes servers. It runs the programs that are used to maintain databases on all the Notes workstations connected to it. A workstation is also known called a *client* because it runs the Notes client software.

For most Notes users, a server appears as another disk drive that each person selects from his or her own workstation. For example, in Windows, the File Manager might display a server as the X or Y drive. Your organization may even maintain multiple servers for different purposes. You would simply click on the appropriate drive icon to access the desired server when you want a particular directory or file.

Notes databases are stored on either an OS/2 or a Windows server or the new Notes 3.1 for Novell NetWare server. They essentially work the same way. The server is physically located near the group of its users and is connected to them by a network. Each user works on a *client* version of Notes, which turns an individual's computer into a workstation. If a Notes server can be considered the central repository of information, the client can be considered the gateway to it.

▶ Notes as Groupware

Notes falls into a new category of applications known as *groupware*. While word processing, spreadsheet, and similar computer application programs are designed for a single user, Notes was created specifically for groups of people who want to organize and share information in a document database.

Groupware enables a group of people in an organization to use the same information in different ways that fit their own specific needs. It can enhance decision-making, and it can encourage the spread of ideas and critical thinking. Using information as a basis for discussion and decision-making lies at the heart of Notes. Figure 1.1 shows an example of the kind of information a Notes database can contain.

To get a more concrete handle on how Notes manages information, let's look at how an insurance company uses Notes to keep track of the thousands of homeowners' policies it underwrites. Its Notes database contains detailed information on individual policies, including a

FIGURE 1.1

A Notes database can contain a variety of information. This database contains the results of financial research on many companies. Each line displays a summary of an individual analyst's research on a particular company.

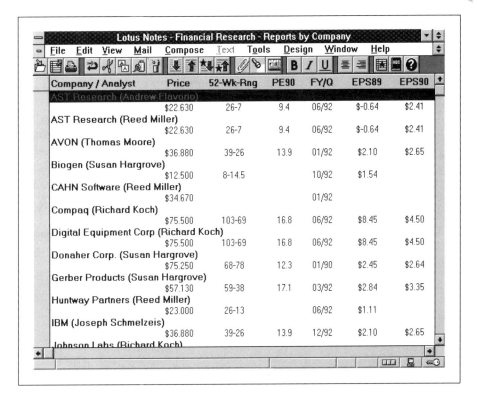

photograph and/or floorplan of the property, the location and age of the home, type of building, fire-protection class (distance from a water source), construction costs, and the number of units (for apartment buildings or condominiums).

Many additional factors are considered before a policy is written or a claim processed, so the database also contains the following information in separate documents:

- Policy quotes from account agents
- Premium evaluations from underwriters
- Construction reports from building inspectors
- Claims from policyholders

All this information is stored in the same Notes database in different formats and is used by many different people in the firm. Policyholder information is updated by account agents. Premiums are calculated by underwriters. Building construction reports are written by inspectors. Claims are tracked by adjusters.

What sets a Notes database apart from other client-server database applications is the complexity of the information it is designed to store and how it relates each piece of information to others: a inspector's building report or a homeowner's claim, for example, and everything from faxes to photos. Moreover, Notes allows an organization fine-grained control of access to this information. Each group in an insurance firm, for example, would view only the information it needed, and would add to or change only the information to which it had access privileges:

Information	Group responsible for maintaining information
Policyholder information	Account agents
Premiums	Underwriters
Building construction reports	Inspectors
Claims	Adjusters

While Notes enables individuals in the company access to just the information they need, it also allows them to share it as appropriate and discuss it among themselves. Through its built-in electronic mail (see Chapter 8), Lotus Notes facilitates communication between workers and between groups of workers. In sum, Notes provides all the tools you need to manage the information shared by groups in your organization.

▶ Notes as E-Mail

As we mentioned previously, Notes features its own sophisticated e-mail system, which is called Notes Mail. (We discuss Notes Mail in detail in Chapter 8.) It's similar to other e-mail systems because it allows you to perform routine tasks such as sending mail messages to named recipients, routing mail messages over the Internet and other gateways to their final recipients, viewing lists of incoming messages, and so on. However, Notes Mail is fundamentally different from other e-mail systems because it's integrated with Notes and becomes a part of much larger database management workgroup applications.

Traditional e-mail systems are designed to send information from one user to another. Lotus refers to the traditional e-mail system as a "send-model" system. This kind of system places most of its emphasis on moving messages quickly from user to user. It's up to the eventual user to manage the received messages.

Lotus calls a system like Notes Mail a "share-model" system because it collects information in a central location where users can access it. The system managing the shared information provides services for managing the collection, including archiving and group access. The electronic mail portion of Notes is implemented as an integrated messaging component for delivering documents. As in traditional e-mail systems, Notes databases are stored on servers that manage the information. Unlike traditional e-mail systems, however, those central servers focus more on document management, structure, and categorizing than on the absolutely fastest way to move messages.

▶ *Notes as a Document Database*

Lotus Development Corporation, the makers of Notes, refers to Notes as a document database, but don't let this terminology lead you to think that Notes is just a version of a traditional database. It's more useful to think of Notes as a way of organizing documents and making them accessible to groups than as a kind of database, in the traditional sense of the word (dBASE, Paradox, etc.). Unlike a traditional database, which requires that you break information into discrete *data* fragments (such as a middle initial or social security number), a *document* is the fundamental unit of information in Lotus Notes. As you know if you've worked with databases, a piece of data doesn't have much meaning outside of the context of the rest of the database; however, documents are meaningful standing alone.

A document can be as long, as complex, and as unstructured as any paper document you already use. A Notes document is something like a paper document, except, of course, that you view it on screen. Like a word-processed document, a Notes document can contain complex formatting, even images. In fact, anything that can be digitized (a fax, an image, a newsfeed, you name it) can be stored in Notes as a document. Figure 1.2 shows an example of a Notes document. Unlike a word-processing document, a Notes document can be read, revised, and responded to by many people. It won't be tossed away accidentally or lost in a file cabinet.

FIGURE 1.2 ►

This is an example of a document from a database that includes financial information on companies from 1989 to the present. It displays a year-end financial report on a well-known company.

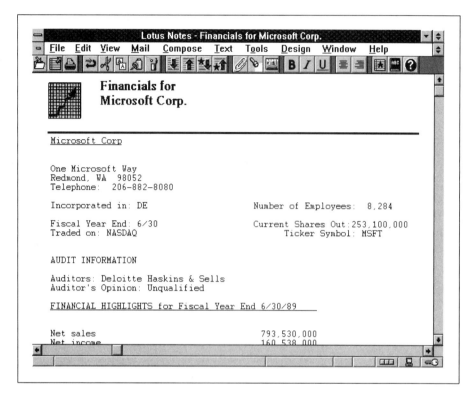

►► *The Benefits of Notes*

Notes' unique database structure lets you keep track of complex, relatively unstructured information, and to make that information available to groups of users on a network. As a result of this structure, Notes offers you these additional benefits:

- Notes keeps your information current.
- Notes keeps your information secure.
- Notes applications accommodate the complex flows of information and divisions of responsibility within your group or even your entire organization.

▶ *Notes Keeps Your Information Current*

A Notes document gives you a convenient way of reading and modifying information. Over time, many people will make changes to documents. At an insurance agency, for example, homeowner policies get added and canceled or premium rates may increase. Because they're centralized, easily accessed, and systematically revised through *replication*, Notes documents remain more current and accurate than a paper document. (You'll learn about replication in Chapter 18.) This is important because the information is shared by individuals and groups of people. Different people use a document database to make decisions. Inaccurate information could hurt an organization and result in bad decisions. Notes gives you and your workgroup the means to keep your organization's information up to date.

▶ *Notes Keeps Your Information Secure*

Notes requires that every user be assigned an *access level*. For example, an insurance adjuster would have access to claim records that an account agent would not; account agents would have access only to their clients' records. Because information is sensitive, Notes enables an organization to build security mechanisms into a database.

An organization needs to protect a database's *design* from unauthorized modification, in addition to protecting the data stored within. It needs to make sure that only certain people can see certain information. It may also want to control the operations that each user can perform within a particular database. For each database the Notes administrator assigns users access levels specifying who can design and manage the database, and who can read, modify, and add documents to it. You'll learn more about the different user access levels and the Access Control List (ACL) feature in Chapter 4.

▶ *Notes Helps Your Group Work Smarter*

The most important benefit is that Notes promotes the efficient flow of information in a group. As we mentioned above, Notes pioneered the concept of *groupware*—software that enables a group of people in an organization to use the same information but in different ways, depending on specific needs. Figure 1.3 shows an example of a database made up of information contributed by different people.

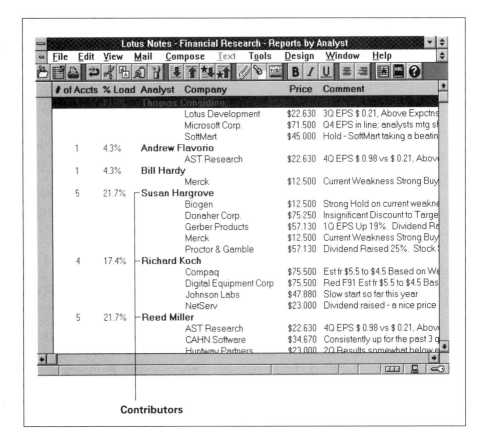

Contributors

A Group in Action

Of the hundreds of people employed by an insurance company, for example, four groups of people work closely together to process homeowner policies:

- Agents, who write the proposed policy for the homeowner
- Underwriters, who approve the policy and set the premium
- Inspectors, who evaluate building structure
- Adjusters, who investigate damage and estimate cost of claim settlement

These people probably don't work in the same location; in fact, most agents establish their own offices and work independently. That's the nature of the insurance business. However, a Notes database provides a central location where information on homeowners' policies is stored. Each one of these people can access and use the information to track policies accurately. By using Notes, they're able to evaluate the status of policies, revise them when necessary, change premium rates, and settle claims.

Account agents use Notes to write policy quotes for homeowners. The policy quote requires information from several other people. Let's say an agent has been approached by a homeowner in earthquake country.

An *underwriter* assigned to California, evaluating the proposed policy, uses Notes to write her evaluation report. Before she can give final approval, she needs to verify in the database that the house was inspected, to make sure it's properly bolted to the foundation and satisfies other building requirements. The underwriter won't give final approval until the inspector determines the house is structurally sound.

After the house is inspected and found to satisfy the insurance company's building requirements, the *inspector* uses Notes to write his building construction report for the underwriter's review. This information is added to the original policy quote, indicating the house passed the inspection. Subsequently, the underwriter approves the coverage and sets the premium rate in the policy quote.

Going with the (Work)Flow

Every organization establishes systems and procedures for people to follow in order to do their work. Each person has a specific job to do. The way you perform your duties can affect the way other people do their work, and the way you share information with other colleagues can help or hinder them.

Notes fosters communication and the flow of information among group members and between groups, thus encouraging people to work together more effectively. *Workflow* is the way a group of people works together to accomplish tasks and achieve their goals. By using Notes to organize, access, track, and share information, your group can devise a more effective workflow. For a good example of how Notes demonstrably improved the exchange of information in one organization, read the sidebar "Open Communication, Better Products: Canyon Corporation."

▶

OPEN COMMUNICATION, BETTER PRODUCTS: CANYON CORPORATION

Canyon Corporation of Arizona, a small company of 45 people, designs and markets HealthClub (™) software for the health and fitness club industry. The program tracks memberships and vital member information, schedules and maintains a calendar of events, manages point-of-sale transactions in equipment shops and restaurants, and interfaces with a word processor and desktop publisher. Canyon has installed and customized the program in almost 2500 health clubs and gyms around the country. However, with sales of more than $10 million, they were concerned that key business information such as customer feedback wasn't flowing through the small workforce as efficiently as it could. There was a lot of duplication of efforts, and good ideas were ignored.

In particular, the Sales Department didn't feel the Product Development group was responsive to feedback from clients. Part of the problem was that salespeople were passing along suggestions to programmers informally; that is, they'd talk to them if they happened to meet in hallways and during breaks. The Vice President of Sales would frequently discuss suggestions with the head of Product Development. But the really useful information that came directly from salespeople in the field—specific suggestions for improving the program's interface and adding new features— wasn't passed along to programmers. In fact, the head of Product Development didn't want salespeople to share the information with her staff because it "created confusion and uncertainty." Friction between Sales and Product Development grew, developing into an old-fashioned turf war.

A Notes application was the solution. By using Notes, each member of the Sales division could share collective knowledge about customers. Using a simple feedback form, each sales person would enter information—suggestions, criticisms, complaints—from clients. The information was shared with the Product Development group, who would analyze the information and evaluate the feasibility of making certain changes. Subsequently, the group began using a feasibility form to discuss among themselves the usefulness and applicability of specific suggestions.

One of the best suggestions resulted in the development of a new product called ClubKit (™), a much less expensive version of HealthClub (™). This version is better suited for smaller clubs and gyms that don't schedule events and classes, track extensive member information, or generate correspondence and produce newsletters. The new product has almost eliminated the expensive and time-consuming work of customizing the original product. Programmers can now direct their efforts to fine-tuning the company's products and developing new products.

The communication between Sales and Product Development has improved greatly through Notes. Discussions are less confrontational because product information is shared online over the company's network. By using two simple database documents, one for collecting customer feedback and the other for discussing the feasibility of the feedback, two groups are working together in a more productive way.

Larry Espinoza, the founder and President of the company, thinks Notes "is a great product. Ultimately we're seeing a savings in product development time, which means we're spending less money. If we can work customer feedback into an application, we're going to produce a better product. Word of mouth is important in the sports club business. Being able to maintain our reputation for providing excellent products makes us successful. If one club likes our product, that's our best advertisement. It helps making a sale at the next club that much easier. More sales is what it's all about."

▶▶ *Resistance to Lotus Notes*

Let's face it. No one really welcomes change when it means doing a job differently. You've probably had to adapt at one time or another to a change in management. Or you've experienced other changes such as the expansion of a division. A new sales commission rate structure. Reductions in departmental budgets. Reporting to a new supervisor. Changing over to a new computer system.

Setting up Notes in an organization means a major investment of time, money, network resources, and people. It can also mean a change in the way a group works: decentralized responsibility and greater accountability, at the very least. Not all users will be happy with these changes, as you can read in "The Benefits (and Threat) of Notes: Path Properties".

▶ ## THE BENEFITS (AND THREAT) OF NOTES: PATH PROPERTIES

Path Properties manages commercial real estate properties in lower Manhattan and New Jersey—office buildings, retail stores, restaurants, and small food concession spaces. The staff of about 30 people oversees nearly 90 properties, valued at $125 million.

The company's president was concerned that maintenance problems were not addressed quickly enough. Minor problems often turned into major ones because managers didn't respond in time. The bigger the repair problems became, the more expensive they were to fix. Many tenants didn't renew their leases. Path's business was in trouble.

Before the implementation of a Notes database, the eight property managers informed the company's president of problems and repairs at weekly meetings. But the information wasn't efficiently disseminated throughout the company, and if a problem wasn't taken care of immediately, only the manager would know and deal with it.

Then Path hired a Notes consultant to help the managers access property information from their homes, so they could respond quickly to problems, and visit properties on their way to the office.

The database the consultant created made it easier for managers to keep track of their properties and stay on top of problems, and it also allowed the President to monitor the managers' perform- ance. By checking the database, she could track the amount of time it took for a specific manager to respond to and resolve a spe- cific problem. The benefits were apparent immediately— the com- pany was doing a better job of tracking problems, monitoring repair work, and keeping tenants—and the President was thrilled with the new system.

Unfortunately, the managers didn't see the new system in quite the same way. They felt that the Notes database forced them to re- spond *too* fast to problems and that their performance was being monitored unfairly. They also resented having to learn to use Notes.

The managers wanted to return to the old system of tracking prob- lems. They admitted that problems weren't fixed as quickly as ten- ants would like under the old system. What they wouldn't admit was that the new Notes system was making them more account- able; they didn't want to feel like they were "on call." But the bot- tom line was that the managers became more productive and Path Properties became more efficient—and the President insisted they use the database.

►► *Developing Notes Applications*

Out of the box Notes doesn't do much (except give you e-mail); to take advantage of its full power you need to build applications—design and construct Notes databases, then create interfaces for the various groups using the databases. You can hire someone to develop applications; or if you're the do-it-yourself type, turn to Parts Two and Three. There you'll find all you need to build Notes applications.

If you do create your own applications, you'll find yourself performing all the tasks done by developers hired by organizations to design and implement database applications. Most Notes developers start by analyzing the way an organization conducts its business and uses information. They watch and speak with clients, customers, managers, and staff to discover the different ways in which people share information throughout an organization. They assess the way people use e-mail, scrutinize the kind of data they share or need to share on a network, and ask staff to articulate what they do with information and how they use it in their jobs.

Once developers understand how people use information in an organization, they can set about designing an application that matches the way people share information in an organization. Ideally the application should streamline workflow. Using Notes helps to coordinate and optimize the use of information that was once decentralized throughout an organization's employees, departments, and divisions.

▶▶ *What's Next?*

As organizations move to network their computers and facilitate communication through electronic mail systems, the ways in which people work together change. Lotus Notes helps organizations put information in everyone's hands, keep the information current and secure, and prevent duplication of effort. Lotus has undertaken studies of its customers showing a very high return on investment among organizations implementing Notes, in some cases on the order of several hundred percent.

The remaining chapters of Part One give you, the Notes user, all the information you need to use Lotus Notes—to navigate the Notes environment, to use views and forms, to print databases, to use e-mail, and to run Notes from your laptop or home computer using a modem. If you're already developing Notes applications, Part One provides a thorough introduction to the realities confronting your users.

▶ ▶ CHAPTER **2**

Understanding Notes Basics

►► *F*AST *T*RACK

▶ ***A document is***   **33**

the basic unit of information in a Notes database. It's
called a document (rather than a record, as in other
databases) because it's analogous to a paper document. A
document can be any length, and it can contain different
types of formatting, much like a document you'd create
with a word-processing program.

▶ ***A network helps***   **34**

users share access to files and programs by storing master
copies in a central location, managing each user's access,
and keeping track of modifications to shared files. This
central repository of files is known as a server. The main
storage area for Notes databases is the Notes server.

▶ ***Replication is***   **34**

a process that allows you and others to work simultaneously on a single database, while ensuring that the database remains up-to-date.

A *database* is a collection of information that's organized in a particular way. You may already be familiar with flat-file and relational database programs. Both types of database organize information in a rigid file-record-field-data structure. Notes, however, is neither one of these kind of databases. It doesn't use a rigid structure to organize information. Instead, Notes uses a unique document structure to organize information, in which a document contains fields that hold data. Although this may sound a bit like a conventional database, in Notes you have more flexibility in the way you design a database. A document's design makes the information easy to read and convenient to use.

In this chapter, we build on the conceptual discussion of Notes from Chapter 1 and describe the basic components of a Notes database that make it different from traditional databases. In particular, we cover the following topics:

- Viewing documents
- Designing forms
- Composing documents
- Replicating databases

▶▶ Notes and Relational Database Programs

Before you get into learning about the basic components of Notes databases, you should understand how Notes terminology differs from traditional database terminology. You may be tempted to compare Notes with a relational database because they use similar terminology such as *document, form, field,* and *view*. This would be a mistake; these terms have different meanings in Notes and relational databases.

The architecture of a Notes database is different from that of a relational database. Notes structures data in documents, whereas relational databases structure data in tables. Notes is much more flexible in its approach to structuring data when you compare it to the rigid table structure of a relational database.

A Notes database and a relational database also perform different functions. A Notes database is a workflow-automation application. It uses an organization's computer network to keep the paperwork flowing among a group of people who are involved in the same business process. Each person in the group can access the same data at the same time, but use the data for their own purposes. In general, this ability to interpret data in different ways encourages discussion, which eventually leads to making decisions. Communication lies at the heart of a Notes database because it brings a group of people together and acts as a catalyst for change. It's an extremely dynamic application.

By contrast, traditional databases restrict you to organizing data in structured tables. For example, in a typical relational database, you might find that a record in one table would appear in another table, thus creating a relationship between the tables. This relationship enables you to perform an operation or *transaction* that affects the data. An example of a transaction would be transferring funds from a checking account to a saving account by debiting the checking account and crediting the savings account. One table would store the data for the checking account and another table would store the data for the savings account.

A relational database program usually provides you with tools to create tables of information. This tabular format enables you to use a query to look up information you need quickly and easily. Although you can perform query lookups from one Notes database to another, Notes doesn't require you to organize the information in a tabular format.

So, if you want an application that allows you and others in your organization to create relatively free-form documents that can be shared among users, Notes is the application for you. On the other hand, if you need to manage information you want organized in one or more neatly formatted tables, Notes isn't the appropriate application.

Now that you know what Notes isn't, let's get a better grip on what it is. The next few sections describe each of the basis parts of a Notes database:

- View
- Form
- Document
- Field

▶▶ *Viewing Documents in a Database*

A *view* is a listing of particular documents in a database. For example, Figure 2.1 shows a view that displays the names of consultants. A database can contain many views that organize documents in different ways, depending on the needs of the organization and the group(s) of

FIGURE 2.1 ▶

This is a view.

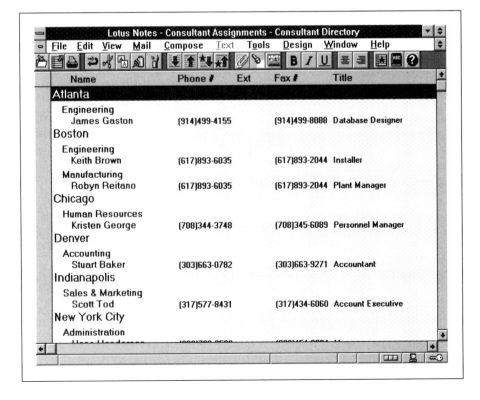

people using them. Figure 2.2 shows another view in the same database.

A view is the first element you see when you open a database. Like the table of contents you see when you open a book, a view summarizes the documents in a database in a particular way. It structures the information by neatly organizing documents into rows and columns. Each row in a view refers to a document, and each column can be based on a specific field or fields in a document. In other words, a column might display the value of a field, a piece of static text, or the results of several fields that have been calculated together.

This structure has nothing to do with the actual structure of the documents themselves (and shouldn't be confused with the structure of relational database tables). It's simply a convenient way to get an overview of documents in a Notes database, so you can find a specific document you need quickly. From a view, you scroll down the list and double-click on the document you want to open.

FIGURE 2.2 ▶

This is a different view in the same database.

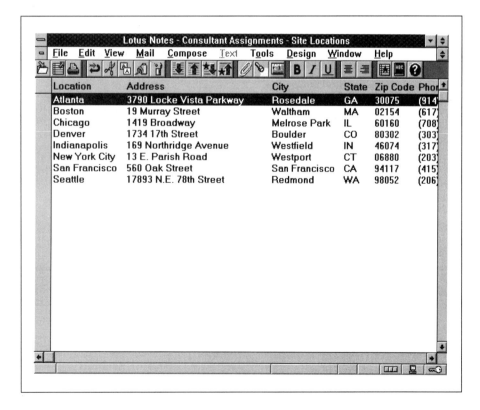

►► **N O T E**

You'll learn about creating views and defining columns in Chapter 14.

►► *Defining Forms*

A *form* is the basic structure of a document. Figure 2.3 shows an example of a form. You can think of a form as the original blueprint for a document and the documents themselves as alternative versions of the blueprint—just like a subdivision of tract houses where the floor layouts are exactly the same, but the houses' exteriors and furnishings differ.

FIGURE 2.3 ►

A form

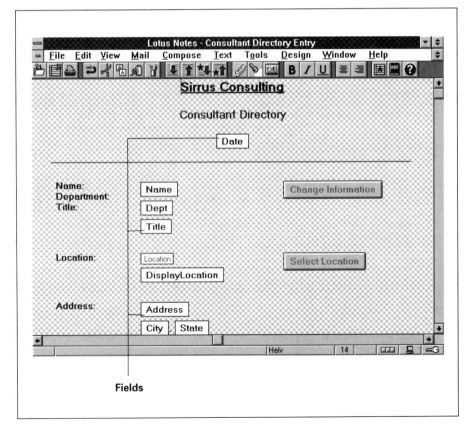

The data in a Notes database is entered on a form according to the way the Notes application designer has designed the form and defined the fields. Each field holds a single piece of data that you or another user enters.

A blank form is the first thing you encounter when you want to create a new document and add it to a database. You fill in—or *compose*—a document by entering data in the empty fields. In fact, you can look at a document as nothing more than a copy of a "fill-in-the-blank" form with a separate field for each item of data. You enter and edit data that constitutes the document's contents directly on the on-screen form, and once you save it you've got a separate document. Each subsequent document gets added to the database.

▶ The Elements of a Form

A form can be formatted on-screen in many ways. The designer can add different design attributes such as boldface and italics, change the color of backgrounds and fonts, and choose from a variety of typefaces and point sizes. A designer can modify a form by using familiar formatting tools, just as you can change the appearance of on-screen text in any other Windows application.

A designer can also place graphics on a form to enhance its appearance, or create tables to display information in a tabular format. Figure 2.4 shows an example of a form that includes a graphic and table. The designer can add popups to present information in dialog boxes, or buttons to execute macros. (A *macro* is a simple way to automate a task; for more information, see Chapter 15).

▶ Who Can Design a Form?

As we've mentioned in passing, forms aren't created as needed by individual users. A person must have a special designer or manager access status to create or modify forms. This person may be your organization's Notes Administrator, but since the Notes Administrator also manages the databases on the network and makes sure the Notes server is always up and running, someone else is probably responsible for developing databases and designing forms. Frequently, organizations hire Notes consultants or train in-house people to design databases.

FIGURE 2.4 ▶

This form includes a graphic and a table.

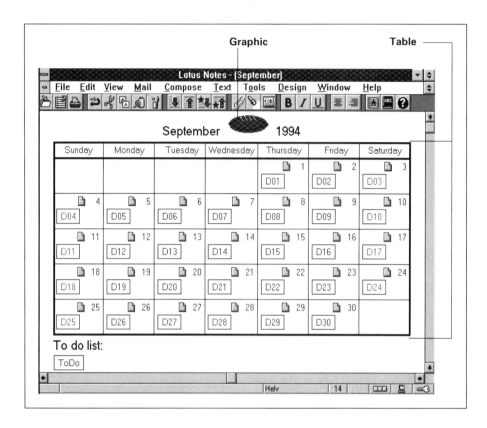

Notes developers assess an organization's information needs, study the "flow" of information from one group to another, and recommend ways to move information through an organization by using Notes. Then developers create forms that attempt to match the way an organization manages the steady stream of information it receives, such as sales leads, customer feedback, or status reports. By defining a form structure that's convenient for people to use, a designer can ensure that Notes is used to disseminate information efficiently throughout an organization. If a form is poorly designed or misconceived, the information contained in the documents won't be of much use.

Notes recognizes that the structure of information should reflect the changing needs of an organization. Therefore, it doesn't restrict a database designer to a particular format. The variety of view and form formats is limited only to the designer's imagination and creativity, and the particular needs of an organization.

If you are interested in creating forms, Parts Two and Three of this book will walk you through the process. However, if you're not yet familiar with the issues Notes users face, you may want to continue with the chapters in Part One before you take the plunge.

▶▶ *Composing a Document*

A *document* is the fundamental unit of information in a Notes database. Figure 2.5 shows an example of a document from the Consultant Assign database. It's called a document (rather than a record) because it's analogous to a paper document.

Documents can include file attachments from other Windows applications, such as word processors or spreadsheets. This can be handy when you send e-mail to someone in your group and want to include a

FIGURE 2.5 ▶

This is a document.

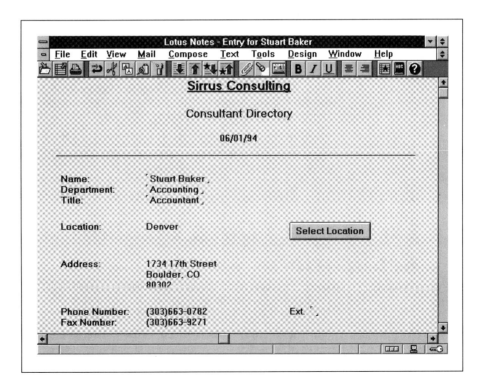

file. You can also embed objects in a document—a graphic, for example—and modify them later on by using OLE (**O**bject **L**inking and **E**mbedding; see Chapter 20 for more information).

Notes uses documents to organize information because the format is familiar to people and reflects the way people work. Relationships exist between documents in the same way we might talk and relate to one another by discussing topics and issues or writing our responses.

For example, you can relate one document to another in Notes with a response. Suppose you write a memo and send it to three people. The people respond to your memo by sending you their replies. By designating the replies as responses, the recipients of your memo create a chronological hierarchy of information that others can track, and if the database is set up properly, your recipients can also incorporate information from your memo in their responses. Your memo is considered the main document and the three replies are considered the response documents.

Another example would be the way the insurance company we introduced earlier uses an underwriter evaluation document to "respond" to the policy quote document that's written for each policyholder. (You'll recall this document summarizes the proposed coverage of the policy and estimates the premium.) Next, an inspector completes an building construction document that "responds" to the underwriter evaluation document. (This document assesses the risk of insuring the building on the basis of its construction.) The information is disseminated over the network and viewed by different people who use the information to make decisions.

▶▶ *Exchanging Data through Replication*

Replication is a process that lets a group of people access a database on a network and work on it at the same time, while ensuring that the database remains up-to-date. How is this accomplished? Briefly, each time you need to work on a database that's stored on a Notes server, you can make a copy of it and then save it to your own computer. You can add or delete information if you choose and regularly send your changes back to the server. Through replication, also known as database exchange, Notes incorporates your changes and the changes made by others, and so keeps the database current.

Notes uses database replication to distribute and update copies of the same database that may also be stored on different servers and workstations. This allows users on different networks, in different time zones, or even different locations to share information. The servers connect to each other at scheduled intervals, and the databases replicate changes to documents.

Notes compares the different copies of the same database and saves the most recent version (according to the date the changes were made) or the version with the most changes. Subsequently, the server stores the most current version of the database for users to continue to access. Replication makes all copies of a database essentially identical over time. If a user makes changes in a copy of the database, replication ensures that those changes are added to all copies, as long as the replication options are set up to do so. The process takes times and requires specific Notes server resources on a network. Your organization's Notes Administrator determines the replication schedule that makes the most sense for the company's system. (You'll learn much more about replicating databases in Chapter 18.)

▶▶ *What's Next?*

Of course, the previous description simplifies the process of replication. But it illustrates the uniqueness of this database program. Notes enables people in an organization to work together more efficiently and productively by allowing them to share information in the same database. Although people can use a database at the same time, each person can actually work with a copy—or *replica*—of the database on his or her own computer. No one needs to use the database that's stored on the server.

We'll discuss the nuts and bolts of replicating databases in subsequent chapters, because making copies of databases identical over time is an important issue. But for now, we're going to put aside our discussion of Notes in conceptual terms and let you get your feet wet using Notes. In the next chapter, we take you on a tour of the Notes environment.

▶ ▶ ▶   CHAPTER **3**

Working in
the Notes
Environment

———

F*AST* T*RACK*

▶ *The Status bar appears*   **43**

along the bottom of your active Notes window. It includes a message area, indicators for network and hard disk activity initiated by Notes, popups, and your access level to the active database.

▶ *You can open up to nine active windows*   **46**

at a time in Notes. When you try to exceed that number, Notes responds by telling you to close a window. You can switch from window to window by pulling down the Window menu and choosing a new window.

▶ *A SmartIcon is*   **48**

a button that executes one or more actions when you click on it. The set of 23 default SmartIcons appears below the menu bar. A SmartIcon can perform a simple action, such as choosing a menu command or navigating to the next document, or more complex actions, such as executing a macro formula. For many tasks, clicking on a SmartIcon is quicker than pulling down a menu or recalling and typing a keyboard shortcut.

►► **W**orking in Notes is a lot like working in other Windows or Macintosh applications. The graphical user interface provides you with a myriad of tools and features that makes getting around Notes easy. In this chapter, you'll learn the basics you need to find your way around in Notes. Specifically, you'll learn how to:

- Start Notes
- Organize the Notes Workspace
- Use the Status Bar
- Work with Notes windows
- Use, customize, and create new SmartIcons

►► Starting Notes

To start Notes, double-click on the icon in the Windows Program Manager. After a few moments, Notes displays the Notes interface, as shown in Figure 3.1, which is known as the *Workspace*. As you can see, the Workspace displays a set of six tabbed folders in which you organize your work. The tabbed folders display the databases in any way you choose, allowing you to systematize (and customize) your Workspace just as you would by organizing paper documents in file folders. You can organize the folders to correspond to the way you organize or use the information you want.

FIGURE 3.1 ▶

The Workspace is where you perform and organize your work in Notes.

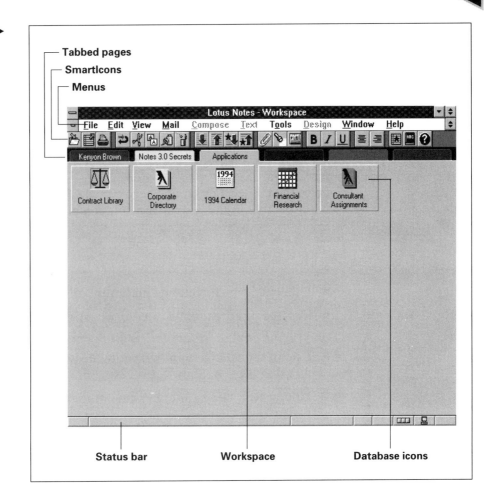

▶▶ *Exploring and Organizing the Notes Workspace*

The Workspace is an active window that displays many important elements. These include:

- Menus
- SmartIcons
- Six tabbed pages (which can display database icons)

- Any other Notes windows you open
- Status Bar

Other elements, such as the control box, window title bar, scroll bars, and minimize and maximize buttons, should be familiar to you from using other Windows applications.

▶ Customizing the Workspace Pages

Each of the tabbed Workspace pages provides you with ways to organize your databases and display information about them. For example, when you start Notes, the database icons display the names of your databases. Altogether, there are four types of information you can display on a database icon:

- Title only, which contains minimum information (the default).
- Number of unread mail documents in a database, which you can display by choosing View ➤ Show Unread.
- Title of the database and server name, which you can display by choosing View ➤ Show Server Names.
- Title, server name, and file name of the database, which you can display by holding the Shift key down while choosing View ➤ Show Server Names.

▶ Adding Names to the Workspace Pages

As you use Notes, you will regularly add and remove database icons and also move them from one page to another to organize your work. So it's a good idea to group similar databases on a page and give the page a descriptive name.

You add a name to a page by double-clicking on the tab at the top of a page. The Workspace Page Name dialog box appears, as shown in Figure 3.2. Enter an appropriate name in the text box.

You can also change a tab's color if you don't care for gray, the default color, or if you want to code the page. Click on a color at the bottom of the dialog box to select it. When you've got a color you like, click on OK to accept the change(s). The tabbed page will display the name and color that you gave it.

FIGURE 3.2

The Workspace Page Name dialog box lets you add a name and color to each tabbed page.

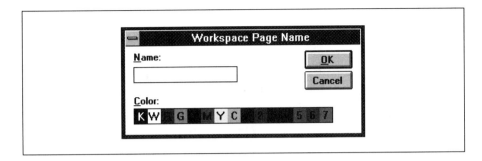

  T I P

To display another Workspace page, you click the tab of the page you want. You can also press ↑ until the current page's tab is highlighted and then press ← or → to reach the page you want.

▶▶ *Using the Status Bar*

The Status Bar appears along the bottom of your active Notes window, as shown in Figure 3.3. It includes a message area, indicators for network and hard disk activity initiated by Notes, a popup for SmartIcons control, and your access level to the active database.

The parts of the Status Bar (from left to right) are described below.

- **Network access indicator:** A lightning bolt indicates network activity. For example, you'll see a bolt when you open a shared database.

- **Message/status area:** Shows messages such as "10 documents selected" and "No more unread documents in this database." These messages display brief descriptions of your activities. The status area also displays the meaning of the user access level and setup indicators (at the right of the Status Bar) when you click those indicators. If you click the status area, a popup shows the nine most recent messages that have appeared. Click the popup again to close it when you've finished reading it.

FIGURE 3.3 ▶

The Status Bar displays important information such as messages, network activities, and your user access level to a particular database

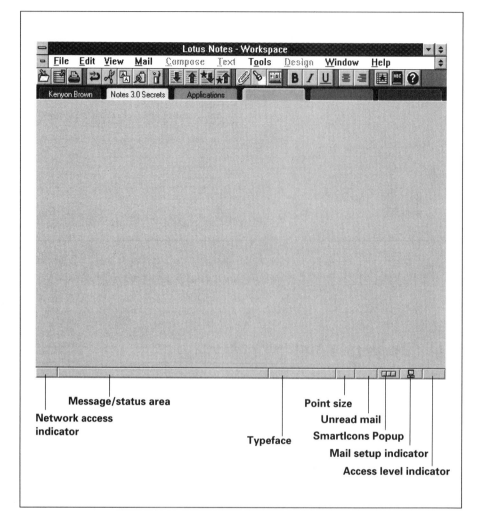

• **Typeface:** Shows the font at the insertion point when you're editing a document. Click this indicator to pop up a menu of all available fonts and choose a different font.

• **Point size:** Shows the size of the font at the insertion point when you're editing a document. Click this indicator to pop up a menu of all available sizes and choose a different size.

• **Unread mail:** Displays an envelope when there is unread mail in your Notes mail file. Click the envelope to open your mail file to the last view you used. If your mail file is already open, Notes brings its view window to the front. This area is blank if you have no unread mail.

- **SmartIcons popup:** Click this indicator to display a popup menu that lets you choose a different SmartIcons set or hide SmartIcons.

- **Mail setup indicator:** Shows whether Notes is set up for server-based mail (message says network-based mail), for work-station-based mail (most commonly used for working off-site, away from your company's computer network), or for non-Notes mail such as cc:Mail.

- **Access level indicator:** Shows your database access level for the active database. Click the icon to see your access level in a message in the status area.

EXECUTING COMMANDS IN NOTES

There are many keyboard shortcuts—combinations of keys—you can use to quickly execute commands in Notes. Using these short-cuts will make you more efficient—and proficient—when you start designing databases.

There are only two Notes tasks that *require* a mouse: using the ruler (to change tab and left paragraph margin settings), and designing a database icon.

Notes supports Windows standards for choosing menus and commands from the keyboard. For example, to choose the View ➤ Show Ruler command, hold down Alt, press V, and press R. This action is represented as Alt+V, R. You can release the Alt key after you press the V. To choose Text ➤ Alignment ➤ Left, press Alt+T, A, L.

You can also use accelerator keys to choose commands automatically from the keyboard. Simply press the key combination shown to the right of a menu item. For example, to choose Edit ➤ Cut, press Ctrl+X.

▶▶ Controlling Notes Windows

You can open up to nine active windows at a time in Notes. When you try to exceed that number, Notes responds by telling you to close a window. Each open window consumes memory (RAM), and Notes likes memory. You'll experience a slowdown in your computer's performance as you open windows, so don't open any more windows than you need to display. To switch from window to window, pull down the Window menu and choose a new window.

Controlling windows means moving, sizing, and closing them, as well as moving among them. You can control all Notes windows by using the mouse or the keyboard. You can also move Notes dialog boxes and most messages (alerts/error messages) the same way you move Notes windows, although you cannot size or scroll dialog boxes and messages. The easiest way to move a window is with the mouse. Just place the mouse pointer on the window's title bar, drag (click and move) the window to the position you want, and release the mouse button.

 ▶▶ **T I P**

You can also use the keyboard to move a window by pressing Ctrl+F7. Use the ↑, ↓, →, or ← to move the window to the position you want and then press ↵.

▶ Sizing a Window

To maximize or minimize all windows with your mouse, do the following:

- To enlarge the window to maximum size, choose Window ➤ Maximize All or click the button in the upper right corner of the window.

- To reduce the window to minimum size, choose Window ➤ Minimize All or click the button in the upper right corner of the window.

▶▶ **T I P**

If you minimize a window, it won't display the maximize button. To maximize the window, double-click its title bar. To maximize or minimize all windows with the keyboard, press F10, W, X. Press F10, W, N to minimize all windows.

There are two additional ways to size the active window with the mouse: by changing horizontal AND vertical dimensions simultaneously, and by changing horizontal OR vertical dimension. To change the horizontal and vertical dimensions at the same time, point to the lower right corner of the window. The pointer changes to a double-headed arrow. Drag the lower right corner to make the window the size you want.

▶▶ **N O T E**

You can't drag a window beyond the boundary of its "parent" window.

To get the same result, point to the size box in the lower right corner of the window. Drag the size box to make the window the size you want. To change the horizontal or vertical dimension, point to either the horizontal or vertical border of the window. Drag the border to the new position. To restore a window to its previous size, either double-click its title bar or choose Restore from the System menu.

You can also resize the active window with a keyboard. Press Ctrl+F10 to toggle the active window between its current size and its previous size. Press Alt+F5 to make the application window smaller. You can't make it bigger, however. To restore a window to its previous size, press Ctrl+F5.

▶▶ T I P

To display a different open window, press Alt+W and then the number shown next to the window title. You can also pull down the Window menu and select another open window by clicking on the name.

▶ Closing a Window

There are a lot of ways to close the active window. As you work with Notes, you will probably develop a preference for one and forget the others, but for now, here's the whole list:

- Choose File ➤ Close Window.
- Press Ctrl+W.
- Press Esc.
- Move the pointer into the window and double-click the *right* mouse button.
- Select Close from the control menu, which you access by clicking the bar in the upper left corner of the window.
- Press Ctrl+F4.
- Click the window's close box.

▶▶ Using SmartIcons

A *SmartIcon* is a button that executes a combination of actions when you click on it. The set of default SmartIcons—all 23 of them—appears below the menu bar, as shown in Figure 3.4.

A SmartIcon can perform a simple action, such as choosing a menu command or navigating to the next document, or more complex actions, such as executing a macro formula. Notes comes with over 100 predefined SmartIcons, including icons for most Notes menu commands. Notes also includes over a dozen custom SmartIcons to which you can assign your own macros.

FIGURE 3.4 ▶

The set of 23 default SmartIcons helps you to automate a myriad of routine tasks in Notes.

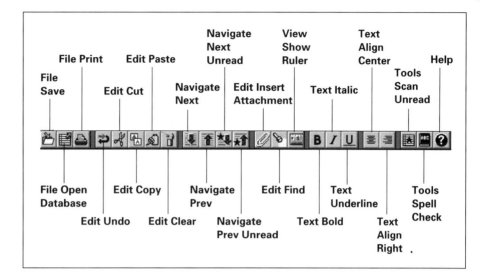

For many tasks, clicking on a SmartIcon is quicker than pulling down several menu options or recalling and typing a keyboard shortcut. For example, if you didn't know that Ctrl+S was the keyboard shortcut for the Save command, you could click on the leftmost SmartIcon (the file folder with the arrow pointing inside it). This is much faster than opening the File menu and clicking on Save.

You can also find out what any SmartIcon does without activating it. Just place the pointer on an icon, and click and hold the right mouse button down while you check the active window's title bar. A description of the SmartIcon appears, as shown in Figure 3.5. If you want to scan all the predefined SmartIcons, choose Tools ➤ SmartIcons. A dialog box appears, as shown in Figure 3.6. Scroll through the left list box.

Obviously, you can save a lot of time by using the default set of Smart-Icons. But if you do specialized work, or if your work leads you to repeatedly use a function that is not in the set of default SmartIcons, you can save even more time by adjusting the SmartIcons to suit your own needs.

You can customize SmartIcons in several ways. You can create new sets of SmartIcons, modify preexisting sets of SmartIcons, and delete sets of SmartIcons you don't use. You can also adjust the size of your Smart-Icons, and if you know how to write macros, you can create custom SmartIcons.

FIGURE 3.5 ▶

Point on a SmartIcon and then click and hold the right mouse button down. A description of the icon appears in the active window's title bar.

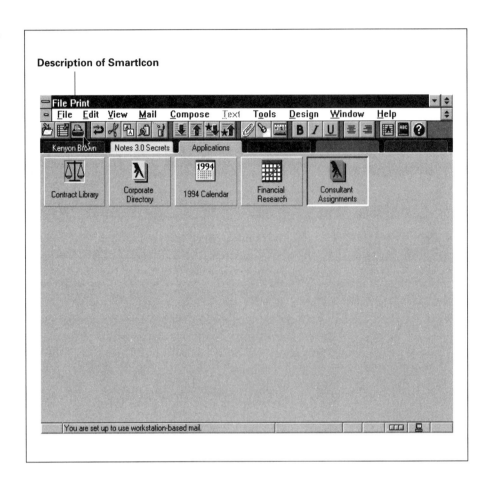

▶ *Modifying an Existing SmartIcons Set*

One of the easiest ways to customize SmartIcons is to modify a preexisting set. To add SmartIcons to a set, choose Tools ➤ SmartIcons to open the SmartIcons dialog box. Then drag the SmartIcons you want (one at a time) from the Available Icons list into the scroll box to the right. You're actually dragging a copy, so nothing's removed from your Available Icons list.

On the other hand, sometimes you only need to use specific icons to perform particular tasks. Why let icons you don't need clutter the screen? To remove SmartIcons from a set, drag them (one at a time) out of the current set and back to the Available Icons list.

FIGURE 3.6

The SmartIcons dialog box displays all the pre-defined icons.

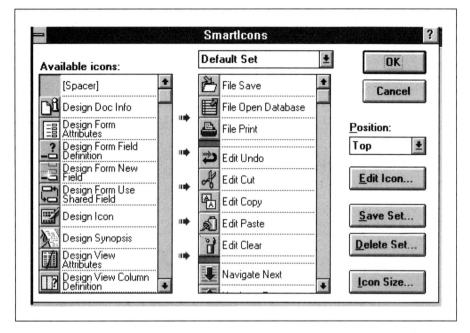

To delete a SmartIcons set you no longer use, choose Tools ➤ Smart-Icons and click on Delete Set. The Delete Set dialog box appears. Select the set you want to delete in the list and then click on OK.

You can also fix SmartIcons when they don't look right on your screen. Ordinarily your operating system displays SmartIcons correctly on any type of monitor supported by Notes. However, some monitors don't communicate their type (EGA, VGA, or SVGA) correctly to the operating system, so you may need to do that yourself in this dialog box.

To adjust your icons to match your monitor, choose Tools ➤ Smart-Icons and select Icon Size. To use the Icon Size dialog box, select the option that matches your type of monitor: EGA, VGA, or SVGA.

▶▶ **N O T E**

> **The options Small, Medium, and Large that appear in the dialog box refer to the size of the SmartIcons, not your monitor.**

►
CHANGING THE POSITION OF SMARTICONS

Some people don't like having the SmartIcons up there, hanging from the top of their screen. If you're one of these people, choose Tools ➤ SmartIcons. The SmartIcons dialog box appears. Click the arrow on the Position list and choose one of these positions:

➢ Floating, which places SmartIcons in a floating window that you can move, close, and resize. (To move the floating window, drag it by its title bar. To close it, click the small white close box in the upper left corner.)

➢ Left, which places SmartIcons along the left edge of your Notes application window.

➢ Top, which places SmartIcons along the top of your Notes window, just under the menu bar (this is the default).

➢ Right, which places SmartIcons along the right edge of your Notes window.

➢ Bottom, which places SmartIcons along the bottom of your Notes window.

Click on OK to confirm your changes (or Cancel, to revert to the previous position).

► *Creating a New SmartIcons Set*

Creating new sets of SmartIcons is one of the best things you can do for yourself if you have certain tasks that lead you to use certain functions all the time. You can define multiple sets of SmartIcons for different purposes, such as one set for reading and writing documents, another for using Notes off-site, and a third for designing databases. To create a set of SmartIcons that you define:

1. Choose Tools ➤ SmartIcons.

> ## CREATING OR EDITING FORMULAS FOR SMARTICONS
>
> You can define custom SmartIcons by creating macros—Notes formulas that accomplish specified tasks—in the Edit SmartIcons dialog box or SmartIcons dialog box. You can save yourself a lot of time by defining custom SmartIcons for your most-used complex tasks.
>
> To edit or create a formula for SmartIcons, choose Tools ➤ SmartIcons. (See Chapter 15 for information on how to write and edit formulas.) The SmartIcons dialog box appears. Select the icon you want to edit in the Custom Icons list. Click on Edit Icon button. Click on the Formula button. Edit the formula.
>
> If you want to create a formula, type the formula into the Formula text box. To add an @function, click on Add @Func, then select an @function from the list. (Chapter 15 also covers @functions.) To add a Notes command, click on Add Command, then select a command from the list. Click on OK (or Cancel, if you don't want to save your formula).

2. Select the set that's closest to the one you'd like to create. Add and remove SmartIcons until you're satisfied with the new set.

3. Select Save Set. The Save Set of SmartIcons dialog box appears, as shown in Figure 3.7.

4. Type an appropriate name for the set into the Name of set box, such as **DB Design** for your set of database design SmartIcons. You can use any characters supported by your operating system, but the name can't be more than 15 characters. This name appears in the SmartIcons popup menu in the Status Bar.

5. Type a file name into the Filename box. You have the option of scrolling the list of current sets to see file names for existing sets in order to avoid reusing a name. The file name must be in DOS

FIGURE 3.7 ▶

The Save Set of Smart-Icons dialog box lets you have your custom icon set.

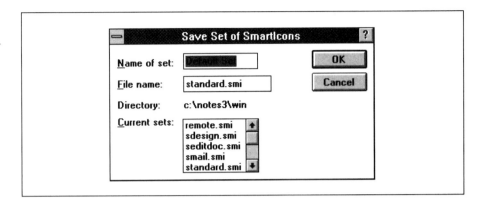

format—that is, up to eight characters (limited to letters, numbers, and underscore), followed by the extension .SMI. (Note: If you skip this step, Notes assigns a file name based on what you entered for Name of set.)

6. Click on OK (or Cancel, if you change your mind about saving this set).

Your new set appears in the right-hand list box in the SmartIcons dialog box, with the new set name above the list. The name serves as both file name and menu name. The new set is automatically stored in your Notes data folder, in the SmartIcons Sets folder.

 ▶▶ **TIP**

To create a blank set that's easy to use as a basis for new sets, just remove all the SmartIcons from a set, and save it under an appropriate name such as MYSET. Whenever you want to create a new set, select this one from the Set popup menu.

▶▶ *What's Next?*

As you use Notes, you'll discover the best way to make SmartIcons work for you. They can save you a lot of time as you perform routine tasks. In the next chapter, we discuss the basics of using a Notes database. Obviously, any Notes database will have some feature that make it unique. However, there are also some features that all databases have in common. The chapter identifies these features to help you become comfortable using any database you have access to.

CHAPTER 4

Accessing
Notes Databases

▶▶ FAST TRACK

▶ **To see your access level in the access control list** **60**

choose File ➤ Database ➤ Access Control. The Database
Access Control List (ACL) dialog box appears. Scroll
down the list to see if you're listed. If you are listed, highlight your name. Your access level appears at the bottom of
the dialog box. If your name is not listed in the database's
ACL, your access level is the default access level, which is
No access.

▶ **Before you add a database to the Workspace** **64**

switch to the Workspace page to which you want to add
the database. Click on the appropriate tab to display the
page. If you don't click on a tab, Notes will add the database's icon to the page that's currently displayed.

▶ **An icon is** **64**

a graphical pointer to the actual location of the database
on a Notes server or your computer.

▶ **To open a database for the first time** **64**

choose File ➤ Open Database. The Open Database dialog
box appears. (If the database file you want to use is stored
on a server, make sure you can access it.) Highlight Local
(or the name of the Notes server) in the Server list and
click on the Open button. (You can also double-click on
Local or the server's name.) The path name of the Notes
directory will appear along with a list of the directory's
files and subdirectories. Double-click on the subdirectory
where the database file is located. The name of the file will
appear in the list box. Double-click on the database's
name. Notes subsequently adds the database's icon to the
Workspace page that's currently displayed.

▶ **To open a database** **64**

click on the Workspace page where the database is located and double-click on its icon.

▶ **To display information about a database** **67**

before you add it to your Workspace, highlight the database you want to read about in the File ➤ Open Database dialog box. Click on the About button. An About document appears.

▶ **To close a database** **69**

press Esc. If a document is open, press Esc until you return to the Workspace. You can also press Ctrl+W to close a window and return to the Workspace.

▶ **To move a database icon around on your Workspace** **70**

simply drag the icon around the page. To move the icon to a different page, drag it to the tab at the top of page you want to move it to. When you see an outline box appear around the tab name, release the mouse button. The icon will appear on the selected page.

▶ **To remove an icon from a Workspace page** **71**

click on the icon you want to remove and then press Delete. When the dialog box appears, click on the Yes button.

▶ ▶ **U**sing a Notes database isn't difficult. Before you can use one, however, you need to add it to your workspace. If you have access to your organization's databases, you can follow the instructions in this chapter to begin using them. If you don't have access to any existing databases, you can use the sample databases and templates that we refer to in our examples. These samples are on the companion disk included with this book. You can copy the databases to your hard disk and use them as they are or modify them to fit your own needs. You might want to check with your organization's Notes Administrator to make sure it's okay to do this. We don't want to get you in trouble.

In this chapter, we explain the basics of accessing a Notes database. You open and close all Notes databases, regardless of their uniqueness, in the same way. You also use the same procedures to organize Notes databases in your workspace, regardless of the organizational principles you favor. This chapter covers all the basics of database access in Notes, including the following topics:

- Access privileges
- Using the sample databases and templates
- Workspace pages
- Opening a database
- Database icons

▶ ▶ Knowing Your Access Privileges

If you have the appropriate access level, you can select one or more databases to add to your workspace. Every Notes database has an access control list (ACL) specifying which users, user groups, and servers can access the database and what tasks they can perform. Both of the ACL's elements—access levels and access roles—are set by the database designer or manager in the Database Access Control List dialog box. You should check the settings in this dialog box for any database that you want to open.

▶▶ **N O T E**

You must be on a database's access control list (ACL) in order to open the database.

If your name is not listed in the database's ACL, either explicitly or as a member of a group, your access level is the default access level, which is No access.

Notes offers seven access levels. The access levels, from highest to lowest, are:

- **Manager**: Can perform almost any operation—reading, writing, or editing—on documents, forms, views, and the database icon. A manager can also record or stop recording user activity, modify the ACL and replication settings, and delete the database. However, a manager can be prevented from deleting documents. A database always has at least one manager, who may or may not be the person who created the database.

- **Designer:** Can perform the same operations as a manager, except for modifying the ACL, User Activity, Replication or "Other" settings (the settings available when you select Other Settings in the Database Information dialog box), and deleting the database. Designers can be prevented from deleting documents.

- **Editor:** Can read, write, and edit all documents in a database, but cannot modify forms, views, or the ACL. Editors can be prevented from deleting documents.

- **Author**: Can read existing documents and create new ones, but can only edit the documents he or she created. Authors can be prevented from deleting documents or creating documents.

- **Reader:** Can read documents but cannot add new ones or edit existing ones.

- **Depositor:** Can add new documents but cannot read existing ones. This level is most often used for mail-in databases as well as databases like ballot boxes or suggestion boxes, since it lets users compose their own documents but not read anyone else's documents. This level is also used for data entry personnel entering new policies in an insurance company.

- **No access:** Users who are assigned this level cannot open the database or mail in documents.

The symbol for your access level appears at the right end of the status bar when you open a database. To see your access level, choose File ➤ Database ➤ Access Control. The Database Access Control List dialog box appears, as shown in Figure 4.1. Scroll down the list to see if you're listed. If you are listed, highlight your name. Your access level appears at the bottom of the dialog box. Click on Cancel to close the box. You'll need to ask your Notes Administrator to change your access level if you want to use a database in a different way than your current access level allows.

If you use Notes mail, you can also discover the names of the managers of a database. Select or open the database, then choose Mail ➤ Compose ➤ Memo to Manager. In the To field of the mail memo, you'll see the users and groups assigned manager access. You can just read the

FIGURE 4.1

The Database Access Control List dialog box. FENDER/Sirrus and GIBSON/Sirrus are servers of the Sirrus organization. Kyle G. Brown/Sirrus is a user in the same organization, Sirrus. Writers is a group, including a list of users involved with the writing of this book. NEXTAGE1/NextAge is another server located at a different company.

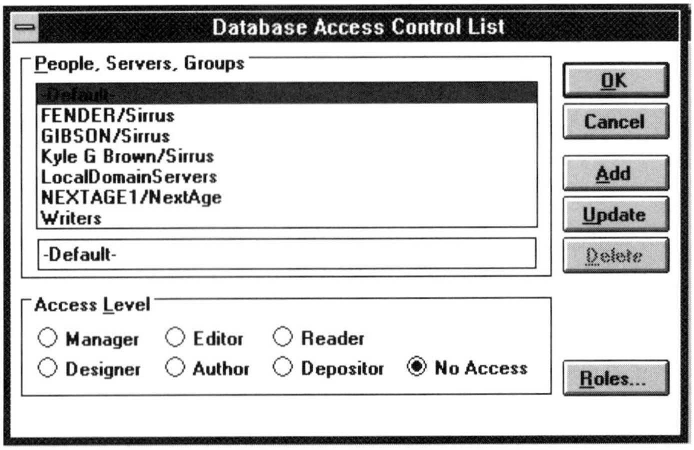

Database Access Control List

People, Servers, Groups

-Default-
FENDER/Sirrus
GIBSON/Sirrus
Kyle G Brown/Sirrus
LocalDomainServers
NEXTAGE1/NextAge
Writers

-Default-

OK
Cancel
Add
Update
Delete

Access Level

○ Manager ○ Editor ○ Reader
○ Designer ○ Author ○ Depositor ◉ No Access

Roles...

list, or you can send the manager(s) a mail memo, if you have suggestions or comments about access to the database. If you don't use Notes mail you can discover the names of the database managers in the Database Catalog, a Notes database that should be available on any Notes server at your organization. If you can't find it, ask your Notes Administrator.

▶▶ *Using the Companion Disk Databases*

The sample Notes databases on the companion disk are included with this book for your convenience. As you follow the book's instructions, you may not feel comfortable applying what you learn to your organization's Notes databases. Therefore, we've provided you with databases that you can analyze and modify. Go ahead and mess around with them!

One of the databases on the companion disk is a Consultant Assignments database, which we'll use in this chapter to illustrate the basics of using Notes. This database stores information on freelance consultants. A training firm uses the information to hire consultants on a contract basis.

In the next few sections, we're going to take you through the steps of opening and using a database so you can get accustomed to the Notes features that are found in the workspace. After you add a database to your workspace page, you can open its views, select documents, and compose new documents. We'll discuss how the Consultant Assignments database was designed in Part Three.

If you haven't yet copied the Consultant Assignments database from the companion disk to your computer (*not* to the Notes server), you should do so now. There are instructions on the inside cover of the book, opposite the disk. You'll work with the database locally; that is, you'll copy and use the database on your computer—or workstation—only.

The Consultant Assignments file (all the files, for that matter) is a compressed (to save floppy disk space), self-extracting archive. This means you don't need a specific decompression program on your hard disk to open the file. However, like any compressed file you expand, it's larger and takes up more room on your computer than it does on the companion disk. So make sure you have adequate space on your hard disk.

▶▶ *Selecting a Workspace Page*

The pages that appear in your workspace are provided to help you organize the databases you use. Each time you open a new database, you can add it to a particular page that includes other databases with similar traits. For example, one page may display sales-tracking databases, while another page may contain group discussion databases. As we discussed in Chapter 3, you can organize the workspace to suit your own needs. (That's why we always refer to the workspace as *your* workspace.) Each of the tabs on the six workspace pages can display a unique label name that you create.

 ▶▶ **T I P**

> **You can always change a tab name and its color later on. Double-click on the tab, enter a new name, select a new color, and click on OK. It's very easy to change page tabs when you want to reorganize your workspace.**

We recommend that you name one of the pages "Applications" or "Sample Databases" (or another appropriate name) and then use the page to organize the databases you copy from the companion disk. From this page you can access the databases and display their icons. At the same time, you may also want to use separate workspace pages for the databases you create or use in your organization.

▶▶ *Opening a Database*

Once you've organized the pages in your workspace the way you want, you can open databases to which you have access. When you open a database for the first time, you need to perform a few special tasks.

After you've added a database to your workspace, it's very easy to open and use it.

1. If you haven't done so already, switch to the workspace page where you want to access the Consultant Assignments database (or any other database).

2. Click on the appropriate tab to display the page. If you don't do this, Notes will add the database's icon to the page that's currently displayed. When you "add a database" you actually place a database *icon* on your workspace. An icon is a graphical pointer to the actual location of the database on a Notes server or your computer.

3. If you've copied the sample databases and templates from the companion disk to your hard disk, you'll need to remember the directory's name where the database is located. To open the database for the first time, choose File ➤ Open Database. The Open Database dialog box appears, as shown in Figure 4.2.

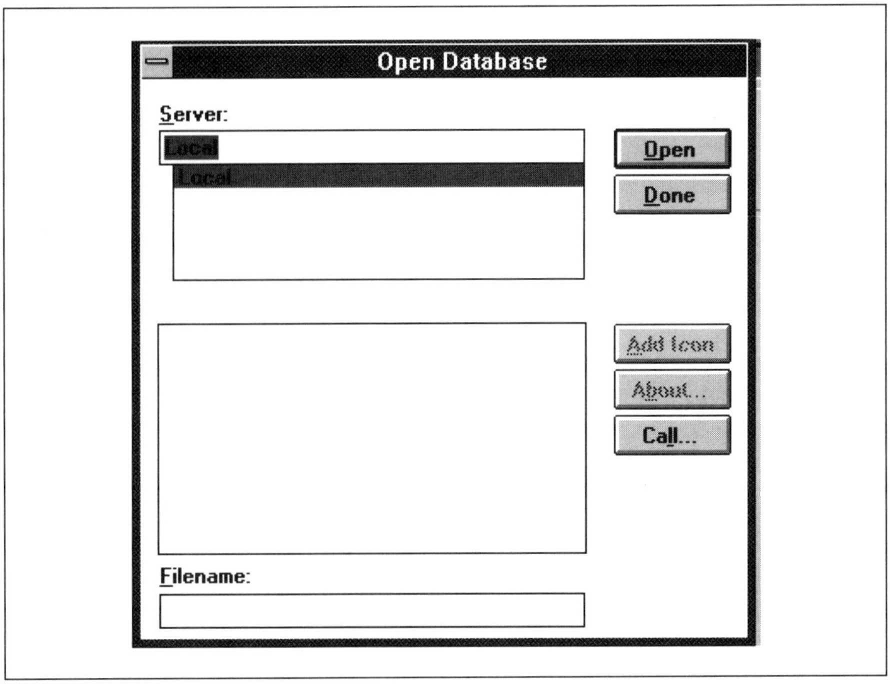

FIGURE 4.2

The Open Database dialog box displays a list of servers where database files are stored. Here, "Local" is highlighted to indicate that a person is working with a copy of a database file locally, that is, on a workstation.

Open Database
Server:
Local
Local
Open
Done
Add Icon
About...
Call...
Filename:

▶▶ **N O T E**

If the database file you want to use is stored on a server, make sure you have rights to access that server (separate from the ACL to the database file itself). You'll need to ask your Notes Administrator if this possible. We discuss access rights and other security issues in Chapter 17.

4. Highlight Local (or the name of the Notes server) in the Server list and then click on the Open button. (You can also double-click on Local or the server's name.) The path name of the Notes directory will appear along with a list of the directory's files and subdirectories. For example, our Notes directory includes an APPS subdirectory, as shown in Figure 4.3.

5. If you want to open the Consultant Assignments database, double-click on the subdirectory where you've copied the database file. The name of the file will appear in the list box (along with the names of other files if you've decompressed them), as shown in Figure 4.4.

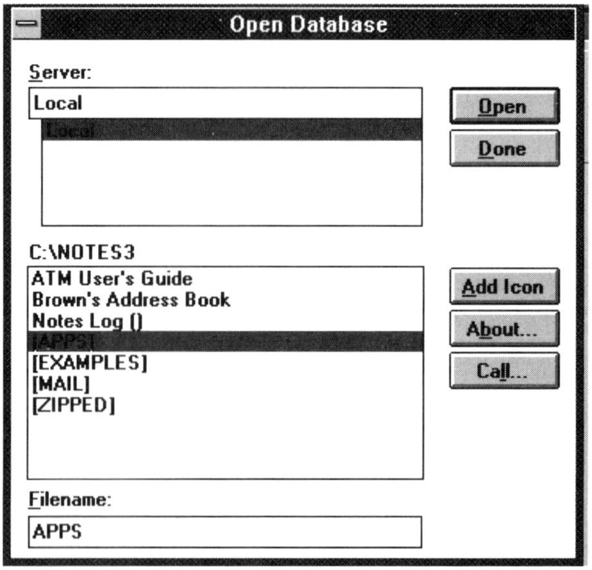

FIGURE 4.3 ▶

After you select a server, the Notes directory's path name appears along with a list of databases and directories.

Open Database
S̲erver:
Local
Local
C:\NOTES3
ATM User's Guide
Brown's Address Book
Notes Log ()
[APPS]
[EXAMPLES]
[MAIL]
[ZIPPED]
F̲ilename:
APPS

Buttons: O̲pen, D̲one, A̲dd Icon, Ab̲out..., Ca̲ll...

FIGURE 4.4

When you select a sub-directory, a list of databases appears.

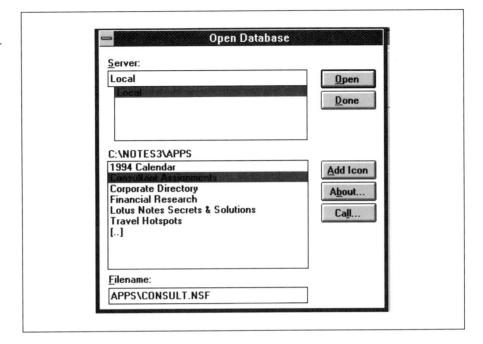

6. Highlight Consultant Assignments. You'll notice the file's path name appears in the Filename text box at the bottom of the dialog box.

7. Double-click on the database's name.

The dialog box closes, and Notes adds the database's icon to the workspace page and opens the database. A view appears automatically, as shown in Figure 4.5.

▶▶ *Browsing through Databases*

Once you get used to opening databases, you can browse through the lists of other databases that are stored on your hard disk (or on your organization's Notes server if you have access). While browsing, you can read a description of the database, its features, and what you can do with it—before you open it and add its icon to your workspace. If you don't like what you read, you don't have to open the database.

FIGURE 4.5 ▶

The default view appears after you open a database.

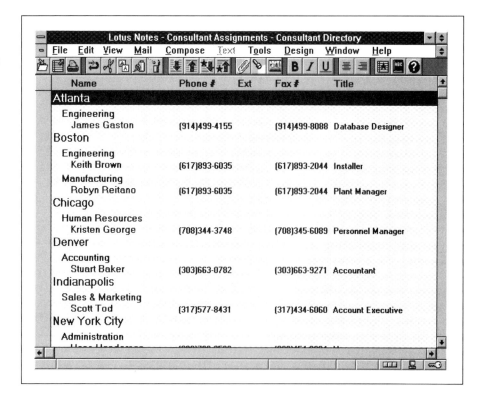

To start browsing, choose File ➤ Open Database. Select the Notes server you want to browse and then click on the Open button. A list of databases from the opened server appears; subdirectories are listed together following the list of databases. The first database on the list is highlighted and its file name appears in the Filename box.

To open a subdirectory where other databases may be located, select it and then click on Open. The databases from the opened subdirectory now appear in the list. You can do one of the following:

- To display information about a database without opening it, select the database and then choose Help ➤ About. You'll see the document that's displayed the first time you open a database. You can display this information at any time by selecting or opening the database and then choosing Help ➤ About <name of database>.

- To add a database icon to your Workspace without opening the database, select the database and then click on the Add Icon button. The selected database's icon is added to your workspace and the dialog box remains open to let you browse some more. Click on the Done button when you're finished.

- To add an icon and open the database in one step, double-click on the database, or select it and then click on the Done button.

▶▶ *Closing a Database*

To close a view or document, press Esc or double-click with the right mouse button. So for now, press Esc to close the view that's displayed and return to the workspace page.

Since views and documents are actually active windows, you can also press Ctrl+W to close a window and return to the workspace. Of the three methods, pressing Esc and using the mouse are definitely faster.

▶▶ *Using Database Icons*

An icon represents a database you have stored on your workstation or a database that's stored on a server. Using icons helps to organize databases on your workspace or on the server's workspace. You click on a database's icon in order to access the database. An icon also displays the database's name, which helps you to locate it quickly. The icon may also display a graphic that helps to illustrate the database's purpose.

▶ *Adding a Database Icon to a Workspace Page*

You can add a database icon to a workspace page without actually opening the database the first time. In the Open Database dialog box, highlight the database and then click on the Add Icon button. (For example, you could have highlighted the Consultant Assignments database and selected Add icon.) Notes adds the icon to the page without opening the database at the same time. Nothing could be easier.

▸ *Moving Database Icons around Your Workspace*

To move a database icon around on your workspace, you simply drag the icon around the page. To move the icon to a different page, drag it to the tab at the top of page you want to move it to. When you see an outline box appear around the tab name, release the mouse button.

  TIP

> **You can select several icons to move at the same time by Shift-clicking them and then dragging them as a group. Click on an icon (any icon), hold down the Shift key, and click on the other icon(s) you want to move. Still holding down the Shift key, point the mouse on any selected icon, press the left mouse button, and drag the icons to the desired location.**

You can also move icons around by using the keyboard. Simply select the icon (or group of icons) you want to move, then begin the drag operation by pressing Shift+Ctrl+*arrow key*. Select the arrow key based on which direction you want to move the icon. Once you've pressed an arrow key, you can release the Shift and Ctrl keys.

The workspace scrolls when you perform an action that would cause icons to be moved off the screen. Scrolling only occurs if there's additional workspace in the desired direction; if your computer is set to make a beep sound, you hear a beep when you can't move icons any farther.

▸ *Moving an Icon to a Different Page*

If you want to move a database icon to a different page, click and drag the icon to the desired page tab until there's a white box around the tab name. Release the mouse button. The icon will appear on the selected page. This is a handy way to move icons from page to page when you want to reorganize them.

You can also hold down Ctrl+Shift and press the arrow key(s) to move the icons to the location you want. Press ↵ when the icons are positioned correctly. If you decide not to move the icons, press Esc.

▶ *Arranging Icons on a Workspace Page*

You can arrange icons into continuous rows starting at the top left of the workspace page. Make the workspace window active and select the page on which you want to arrange icons. Choose View ➤ Arrange Icons.

If the icons are already in rows with no spaces between icons, this command has no effect. If you place more icons on a page than would fit the screen, a scroll bar will appear on the right side of the window.

▶ *Removing an Icon from a Page*

You can also remove an icon from a workspace page easily. Let's say you accidentally add a database icon to a page twice. Click on the icon you want to remove and then press Delete. A dialog box appears, asking if you want to remove the selected icon from the workspace. Click on the Yes button. Notes removes the icon from the page.

 ▶▶ **N O T E**

> **Don't confuse removing an icon from the workspace with deleting a database from your computer. They are different actions and they serve different purposes. Removing an icon is simply a "housecleaning chore" and helps to keep your workspace pages uncluttered and organized (not to mention dusted and vacuumed). Deleting a database permanently erases it from your hard disk.**

▶▶ *What's Next?*

In the next chapter, we discuss viewing the contents of a database. We'll explain how you access the data that a database contains, as well as selecting specific data.

► ► **CHAPTER** **5**

Viewing
the Contents
of a Database

►► *F*AST *T*RACK

a list of the documents that are stored in a Notes database. Without a view, you wouldn't be able to access the information in the database.

you must display a view window, open a document, or click on the database icon to select it in the Workspace. After you click on the icon pull down the View menu. The views for the database are listed in the last section of the menu.

highlight the document of your choice and press ⏎. The document opens.

▶ **To close a document**   **78**

> press Esc. The active document window closes. Press Esc
> again in order to close the view. (The view window closes.)

▶ **To refresh a view**   **83**

> or to show added documents and confirm deletion of
> documents, simply press F9.

▶ **To select (checkmark) a single document**   **85**

> click to the left of its title. To select multiple documents,
> drag through the column to the left of their titles, or hold
> down the Shift key and click to the left of each title in turn.

▶ **To delete selected document(s)**   **86**

> press Delete so that you see a trash can next to each docu-
> ment you want to remove. Refresh the view by pressing
> F9, and click on OK when Notes asks whether you want
> to delete.

▶▶ **A** **_view_** is a list of the documents stored in a Notes database. Figure 5.1 shows an example of a view. Without a view, you wouldn't be able to access the information in the database. Every view is unique because it's based on the information that's contained in the documents.

When you go looking for information in a database, a view is the first element you'll see. A database always has at least one view, but it will probably have several: Each view displays documents in a different way.

FIGURE 5.1 ▶

A view lists the documents stored in a database.

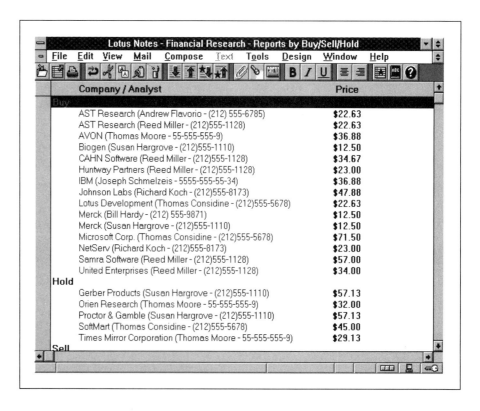

These listings are displayed on your screen according the way a designer defined them.

In this chapter, we'll discuss several topics having to do with views, including:

- What a view is
- Using a view
- Displaying a view
- What the elements of a view are
- Selecting documents in a view

▶▶ *Using a View*

A view is used for opening the documents in a database. After you get information into a Notes database, you need to be able to get information back out easily. A view allows anyone in an office, department, or division to pull out of the database the specific data they need. A view displays the information an organization has collected, and it enables individuals or a group of people working together to use the information to do their work and to make decisions based on the data.

Usually you'll use views to access documents, but you can also use views to perform the following tasks:

- Navigate to specific documents
- Find unread documents
- Select documents to act on as a group
- Delete documents
- Switch to another view
- Update the view
- Find text in any documents in the view
- Close the view window

A view's design reflects how different groups of users in an organization need to access the information. For example, account agents for an insurance company only need to view policy quotes; underwriters only need to view inspection reports; adjusters only need to view claims. Any database these individuals work with in common should contain views that reflect their individual needs. In other words, you can think of a view as a unique display of particular documents that summarizes the information in a special format for a specific group of people.

The designer of the database creates the view(s) you access. For a user, a view is the first thing he or she sees when using a database; but a designer creates a view only after creating the forms on which the documents are based. That's because the designer has to have a good idea of how the information in a database is structured before he or she can create a view. Ideally, the designer creates a view in a way that makes the information in the documents easy to access. Each row in a view refers to the value of a field or combination of fields a specific document in a database, and each column refers to a field in the document.

▶▶ *Displaying a View*

To see a list of view(s) in a database, you must display a view window, open a document, or click on the database icon to select it in the Workspace. For example, click on the Consultant Assignments database icon and then pull down the View menu. The views for the database are listed in the last section of the menu, as shown in Figure 5.2. There are two views in the database, the Consultant Directory view and the Site Locations view.

From the View menu, click on Site Locations. The Site Locations view opens, as shown in Figure 5.3.

From a view, you can select a document and open it. For example, with the Site Locations view displayed, highlight the document of your choice and press ↵. The document opens, as shown in Figure 5.4.

To close the document, press Esc. The active document window closes. Press Esc again in order to close the Site Locations view. (The view window closes.) Now pull down View menu again and select the Consultant Directory view. The view opens, displaying the list of documents shown in Figure 5.5.

FIGURE 5.2 ▶

The View menu displays two views for the Consultant Assigments database.

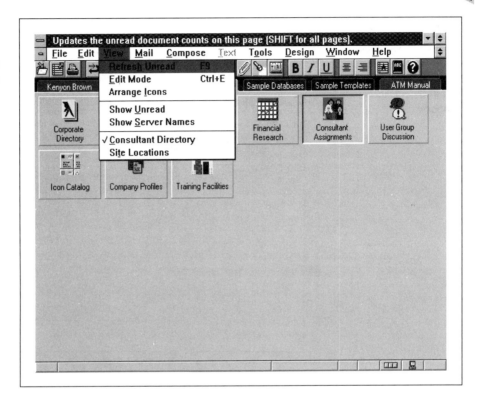

▶▶ *The Elements of a View*

A view's design should reflect how people use the information in a database. Therefore, a view can contain different elements, depending on how an organization wants the list of online documents to appear. The information displayed in a view should be organized and formatted attractively, and it should be easy to read. If you don't understand the organization of information in a view, the designer hasn't done a good job of presenting it.

A database can have many views, each of which selects, sorts, or groups the documents in the database in a specialized way. However, the basic structure of a view is the same: Each row refers to a document and each column refers to the value of a field (or combination of fields) in a document. By *value*, we mean the data in the field(s) that the documents

FIGURE 5.3 ▶

The Site Locations view displays location entry documents in the Consultant Assignments database.

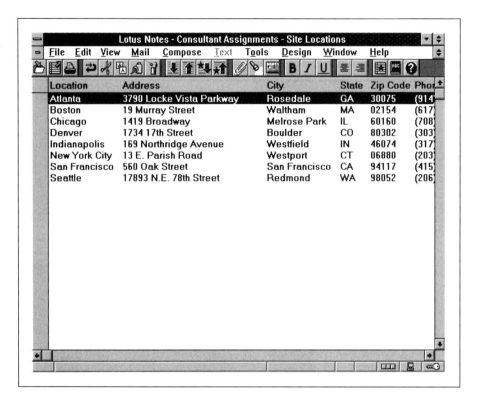

returns (displays). For example, the Location view displays seven columns:

- Location
- Address
- City
- State
- Zip Code
- Phone #
- Fax #

Each column corresponds to a field in the Consultant Directory Entry document. Each row in the list of documents displays the data in each field. As you can see, the organization of this view enables you to read quickly through the list of documents to find the information you want.

FIGURE 5.4

Highlight a document in a view and then press ↵ to open it.

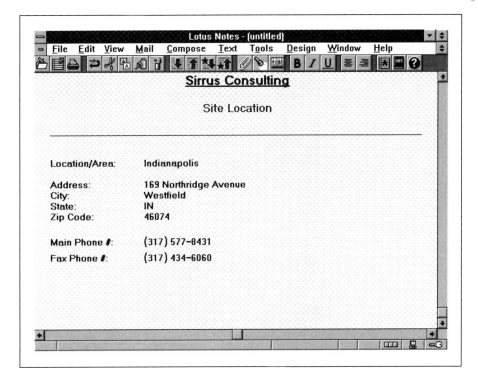

The designer defines the columns in a view by applying various attributes to the view. For example, one attribute might specify that the view's name appear in the title bar, another might designate access levels (who can look at the view), and another might format the appearance of the text in each column.

The designer also identifies which documents are displayed in the view by writing a selection formula. This formula is important because it allows the designer to select specific documents. Not all documents need to be displayed in a particular view.

▶▶ *Moving through a View*

A view can list hundreds of documents from the database. Moving through a view to locate a particular document could become tedious

FIGURE 5.5 ▶

The Consultant Directory view displays a list of documents.

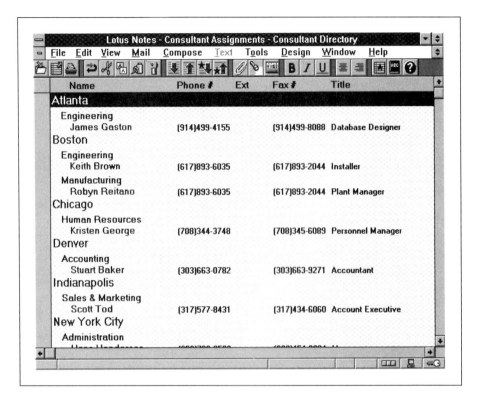

and time-consuming. However, there are several shortcuts you can use to peruse a listing.

Press	To move
Home	To the left edge
End	To the right edge
Ctrl+Home	To the top of the document
Ctrl+End	To the bottom of the document
↑ or ↓	Up/down one line
← or →	Left/right one character
Page Up/Page Down	Up/down one screen
Tab	To the next unread document
Shift+Tab	To the previous unread document

You can also scroll with a mouse to move to an approximate position within a window. Simply drag the scroll box to the position in the scroll bar corresponding to the desired location in the window. For example, to move halfway through the information, drag the scroll box halfway down the scroll bar.

To move up or down (or left/right) one line (or character) at a time, click the up or down (left or right) arrow at the ends of the scroll bar.

To move forward or backward one screen at a time, click within the scroll bar above the scroll box to move one screen backward, or below it to move one screen forward.

▶▶ *Working with Views*

Although you'll use views mostly to look up information, you're not limited to passively scrolling around a database's views. You can manipulate your views and customize them, to a degree, so that they work for you. The following sections show you some keyboard shortcuts for managing your views in Notes.

  T I P

If you prefer to use the mouse, you can also use SmartIcons for most of the actions described.

▶ *Refreshing a View*

After you make changes to a document, you'll want the view to reflect the changes. For example, you might add documents or want to delete documents, or you might revise the data within a document. However, changes don't appear automatically in a view after you make them. You have to *refresh* a view in order for the changes to appear. To "do a refresh" means to recalculate the data or confirm changes that you've made. To refresh a view, press F9.

► *Collapsing and Expanding*

Sometimes you won't want to see all the document titles that are displayed in a view at one time. As a database grows, you'll only be able to see those document titles that can fit in a window. It may be faster for you to see just the main titles in order to locate a particular document. In that case, you can *collapse* a view. Collapsing a view refers to limiting the titles that appear in the view.

If you decide you want to see all the documents at the same time, you can *expand* the view. Expanding a view refers to displaying all the document titles in a view if it's been collapsed. You can only expand a view that's been collapsed. In this way, you can display all the titles at one time.

To expand and collapse document titles in a view, you can

- Press Shift++ (Shift+plus) to expand all document titles.

- Press + (plus) to expand only the document titles under the selected document.

- Press Shift+- (Shift+minus) to collapse all document titles.

- Press - (minus) to collapse only the document titles under the selected document.

In many views, documents are grouped by category or by hierarchy. In a categorized view, documents are sorted so they appear under the category to which they've been assigned. In the Consultant Directory view you saw back in Figure 5.5, documents were categorized by location.

In a hierarchical view, you can control what level of documents you want displayed in a view at any time—all documents, only documents at a certain level, or only documents within certain categories. Sometimes you don't want to display all levels because too much would appear in the view at the same, making the screen appear cluttered and difficult to read.

For example, highlight the Location category, such as Boston, and press ↵. This action *collapses* the category (main document) so only the location name appears in the view, as shown in Figure 5.6. Press ↵ again. This action *expands* the next category, which is Title. Press ↵

FIGURE 5.6

Highlight a category in a view and press ↵ to collapse the category/ main document.

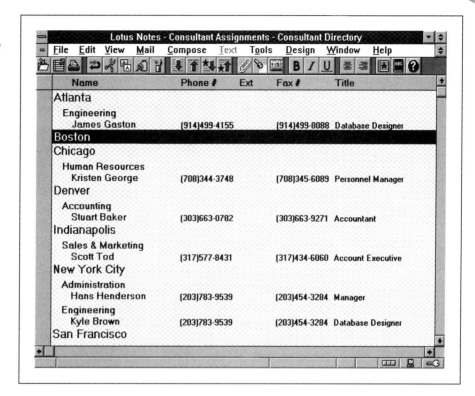

once again to expand the next category, which is the Name of a person in the directory. You can also double-click on a category instead of pressing ↵. To toggle between expanding and collapsing a category, simply double-click it or press ↵.

▶ Marking and Unmarking

A checkmark will appear next to a document when you select it in a view. "Selecting" refers to highlighting a document and then pressing the spacebar or Delete key to mark it. To select a single document, click to the left of its title or press the spacebar. To select (checkmark) multiple documents, drag through the column to the left of their titles, or click to the left of each title in turn, or hold the Shift key and press ↑ or ↓.

T I P

**If you find a document in one view and want to find it
again in a different view, select the document (highlight it in the first view), then hold the Ctrl key while
you switch to the other view. The document will be
highlighted in the second view. If the document isn't
included in the second view, you'll hear a system beep.**

Notes marks the documents you haven't opened yet with a star in the
left margin. Notes removes the star after you open the document. In
some databases, the database designer also makes unread documents
appear in colored text in a view.

You can mark documents read without opening them, and mark documents unread that you've already opened, perhaps to draw your attention to them later. To mark *all* documents in databases read or unread,
choose Tools ➤ Unread Marks ➤ Mark All Read (or Mark All Unread)
from a view, from within a document, or with one or more databases selected on your Workspace. All documents in the active or selected data-
base(s) are marked Read (or Unread).

You can also mark *selected* documents in a database as read or unread.
In a view, select the documents you want to mark read or unread. You
can select by date or select documents individually. Choose Tools ➤
Unread Marks ➤ Mark Selected Read (or Mark Selected Unread). All
selected documents are marked read or unread. To deselect the selected documents when you're done, choose Edit ➤ Deselect All.

▶ *Deleting Documents*

When you delete a document from a view, the document is permanently removed from a database. Therefore, you need to be careful
when deciding to delete any document. In order to perform a deletion,
you must be assigned the proper access in order to do this—the action
is irreversible; you can't perform an undo delete document as you can
with other undo actions. Obviously, not everyone in an organization
can delete database documents willy-nilly. Think of the havoc this
would cause an organization, since any organization depends on secure
data to help it remain successful. Your Notes Administrator has taken

precautions to limit who can delete documents from a database. Since your organization's databases are located on a server, you may be working with a copy of the database on your workstation. If you are, you may be able to remove documents from the copy you're working with. If you don't know your access level, ask your Notes Administrator.

To delete selected document(s) from a view, press Delete so that you see a trash can next to each document you want to remove. Refresh the view by pressing F9 and click on OK when Notes asks whether you want to delete.

►► *Reading Documents*

People read documents on screen primarily to find the data they need. After you open a document, you'll need to spend some time reading through a document until you locate the information you want. Documents can be long. Sometimes they are too large to display their entire contents in a window, as in Figure 5.7.

You can scroll within windows horizontally or vertically when there's more information that needs to be displayed. Simply drag the scroll box to the position in the scroll bar corresponding to the desired location in the window, or click on the arrows at the ends of the scroll bars.

To see how this works, open a document in the Consultant Directory view by selecting it and pressing ↵. A document appears, as shown in Figure 5.7. To move halfway through the information in the document window, drag the scroll box halfway down the scroll bar. Click on the arrows at the ends of the scroll bar to scroll in the direction the arrow indicates. To move forward or backward one screen at a time, click within the scroll bar above the scroll box (to move one screen back), or below it (to move one screen ahead).

Press Esc to close the document and to return to the view. Press Esc again to close the view. The Workspace appears.

FIGURE 5.7 ►

Sometimes the data contained in a document can't appear on screen at the same time, which makes the document difficult to read.

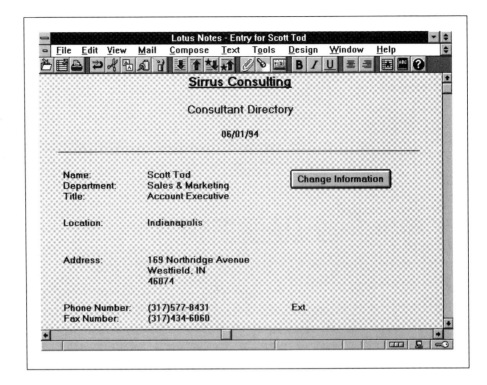

►► *What's Next?*

As you saw in this chapter, a document appears in a view once it's been created. In the next chapter, we take you through the steps of actually composing a document. A document contains the data that becomes part of a Notes database.

▶ ▶   CHAPTER **6**

Creating a
Document

▶▶ *F*AST *T*RACK

▶ **To apply a format to selected text or paragraphs** **102**

highlight the text or paragraph(s) and choose commands from the Text menu. If you specify a new *paragraph* format without selecting any text, the current paragraph (the one in which the insertion point is located) is reformatted.

▶ **To increase or decrease text size one point at a time** **103**

press F2 or choose Text ➤ Enlarge to increase text size. To reduce text one point size, press Shift+F2 or choose Shift+Text ➤ Enlarge.

▶ **To display the ruler** **105**

switch to Edit mode and then choose View ➤ Show Ruler. The ruler appears at the top of the document.

▶ **To set the alignment** **107**

switch to Edit mode. Select the text or place the insertion point within a paragraph. Choose Text ➤ Alignment and then select the desired alignment.

▶ **A button performs** **108**

Notes commands or other actions automatically. Click on a button to execute its associated action(s).

▶ **A doclink provides** **109**

direct access from one Notes document to another. Double-click on a doclink icon to open the document the doclink linked to.

►► **W**hen you're ready to create a document to add to a database, you use a form that you select from the Compose menu. As we discussed earlier, a database's designer creates forms for entering information into predefined fields. You *compose* a new document by entering information in the predefined fields of the form you've selected.

Each database will have its own unique form(s). For example, a call tracking database would use a form for logging calls and tracking their resolution. A support conference database would use a form for sharing information among members of a workgroup. A news database would use a form for entering news from different sources. These are just a few of many ways forms are used in databases. In this chapter, we show you how to create a document that's based on a form. We discuss:

- Composing a new document
- Editing a document
- Formatting a document
- Using Notes default text attributes

►► Composing a New Document

To compose a document for the Consultant Assignments database, make sure the database is selected by either opening it or clicking on its icon in your Workspace. (Of course, you can also use another database.) Pull down the Compose menu. You'll see the forms you can choose from when you want to compose a document, as shown in Figure 6.1. If a database doesn't provide any forms, "None Available" appears on the menu when you pull it down.

▶▶ **N O T E**

> Some databases, especially group schedule and calendar databases, will provide a fixed number of forms that you simply fill out. You enter information in these forms, but you don't actually compose new documents. For example, a calendar database could provide 365 forms, one for each day of the year, that a manager could use to track project schedules or employee vacations and leaves. A schedule database might provide a form for each day of the week, which displays the hours between 8:00 AM and 6:00 PM, that individuals could use to schedule their daily appointments. The designer's rationale is to make it easy for people in a workgroup, who need to keep track of appointments and schedules, to use the same form for displaying information (in these cases, scheduling information) that the group needs to constantly access and maintain. Chapter 23 features just such a database, which we explain in detail.

The Consultant Assignments database provides two forms from which you choose to create new documents: a Consultant Directory Entry form and a Site Location Entry form. You enter information in the documents by either typing or by using data created in other applications.

▶▶ **N O T E**

> Most documents display or at least store the date and time they were created and/or modified. For example, the Consultant Directory Entry form contains a Date field, which will display the current system date. Documents created locally (in databases on your hard disk) use your workstation's time. Documents created in databases that are located on servers use the server's time.

FIGURE 6.1 ▶

The Compose menu displays the list of the database's forms.

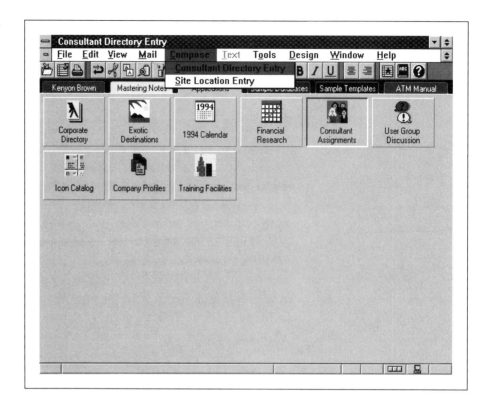

Let's compose a new document in the Consultant Assignments database. Choose the Consultant Directory Entry form from the Compose menu. The form opens, as shown in Figure 6.2. Type text into the fields of the document. You can enter text just as you would with a word processor.

 ▶▶ N O T E

Each field in a document is indicated by small angle brackets. When the brackets are red, the field is encryptable. This means the designer has provided you with a way to scramble the information in the particular field so no one can read the information except you (or another designated person). See Chapter 18 for more information on encryption and setting system security.

FIGURE 6.2 ▶

To compose a document, you select the form name from the Compose menu.

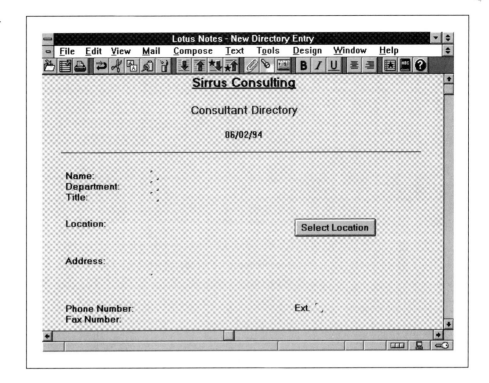

The keystrokes you'll use most often in text entry are:

To	Do this
Enter text	Type
Remove text	Backspace erases the character to the left of the insertion point. Delete erases the character to the right of the insertion point. Ctrl+Backspace erases the *word* to the left of the insertion point (except in text boxes within dialog boxes). To erase a block of text, select it, then choose Edit ▶ Clear. When a message asks for confirmation, select Yes.
Change text	Select some text, then type over it. The new text replaces the old.

To	Do this
Insert text	Move the cursor to the position where you want to insert the new text and type.
Start a new paragraph	Press ↵. The new paragraph is formatted like the old one. You can change the new paragraph's format after you press ↵ and before you start typing, or change it later.

▶▶ **T I P**

Oops! Make a mistake? Don't worry, you can reverse most actions in Notes. To undo your last text entry, command, or other action, choose Edit ➤ Undo <action>, or press Ctrl+Z. The Undo command's name depends on your last action; for example, if your last action was deleting something (except for deleting a document), the command is Edit ➤ Undo Delete. If Notes can't undo the last action, the Undo command is dimmed (unavailable).

Press Ctrl+S or choose File ➤ Save to save the document, or press Esc if you don't want to save the document. A dialog box, such as the one in Figure 6.3, will ask you if want to save your changes. Click on the No button. The document window closes and you return to either the view or the Workspace.

It's a good idea to save a document you're writing or editing every few minutes. You don't need to close the document when you save it. When you're finished, save and close the document.

▶▶ **T I P**

With the pointer anywhere in the document, double-click the right mouse button. A dialog box asks if you want to save the changes. Click on the Yes button.

FIGURE 6.3 ▶

If you don't want to save the information you've entered in a document, press Esc. When the dialog box appears, click on the No button.

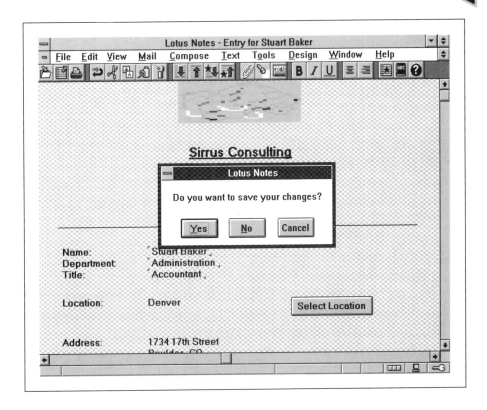

▶ SETTING YOUR OWN PERSONAL ACCESS LEVELS

Sometimes you'll want only specific people to read your documents. You may not want just anyone to access a document; the information might be personal or it could be misinterpreted by someone. Privacy is difficult to maintain in any organization. People talk; they gossip. While Notes encourages people to work together by sharing information and maintaining it in a central database, it also provides a feature that enables you to limit access to certain documents you compose or edit.

You can create a list of authorized "readers" for a document. Only the users named in your list can read the document; they must already have at least Reader access to the database. Other users may have Reader access (or better), but if they are not included in your readers list, they cannot read, edit, or even copy the document.

If the document already contains a Reader Names field that lists authorized readers, your list is combined with that list—any user named on either list can read the document. In addition, if the document contains an Author Names field that lists authorized editors for the document, all users listed in that field automatically receive reader access to your document.

It's very easy to create a list of authorized readers. Choose Edit▶ Security▶Read Access and fill in the Read Access Control dialog box. That's all there is to it. For example, if the document you're composing or editing contains an Author Names field, you can create a list of "authors" for the document by storing their user names in this field.

Any user who has at least Author access to the database and who is named in this field can edit the document (even if the person didn't create it). Any user who is excluded from this field cannot edit the document, regardless of his or her access level.

In the document, the field might not be titled "Author Names," it might have a title like "Author" or "From." When you're creating a document, you can usually tell whether a field is an Author Names field if:

> ➤ The field contains one or more user names.

> ➤ The field's title indicates that this is an Author Names field.

> ➤ The field's help description (above the Status Bar) indicates that this is an Author Names field.

If the document already exists, you can tell if a field is an Author Names field by viewing the document in read mode or clicking the field and holding it. If a box appears, displaying one or more user names, this is an Author Names field. Anyone who can edit the document can modify the list of names in the Author Names field. To remove a name from the list, just delete it. To add a name to the list, just type it in. Be sure to use the same separator used in the rest of the list. For example, if the list displays names separated with semicolons, be sure to use a semicolon as the separator when you add a name.

▶▶ *Editing a Document*

Editing means adding, deleting, or replacing text, and specifying text attributes. Although a database designer creates and formats the form on which a document is based, you can still change various text attributes. Text attributes include font, size, special emphasis (like bold and italics), and color. When you specify text attributes, keep these points in mind:

- You can format text and paragraphs only in Rich Text fields. A Rich Text field is a special kind of field that can contain formatted data, graphics, and objects. (We discuss the differences between Rich Text and Plain Text fields in Chapter 12.) Text menu commands are unavailable when you write or edit any other type of field.

- A document must be in Edit mode in order to change it in any way. To put a document in Edit mode, choose Edit ➤ Edit Document or press Ctrl+E. This command is a toggle—choose it again to turn off Edit mode.

►► N O T E

If you're composing a document, it's already in
Edit mode.

►► Formatting a Document

In Notes, you have an abundance of tools for improving the appearance of your documents. You can format paragraphs by specifying attributes such as margins, tab stops, interline and interparagraph spacing, and alignment (justification). You can format text by choosing different typefaces, font sizes, or text attributes. Whether you are formatting text or paragraphs, your document must be in Edit mode.

To apply a format to selected text, just choose the appropriate command from the Text menu. You can also specify a format without first selecting any text. If you specify a new *paragraph* format without selecting any text, the current paragraph (the one in which the insertion point is located) is reformatted. However, if you select a new *text* format without selecting any text, no existing text is reformatted, but subsequent text that you type has the new attributes.

 ►► N O T E

You can format text and paragraphs in Rich Text fields
only. Many fields in Notes are plain text. For example,
the To field in a Notes mail memo and the Subject field
in most discussion documents are Plain Text fields. The
Text Font command is dimmed when your pointer is in
a Plain Text field.

► Formatting Text

The default text font in Notes is 10-point Helvetica, plain and black. (A font, such as Helvetica, Geneva, or Times Roman, is a set of characters distinguished by their shapes, and a size is a measurement in points of the height of the characters.) Default character spacing is proportional. If you like the appearance of the default text formats, feel free to leave them as they are; but if you want to change text formats, you have several options.

The simplest is to select commands from the Text menu. You can also choose Text ➤ Font to bring up the Font dialog box, as shown in Figure 6.4. You can use this Font dialog box to review or change text attributes such as font, size, color, and special attributes like bold, underline, and superscript.

The Font Name & Size list box displays all the fonts and point sizes available to you. Select the typeface and type size that you want from the lists; or type a size into the Size box. Display Fonts displays only the typefaces and sizes available for your type of display in the Font Name and Size list boxes (this is the default). Printer Fonts displays only the typefaces and sizes available for the printer you selected.

 ▶▶ **T I P**

To increase text size one point at a time, highlight the text and press F2 or choose Text ➤ Enlarge. To reduce text one point size, press Shift+F2 or choose Shift+Text ➤ Enlarge. For example, if text is in 10-point Helvetica, selecting Enlarge changes it to 12-point if that's the next available size.

FIGURE 6.4

The Font dialog box lets you choose different typefaces and point sizes, select attributes, and apply colors to text.

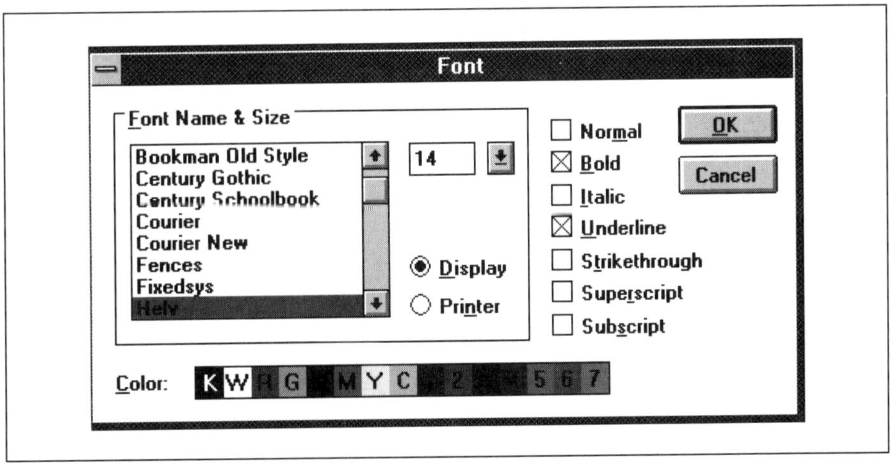

Font
Font Name & Size
Bookman Old Style   14
Century Gothic
Century Schoolbook
Courier
Courier New
Fences
Fixedsys
Helv

- ⦿ Display
- ○ Printer

- ☐ Normal
- ☒ Bold
- ☐ Italic
- ☒ Underline
- ☐ Strikethrough
- ☐ Superscript
- ☐ Subscript

OK
Cancel

Color: K W R G B M Y C 2 5 6 7

You can select other text attributes, such as bold, strikethrough, or superscript, by clicking in the box to the side of the option you want. You can also use a different text color by clicking on the color you want.

When you finish selecting attributes, click on OK to accept the changes.

▶ *Formatting Paragraphs*

As with text formats, you can either accept the default paragraph formats or change them to suit your needs. To change such paragraph attributes as margins, tab stops, and interline and interparagraph spacing, choose Text ▶ Paragraph. You'll see the Text Paragraph dialog box that appears in Figure 6.5. You can apply the attributes from this dialog to paragraphs you've already selected, or you can select attributes at any point and the paragraph that contains the insertion point will take on the attributes you specified.

The default formats are:

- **Indents, tab stops, headers and footers:** Every 0.5 inch, although these do not appear in the Tabs box or on the ruler

- **Alignment:** Left

- **Line spacing:** Single

- **Paragraph spacing:** Single line

FIGURE 6.5 ▶

The Text Paragraph dialog box lets you change the paragraph settings for margins, tabs, and other attributes.

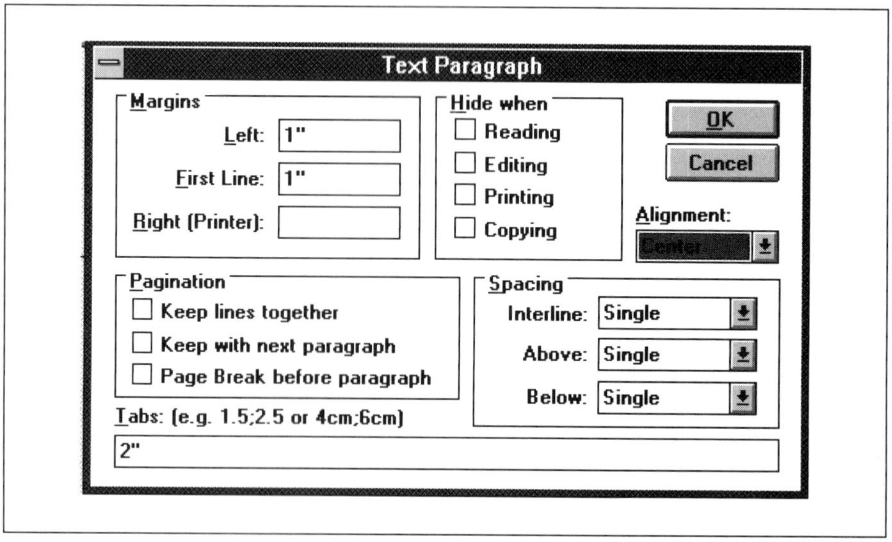

You can also change the following default settings by choosing and displaying the Page Setup dialog box shown in Figure 6.6:

- **Paper size:** Specified by your print driver
- **Margins:** 1-inch top and bottom; 1-inch left and right
- **Header position:** 0.5 inch from top
- **Footer position:** 0.5 inch from bottom
- Start page numbers at 1

FIGURE 6.6

The Page Setup dialog box lets you change the default settings for a page.

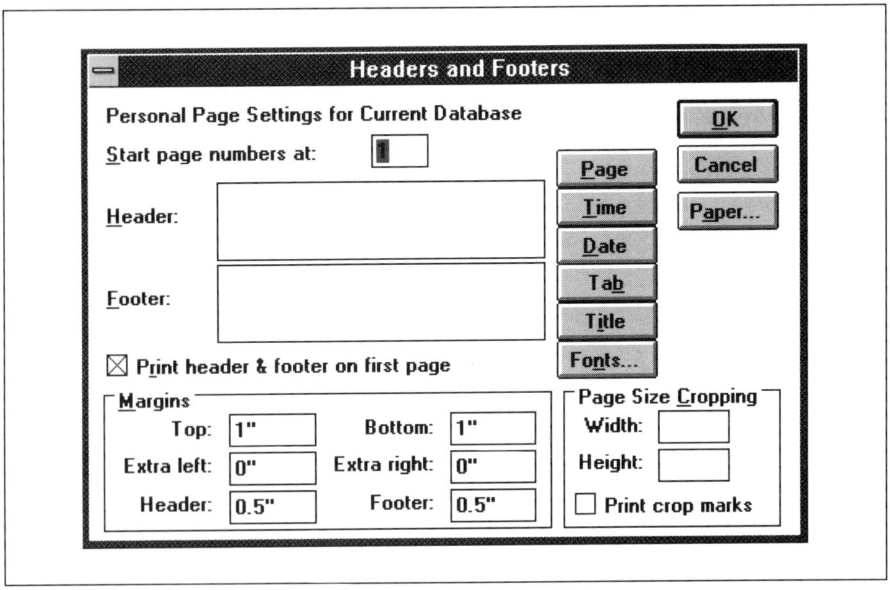

Headers and Footers		
Personal Page Settings for Current Database		

Start page numbers at: [1]   [**Page**] [**OK**]
[**Time**] [**Cancel**]
Header: [ ]   [**Date**] [**Paper...**]
[**Tab**]
Footer: [ ]   [**Title**]
☒ Print header & footer on first page   [**Fonts...**]

Margins
Top: [1"]   Bottom: [1"]   Width: [ ]
Extra left: [0"]   Extra right: [0"]   Height: [ ]
Header: [0.5"]   Footer: [0.5"]   ☐ Print crop marks

Page Size Cropping

Changing Tabs and Margins Using the Ruler

To display the ruler, switch to Edit mode and then choose View ➤ Show Ruler. The ruler appears at the top of the document, as shown in Figure 6.7. You can also bring up the ruler by clicking on the Smart-Icon that shows a small picture of a ruler.

When you open a new document, the position and number of markers on the ruler depend on the settings specified by the database designer in the form used to create the document. If no settings were specified,

FIGURE 6.7 ▶

Display the ruler when you want to change a document's margins and tabs.

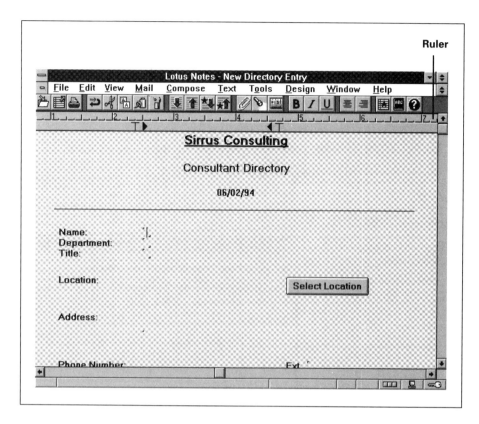

the default left margin is 1 inch and there are default tab stops every 0.5 inch. You can override any default margin and tab settings.

If you're using a color monitor, black arrows determine the tab stops. Click the ruler where you want a tab stop. To remove a tab stop, click the arrow on the ruler.

  TIP

> **To remove all tab stops from one or more paragraphs, select the paragraphs, then add a single new tab stop and then remove it. All tab stops will be removed.**

Indenting and Outdenting Paragraphs Using the Keyboard

When you indent or outdent a paragraph, you are changing its left margin relative to the left margin of the rest of the document. You can use keyboard shortcuts to adjust paragraph indents and outdents in $1/4$-inch increments; each additional indent or outdent moves the paragraph another $1/4$ inch in the appropriate direction.

To indent only the first line of a paragraph, place the insertion point anywhere in the line, then press F7. Subsequent lines in the paragraph wrap to the left margin.

To indent an entire paragraph, place the insertion point anywhere in the paragraph, then press F8. This indents every line in the paragraph.

To outdent the first line of a paragraph, press Shift+F7 anywhere on that line. All subsequent lines in the paragraph will wrap to the normal left margin. To outdent an entire paragraph, press Shift+F8 anywhere in the paragraph. Every line in the paragraph will be outdented.

You can create a hanging indent, often used for bullets or numbered list items. Press Shift+F7, then press F8. Type the number or bullet, press Tab, and type the text for the item.

Setting Alignment (Justifying Text)

Alignment (justification) is the position of text relative to the left or right edges of a window on your screen or of a printed page. For example, this paragraph is left-aligned. To set the alignment, switch to Edit mode. Select the text or place the insertion point within a paragraph. Choose Text ➤ Alignment and then choose one of the following:

- **Left** to align text on the left margin (the default)
- **Right** to align text on the right margin
- **Center** to center each line of text
- **Full** to align on both left and right margins
- **None** to turn off word wrapping and display the paragraph as one line

▶▶ *Activating Buttons and Doclinks*

Buttons and doclinks are graphical elements you insert in Notes documents for executing commands or automating tasks. Each element is suited for performing specific actions. We discuss them in greater detail in Chapter 11, but we wanted to introduce them here since you can add them to documents.

▶ *Adding a Button to a Document*

Buttons automatically execute Notes commands or perform other actions. You use the mouse to click on a button to execute its associated action(s). Clicking on buttons should be familiar to you because you find them in almost every Windows application.

> **Buttons are a new feature in Lotus Notes version 3.X. Earlier versions of Notes can't interpret buttons. For instance, if you're using version 2.X and try to open a document or form that includes buttons you created in version 3.X, Notes will warn you the buttons are a feature that can't be displayed. You won't see them.**

You can add a button to a form or a document. If you add one to a form, every document that's created with the form will include a button on it. (We discuss adding a button to a form in Chapter 11.) When you add a button to a document, only that particular document will display the button. To create a button, follow these steps:

1. Open the document where you want the button to appear.

2. Place the insertion point in the desired location on the document.

3. Choose Edit ➤ Insert ➤ Button. The Insert Button dialog box appears.

4. Enter the text in the Button text box that you want displayed on the button.

5. Change the word wrap dimensions or leave the text box empty. (The default dimensions will be used automatically if you leave the box blank.)

6. Enter a formula in the Formula box. The formula defines the command or macro that's executed when you activate the button.

7. Click on OK.

▶ Creating Doclinks

Doclinks are handy to use because they enable you to relate documents between databases. They provide direct access from one Notes document to another, and the documents don't have to be part of the same database. They don't even have to be located on the same server or workstation. You create doclinks when one document depends on information that may change in another document. For example, you can make doclinks when you want one document to refer to another document that's very large, such as a Sales Account Profile. You could also make doclinks when you want one document to refer to another document that's used infrequently. An example might be an IRS warning or a Wall Street article on a company that's featured in the same Sales Account Profile that we mentioned above.

You need to always keep in mind when you create doclinks that they are "hardwired" to a specific name of a database. If the file name of a database is changed or if the database is deleted, you will need to either recreate the doclink or remove it from the document. To create a doclink, follow these steps:

1. Open the document that you want the doclink to go to. You can also select the document in a view.

2. Choose Edit ➤ Make Doclink. This places the doclink on the Clipboard.

3. Open the document where you want the doclink to appear.

4. Place the insertion point where you want the doclink icon to be located.

5. Choose Edit ➤ Paste or press Ctrl+V. The icon will appear, as shown in Figure 6.8.

FIGURE 6.8 ▶

A doclink enables you to access one document from another.

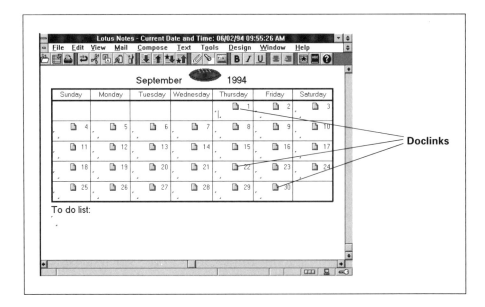

You use the mouse to double-click on a doclink icon, which opens the related document for you to use. You can also position the cursor on the doclink or button while in Edit mode and press spacebar.

 ▶▶ **TIP**

You can activate buttons or doclinks from the keyboard even when you're not in Edit mode. Just press the spacebar. If you are in Edit mode, press Ctrl+E or the spacebar to toggle to read-only mode.

▶▶ *What's Next?*

In the next chapter, we'll discuss printing documents and views in Notes. There will be times when you'll need a hard copy of data in a particular database. You'll also discover that reading a printout of information is easier than reading it on a monitor.

► ► CHAPTER **7**

Printing Views
and Documents

▶▶ *F*AST *T*RACK

▶ **To specify a page layout**   **120**

    for documents and views in the current database, choose
File ➤ Page Setup. The Headers and Footers dialog box
appears. Choose the desired options. Click on OK when
you're satisfied with your settings, or Cancel if you change
your mind.

▶ **To see page breaks**   **123**

    open the document. Choose View ➤ Show Page Breaks.
This command is a toggle. To exit Preview mode (deselect
Show Page Breaks), choose View ➤ Show Page Breaks
again, or close the document by pressing Esc.

▶ **To specify the type of paper**   **123**

    you want to use to print your document, choose File ➤
Page Setup. Click on the Paper button. The Page Setup -
Paper Source dialog box appears. Select Paper and then
select the Manual Feed, Auto Sheet Feeder, or Tractor
option for First Page and for Other Page. If necessary,
select Reset to revert to the original settings. Click
on OK, or Cancel if you change your mind.

▶▶ **S**ometimes you might want to print a view's listing of documents in a database, because a piece of paper is easier to refer to than a screenful of text. Sometimes you might need printouts of particular documents because a situation calls for you to refer to the information and you can't access the database easily. Sometimes you might just get tired of reading information on your computer's screen.

Whatever your reasons, Notes lets you print an open or selected view, part of a view, an open document, or document(s) you select in a view. In this chapter, you'll learn all the ins and outs of printing with Notes, including:

- Selecting what you want to print
- Printing documents
- Printing views
- Choosing settings for your printer
- Choosing page setup options

▶▶ Printing Documents

Printing a document means printing a selected document from a view or printing the entire contents of an open document. To print a document from a view, follow these steps:

1. Open a view.

2. Highlight the document and then press the spacebar to select it. A checkmark will appear to the left of the document title. You can select one or more documents at a time.

3. Choose File ➤ Print or press Ctrl+P. The File Print dialog box appears, as shown in Figure 7.1.

4. Enter the number of copies you want to print or accept the default number, which is 1.

5. Select a Page Range option:

- All prints all the pages in the document (the default)
- From/To prints the range of pages you specify in the text boxes

6. Select the Print Selected Documents option.

7. You don't have to type a To (last) page. If you leave this box blank, Notes prints all remaining pages in the document, starting with the From page.

8. If you want, select Draft Quality to print a draft-quality version of your document (not available on all printers). Draft quality prints faster on most printers, but with reduced print quality.

9. Click on Setup if you need to specify additional printer options, such as paper source, paper size, and paper orientation.

10. Click on OK.

FIGURE 7.1

The File Print dialog box allows you to print a selected document directly from a view.

File Print
Copies: 1
Page Range
⦿ All
○ From: To:
OK
Cancel
Setup...
Printer: Panasonic KX-P1124 on LPT1:
☐ Draft Quality
⦿ Print View   Form Override...
○ Print Selected Documents
Document Separation:
☐ Reset Page Numbers

The following options also apply when you print a selected document from a view:

Page Break	Each document starts on a new page.
Extra Line	An extra blank line is inserted between documents, and page numbering is continuous.
No Separation	One document follows another without a separator, and page numbering is continuous.
Form Override	Displays the Print Form Override dialog box, where you can print a document using a form other than the one used to compose the document. This advanced option is used when the database designer has created a form or a set of forms specially designed for printing reports, as opposed to reading or editing documents.
Reset Page Numbers	Numbers the first page of each document as page 1 or as specified with Page Setup and prints the headers and footers on every page. Available only when you select Page Break as the document separator.

You print an open document in the same manner as you print from a view. All you do is display a view, select a document, and press ↵ to open it. With the contents of a document displayed, choose File ➤ Print. The File Print dialog box appears. As you can see, it looks different from the File Print dialog box that appears when you want to print a document from a view. However, you can follow the same procedures as above.

▶▶ *Printing Full and Partial Views*

Printing a view means either printing all the document titles that you see on the screen when you display a view (a full view), or printing selected document titles in the view (a partial view). To print a full view, follow these steps:

1. Display a view.

2. Choose File ➤ Print. The File Print dialog box appears.

3. Select any, all, or none of the following options: Copies, Page Range, Draft Quality, and Setup. These are the same options for printing an open document that we described above.

4. Select Print View. This option prints the entire list of documents in the view (not their contents, just the list as it appears in the view).

5. Click on OK.

To print the names of some rather than all the documents in the view, follow these steps:

1. Open a view.

2. Highlight a document title and then press the spacebar to mark it. A checkmark appears to the left of the document name. You can mark as many document titles as you like to appear in the printout.

3. Choose File ➤ Print. The File Print dialog box appears.

4. Select the Print View option.

5. Click on OK.

Only the names of the documents you selected will appear in the printout.

▶▶ *Choosing Printer Settings*

You can specify printer settings, such as how many copies to make, which paper source to use, paper size, and print orientation.

▶▶ **N O T E**

Printer settings may vary for different types of printers.

Choose File ➤ Print Setup. The Printer Settings dialog box appears, as shown in Figure 7.2. This dialog box displays a list of the printers you (or the Notes Administrator) specified when setting up Notes on your workstation, or that you installed using the Windows Control Panel.

FIGURE 7.2 ▶

The Printer Settings dialog box lets you specify settings, such as how many copies to print, orientation, and so on.

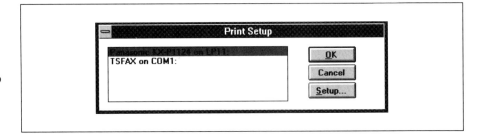

Select the printer you want to use. If you want to check or change specifications for using this printer, choose Setup. The Printer Settings dialog box is displayed. Click on OK, or Cancel if you change your mind.

▶▶ *Choosing Page Setup Options*

You can specify page layouts for documents and views for the current database. Options include headers and footers, page numbering, margin settings, page cropping, and special page source specifications.

Choose File ➤ Page Setup. The Page Setup dialog box appears, as shown in Figure 7.3. Options set in this dialog box remain in effect until you change them.

FIGURE 7.3

The Page Setup dialog box lets you specify page layouts for documents and views in the selected database.

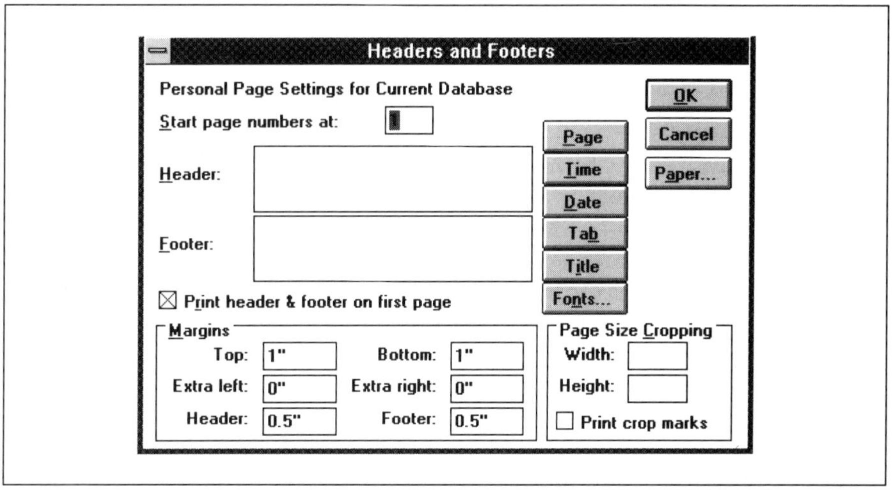

Headers and Footers
Personal Page Settings for Current Database
<u>S</u>tart page numbers at: [ ]
Header: [ ]
Footer: [ ]
☒ P<u>r</u>int header & footer on first page

Buttons: <u>P</u>age, <u>T</u>ime, <u>D</u>ate, Ta<u>b</u>, T<u>i</u>tle, Fo<u>n</u>ts..., <u>O</u>K, Cancel, Pa<u>p</u>er...

Margins
Top: [1"] Bottom: [1"]
Extra left: [0"] Extra right: [0"]
Header: [0.5"] Footer: [0.5"]

Page Size <u>C</u>ropping
Width: [ ]
Height: [ ]
☐ Print crop marks

Select the page setup options you want:

Start page numbers at	Lets you use a page number other than 1 for the first page. Type the number you want to start with into the text box. Pages are numbered sequentially, starting with the number you specify.
Header and Footer	Lets you create headers and footers for your printouts. You can type in text or choose from the Page, Time, Date, Tab, Title, and Fonts options. See Help on the Edit Headers/Footer dialog box to learn about these options.
Print header & footer on first page	Prints the header and/or footer on the first page; otherwise they begin printing on the second page. This is useful when the first page is a cover page or other special page.

Margins	The margins are the top, bottom, right, and left edges of the page (which is the printing area, not the paper size). If you specify a page size, Notes calculates the printing area based on the page size and your margin settings.
Page Size Cropping	Lets you reduce the size of the printing area of the paper. Type the width and height of the area you want into the Width and Height text boxes. This area is measured from the upper left corner. Tell Notes the size of the paper in your printer in the Printer Settings dialog box. See "Choosing Printer Settings" above.
Print crop marks	Prints page boundary indicators in the lower right corner of each page that show the edges of the image. This is useful when you're sending documents to your organization's print service.

Click on OK when you're satisfied with your settings, or Cancel if you change your mind.

 ▶▶ **N O T E**

You can fine-tune the defined print area by changing the page size settings and adjusting the margins as well as the cropping area. Experiment to find the appropriate settings for your needs.

▶▶ *Adding Page Breaks*

When you print a document, it usually looks somewhat different from what you see on the screen. To see where lines will wrap and pages will "break" in the printed version, you can enter Preview mode. If you see things you don't like in the preview, you can easily revise the document without printing it first.

To enter Preview mode, open the document and choose View ➤ Show Page Breaks. You should now be able to see where the lines wrap, and you can also see the page breaks, which are indicated by a solid line across the screen. To exit Preview mode, choose View ➤ Show Page Breaks again, or close the document by pressing Esc.

 ▶▶ **T I P**

To force text onto the next page, try these paragraph attributes in the Text Paragraph dialog box: keep lines together, keep text with next paragraph, and page break before paragraph.

▶▶ *Selecting the Type of Paper*

You can specify the type of paper you want to use to print your document. Choose File ➤ Page Setup. The Page Setup - Paper Source dialog box appears, as shown in Figure 7.4.

FIGURE 7.4

The Page Setup - Paper Source dialog box lets you choose the source of paper used for printing.

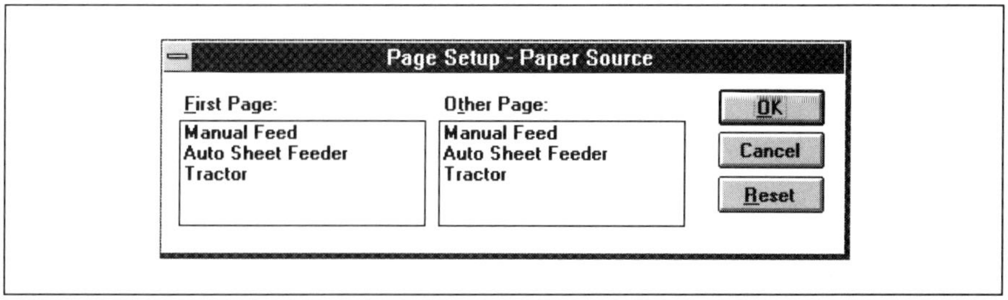

Page Setup - Paper Source		
First Page:	**Other Page:**	OK
Manual Feed	Manual Feed	Cancel
Auto Sheet Feeder	Auto Sheet Feeder	Reset
Tractor	Tractor	

Select Paper and then select one of these options for First Page and for Other Page:

Manual Feed	Pulls paper from the printer's manual input slot. If no paper is loaded, displays a message and waits for you to insert pages in the printer's manual input slot.
Upper Tray	Uses paper loaded in the printer's upper tray.

If necessary, select Reset to revert to the original settings. Click on OK to accept the settings, or click on Cancel if you change your mind.

▶▶ *What's Next?*

In the next chapter, we discuss using Notes Mail, which is a powerful e-mail system that's fully integrated with Notes databases. You can use Notes Mail just like you would any other e-mail system. The major difference between Notes and other e-mail systems is that Notes Mail *is* a database application that provides you with unique communication features to support workflow throughout an organization.

▶ ▶ **CHAPTER 8**

Importing and Exporting Data

▶▶ *F*AST *T*RACK

▶ **To import a word processing file into a Notes document**   **131**

open the document you're importing into and choose Edit
➤ Edit Document, or press Ctrl+E. Place the insertion
point in a rich text field where you want the imported file
to begin. Choose File ➤ Import. Select the file type (the
default is ASCII), drive, and directory. Enter the name of
the file you're importing. Select Import to start importing.

▶ **To import a graphic files into Notes document**   **135**

highlight the document in a view. Choose Edit ➤ Edit
Document (or press Ctrl+E) to open the document in edit
mode. You can also choose Compose ➤ <Form Name> to
create a new document to hold the imported graphic.
Place the insertion point in a rich text field where you
want the imported file to begin. Choose File ➤ Import.
Enter the name of the file you want to import, and its file
type and location. Click on Import.

▶ **To import a spreadsheet file into Notes document**   **137**

select a document in a view. Choose Edit ➤ Edit Document (or Ctrl+E). Place the insertion point in a rich text
field where you want the imported file to begin. Choose
File ➤ Import. Select the file you want to import, and select 123 Worksheet as the file type. When you click on Import, the 123/Symphony Worksheet Import dialog box
appears. You can import either all the data in the worksheet file, or just the data in a named range. Select the desired option. Click on OK to perform the import.

▶ ***To export a Notes document to a word processing file*** **145**

open the document you want to export. Choose File ➤ Export. Select a file type under Save File as Type. Select a drive under Drives, if necessary. Open the directory you want in the Directories box by double-clicking it. Type the file name into the File Name box, or type the complete path and file name into the File Name box. To export to an existing file, select the file's name from the list or type its file name and path into the text box. Notes asks if you want to overwrite the existing file or append the export material to it. Click on Export to perform the export.

▶ ***To export graphics to picture files*** **146**

open the document and select the graphic. Choose File ➤ Export. Select a file type from the Save File as Type list box. To export the picture into an existing file, select the file from the list of file names. The file name appears in the text box. To export the picture into a new file, type the file name into the text box. The file is created in the selected directory. Click on Export to perform the export.

▶ ***To export a view to a 1-2-3 file format*** **147**

open the view you want to export. The entire view will be exported unless you select specific documents for export. Choose File ➤ Export. Select the 123 Worksheet option in the Save File as Type list box. To export the view into an existing spreadsheet file, select the file from the list of file names. To export the view into a new spreadsheet file, type the file name into the text box. The file is created in the selected directory. Click on the Export button. Specify which documents you want to export. Click on OK to perform the export.

► ► **N**otes supports a wide variety of file formats for importing and exporting data to and from other applications. By importing data into Notes, you can increase a database's value by integrating information from a variety of outside sources without having to enter it manually. Conversely, exporting data from Notes can aid you in making presentations and writing reports that rely on the information from a database. This chapter shows you how to import and export information, and discusses the following topics:

- Importing different file formats into documents and views
- Exporting documents and views to different file formats
- Using rich text format

► ► *Importing Data*

Importing means converting non-Notes data into a form that can be used in a Notes document or view. Importing and exporting map one document or view format onto another, so before you start importing or exporting on a large scale, you may want to review Chapters 14 and 15 on Notes form and view design, respectively.

You can import word processing, graphics, spreadsheets, and ASCII text files into Notes documents. Similarly, you can import spreadsheets and ASCII text files into Notes views.

 ► ► **N O T E**

You cannot import executable files—that's any file with the .EXE extension.

In general, to import data into a Notes database, you follow these steps:

1. Open the view or document you're importing into.

2. Choose File ➤ Import. The Import dialog box appears, as shown in Figure 8.1.

3. Select a file type under List Files of Type. For example, you could select a 1-2-3 worksheet. The items on the list depend on whether you're importing into a view or into a document. If you're importing into a document, the default file type is Structured Text. If you're importing into a view, the default is Structured Text. Be sure to change the default to match the file you're importing. In particular, be sure *not* to select ASCII Text for non-ASCII files. When you select a file type, Notes displays only those file names in the File Name list box that end with the extension corresponding to the file type. For example, when you choose a 1-2-3 worksheet, only files with spreadsheet extensions are displayed.

4. Select a drive under Drives, then open the directory you want in the Directories box by double-clicking it.

5. Do one of the following:

   - Select a file from the File Name list box. The File Name list box displays all files of the file type you selected that are stored in the directory that you selected. When you select a

FIGURE 8.1 ▶

The Import dialog box enables you to specify settings for importing many different file formats into Notes.

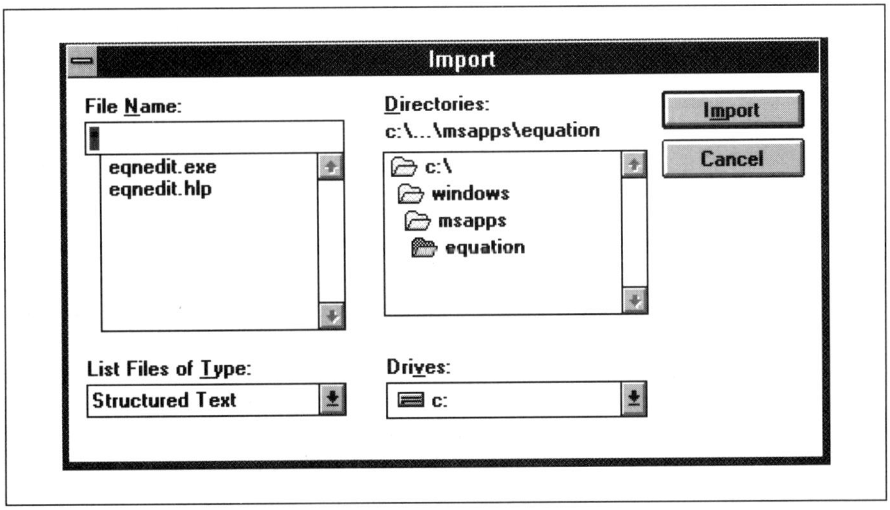

file, Notes displays its last modification date and time, as well as its size, at the bottom of the dialog box.

- To select several files in a row, select a file at one end of the group, then press Shift and select the file at the other end. Both of these files, and all files between them, will be selected.

- If you know the exact name and location of the file you want, you can skip the steps above and just type the file and path into the File Name text box—for example, type **c:\123w\sample\sales.wk3**.

6. Click on Import to perform the import.

▶ Using Rich Text as an Intermediate File Format

When you import data into Notes from other applications, more than likely it will include formatting attributes such as boldface, italics, and different fonts. Notes allows you to retain many formatting attributes because it uses Microsoft Rich Text Format (RTF) as an intermediate file format for importing and exporting files. As we've discussed previously, a Notes document *is* a rich text field that can contain formatted data, graphics, and objects, as well as other rich text fields. This enables a Notes database to import (and export) data in rich text format. (See Chapter 11 for more information on rich text fields.)

For example, when you import a WordPerfect file, Notes calls the MasterSoft® libraries to translate the file to an RTF file, and then imports this RTF file into Notes. Similarly, when you export from Notes to Lotus Manuscript format, Notes outputs an RTF file and then calls the appropriate MasterSoft libraries to convert it to the Manuscript file format.

For importing and exporting, Notes uses version 1 of the Rich Text Format standard, the same version used in Microsoft Word for Windows 1.0. RTF version 1 supports tables, fields, annotations, and other features of high-end word processors.

You might wonder what happens to certain features of word processing files that Notes translates using an intermediate RTF file. The Windows ANSI, Macintosh, IBM PC, and IBM 850 character sets are fully supported for import. When exporting, Notes uses the IBM 850 character set.

When importing, Notes maps each font to one of the three basic Notes fonts. For documents that support changeable fonts, serif fonts are mapped to Times Roman, sans-serif fonts to Helvetica, and fixed-pitch fonts are mapped to Courier. Other fonts default to Helvetica. On the PC, the three basic Notes fonts are Helvetica, Times Roman, and Courier. Roman is mapped to Tms Rmn, and Modern is mapped to Courier. Other fonts are mapped to Helv.

The character attributes of bold, italic, and strikethrough are fully supported. Small caps, caps, and shadow attributes are imported as bold text. Outline is imported as italic, and any hidden text is imported as plain text. Notes has only one kind of underline, so continuous, dotted, and word underlining all import as underlined text. Superscripts and subscripts are supported.

Font sizes and colors are imported correctly. Each color is mapped to the closest Notes color—that is, black, white, red, green, blue, cyan, magenta, and yellow. The dark versions of these colors don't import or export.

In Notes, paragraph left, first line indents, and tabs are relative to the left edge of the page, whereas in word processing packages they are relative to the document margins. When Notes imports, it calculates the left margin of a paragraph by adding the document left margin to the paragraph indent. When exporting, Notes checks all paragraphs and sets the document left margin to be equal to the left margin of the leftmost paragraph.

For example, if you import a paragraph with a 0″ left margin and a .5″ tab setting, the document under Notes will have a 1″ left margin and a 1.5″ tab. To set the right margin when importing and exporting, Notes wordwraps appropriately, depending on the window size. The printer right margin is set to 7.5″ in the Text Paragraph dialog box.

Notes also imports left, right, full, and center justification. It converts all line spacing into 1, $1\frac{1}{2}$, and 2 lines.

A section break is imported when the section is also a page break. Otherwise a section break is imported as a paragraph break.

Notes doesn't import or export header or footer information into Notes headers and footers. Instead, header or footer text is inserted into the body of the document at the position in the document where the control code for header or footer exists in the original document.

▶▶ **N O T E**

Notes doesn't translate revision marks, style sheets, footnotes, annotations, expanded or compressed text, or bookmarks.

▶ *Importing Word Processing Files into Documents*

You can import word processing files that have been created using:

- Lotus AmiPro
- Lotus Manuscript
- IBM DisplayWrite (DCA format)
- Microsoft Rich Text Format (RTF)
- Borland Multimate
- WordPerfect
- MicroPro WordStar

▶▶ **N O T E**

Lotus AmiPro, DisplayWrite DCA, MultiMate, WordStar 5.0, and Manuscript support line spacing. Lotus AmiPro, DisplayWrite DCA, and MultiMate also support enlarged text.

To import a word processing file into a Notes document, follow these steps:

1. Open the document you're importing into and choose Edit ➤ Edit Document or Ctrl+E.

▶▶ **N O T E**

If you place the insertion point in a field that isn't rich text, the Import command on the File menu will be dimmed and unavailable.

2. Place the insertion point in a rich text field where you want the imported file to begin.

3. Choose File ➤ Import. The Import dialog box appears. Select the file type (the default is ASCII), drive, and directory.

4. Enter the name of the file you're importing.

5. Select Import to start importing.

▶ Importing Graphic Files into Documents

Each picture must be imported into Notes (and exported from Notes) as a separate entity; also, Notes can't import a picture that is embedded in a text file, such as a .PIC file in a WordPerfect document. (The same is true for export.) If a file contains more than one picture, only the first picture is imported.

Notes supports the following graphics file formats for import (see the product documentation for specific information on these file types):

- Lotus 1-2-3 and Symphony .PIC Files (graphs).

- American National Standards Institute (ANSI) Metafiles (.CGM), which are graphic objects represented by their positions on a two-dimensional grid. The objects can be text, linear, or closed, and can have attributes such as a specified line thickness or font. Metafiles can be imported from applications such as Lotus Freelance Graphics, Lotus 1-2-3 Release 3.X, and Lotus Graphwriter.

- Tagged Image Format Files (TIFF), such as scanned bitmap images of photographs and other artwork. The image must be transferred by software that supports the TIFF format. (TIFF files must use the CCITT 3D compression scheme.)

- PCX files that are generated by various software packages.

To import a graphic files into Notes document, follow these steps:

1. Highlight the document in a view.

2. Choose Edit ➤ Edit Document (or press Ctrl+E) to open the document in Edit mode. You can also choose Compose ➤ <Form Name> to create a new document to hold the imported graphic.

3. Place the insertion point in a rich text field where you want the imported file to begin.

4. Choose File ➤ Import. The Import dialog box appears, where you enter the name of the file you want to import, and its file type and location.

5. Click on Import.

 ▶▶ **T I P**

> **When importing scanned images, save scanned images in PCX or TIFF format for import into Notes. Then follow the usual Import procedure, making sure to choose PCX Image or TIFF 5.0 Image format. If you're not satisfied with the appearance of your scanned images, try adjusting the dpi (dots per inch) setting or the image size setting in your scanner software, if that's possible. Start with 75 dpi and 100% size, increasing the dpi and de-creasing the size until you're satisfied with the results. In general, higher dpi settings result in larger images in Notes. Remember that different monitors may display the scanned image differently.**

▶ *Improving the Appearance of Graphics*

Imported pictures may look different in Notes than in their source applications because their fonts, colors, text sizes, and overall size are mapped to Notes equivalents. Since you can't create or edit imported graphics in Notes except to resize them, you may want to experiment with the picture in the original application.

You can adjust the shades of colors used to display or print imported pictures with the Color Setup dialog box. Picture colors affect some imported or displayed graphs and pictures, such as those in .PIC files and Freelance metafiles. When the files contain color information, Windows interprets the colors as defined in the original file. If the files don't contain color information, Notes maps the colors.

▶ *Importing Spreadsheet Files into Documents*

To bring spreadsheet data into a document, import the worksheet into a rich text field. To import spreadsheet data as a *database*, import it into a view. Each worksheet row becomes a document, and each column becomes a field whose contents are the original cell contents.

  T I P

> **Import a named range of several rows and columns for test purposes before you import the entire spreadsheet. While 1-2-3 Release 3 for Windows can display multiple spreadsheets at one time, only the specified range in the current worksheet is imported. A range name used for a range to be imported cannot span multiple worksheets.**

The default font for spreadsheet imports is Courier. Notes ignores any fonts defined for the field into which you are importing the worksheet. (After the worksheet is imported, you can change its fonts to Notes fonts.)

Notes doesn't wrap the lines of an imported spreadsheet. If the spreadsheet has more columns than a Notes window can display, use the horizontal scroll bars to see what's out of view. Notes can handle a maximum text width of 22.75 inches in a document. Additional text is truncated.

If you aren't sure how you want the database structured, use the Worksheet Title Defined option in the Worksheet Import Settings dialog box. It maps the existing worksheet column titles and contents to the fields in a Notes document. To import a spreadsheet file into Notes document, follow these steps:

1. Select a document in a view.

2. Choose Edit ➤ Edit Document (or Ctrl+E).

3. Place the insertion point in a rich text field where you want the imported file to begin.

4. Choose File ➤ Import. Notes displays the Import dialog box.

5. Select the file you want to import, and select 123 Worksheet as the file type.

6. When you click on Import, the 123/Symphony Worksheet Import dialog box appears, as shown in Figure 8.2. You can import either all the data in the worksheet file, or just the data in a named range.

7. Select one of these options:

   • To import the entire worksheet, select Entire Worksheet.

   • To import a named range of data, select Named Range and type the name of the range in the Range Name box.

8. Click on OK to perform the import.

FIGURE 8.2

The 123/Symphony Worksheet Import dialog box lets you import an entire worksheet or a named range.

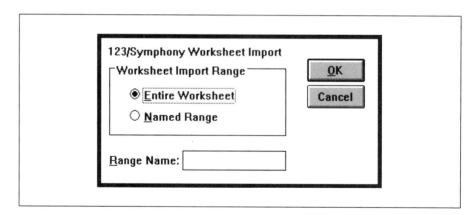

▶ *Importing Spreadsheet Files into Views*

When you import a spreadsheet into a view, each row becomes an individual document and each column becomes a field with the original cell contents as its field contents. To import at the view level, you must create a form and a view that can accommodate the format of the worksheet you are importing.

While 1-2-3 Release 3 can display multiple spreadsheets at one time, only the entire current spreadsheet or a specified range in the current worksheet is imported. A range name used for a range to be imported cannot span multiple worksheets.

Notes uses a character translation (CLS) file to translate foreign symbols and characters. This file must be in your Notes program directory.

Notes doesn't wrap lines of an imported worksheet. If a worksheet has more columns than a window can display, use the horizontal scroll bars to see the full width of the worksheet. Notes can handle a maximum text width of 22.75 inches; additional text is truncated.

▶▶ **N O T E**

Before importing an entire spreadsheet, consider importing just a named range of several rows and columns for test purposes first.

To import a spreadsheet file into a view, follow these steps:

1. Click on the database's icon to select it and switch to the view that will receive the spreadsheet data.

2. Choose File ➤ Import. The Import dialog box appears.

3. Select the files you want to import on the left, and select 123 Worksheet as the file format in the right list box if it isn't already selected.

4. Select Import. The Worksheet Import Settings dialog box appears, as shown in Figure 8.3.

5. Select a form to use for the imported data under Use Form. The forms listed are those available in the database you're currently using.

6. Select one of these options under Column Format:

   • **View Defined:** Select this option if the format of the worksheet columns exactly matches the format of the columns in the view. The column names and column widths must be identical.

FIGURE 8.3 ▶

The Worksheet Import Settings dialog box lets you select a database form to use for the imported data, as well as define a view and select the labels in the cells in the first row of the worksheet as the column names and fields.

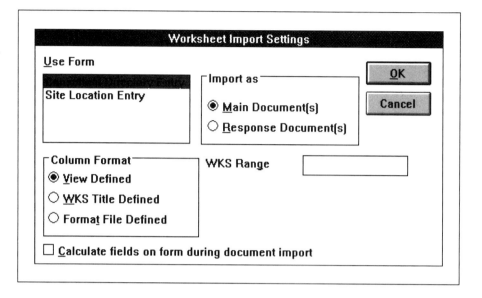

- **WKS Title Defined:** Select this option if the cells in the first row of the worksheet file are to be column headers and fields. These cells must be labels. They can be used as the view column names, but will not be imported. Field names will be created from the column titles and can be used in the database form.
- **Format File Defined:** Select this option if you're using a Column Format Descriptor File, and enter the name of the file in the COL File Name text box that appears when you select this option.

7. Select one of these options under Import As:

- **Main Document(s):** Select this option in all cases when you want to import the file as a document-type document.
- **Response Document(s):** Imports the file as one or more response documents.

8. If you're importing a named range from the worksheet file, select the check box and type the range name in the WKS Range text box.

9. Click on OK to start importing.

> To update the view to show column headings and the
> data from the import, choose Design ➤ Views. When
> the Design Views dialog box appears, select the view
> you want to modify.

When import is complete, all documents produced by the import are
displayed in the view.

▶ Importing ASCII Text into Documents and Views

You can import ASCII files into either documents or views. To import
an ASCII file into a document, follow these steps:

1. Select a document *in a view.*

2. Choose Edit ➤ Edit Document.

3. Place the insertion point in a text field (or rich text field) where
you want the imported file to begin.

4. Choose File ➤ Import. The Import dialog box appears.

5. Select the file you want to import.

6. Click on Import. A Lotus Notes message box asks if you want to
preserve the line breaks in the file, as shown in Figure 8.4.

FIGURE 8.4

*This Lotus Notes mes-
sage box asks you if
you want to preserve
the line breaks in an
imported file.*

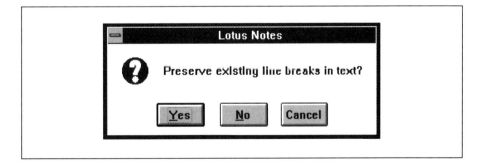

7. Select one of these options:

- **Yes:** To preserve the existing line breaks. This is useful when the original file contains tables or columns.
- **No:** To make the text wrap at the end of each line when displayed in a window.

8. Click on Yes or No to continue the import.

The ASCII file is imported and inserted into the Notes document at the insertion point. To import an ASCII file into a view, follow these steps:

1. Open the view into which you want to import the file.

2. Choose File ➤ Import. The Import dialog box appears.

3. Select the file(s) you want to import.

4. Select the format Structured Text, if it isn't already selected.

5. Select Import. The Structured Text Import dialog box appears, as shown in Figure 8.5.

FIGURE 8.5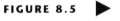

The Structured Text Import dialog box

Structured Text Import

U̲se Form

Consultant Directory Entry
Site Location Entry

OK

Cancel

Inter-Document Delimiter

○ F̲orm-feed
◉ C̲haracter Code: 12

Import as: Main Document(s) ⬆

For b̲ody text: Justify ⬆

☐ C̲alculate fields on form during document imp

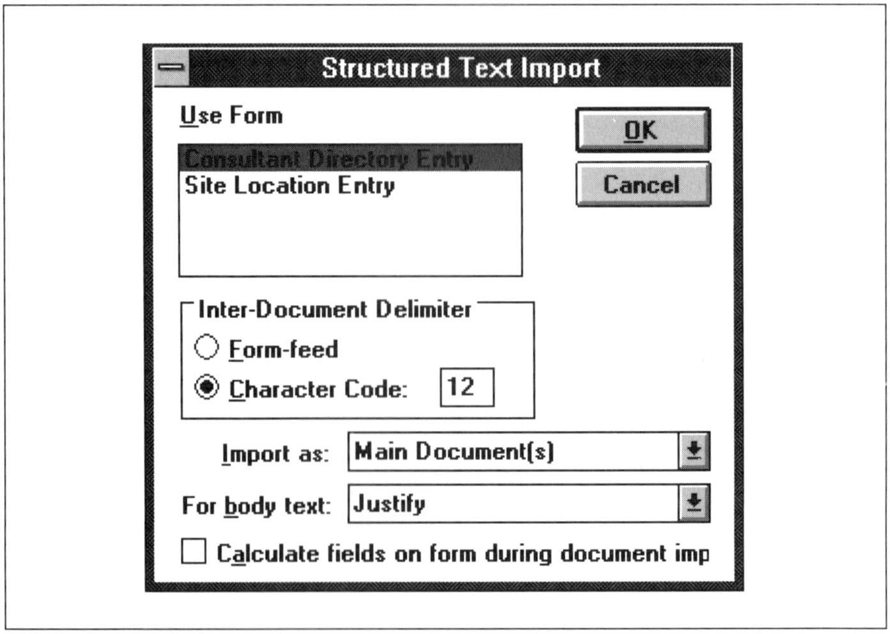

6. Select the form into which you want to import the ASCII text file.

7. Choose the desired options.

8. Click on OK to perform the import.

When the import is finished, the view is automatically updated to show the new documents.

►► *Exporting Data*

Exporting means translating Notes documents or views into a format that other applications can use. You can also use Export to export a Notes view and then import it into a Notes document. The details depend on what you're exporting, but you always use the Export dialog box for exporting documents and views.

Notes lets you export to the following file formats:

- Word processing formats
- Character and Language Services files (CLS files) for character translation and collation
- Microsoft's Rich Text Format (RTF) as an intermediate format for import and export

You can also specify the type of format you want to export documents and views to:

- Documents to word processing files
- Graphics to picture files
- Views to spreadsheets
- Documents to ASCII text files
- Views to tabular text files
- Views to structured text files
- Documents to Lotus Agenda files

▶ *Exporting a Document to Another Application*

In general, to export a document to another application, you would follow these steps:

1. Open a view and select or open the document you're exporting.

2. Choose File ➤ Export. The Export dialog box appears, as shown in Figure 8.6.

3. Select a file type under Save File as Type. The options listed depend on whether you're exporting a view or a document. If you're exporting a view, the default file type is Structured Text. If you're exporting a document, the default file type is ASCII Text.

4. Select a drive under Drives, if necessary.

5. Open the directory you want in the Directories box by double-clicking it.

6. Type the file name into the File Name box, or type the complete path and file name into the File Name box.

FIGURE 8.6 ▶

The Export dialog box enables you to choose settings for exporting Notes documents and views to other applications.

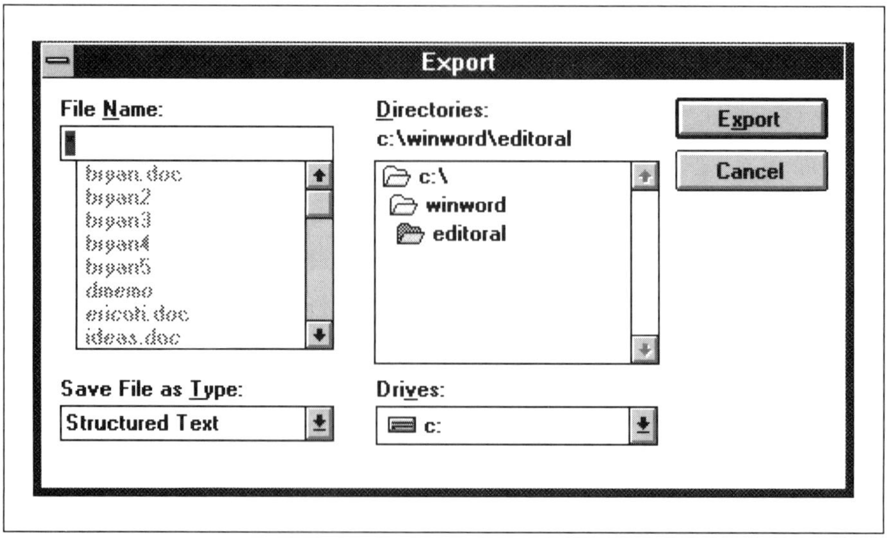

7. To export to an existing file, select the file's name from the list or type its file name and path into the text box. Notes asks if you want to overwrite the existing file or append the export material to it.

8. Click on Export to perform the export.

► *Exporting Documents to Word Processing Files*

You can export Notes documents to all releases of the following word processing applications and file formats:

- ASCII
- IBM DisplayWrite (DCA format)
- Lotus AmiPro
- Lotus Manuscript
- Microsoft Rich Text Format (RTF)
- MultiMate
- WordPerfect
- WordStar

Other word processors do not support some of the paragraph and text attributes supported by Notes.

To export a Notes document to a word processing file, follow these steps:

1. Open the document you want to export.

2. Choose File ➤ Export. The Export dialog box opens.

3. Select a file type under Save File as Type. The default file type for exporting a document is ASCII Text. You can also choose Rich Text Format, which will retain all the formatting in the document when it's exported.

4. Select a drive under Drives, if necessary.

5. Open the directory you want in the Directories box by double-clicking it.

6. Type the file name into the File Name box, or type the complete path and file name into the File Name box.

7. To export to an existing file, select the file's name from the list or type its file name and path into the text box. Notes asks if you want to overwrite the existing file or append the export material to it.

8. Click on Export to perform the export.

If you choose to export a Notes document in the default ASCII Text format, the Text File Export dialog box appears, as shown in Figure 8.7. You can set the line length of exported text; the default is set to 75 characters. Words that extend beyond that length wrap to the next line. To change the line length, type a number. Click on OK to export the document(s) using the specified line length.

FIGURE 8.7

The Text File Export dialog box lets you set the line length of exported text.

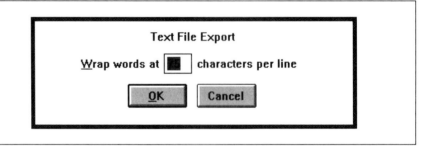

▶ Exporting Document Graphics to Picture Files

You can export Notes graphics in the following formats on any platform:

- Any picture with a valid ANSI metafile format can be exported to an ANSI Metafile.

- Any .PIC file can be exported to an ANSI Metafile.

To export graphics to picture files, follow these steps:

1. Open the document and select the graphic. If you don't select a graphic, the first graphic in the document is selected by default.

2. Choose File ➤ Export. Notes opens the Export dialog box.

3. Select a file type from the Save File as Type list box.

4. To export the picture into an existing file, select the file from the list of file names. The file name appears in the text box.

5. To export the picture into a new file, type the file name into the text box. The file is created in the selected directory.

6. Click on Export to perform the export.

If you're exporting to a new file, the Export dialog box closes and a wait cursor is displayed until the export is complete. For some file types, if you're exporting into an existing file, Notes opens the Export Warning dialog box, where you specify whether you want to replace the existing file or add to it. The dialog boxes close and a wait cursor is displayed until export is complete.

▶ *Exporting Views to Spreadsheets*

You can export a view to a 1-2-3 spreadsheet file. Each column in the view becomes a column in the worksheet, and each row in the view becomes a row in the worksheet. You can also include the column headings in a view in the first row of the worksheet. To export a view to a 1-2-3 file format, simply follow these steps:

1. Open the view you want to export. The entire view will be exported unless you select specific documents for export.

2. Choose File ➤ Export. Notes opens the Export dialog box.

3. Select 123 Worksheet option in the Save File as Type list box.

4. To export the view into an existing spreadsheet file, select the file from the list of file names. To export the view into a new spreadsheet file, type the file name into the text box. The file is created in the selected directory.

5. Click on the Export button. The Worksheet Export Settings dialog box appears, as shown in Figure 8.8. Here you specify which documents you want to export. (If you're exporting the view to a new file, the Export dialog box closes and a wait cursor is displayed until export is complete. If you're exporting to an existing file, Notes opens the Export Warning dialog box, as shown in Figure 8.9. Here you specify whether you want to replace the existing file.)

6. Click on OK to perform the export.

The dialog boxes close and a wait cursor is displayed until export is complete.

FIGURE 8.8

The Worksheet Export Settings dialog box lets you specify the document you want to export.

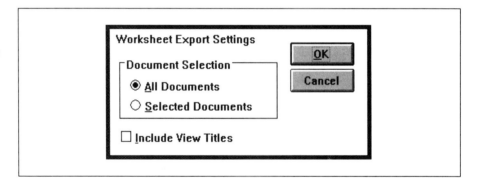

FIGURE 8.9

If you're exporting to an existing file, the Export Warning dialog box lets you specify whether you want to replace the file.

▶ *Exporting Documents and Views to ASCII Text Files*

You can perform a process similar to that above to export documents and views to structured ASCII text files. To perform the export, just follow these steps:

1. Select a database in your Workspace.

2. Choose a view that you want to export.

3. Select the document(s) you want to export if you don't want to export the entire view. (A document doesn't have to be in Edit mode.)

4. Choose File ➤ Export. The Export dialog box appears.

5. Specify where to store the exported file.

6. Enter a new file name or select an existing one to which you want to export the view.

7. Select the default ASCII Text as the file type.

8. Click on the Export button. If you're exporting the view to a new file, the Export dialog box closes and displays the Text File Export dialog box. (If you're exporting to an existing file, Notes opens the Export Warning dialog box, where you specify whether you want to replace the existing file or append it.)

9. Choose the desired options.

10. Click on OK. The dialog boxes close and a wait cursor is displayed until the export is complete.

▶▶ *What's Next?*

The means to import data from other applications into Notes and to export data from Notes to other applications shows how flexible Notes is. When importing data into Notes, you can increase a database's value by integrating information from a variety of outside sources. Furthermore, you won't need to recreate data by manually entering it again. Conversely, exporting data from Notes can aid you in making presentations and writing reports that rely on the information from a database.

In the next chapter, we discuss using Notes Mail, which is a powerful e-mail system that's fully integrated with Notes databases. You can use Notes Mail just like you would any other e-mail system. The major difference between Notes and other e-mail systems is that Notes Mail *is* a database application that provides you with unique communication features to support workflow throughout an organization.

► ► CHAPTER **9**

Communicating
with Notes Mail

———

FAST TRACK

full name of each person in the group. Choose File ➤
Save, or press Esc, to exit and confirm.

▶ ***To send a mail message and any attachment*** **176**

you can either click on the Send button, choose Mail ➤
Send, or press Esc.

▶ ***To save your memo without sending it*** **178**

choose Mail ➤ Send. The Mail Send dialog box appears,
displaying the Sign and Encrypt options and Send button.
If you press Esc, the Document Save dialog box appears.
Deselect the Mail option and then click on the Yes button.

▶ ***To sign outgoing mail*** **179**

choose Mail ➤ Send, or press Esc. Select the Sign option
and then click on OK. To sign all documents by default
when you send them, choose Tools ➤ Setup ➤ Mail.
Select Sign Mail and then select OK.

▶ ***To read your mail*** **182**

choose a particular mail view, select a memo, and then
open and read it.

▶ ***To reply to a mail memo*** **185**

open the memo you're replying to, or highlight it in a view.
Choose Compose ➤ Reply to reply to the sender of the
memo, or choose Compose ➤ Reply to All to reply to all
users listed in the To and cc recipient fields of the memo.
Complete the reply memo just as you would any other
mail memo, then send it as usual.

► ►	**M**any people use Notes for its e-mail capabilities alone. With Notes Mail, you can communicate quickly and easily with other electronic mail users, and not just people on the same Notes network. You can send and receive mail memos— from simple one-line messages to complex, multipage reports. You can attach files, or even an entire Notes database, to a mail memo. You can forward or receive documents from any Notes database. You can even send files created with other Lotus Windows products, such as 1-2-3 and Improv, as if they were Notes mail memos.

This chapter covers everything you need to know to use Notes Mail. You'll learn how to:

- Create mail messages
- Send mail
- Create address books for frequent correspondents
- Reply to and forward mail

► ► *Using Your Notes Mail Database*

Every person who uses Notes as part of a company-wide system has a *mail database*. Your mail database is like any other Notes database that's located on a server. (Remember that the *server* is used to designate whether your system is local or remote.)

You should see two mail database icons in your Workspace; one is for your Name & Address Book and the other is for your mail database, as shown in Figure 9.1. The mail database stores your incoming and outgoing mail. All Notes mail users have their own mail database, unless they're using an alternative mail system such as cc:Mail. The Name & Address Book stores the names of individuals and workgroups you send mail to.

FIGURE 9.1

Your name will appear on your mail database icon.

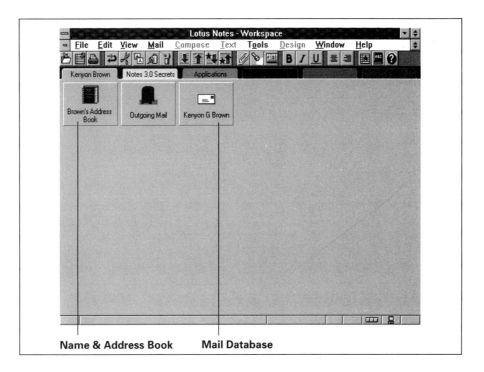

Name & Address Book   Mail Database

▶▶ *Accessing Notes Mail from the Workspace*

You open your mail database as you would open any other Notes database. Simply double-click on its icon in the Workspace. You can also access your mail from any other Notes database that you might have open. Choose Window ➤ 1. Workspace and switch to the tabbed folder that contains your mail database (if it's not displayed already). Click on the mail database to select it and then pull down the Compose menu. As you can see in Figure 9.2, there are five predesigned forms you can choose from to send a mail message.

You also have complete access to your mail database anytime while you're using Notes. For example, if you want to send a memo while

FIGURE 9.2 ►

Notes provides five pre-designed mail forms that you can use to send messages.

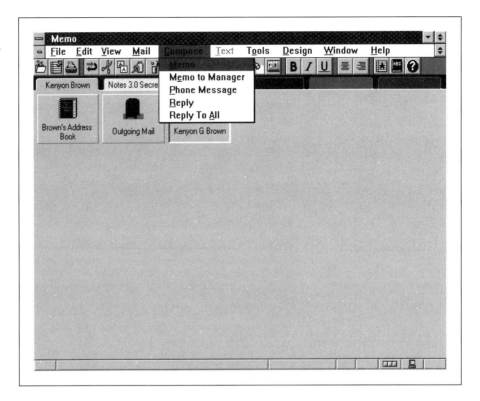

you have a database open, choose Mail ➤ Compose and then select one of the five predesigned forms from the menu as shown in Figure 9.3. You can also choose the Custom Forms option from the menu in order to select one of the four custom forms that Notes provides (more on predesigned forms and custom forms in a minute).

►► *Composing Mail*

When you click on your mail database in the Workspace, the Compose menu usually displays the five predesigned mail forms (unless your organization has its own standard forms) and any custom forms you've added yourself. As we discussed in the previous section, Notes also provides four custom forms. However, you can only access these forms when you open the Mail menu and then choose Compose while you have another database open.

FIGURE 9.3

You can choose one of five predesigned forms to compose mail while you have another database open.

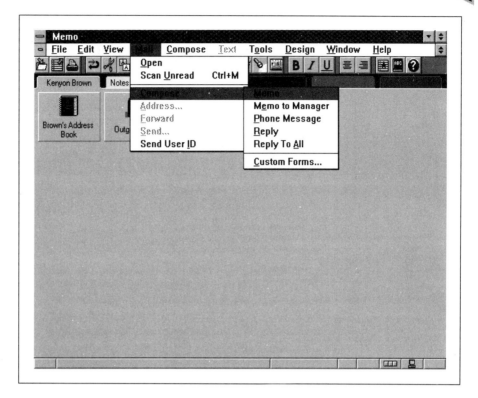

▶ *Using Predesigned Forms*

After you select your mail database and choose a form from the Compose menu, Notes displays the appropriate form to fill out. Since they've been predefined for you, using a form can save you the time it takes to create one. Let's look more closely at each of the five forms and the buttons associated with them.

- **Memo:** Figure 9.4 displays the standard Memo form. As you can see, it includes your name and the current date and time. This form lets you write and send (or just save) a regular mail message.

- **Memo to Manager:** As you can see in Figure 9.5, the Mail to Manager form displays the name of your server in the To line. This form lets you write and send a mail message to the manager(s) of the active database.

- **Phone Message**: The Phone Message form, as shown in Figure 9.6, is extremely useful for taking others' phone messages. You

FIGURE 9.4 ▶

The Memo form

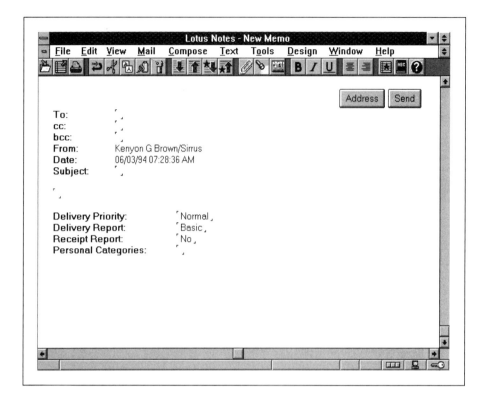

just fill in the blanks and send the message note immediately. You'll never have to fill out one of those "While You Were Away" slips again.

- **Reply**: You can use this form to create a response to an open or selected document and then send it to one person. If you try to open a Reply form without first selecting the mail message you want to respond to first, Notes beeps and displays a message telling you to select (or open) a document. Figure 9.7 displays the Reply form.

- **Reply to All:** Just like the Reply form, the Reply to All form requires you to select a document to respond to, or you'll get a beep and a message telling you that no document is selected. Once you select a document, you can use this form to create a reply to all users listed in the To and cc recipient fields of the open or selected mail message, as you can see in Figure 9.7 above. Users in the bcc (blind carbon copy) field receive a Reply to All only if they were listed in the bcc field of the original message.

FIGURE 9.5

The Memo to Manager form

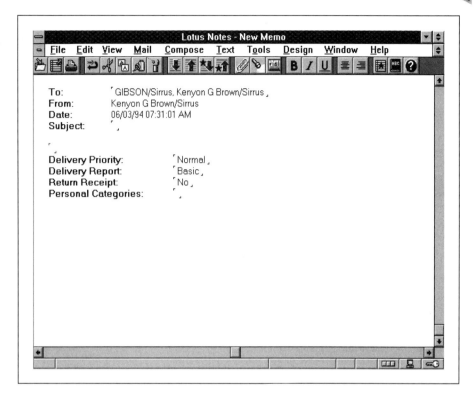

- **Address**: When you have another database open, each of the forms includes an Address button, which is also accessible from the Mail menu. After you click on the button, the Mail Address dialog box appears, as shown in Figure 9.8. You can fill in the mail address fields by selecting names from a Name & Address Book instead of typing them in the text boxes.

- **Forward**: The Forward command is only accessible from the Mail menu when you have a database open. By choosing this command, you can forward a copy of one or more selected Notes document(s) to the people you specify. As you can see in Figure 9.9, the selected document(s) become the body of the memo; you can edit and add to this information if you desire.

- **Send**: The Send button also appears on each of the mail forms only when another database is open; however, you can also access the command from the Mail menu when you have a database open. By clicking on the Send button, you can send an open mail

FIGURE 9.6 ▶

The Phone Message form

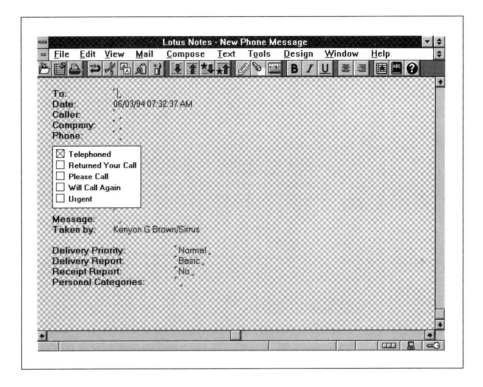

memo (or the highlighted memo in a view) to the people you specify. The Send command also lets you sign and encrypt a mail message.

▶ Using the Notes Custom Mail Forms

You can also use the custom mail forms that Notes provides for composing mail memos. These forms are useful in a variety of applications.

▶▶ **N O T E**

If you try to open the Custom Mail Forms dialog box and see the message "Server error: file does not exist," ask your Notes Administrator to put the custom forms (FORMS.NTF) on your mail server.

FIGURE 9.7

*The Reply form allows
you to respond to a
specific mail message,
which might be a docu-
ment that someone
sent to you.*

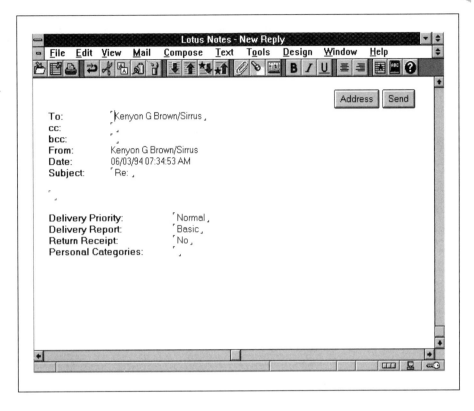

FIGURE 9.8

*The Mail Address dia-
log box appears when
you click on the Ad-
dress button that's
displayed on each of
the mail forms (when
another database is
open).*

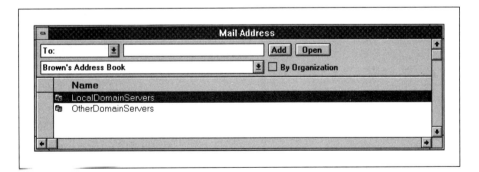

To use a custom mail form while a database is open, choose Mail ➤
Compose ➤ Custom Forms. The Custom Mail Forms dialog box appears, as shown in Figure 9.10. Select the form you want to use by double-clicking on it, or by selecting it and then clicking OK. For example,
choose the Weekly Time Record form that's shown in Figure 9.11.

FIGURE 9.9

The Forward command enables you to forward a selected document to another person.

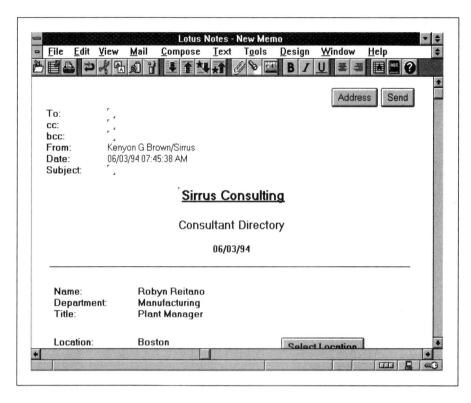

FIGURE 9.10

You can select one of the custom mail forms that Notes provides when you choose the Compose command from the Mail menu.

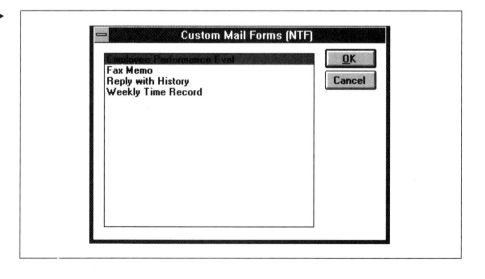

FIGURE 9.11

*The Weekly Time re-
cord form is one of
several custom mail
forms that Notes
makes available.*

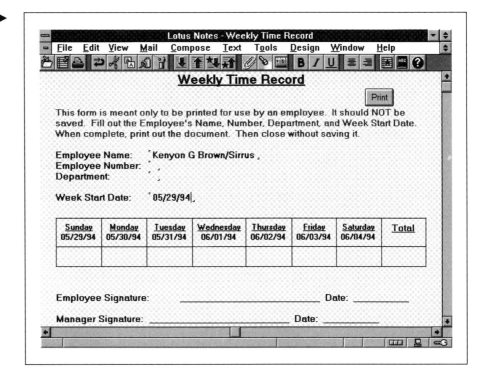

Click on the Print button if you want a printed copy of the form. (Note:
You do not compose this mail form on the screen; you print a copy of
the form first and then fill in the blanks.) Go ahead and fill the form
out. As you can see, it provides a handy way to keep track of your
weekly hours. Press Esc to close the form.

▶▶ N O T E

> **Remember that the custom forms are only available
> on the Mail menu while you have a database open.
> If you try to access the forms after you click on your
> mail database, they won't be available on the
> Compose menu.**

▶ *Creating the Message*

Whether you're using a predefined form or a custom form, the final step in composing a message—actually writing it—is pretty straightforward. Just type into the blank fields on the on-screen form the same information you'd type into the corresponding spaces on a paper memo. To move from one field to the next in any one of the mail forms, press Tab. To move to the previous field, press Shift+Tab.

Most of the fields you'll be using are self-explanatory, but let's take another look at the standard mail memo form anyway. (Look back at Figure 9.4 if you need a reference.) The following fields appear on this form:

- **To:** The To field allows you to enter the name(s) of the primary recipient(s). You can type many names into this field. However, by using group names, you can send a single message to all recipients at the same time. When sending a message to an individual, you can enter just a first name (David) or last name (Peal) if the name is unique in your Name & Address Book; or a first and last name (Kristen Tod) or a group name (Sales Dept) listed in a Name & Address Book. If a name is misspelled, Notes prompts you for the right name.

- **cc:** The cc field allows you to enter the name(s) of secondary recipient(s). The same limitations apply to this field as to the To field.

- **bcc:** You enter the name(s) of secondary recipient(s) in this field, but primary and secondary recipients won't see the bcc names (bcc means blind carbon copy). If you enter more than one name in the bcc field, bcc recipients will see only their own name in that field; that is, their names are hidden from each other. If you enter a group name, members of the group won't see *any* names belonging to the group, not even their own.

- **From:** Notes automatically enters your name in the From field.

- **Date:** Notes automatically enters the current date and time in this field.

- **Subject:** Enter a brief description of the memo in this field. It's a good idea to always fill in the Subject field because it will appear in the Subject column in the standard mail view. A specific, accurate Subject column acts as an advertisement encouraging the recipient to actually open the mail document and read on. A person can read the memo's description immediately. If you don't enter a subject, the Subject entry for this document will appear blank in the view.

- **Body**: You type your memo in the Body field, which is the unlabeled field following the Subject field. You can use text and paragraph formatting features by choosing the appropriate commands from the Text menu. You can also add graphics, make doclinks to other Notes documents, and insert DDE, OLE links, or objects. You'll notice the red brackets that are displayed on the screen. These brackets surround the Body field and indicate that you can apply an encryption key to this field to keep it private from some readers.

▶▶ *Addressing Mail*

When you write a mail memo, you typically type the names of the recipients into the To, cc, and bcc fields. This is called, sensibly enough, addressing your mail. As you saw in the illustrations of the predefined forms that we discussed earlier, Notes automatically enters your name and the current date in the memo. However, you must enter the name of at least one recipient in the To field. All the other field entries are optional.

You can also enter your addressees' names by choosing them directly from a Name & Address Book when you select the Address command from the Mail menu. (The Mail Address dialog box appears.) This is useful when you're unsure of a name or its spelling, or if you prefer to point and click rather than type. You can also use this feature to add correctly spelled user names and group names to the body of a Notes document. (If you don't know what a Name & Address Book is, skip ahead to "Using Name & Address Books" section.)

To use the address feature:

1. Open one of the mail documents in Edit mode and place the insertion point in a field that will accept names (such as the To field), then choose Mail ➤ Address or click the Address button on the standard mail form. The Mail Address dialog box appears.

2. Select where you want the names inserted from the first ("To") list. The options are To, cc, bcc, and At the Cursor.

3. Select the Name & Address Book you want to search. The options are your public and your personal Name & Address Books.

4. Select which types of names you want to see.

   • If you're searching your personal Name & Address Book, your options are People and Groups (the default) and People and Groups Hierarchical.

   • If you're searching the public Name & Address Book, the options depend on whether your home server is running Notes Release 3 or an earlier release. If it's an earlier release, the options are People (the default) and Groups. If it's Release 3, the options are the same as the ones for your personal Name & Address Book.

5. Select the name you want (scroll down the list if necessary), or type the first letter(s) in the name.

6. Click the Add button, or just double-click the name. The name appears in the Names box and in the document location you specified.

If you change your mind, you can select and delete the name from your document. If you want to select more names, you can repeat the steps. Just remember to separate any names with commas (,) or by pressing ↵. When you're done, press Esc to close the dialog box.

  TIP

Before actually sending the message, you can press F9 at any time to see the way Notes interprets the address you've entered so far.

▶ Using the Name & Address Books

After you've physically entered a long list of recipient addresses a few times, you'll rejoice in using the Notes Name & Address Books. These books are special Notes databases that list users, user groups, servers, and server connections. Why use these books? Name & Address Books help you to locate recipients' addresses quickly, allowing you to select the addresses to which you want to send mail so you don't have to actually type the addresses yourself. Name & Address Books can save you a lot of time.

Notes creates two kinds of Name & Address Books for you, one that's public and one that's personal. When you registered as a new user, your name was added to the *public* Name & Address Book. During the Notes setup procedure, your *personal* Name & Address Book was created. The file name of the public Name & Address Book is NAMES.NSF. Where multiple books are used, they are usually called NAMES1.NSF, NAMES2.NSF, and so on. The file name of your personal Name & Address Book is usually your name or a portion of your name, such as KENBROWN.NSF.

Using the address books isn't without its limitations. For instance, you can't use the Mail ➤ Address command to look up or add an address that begins with a number. The reason is because access to addresses in the Mail Address dialog box is by first *letter* only. Notes addresses can't handle addresses that begin with numbers. So if your organization has group names that begin with numbers, such as "2nd Building," you may want to distribute a separate list of these mail addresses, or write out the numbers, as in "Second Building."

Using the Public Name & Address Book

Your name and Notes mail address must appear in the public Name & Address Book before you can send and receive mail. You can update your listing if your name or mail address changes. To see your listing, open the Name & Address Book, choose View ➤ People, and find your personal document (your name) in the view.

There's only one public Name & Address Book per domain (most organizations have only one domain), although there's a replica of it on every Notes server in that domain. What does domain mean? If your organization uses only one Notes server, the domain is the group of users with the same Name & Address Book. A domain can also be a group of Notes servers with the same public Name & Address Book.

If your public Name & Address Book is large, you can omit it from the Workspace. The only reasons to have the public Name & Address Book on your Workspace are to make use of the Mail Address feature and to get instant notification when you've entered a user's name incorrectly (otherwise you'll receive a Delivery Failure notice at the time of the next scheduled replication).

However, you can avoid these limitations by copying the People, Groups, and Remote Connection records that you need into your personal Name & Address Book. Select the documents you want to copy at the view level in the public Name & Address Book, then paste them into your personal Name & Address Book. To make sure they "arrive safely," be sure to look at the correct view; for example, switch to the People view to look for the People documents.

You can also use the public Name & Address Book to look up user groups to whom you want to send mail. Open the Name & Address Book database, then choose View ➤ Groups.

Using Your Personal Name & Address Book

You have a unique personal Name & Address book (also called NAMES.NSF) that you can use for storing any of the following:

- Private mailing lists (for your own use)
- Names and mail addresses of people on other electronic mail systems (such as cc:Mail) that can communicate with Notes over a gateway
- Names of users and groups in your domain when you don't keep the public N&A Book icon on your Workspace
- Nicknames and mail addresses of users in your domain (so you don't have to type long names)
- Remote Connection documents for calling servers via modem

Your personal N&A Book entries don't appear in any public Name & Address Book, or in any other users' personal Name & Address Books. Your personal N&A Book shouldn't be used to duplicate entries in the public Name & Address Book. This database is located on your workstation's hard disk, or on a Notes server if you have a diskless workstation.

Your personal Name & Address Book must be stored in the data directory specified in the User Setup dialog box. If you can't find the database's icon on your Workspace, see your Notes Administrator.

You can save nicknames for the people you send mail to frequently. Open your personal Name & Address Book, choose View ➤ People, open a document for a specific person listed in the view, and type the nicknames into the First Name field and the full Notes name into the Full Name field.

➤ *Defining User Groups*

If you often send mail to the same groups of people, you can save time and typing by creating user groups. Once you've defined a group in your personal Name & Address Book, you can type the group name instead of the individual names in any of the recipient fields of a mail document. A group can include people or other groups from your own domain, a domain other than your own, or from mixed domains.

 ▶▶ **N O T E**

> **Only users with Author access to the *public* Name & Address Book can define user groups for everyone in your domain to use. To see a list of these user groups, open the public Name & Address Book and choose View ➤ Groups.**

To define a user group, do the following:

1. Open your personal Name & Address Book database.

2. Choose Compose ➤ Group. A Group document appears, as shown in Figure 9.12.

3. Type a name for the group into the Group Name field. For example, if you often send marketing reports to the same group of people, you might name this group MktReport. The group name specified here is the name you will type into a recipient field of a mail document. (Notice that the Owner field contains your name.)

4. You have the option of typing a brief description of the group into the Description field, but you can skip it. In the Members field, type the full name of each person in the group. Separate each name with a comma (,), semicolon (;), or carriage return (press ↵). You can use names of other user groups as well as names of individuals.

FIGURE 9.12 ▶

A Group document

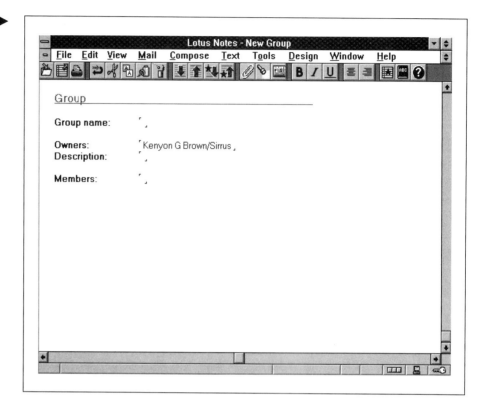

5. Press Ctrl+S t save the changes, or press Esc, to exit and confirm. Close your personal Name & Address Book database.

 ▶▶ N O T E

> **You can enter names of other user groups as well as names of individuals. Groups can be nested five levels deep.**

As you can see, user groups can be a big time-saver. They do have their limitations, though. If you send a document to a *personal* (as opposed to public) user group, the recipients cannot use the Mail ➤ Reply to All command to send a reply to everyone in the group because personal user groups aren't listed in the public or the individual recipients' personal Name & Address Books. You could include the names of your user group in the body of the document if Replies to All may be needed.

Also, if you send mail to a user group that includes yourself, you won't receive the memo unless you choose Save when you send the memo, or you have Save Sent Mail selected in the Mail Setup dialog box.

▶ *Resolving Name Conflicts*

When there's a name conflict between identical names *within* your public or private Name & Address Book or *between* your public and private Name & Address Books, Notes displays all the possible names for you to select from when you choose Mail ➤ Send. For example, if you type David, Notes displays all the Davids in your public and private Name & Address Books so you can select the one you want.

When there's a conflict between multiple public Name & Address books, Notes sends your message to the person in your *primary* public Name & Address Book, without displaying the alternatives. For example, if you type **David** and there's only one David in your primary Name & Address Book, Notes will send your message to him without displaying alternatives, even if your secondary Name & Address Book includes a David. However, if there are several Davids in your primary public Name & Address Book, Notes displays all of them, but any Davids in your secondary Name & Address Book will not be included on this list. When you want to send mail to David in your secondary Name & Address Book, type his last name instead, if it's unique, or type his full name.

 ▶▶ **N O T E**

> **When you send mail to someone who is *not* listed in *any* Name & Address book on your mail server, you must type @ followed by the domain name after the recipient's name. For example, to send a message to Kristen in Sales, you would type Kristen Tod@Sales (assuming Sales is on another server).**

The dialog box appears automatically if Notes finds more than one match for the name of a mail recipient specified in the To, cc, or bcc fields. For example, it appears if you address a message to David and there are three Davids in the Name & Address Book. If this happens, the dialog box lists all Davids in the Name & Address Book and presents three options.

► Using Distinguished Names

Notes can use, and your organization might use, distinguished names to differentiate people in the same organization who have exactly the same full name. If your organization began with Notes Release 3, it's probably using distinguished names; if earlier releases were installed, there may or may not be distinguished names.

Distinguished names include extra information (such as department names) separated by slashes (/). For example, to distinguish three John Smiths working in the same company, each name could include extra information such as:

John Smith/Technical Writer/Sirrus

John Smith/Trainer/Sirrus

John Smith/Editor/Sirrus

If your organization uses distinguished names, and you know the full distinguished name of the person (for example, John Smith/Editor/Sirrus), you can type it directly into the Address field. You must type the full distinguished name including all slashes. You can also mix distinguished and nondistinguished names in the Address field.

If two people have the same full name and you don't know the distinguished name of the person you want to send a message to, Notes can provide the distinguished name. To send the message, enter a non-unique full name in the Address field and either choose Mail ➤ Send or press F9. The Ambiguous Names dialog box appears to help you select the correct person. If your company doesn't use distinguished names, the Ambiguous Names dialog box differentiates between people with the same full name by location, for example:

Marcus Aurelias (Sonoma Street)

Marcus Aurelias (Hayes Valley)

Marcus Aurelias (San Francisco)

To help you find people with non-unique names, you can select one of the following three options:

OK	If the name you want appears in the list, select that name, then select OK to send the message.
Skip Name	This option sends the message to all the other names specified in the field. Select this option if you're sending the message to a group which contains the problem name.
Cancel Sending	This option cancels sending the message to any of the recipients. Select this option if you see an obvious mistake you made in one of the names and want to correct it and try again.

The dialog box appears if you misspell a mail recipient's name and try to send the message. If the name doesn't appear in any Name & Address Book, Notes looks for alternative spellings that "sound right." If any are found, they appear in a list where you can select the correct one. For example, if you try to send mail to Marcus Aurelias but type Aurleius, Notes responds:

No match was found for name: Marcus Aurleias
If you intended one of the following name(s) choose one...

The list shows possible alternatives, among them Marcus Aurelias. When you select the correct name from the list, Notes makes the correction and delivers the mail. If the misspelled name is also in the Name & Address Book, Notes delivers the message even though that recipient is the wrong one. For example, suppose the Name & Address Book contains David Clark and David Clarke. If you want to send mail to Clark but you typed Clarke, the mail is delivered to the wrong recipient.

The dialog box has two other options to help you out in this situation:

Skip Name | This option skips sending the message to the name indicated. This is useful if you're unsure about one name in a list, since it lets you send the message to everyone else without having to retype the entire list.

Cancel Sending | This option cancels sending the message to any of the recipients.

►► *Sending Mail*

Once you've composed and addressed your mail message, sending it is a simple matter. You can either click on the Send button, choose Mail ➤ Send, or press Esc. The Mail Send dialog box appears, displaying the Sign and Encrypt options and Send button, as shown in Figure 9.13.

Although sending mail is usually a one-step process, there are several options related to sending mail that will help you keep your mail messages secure and ensure that they get to their intended recipients. You can save copies of your mail messages, you can sign them, and you can encrypt them to keep their contents from prying eyes. Each of these options is described in the sections that follow.

FIGURE 9.13 ►

The Mail Send dialog box

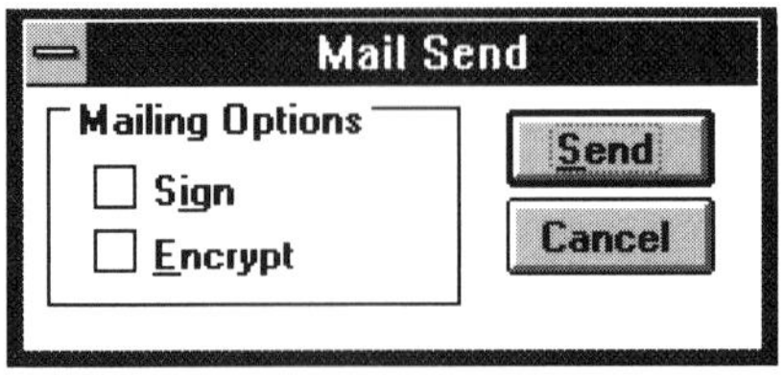

▶ # TRANSMISSION AND DELIVERY PROBLEMS

Transmission problems and delivery failures fall into two categories: those that occur when you send a message, and those that occur when Notes delivers it. In either case, Notes displays a message to help you deal with the problem.

As you learned in "Distinguished Names" above, transmission will fail if you type a name incorrectly or you type a non-unique name. Notes usually displays the error message when you try to send the document. However, recipient names that include explicit domain names (such as Kristen Tod@MicroAge) are not validated when you send them. Instead, Notes verifies the names when the document reaches the specified domain. If delivery is unsuccessful, you will receive a delivery failure report at that time.

In other situations where Notes can't deliver a mail memo, you receive a delivery failure report containing the recipient's name and the reason for the failure. Once you know what caused the problem, you can resend the document. When you succeed, the delivery failure report is removed from the mail document.

Some of the most common reasons for a delivery failure (and related error messages in the report) are:

➢ **User Name Not Unique**, which means that Notes found two people with the same name in the Name & Address Book This message appears only when sending mail across domains, and usually occurs if you use just a first name (David @Editorial) rather than a full name (David Peal @Editorial).

➢ **User Not Listed in Address Book**, which mean that the recipient is outside your domain. (If the recipient was in your domain, a message stating that the user name did not exist would appear when you tried to send the document.)

➤ **No Route Found to Server X from Server Y, which means
that Notes can't find a route on the network to the recipient's mail server. If the address is correct, report the problem to your Notes administrator.**

➤ **Delivery Time Expired, which means that mail delivery
was delayed somewhere along the delivery path, usually
for longer than 28 hours. Report this to the Notes
administrator.**

➤ **Recipient's Name & Address Book Entry Does Not Specify a Mail File, which means that the recipient's mail
database as specified in the public Name & Address Book
doesn't exist. You should report this to your Notes
administrator.**

**To resend a mail document that was returned with a delivery fail-
ure report, open the delivery failure report, or select it in a view.
Choose Mail ➤ Send. The Mail Resend dialog box opens. Use this
dialog box to resend a mail message that Notes was unable to deliver (and that is now marked DELIVERY FAILURE).**

**The To: text box lists the recipients who didn't receive the original
message. Correct or delete their names as necessary. Select Sign
or Encrypt to sign or encrypt the message. However, these are optional. Click on the Send button. The message will be sent, without
the delivery failure report.**

► *Saving Mail*

You can save a mail memo and continue to work on it by choosing File
➤ Save or pressing Ctrl+S while your memo's in progress.

To save a memo-in-progress and go on to other tasks, choose Mail ➤
Send. The Mail Send dialog box appears. If you press Esc, the Document Save dialog box appears, shown in Figure 9.14. Deselect the Mail
option and then click on the Yes button.

FIGURE 9.14

*The Document Save
dialog box*

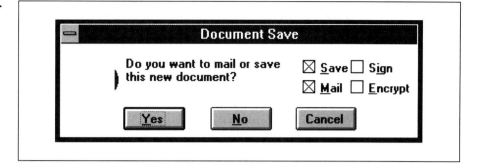

▶ *Signing Mail*

When you send mail, you can "sign" it to assure the recipient that you
are the author of the document. Signing a document in Notes attaches
a unique electronic signature derived from your User ID to that
document.

There are two main ways to sign outgoing mail:

- Choose Mail ➤ Send, or press Esc. Select the Sign option and
  then click on OK.

- To sign all documents by default when you send them, choose
  Tools ➤ Setup ➤ Mail. Select Sign Mail and then select OK.

▶▶ N O T E

**You can still deselect signing for any document when
you send it.**

What if you want to sign and encrypt every document that you send
but don't want the inconvenience of selecting the options each time?
You could do the following:

- To perform these actions automatically, open your NOTES.INI
  file and add the line **SecureMail=1**. Exit and restart Notes (in
  order to make the change to NOTES.INI take effect). Adding
  SecureMail=1 to your NOTES.INI file removes the Sign and
  Encrypt check boxes from all dialog boxes.

The situation now is that Notes will automatically sign and encrypt each mail document. To stop automatic signing and encryption of documents, just remove **SecureMail=1** from your NOTES.INI file and then restart Notes.

▶▶ **W A R N I N G**

If you aren't accustomed to working in files like NOTES.INI, ask your administrator or someone who's knowledgeable for assistance.

▶ Encrypting Your Outgoing Mail

You can stop all those prying eyes from reading your incoming or outgoing mail by using the Notes encryption feature. *Encryption* is a technique by which Notes scrambles your outgoing and incoming messages so that only you (or the designated recipients) can read them. When you send mail, you can encrypt it to ensure that nobody except your recipients can read your memos while in transit, when stored in intermediate mail boxes, and on arrival in the recipient's mail file. You can also encrypt all of your saved mail and incoming mail automatically.

When you encrypt a document, Notes scrambles the information using the recipient's public key so that it can be decoded only by the recipient. A user's *public key* is a 600-character string of apparently random letters and numbers that's assigned to each new Notes user. Your public key is listed at the bottom of your Person record in your organization's Notes Address Book. When you tell Notes to encrypt a message to another user, the contents of the message are manipulated mathematically using the recipient's public key, producing a scrambled and indecipherable message.

When you want to send a person encrypted information or someone wants to send you encrypted information, Notes gets the recipient's public key from the Name & Address Book. If the recipient's public key isn't stored in the book for some reason, information can't be encrypted. In that case, you should send your key to the Notes Administrator, who will paste it in the book.

There are three ways you can encrypt outgoing mail:

- To encrypt a document when you send it, choose Mail ➤ Send, or press Esc. Select Encrypt and then click on OK.

- To encrypt all documents by default when you send them, choose Tools ➤ Setup ➤ Mail. Select Encrypt Sent Mail and then click on OK.

 ▶▶ **N O T E**

You can still deselect encryption for any document when you send it.

- To encrypt and sign every document you send, add **Secure-Mail=1** to your NOTES.INI file. Exit and restart Notes (to make the change to NOTES.INI take effect). Adding **SecureMail=1** to NOTES.INI removes the Sign and Encrypt check boxes from all dialog boxes, but automatically encrypts and signs all outgoing mail.

If you want to stop automatic signing and encryption of documents, just remove **SecureMail=1** from your NOTES.INI file, and then restart Notes.

 ▶▶ **N O T E**

As we stated earlier, if you aren't accustomed to working in files like NOTES.INI, ask your administrator or another knowledgeable person for assistance.

You can also encrypt your incoming mail and saved mail. To encrypt saved mail, choose Tools ➤ Setup ➤ Mail. Select the Encrypt Saved Mail option. Click on OK. The Encrypt Saved Mail option allows privacy-minded users to automatically encrypt all mail memos they save. When you enable Encrypt Saved Mail, your saved copy is always encrypted whether or not you send it to others encrypted. Encrypting saved mail effectively prevents anyone from reading your mail on the server, even the server administrator or others with access to the server.

The Encrypt Incoming Mail option provides additional security for incoming mail from outside your system to your mail server. This prevents any access to your mail when it reaches your mail server, either by administrative access to your mail database or by unauthorized access to the server. Incoming mail cannot be encrypted when using the following gateways: SSW (SoftSwitch), MHS, and cc:Mail.

To encrypt incoming mail, follow these steps:

1. Open your public Name & Address Book.

2. Choose View ➤ People and then open the document with your name.

3. Choose Edit ➤ Edit Document, and select Yes for the Encrypt Incoming Mail option.

4. Click on OK, close the document, and close the Name & Address Book.

The Notes Administrator can also set this option for all users. This selection takes precedence over the setting of an individual user.

▶▶ *Receiving Mail*

Reading your mail is like reading any Notes document. You choose a particular view, select a memo, and then open and read it. Once you click on your mail database to select it, there are eight standard mail views available under the View menu, along with any private views you may have added. The views are shown in Figure 9.15. Any unread memos are displayed in red text and have an asterisk next to them in the left margin of the view.

The standard views can display your mail memos in the following ways:

All by Category　　This view lists all mail memos sorted by their assigned categories, including (Not Categorized). One memo can appear in multiple categories, and one category can contain any number of memos.

FIGURE 9.15

You can read your mail using eight different views that are available.

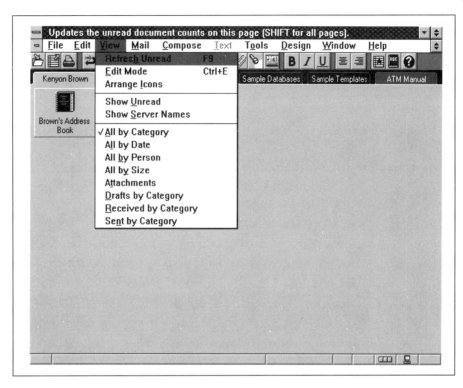

All by Date	This view lists all mail memos in chronological order, with the oldest appearing first. You cannot categorize mail in this view.
All by Person	This view lists all mail memos, sorted by who sent and received them. You cannot categorize mail in this view.
All by Size	This view lists all mail memos in size order, with the largest appearing first. You cannot categorize mail in this view.
Attachments	This view lists all the mail documents that have attachments in chronological order, with the oldest appearing first. You cannot categorize mail in this view.
Drafts by Category	This view lists all mail memos that you saved but didn't send, sorted by category.

| Received by Category | This view lists all mail memos that you have received, sorted by category. |
| Sent by Category | This view lists all mail memos that you have sent, sorted by category. |

▶ RESOLVING COMMON MAIL VIEW PROBLEMS

You may sometimes receive the same memo twice. The reason is usually because you're listed in at least two user groups. When someone sends a message to two of these groups, you receive the memo twice. Unfortunately, Notes doesn't compare the groups to remove duplicate names. This is because groups are used for several purposes besides mail. For example, a member of both the Finance and Executive groups might have his mail filtered so that his assistant reads incoming Finance memos but not Executive memos. Removing duplicate names might inadvertently remove this user's name from the wrong list.

Also, the computations needed to remove duplicate names can easily grow beyond the system's capacity. For example, suppose the group Finance contained the subgroups Accounting and Control and the group Executive contained Officers and Management. The number of possible combinations to check could grow very fast, affecting system performance.

Sometimes you may wonder why new mail doesn't always appear when you receive a New Mail message. This happens when you receive a new mail memo while a Mail view is open. You must refresh the view to see any new memos. To do so, simply press F9 (or choose View ➤ Refresh). Any new memos will then appear in the view; also, any memos you had marked for deletion will disappear.

▶ *Replying to Mail*

Of the many conveniences that Notes Mail provides, the ability to reply *immediately* to mail you receive is foremost. Some people might argue that an "organized" person always performs those tasks that can be completed immediately, leaving the more complex ones for later. The same people might also say that since you send and receive mail through your computer you don't have any excuse for delaying your replies. Mail is stored on your system, waiting for your responses.

You may decide not to reply right away—or not at all—to a mail memo. However, be forewarned that Notes will notify the sender when you receive the mail and when you open it. Unfortunately, this is another handy feature that Notes Mail provides.

Replying to a mail memo is very easy. Open the memo you're replying to, or highlight it in a view. To include excerpts from the original memo, copy and paste them into the body field of your reply. To include the entire memo in your reply, press Ctrl+A for Select All, press Ctrl+C for Copy in the memo you're replying to, and press Ctrl+ V for Paste in your reply. Choose Compose ➤ Reply to reply to the sender of the memo, or choose Compose ➤ Reply to All to reply to all users listed in the To and cc recipient fields of the memo. The subject line of the memo to which you're replying is automatically entered into the subject field, preceded by Re. You can edit this subject line if you desire to do so. Complete the reply memo just as you would any other mail memo, then send it as usual.

 ▶▶ **N O T E**

> **Reply to All includes the users in the bcc (blind carbon copy) field only if *you* were listed in the bcc field of the original message.**

▶ *Forwarding Mail*

The Mail ➤ Forward command lets you forward a copy of any open or highlighted documents to one or more Notes users. Forwarding a document is just like writing any other mail memo, except that Notes automatically inserts the open (or selected) document into the body of the forwarding document.

To forward a Notes document, open the document you want to forward, or select one or more documents in a view. Choose Mail ➤ Forward, and complete the address fields as you would in any mail memo. Edit the body of the document if you wish and then send as usual. If you want to save a copy for yourself, you must add your name to one of the recipient lists (To, cc, or bcc). The Save option in the Document Save dialog box only works for ordinary mail.

 ▶▶ **TIP**

If you want to combine several short documents in your mail database, select them all in the view, choose Mail ➤ Forward, enter yourself as the To recipient, and save. Notes copies all the documents, one after another, into one new document.

▶ New Mail Notification

You can choose if and when to be notified when you receive new mail. If you so choose, your computer will beep and Notes will display a mail notification message when you receive new mail.

To set up new mail notification, choose Tools ➤ Setup ➤ Mail. Select the Check for New Mail Every <number> Minutes option and enter a number (of minutes) that Notes should wait before notifying you. Click on OK.

When this option is enabled, the following actions occur:

- A multinote beep sounds when new Notes mail arrives.

- The Status Bar displays the message "New mail has been delivered to you" when you receive new Notes mail.

- Whenever you have unopened mail (even if it isn't new), a small envelope icon appears in the Status Bar between the point size control and the SmartIcons palette control. You can open your mail file by clicking the envelope.

- If you minimize the Notes window, the Notes icon changes to a small envelope when you receive new mail.

To stop Notes from notifying you, deselect the Check for New Mail Every <number> Minutes option in the Mail Setup dialog box. Deselection takes effect after 30 seconds, providing time to adjust your Ports settings if necessary. Please ask your Notes Administrator to help you since you probably won't be familiar with the Ports settings on your workstation and how you're connected to your Notes server.

▶▶ Sending Mail from Lotus Products That Run in Windows

You can send Notes mail from within any Lotus product that runs under Windows, as well as from within other products that make use of Dynamic Data Exchange (DDE). You must be running Notes Release 2.1 or later, plus at least one of the following products:

- Lotus 1-2-3 for Windows

- Lotus Freelance Graphics for Windows

- Lotus AmiPro Release 2.0 or later

- Lotus Organizer
- Lotus Improv for Windows Release 2.0 or later

You can install these products in any order, following the instructions that come with each product. You don't have to do anything extra.

To send mail from a Lotus product that runs in Windows, start the product and then follow these steps:

1. Open the file you want to send or copy text from. If you just want to send a message (without attaching a file to it or copying anything from it), skip ahead to the next set of numbered instructions. If you want to attach an existing spreadsheet, graphics, or word processing file to your mail message, or if you plan to copy part of a file and paste it into your message, open that file now. If you want to create a new file and attach it to a mail message, you should create the file now.

 ▸▸ **T I P**

In AmiPro, you don't actually have to copy the text; just make sure it's selected before you continue. If you use this shortcut, however, you won't be able to attach a file, nor add to or edit the message text.

2. Select text from the open file you want to copy to the Windows Clipboard.

3. Press Ctrl+C to copy to the Clipboard. You'll be able to paste the text from the Clipboard into your mail message later on.

4. Choose File ➤ Send Mail. The Send Mail dialog box appears. (If the Send Mail command doesn't appear on the File menu, make sure you've installed the appropriate release of the product.)

5. If you want to attach the current file to your mail message, select the Attach checkbox.

6. Click on OK.

▶▶ **T I P**

> **For 1-2-3 users, if a format file exists for your spreadsheet, it is attached to your message along with the spreadsheet. In your message, you should include a reminder to extract both files.**

The Send Mail dialog box varies depending on whether the file has been saved. If the file has been saved since it was last modified, select the Attach checkbox to attach the file to your message, or leave it alone if you want to send only the message itself.

If the file has *not* been saved since it was last modified, select the Save and attach checkbox to save the file and attach it to your message. Don't select Save and attach if you only want to send the message. If the file is empty, the Attach checkbox is dimmed because you cannot mail an empty file (in 1-2-3, the checkbox doesn't even appear). If you selected text in an AmiPro file, the Attach checkbox is dimmed because you cannot attach a file when text is selected.

Now you're ready to send your Notes Mail message. If Notes isn't already running, and you have a password for your User ID, you'll see the Enter Password dialog box:

1. Enter your password.
2. Click on OK. The Lotus Notes dialog box appears.
3. Enter the recipient's name.

▶▶ **N O T E**

> **If you have Save Sent Mail selected in the Mail Setup dialog box in Notes, a copy of the mail message will be saved in your Notes mail database.**

4. Write your mail message, or press Ctrl+V to paste the text you copied to the Clipboard in the section above.
5. Select Send to mail the message and attached file. The message is mailed, and the dialog box closes.

▶▶ **N O T E**

> If you're working in AmiPro, you can send text in the
> active document as the body of the Notes mail memo
> by selecting the text before choosing File ➤ Send Mail.
> The Lotus Notes dialog box you see doesn't have a
> Memo box, because your selection becomes the memo.

▶▶ Converting Mail from cc:Mail to Notes and Notes to cc:Mail

A Notes mail database can be converted to a cc:Mail mailbox, and vice versa. This conversion is generally performed by your Notes or cc:Mail Administrator, but the process may have been set up so that you can perform your own conversion. Add the Mailbox Conversion database to your Workspace, and open it. (Ask your Notes Administrator where you can find the database.) Then follow these steps:

1. Choose Compose ➤ Conversion Request. The Conversion Request document appears. Select one of these options:

   - cc:Mail to Notes, which converts your cc:Mail mailbox to a Notes mail file.
   - Notes to cc:Mail, which converts your Notes mail file to a cc:Mail mailbox.
   - Notes Name & Address Book to cc:Mail, which converts Notes Group lists in your personal N&A Book to cc:Mail private mailing lists. You should do this after you convert your Notes mail database to cc:Mail.

2. Specify the date and time to start the conversion. Use the same format as the default date and time. Choosing a nonpeak time (such as overnight or on the weekend) is less disruptive than converting during peak hours. Specify the earliest date of mail messages to convert. However, this is optional. The feature is known as Message Cutoff Date. If no date is entered, all messages are converted.

3. Enter your full name as it appears in the Notes Name & Address Book.

4. Enter your cc:Mail password.

5. Press ↵.

6. Select the name of your cc:Mail Post Office.

7. If you are converting your Notes personal Name & Address Book to a cc:Mail mailing list, choose File ➤ Attachment and attach the personal N&A Book database. However, this is optional.

8. Press Esc to save and exit the document.

9. Open the Conversion Status view of the Mail Conversion database at any time to see whether your mail file is in the Pending, Processed, or Failure category.

▶▶ *Using Notes with cc:Mail and Other VIM-Compliant Mail Systems*

You can use Notes and any Windows mail program separately. However, if you want to use the products together (to access your mail program from within Notes, and send Notes documents using your mail program), you must use Notes with a VIM-compliant mail system, such as cc:Mail.

What's VIM? VIM stands for Vendor Independent Messaging. When a product supports VIM, it offers certain mail functions and complies with specific technical standards for performing them.

 ▶▶ **W A R N I N G**

> **Your workgroup can support the use of Notes mail along with multiple VIM compliant mail systems, but only one mail product should be installed on your workstation at a time. You can install the mail product either before or after you install Notes.**

▶ *Changing Your Mail System*

When Notes was installed on your workstation, you or your Notes administrator had the opportunity to select either Lotus Notes Mail, cc:Mail, VIM-compliant mail, or None. However, you can change your mail system at any time. Install your new mail product (skip this step if you're changing from an alternative product to Notes mail, or from any mail product to none). Launch Notes, and choose Tools ▶ Setup ▶ Mail. Under Mail Program, choose the mail product you want to use.

▶ *Reading and Sending Mail*

When you use a VIM-compliant mail system, you'll see the following commands on the Notes Mail menu (some mail systems may not use all three commands):

Open	Launches the mail product. Notes remains open.
Forward	Converts the contents of open or selected Notes documents to text or rich text (text with style attributes), and opens the mail product's standard window or dialog box so you can address and send the text as a mail memo.
Forward as Attachment	Converts the open or selected Notes documents to a database and attaches the database to the message you're sending. You see a dialog box in which you can provide additional information about the attached database (for example, in cc:Mail, you see the Addressing dialog box).
Send	Converts the current or selected Notes document(s) into an encapsulated Notes database and attaches it to a mail memo that you address and send as usual.

▶ *Opening Encapsulated Databases Sent to You*

Encapsulation is the process Notes uses to store a Notes document in a database attachment when you send a message to cc:Mail or another VIM-compliant mail system. If you're using cc:Mail as your mail system in Notes, the cc:Mail recipient normally receives the message in a Notes database attachment.

If you want the cc:Mail user who's receiving your message to see the message in rendered text format, you can use a special Notes field called MailFormat. Check with your Notes Administrator for information on using the MailFormat field.

Notes can encapsulate a database within an attachment. If your mail program supports direct launching of attachments (as cc:Mail does), double-click the attachment icon within the message. The mail product copies the attachment, launches Notes, and opens the encapsulated database. You can also copy the attachment to disk, and at the DOS command line, start Notes and specify the file with the Notes database extension .NSF. For example:

```
NOTES C:\DATA\DOCUMENT.NSF
```

You can create a database just for storing these documents and then copy the documents from encapsulated databases to this new database (or to any other database on your Workspace).

Finally, we should emphasize that several Notes features aren't available to you when you don't use Notes Mail. For example, the Mail ➤ Address command isn't available. However, your mail product probably has a similar capability. The Send User ID commands aren't available either. (These commands include mailing encryption keys and requesting certificates by mail.) However, you can export an encryption key by using the Tools ➤ User ID ➤ Encryption Keys, Export command, and you can get new certificates by delivering a safe copy of your User ID to your certifier using Tools ➤ User ID ➤Create Safe Copy. You can also send and receive Notes encryption keys as cc:Mail attachments.

The Tools ➤ Scan Unread commands are not available for use in your mail file. These Tools ➤ Setup ➤ Mail options are not available in the

Mail Setup dialog box: signing and encrypting mail, new mail notification, and mail file location.

Dial-up mail (including the Tools ➤ Call and Tools ➤ Hang Up commands) aren't available. However, cc:Mail users have a similar remote use capability. The Signing a memo option isn't available when the Forward command is used. However, Notes documents sent using the Send command can be signed if the mail product supports it.

Notes rich text is converted to rich text format (RTF), except with cc:Mail where Notes rich text format is maintained very closely. However, tables and DDE links are converted to ASCII text (plain text).

▶▶ *Managing Your Mail*

As soon as you've saved a few dozen mail memos and then tried to find a specific memo, you'll want to manage your mail for easier retrieval. There are several ways to manage your mail:

- Sort your saved memos by creating categories for them.
- Change the subject lines of saved mail memos.
- Keep down the size of your mail file.
- Create personalized views for your mail database, which we discussed in an earlier section.

▶ *Categorizing Your Mail*

You can create categories in which to sort your saved mail memos, and assign one or more of them to each memo. Of the standard mail views, only All by Category, Received by Category, and Sent by Category can display your mail categories. Memos that you haven't assigned to any categories are listed under "(Not Categorized)" at the end of the view.

Personal Categories lets you create a simple filing system for mail documents that you save. A category can be any word or phrase, and you can save a memo in more than one category. You would enter the category name. If you enter multiple categories, separate them with commas. For example, you could save a memo about a new employee under both the Memos and Personnel categories. Categories are displayed only in the Composed by Category and All by Category views; they aren't seen by the recipient(s) of your memos.

▶▶ **N O T E**

Categories are case-sensitive. For example, "sales report" is a different category from "Sales Report".

To categorize a mail memo, follow these steps:

1. Open a memo from your mail database, or select one or more memos in the view.

2. Choose Tools ➤ Categorize. The Categorize dialog box appears. It lists your existing mail categories and allows you to create new ones.

3. Assign one or more existing categories to the open or selected memo(s) by selecting categories from the list. You can also create a new category by entering the name into the text box.

4. Click on OK. The selected document(s) will appear under the assigned category in the view.

▶▶ **T I P**

When you assign more than one category to a memo, it appears in the view under each category. Don't use the backslash character (\) within a category name, because Notes uses that to create subcategories. If you know category names and don't want to scroll through the list, you can type multiple categories into the text box by separating them with commas.

▶ *Changing and Removing Categories*

Removing a memo from a category can only be accomplished by opening the memo or selecting one or more memos at the view level. Choose Tools ➤ Categorize. Deselect the highlighted category you want to remove from assignment to the memo(s) and then click on

OK. If you remove all category assignments from a memo, the memo will appear under (Not Categorized) when you return to the view.

▶▶ **WARNING**

You *cannot* delete a memo from a category by selecting the memo under the category and then choosing Edit ➤ Cut or pressing Delete. These actions *delete* the memo from your mail database, which you may not want to do. It helps to remember that assigning a category to a document is an *attribute* of a document, an attribute that you can change any time in your mail database.

A category exists only as long as it contains documents. To eliminate a category, all memos assigned to it must be deleted or must have their assignment to this category removed. Any of these documents that are not assigned to other categories will be listed under Not Categorized.

▶▶ **NOTE**

The category will not disappear from the category list box until you close and reopen the database.

To change the name of a category at the view level, select all the memos in the category. Choose Tools ➤ Categorize and deselect the category you want to change. Enter the new category name into the text box, and click on OK. All the documents you selected are now categorized under the new name. To create subcategory names, type the category and subcategory into the text box in this form:

    Category\Subcategory

For example:

    Customers\West
    Customers\Southeast

You can create additional levels of subcategories by specifying:

    Category\Subcategory\SubSubcategory (and so on)

For example:

Customers\West\Menlo Park\Downtown
Customers\West\Menlo Park\Suburbs

Subcategories aren't listed in the Categorize dialog box. To assign a subcategory to subsequent memos, you need to enter it into the New Categories text box in the above format each time.

N O T E

If you create a category by entering it as a Personal Category when composing a mail document, you must save the document in order to save the category.

For further convenience, you can design macros that manage your mail by categorizing documents automatically. For example, suppose you often receive press releases which you want to save in your mail database under the category "Press Release." You can design and run a macro that automatically places all incoming mail from the industry newswire in the "Press Release" category. We discuss macros in Chapter 16, "Writing Formulas and Macros."

▶ *Changing the Subject Line of a Mail Memo*

Why would you want to change the subject line of a mail memo that someone sends you? When you receive a memo with no subject line or a nonspecific subject line, it's hard to tell from the view what information the memo contains. The subject line appears in the view. So the more specific you make the subject line, the easier it will be for you to find the memo in the view.

To change the subject line of a mail memo, select the document in the view and press Ctrl+E (or choose Edit ➤ Edit Document) to edit the document. At this point, you can enter some meaningful text into the subject field. For example, change the subject line:

Date: 08/13/98 10:30:23 AM
Subject: Presentation

to this:

> Date: 08/13/98 10:30:23 AM
> Subject: Marketing presentation—results of product focus groups

You can then save the memo without sending it by pressing Ctrl+S (or choosing File ➤ Save) and exiting from the memo by pressing Esc. Days, weeks, or months later, you'll be able to find this memo fast with a glance at the subject that appears in the view.

▶ Keeping Down the Size of Your Mail Database

Mail databases can get very big, very quickly, and can take up valuable space on your computer. You might even notice that as your mail database grows—and this applies to any database—the system takes longer to open views and documents. Your system starts performing sluggishly. However, you can keep down the size of your mail database by performing these housekeeping tasks routinely:

- Periodically browse through the mail you've saved and delete those memos that you no longer need.

- Save large attachments on the mail server rather than locally on your hard drive.

- Cut memos that are very large or have large attachments from a local database on your system and paste them into a database on the server.

- Export large "goodies"—such as scanned images, graphics, and especially sound and video clips—from your computer to the server.

- If you're a dial-up Notes user, select the Truncate large documents option and remove attachments in the Tools Replicate dialog box.

▶▶ What's Next?

In the next chapter, we discuss Dial-up Notes. As a Notes workstation or laptop user, you can connect to a Notes server either through a direct LAN connection or through a remote, dial-up connection using

Dial-up Notes. However, Dial-up Notes isn't a separate product; instead, the term describes the new remote communications features of Lotus Notes version 3.X. You'll be able to take advantage of these features whenever you are using Notes on your workstation to connect to a server over a telephone line. For a person working off-site or on the road, Dial-up Notes can help you to keep your Notes databases current.

Dial-Up Notes

▶▶ *F*AST *T*RACK

▶ ***To create a new database replica***   **215**

choose File ➤ New Replica. The New Replica dialog box
appears. Choose the server where the original database
you want to copy is stored. Enter the file name, if Notes
hasn't filled it in for you. Choose the server where your
replica will be stored in the New Replica, Server box.
Choose Local to store it on your hard disk. Type a file
name (up to eight characters) for the new replica. Notes
adds the .NSF extension for you. Click on the New button
to create the replica. Click on OK to confirm the changes
you made.

▶ ***To call a Notes server and replicate a database***   **219**

display the Workspace and then click on the database icon
to select it. Choose Tools ➤ Replicate. The Tools Replicate
dialog box appears. Enter your password if you've set one
for yourself. Select a Notes server from the Server list box.
Click on OK.

▶ ***To replicate workstation-based Notes mail***   **224**

choose Tools ➤ Setup ➤ Mail. The Mail Setup dialog box
appears. Select the Workstation-based mail option. Click
on the Replication button. The Local Mail Database Replication Options dialog box appears. Click on OK to accept
the changes. Click on OK to close the Mail Setup dialog box.

▶ ▶   **I**f **you** often work outside your office, at home, or on the road, and still want access to your organization's databases, you're going to appreciate Dial-up Notes. Dial-up Notes is a set of Notes features that lets you access Notes via modem when your workstation isn't connected to a local area network (LAN). You can use Dial-up Notes on any computer running the Notes workstation software, including desktop computers and many laptops and notebooks.

You can use Dial-up Notes to work *locally*, wherever you are, because you can make local replicas (exact copies of shared databases) and then work on these replicas. You can also send and receive Notes mail by working in a local replica of your mail database and then exchanging documents (replicating) with your mail database on the server.

In this chapter you'll learn how to set up a remote Notes connection so you can get all the benefits of working off-site. Specifically, you'll learn how to:

- Set up your modem for Notes
- Use Notes scripts
- Call your server
- Use database replicas

▶ ▶ Getting Started with Dial-Up Notes

Before you set up a dial-up workstation, be sure that:

- Notes is completely installed on your workstation.
- A Notes-compatible modem is connected to your workstation, as discussed in the next section.

▶ *Setting Up the Remote Connection*

Before you can use your modem to send and receive mail or exchange data between databases, you must "prepare" Notes by identifying some important communication settings:

1. Choose Tools ➤ Setup ➤ Location. The Location Setup dialog box appears.

2. Identify your home server.

3. Select a time zone.

4. Specify the telephone dialing prefixes you need to use in order to call the Notes server.

5. Click on OK.

6. Choose Tools ➤ Setup ➤ Mail. The Mail Setup dialog box appears.

7. Select the Workstation-based mail option to work locally on your computer (rather than interactively with a server).

8. Click on the Replication button to select replication options.

▶ *Creating a Remote Connection Document*

You also need to create a Remote Connection document in your personal Name & Address Book for each Notes server that you call. You use Remote Connection documents to set up modem connections from your workstation to Notes servers. Windows users can also use Remote Connection documents to schedule calls that take place automatically in the background.

▶▶ **N O T E**

If you chose the Dial-up Workstation option during Notes setup, Notes has already created a Remote Connection document for your home server. If all the databases you'll use are on that server, you don't need to compose any additional Remote Connection documents.

Remote Connection documents are created and stored in your personal Name & Address Book. If you specify your modem settings, Dial-up settings, and Remote Connection document properly, you can place a call to a server on demand by using the Tools ➤ Call or Tools ➤ Replicate commands. (The server names that appear in the Tools ➤ Call and Tools ➤ Replicate lists are taken from your Remote Connection documents.)

To create a new Remote Connection document, follow the steps below. If you don't quite understand what we're doing here, we'll explain everything over the course of the chapter.

1. Click on or open your personal Name & Address Book that's located on a page in your Workspace.

2. Choose Compose ➤ Connection ➤ Remote. The Remote Connection Document appears, as shown in Figure 10.1.

FIGURE 10.1 ▶

The Remote Connection document

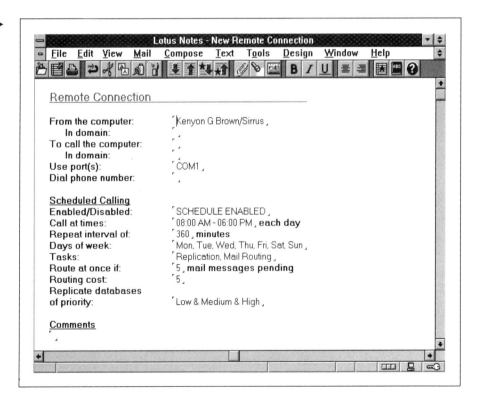

3. Enter the name of the Notes server you want to call. (This document is the Remote Connection record for the server you name here.)

4. Enter the name of the communication port you specified in Tools ➤ Setup ➤ Ports. It should be a COM port.

5. Enter the server's telephone number. Parentheses and hyphens are ignored, so feel free to use them to make the phone number readable. Use a comma to force a 2-second delay. This is useful for separating credit card numbers and digits that access outside phone lines. For example, it is common in the U.S. to use 9 to access an outside line from a business telephone. If the server has more than one number, you can enter each number separated by semicolons (;). If the first number is busy, your modem will try each number in turn until a connection is established. If you entered a Phone Dialing Prefix in the Location Setup dialog box, enter only the part of the number that follows the prefix. For example, if you entered the area code and exchange as a prefix, enter only the last four digits of the telephone number.

6. Press ↵ to change your selection in the Enabled/Disabled field (it's a toggle). Disabled turns off background exchange for this server; otherwise leave Enabled selected. You might want to select Disabled when you won't have a chance to read new documents from this server for a day or two, or when you know the server will be unavailable for the next couple of replications.

7. Specify a particular time or a range of time to call the server. If you enter a range, your modem will call at the beginning of the range and will keep calling every so often until a connection is made. It will stop calling the server at the end of the range. If you enter a single time, your modem will call periodically for up to an hour until a connection is made.

8. Specify how soon your workstation should call the server again after a successful call. Enter 0 (zero) to call once only.

9. Specify which day(s) of the week to call this server.

10. Select one or both task(s)—Mail Routing and Replication. The task(s) you select will be performed each time this server is called. Mail Routing applies to Notes mail users only: Select it for your mail server Remote Connection document if you use workstation-based mail. Replication exchanges data with all databases for which you have local replicas, including Notes mail if you use it.

11. Specify the number of outgoing mail messages that automatically trigger a call to the server (applies only when Mail Routing is selected under Tasks).

  T I P

> To prioritize databases for scheduling replication, use the default entry of Low & Medium & High, unless you want to create separate Remote Connection documents for databases of different priority. For example, you could set the priority of your mail database to High and other databases to Medium or Low, then specify two Remote Connection documents: one to call the server to replicate High priority databases every hour, and one to call the server to replicate Low and Medium priority databases once a day. Click on a database to select it and then choose File ➤ Database ➤ Information. Click on the Replication button. Select the Priority setting you want for this database (Low, Medium, or High). Repeat for all the local database replicas you have in common with this server. Create a separate Remote Connection document for each priority level (or perhaps one for High and another for Medium & Low).

▶ Setting Up Your Modem

You can set up any Notes-compatible modem to use Dial-up Notes. However, before you do, we recommend that you refer to your modem's documentation for further advice. Modems that aren't Hayes-compatible sometimes have problems running Dial-up Notes. To set up your modem, follow these steps:

1. Choose Tools ➤ Setup ➤ Ports. The Port Setup dialog box appears, as shown in Figure 10.2.

2. Highlight a communication port to use with your modem (a COM port on the PC).

FIGURE 10.2 ▶

The Port Setup dialog box enables you to se-lect a communication port and connect your modem to it.

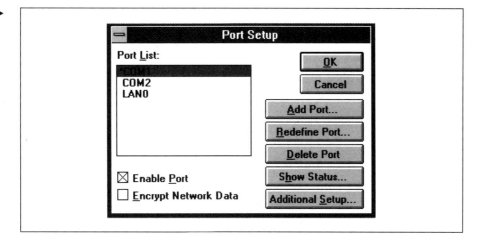

3. Click on the Show Status button to see if another device is using the same port. The Show Status dialog box appears, as shown in Figure 10.3.

FIGURE 10.3 ▶

The Show Status dia-log box lets you see what tasks are running on the port you select.

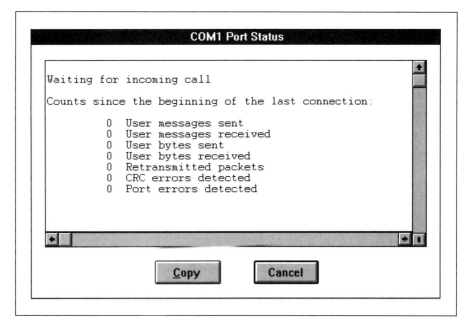

4. From here, you can do any of the following:

- Review the information displayed.
- Click on the Copy button to copy the information to the clipboard.
- Click on Cancel to close the dialog box.

As you can see in the Port Settings dialog box, there are a number of option buttons. Click on the Additional Setup button. The Additional Setup dialog box appears, as shown in Figure 10.4.

You use this dialog box to select a modem, configure dialing options for it, or monitor your modem's activity during dial-up operations. To finish configuring the type of modem you're using, follow these steps:

1. Select a modem command file (.MDM file) for your modem from the Modem Type list. Its file name appears beneath the list (in this example, it's HAYES24.MDM).

2. Set your modem's speaker volume to High, Medium, Low, or Off, depending on your work environment. The default setting is Off, meaning you won't hear the modem. Turn on the Speaker Volume so you can monitor call progress while attempting server connection. This is most useful when using internal modems which do not have lights to monitor the activity of the modem.

FIGURE 10.4

The Additional Setup dialog box enables you to select a specific modem and configure dialing options for it.

```
┌──────────────────────────────────────────────────────────────┐
│  ─                    Additional Setup                        │
│  Modem Type                                      ┌─────────┐   │
│  ┌──────────────────────────────────────────┬─┐ │   OK    │   │
│  │ DSI 9624LE/PC (no RTS/CTS)               │▲│ └─────────┘   │
│  │ Generic V2 9600 bps Modem File (with instr)│ │ ┌─────────┐ │
│  │ GRiD Internal 2400                        │ │ │ Cancel  │ │
│  │ Hayes Smartmodem 1200                     │ │ └─────────┘ │
│  │ Hayes Smartmodem 2400                     │▼│ ┌─────────┐ │
│  └──────────────────────────────────────────┴─┘ │ Edit... │ │
│  Command File:    HAYES24.MDM                    └─────────┘ │
│  ┌Speaker Volume─┐ ┌Maximum Speed──┐  ☒ Log Modem I/O       │
│  │ ⦿ Off ○ Medium│ │○ 1200  ○ 19200│  ☒ Rts/Cts Flow Control│
│  │ ○ Low ○ High  │ │⦿ 2400  ○ 38400│  ☐ Log Script I/O      │
│  └───────────────┘ │○ 4800  ○ 57600│  ┌─────────┐           │
│                    │○ 9600  ○115200│  │ Scripts...│          │
│  ┌Dial Mode──────┐ └───────────────┘  └─────────┘           │
│  │⦿ Tone ○ Pulse │    Dial Timeout │60│ seconds             │
│  └───────────────┘    Hangup if idle│15│ minutes            │
└──────────────────────────────────────────────────────────────┘
```

3. Set your modem's dial mode to Tone or Pulse. Select Pulse if you use a rotary phone or if your modem doesn't support Tone (touchtone) dialing; otherwise select Tone (the default).

4. Change the Maximum Speed of data transmission for your modem if there are problems communicating at higher speeds, as on a noisy phone line. You can always use a lower setting to reduce the speed. Otherwise, Notes determines the maximum data transmission speed from the type of modem you are using. The speed actually used will be the *lesser* of the maximum speed you select here and the maximum speed specified in the .MDM file. For example, if you select 38400 bps here and the .MDM file specifies 19200 bps as the maximum, you will see a warning similar to the following:

   The selected Modem command file only allows speeds as high as: 19200

5. Specify the maximum number of seconds your workstation tries to establish a connection to a Notes server. When this number is reached, the call "times out" (terminates) and your modem returns to its initial state. You can increase or decrease Dial Timeout to meet specific calling conditions before you try calling the Notes server again.

6. Specify the maximum time your workstation maintains a connection to a Notes server before it "hangs up" (terminates the connection). Selecting this option disconnects your workstation from the server when you aren't transmitting or receiving data beyond the specified time. If the Notes Administrator has specified a different Hangup if idle time for the server's modem, the shorter time period takes precedence.

 ▶▶ **N O T E**

The Hangup if idle option works only if the value you set is less than the value set for the mail polling interval in the Mail Setup dialog box.

7. Select the Log Modem option to tell Notes to record modem control strings and responses in the workstation's Notes Log. In this way, you can determine or anticipate modem communication problems. You can then review the Phone Calls, Replication Events, and Miscellaneous Events views of the log. Deselect this option when problems are corrected.

8. Select the Rts/Cts Flow Control option. Rts/Cts stands for **Re**quest **T**o **S**end, **C**lear **T**o **S**end. This enables Notes to control hardware flow between the server's modem and your modem. You specify this option when using data compression.

 ▶▶ **N O T E**

Some serial cards and modems don't support this feature—if it isn't mentioned in your serial card or modem documentation, it's probably not supported.

You can also click on the Edit button to open the Edit Modem Command File dialog box if you want to change your modem command file. Scroll to the setting(s) you want to change and make your changes. Click on the Save or Save As button. The Save option saves your changes to the command file, which is stored on your hard disk. The Save As option saves the edited command file to your hard disk under another name that you specify in a standard Save File dialog box, and doesn't affect the command file you originally opened.

 ▶▶ **W A R N I N G**

Record your modem's current configuration before editing command or script files, or save edited command and script files under a new name.

Click on the Exit button to close the window. The Exit option closes the dialog box. If you haven't selected Save or Save As after making changes, a message asks if you want to save your changes. Select Yes to save your changes, No to close the dialog box and revert to the previous version of the modem command file, or Cancel to return to the dialog box.

▶▶ *Calling a Server*

After you set up your workstation and modem to use Dial-up Notes, you're ready to call a Notes server. You might want to call a server to exchange data between your local database replicas and their corresponding shared databases, or to work interactively with databases on the server.

You can use the Call Server dialog box to call a Notes server immediately, or you can set up a schedule for automatic dialing by using the Scheduled Calling part of the Remote Connection document for a server.

To call a Notes server, do the following:

1. Choose Tools ➤ Call. The Call Server dialog box appears, as shown in Figure 10.5.

2. Select a server from the Server list. The servers that are listed here are the ones for which you have Remote Connection documents in your personal Name and Address book.

3. Type the server's telephone number as it appears in the Remote Connection document in your personal Name & Address Book.

FIGURE 10.5 ▶

The Call Server dialog box

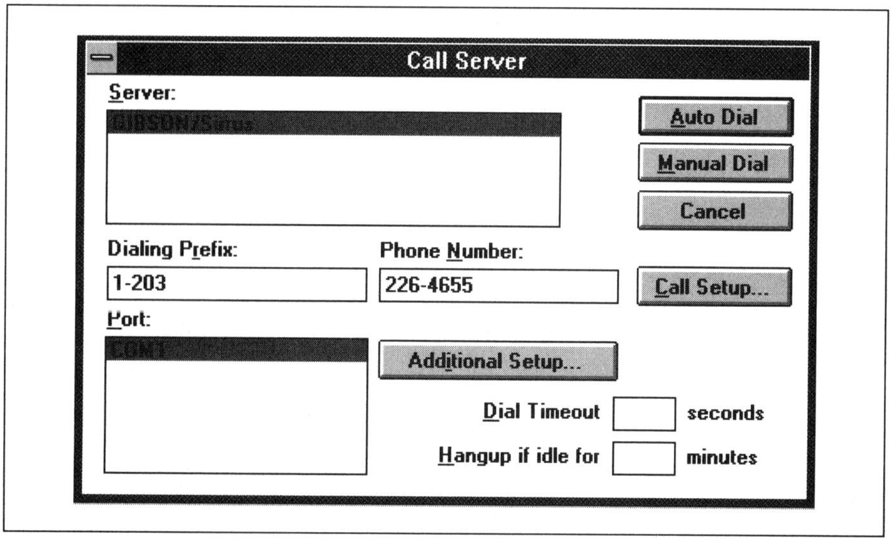

4. Specify the maximum number of seconds to wait for a connection to a server before canceling the attempt. The default is 60.

5. Specify the maximum number of minutes your system will stay connected to a server without activity (data transmission). The default is 15. The Hangup if idle option works only if the value you set is less than the value set for the mail polling interval in the Mail Setup dialog box.

6. Select Auto Dial or Manual Dial. The Auto Dial option automatically dials the specified telephone number. The Manual Dial option prompts you to pick up the phone and dial the number. Use this option when you require an operator to complete the call, for example, when you're calling from a hotel room.

When a connection is made, the dialog box closes and the your Workspace reappears.

▶▶ *Making a Database Replica with Dial-Up Notes*

As we discussed in earlier chapters, a replica is a copy of a shared database that you store either on a network server or on your hard disk. It can be displayed in your Workspace just like the source database. When you create a replica, changes to the original database (source database) or to the replica will be reflected in the other. To update a database replica with information from the source database (and to update the shared database with information that you create locally), you perform replication. To do this, you can use a Remote Connection document or call the server directly using the Call Server dialog box.

Before you can use the database exchange feature of Dial-up Notes to replicate regularly, you must first create a local replica of the shared database you want to use. By creating a local database replica, you can use the database without being connected to a Notes server on a LAN or being connected to a modem all the time.

▶▶ **N O T E**

You must know the name of the server and the file name of the database you want to replicate before you attempt replication.

To create a new database replica:

1. Choose File ➤ New Replica. The New Replica dialog box appears, as shown in Figure 10.6.

2. Choose the server where the original database you want to copy is stored. Notes fills this box in for you automatically if you selected a database on your Workspace before you chose the command.

3. Enter the file name, if Notes hasn't filled it in for you.

4. Choose the server where your replica will be stored in the New Replica, Server box. Choose Local to store it on your hard disk.

5. Type a file name (up to eight characters) for the new replica. Notes adds the .NSF extension for you.

FIGURE 10.6

The New Replica dialog box enables you to make a replica copy of a database.

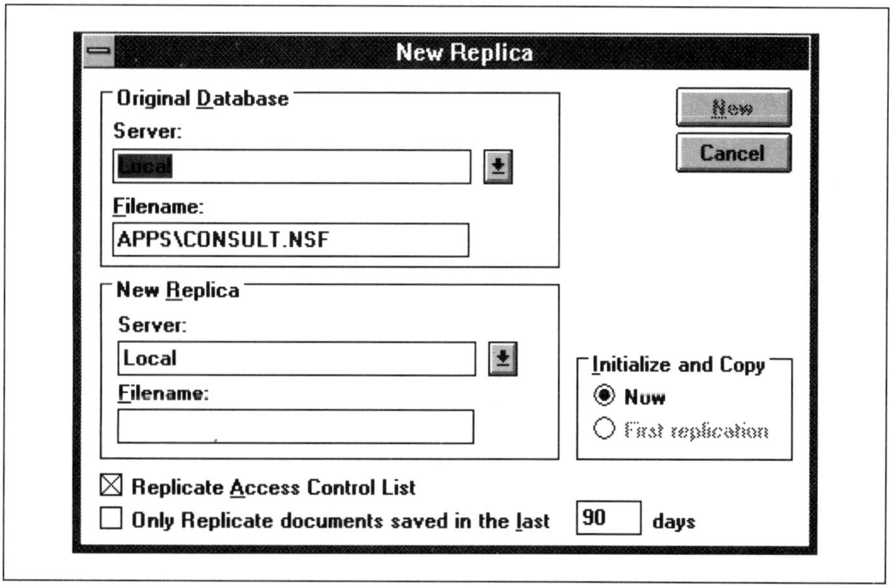

New Replica

Original Database

Server:
Local ▼

Filename:
APPS\CONSULT.NSF

New Replica

Server:
Local ▼

Filename:

⊠ Replicate Access Control List
☐ Only Replicate documents saved in the last 90 days

New
Cancel

Initialize and Copy
◉ Now
○ First replication

6. Select one, both, or neither of these options:

- **Replicate Access Control List (ACL)**: This option copies the ACL. However, this is selected by default. We recommend that you keep the default, at least until you have reviewed Chapter 18, on security issues.
- **Only replicate documents saved in the last [ ] days**: Fills the new replica with those documents created in the time period you specify. Selected by default. This option is especially useful for Dial-up Notes users who create smaller subsets of shared databases to use on a laptop workstation.

7. Select one of the options under Initialize and Copy:

- **Now**: Fills the replica with documents as soon as you select New and attempts to make a phone call to that server right away.
- **First replication**: Fills the replica with documents at the first scheduled or forced replication. Until that time, the replica is called a "replica stub" because it consists of a blank database icon and a database ID number only. There is no design or data.

8. Click on the New button.

Notes creates the replica. The next time you replicate, you can select several options to refine the replication settings according to your needs. To limit the number of documents that will be copied to a database replica during the first replication, choose File ➤ Database ➤ Information. The Database Information dialog box appears, as shown in Figure 10.7. Click on the Replication button. The Replication Settings dialog box appears, as shown in Figure 10.8. Select a Priority level. The priority level is used for scheduling database replication. The default is Medium.

Select any of the following options:

- **Do not replicate deletions to replicas of this database**: To prevent deletions to local replicas from being propagated to other replicas of this database. This option is selected by default. In other words, if you delete documents in the replica database located on your Dial-up machine, these deletions won't propagate back to the main server database when you get reconnected.

FIGURE 10.7

*The Database Informa-
tion dialog box*

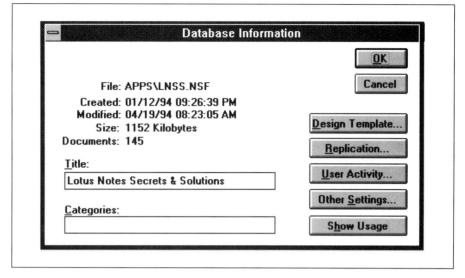

FIGURE 10.8

*The Replication Set-
tings dialog box*

Choose this option when you have Author access or higher to a
database and need to delete documents to manage space on your
Dial-up machine, but these documents are still of relevance to the
other users of the database.

- **Disable replication of this database**: To prevent replication of this database during any replications you perform, even if it is included in the databases selected for the replication.

- **Remove documents saved more than <number> days ago**: To remove documents saved longer than the number of days specified. You will be prompted each time you open the database until you answer Yes to delete the documents, change the number of days specified, or turn this option off.

- **Truncate large documents and remove attachments**: To remove bitmaps and other large objects and all attachments from documents being received over a dial-up connection. Select this option to avoid long connect times when it isn't practical to receive large files over a dial-up connection. A truncated file appears with the word *Truncated* as part of document name.

- **Replicate database Title, Categories, and Template Names**: To give this database the same title, categories, and template names as the original database.

Select Selective to display the Selective Replication dialog box. (We discuss selective replication in more detail in Chapter 19.) Select options in this dialog box to replicate only certain types of information from the source database. Select View history to display the Replication History dialog box. The information you see in this dialog box lets you check when and with which server this database last replicated. Click on OK to confirm the changes you make.

▶▶ *Replicating a Database on a Regular Basis*

After you make a local replica of a database the first time, you can use Dial-up Notes to work locally. This means you share databases on your workstation by calling a Notes server regularly and then exchanging data between your local replicas and the shared databases. In other words, you replicate databases when you want to exchange information between an original and a replica of a database. Replicating databases is an easy procedure.

Why do you want to replicate databases on a regular basis? You save time because your Notes runs faster with local databases. You also save money because your telephone calls are shorter when you work locally. It's more convenient and less expensive to move data over telephone lines all at once. Furthermore, you can work whenever and wherever you want, even when a telephone line is unavailable. You already have a replica of a database on your computer.

To call a Notes server and replicate a database, display the Workspace and then click on the database icon to select it. Choose Tools ➤ Replicate. Enter your password if you've set one for yourself. The Tools Replicate dialog box appears, as shown in Figure 10.9. Select a Notes server from the Server list box. Select the Replicate options you want as follows:

- **All databases in common**: Exchanges documents between all databases in common between your workstation and the server.

- **Selected databases**: Exchanges documents between the local database(s) you selected on your workstation and their counterparts on the server. You must select the databases before you open this dialog box.

FIGURE 10.9

The Tools Replicate dialog box lets you choose replication options for refining data exchange between the server and your machine.

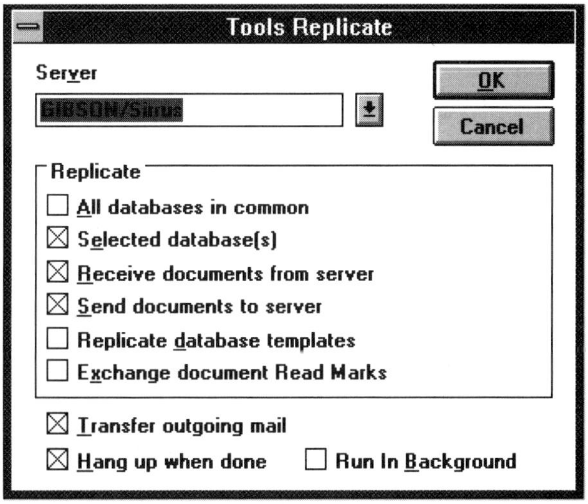

Tools Replicate

Ser**v**er

GIBSON/Sirus

☐ **A**ll databases in common
☒ S**e**lected database(s)
☒ **R**eceive documents from server
☒ **S**end documents to server
☐ Replicate **d**atabase templates
☐ E**x**change document Read Marks

☒ **T**ransfer outgoing mail
☒ **H**ang up when done   ☐ Run In **B**ackground

OK

Cancel

- **Receive documents from server**: Pulls new information from databases on the server to their counterparts on your workstation, for all databases in common or for selected databases (whichever option you selected above).

- **Send documents to server**: Pushes new information from your local databases to their counterparts on the server, for all databases in common or for selected databases (whichever option you selected above).

- **Replicate database templates**: Updates database templates.

- **Exchange document Read Marks**: Exchanges the read marks on documents in all replicated databases. A read mark is a star in the left margin of a view that indicates which documents you haven't opened (read) yet.

- **Transfer outgoing mail:** Applies only if you use Notes mail and hold mail locally until you call your mail server. Sends documents from your local Outgoing Mail database (MAIL.BOX) to the server. Notes deletes these documents in MAIL.BOX after sending them to the server. Note that if your company has more than one server accessible via dial-up, you can transfer outgoing mail to any server in your company's domain, not just your home (mail) server.

- **Hangup when done**: Automatically disconnects from the server when replication is complete. Use this option to reduce your telephone charges.

- **Background Exchange**: Performs data exchange in the background so you can continue using your workstation for other tasks. Selecting this option does not perform scheduled tasks; to do so, use the Background Program option in the User Setup dialog box.

Click on OK to accept the changes. Notes then calls the server. When a connection is made, the dialog box closes and the Notes Workspace reappears.

> **Make sure that the database you're replicating and its counterpart on the server both have either LocalDomain-Servers or the name of the specific server you're replicating with in their access control lists, with Manager access.**

After Notes completes the replication process, the Replication Statistics dialog box appears. (It opens automatically after replication.) This dialog box displays details about the database documents and mail messages that are affected during database replication:

- **Additions:** Reports the number of new documents that are added (Sent) to the original database, or added (Received) to the database replica.

- **Deletions:** Reports the number of documents that are deleted (Sent) from the original database, or deleted (Received) from the database replica.

- **Updates:** Reports the number of documents that are changed (Sent) in the original database, or changed (Received) in the database replica.

- **Databases replicated:** Reports the number of databases that are replicated.

- **Databases initialized:** Reports the number of databases that are initialized.

- **Mail messages transferred:** Reports the number of Mail messages that are transferred from your Outgoing mailbox to your mail server.

- **Replication exception conditions logged:** Reports the number of possible error conditions that occurred during replication. Information about these conditions appear in your Notes log file (LOG.NSF).

Click on OK to close the dialog box and return to the Notes Workspace. If you didn't select the Hang up when done option in the Tools Replicate dialog box, you need to manually break the connection to the server. To end a modem connection to a Notes server, choose

Tools ➤ Hang Up. The Hang Up dialog box appears, as shown in Figure 10.10. Select the port you want to disconnect. Click on the Hangup button, or Cancel if you change your mind.

To check when and with which server a database last replicated, choose File ➤ Database ➤ Information. Click on the Replication button. Click on the View History button. The Replication History dialog box appears, as shown in Figure 10.11. You can do any of the following:

- To sort the information by date, select By Date.

- To sort the information by server, select By Server.

- To delete all history, select Clear. This option is useful if you think your replica doesn't contain all the documents it should or if time/date stamps are out of sync between your replica and others. This deletes the replication history for all servers which the server replicates.

Select Cancel to close the dialog box.

FIGURE 10.10 ▶

The Hang Up dialog box

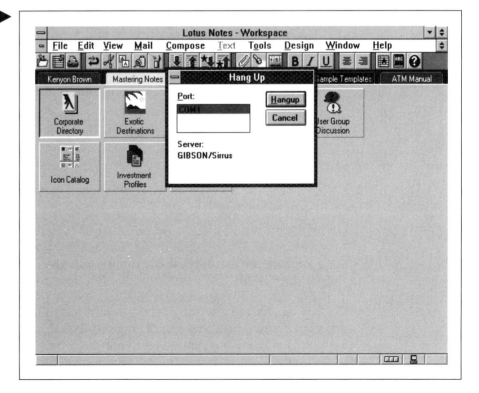

FIGURE 10.11 ▶

The Replication History dialog box enables you to check when and with which server a database last replicated.

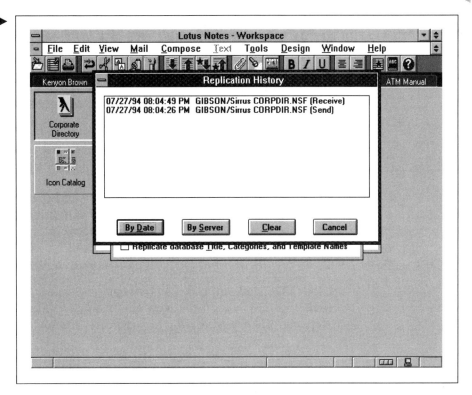

 ▶▶ **N O T E**

If you clear the history, Notes will no longer have a record of when replication occurred last. The next replication will invoke a *full* search for documents to replicate, not just a normal (incremental) search. That means Notes will look at the "last modified time" for all documents in the source database and replicate any changes that the destination database doesn't have. Use this option only if you're sure it's needed; full replications create more network traffic and take longer than incremental replications.

▶▶ *Replicating Mail with Dial-Up Notes*

If you selected either the Remote-connection (via modem) option or the Network and remote connection option during Notes setup, Notes created both the local mail replica and the local MAIL.BOX. This is your outgoing mailbox for storing your mail. Notes added the icons to your Workspace.

As you can see, Notes doesn't add the icon for the server-based mail file, even when you switch to server-based mail. If you want to switch to server-based mail, you must manually add the icon by connecting to the server first and then selecting File ➤ Open Database for your server before you can work with mail interactively.

You can also replicate mail to your server so you can access it locally. To replicate workstation-based Notes mail, choose Tools ➤ Setup ➤ Mail. The Mail Setup dialog box appears. Select the Workstation-based mail option. Click on the Replication button. The Local Mail Database Replication Options dialog box appears, as shown in Figure 10.12.

Use the "Do not copy local changes or deletions back to server" option when you want to make changes in or remove documents from the local version of your mail database, but don't want these changes to affect the documents on the server version. Use the "Only copy first part of large documents from server" option to limit the size of the documents you receive from the server. The advantage is that it keeps the local replica of your mail database small, so it opens more quickly. Don't use this, however, if you need to work with entire documents or use attachments in your local location. The "Remove documents saved more

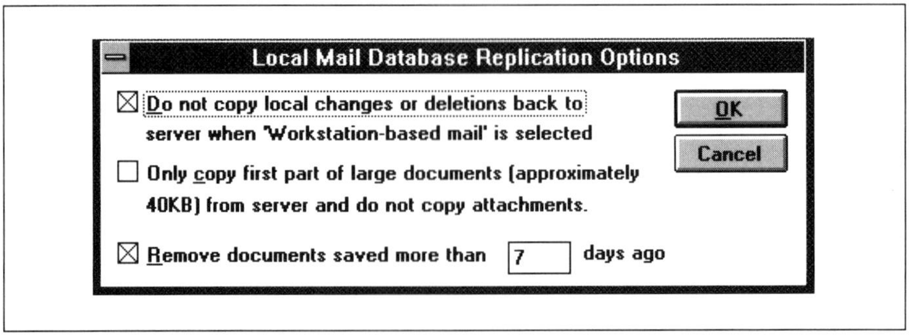

FIGURE 10.12 ▶

The Local Mail Database Replication Options dialog box enables you to select replication options for workstation-based mail.

Local Mail Database Replication Options

☒ <u>D</u>o not copy local changes or deletions back to server when 'Workstation-based mail' is selected

☐ Only <u>c</u>opy first part of large documents (approximately 40KB) from server and do not copy attachments.

☒ <u>R</u>emove documents saved more than [7] days ago

OK

Cancel

than n days" option lets you work locally with only your most recent mail.

Click on OK to accept any changes you make. Click on OK to close
the Mail Setup dialog box.

►► *Using Your Outgoing Mail Database*

Your Outgoing Mail database (called MAIL.BOX) is a temporary storage area on your workstation for your outgoing memos. It is not used
in the same way as your Mail database. Do not try to compose mail
from your Outgoing Mail database. You should use your Mail database
instead.

The documents you send are dropped in the mailbox and held for
pickup like letters dropped in a mailbox but not yet picked up by the
Post Office. Pickup occurs when:

- You perform replication with your mail server by selecting the
  Transfer outgoing mail option in the Tools Replicate dialog box, or

- You close the Workspace and exit Notes. When you do, Notes displays a dialog box telling you that you have outgoing mail. You're
  asked if you want to transfer it now. When you click on the Yes button, you're prompted to call your mail server. Once the mail is
  sent, your documents are taken from the Outgoing Mail database
  and delivered to the server's mailbox. From there, the server delivers the mail to the recipients.

When the data exchange is completed successfully, your Outgoing Mail
database is empty.

►► *Addressing Mail for Replication*

For your outgoing mail to be delivered properly, the recipients listed in
the To field of a document need to be included in your personal Name
& Address Book or the server's Name & Address Book.

When Workstation-based mail is selected, Notes looks up recipient
names in your personal Name & Address Book first. If the recipient

isn't there, it transfers the document anyway during mail replication, assuming the server will look for the recipient in its Name & Address Book. If the server can't find the name, it sends a nondelivery report to your mail file on the server to let you know who didn't receive your document. Therefore, you may not be aware that the document was not delivered until the next time you replicate your mail database.

▶▶ *What's Next?*

If you work off-site, whether at home or on the road, Dial-up Notes can help you to work *locally*, wherever you are, because you can make local replicas (exact copies) of shared databases and then work on these replicas. You can also send and receive Notes mail by working in a local replica of your mail database and then exchanging documents (replicating) with your mail database on the server. With Dial-up Notes, you can work in a different location, and continue to exchange data with your organization's databases. Updates are literally a telephone call away.

In Part Two, we'll show you how to design Notes databases for users, and we'll examine all the issues involved in developing workflow-automation applications. In Chapter 11, we'll explain how all the basic components of a Notes database work together. From there, you'll have a good foundation for building applications that integrate a database's functionality with ease of use.

PART TWO

▶ ▶ **P**art Two guides you, the developer, through the steps of designing a Notes database, which includes creating forms and views, and writing formulas and macros. Chapter 11, "Learning the Notes Building Blocks," discusses the types of forms you can create, fields, static text, and buttons and popup annotations. Chapter 12, "Basing a Database on a Design Template," suggests a process you might follow as you analyze a database's requirements and the needs of the people who'll use the database. Chapter 13, "Using Notes Templates and Databases," describes the application templates and example databases that are included with Notes.

Chapter 14, "Designing a Form," takes you through the steps of designing the forms for a Corporate Directory database. The chapter covers form design considerations, including a form's basic components, defining a form's attributes, and formatting a form. Chapter 15, "Creating a View," takes you through the steps of creating a view, and discusses defining view attributes and writing a selection formula. Chapter 16, "Writing Formulas and Macros," shows you how to use formulas in a database, and discusses defining formulas for different field types and creating macros.

Chapter 17, "Applying Workflow to a Database," explains how to apply workflow to a Notes application, showing you how to incorporate workflow automation features into the structure of a database. Chapter 18, "Building Security into Notes Databases," shows you how you can incorporate security features into your Notes databases. Chapter 19, "Replicating Databases," explains what replication is, including how to create and update a database replica, and handle replication conflicts.

Chapter 20, "Indexing a Notes Database," explains the differences between using plain-text and full-text search methods. Chapter 21, "Linking and Embedding Objects in Notes," discusses how to link and embed objects, and insert objects in forms and documents. Chapter 22, "Managing Databases," discusses the tasks involved in managing multiple databases.

11

Learning the Notes Building Blocks

▶▶ *F*AST *T*RACK

▶ **Forms are designed for entering information** **234**

that's stored in a Notes database. Forms define the format and layout of documents. Each form can contain fields, static text, graphics, and objects such as buttons and popups. These elements determine how users enter information as well as how that information is processed and displayed.

▶ **Information is contained in fields** **235**

that you place on a form; the information is then saved as a document and becomes part of a Notes application. When you open a document, you see the data through the form. The form dictates the structure of the document and how the data appears on the screen.

▶ **There are three types of forms** **236**

that can exist in any Notes database; they are arranged in the following hierarchical order: Document, Response to Document, and Response to Response. If you don't designate the form as a specific type, it will automatically be assigned the default form type, which is *Document*. If you've created only one form in the database, it must be of Document type.

▶ **The relationship between a Document and a Response is** **238**

created by first highlighting the appropriate document in a view before composing the response. In order to create any *Response*-type documents, you must first create a form of the Document type in the database. In other words, a person needs *something*—in this case, a document—to respond to. If you don't choose a document to respond to, Notes will tell you to select a document before you can compose a document of this type.

▶ ***A field's data type specifies***   **245**

the type of information that can be entered in it. The field data types you encounter in Notes are: Text, Number, Time/Date, Keywords, Rich Text, Names, Author Names, Reader Names, and Section. In addition, you can specify certain fields as editable or computed.

▶ ***An Editable field allows***   **245**

a user to enter or change information.

▶ ***A Computed field supplies***   **245**

information automatically. In most cases, a user can't change the information in a Computed field.

▶ ***Static text is***   **246**

text that is displayed on every document you create. It's referred to as "static" text because it doesn't change. This text can be placed on the form to act as labels for fields or as titles.

▶ ***Buttons and popups are***   **249**

objects you can insert in forms to automate tasks, perform actions, or provide additional information. A *button* executes instructions that you write, which in turn perform specific actions. They are handy because they perform actions automatically, thus saving a person time when they read a document. A *popup* is a block of text that's associated with a specific area in the form. It can be used to annotate or supply additional pertinent information, a definition, or a reference. A popup appears as a green outline around the area it's associated with. When the person points to a popup with the mouse and presses the button, the popup displays the information.

▶ ▶ **S**o far we've been discussing the uses of Notes databases in broad terms. However, the real value of Notes lies in its powerful set of design features that let you build new applications with ease. Since most of your work as a designer will be devoted to creating databases from the ground up, you should familiarize yourself with the building blocks, or basic components, of a Notes database. This chapter will help you along the way, with discussions of the following topics:

- Types of forms you can create
- Types of fields you can use
- Static text
- Buttons and popup annotations

▶ ▶ The Process of Creating a Notes Database

By now you should be comfortable using a Notes database. If you've been using the sample databases that are included on the book's Companion Disk (or one of your own), you've seen firsthand the ingenious ways a Notes database can be designed to organize and present information. You've also seen how the structure of a Notes database is uniquely different from other Windows databases, such as FileMaker Pro, Access, or Approach, that utilize the traditional field-record-file database structure.

As we described way back in Chapter 1, Lotus Notes uses a document database structure, where information is presented in documents that are accessed by a group of people. This structure provides you with new ways to work and collaborate with other people on different projects.

Up until now we've tried to emphasize in a conceptual way the importance of workflow management and the gains in productivity that can be achieved by using Notes. Now, we roll up our sleeves and show you how to do it.

You start creating a database in Notes by designing a form that people in an organization will use to organize and collect data. We'll take you through the steps of designing a form in Chapter 14. However, before you start, you need to understand the function of a form and the way you put a form together.

The process of building a Notes database involves:

- Creating a form
- Defining fields
- Defining attributes
- Formatting text
- Writing formulas

When your users begin composing documents, only the forms that you have created will be visible. It is through documents that users input and capture information that becomes part of a Notes application.

▶▶ *What Is a Form and What Do I Do with It?*

As we discussed in Chapter 2, you design *forms* for entering and displaying information. Forms define the format and layout of documents. Each form can contain fields, static text, graphics, and buttons. These elements determine how users enter information as well as how that information is processed and displayed.

Information—data—is stored in the fields that you place on a form; the information is then saved as a document and becomes part of a Notes application. When you open a document, you see the data "through" the form. The form dictates the structure of the document and how the data appears on the screen. Figure 11.1 is an example of a form that's used in a Travel Guide database.

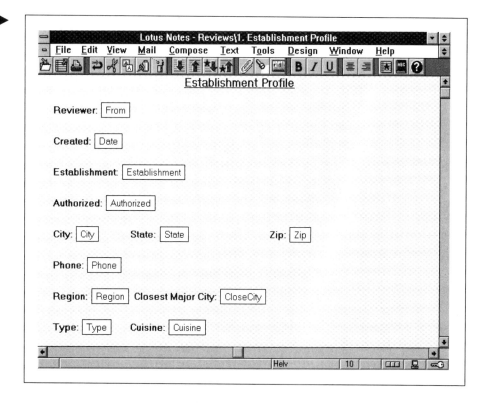

▶ Types of Forms

Each form that you create for any application has a *type* associated with it. The type assignation you give a form dictates how other people will use it. For example, the Travel Guide database uses three different forms: Establishment Profile, Visit, and Comments. Each one serves a different purpose. The Establishment Profile form includes the location and description of a particular hotel, motel, or inn. The Visit form includes a rating of the establishment. The Comments form includes a review of the establishment.

The three forms that are used in the Travel Guide database coincide with the three *types* of forms that can exist in any Notes database. These types are arranged in the following hierarchical order:

- Document
- Response to Document

- Response to Response

In the Travel Guide database, the Establishment Profile form is a Document type. The Visit form is a Response to Document type, and the Comments form is a Response to Response type. There is a connection between the three types of forms, which can be described as follows: A person uses the Establishment Profile form to compose a a simple profile on a particular establishment. The information is used as a basis for rating the establishment on several criteria. A person subsequently uses the Visit form to compose a document that assigns a rating to the establishment. If a person wants to compose a detailed review of an establishment, he or she uses the Comments form.

You assign a form a type in the Design Form Attributes dialog box (Design ➤ Form Attributes), which is shown in Figure 11.2.

If you don't designate the form as a specific type, it will automatically be assigned the default form type, which is *Document*. If you've created only one form in the database, it must be of Document type. In order to create any *Response*-type documents, you must first create a form of the Document type in the database. In other words, a person needs *something*—in this case, a document—to respond to.

FIGURE 11.2 ▶

When you design a new form, you assign a type to it by selecting one of the choices in the Design Form Attributes dialog box.

Design Form Attributes

Name: Reviews\1. Establishment Profile | Profile

Type: Document

- ☒ Include in **C**ompose Menu
- ☒ Include in **Q**uery by Form
- ☒ **D**efault database form
- ☐ **A**utomatically refresh fields
- ☐ **S**tore form in documents
- ☐ **I**nherit default field values
- ☐ **M**ail documents when saving
- ☐ **U**pdates become responses
- ☐ Prior **v**ersions become responses

OK
Cancel

Read Access...
Compose Access...
Encryption...
Object Activation...

Co**l**or: A B C D E F G H I J K L M N O P Q R S T U

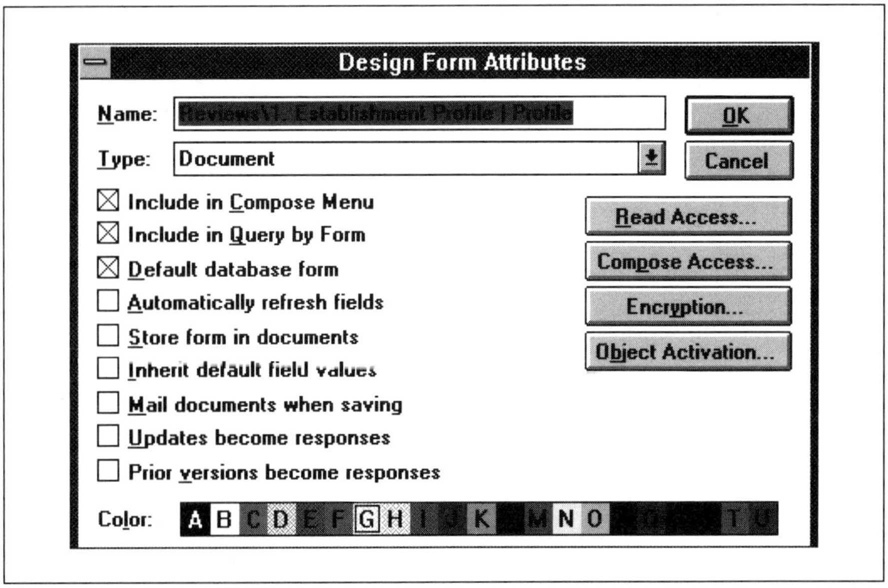

A *Response to Document* form is used to create a response document, which is exactly what the name says it is: a response to a document. Responses can be comments, further thoughts on a topic, additional information that isn't contained in the original, or main, document; however, these responses will always be associated with the document. Figure 11.3 shows the Visit form in the Travel Guide database, which is a Response to Document form.

When you design a Response form, you will frequently want it to *inherit*—or use—data from the main document. You don't have to design it in this way, but inheritance can save you the time of entering—and duplicating—the same information that appears in the main document.

The relationship between the document and the response is created by first highlighting the appropriate document in the view before composing the response. If you don't choose a document to respond to, Notes will tell you to select a document before you can compose a document of this type. A view makes it easy for you to locate the document(s) that you need. Response documents create a hierarchy in a view where the response appears below the document and is indented three spaces.

FIGURE 11.3 ▶

The Visit form in the Travel Guide database is an example of a Response to Document form.

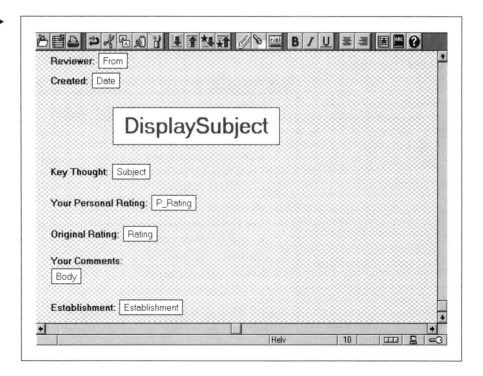

Figure 11.4 shows an example of a response to a document in one of the views in the Travel Guide database.

A *Response to Response* type form provides a user with even more flexibility when composing documents. Figure 11.5 shows the Comments form in the Travel Guide database, which is a Response to Response form. The form can be associated with either a Document or any Response-type document.

A Response to Response document appears below the document (whether a Document or Response to Document) that was highlighted when the user opened the Compose menu and is indented three spaces more than its *parent*, the document it is responding to. Figure 11.6 shows how a Response to response form would appear in one of the Travel Guide database's views.

FIGURE 11.4 ▶

A Visit document appears indented below an Establishment Profile document in a view because it's a Response to Document form.

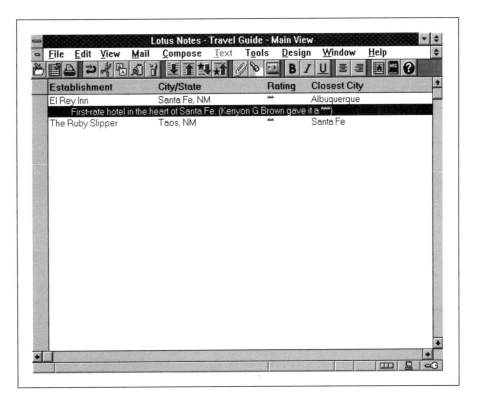

FIGURE 11.5 ►

The Comments form in the Travel Guide database is a Response to Response form.

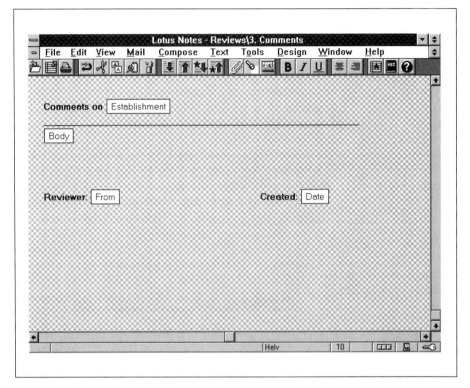

We'll discuss the creation of Response forms in detail in Chapter 14, "Designing a Form," but we wanted to mention them here because they are a basic component of using Notes. Here's summary of the different form types:

Type of Form	Description of Form
Document	Is the default form type that is assigned to any main document. This form type is independent of all other documents.
Response to Document	This form type is assigned to a form that is used to respond to a main document. It is dependent on the main document. It appears indented three spaces beneath the main document in a hierarchical view.

FIGURE 11.6

A Comments document appears indented below a Visit document in a view because it's a Response to Response type form.

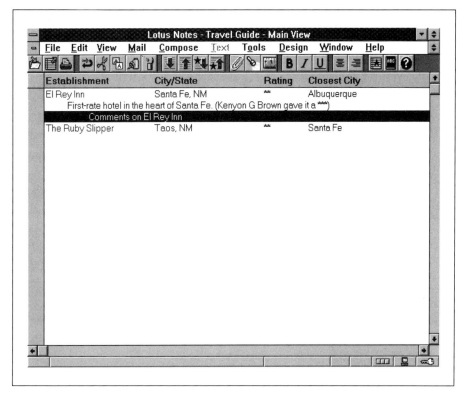

Type of Form	Description of Form
Response to Response	This form type is assigned to a form that is used to respond to either a main document or another response. It appears indented three spaces under its parent in a view hierarchy.

▶ *Planning a Form on Paper*

Before you actually start creating a form, we suggest you take the time to plan it out on paper. Certainly you can create a new database by placing static text, fields, and other items on the form and then moving the items around, but you'll probably leave out something important. You should spend as much time as you need considering how people will use the form and the information they will want to capture. The results will be the form(s) you design for the database. Figure 11.7 shows an example of a preliminary sketch for a form, indicating the placement of static text and fields.

As you design a new form, you use *Form Design* mode. When you begin, you are presented with a single, large rich text field to which you can add whatever fields, graphics, buttons, and static text that you want on your form. After you place an item on the form, you can always move it around if you're not satisfied, or delete it.

FIGURE 11.7 ▶

The sketch for a form should indicate the placement of static text and fields, and graphics and buttons (if any). Also indicate the colors for the background and typefaces.

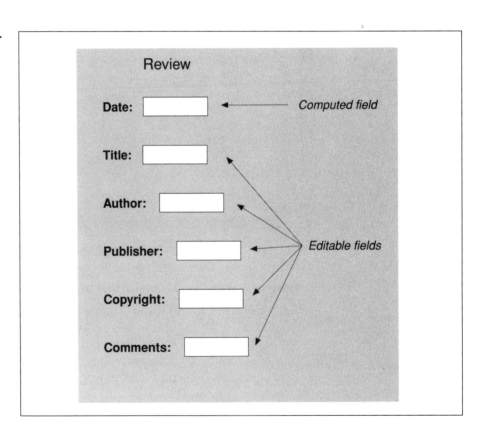

▶▶ *What Is a Field?*

When you enter text information in a form, you enter it in *fields*. A field can be either *plain text* or *rich text*. The names give you a clue as to the kind of data the fields can contain. Briefly, a plain text field can't contain *formatted* data; by formatted, we mean any data whose appearance

THE DIFFERENCES BETWEEN PLAIN TEXT AND RICH TEXT FIELDS

There are two kinds of fields you can insert on a form: *plain text* and *rich text*. Actually an empty form is a gigantic rich text field. The creators of Lotus Notes defined a form in this way because forms must be able to contain an assortment of elements whose appearance can be formatted and modified. A form can contain graphics, objects such as buttons, doclinks, and popups, embedded objects that are linked to other Windows applications, other rich text and plain text fields that contain data, and text that you can format to appear any way you choose by changing its font, point size, and color.

A *rich text field* is named as such because a person can enter text and format it. As we stated above, you can enter many kinds of elements in a rich text field. You can also insert tables and attachments. For example, you might want to attach a file to a mail memo you send to someone. A *plain text field* is a field that can only contain text with no formats applied to it; you can't change the appearance of the text. You use plain text fields when formatting the appearance of text serves no purpose or when you need to design computations based on string or numerical values contained within.

You'll discover that you can't tell whether an empty field is plain text or rich text by simply looking at it. Furthermore, you can't easily tell the difference when you edit a document that contains information in fields. Sometimes the only way you can tell is to try changing the appearance of the text in some way. If Notes doesn't let you, the field is a plain text field. Another way to distinguish the two is to place the insertion point in the field and pull down the Text menu. If formatting commands such as Bold, Italic, or Enlarge are dimmed and unavailable, the field is plain text.

can be changed by using different attributes such as boldface, color, and so on. Thus, the data looks "plain." Conversely, a rich text field can contain formatted data. A rich text field can also contain linked objects, graphics, and file attachments. In other words, a rich text field can hold "an assortment of riches." For more information, read the section "The Differences between Plain Text and Rich Text Fields." Whether it's plain text or rich text, a field contains a single type of information. A form can have many fields, each with a different data type and an assigned name.

A field's data type specifies the type of information that can be entered in it. In addition, you can specify certain fields as editable or computed. A field's name appears inside the field. For example, the Establishment Profile form that appears in Figure 11.8 displays the names of the fields in the form. You can use a field's name to refer to that field in formulas when Response-type documents inherit data from a main document. The Field Definition dialog box, which is shown in Figure 11.9, displays the Field Type area where you designate the specific field type.

FIGURE 11.8 ▶

After you name a field, its name appears inside the field box.

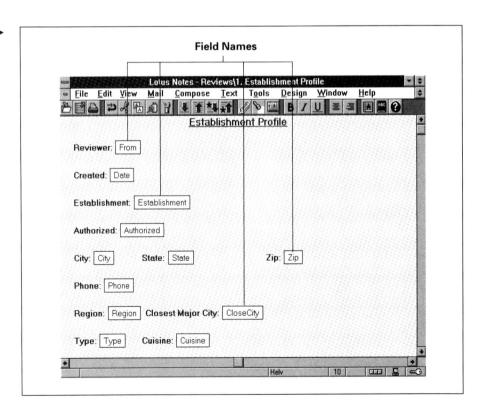

FIGURE 11.9

The Field Definition dialog box lets you specify a field's type.

Field Definition

Name:

Help Description:

Displays the document author

Data Type: Author Names

☐ Allow Multi-Values

Field Type
○ Editable   ○ Computed for display
○ Computed   ● Computed when composed

[Formula...] [Format...] [Separators...] [Security...]

[OK]
[Cancel]

▶▶ *Types of Fields*

An *Editable field* allows the user to enter or change information. A *Computed field* supplies information automatically. In most cases, a user can't change the information in a Computed field. The name of the author of a document and the date a document was composed are examples of information that might be contained in this type of field. The Date field that appears in the Establishment Profile form in Figure 11.10 is a Computed field. So is the From field. The other fields are Editable fields.

In addition to these two broad types of fields, there are also fields that are categorized by the type of data they can contain. As you can see in Figure 11.9, the Field Definition dialog box displays the Data Type list box from which you choose the data type. The data type of field not only determines what data the field can contain, but also how you can enter that data. The field data types you encounter in Notes are:

- Text
- Number
- Time/Date

FIGURE 11.10 ►

The Date field on the Establishment Profile form is a Computed field. Your ocmputer system's date and time appears automatically in the field.

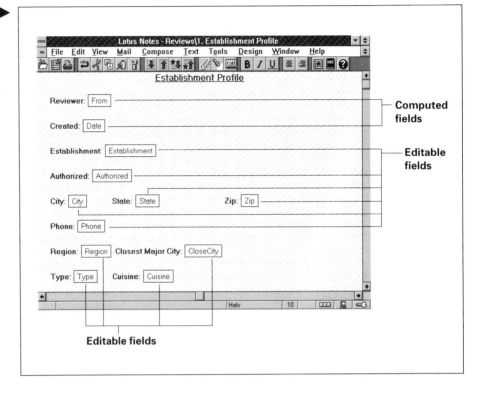

- Keywords
- Rich Text
- Names
- Author Names
- Reader Names
- Section

Chapter 14, "Designing a Form," will discuss these different field data types in detail as you follow the steps in creating a form.

►► *Using Static Text*

Static text is text that is displayed on every document you create. It's referred to as "static" text because it cannot be changed by users of the applications. This text can be placed on the form to act as labels for fields or as titles. Fields, on the other hand, are the areas in which users actually enter information or the application performs actions automatically by using formulas. If you want text to change under different conditions, you need to use fields.

Figure 11.11 shows examples of static text that appears next to fields on a Visit document.

A nice feature of static text is that you can format it in order to change its appearance. The default font for static text on new forms is Helvetica 10-point. The default text color is black. It's a good idea to display static text in a different color or size than the defaults in order to set it off from the field contents it identifies. You can also make the text appear boldface or in italics.

You make changes to static text by accessing the commands on the Text menu or opening the Font dialog box (Text ➤ Font), which is shown in Figure 11.12. You can change the size, color, and other

FIGURE 11.11 ▶

You use static text to identify fields and to act as titles.

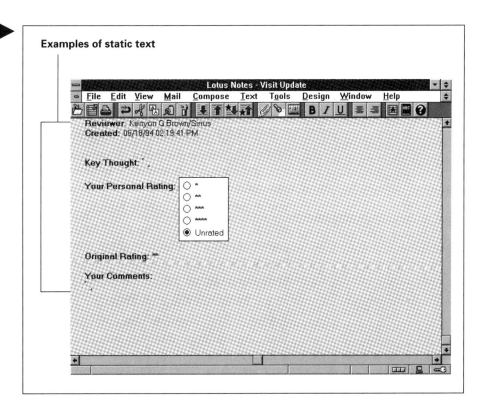

Examples of static text

FIGURE 11.12 ▶

You format text on a form by accessing the Text menu and opening the Font dialog box.

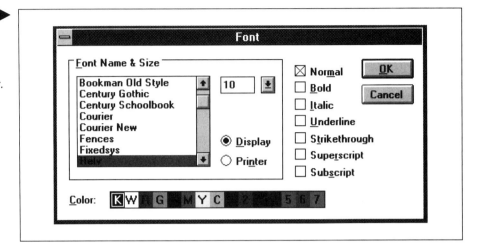

attributes of static text. To change the text attributes without using the menu, use the Ctrl+K keystroke combination to display the Font dialog box. (You can always use accelerator keys or keystroke combinations to choose commands in Notes, just as you would in any Windows program.)

 ▶▶ **T I P**

We suggest you limit the number of colors and fonts you use to format static text. Other people will probably use the form you've created, and you don't want to give them headaches by subjecting them to your artistic touch. Choose colors carefully; you can change the background color of a form as well as the color of the font. So be sensitive to the combinations of colors you use. Try not to mix too many different fonts and point sizes. Stick to using no more than two fonts on a form. For labels, keep the size to 10 or 12 points. For titles, use 18 to 24 points. A rule of thumb is to label every Editable field clearly so a person knows the purpose of each one. Use concise, descriptive identifiers so a person doesn't have to guess what to input in a field.

►► *Inserting Objects in a Form*

In Chapter 6, we discussed using doclinks in documents to provide access to information stored in other documents. The other documents may be in the same database or another database. The other database can even be stored in another server. By double-clicking on a doclink, you go directly to the linked document.

Doclinks are convenient to use because they help people locate related information easily. However, you can only add doclinks to documents as you compose them; you can't add doclinks to forms as you design them. If you try, you'll notice that the DocLink command is dimmed and unavailable.

There are other kinds of graphical objects in addition to doclinks that you can use in forms to automate tasks, perform actions, or provide additional information. They are called *buttons* and *popup annotations*. Although we've already discussed using buttons in an earlier chapter, we wanted to mention them here because you can add buttons to forms as you design them, as well as when you compose documents.

► *Adding Buttons*

You use *buttons* to execute instructions that you write, which in turn perform specific actions. Like other items you might place on a form, you can also place buttons, move them around, and delete them if necessary. The buttons are duplicated on all documents that are composed with that form. Buttons are handy because they perform actions automatically, thus saving a person time when they read a document. You use buttons the same way you would in any Windows applications that utilizes buttons. Figure 11.13 shows an example of a button (the Select Profile button) that's been inserted on the Establishment Profile form in the Travel Guide database.

The new Select Profile button is used to automate the steps of selecting all the data in the document. Instead of manually pulling down the

FIGURE 11.13 ►

This button was inserted on the Establishment Profile form in the Travel Guide database.

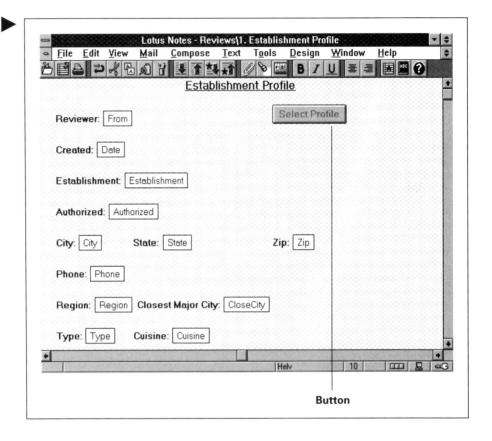

Button

Edit menu and choosing the Select All command, the user needs only to click on the Select Profile button to select all data. With all the data selected, the user can perform different actions on the data, such as pressing the Delete key to mark the document for deletion from the view, pulling down the Text menu and choosing the Font command to change the text's font and point size, or display the text in a different color, and so on.

To insert this button on the form, you must include a formula in the Insert Button dialog box that's shown in Figure 11.14. The line

```
@Command((EditSelectAll))
```

that appears in the Formula text box performs the action of selecting all the data on the form.

FIGURE 11.14 ▶

The Insert Button dialog box

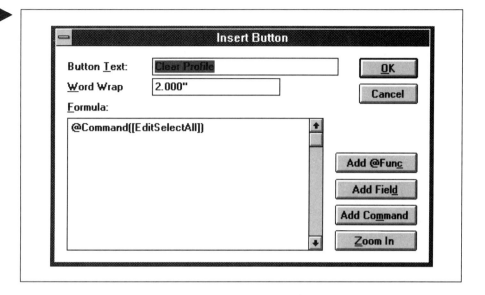

 ▶▶

Buttons are a new feature in Notes 3.x. If you want to use documents that were created in an earlier version of Notes and bring them into a database that was created in Notes 3.x or later, the older documents won't display the button that's included on the newer form. Since the older documents weren't composed with the form, the button won't be duplicated on the documents.

▶ Adding Popups

A popup is another kind of object you can insert in a form or a document. A popup is a block of text that's associated with a specific area in the form. It provides a designer with a way to annotate a feature or supply additional pertinent information, a definition, or a reference. For example, a popup could provide directions for composing a document or a reminder to enter data in a particular field.

A popup appears as a green outline around the area it's associated with (in this case, the form's title, Establishment Profile), as shown in Figure 11.15. A popup is displayed when a user edits or reads a document. When the user points to the popup with the mouse and presses the button, the popup displays the information.

To insert a popup, choose Edit ➤ Insert ➤ PopUp. The Insert PopUp dialog box appears, as shown in Figure 11.16. You must enter the text you want displayed in the popup.

FIGURE 11.15 ▶

When you insert a popup on a form or document, it appears as a green outline around the area it's associated with.

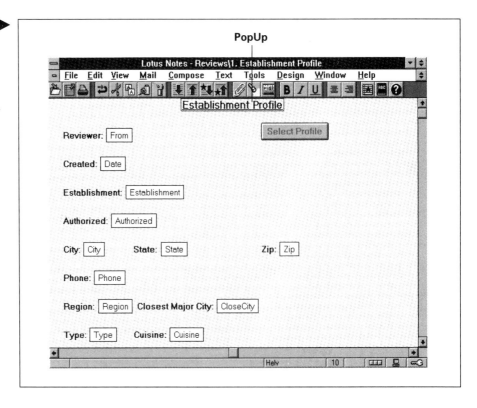

FIGURE 11.16

The Insert PopUp dialog box

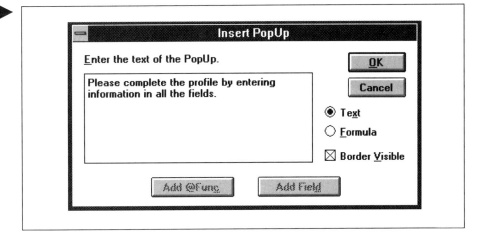

▶▶ *When Do I Create a View?*

You create a view *after* you design a form you want people to use for composing documents in a database. You can't create a view until you've designed a form and decided on what information from the form you want displayed in the view. As you've already learned, a *view* is a summary of the documents in the database. A view provides an easy way for a person to locate a particular document.

When you select a database and pull down the View menu, the views in the database are displayed at the bottom of the menu. For example, the Travel Guide database includes the three views that are shown in the View menu in Figure 11.17: Main View, By City/Cuisine, and By Region. Figure 11.18 shows an example of the By City/Cuisine view in the Travel Guide database.

As in any view, each row represents a single document. A row may be divided into one or more columns. Each column displays the information that's contained in a field (or from a combination of fields) from the document. A view can include various symbols that indicate further information about the document. Markers in the left column can indicate that you have not yet read a document; similarly, icons in a column can represent a document, folder, person, group, or attachment.

FIGURE 11.17 ▶

The Travel Guide data-base's View menu displays three views.

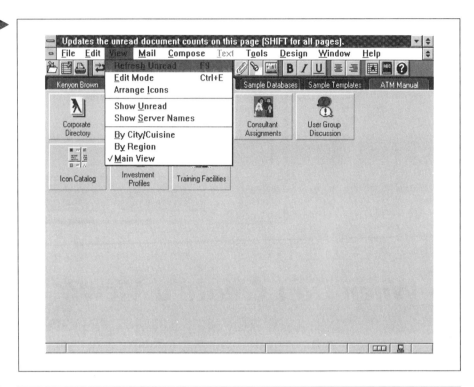

FIGURE 11.18 ▶

This is the By City/Cui-sine view in the Travel Guide database.

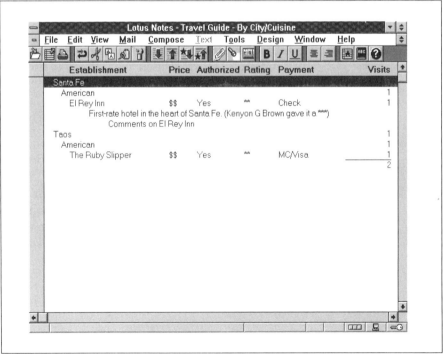

▶▶ *When Can a Person Compose a Document?*

Once you design a form and create a view, users can start composing documents. You'll recall that a *document* is the main unit of storage in a Notes application. It is the finished product that has been derived from a form. In other words, a document contains the information that has been entered into a form.

Each document in a database corresponds to a particular form that you've designed. For instance, in the Travel Guide database there are three kinds of documents that a person can compose. After the database is selected, a person can pull down the Compose menu to display the three choices, as shown in Figure 11.19.

FIGURE 11.19 ▶

The Travel Guide database's Compose menu displays the three kinds of documents that are available.

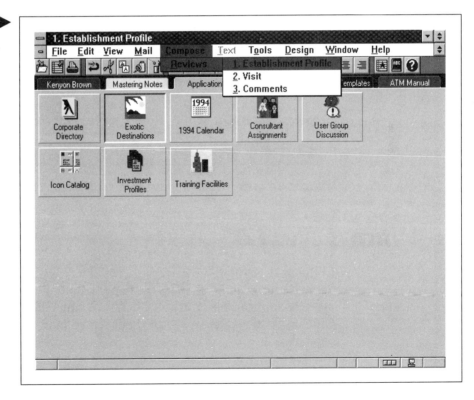

The information in a document can be manually entered by an end user, calculated by formulas, or imported from other applications. Figure 11.20 shows an example of the Visit document in the Travel Guide database.

FIGURE 11.20 ▶

This is the Visit document in the Travel Guide database.

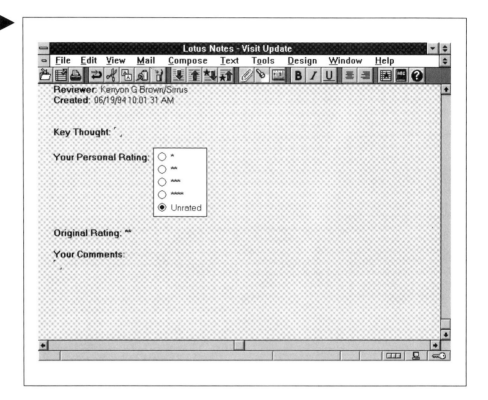

▶▶ *What's Next?*

In the next chapter, we discuss the value of customizing an existing database template to fit your own application needs rather than creating new applications. You can often save yourself a lot of time by modifying an existing database instead of spending the time to build a new database.

CHAPTER 12

Basing a Database on a Design Template

FAST TRACK

▶ **A Notes template is** 266

a prefabricated frame from which an application may be initiated. It contains skeletal design elements, such as forms, fields, views, macros, icons, but no documents.

▶ **To create a new database that's based on a template** 272

choose File ➤ New Database. Select the template from which you will initiate your new database. Select Inherit Future Design Changes if you want design changes made to the template to automatically propagate to the new database. Fill in the Filename and Title text boxes. Click the New button.

▶ **To extract the design elements of your application** 277

and create a template from them, select your database by pointing and clicking on its icon in the Notes Workspace. Choose File ➤ Database ➤ Copy. Fill in the Server, Filename, and Title text boxes. Be sure to give the file name an extension of .NTF to designate it as a template file. Select Design Only in the Copy section of dialog box. This will ensure that only the design elements of the application are copied and not the data. Click on OK. Copying will proceed. A new template will be created and added to your Workspace automatically.

▶ ***To designate the new template as a design template***   **278**

select the new template by pointing and clicking on its
icon in the Workspace. Choose File ➤ Database ➤ Information. Click the button that's labeled "Design Template."
Select Database is a Design Template and fill in the Template Name text box. This name should be different from
the name you assigned to the template previously. Click
on OK.

▶ ***To link the application to the template***   **279**

so the design of the application remains synchronized to
that of the template, select your database by pointing and
clicking on its icon in the Workspace. Choose File ➤ Database ➤ Information. Click on the Design Template button.
Select Inherit Design from Template and fill in the text
box under Based on Template with the name of the design
template you established previously. Click on OK.

▶ ***To synchronize changes between the template and
database***   **281**

select your database by pointing and clicking on its icon in
the Workspace. Choose Design ➤ Replace Design. Select
the name of design template from the list. If the design
template resides on a different server, click on the button
labeled "Template Server" and choose the correct Notes
server and design template. Choose Replace.

▶ ▶ **W**_hile_ there are surely applications whose beginnings consisted merely of a person uttering the words "Wouldn't it be nice if?…," as a novice Notes application developer you'll need to be clearer on what your final objective is. A Notes database should address specific needs and solve specific problems. However, because Notes allows you to do so much, particularly in terms of exploiting its graphical user interface (GUI) capabilities, you can easily find yourself drowning in a sea of buttons, colors, fonts, and graphics and forgetting what your original purpose was.

One way to avoid this problem is to base your database's design on a preexisting design, or template. This chapter takes you through the process of analyzing the needs of the people who will use your database, planning that database's design based on users' needs, and deciding whether to use a template. Along the way, we'll cover the following topics:

- Deciding whether to use a design template
- Initiating a database from a template
- Linking a database to a design template
- Synchronizing changes between a design template and an application

▶ ▶ *Planning Your Database*

At its heart, Notes is a database development/management environment. Those of you with a background in relational database development might be tempted to model Notes databases on relational database concepts. Save yourself the headache! Notes is not a relational database management system (RDBMS), although there are some lukewarm similarities. The Notes database paradigm is sufficiently unique from any other database model as to demand a new approach to database development. Not having prior experience in database development might, in fact, be more of a help than a hindrance when it comes to Notes development since your perspective will not have been colored by your previous experience. On the other hand, any experience you have thinking through the design and organization of a database (whatever its type) will come in handy.

In the typical systems development cycle, there are at least five distinct phases you would complete before the actual delivery of a finished product:

- **Analysis**: Gather requirements from users. Ask them "What type of system would you like to see implemented?" "What should this system do?" "How should the system look and feel?" Consolidate the requirements into a clear definition of the problem or identify the need that the application is intended to address. These steps should act as your guiding light as you proceed through the development of a system.

- **Feasibility**: Determine the feasibility of developing a system. Ask "Can we actually develop and implement the system given the associated costs, level of resources (human and otherwise), and state of technology?" Create specifications for a system that will address the problem or need. You need to say to yourself, "Okay, we understand the problem and need, and we're confident we have the resources and technology to develop a system to address it. Here's exactly what the system should do…"

- **Design**: Formulate a design for the system based on the specifications.

- **Development**: Build a system that is based on the design and test it.

- **Delivery**: Roll out the system to end users and train them to use it.

Sounds easy, doesn't it? Actually, developing a Notes application can be relatively simple, but only if it's been well-planned and executed. That's why it's so important to analyze the needs of your users.

The role of the analysis phase cannot be overstated, particularly with a product like Notes. Thus, while we will spend most of the rest of this book talking about design and development, let's take a moment to talk about analysis. Why is analysis so important? Ironically, the answer lies in one of Notes' strongest features, the ease with which it allows systems development. Notes puts systems development in the hands of people who might not have a classic programming or systems analysis background; indeed, you may fall into this category yourself. The potential danger in this is the infamous "hurry up and code" syndrome: In a mad rush to get a system developed, you start straight into writing the application without actually planning it. Then, somewhere toward the end of the project, you realize you've forgotten to include a key element and the application falls on its face.

So, does the fact that Notes makes systems development easier (and perhaps fun) necessarily translate into a proliferation of poorly designed, unmaintainable systems? Of course not, if you follow some common-sense rules. Ultimately, the bottom line is this: Spend a healthy portion of your time developing the blueprint of your system before actual construction begins. With a set of clear specifications in hand, a thorough design will be much easier to create. In turn, with a thorough design to work from, the application should essentially "write itself," assuming that the development tool you are using (Notes) allows you to express the elements embodied by the design in straightforward fashion.

So take a moment (or two or three...), clear your mind and simply think about the system you intend to implement (and, if you wish, all the pats-on-the-back, applause, and accolades you'll receive because of its success). Consider the following:

- **What will be the measure of success for your system?** Answering this question requires a very clear understanding of what you are trying to accomplish. State the goal(s) of the system in measurable, quantifiable terms, e.g. faster performance, increased revenue, more widgets per hour, etc.

- **Let your users drive the requirements-gathering phase.** Act as a facilitator in order to draw input from the user community on how they want the system to work. This makes them an active participant in the development of the system and goes a long way toward their acceptance.

- **Spread the word: WORKFLOW!** Remember, as a groupware product you don't simply use Notes, you buy into it. The "workflow" model upon which Notes is based works only when users are faithful to it. Make sure your users understand exactly what workflow means and what their place is in the workflow process. If you're having trouble convincing your users of Notes' value, check out "Selling People on Notes' Workflow Philosophy" for some tips.

SELLING PEOPLE ON NOTES' WORKFLOW PHILOSOPHY

As we've stated several times, any workflow that is currently based on disseminating paper from person to person, department to department, and so on, according to some sort of timetable or schedule, can be streamlined and automated in Notes. Notes centralizes information in a single application where it may have been previously decentralized among many people in many different formats. A Notes application enables people to see information in its entirety, thus giving them the big picture to aid them in making decisions.

People need to understand that Notes is good for automating workflow for a couple reasons. Notes can track what's been done and what hasn't in an organization by integrating particular information in a database. It also will integrate the same database with e-mail, which can help people notify each other that something needs to be done or move a document from one database to another. E-mail facilitates communication and keeps people abreast of new developments that occur frequently in an organization.

As a Notes database designer, you have to be a workflow cheerleader because you're affecting the way people use information in an organization and ultimately how they do their jobs. People, unfortunately, don't often see the value of using Notes because they have to work differently than the way they did before they used Notes. Some Notes application developers like to refer to this change in peoples' work habits as *before Notes* and *after Notes*— BN and AN, respectively.

When you tell people that they'll become more "productive" and "efficient," you're not giving them good reasons to use the product. People will interpret your statement to mean you think they weren't as productive or efficient before Notes entered the scene. The most compelling reasons you can give people for using Notes is to show them how it will make doing their jobs easier and how it will improve communication. As a database designer, this is an ongoing process that'll present you with many challenges. However, it will also offer you many opportunities to get people to rethink the way they work.

▶▶ Deciding Whether to Use a Design Template

In Notes, instead of building a database from the ground up, you can base your database on an existing template and modify it. With a template, you can assemble your database from preexisting pieces—forms, fields, views, etc.—and customize it or add design elements as you need to.

In a way, a template is a lot like a prefab house. Just as you can save a lot of time and money by building a prefab house instead of building it from the ground up, so can you save a lot of time and effort (and of course, money) by using a template.

DO YOU MIND IF I USE YOUR DATABASE TEMPLATE?

A template can serve as a powerful learning tool. If you've ever seen a Notes application in action and a particular feature really caught your eye, you may have thought to yourself "Wow! I wonder how that works?" As politely and diplomatically as possible, request a template of the database! Since it will contain only design elements and no documents, there is no possibility that you might inadvertently receive actual data.

Of course, many businesses may be skittish about revealing how their data is recorded and maintained within Notes (for competitive reasons). So don't be surprised if your request is denied. However, if you are lucky enough to get your hands on a well-designed, interesting, and useful template, it's time to put your engineer's (actually, reverse engineer's) hat on and pry the design apart.

Lotus provides over a dozen templates with version 3 of Notes and gives users permission to modify them for their own purposes. Another excellent source of Notes templates is the LotusComm Forum on CompuServe. To access the forum through the Windows CompuServe Information Manager, follow these steps:

1. Choose Services ➤Go.

2. Type LotusComm—case isn't important—in the dialog box.

3. Choose Library ➤ Browse. The Library Section dialog box appears.

4. Double-click on Notes Applications.

The Notes Applications dialog box appears. Scroll down the list to get an idea of the different kinds of applications that are available.

Lotus also sponsors a database design contest for all you developers out there. This is a great way to present your applications to the Notes user community.

Discovering how a particular form, view, or macro operates by taking the finished product and stepping back through its structure is a fantastic (and the quickest) means of sharpening your own programming skills and adding tricks to your Notes programming repertoire.

▶ When Should I Use a Template?

If you can find a template that resembles the application you intend to build, then use it! The trick is to discover if a template does indeed fit. Determining the usefulness of a template requires a fair amount of investigation on your part and is based largely on visual evidence. Use the following steps as guidelines for your investigation:

1. Create a new database based on a template. For example, if you had a template showing the structure of a form for a service request tracking database, as in Figure 12.1, you could create a document from the same form, as in Figure 12.2.

2. Compose several documents based on each defined form to get a feel as to what the data-entry interface is like and what type of information is being captured. Note the layout of each form.

3. Examine the various resulting views and decide if they present the database contents in a desirable fashion.

4. Execute any macros and view their results.

▶ Understanding a Template's Limitations

As you proceed through your investigation, put yourself in the shoes of an end user of the application. Is it easy to use? Is it intuitive? Think about how you might modify the design of the database for the purposes of your organization and how much effort that would entail. It

FIGURE 12.1

Editing a form reveals the structure of a database template. Only a portion of the Service Request form from the Service Request Tracking database is shown.

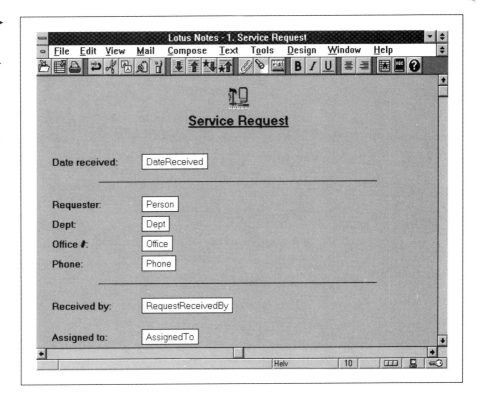

might actually be easier to build the application from scratch if it appears that there is extensive redesign work to be done.

If the design includes a lot of excess items that you don't find useful, it is a fairly simple matter to remove them from the design. If you conclude that the database fits your needs, or at least comes close, you may then use it as is or as a platform from which to build a more full-featured application.

But don't reinvent the wheel if you don't have to. If you're really lucky, a database initiated from a template may require no modification. Practically speaking, however, it's highly likely that you'll have to make some modifications to tailor the database to the precise requirements of your application. At this point, however, pay more attention to how the database operates than to why the database operates as it does.

FIGURE 12.2 ▶

The document displays a service request for July 30.

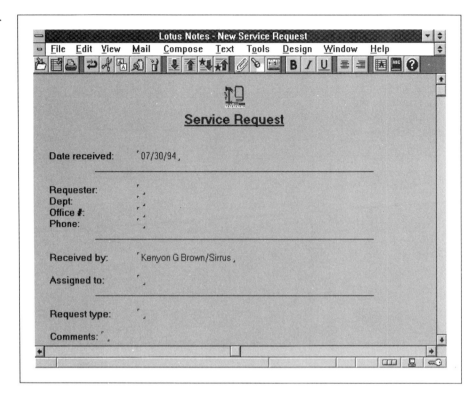

▶ *Borrowing Elements from a Template*

You should also keep in mind that the utility of a template is not necessarily an all-or-nothing proposition. It is possible to utilize only specific elements of the template rather than the entire template. Ask yourself the following questions when deciding the extent of a template's usefulness:

- Does the template's entire design closely resemble the intended design of my application?

- Does the template contain only particular design elements which appeal to me, and other elements that do not?

Finding a template which satisfies your requirements (either fully or something just shy of fully) is obviously a best-case scenario and translates into less work for you as a developer. However, a template might contain only specific items which you find useful—a particular form (or perhaps just a particular field on a form), a particular view, etc. In that case, it is possible to pull just those items into your new application. The process would be similar to building a house from prefabricated pieces of different origin! For instance, you might say "I want the master bedroom of prefab style #1 but the kitchen of prefab style #2." While this might be impossible in terms of house-building, it's quite easy in terms of Notes application-building.

 ▶▶ **T I P**

> **When piecing an application together from design elements found in different templates, add the templates to a single Workspace page (the same one as your new database). Click on a template to make it the active database and then go to the Design menu and select the view, form, or macro from which you want to take design elements. While still in Design mode, go the Window menu and select 1.Workspace to go back to the Workspace page. Repeat the process for each template. As you open new design windows, notice that previous ones are listed in numerical order under the Window menu, so you can switch back and forth between your application and the design elements of the various templates easily.**

▶▶ *Initiating a Database from a Template*

Let's say that after exploring a particular template you come to the conclusion that its design suits your purposes. The next step is to actually create the new database, indicating that it will inherit its design from the template of choice. Follow these steps:

1. Choose File ➤ New Database. The New Database dialog box appears, as shown in Figure 12.3. You'll notice the Design area and the Template scroll box. It is here that you designate the template on which the new database will be patterned after. The default selection is -Blank-, which means that your new database will not take its design from a template at all and will be developed from scratch.

2. Select the template from which you will initiate your new database. If the template you want resides on another Notes server, click Template Server, select a server from the list, and choose your template.

3. Select Inherit Future Design Changes if you want design changes made to the template to automatically propagate to the new database.

4. Fill in the Filename and Title text boxes, respectively.

5. Click the New button.

For a description of template-to-database inheritance, see "Maintaining a Database by Linking It to a Template" later in this chapter.

FIGURE 12.3 ▶

The New Database dialog box lets you select a template on which to base a new database.

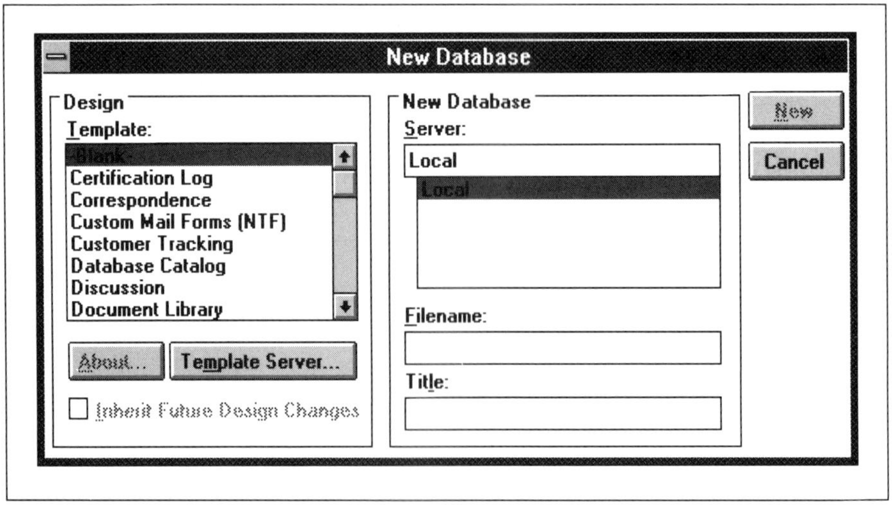

▶▶ *Taking Specific Design Elements from a Template*

You have essentially two methods by which you can take specific design elements from a template. One we'll call the "strip-down" method and the other we'll call the "build-up" method.

Regardless of the method, you'll utilize the standard cut-and-paste features of Windows together with specific Notes features that allow you to build your database by using the design elements from other databases.

▶ *Using the Strip-Down Method*

In the strip-down method, you initiate your new database from a template in the normal way (described above) and then proceed to strip out those design elements you don't need. This method assumes that you have initiated your application from a template that had all (or most) of the design features you wanted, plus some that you didn't. You will then eliminate the unwanted design elements such as:

- Forms
- Views
- Macros
- Specific fields in forms
- Specific columns in views

With this method, you should try out the application frequently to make sure you didn't remove something vital to its functioning.

▶ *Using the Build-Up Method*

In the build-up method, you cut and paste design elements between template(s) and your new database. You could even employ both methods in hybrid fashion—initiate the database from a template, strip out unwanted design elements, and cut and paste design elements from other templates. This method assumes that there are only a few design elements in the template that appeal to you and you want to take just those elements for your database.

▶▶ *Linking a Database to a Design Template*

How do you make modifications to the design of a database without disrupting usage of that database? Making design changes while users are actively engaged with the database can lead to unpredictable results and is definitely not good policy. One possibility would be to simply wait until the database is quiet (no activity related to the database is occurring) and then make design changes. But a quiet Notes database might be something of a rarity given standard end-user access, replication, and other database-oriented activity.

The answer is to link the database to a design template. A design template is like a standard template in all respects except that the design of the design template actually controls (either fully or partially) the design of databases linked to the template. By utilizing a design template you are able to maintain the design elements of a database off-line, where you can make modifications to the design template and then test those modifications, neither of which is intrusive on the production database. The production database then inherits the modifications made to the design template on a continuing basis, as illustrated in Figure 12.4. This process of database-to-design template synchronization may occur at regular intervals or may be forced on an as-needed basis.

For all intents and purposes a design template represents a repository for the definition of design elements (what could loosely be called a "data dictionary") upon which a database relies. As changes are made to the definitions, those changes are propagated to databases linked to the design template. In plain terms, change the template and you've changed the database! Another way of thinking about a design template is as a "master overlay." You place the design template over the existing design of the production database, thereby changing its look, feel, and functionality while retaining the underlying data. You can think of it as a facelift for your database!

FIGURE 12.4 ▶

A production database can "inherit" changes made to the design template on a regular basis.

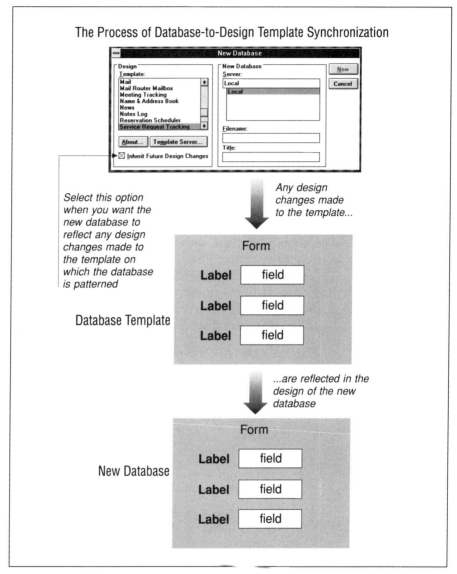

The Process of Database-to-Design Template Synchronization

Select this option when you want the new database to reflect any design changes made to the template on which the database is patterned

The synchronization of a database to a design template can take two distinct forms, depending on the extent of the synchronization:

• You can fully synchronize the database to a single design template. Any change made to the template is applied to the database.

- You can synchronize selected design elements of a database to the corresponding design elements of a single design template or a series of design templates. Only changes made to those design elements in the template are applied to the database.

Consider the extent of the synchronization between a database and a design template in terms of scope of reference. When a database is synchronized to a design template, we can think of the database as referring to the design template for the definition of its own design elements, either completely or partially. A design template with which a database is completely synchronized we'll call a *fully referenced* design template. Any changes to any of the design elements of the template are propagated to the linked database.

A design template with which a database is only partially synchronized we'll call a *partially referenced* design template. Only changes to specific design elements, as set forth by you as you design the database, will propagate to the linked database. In fact, a database may be linked to several partially referenced design templates, in effect, pulling different design elements from a distributed repository of definitions.

There are two general methods for establishing design templates:

- If the database was originally based on a template, you can designate the template as design template (assuming it has not already been designated as such) and then link the database, or selected design elements of the database, to the template. Changes made to the template are propagated to the database.

- If the database was developed from scratch, or was originally based on a template but has been significantly modified since, you can "extract" the design of the database to a new template, designate the template as a design template, and then link the database, or selected design elements of the database, back to this template. Changes made to the template are propagated to the database.

▶▶ *Establishing a Fully Referenced Design Template*

The process of establishing a fully referenced design template entails the following basic steps:

- Extract the design of your application to a separate (new) template.
- Designate the template as a design template.

"Extract the design" means you take only the design elements of your application and create a template from them. To accomplish this step, do the following:

1. In the Notes Workspace, select your application/database by pointing and clicking on its icon.

2. Choose File ➤ Database ➤ Copy. The Database Copy dialog box appears, as shown in Figure 12.5.

FIGURE 12.5 ▶

The Database Copy dialog box lets you select a database and create a new design template from it.

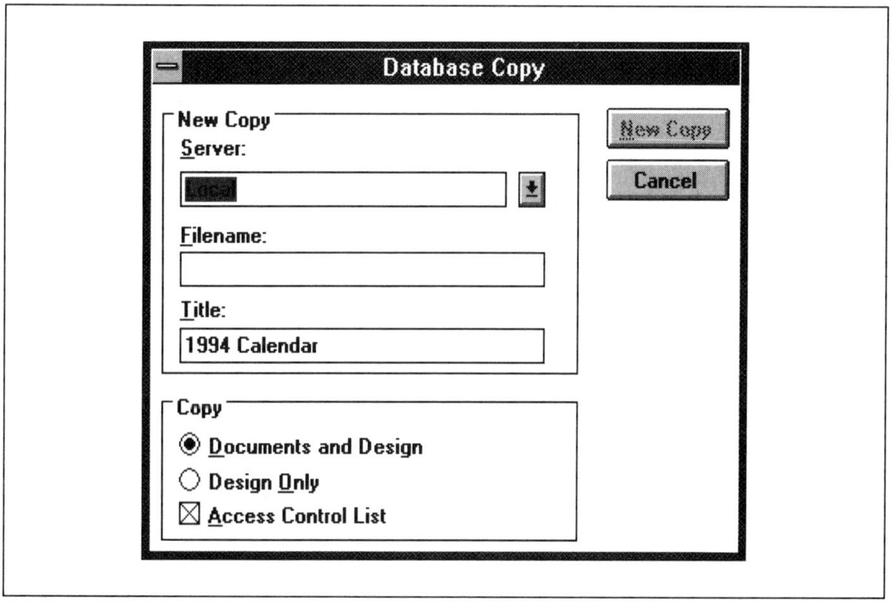

Database Copy

New Copy

Server:

Local

Filename:

Title:

1994 Calendar

Copy

● **Documents and Design**
○ **Design Only**
☒ **Access Control List**

New Copy

Cancel

3. Fill in the Server, Filename, and Title text boxes, respectively. Be sure to give the file name an extension of .NTF to designate it as a template file. The title should be something that distinguishes the item as a template. (This will avoid confusion when both the application and template appear in the Workspace.) For instance, if the original application was titled "Client Tracking" you might give the new template the title "Client Tracking - Template."

4. Select Design Only in the Copy section of dialog box. This will ensure that only the design elements of the application are copied and not the data.

5. Click on OK.

Copying will proceed. A new template will be created and added to your Workspace automatically.

Once this procedure is completed, you must next designate the new template as a design template. To accomplish this, you do the following:

1. In the Workspace, select the new template by pointing and clicking on its icon.

2. Choose File ➤ Database ➤ Information. The Database Information dialog box appears, as shown in Figure 12.6.

FIGURE 12.6 ▶

The Database Information dialog box lets you designate a new database template as a design template.

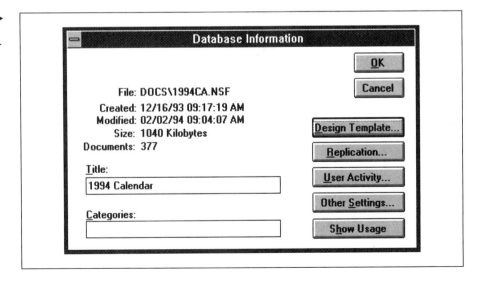

3. Click the button that's labeled "Design Template." The Design Template Options dialog box appears, which is shown in Figure 12.7.

4. Select the Database is a Design Template option.

5. Enter a name in the Template Name text box. This name should be different from the name you assigned to the template previously.

6. Click on OK.

You have now extracted the design of your application to a design template. The next step is to link the application to the template so the design of the application remains synchronized to that of the template.

FIGURE 12.7 ▶

The Design Template Options dialog box

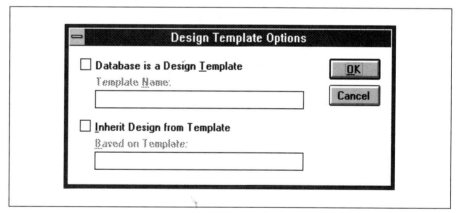

▶▶ *Linking an Application to a Design Template*

After you establish a design template, you must link the application to the design template. Just follow these steps:

1. In the Workspace, select your original application/database by pointing and clicking on its icon.

2. Choose File ➤ Database ➤ Information. The Database Information dialog box appears.

3. Click on the Design Template button. The Design Template Options dialog box appears.

4. Select Inherit Design from Template and fill in the text box under Based on Template with the name of the design template you established previously.

5. Click on OK.

▶▶ **W A R N I N G**

You should understand that linking an existing database to a template can effect your existing design adversely. You may lose some of the information in the current forms or views. Therefore, only use an existing database whose design can be modified without causing much damage, resulting in a loss of data.

You have now tied your application to a design template in a fully referenced fashion. Any changes made to the design elements of the template will propagate to the application either on a scheduled basis, or when forced, or both.

▶▶ *Synchronizing Changes between a Design Template and an Application*

If the application and "linked-to" design template reside on a server, the process of synchronizing changes between the template and application can be handled on an automated, scheduled basis. By default, a Notes server will apply changes made to a design template to all fully referencing applications at 1:00 a.m. (This is controlled by the **[ServerTasksAt1=Design]** parameter you'll find in the NOTES.INI file in the NOTES directory.). You may change the scheduling of synchronization through the NOTES.INI file if you wish.

If the application and template are server-based or reside on a local drive, you can also force synchronization manually. To force replication:

1. In the Workspace, select your application/database by pointing and clicking on its icon.

2. Choose Design ➤ Replace Design. The Replace Database Design dialog box appears, as shown in Figure 12.8.

3. Select the name of design template from the list. If the design template resides on a different server, click on the button labeled Template Server and choose the correct Notes server and design template.

4. Choose Replace.

The changes made to the design template will now propagate to the selected application.

FIGURE 12.8 ▶

The Replace Database Design dialog box

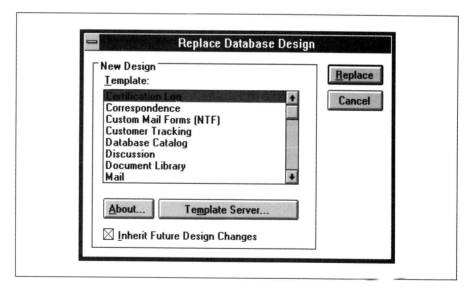

▶▶ What's Next?

Basing a database on an existing design template can save you the time of creating a new database, especially if the template contains elements you want to use. If you don't like some of the elements, you can choose only those you want. However, you might discover that using a template is time-consuming when you have to make many modifications to suit your needs. Therefore, in the long run, you might decide that creating a new database might be more productive.

In the next chapter, we'll describe all the sample design templates and example databases that Notes provides. These files are installed during the Setup process, so you'll have to find out from your Notes Administrator if the files are available to you. Lotus allows you to use the templates and databases "as is" and to make modifications to them to fit your own applications goals. They're a great source of ideas.

CHAPTER 13

Using Notes Templates and Databases

▶▶ **F**AST **T**RACK

▶ **A Notes template is**   289

a prebuilt database that has no data. That is, it has forms, views, an icon, Help documents, and possibly some macros. But there are no documents. You use the template to create a new database—Notes makes an identical copy that you can then use any way you like. The new copy is ready for you to enter your own documents. You can also modify parts of the newly created database structure before you use it.

▶ **There are two varieties of templates:**   289

application templates and system templates. *Application templates* are the ones you will most likely use. They include Correspondence, Discussion, Customer Tracking, and other databases for typical group applications. The *system templates* include Name & Address Book, Certification Log, Mail Router Mailbox, and others that are of interest to the Notes Administrator. Files that are based on these templates are usually created by the Notes Administrator or by the Notes system during installation.

▶ **To create a new Notes database from a template**   290

choose File ➤ New Database. The New Database dialog box appears. On the left of the New Database dialog box you will see a list of templates. These are the .NTF files Notes found in your personal Notes data directory. Click on the Template Server button and select the server that contains the template you want to use if you want to access templates from a server. Specify the server and directory. Enter an appropriate name in the Filename text box. Enter an appropriate name in the Title text box. Click on New to make the database.

▶ **A Notes example database is** **306**

a fully functional database that includes artificial data. The example databases demonstrate many of the advanced application development features of Notes by taking simple databases and customizing them.

▶ **To make a new database based on an example database** **306**

add the example database to your Workspace and then click on the database to select it. Choose File ➤ Database ➤ Copy. The Database Copy dialog box appears. Select the server where you want to store the copy of the database. Enter an appropriate name in the Filename text box. Enter an appropriate name in the Title text box. Choose either the Document and Design option or the Design Only option. If you choose the former, the documents will include data, which you may or may not find useful for your purposes. Select the Access Control List (ACL) option if you want to use the same ACL. Otherwise, don't select the box. Click on the New Copy button.

▶▶ *There* are many templates and example databases provided with Notes that can help you get started in building your own Notes applications. These templates and databases typify the different kinds of applications you can create in Notes. We've identified five general categories and some of the routine tasks you might accomplish:

- Discussion, which would include customer support, group feedback, and brainstorming

- Tracking, which would include servicing clients, and status reports

- Reference, which would include libraries and catalogs

- Scheduling/Workflow Automation, which would include reservations, calendars, and routing information

- News/Reports, which would include meeting agendas, minutes, and newsfeeds from outside services

 ▶▶ **N O T E**

The template and example database files are included with all versions of Notes.

In this chapter, we describe the templates and example databases that are included with Notes. You can look over the ones that interest you and make your own decisions on whether they're appropriate for your needs. We also identify some of the important features of the templates and databases. These features may or may not be suited to the particular demands of the database you have in mind. The descriptions should help you to decide if a template or example database comes close to meeting your application goals.

Anyone who wants to create Notes applications can benefit from using the templates or example databases as starting points for developing new databases. The template and example databases are also useful for anyone who wants to learn more about how the many Notes application features are used. You can study the forms, views, and macros of the templates and example database.

▶▶ *Using the Built-In Application Templates*

A Notes *template* is a prebuilt database that has no data. It has forms, views, an icon, Help documents, and possibly some macros, but there are no documents. You can use a template to create a new database—Notes makes an identical copy that you can then use any way you like. You can use the new copy unaltered—it is ready for users to enter their own documents—or you can also modify parts of the newly created database structure before you use it.

There are two varieties of Notes templates: *application templates* and *system templates*. Application templates are the ones you will most likely use. They include the Correspondence, Discussion, and Customer Tracking databases, plus other databases for typical group applications.

The system templates include Name & Address Book, Certification Log, Mail Router Mailbox, and other templates that are of interest to the Notes Administrator. Files based on these templates are usually created by the Notes Administrator or by the Notes system during installation.

 ▶▶ **N O T E**

> **You are free to create new databases based on any template. You are not restricted from using the system templates—it's just that the databases these templates are based on will be less likely to match your application needs.**

To help you with developing Notes applications, there are several template databases that come with Notes. If you choose to have these copied to your personal Notes directory during installation, then you will have your own copies. You can find them by looking for files with the .NTF extension. (Regular Notes databases have the .NSF extension; the *T* in NTF stands for **T**emplate.)

If you do not have the templates in your local Notes directory, they will likely be on your organization's Notes server. These public templates can be accessed as well (see instructions below). Whatever the location of your template files, you will most likely not want to modify these databases directly. They are design templates that you use when creating new Notes databases. In other words, you normally don't use template files directly. When you create a new database, Notes uses the template as the master. Your new database will inherit all the design features from the template you choose.

▶▶ *Creating a New Database from a Template*

To create a new Notes database from a template, simply follow these steps:

1. Choose File ➤ New Database. The New Database dialog box appears, as shown in Figure 13.1. On the left of the New Database dialog box you will see a list of templates. These are the .NTF files Notes found in your personal Notes data directory.

2. If you want to access templates from a server, click on the Template Server button and select the server that contains the template you want to use.

3. Specify the server and directory.

4. Enter an appropriate name for your new database in the Filename text box.

5. Enter the name you want displayed on the database's icon in your Workspace in the Title text box.

6. Click on New to make the database.

You need to distinguish between the original template itself and the database that you can create based on a template. In general, you will

FIGURE 13.1

The New Database dialog box lists the design templates that are provided with Notes.

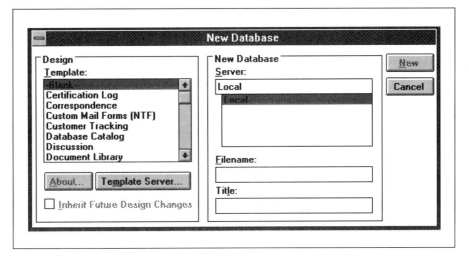

probably need to make the following changes to your new database:

Set the access control list

Identify the users of the application and the access level each will need. List the name of each user and user group in the access control list accordingly.

Edit the About Database document

When you implement this database, you should remove the For Database Managers section of the About document. It contains information for the database implementer, not for the users of your application. You may also choose to remove the For Developers section. This depends on the needs and interests of the users of the database. If you think the For Developers section contains information that is interest-ing and important for your users, you can either leave the section as is or combine it with the For Database Users section. You'll need to use your judgment.

Customize the allowable keywords in the keyword fields	You will need to customize the keyword list of keyword fields in the database you create from a template. There are no default keyword lists for keyword fields in templates. This list must be customized by the database designer.
Customize the database design	Make any design changes that are necessary for your particular application. Of course, you may not have to do anything. If you do make design changes and they add new functionality to the database, be sure to describe what it is in the "What does this database do?" section of the About document and how to use it in the "Functions of the Database" section of the Using document.

Now that you know in general what you need to do to use a Notes template, let's look at some example templates. Each section in the remainder of this chapter describes a different Notes template.

► Correspondence

This database provides a shared repository for names and addresses. It also gives you easy-to-use mechanisms for creating letters, mail merge documents, and faxes. Anyone who wants to contribute names or wants to send a letter or fax will find this database handy. You benefit by having a central place to keep names and addresses that many people may need. You also get a simple and quick way to create both printed and electronic correspondence.

Important Features of the Template

The template provides the following features that you might find useful:

- Tables are used for attractive display of information.
- Different form appearance for editing versus viewing the Person documents.

- Scanned photos and signatures can be inserted in documents.
- Mail merge function using Form Override.
- Fax capability.

> **▶▶ N O T E**
>
> **Users must have at least Designer access to create or edit forms necessary for mail merge letters.**

This template has a hidden form called (FAX) that can be used to send letters via the Notes Fax Gateway. The Fax Gateway is a separate Notes product. If your Notes installation does not have a Fax Gateway, ignore the (FAX) form. If the Fax Gateway is installed, edit the name of the form by removing the parentheses from around the name. This will make the form visible on the Compose menu. Instructions for using the form are included in the database's Help document.

▶ Customer Tracking

You can use this template to track activity between your company and its customers and prospects. Figure 13.2 shows an example of a form that's included in the template. For each new customer, you must first describe your customer and any contacts you have with the customer. Then you can track all activity you might have with that customer. You can track many different kinds of activity between your company and a customer:

- Action items
- Call reports
- Incoming correspondence
- Outgoing correspondence
- Meeting reports
- Miscellaneous activity

Over time, you will build up a history of this activity with all your customers.

FIGURE 13.2 ▶

This form is included in the Customer Tracking database template.

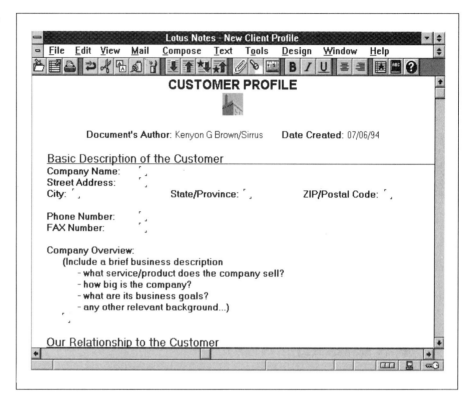

> ▶▶ **TIP**
>
> **The Wholesale Customer Tracking example database, which is described later in this chapter, is based on the Customer Tracking template. You should open the database in order to see examples of the kind of data you can store within it.**

Anyone in your company who has information on a customer can use this database to enter that activity and thereby inform the rest of the company. The sales team that sells to a customer would certainly have important information to record in this database. But product support, legal, credit, senior management, and others might also have information to add.

Thereafter, anyone in your company who has a relationship with a customer can come to this database to review the history of activity between your company and the customer. A sales person might review the latest activity before making a sales call. Management might track action items from the time they are specified, to the assignment of a person responsible, and finally to their ultimate resolution.

Important Features of the Template

The template provides the following features that you might find useful:

- Consolidates all information on your customers in one place.
- Outgoing correspondence can be composed in this database and then faxed or e-mailed.
- Allows you to set up an action item, assign it to an individual, and track it to completion.
- Allows you to report on meetings with a customer.

▶ Custom Mail Forms

This database is a template database (.NTF) that is used in conjunction with Notes Mail. Each Notes Mail server will contain a copy of this template database. The forms in this database are available to the Notes Mail user in addition to the forms in the user's Mail database. When a Notes Mail user chooses the menu option Mail ➤ Compose ➤ Custom Forms, the forms in this database are displayed for use.

This Custom Forms database is an example of the use of Custom mail forms for any organization using Notes Mail. It is a central forms bin available to all Notes Mail users. A user's Notes Mail database contains standard mail forms such as Memo, Reply, etc. This database, which is accessible through the Mail menu, contains additional corporate standard forms that can be used by all Notes users.

With this database, users can access forms, (request forms, order forms, tracking forms, etc.) from a central repository rather than having a Workspace full of databases that are accessed only to use specific forms.

Many of these forms will be mail enabled, and after entry is completed, will route to other users for approval, or to repository databases for tracking.

The database will be accessed by any Notes Mail user in the organization. They will have access to the forms, but will not have general access to the views or documents. The forms that are available are designed to fill specific needs within the organization.

Important Features of the Template

The template provides the following features that you might find useful:

- Several mail options enable you to route documents that require approval from "approver to approver."
- Popups provide information to the user.
- Automatic field refresh force fields within the form to recalculate when a user moves from field to field.

▶ *Discussion*

A workgroup can use this database template to share their thoughts and ideas. Figure 13.3 shows an example of a form that's used by the database. Almost any group that has information to share among its members can use a discussion database. An engineering group can discuss the products they are designing. An advertising agency can discuss the ad campaigns they are developing. A special interest group can share ideas and opinions on their common interests.

To get started, a user can simply browse through the topics for discussion and responses that others have contributed. This is particularly useful for new members of a workgroup who need to come up to speed on the important issues that the group is working on. The history of discussion about these issues is preserved in the group's discussion database.

A user can also take a more active role in the discussion by composing his own responses to others' comments and by proposing new main topics for discussion.

You can think of a discussion database as an informal meeting place, where the members of a workgroup can share ideas and comments. As

FIGURE 13.3

This form is part of the Discussion database template.

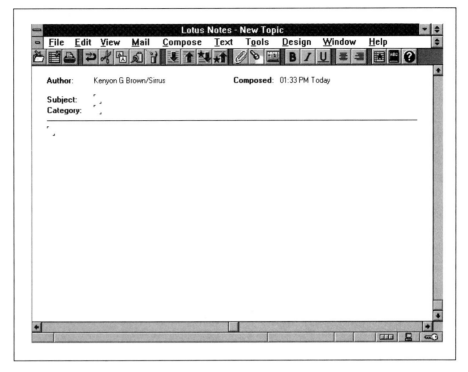

in a physical meeting, each member of the workgroup listens to what others have to say and can voice his or her own opinions. However, unlike a physical meeting, the participants do not have to be in the same room at the same time to share information. People can participate when it is convenient for them to do so. And because it is easy for them to share information, they will do so.

All the members of a workgroup should use the group's discussion database. Some users will just follow the main topics and responses that other members have contributed. More active users will compose their own main topics and responses.

Important Features of the Template

The template provides a virtual meeting place where participants in the discussion can share information without having to travel to an agreed-upon location at an agreed-upon time to discuss a limited agenda. This is particularly important to workgroups whose members do not all sit next to each other. The members of a workgroup may travel frequently; they may not all work for the same boss, in the same department, or even the same company! Members do not have to wait for the next group meeting to raise, discuss, and resolve important issues.

▶ Document Library

A Document Library application is an electronic filing cabinet that stores reference documents for access by a workgroup. Figure 13.4 shows an example of a form that's part of the database. The database might contain anything from environmental impact statements for a group of engineers to financial statements for a group of loan officers. Anyone who wishes to create a record of a document or review available documents can use this database.

FIGURE 13.4 ▶

This form is part of the Document Library database template.

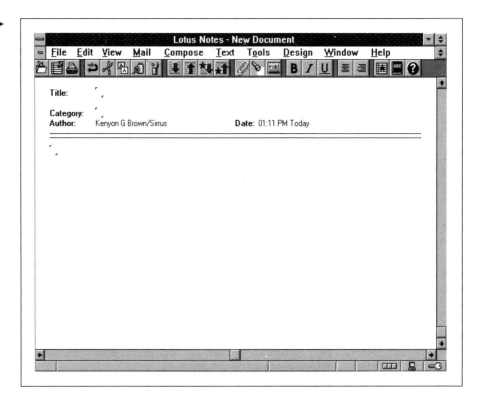

▶▶ **T I P**

> **The Electronic Library example database, which is described later in this chapter, is based on the Document Library template. You should open this database in order to see examples of the kind of data you can store within it.**

Important Features of the Template

The template provides the following features that you might find useful:

- Popup annotations are used to display additional help in the Response to Response form.

- An @DBColumn keyword formula is used to automatically generate a list of keyword values for the Document form's Categories field. The keyword list will not be dynamically refreshed if you compose a new document in a view other than the By Category (Main View); if you enter new category values while composing a new document from the By Author or By Title views, you must close and reopen the database before the new keyword values will appear in the keyword list.

▶ Meeting Tracking

This database allows you to generate a meeting agenda prior to a meeting and send it to all invitees. You can also publish meeting minutes after the meeting, assign and track action items, and reuse the information generated as a knowledge base.

Members of a workgroup, who conduct regular or occasional meetings where formal agendas, minutes, and action items are generated, can follow up on recommendations that were made or consider ideas that were discussed. Meeting leaders can publish agendas and minutes, and follow up on commitments made during the meetings. Attendees can access the minutes generated, and be reminded of the action items that they were assigned. Others can use this database to follow activities from meetings they may have missed, or use the information generated as a knowledge base.

This database can be used in two primary ways. For a department or task force that meets on a regular basis, it can be the primary place where those meetings are chronicled. For people who interact in multiple, overlapping subgroups, it can be the place where meeting minutes and action items are assembled across these different groups.

Important Features of the Template

The template provides the following features that you might find useful:

- Agenda documents are automatically mailed to invitees, by including the document in the text of the mail message.

- Hidden sort columns force the following sort order: Agenda, Minutes, Action Item.

- The "Open Action Items by Due Date" view highlights late action items.

- Field inheritance is used heavily to save unnecessary typing and to ensure that related items are sorted together.

- Tables are used for attractive display of information.

▶ News

This database template is used to distribute news throughout an organization. Figure 13.5 shows an example of one of the forms that's included in the database. Internal news items, news articles, and issues of an internal newsletter are posted in this database. Then employees can review this news to keep informed about goings-on in their industry with competitors and customers—the things that affect their work and the success of your organization.

 ▶▶ **T I P**

The Notes News example database, which is described later in this chapter, is based on the News template. You should open this database in order to see examples of the kind of data you can store within it.

FIGURE 13.5 ▶

This form is from the News database template.

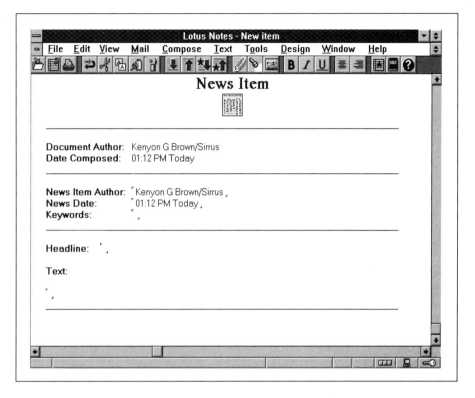

News from three different sources can be published in this database. First, employees can post individual News Item documents. These items might be news about a project or individual inside your organization or a summary of an external news article. Second, news articles from the press can be imported into this database from newswire services with the help of a news retrieval software package. Third, periodic issues of an internal newsletter can be entered into this database and distributed throughout your organization.

 ▶▶ **N O T E**

> **Various third parties have developed news retrieval software packages that capture articles from newswires and import them into Notes databases. See the appendix for a description of products.**

An editor will manage the flow of news into this database. The manager of a small staff of editors would be responsible for posting internal news items and issues of the internal newsletter in this database. The editor would also work with the news retrieval software company to develop a custom profile that specifies the news articles that are important to your organization. Only news articles that meet these criteria would be selected from the newswires and posted in this database. Readers will come to this database to read the news. The news articles in this database have been selected because they cover topics that are important to readers.

Important Features of the Template

The template offers the following benefits that you might find important:

- Integrates many news sources in one database. It can accept and organize news from various sources: articles selected and imported from newswires, individual news items, and issues of an internal newsletter. Information from all these sources is consolidated in one place.

- The Notes environment takes care of news distribution and access. It is perfect for distributing information throughout an organization. Notes is the infrastructure that handles the communications, distribution, and access issues. You need only worry about the information itself.

- From the user's perspective, it is easy to refer to the latest news in this database. You are probably using Notes to track the status of the projects you are working on, to participate in group discussions, to route and approve documents. Reading the latest, preselected, relevant news is as easy as clicking on the news database icon. You do not have to leave your desk or make a special request for information.

- An informed work force makes intelligent decisions. The entire work force has easy access to important information about the company and its competitors. With this information in mind, employees will make more intelligent decisions.

▶ Reservation Schedules

This database serves as a reservation scheduler for any entity, such as a conference room or special piece of equipment. Figure 13.6 shows an example of a form that's included in the database. Anyone who wants to reserve a time slot will use this database. People can check for available time slots and reserve them without a lot of typing or telephone calls.

Important Features of the Template

The template provides the following features that you might find useful:

- All reserving/unreserving is done using macros.
- No composing is required because all date/time documents are set up with a macro.
- All information is available from the views.

FIGURE 13.6 ▶

This form is included in the Reservation Schedules database template.

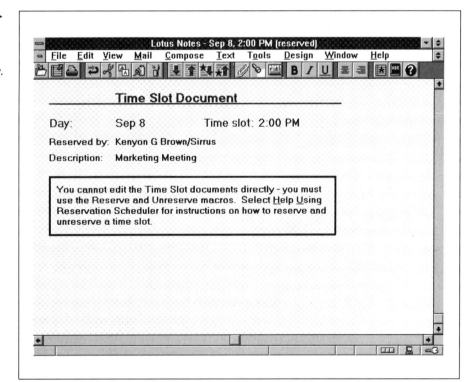

- User cannot change others' reservations (this is because you cannot edit the documents directly, only through the macros).

- Automatically captures user's name.

- Users enter event descriptions by opening an @Prompt dialog box.

► *Service Request Tracking*

A Service Request Tracking application provides service and support departments with a tool to manage their workload effectively. This application can, for example, help an MIS department track requests for software upgrades or enable a maintenance department to track requests for equipment repairs.

The application calculates the length of time that each request is open. It provides a history of requests, so that managers can spot trends—such as seasonal variations, or the departments that require the most service. The database provides quick access to historical information that can save the service providers time when responding to recurring requests.

The people responsible for accepting service requests will compose new documents. Managers can examine the views to analyze service performance.

Important Features of the Template

The template provides validity checks. Many fields within the Service Request form require values. The DateCompleted field includes a validity check that specifies that the DateCompleted may not precede the DateReceived value.

► *Status Reports*

This database template application can track the progress of people on any type of project. It keeps team members up-to-date on project status and issues. Anyone who needs to share their objectives and/or status reports can do so in this database. Managers can use status reports to analyze workflow across multiple projects, departments, or divisions. The application captures valuable historical information for the workgroup's future reference.

Important Features of the Template

The template provides the following features that you might find useful:

- Response documents can be mailed, since the Response form contains a feature called MailOptions, which bypasses the usual mail interface and mails documents automatically.

- The Status Report and Objectives forms use automatic versioning; when a Status Report or Objectives document is edited, the prior version is saved as a response.

▶ Things To Do

This template serves as a reminder list of tasks that you are working on. It can be used by an individual or by a group. Someone who wants to organize projects (or smaller items) that need to be done will find the template useful.

You can be sure that all your tasks, both large and small, are being tracked. You can check for overdue items, as well as get a summary of activities already completed.

Important Features of the Template

The template provides the following features that you might find useful:

- Multiple views let the users look for open items, completed items, or all items, with various sorting and categorizing criteria.

- Project and Category are self-referencing keyword fields. The keyword list for Project(s) always shows all current projects, and the keyword list for Category(s) always shows all currently used categories. In both cases, you can add a new entry to the list just by creating a task with that new project or category.

►► *Taking Advantage of the Example Databases*

A Notes *example* database is a fully functional database that includes artificial data. The power of Notes really comes through when you customize your applications. The example databases demonstrate many of the advanced application development features of Notes by taking simple databases and customizing them.

Some of the examples are based on templates, while others are completely new and different. Also, by including sample data, the example databases give you a better feel for how the applications really work. As with templates, you are welcome to copy any example database and modify it for your own use.

►► *Making a New Database Based on an Example Database*

The Notes Example files are installed in an EXAMPLES subdirectory in your Notes data directory. With Example files, the standard procedure is to copy the database, thereby creating a new one of your own that you can modify. This also protects you against making changes to the original database.

To make a new database that's based on an example database, follow these steps:

1. Add the example database to your Workspace.

2. Click on the database to select it.

3. Choose File ➤ Database ➤ Copy. The Database Copy dialog box appears, as shown in Figure 13.7.

4. Select the server where you want to store the copy of the database or choose Local to copy the database to the hard disk on your workstation.

5. Enter an appropriate name in the Filename text box.

FIGURE 13.7 ▶

The Database Copy dialog box lets you make of copy of an example database on another server or on your workstation.

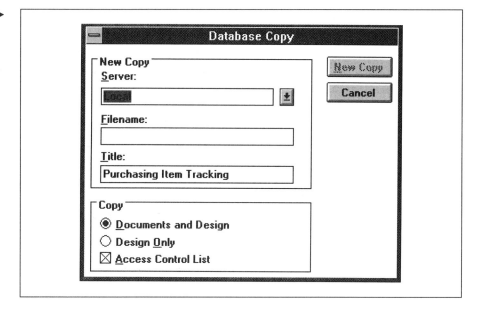

6. Enter an appropriate name in the Title text box.

7. Choose either the Document and Design option or the Design Only option. If you choose the former, the documents will include data, which you may or may not find useful for your purposes.

8. Select the Access Control List (ACL) option if you want to use the same ACL. Otherwise, don't select the box.

9. Click on the New Copy button.

Notes provides the following example databases for you to use and modify to fit your own needs.

▶ Business Card Request

This is a repository and management database for a collection of business card requests. An originator will create and save the request. The originator and the cardholder will be notified, via a mail message, that the request has been entered. A database administrator will update the request status as the request is processed. Whenever the request status is changed, the originator and the cardholder will be notified.

Requests can be initiated by anyone with access to the database. Any user can access the database. Administrators responsible for the ordering and tracking of business cards will use this database interactively. These users can view any request in the database, and can change the status of any request.

Important Features of the Database

The database provides the following features that you might find useful:

- Most keyword lookups have been externalized, and are accessed through the @DbLookup command embedded in formulas and keyword lists. This methodology allows users to review keywords and codes outside the form or application, allows nondesigners to update keyword lists, allows the design of the database to be hidden (choose File ➤ Database ➤ Information and click or and Other Settings) without limiting maintenance of keyword lists, and allows quick customization and translation to other languages.

 ▶▶ **N O T E**

> To use the @DbLookup feature, the example file **Lookup Keyword Library (LOOKUP.NSF) must be installed.**

- A notification (with an embedded doclink) is automatically mailed to the originator and the cardholder whenever the request is changed.
- Computed fields on the form are automatically refreshed (recomputed) whenever the user moves from one field to the next or uses any buttons.
- Popup annotations are used to provide extended help and information text to the user.
- Special buttons are used to simplify several processes in the system.

▶ Call Tracking

This Call Tracking database is an example Notes application that's based on a system used to track calls to the Lotus Notes Support

Organization. It records organization, user, and support call information. Support calls are logged and are tracked to their resolution. The database contains problems and their solutions to provide a knowledge base that support personnel can refer to at any time.

The tracking database is aimed at a central support group, so it would normally have limited access for the adding and editing of documents. The database will be used by two categories of users: support personnel and end users. Support personnel will use this database interactively as part of their job. End users may be allowed Reader access to the database so that they can follow the progress of their calls, or to research their own problems using the knowledge base created by support.

When an organization signs up for support, an Organization document is created. When a user first calls in with a request for support, his or her name and system configuration information are placed into a User document. Each call is assigned to a specific support person using the appropriate field in the Call Tracking document. User information is inherited from the User document to simplify the gathering of information by the support person. The call is assigned to a support person who is responsible for resolution or escalation of the problem. Whenever the Call Tracking document is modified, a notification message is mailed to the assigned support person and to the caller. (These messages will be sent to the caller *only* if their full mail address has been entered into the document.) When a call is resolved, a Technote should be written up with details of the problem and resolution. This Technote should be doclinked to the Call Tracking document. These Technotes serve as a knowledge base for all support personnel.

Important Features of the Database

The database provides the following features that you might find useful:

- The values that are made available in keyword lists can be stored inside the individual fields on a form or they may be stored outside the form as documents in a database. Keyword fields can access keyword lists outside the form using the @DbLookup and @DbColumn commands. These @functions obtain lists of keywords from documents (@DbLookup) or from views (@DbColumn), either of which can be located in the current database or external databases.

- The Call Tracking form is automatically mailed to the support person and the call originator whenever an action is recorded for the call.

- Special buttons are used to simplify several processes in the system. For example, when top level information changes in the Organization document, a Synchronize button forces these changes to all the other documents for the organization. An Escalate or Close button will prompt the user for the new status, and will update all the appropriate fields in the document in one step. When the user pushes a Create a User Profile button from the Organization document, a new User Profile is composed. When the user pushes a Log a Call button from the User Profile document, a new Call Tracking document is composed.

▶ Contract Library

This database provides a central place to consolidate and organize master legal agreements. You can create the text of the agreements in any word processor that supports OLE. These word processing documents will be used as embedded object(s) in the Contract form. You will use the Contract form to compose contracts for specific individuals or companies. The views will track the contracts by attorney responsible, revision date, description, country, and category.

The audience for this database is a corporate legal department, or any group that needs to create and share copies of legal agreements. You would use this database to store the copies of agreements so everyone can reference or modify them. Also, attorneys can use this database to reuse relevant text from previous agreements.

Important Features of the Database

The database provides the following features that you might find useful:

- Documents can be linked from a variety of OLE word processors (the current Contract form uses AmiPro).

- There is only one form on the Compose menu—macros in the word processing document let you choose the type of contract and enter contract-specific information.

- Edit history is automatically stored for each document, and the last five edits are displayed at the bottom of the form.

▶ Electronic Library

The Electronic Library database is an electronic filing cabinet that stores reference documents that can be accessed by a workgroup. The database might contain anything from environmental impact statements for a group of engineers to financial statements for a group of loan officers. The audience for this database is anyone who wishes to create a record of a document or review available documents.

 ▶▶ **T I P**

> **The Document Library template, which is described earlier in this chapter, is the basis for the Electronic Library database. The database is a good example of the amount of development time you can save by using one of Notes built-in templates.**

Important Features of the Database

The database uses an @DBColumn keyword formula to generate a list of keyword values for the Document form's Categories field automatically. You should understand that the keyword list will not be dynamically refreshed if you compose a new document in a view other than the By Category (Main View). If you enter new category values while composing a new document from the By Author or By Title views, you must close and reopen the database before the new keyword values will appear in the keyword list.

▶ Jim Hansen's Mail

This database is one of the five databases which make up the Purchase Requisition example application. You should refer to the Help About document for the Product Catalog & Requisitions database for a complete description of the Purchase Requisitons application, including details on the role of Jim Hansen's Mail database.

► *Lookup Keyword Library*

One of the new Notes Version 3 features is the ability to reference information outside the current form. This is done using the @DbLookup and @DbColumn commands in formulas and keyword format statements. The information that is referenced may be contained within the current database or external to the current database. This Lookup Keyword Library database is designed to be central library of reference information accessed by other Notes database applications.

This database is also used as an external lookup reference library by forms in the Business Card Request database. To give the user a better feel for the use of a lookup database, several types of groups of codes are contained in this example; only two of the groups are used by the Business Card example. The codes listed are:

- Departments
- Locations of Offices
- Product Categories (for a purchasing function)
- Region Codes (with additional information)
- Standard Industrial Codes (SIC)
- State Codes (with additional information)

This is a centrally maintained reference database. As such it will have *very* limited Author and Editor access. It will be restricted to a small group of administrators who will maintain the codes. End users will require Reader access to the database in order to be able to access the documents. Users will not need to keep this database on their Workspace.

Important Features of the Database

You can look up keywords with the use of the @DbLookup command. The values that are made available in keyword lists may be stored inside the individual fields on a form or they may be stored outside the form as documents in a database. Keyword fields can access keyword lists outside the form using the @DbLookup and @DbColumn commands. These @functions obtain lists of keywords from documents (@DbLookup) or from views (@DbColumn) which can be located in a separate database such as LOOKUP.NSF. This methodology eliminates the need for duplication of keyword lists, allows users to review Keywords & Codes outside the form or application, allows nondesigners to update keyword lists, allows the design of the database to be hidden (choose File ➤ Database ➤ Information and click on Other Settings) without limiting maintenance of keyword lists, and allows quick customization and translation to other languages.

▶ Notes News

We discussed the News template earlier in the chapter. Users may choose to browse through information in this database from just one of the available news sources or from all of them. You can even design a customized, private view of the news which selects news about the specific issues, companies, or products you track.

Consider the alternatives for getting this news to employees. Some employees would spend a lot of time getting this information from various print publications. Not only would this take time but it would also be expensive. How many subscriptions do the various members of your organization have to a given publication? Other employees would simply not get the information. The time, money, and effort to keep up is considerable.

Because this database contains news from many sources and because it contains only relevant information, it can serve as a one-stop complete news source for many employees in the company. If necessary, individual employees can supplement this information with specialized news sources that are not included here.

It is also an advantage to provide news in an electronic format. The news can be sorted by source, date, or keyword. This makes it easier to find articles of interest quickly. And once you find something interesting you can forward the information to colleagues via e-mail, or you can cut and paste sections into word processing documents.

Important Features of the Database

This database can integrate many news sources. It can accept and organize news from various sources: articles selected and imported from newswires, individual news items, and issues of an internal newsletter. Information from all these sources is consolidated in one place.

The Notes environment is perfect for distributing information throughout an organization. Notes is the infrastructure that handles the communications, distribution, and access issues. You need only worry about the information itself.

From the user's perspective, it is easy to refer to the latest news in this database. You are probably using Notes to track the status of the projects you are working on, to participate in group discussions, to route and approve documents. Reading the latest, preselected, relevant news is as easy as clicking on the news database icon. You do not have to leave your desk or make a special request for information.

The entire work force has easy access to important information about the company and its competitors. With this information in mind, employees will make more intelligent decisions.

▶ *Product Catalog & Requisitions*

This is the first database from the Purchase Requisitions example application. This application automates all aspects of composing, approving, and fulfilling purchase requisitions inside an organization. Requisitioners can browse through a catalog of products approved for ordering, compose a purchase requisition containing selected products, and then send that requisition around for management approval. Managers who need to approve the requisition are assigned automatically, based on the amount of the requisition and the requisitioner's organizational level and the personal authorization limit associated with it.

This application implements a serial model of approval. First, the requisitioner's immediate manager is tapped to approve the requisition, then the manager's manager, then the manager's manager's manager, and so on until all required approvals have been obtained. Of course, a manager can also reject a requisition. In this case, an e-mail is sent back to the requisitioner indicating the manager's reason for rejecting the requisition.

Ultimately, after a requisition has been approved by all required managers, it is routed to the Purchasing Item Tracking database. There, a purchasing agent is assigned to each item on the requisition. The agent selects a a vendor from whom to order the item, and places the order. When an item has been ordered and received, an e-mail is sent to the person who requisitioned the item, indicating that the item has come in.

Important Features of the Database

This is a workflow application. Documents are routed from one database to another automatically, as their status changes. Individuals are assigned to documents based on rules maintained in a table. Mail messages are sent out to inform users that a document is waiting for their review, approval, or other input. All the while, the process is centrally managed so that information on the status of an item is always available and up-to-date. The key Notes technical features which are used to implement this workflow are the @DbLookup function, buttons, background and paste/mail-in macros, and the @MailSend function.

Each Notes user is identified by a Notes User ID. When a user enters Notes and tries to access a shared database on a Notes server, he or she required to type in the password associated with his or her Notes User ID (if the user has set a password on his ID). Knowing this password ensures that the user is who he or she claims to be. Thereafter, an application can be set up to consider the identity of the user who is attempting to access the data in the application and decide what the user will be allowed to see and do in the application.

In the Purchase Requisition application, the default values for the RequisitionedBy and RequisitionedFor fields in a new Purchase Requisition document are the Notes User Name of the person composing the document. The application then looks in the Notes Name & Address Book database to locate the user's position in the organization and determine from it what managers need to approve the requisition. This calculation is made automatically, based on the requisitioner's User Name.

The Purchase Requisition application also sends mail messages to managers who must approve requisitions. Notes makes this easy, because e-mail is integrated in the Notes environment. An application can send out e-mail to notify users of important information. A user can read that mail and quickly and easily refer to the detailed information in the shared application database.

This Purchase Requisition application demonstrates one way to implement an approval process in Notes. The list of approvers is calculated based on the rules implemented in Notes formulas referring to the organizational information stored in the Notes Name & Address Book.

Requests for approvals are sent to the assigned approvers as e-mail messages, containing a doclink to the centrally located Purchase Requisition document. Approvers do not have to remember to check the central database to see what requisitions require their signature; they just need to read their e-mail! Actually approving or rejecting a requisition is a simple as clicking on the appropriate button. By receiving informational e-mails and referring to the shared Requisition Approvals database, all parties involved are kept up-to-date on the status of requisitions.

From within one document, Notes allows you to look up values stored in another document. In this application, information about the personal authorization limit for an individual in the organization is maintained centrally and looked up when that individual composes a new purchase requisition. Because this information is centrally maintained and accessible, all applications can refer to it when it is needed.

▶ Pur Req Example N&A Book

This database one of the five databases which make up the Purchase Requisition example application. You should refer to the Help About document for the Product Catalog & Requisitions database for a complete description of the Purchase Requisitons application, including details on the role of the Pur Req Example N&A Book database.

▶ Purchasing Item Tracking

This database is one of the five databases which make up the Purchase Requisition example application. You should refer to the Help About document for the Product Catalog & Requisitions database for a complete description of the Purchase Requisitons application, including details on the role of the Purchasing Item Tracking database.

▶ Requisition Approvals

This database is one of the five databases which make up the Purchase Requisition example application. You should refer to the Help About document for the Product Catalog & Requisitions database for a complete description of the Purchase Requisitons application, including details on the role of the Requisition Approvals database.

▶ Support Conference

This database is based on the Discussion template that we discussed earlier in the chapter. A workgroup can use this database to share their thoughts and ideas as they might in a conference or other large forum. The main difference between this database and the template on which it is based is that information from other workgroups can be brought into the database, thus expanding a discussion's scope beyond the members of one workgroup.

▶ Template & Example Card Catalog

This Template & Example Card Catalog lists in one database detailed information on all the standard Template and Example files that come with Notes.

Important Features of the Database

This database provides the following features that you might find useful:

- Multiple views give you different ways to find the template or example database that fits your needs.
- The Demo Scripts view provides the full demo script for the multidatabase demo.

▶ Travel Authorizations

This database is used to track and update the status of travel authorization requests. It is a central repository for the creation, approval/rejection, and tracking of travel authorization requests. Travelers and originators will use the views in the database to check the current status of their requests. Approvers will use the database to check their outstanding work, and to approve or reject requests.

The originator of the request (either the traveler or an administrative assistant) fills out and saves a travel authorization request. A notification message is sent, via mail, to each person on the approval list when the request is saved. This message will inform them that there is a request for their review.

This notification message contains a doclink to the request. The approver double-clicks on the doclink, and the Travel Request document is displayed. The approver then edits the request document and marks it as either approved or rejected by clicking on the appropriate button. When all approvals have been received, the request status is changed to approved.

When the request is completely approved or rejected, a periodic macro sends a notification to the traveler and the originator informing them of the request disposition.

Important Features of the Database

This database provides the following features that you might find useful:

- Popup annotations are used to provide extended help and information text to the user.

- Special buttons are used to simplify several processes in the system.

▶ *Wholesale Customer Tracking*

This database is based on the Customer Tracking template that we looked at earlier in the chapter. You can use this database to track activity between Wholesale Inc. and its customers and prospects. For a new customer, you must first describe your customer and any contacts you have at the customer. Then you can track all activity you might have with that customer.

▶▶ *What's Next?*

Using the templates and example databases that Notes provides can save you the time and effort required to build a new database, especially if an existing one comes very close to fitting your needs. However, the design of a particular template or database might not be ideal for your purposes. You might have to make many modifications. Therefore, in the long run, you might be better off designing a new database that fits the needs of your organization and the people using it. In the next chapter, we take you through the steps of creating a database from scratch. We show you the process involved in creating a *form*, the basic element for structuring data in a Notes database.

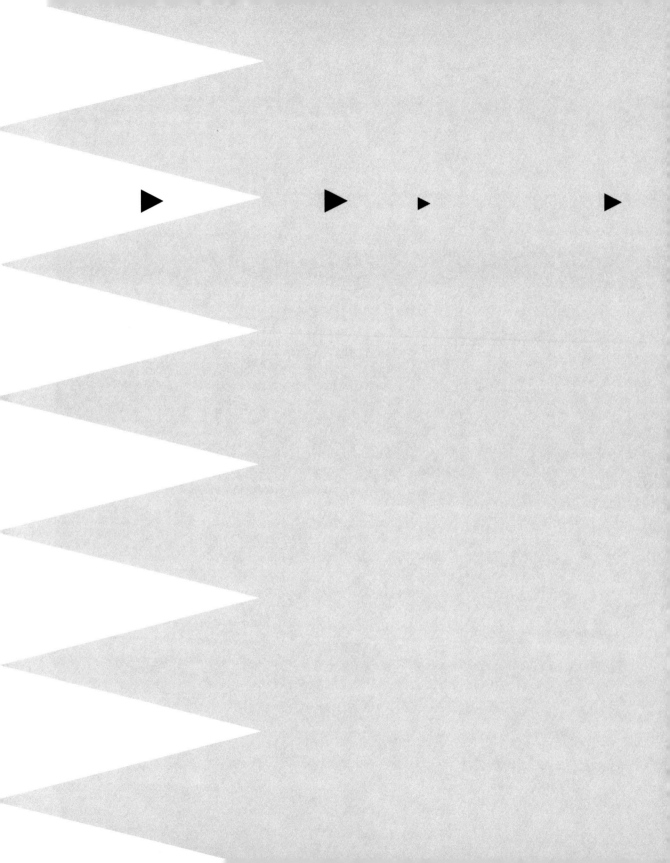

▶ ▶ CHAPTER **14**

Designing
a Form

___

▸▸*F*AST *T*RACK

▶ ***To add a field to a form***　　　　　　　　　　　　　　**348**

> position the cursor at the location where the field is to be placed. Choose Design ➤ New Field. The Design New Field dialog box appears. Make sure one of the options is selected. Click on OK. The Field Definition dialog box appears. Enter a name in the Name text box. You may also enter a brief description in the Help Description text box. Select a data type from the choices in the the Data Type list box. Select a field type. Click on OK to accept the changes.

▶ ***To designate the data type of a field as Keyword***　　　**362**

> and then create a list of allowable keywords for the field, double-click on the field. The Field Definition dialog box appears. Select Keywords as the data type. Click on the Format button. The Design Keyword Format dialog box appears. Enter a list of words in the Allowable Keywords text box. Select Standard, Check Box, or Radio Button from the User Interface list box. Click on the Sort button if you want to sort the list of departments alphabetically. Click OK to accept the changes and to close the dialog box. Click OK again to save the changes.

▶▶ *U*sers will interact with the forms you create more than any other component of a Notes database. Forms become the basis for documents that users will compose and add to a Notes database, and users need forms to read any data that's stored in the database. Therefore, the design of a form—its look, feel, and function—plays a major role in the day-to-day usage of the database. A well-designed form makes life easier for your users. A poorly designed form causes confusion and frustration.

This chapter takes you through the steps of designing the forms for the Corporate Directory database. It assumes you have been given either Designer or Manager access designation, so you can create databases. The chapter covers:

- Form design considerations
- A form's basic components
- Defining a form's attributes
- Identifying the form's type
- Adding fields
- Designating field types
- Formatting a form

▶▶ *Structuring Data in a Notes Database*

The importance of forms can be understood by considering the meaning of the word *form* itself: A form is something that gives raw material shape and structure. Without form, most raw material is without shape or structure, and is probably not too useful.

So it is with Notes databases and forms. At a rudimentary level, a Notes database is a container for raw data—information is put in and information is taken out. The data that is collected in a database—text, numbers, dates—has no structure in and of itself, at least at the user-interface level. (Of course, the raw data has structure at the machine level, but this is not our concern.)

It is the role of the application developer to give the raw data structure (i.e., a form) from the perspective of both the user adding the data to the database (putting information into the container) and the user reading the data from the database (taking information out of the container). The form provides the filter through which we input data and subsequently view it.

The simplest Notes application would consist of a single database with a single form (and a single view). Such a simple setup may be sufficient for some uses; however, it's more likely that your applications will require multiple forms in which each form captures a unique set of related data. Typically, certain forms are used for data entry and viewing by your general user community, while other forms can be used only by specific users (perhaps just yourself) for maintaining information that another form incorporates for lookup purposes.

▶▶ *Form Design Considerations*

The problem with discussing form design is that the aesthetics of form design are highly subjective. That being the case, we will avoid some aspects of the topic. Whether the form background is blue or yellow, the font is Helvetica or Times Roman, or the point size is 10 or 12 is ultimately up to the designer (taking into account users' preferences, of course). What we will discuss is the actual creation of a form along with some general design guidelines related to the usability of your forms. We'll leave the details to your own sensibilities.

When designing a form, you need to keep in mind that it is a vehicle for both *data input* and *data presentation*, and it must handle both functions satisfactorily. On the data input side, your users will compose new documents based on your form, and they will edit previously composed documents in order to change or update the information. On the data presentation side, users will need to read specific documents in the database and perhaps print them. So we've identified two categories of interaction related to form design, and two tasks within those categories:

- Data Input
  - Initial Composition
  - Editing
- Data Presentation
  - Reading
  - Printing

In all cases, it is the underlying form of a document that dictates the structure, and thus the efficiency, of this interaction.

▶▶ *Creating a Form*

You have two basic options when creating a new form:

- You can create the form from scratch.
- You can create the form by copying its design from another form.

If you want to base your form on an existing form, you can turn to Chapters 12 and 13 for full discussions of creating forms from preexisting templates. In this chapter, however, we'll assume that you are creating a form from scratch. Before you begin, you need to select an existing database that will include the form or create a new database. To select an existing database, simply click on its icon in your Workspace.

In this example, you're going to create a new database and name it "Corporate Directory." The database functions as a directory of all employees in an organization. As a workflow-automation application, it provides the means for an administrator or manager (probably the Personnel Manager) to track and update information on each employee.

Since the organization transfers employees to its other regional offices around the country, changes in an employee's status, such as title and address, can be forwarded to the manager for input. In this way, a current personnel file on every employee can be maintained easily. To create the new Corporate Directory database, follow these steps:

1. Choose File ➤ New Database. The New Database dialog box appears, as shown in Figure 14.1.

2. Make sure that -Blank- is highlighted in the Template list box.

3. Highlight the appropriate server name in the Server list box or choose Local to store the database on your workstation.

4. Enter **CORPDIR**, or another appropriate name, in the Filename text box. There's no need to include an extension because Notes appends .NSF to the file name automatically.

5. Enter **Corporate Directory**, or another appropriate name, in the Title text box. Just make sure the name is descriptive.

6. Click on OK. By default, a blank view appears.

7. Press Esc to close the view. You'll return to the Notes Workspace, which displays the new Corporate Directory title on the database's icon, as shown in Figure 14.2.

FIGURE 14.1 ▶

The New Database dialog box lets you name a new database and indicate where the database should be stored, on a server or on your workstation.

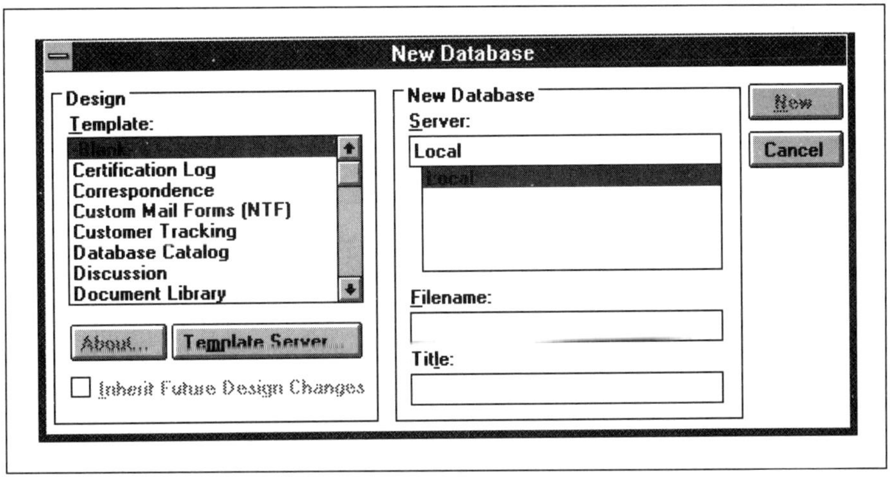

FIGURE 14.2 ►

The Notes Workspace displays the title on the new Corporate Directory database icon.

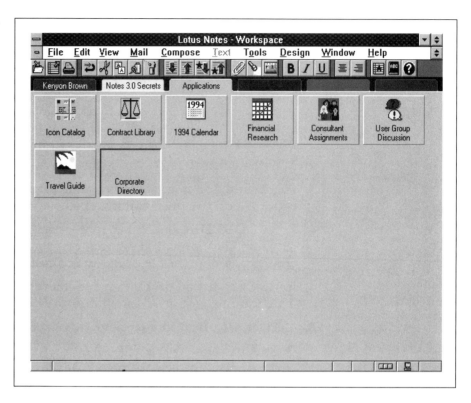

 ►► **N O T E**

An icon always appears in the Workspace, with the title you give the database. This icon is just a blank square until you create a graphic for it. You need to make sure the icon is always selected by clicking on it *before* you start creating any forms or views. Otherwise, you'll either save the forms or views to a database that you unknowingly selected or you won't be able to create the forms or views because you haven't selected a database. If a specific database isn't selected, the Design menu will appear dimmed. Subsequently, you won't be able to access the Views or Forms commands.

To create a new form, follow these steps:

1. Return to the Notes Workspace (if you aren't there already) and click on the Corporate Directory database icon to select it.

2. Choose Design ➤ Forms. The Design Forms dialog box appears, as shown in Figure 14.3.

3. Click the New button. A blank form appears, as shown in Figure 14.4.

You are now in Form Design mode, or just Design mode. The form is entirely blank because it is actually a large rich text field, which we discussed in Chapter 11. You'll recall that a rich text field can contain graphics and objects as well as the formats you apply to text. It is like an artist's canvas before she or he applies the first brush stroke. From here you are now free to "paint" your form any way you wish. As an example, let's put together a simple Directory Entry form that we'll use in our corporate directory of personnel. This form will include each person's name, department, title, location, phone and fax number, and various other pieces of information. Later on in Chapter 15 we'll build a series of views, which will present the directory in a variety of ways.

FIGURE 14.3 ▶

You begin designing a new form by opening the Design Forms dialog box.

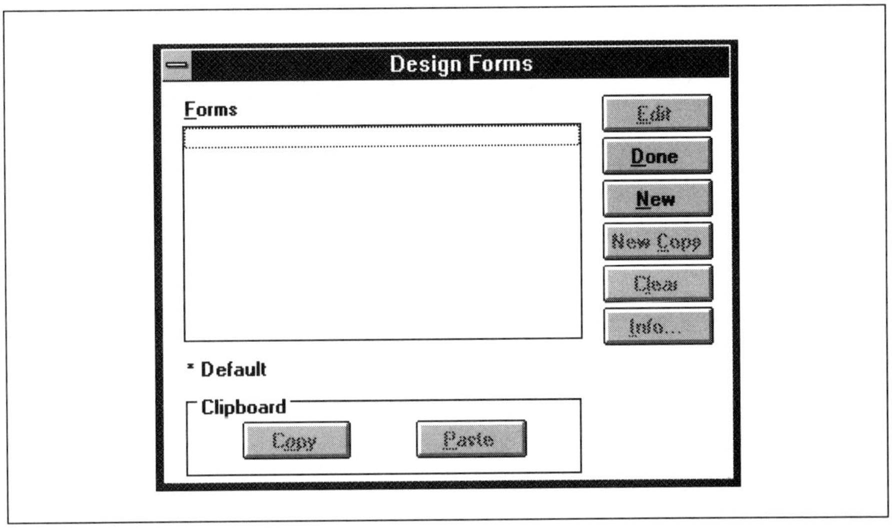

FIGURE 14.4 ►

When you click the New button, a blank form appears.

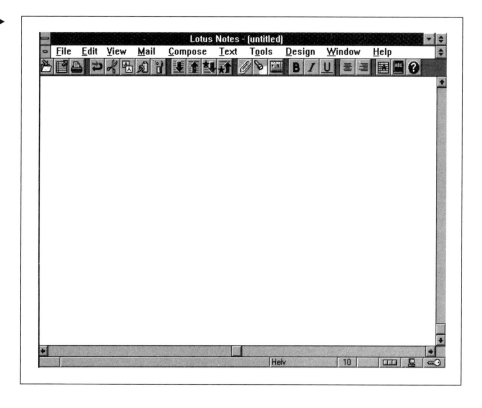

►► *A Form's Basic Components*

There are two primary interrelated components that make up a form:

- A list of general characteristics concerning the form, which are referred to as *form attributes*. These characteristics describe the overall behavior of the form (and documents based on the form) as it relates to the database in general.

- The actual substance of the form, including labels, fields, buttons, and other design elements.

While the substance of the form is certainly the more glamorous side of form design, don't overlook the importance of a form's attributes. You'll be amazed at the effect an incorrectly set attribute can have on the operation of your database. At the very least, you'll want to establish some basic attributes for your form—its name and type—at the outset of the form design process. You may choose to establish other attributes later as dictated by the functionality required of your application.

▶▶ *Defining a Form's Attributes*

A form may have a number of characteristics or attributes associated with it that give the form identity and establish important overall qualities of the form. An attribute can be as simple as the form's name, or it can be more sophisticated. For example, an attribute can specify whether or not information may be passed from another document to a document based on this form. Certain attributes are mandatory. For these attributes you must provide a value, or sometimes Notes provides a default value for you. Other attributes can be ignored entirely since they are used only in more obscure implementations.

To define the Directory Entry form's attributes, follow these steps:

1. Choose Design ➤ Form Attributes. The Design Form Attributes dialog box appears, as shown in Figure 14.5.

2. Enter **1. Directory Entry** in the Name text box. (Make sure you include the number.)

FIGURE 14.5 ▶

The Design Form Attributes dialog box lets you specify a form's name, type, and other attributes.

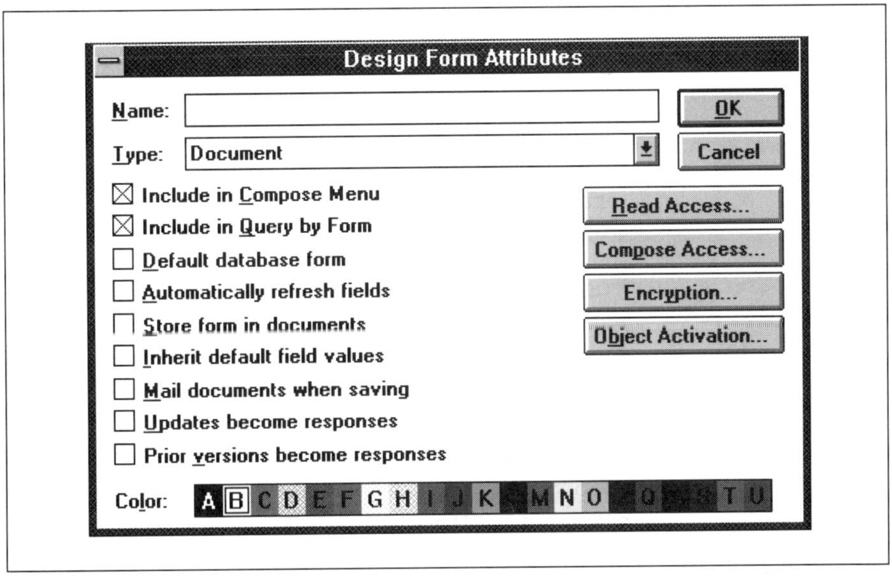

Design Form Attributes

Name:

Type: Document

OK

Cancel

☒ Include in **C**ompose Menu
☒ Include in **Q**uery by Form
☐ **D**efault database form
☐ **A**utomatically refresh fields
☐ **S**tore form in documents
☐ **I**nherit default field values
☐ **M**ail documents when saving
☐ **U**pdates become responses
☐ Prior **v**ersions become responses

Read Access...

Compose Access...

En**c**ryption...

Object Activation...

Co**l**or: A B C D E F G H I J K L M N O P Q R S T U

►► N O T E

When you precede the name of a form with a number, you are indicating that you want the form to appear on the Compose menu in a specific sequence. Otherwise, the names of the forms will appear in alphabetical order. Generally, you want the main document-type forms to precede the response-type forms in hierarchical order.

3. Make sure that **Document** appears in the Type box.

4. Select the following options (nothing else should be checked):

- Include in Compose Menu
- Include in Query by Form
- Default Database Form

5. Click OK to accept the changes.

Let's examine the attributes we have at our disposal.

► Naming a Form

A requirement of any form is that it have a name, which we'll call a "proper name." If you attempt to save a new form without assigning it a proper name, Notes will prompt you for one. Form names usually, though not always, appear on the Compose menu. As such, the name of a form should clearly reflect its use to the end user. The length of a form's proper name cannot exceed 64 characters (contrary to what some Lotus Notes documentation states).

Forms may actually be given more than one name. Beyond the proper name, a form may be assigned "aliases" known as *synonyms*. Synonyms serve a couple of important purposes. First, they give you, the application developer, a shorthand method of referring to the form in formulas. Assuming you keep the length of synonyms down to just a few characters (and you should) you'll find them much easier to work with in formulas where a form name is required—you simply substitute the synonym for the proper name. Later, if you decide to change the proper name of the form, be sure to maintain the same synonym. This way all formulas that reference the form name *via the synonym* will continue to function correctly. On the other hand, if you use proper names themselves in formulas you'll have to manually edit each formula any time you change the proper name, which can be both time-consuming and error-prone.

Secondly, synonyms allow you to change the proper name of the form (as it appears in the Compose menu) without disrupting access to documents previously composed with the form under its original name. When you compose a document, the *name* of the form with which it was composed is stored with the document, rather than storing the form itself with the document. (Notes normally maintains design elements separately from data.) The internal field FORM is used to store the name of the form in the document. This field is automatically created by Notes in each document in the database. Later, when you open the document again, Notes attempts to display the contents of the document through the same form *if it still exists.*

If you change the proper name of the form, a document that's composed with the form under its *original* name (remember, this name is stored with the document in the FORM field) will now reference a form which essentially no longer exists! You've inadvertently "orphaned" the document by changing a form name. When a form has been assigned a synonym, it's the synonym (not the proper name) that will be store with documents composed with that form. Now, you can freely change the proper name of the form as long as you maintain the same synonym.

The synonym acts as a universal pointer to the form regardless of its proper name. Like the proper name, synonyms cannot exceed 64 characters in length. You are allowed to assign as many synonyms to a form as will fit in the Name box. You should get into the habit of assigning synonyms to forms!

Another feature of the form name is the ability to group several forms under a common heading in the Compose menu. This effect, known as "cascading," keeps the Compose menu more manageable by creating a two-tiered selection scheme. Rather than choosing a form name directly from the Compose menu, you first choose a heading which, in turn, displays a submenu of proper form names.

You are only allowed a single level of cascading. The heading may be up to 64 characters in length and is separated from the proper name by a \ symbol. For all forms that you wish to group under a common heading, make sure that the heading portion of the form name is identical.

▶ Identifying the Form's Type

All forms have a type associated with them. A form's type establishes where a document based on the form will reside in the Notes document hierarchy. You'll recall from Chapter 11 that many Notes applications are based upon a discussion style of interaction between users in a workgroup—a user initiates a discussion of some topic, which is then followed by a series of responses, and responses to those responses. (This type of back-and-forth interaction can be applied to any Notes application where group participation is required to produce a final result.)

To accommodate this interaction, Notes gives you the ability to classify forms based on where they fit in the hierarchy, as shown in Figure 14.6. For instance, a particular form is designed for "discussion initiation" and another for "response formulation" and still another for "response-to-response formulation."

Typically, data is passed from documents higher in the hierarchy to documents below, allowing for a consistent thread to be maintained in all of the documents throughout the life cycle of the discussion. (This concept, known as data inheritance, will be discussed later in the chapter.) The three supported form types are as follows:

- *Document* is the default form type for all new forms. Notes documents based on this form type are considered "main" or "lead" documents in that they are not in response to another document; that is, they occupy the topmost position in the document hierarchy.

- *Response to Document* form type is, by definition, composed in response to a lead document. A link is established between lead and response documents that persists as long as the documents remain in the database. In a view, response documents typically appear beneath the lead document to which they are related and are indented a number of spaces.

FIGURE 14.6 ▶

This diagram shows the hierarchy of document types.

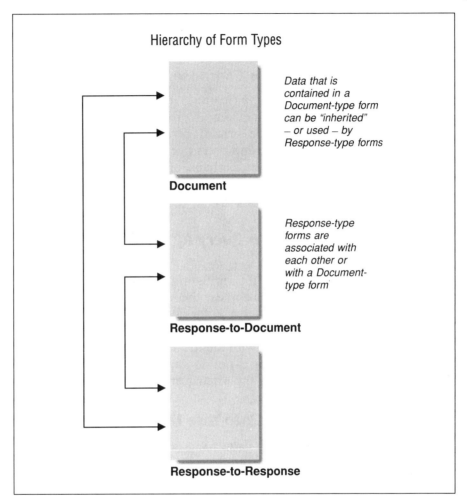

Hierarchy of Form Types

Data that is contained in a Document-type form can be "inherited" – or used – by Response-type forms

Document

Response-type forms are associated with each other or with a Document-type form

Response-to-Document

Response-to-Response

- *Response to Response* form type, as the name implies, is composed in response to a response document, a lead document, or another response to response document. Like response documents, response to response documents appear beneath the documents to which they are related.

▶ Selecting Other Attributes

In the Design Form Attributes dialog box, you'll notice several other attributes that you may select in check-box fashion. None of these attributes are required, but there are a few that are used often in Notes databases. You should certainly be familiar with all of them.

Include in Compose Menu

The *Include in Compose Menu* option determines if the form name will appear in the Compose menu so that users may compose documents based on the form. In certain cases you may not want a form to be available to end users because it is used for some specialized purpose (by you alone, perhaps, or for query only or mail-in documents). This attribute operates in conjunction with the Compose Access attribute (discussed below).

Include In Query by Form

The *Include in Query by Form* option makes the form available as a query tool in formulating full text searches on the contents of the database. In this context the form acts as a mechanism for gathering search criteria rather than for document creation. The values that a user enters in the fields of the form become the basis of the full text search; all documents with identical values in the same fields will be returned in the resulting list of documents. (See Chapter 20, "Indexing a Notes Database," for the discussion of performing a full text search.)

Default Database Form

The *Default database form* option specifies that the form is to be considered the default form in the database. This means that if there is a document in the database that was composed with a form that has since been renamed (and has no synonym) or has been entirely deleted, the document can still be viewed through the default form. This assumes that the fields of the renamed/deleted form and the default form are similar, which is rarely the case.

Automatically Refresh Field

The *Automatically refresh field* option forces Notes to refresh the computed fields of the document when a user navigates from one field to another. While this relieves the user from having to manually press F9 to refresh the document as they edit it, selecting this option can have the adverse effect of severely slowing down the editing process, particularly in documents with many computed fields. (Basically, as the number of computed fields increases the overall performance of the form decreases.) Be sure to enable this attribute only if it's critical that a user immediately see the results of a recalculation before moving to the next field.

Store Form in Documents

The *Store form in documents* option instructs Notes to store the form in the document along with the data. Normally, Notes stores just the *name* of the form in the document, in the internal field FORM. (You should refer to the discussion about using synonyms earlier in the chapter.) The document now becomes a self-contained unit with both data and form.

This ensures that the contents of the document will always be displayed in its original form even if the form has been renamed or deleted from the source database entirely, and when the document is mailed or pasted to another database where the form does not exist. The name of the form, normally stored in the FORM field, is now stored in an internal field named $TITLE.

Inherit Default Field Values

The *Inherit default field values* option enables a key feature in the Notes architecture, which is the ability for field values to be passed from one document to another. This process, known as "inheritance," can be applied to a document of any form type, but is often used in response-type documents where specific values in the responded-to document are inherited by the response document. This allows for a consistent thread to be maintained across related documents. Besides enabling this attribute, you have to do additional work on the form for inheritance to occur. (You can also refer to Chapter 12, "Basing a Database on a Template," for a discussion of inheritance.)

Mail Documents When Saving

The *Mail documents when saving* option is useful in workflow applications where you want a document to be mailed to another database when it is saved. When this attribute is selected, Notes gives the user the option of mailing the document upon saving it. "Mail-enabling" your documents through this feature is a common aspect of workflow automation which we discuss in Chapter 9, "Communicating with Notes Mail." You often use this attribute in conjunction with the Store form in document attribute so that the document can be properly displayed in the receiving database (unless the form has been defined there as well).

Updates become Responses

The *Updates become responses* option is a "version-control" feature that lets you maintain a history of all modifications to a document. Normally, when you update the information in a document and save it, Notes simply overwrites the previous information. Now, Notes will not overwrite the previous information but will actually create a new version of the original document with the updated information and assign it as a *response* to the original document, leaving the original intact. Even updates to the updates themselves are treated as responses to the *original*, resulting in what amounts to an audit-trail of changes from initial composition to the present state.

Prior Versions Become Responses

The *Prior versions become responses* option is essentially the inverse of Updates become responses. As with that attribute you are implementing version-control but with the opposite effect—updating the original results in the updated version becoming the "main" document while the original becomes the response. Going forward in time, the *last* update (either to the original or to other previous updates) will occupy the main document position with all previous versions, including the original, as responses.

▶▶ *Limiting Access to Forms and Documents*

When the Form Attributes dialog box was open, you may have noticed two buttons: *Read Access* and *Compose Access*. These commands enable you to limit access to reading documents and using forms to compose documents, respectively. As a security precaution, you may want to identify individuals who can read documents composed with a particular form, and individuals who can compose documents with the form.

A workgroup may only want its members to be able to use specific documents and forms. Therefore, it can set read and compose access. Similarly, individuals within the group may also want to further limit access to particular documents and forms among themselves. For example, the manager of a project development team may want to limit the access to status reports only to individual team leaders who are responsible for overseeing specific components of the project.

 ▶▶ **N O T E**

> **We discuss access levels and roles in Chapter 4, as well as using other security precautions in Chapter 18. However, setting access levels and roles for a particular database is very different from limiting read and compose access to specific documents and forms. The former limits accessing a particular database on a server, thus providing an effective means of security. The latter provides security for limiting access to docu-ments and forms in a database. A person may be allowed to access a database, but can only read specific documents or compose documents with a specific form.**

You can set a form's read access and compose access at the time the form is created, or later on if the need should arise. If you want to limit access at a later time, click on the database's icon to select it and then choose Design ➤ Forms. When the Design Forms dialog box opens, double-click on the form's name to open it. (You can also highlight the form's name and then click on the Edit button. Either method puts you in Design mode.) Choose Design ➤ Form Attributes to open the Form Attributes dialog box.

▶▶ **N O T E**

You can set either read access or compose access, or both, at the same time. You can also set one now, and the other later on. If you should change your mind, you can remove access limitations and allow all users to access documents and forms. Notes provides you with a flexible way to set access and to remove access limitations because the needs of people using the documents and forms in a database will change over time.

The following instructions assume you want to set both read access and compose access. (However, you can choose to set only one at this time.) Follow these steps:

1. Click on the Read Access button. The Read Access Control List dialog appears.

2. Select the Only the following users option (the default is All Users).

3. Enter the names of the people who can read the documents composed with the form.

4. Click on OK to accept the changes and to return to the Form Attributes dialog box.

5. Click on the Compose Access button. The Compose Access Control List box appears.

6. Select the Only the following users option (the default is All Users).

7. Enter the names of the people who can use the form to compose documents.

8. Click on OK to accept the changes and to return to the Form Attributes dialog box.

9. Click on OK again.

▶ ▶ *Creating a Title for a Form's Window Bar*

You'll want to display a title in a form's window bar because it helps users to identify the form's name as they compose new documents. The title can also display useful information, such as the date and time, or a name or subject that is significant to the database.

To create a title that'll appear in the window's title bar, follow these steps:

1. Choose Design ➤ Window Title. The Design Window Title dialog box appears, as shown in Figure 14.7.

2. Enter the following statement in the Window Title Formula box. (This statement returns and displays in the window's title bar the name of the form and the name of the person that is entered in the Name field.)

@If(@IsNewDoc; "New Directory Entry"; "Entry for " + FirstName+""LastName)

3. Click OK to confirm.

Each time a user composes a document using the Directory Entry form, the title "New Directory Entry" will appear in the window bar (without the quotation marks). When the user opens a view and selects

FIGURE 14.7

The Design Window Title dialog box lets you display a title in a form's window bar, which can help users to identify the form's name as they compose new documents.

Design Window Title
OK
Cancel

Window Title Formula:

| Add @Func | Add Field | Zoom In |

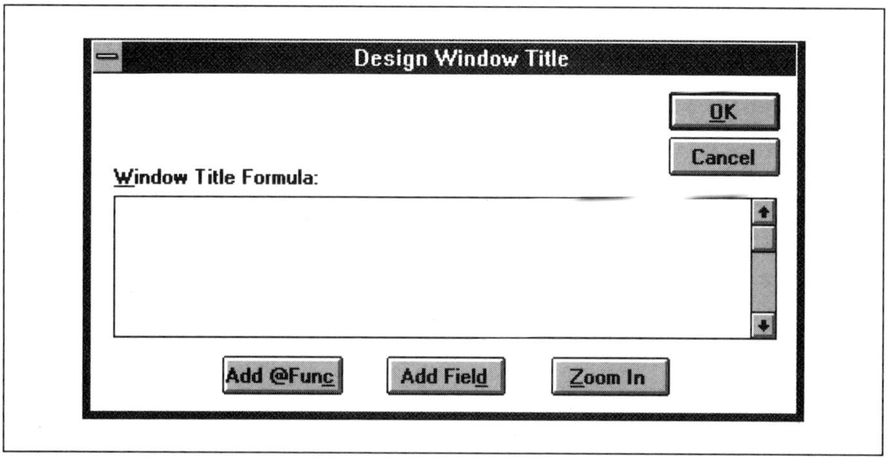

a document to read or edit later on, the window bar will display the title "Entry for [*name of person entered in the form's FirstName and Last-Name field*]." The formula helps the user to quickly identify the subject of the document, which in this case is a person.

You might have noticed the Add @Func button in the Design Window Title dialog box. When you click on it, the Paste Function dialog box appears, as shown in Figure 14.8. Whenever you open a dialog box in which you enter a formula, Notes provides this option. The Paste Function dialog box provides a complete list of all the available functions in

USING FORMULAS AND FUNCTIONS IN A FORM

Sometimes a formula will include more than one function. You can certainly type all the functions, but this becomes especially tiresome because of the @ sign. Furthermore, you may not remember the correct spelling of a function or even that a particular function exists. If you don't have a copy of the Notes reference documentation at your disposal or the System Administrator didn't install the Help files on your system or the server (which include a complete listing and explanation of the functions), you're sunk. However, don't fret.

Another way to enter functions in the Window Title Formula box is to click on the Add @Func button that appears at the bottom of the Design Window Title dialog box. A list of functions appears. You can either double-click on the selected function to paste it in the formula box automatically, or click on the function to highlight it and then click on the Paste button. The function appears in the formula box. You can repeat this method for as many functions as you need pasted in a formula. Just remember: the more functions you use in a formula, the better you'll need to understand how they work together. Otherwise, they might conflict and result in error messages. For a more thorough discussion of writing formulas (and macros), see Chapter 16.

FIGURE 14.8

The Paste Function dialog box provides a complete list of all the available functions in Notes. This list is handy to use because it saves you time as you enter formulas.

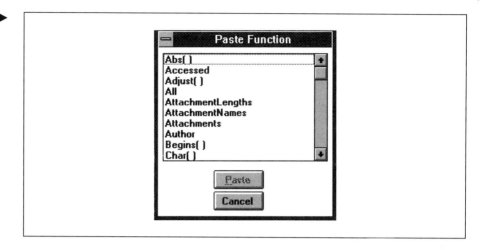

Notes. This list is handy to use because it saves you time as you enter formulas; scroll through the list, highlight a function, and click on the Paste button. Notes pastes the name of the function in the formula text box automatically. Although we discuss writing formulas (and macros) in Chapter 16, we wanted to mention this feature as you create the form.

▶▶ *The Anatomy of a Form*

Before you start adding elements to the form that will become part of the Corporate Directory database, you need to consider the information you need to capture on the form. Since this is a directory, the following information would be appropriate:

- Name
- Department
- Title
- Location
- Telephone number/extension
- FAX number

▶▶ *Adding Labels*

You'll recall from our earlier discussions that the two basic elements of a form are *labels* and *fields*. A label is a piece of static text which is used to indicate the type of information that a nearby field shall contain, either as a result of input or automatic calculation. By using the list of items above, you could draw a series of labels on the form, as shown in Figure 14.9.

There's nothing mysterious about creating labels on a form. Just position the cursor and start typing. Move the insertion point to the top of the form. Type *FirstName*. That's it! The static text you add to a form will appear on documents composed with the form. Realize that there is no formal relationship between a label and a field. We place labels near fields in a form to convey to the user the kind of data we're looking for them to input.

FIGURE 14.9 ▶

A drawing for a form displays labels that will identify fields.

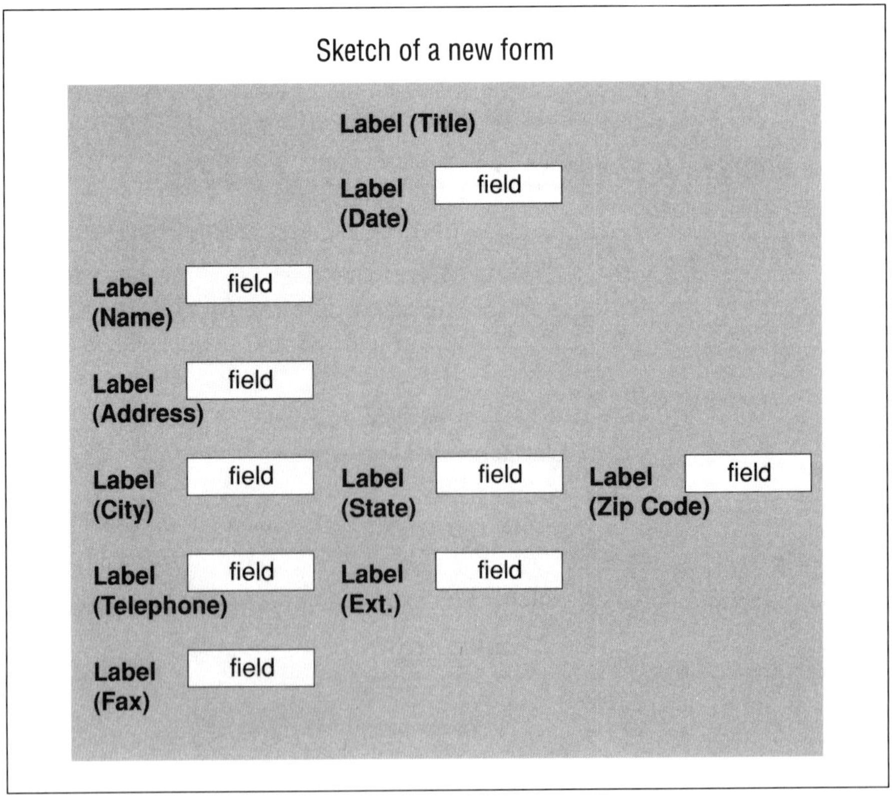

Sketch of a new form

Label (Title)

**Label
(Date)**   field

**Label
(Name)**   field

**Label
(Address)**   field

**Label
(City)**   field   **Label
(State)**   field   **Label
(Zip Code)**   field

**Label
(Telephone)**   field   **Label
(Ext.)**   field

**Label
(Fax)**   field

▶▶ *Defining Fields*

Placing fields on a form is somewhat more involved, but it is the fields of a form that give it meaning. You can think of a field as a container for a single piece of data—a string of text, a number, a date and time, an embedded object, etc. Your forms will include several of these containers, into which users will place specific types of data. In thinking about our directory then, let's classify the information we'll include by *data type*:

Label Name	Data Type
First Name	Text
Last Name	Text
Department	Text
Title	Text
Location	???

Depending on how detailed we want to be, a location might be made up of several components, each of which can be broken out into a separate field. This is important if we want to build views of the directory that are based on city, state, or zip code. With this in mind let's introduce the following items as components of "Location":

Label Name	Data Type
Address	Text
City	Text
State	Text
Zip Code	Text

Yes, we're classifying zip code as text rather than as a number. The reason? If we were to classify the zip code as a number, zip codes which begin with zero would have this leading zero stripped off automatically, since a whole number cannot technically begin with zero. This would leave us with an incorrect, 4-digit zip code.

▶▶ N O T E

As you place labels and fields in your form it may occur to you to align these items in columns. A user who's composing a document based on the form would then use the tab or arrow keys to navigate from field to field, thus changing a field's focus. This navigation process can result in some unusual behavior, however. For instance, if there are two fields vertically aligned with each other, each with a single field to the right (vertically aligned as well), using the down-arrow key to navigate to the field directly below the current field might end up putting you in the field below *and to the right* if you have input data in the current field and there is none in the field directly below. There is no way around this navigational behavior. Therefore, aligning fields in columns doesn't guarantee that a user will be able to use the Tab key to move from field to field in a logical direction. Manually placing the insertion bar in a field by clicking on it is the only consistent way of changing a field's focus.

Let's continue with our classification:

Label Name	Data Type
Main Phone #	Text or Number
Extension	Text or Number
Main Fax #	Text or Number
Direct Phone #	Text or Number
Extension	Text or Number
Direct Fax #	Text or Number

Whether a telephone number, extension, and/or fax number is classified as text or number depends on if we want to put the formatting of these numbers in the hands of the user or handle the formatting ourselves. All three of these items usually include certain formatting elements.

For instance, phone numbers include parentheses and dashes to break up the number into area code, exchange, and ID fields (e.g., (555) 555-5555). The formatting elements, "(", ")", "-", are obviously nonnumeric (i.e., text) and if we require the user to supply these as part of the field value we are essentially forcing the classification of "text" for the phone number. If, on the other hand, we want our application to insert the proper formatting elements for the user whereby they simply supply a number (e.g., 1234567890) which is then *automatically* formatted (e.g., (123) 456-7890), we could classify the phone number as text or number.

The process of automatically formatting the numbers requires a little razzle-dazzle using formulas (known as input translation), which we'll explore later. Whatever data type you choose, it's best to be consistent, that is, make the phone number, extension, and fax number either *all* text or *all* number. For our purposes, we'll stick with text.

▶ Identifying a Field's Type

Next, let's determine the *field type* for each of the data items. This turns out to be extremely easy (at least for the moment). For now, we'll say that all of the fields are available for input and we'll indicate the field type as *Editable* or *Computed* in all cases. (We discussed Editable and Computed fields in Chapter 11.)

Label Name	Data Type	Field Type
First Name	Text	Editable
Last Name	Text	Editable
Department	Text	Editable
Title	Text	Editable
Location	Text	Editable
Address	Text	Editable
City	Text	Editable
State	Text	Editable
Zip Code	Text	Editable
Main Phone #	Text	Editable

Label Name	Data Type	Field Type
Main Fax #	Text	Editable
Direct Phone #	Text	Editable
Extension	Text	Editable
Direct Fax #	Text	Editable

This is just the beginning! The intent is to "evolve" the form (and the whole application) from very basic to very sophisticated. As we proceed along this course, we'll make modifications to this form, introduce new forms (and views), and finally spice things up with some workflow automation features. Ultimately, the goal is to streamline the usability and maintenance of the Corporate Directory database. For the moment, however, let's use what we have and actually start adding fields to the form.

►► *Adding Fields*

Having plotted out the information you want to capture with the form, you can now add the fields necessary to accomplish your goal.

To add a field to a form, follow these steps:

1. Position the cursor at the location where the field is to be placed. This is typically to the right of a label that indicates what goes into the field. If necessary, open up some white space between the FirstName label and the field by using the spacebar or Tab key.

2. Choose Design ➤ New Field. The Design New Field dialog box appears. Make sure the Create field to be used only within this form is selected.

3. Click on OK. The Field Definition dialog box appears, as shown in Figure 14.10.

4. Enter **FirstName** in the Name text box.

5. You can also enter a brief description in the Help Description text box. This field description (known as "field help") will appear on the Status Bar at the bottom of the screen when a user positions the cursor on the field.

FIGURE 14.10 ▶

The Field Definition dialog box lets you define each field on a form.

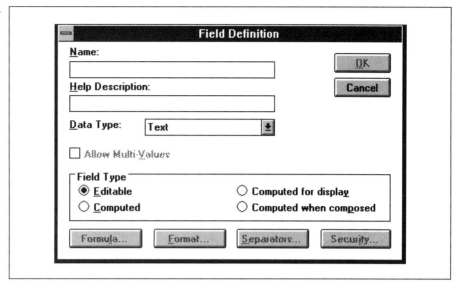

Field Definition

Name:

Help Description:

Data Type: Text

☐ Allow Multi-Values

Field Type
◉ Editable ○ Computed for display
○ Computed ○ Computed when composed

Formula... Format... Separators... Security...

OK Cancel

  TIP

Don't overlook using this help line. It can be a very efficient means of explaining the purpose of a field, in a way that is more informative than the label you include to identify the field. For the FirstName field, you might include something like "Enter the first name of the individual" in the Help description text box.

6. Choose Text from the Data Type list box.

7. Select Editable as the Field Type.

8. Click on OK to accept the changes.

You'll need to repeat the above steps in order to create the rest of the fields that appear on the form. You can refer to Table 14.1 for help in defining all the other labels and fields on the form. When you're finished, press Ctrl+S to save the form. The completed Directory Entry form appears in Figure 14.11.

▶ **TABLE 14.1:** *A complete summary of the labels and fields that appear on the Directory Entry form.*

LABEL NAME	FIELD NAME	DATA TYPE	FIELD TYPE
XYZ Corporation			
Corporate Directory Entry			
Date	Date	Time (Format: mm/dd/yy)	Computed for display
First Name	FirstName	Text	Editable
Last Name	LastName	Text	Editable
Department	Dept	Text	Editable
Title	Title	Text	Editable
Location	Location	Text	Editable
Address	Address	Text	Computed for display
	City	Text	Computed for display
	State	Text	Computed for display
	ZipCode	Text	Computed for display
Main Phone #	MainNum_P	Text	Computed
Main Fax #	MainNum_F	Text	Computed
Direct Phone #	AreaCode_P	Text	Editable
	Exchange_P	Text	Editable
	ID_P	Text	Editable
	DirectNum_P	Text	Computed
Extension	Extension	Text	Editable
Direct Fax #	AreaCode_F	Text	Editable
	Exchange_F	Text	Editable
	ID_F	Text	Editable
	DirectNum_F	Text	Computed

FIGURE 14.11

The completed Directory Entry form displays the placement of the labels and fields. You'll notice the labels at the top are used to identify the name of the organization and the name of the form.

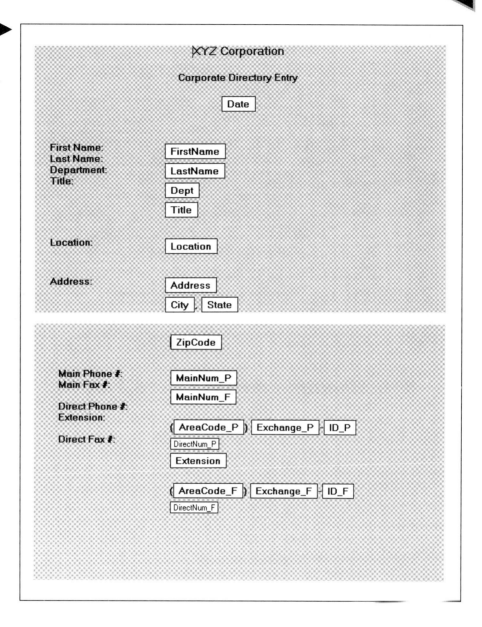

▶

ANOTHER LOOK AT EDITABLE AND COMPUTED FIELDS

For Editable fields, you have the option of establishing a series of formulas associated with the field by clicking the Formula button. For any type of Computed field you *must* establish a formula by clicking the Formula button. Notes will not let you save the form until you've done this.

For certain data types—Number, Time, and Keywords—you may choose to alter the default formats associated with these data types by clicking the Format button. For Keyword fields, you may select an input and display separator by clicking the Separators field. This is important for fields in which multiple values may be expressed.

▶ Designating a Field's Data Type

You'll recall from Chapter 11 that there are nine unique data types for fields:

- Text
- Number
- Time/Date
- Keywords
- Rich Text
- Names
- Author Names
- Reader Names
- Section

Let's look at them in detail since you're involved in the process of creating fields for the form.

Text

The Text data type indicates that the field will contain alphanumeric characters (letters and numbers), punctuation symbols, and spaces. The contents of a text field cannot be formatted because it's not a rich text field. Furthermore, the contents of a text field cannot be directly involved in a mathematical calculation. Even if a text field is comprised entirely of numbers, Notes does not view the contents as numeric data but rather as "text." You would have to convert the contents to a number to use it in a calculation.

  TIP

> Though it may sound strange, you should probably classify fields that will contain numeric data as text unless you need to perform mathematical calculations on the data or require that the data have a specific numeric format (such as a percentage or currency). The reason is that you often use standard text and numbers together in string concatenations and various other string manipulation formulas. As a result, you wind up having to convert numbers to text anyway (see the @TEXT function, discussed in Chapter 16). Classifying numeric data as text simply saves you the effort. The downside to this is that text representations of numbers require more storage space on your disk drive. Unless space is an issue this should not cause a problem.

Number

The Number data type indicates that the field will contain numeric data including the mathematical symbols **+**, **-**, **.**, **E**, and **e**. The format characters **%** and **$** are also permitted. Number fields are typically involved in mathematical calculations and/or format conversion operations. Notes accepts numbers from 2.225E-308 to 1.798E308 with 14-digit accuracy.

Time/Date

The Time/Date data type allows for time and date information to be captured and displayed in a variety of formats, including:

- 04/01/94
- 04/01
- 04/94
- 04/01/94 12:30:01 PM
- 04/01 12:30 PM
- 12:30:01 PM
- 12:30 PM
- 12:30 Today
- Yesterday

Both 12-hour and 24-hour formats are supported. Dates may range from 1/1/0001 to 12/31/9999.

Keywords

Keyword fields allow you to establish a predetermined list of values that the field may take on. Users simply choose a predefined value from a list rather than manually entering a value. This has the effect of eliminating invalid input (as may be the case in free-form editable fields) and can make the task of data input more streamlined.

 ▶▶ **TIP**

You can only format a Keywords field when you select Keywords as the data type. Otherwise, the Format button will appear dimmed and will not be available. When you want to format a Keywords field, click on the Format button and then enter the list of keywords in the list box. Make sure to select either Standard, Checkbox, or Radio Button box. You can also choose to sort the keywords so they appear in the list in alphabetical order. Click on OK to accept your choices.

Keyword fields come in three varieties:

Standard	This type of Keyword field presents a list of choices in a dialog box. The user can pick one or more of the items by either typing the first letter of one of the keywords or pressing ↵, which will display a list of choices.
Check Box	This type of Keyword field presents a list of choices in check box format where a user can check one or more items.
Radio Button	This type of Keyword field presents a list of choices in radio button format where a user may choose ONLY one of the items.

  T I P

> **You should make use of Keyword fields in your forms where they're appropriate. By reducing the amount of free-form input a user has to perform, you make the input process less error-prone and faster (once users get the hang of it).**

Rich Text

The Rich Text data type includes all the functionality of the Text data type in addition to accepting format attributes, such as boldface and italics, and supporting graphical data—pictures, bitmaps, graphs—different fonts and point sizes, and OLE objects. For example, you could cut and paste a range of spreadsheet cells or embed an entire spreadsheet into a Rich Text field in a document. (The Rich Text data type, however, doesn't permit computations on strings or numbers.)

Names

You use the Names data type for fields which will be used to capture and display user and server names.

Author Names

Author Names is a text list of designated users names that you identify can edit a particular document. The list becomes very useful in work-flow automation applications where a document is passed from user to user in a workgroup, and each person is subsequently responsible for updating information in the document.

Reader Names

The Reader Names data type is a text list of designated user names that you identify can read a particular document. Although any user on the list may have Reader access to the database, the person cannot read the document.

Section

A section field allows you to define a particular area on a form and then place others fields and static text within the area. In this way, you can group the fields as part of a workflow automation application. You can subsequently limit access to the fields in this area by specifying the users who can read or edit those fields. However, using a section field doesn't limit a larger number of users from accessing the rest of the document.

▶▶ *Understanding Field Types*

The fact that a field may contain text, a number, or some kind of date/time value is a function of its data type. Data type defines *what* will go into the field. Equally important is the issue of *how* the information will actually get put there.

You may be under the assumption that it's the responsibility of the user to supply all the information to be captured in a document, but that is not the case at all. The value of a field may be the result of an automatic calculation over which the user has no direct control (although they will very likely have some indirect control). You can think of this type of field as a "read-only" field. This field simply *shows* the user some information that the person may not directly alter, as opposed to a read/write field where the user provides a value. In Notes terminology, the former is called a *Computed* field and the latter an *Editable* field.

The question of whether a field is editable or a field's value is computed depends precisely on the function of the field as an element in the overall design of the form. A field is either editable or computed, never both.

▶ Designating Editable Fields

When defining a new field, you'll notice that its field type defaults to Editable. This is appropriate for fields where you want the user to supply a value. Notes allows you to establish an initial value in an Editable field for the user to ensure that *something* is in the field during the composing of a document. (It's a subtle point, but you should realize that although a default value appears in a field of a newly composed document the field will not actually assume that value until you save the document. Prior to this, the value is simply a placeholder that can be changed to something else.)

A user-supplied value in an Editable field may have some action taken upon it, including a variety of transformations (e.g., a text value might be converted to all uppercase characters) and/or a validity check which could ensure that supplied value satisfies specific criteria (e.g., a numeric value is checked to see if it falls within an acceptable range of values). The Editable field type is available with all data types.

▶ Designating Computed Fields

A Computed field derives its value from some form of calculation as set forth by a formula associated with the field. Table 14.2 includes a summary of the field formulas that are used in the Directory Entry form. You can input the formulas now or wait until Chapter 16. (We explain how the formulas work in Chapter 16.) The value cannot be altered by the user, at least not directly. Frequently the value of a Computed field is based on the value of an Editable field (or perhaps several Editable fields), which gives the user a degree of control over the computed value.

▶ **TABLE 14.2:** *A complete summary of field formulas used in the Directory Entry form.*

LABEL NAME	FIELD NAME	FORMULA
Date	Date	@Today
First Name	FirstName	Input Translation Formula: @ProperCase(FirstName)
		Input Validation Formula: @If(FirstName = ""; @Failure("You must enter a first name before saving this document!");@Success)
Last Name	LastName	Input Translation Formula: @ProperCase(LastName)
		Input Validation Formula: @If(LastName = ""; @Failure("You must enter a last name before saving this document!");@Success)
Title	Title	Input Translation Formula: @ProperCase(Title)
Address	Address	@If(Location != "";@DbLookup("";"";"Locations";Location;"Address");"")
	City	@If(Location != "";@DbLookup("";"";"Locations";Location;"City");"")
	State	@If(Location != "";@DbLookup("";"";"Locations";Location;"State");"")
	ZipCode	@If(Location != "";@DbLookup("";"";"Locations";Location;"ZipCode");"")
Main Phone #	MainNum_P	@If(Location != "";@DbLookup("";"";"Locations";Location;6);"")
Main Fax #	MainNum_F	@If(Location != "";@DbLookup("";"";"Locations";Location;7);"")
Direct Phone #	AreaCode_P	@If(AreaCode_P = ""; @DbLookup("";"";"Locations";Location;"AreaCode_P"); AreaCode_P)
	Exchange_P	@If(Exchange_P = ""; @DbLookup("";"";"Locations";Location;"Exchange_P"); Exchange_P)

TABLE 14.2: *A complete summary of field formulas used in the Directory Entry form. (continued)*

LABEL NAME	FIELD NAME	FORMULA
	ID_P	@If(ID_P = ""; @DbLookup("";"";"Locations";Location;"ID_P"); ID_P)
	DirectNum_P	"(" + AreaCode_P+")" + Exchange_P + "-" + ID_P
Direct Fax #	AreaCode_F	@If(AreaCode_F = ""; @DbLookup("";"";"Locations";Location;"AreaCode_F"); AreaCode_F)
	Exchange_F	@If(Exchange_F = ""; @DbLookup("";"";"Locations";Location;"Exchange_F"); Exchange_F)
	ID_F	@If(ID_F = ""; @DbLookup("";"";"Locations";Location;"ID_F"); ID_F)
	DirectNum_F	"(" + AreaCode_F+")" + Exchange_F + "-" + ID_F

►► **TIP**

To edit a field's formula, open the form in which it appears and then double-click on the field. (The longer method would be to highlight the field and then choose Design ➤ Field Definition.) The Field Definition dialog box appears. After you designate the field's field type, click on the Formula button. Enter the formula(s), depending on the field's type. When you're finished, click on OK to accept the formula. If the formula's syntax is incorrect, Notes will display a message telling you so. Correct the formula if necessary. Click on OK to save the changes and to close the formula dialog box. Click on OK again to accept the changes in the Field Definition dialog box and to return to the form.

For example, a user inputs a value into an Editable field, which is then used as part of a formula for a Computed field. When in Edit mode, a user will not be able to position the cursor in a Computed field. Notes actually defines four different types of Computed fields, each of which is appropriate in certain circumstances. In all cases, the value of the field is the result of a formula (not user input). Notes will not let you save the form until you have specified the formula.

Computed

A Computed field type may be used in conjunction with any data type except Rich Text. The value is stored in the document and can be referenced in views and macros. Each time a document with Computed fields is opened, refreshed, or saved the values in those fields are recomputed. A Computed field is appropriate for fields whose values will change over time. Typically, the formula associated with a Computed field makes reference to other Editable fields in the document. As the values of those fields change, so changes the value of the Computed field.

  ▶▶ TIP

When designing a form it is possible to define a Computed field whose value is based on the value of another field (either editable or computed) in the *same form*. The formula for the Computed field is simply the name of the other field. Whatever value appears in the other field is fed to the computed field. This is particularly useful when you want to link an input (Editable) field to a presentation (Computed) field where the value that is input is displayed elsewhere in the document with special formatting characteristics. For example, an editable field labeled "Client Name" appears on the form and is used to store the name of a client. Another field (typically unlabeled) at the top of the form has its value computed (for display only) as the value of the client name field below and has format attributes— font, point size, etc.—that make it stand out. The idea is to prominently display the client name at the top of form for the benefit of anyone reading the document.

Computed For Display

A Computed For Display field type may be used in conjunction with any data type except Rich Text. Unlike a Computed field, the value is *not* stored in the document. Rather, the value only exists when the document is opened and is essentially discarded when the document is closed. This is appropriate for computed fields that will never be referenced outside the document, such as in views and macros.

If you think of a field in terms of its scope, a Computed For Display field's value is not usable beyond the document level—for instance, in a view. The value of the field is recomputed when the document is opened or refreshed. As a performance mechanism, Computed For Display fields can make your database more streamlined in terms of speed (since the value is discarded when the document is closed, there is no disk access necessary to store the value) and size (no value stored, no disk space required).

Computed When Composed

A Computed When Composed field type may be used in conjunction with any data type except Rich Text. It is similar to a Computed field except that the value is calculated only once when a document is composed and never again. From that point forward, the value is static and will not change. Like the Computed field type, the value is stored in the document and may be referenced in views and macros.

A Computed When Composed field is appropriate in instances where you wish to simply "hard-code" a value for a field at composition-time and leave it intact.

Non-Editable

The Non-Editable field type is a form of computed field used in conjunction with Rich Text data types only.

▶ ▶ *Modifying the Dept Field in the Directory Entry Form*

Now that you have some familiarity with the Keywords data type let's make our first modification to the Directory Entry form. In the case of the Dept field, it's safe to assume that the choices for department are fairly limited and consistent. Rather than making the user type the name of the department when composing a Directory Entry document, we'll modify the field definition of the Dept field by changing its data type from Text to Keywords and create a list of possible departments to choose from.

To make this modification to the Directory Entry form, follow these steps:

1. In the Directory Entry form, double-click on the Dept field. The Field Definition dialog box appears.

2. Change the data type from Text to Keywords.

3. Click on the Format button. The Design Keyword Format dialog box appears, as shown in Figure 14.12.

4. Enter the following list of departments in the Allowable Keywords text box:

   - Accounting
   - Executive
   - Sales & Marketing
   - Manufacturing
   - Administration
   - Human Resources
   - Research & Development
   - Engineering

5. Select either Standard or Radio Button from the User Interface list box. (Check Box is not appropriate since we want to allow a single department per directory entry.) In this example, we'll use Standard.

6. Click on the Sort button to sort the list of departments alphabetically.

7. Click OK to accept the changes and to close the dialog box.

8. Click OK again to save the changes.

Now, when a user wants to supply a value in the Dept field, he or she can simply press ↵ to display a list of departments from which to choose. Alternatively, a user may press the Spacebar repeatedly to cycle through the list of departments.

FIGURE 14.12

The Design Keyword Format dialog box lets you create a list of keywords that a person can choose from when entering data in a field whose data type is Keywords.

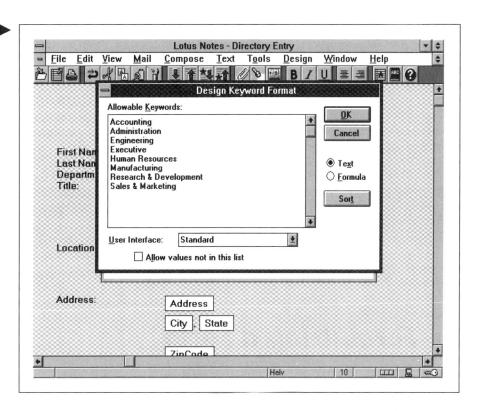

▶▶ *Saving a Form*

When you're finished creating a form (and after modifying a form), press Ctrl+S to save it. If you press Esc or Ctrl+W to close the window *before* saving the form, Notes will ask you if you want to save your changes. Click on Yes. You'll return to the Workspace.

We've already taken you through the steps of naming a form by entering its name in the Form Attributes dialog box. (You'll recall that a name is one of many attributes you can set for a form.) This name will appear on the Compose menu when users start composing documents with the form. However, while you're creating a form, you can place labels and fields and then save your work *before* you identify other specific attributes in the Form Attributes dialog box. (You can do this at a later time. However, until you specify the attributes you want, you'll have to be satisfied with using the default options.)

If you want to save a form without going through the steps of opening the Form Attributes dialog box and setting attributes (specifically, the form's name), press Ctrl+S. The Save Form dialog box appears. Enter a name in the Name text box and then click on OK. The name will appear on the Compose menu and in the Form Attributes dialog box. Just remember, however, that all you've done is saved the form under a specific name. You haven't set any other form attributes.

The change will take effect immediately. With the form window still open (you don't have to close it), you can pull down the Compose menu and click on the form's name. A blank document will open in which you can enter data in the fields. (We describe the steps in the "Testing the Functionality of a Form" section below.) When you're finished composing the document, press Ctrl+S to save the information. To close the document's window, press Esc. Press Esc again to close the form's window and to return to the Workspace.

▶▶ *Formatting a Form*

You format a form in order to change and enhance its appearance. Formatting allows your creative side to come out. By applying different formatting attributes, you help users to distinguish one form from another in the same database, and you give each form a distinctive look and feel. You can format a form after you've created it, or you can apply formats to a form while you're designing it. Some designers like to place the labels and fields and then format the form; others prefer to format a form as they go along.

Notes provides a set of formatting tools that are similar to those found in other Windows applications. For instance, you can change the background color of a form as well as format the labels and the text that users will enter in fields. The choices you make will be purely subjective, so keep in mind that a person will be using the form for data input. You don't want to overwhelm the user with a form that appears too busy.

You shouldn't clutter a form with too many different fonts and point sizes. You should keep the number of colors you use to a few and consider if they complement each other. If you decide to add a background color to the form (instead of white, the default), make sure the color of the labels and the field text contrast with it. You don't want the text to appear too light against the background.

The following instructions assume that you have created the Directory Entry form and want to format it. We also assume that you placed all the labels and fields that we described earlier in the chapter. To change the form's background color, follow these steps:

1. If the form isn't open, click on the Corporate Directory database icon to select it.

2. Choose Design ➤ Forms. The Design Forms dialog box appears.

3. Double-click on Directory Entry (or highlight the form and click on the Edit button). The form window opens.

4. Choose Design ➤ Form Attributes. The Design Form Attributes dialog box appears.

5. To change the background color of the form from the default color, white, select another color from the bar at the bottom of the dialog box.

6. Click on OK to accept the change. The form's background color will reflect your choice.

7. Press Ctrl+S to save the form.

 ▶▶ **TIP**

When you highlight a label (any static text) on a form in order to apply formatting attributes, you can pull down the Text menu and choose one of several attributes directly from the menu. Just click on the command. You can also use the available keystroke combinations to execute the same commands.

To format the labels, follow the steps below. You can format all the labels at one time, but you will affect the format of the fields.

1. Choose Edit ➤ Select All to highlight all the labels (and the text fields) at the same time.

2. Choose Text ➤ Font. The Font dialog box appears.

3. Change the font and point size if you wish.

4. Select one or more of the attribute options on the right, such as Bold.

5. Select a color for the text from the Color Bar at the bottom.

6. Click on OK to accept the changes. The labels will reflect your choices.

7. Press Ctrl+S to save the form.

▶▶ *Creating Other Forms for a Database*

A Notes database will usually include more than one form; one of the forms will probably be a response-type form that responds to the main document-type form. For example, in the Corporate Directory database, you can create two other forms: the Location Entry form and the Change Request form.

The Location Entry form is another document-type form, which will be used to create a lookup table of company location in the Corporate Directory database. We'll tie this lookup table back to the Directory Entry form so that the Address, City, State, Zip Code, Main Phone #, and Main Fax # fields can be automatically filled in by selecting a location. We'll show how this is accomplished at the end of the next chapter. The Change Request form is a response-type form. You'll see how the Change Request form is displayed when you create the database's views in the next chapter.

In the meantime, to create the Location Entry form, follow these steps:

1. Select the Corporate Directory database.

2. Choose Design ➤ Forms.

3. Click on the New button. A blank form appears.

4. Choose Design ➤ Form Attributes.

5. Enter **2. Location Entry** in the text box (including the number).

6. Select Document as the type.

7. Select the Include in Compose Menu and Include In Query by Form options. (Don't check any other options.)

8. Click on OK to save the new attributes.

9. Press Ctrl+S to save the form.

10. Press Esc to return to the Workspace.

To add the labels and fields to the Location Entry form, refer to Table 14.3. The table includes a summary of all the field definitions and formulas. The completed Location Entry form is shown in Figure 14.13.

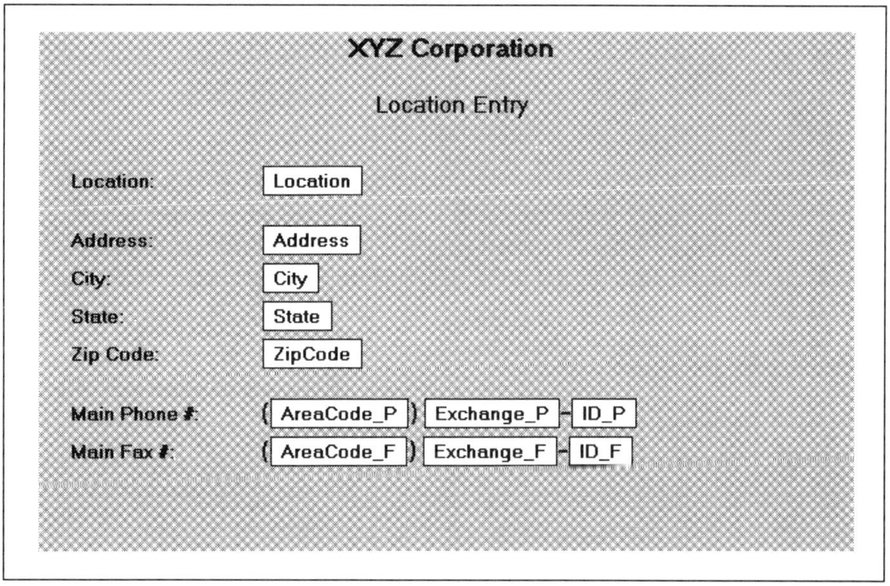

FIGURE 14.13 ▶

The Location Entry form allows the user to enter the locations of an organization's regional offices, which is reflected in the Directory Entry form.

XYZ Corporation
Location Entry

Location: [Location]

Address: [Address]
City: [City]
State: [State]
Zip Code: [ZipCode]

Main Phone #: [AreaCode_P] [Exchange_P] [ID_P]
Main Fax #: [AreaCode_F] [Exchange_F] [ID_F]

▶ **TABLE 14.3:** *A complete summary of the labels, fields, and field formulas that are included on the Location Entry form.*

LABEL NAME	FIELD NAME	DATA TYPE	FIELD TYPE	FORMULA
XYZ Corporation				
Location Entry				
Location	Location	Text	Editable	
City	City	Text	Editable	
State	State	Text	Editable	
Zip Code	ZipCode	Text	Editable	
Main Phone #	AreaCode_P	Text	Editable	Input Validation Formula: @If(AreaCode_P = "" & (Exchange_P != "" | ID_P != ""); @Failure ("You must supply the Area Code portion of the phone number");@Success)
	Exchange_P	Text	Editable	Input Validation Formula: @If(Exchange_P = "" & (AreaCode_P != "" | ID_P != ""); @Failure ("You must supply the Exchange portion of the phone number");@Success)
	ID_P	Text	Editable	Input Validation Formula: @If(ID_P = "" & (AreaCode_P != "" | Exchange_P != ""); @Failure ("You must supply the ID portion of the phone number");@Success)

TABLE 14.3: A complete summary of the labels, fields, and field formulas that are included on the Location Entry form. (continued)

LABEL NAME	FIELD NAME	DATA TYPE	FIELD TYPE	FORMULA
Main Fax #	AreaCode_F	Text	Editable	Input Validation Formula: @If(AreaCode_F = "" & (Exchange_F != "" | ID_F != ""); @Failure ("You must supply the Area Code portion of the fax number");@Success)
	Exchange_F	Text	Editable	Input Validation Formula: @If(Exchange_F = "" & (AreaCode_F != "" | ID_F != ""); @Failure ("You must supply the Exchange portion of the fax number");@Success)
	ID_F	Text	Editable	Input Validation Formula: @If(ID_F = "" & (AreaCode_F != "" | Exchange_F != ""); @Failure ("You must supply the ID portion of the fax number");@Success)

The Change Request form is used as a means to keep the data in the Corporate Directory database current. It provides the workflow component of the application. Inevitably, employees will get promoted, change job titles, departments, locations, or they leave the company entirely. It's important that the Corporate Directory database keep pace with these changes and not become outdated. The theory behind the database is that only the database manager(s) should be allowed to update the Directory—if anyone could update the Directory at any time, that would very likely lead to gross inaccuracies.

Placing the burden of maintaining the Directory solely on the database manager, however, assumes that the person will always be aware of changes in employee status. While this is feasible in a small company, it's virtually impossible in a large company. Therefore, to assist the database manager in this effort we'll make all other users of the Directory active participants in its maintenance through the Change Request form.

Any person in the organization can compose a Change Request document and forward it to the person who is responsible for managing the database. A Change Request notifies the database manager that an entry in the Corporate Directory needs to be updated and indicates exactly what should be changed. However, the database manager decides whether to approve or deny the request. If a specific request is approved, the information in the corresponding Directory Entry document is updated automatically. To create the Change Request form, follow these steps:

1. Select the Corporate Directory database if it isn't selected.

2. Choose Design ➤ Forms.

3. Click on the New button. A blank form appears.

4. Choose Design ➤ Form Attributes.

5. Enter **3. Change Request** in the text box. (Include the number.)

6. Select Response to Document as the type.

7. Select the following options (don't check any other options):

   - Include in Compose Menu
   - Include In Query by Form
   - Inherit Default Field Values

8. Click on OK to save the new attributes.

9. Press Ctrl+S to save the form.

10. Press Esc to return to the Workspace.

To add the labels and fields to the Change request form, refer to Table 14.4. The table includes a summary of all the field definitions and formulas. The finished Change Request form is shown in Figure 14.14.

▶▶ *Testing the Functionality of a Form*

In order to test the functionality of a form, you'll need to perform a standard "Compose" by using a form and entering information into the Editable fields just as a regular end user would. If the form contains a lot of Editable fields the process of repeatedly filling in each field as you proceed through several test iterations can be tedious. You might consider assigning a default value to the Editable fields, which is similar to the actual data an end user would input.

If you anticipate designing several forms with similar functionality (either generally or as it relates to the implementation of a specific feature you intend on incorporating in each of the forms) you should consider concentrating on one of the forms only, making it the prototype. This way you can work out the logic of any complex formulas and/or calculations in a controlled manner and then propagate that logic to the other forms. You'll find this easier than designing the forms in parallel and trying to maintain logic changes across them all.

After you work with Notes for a while you'll discover that there is usually more than one way to implement a particular feature in your application. Chances are pretty good that you'll change your mind on how to accomplish the implementation of a complicated feature (even if it's a subtle change) at least once. With one form serving as a prototype, you can confine your changes to that form rather than attempting to synchronize changes across several.

FIGURE 14.14 ►

The Change Request form allows the user to request that specific changes be made to the Directory Entry form. The document is forwarded to a manager who approves or denies the request.

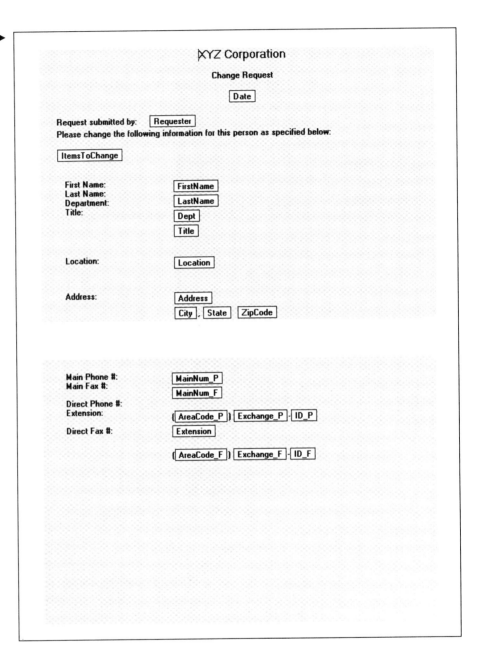

TABLE 14.4: A complete summary of the labels, fields, and field formulas that are included on the Change Request form

LABEL NAME	FIELD NAME	DATA TYPE	FORMAT	FIELD TYPE	FORMULA
XYZ Corporation Change Request					
Date	Date	Time	mm/dd/yy	Computed for display	@Created
Request submitted by	Requester	Text		Computed	@Name([CN]; @UserName)
Please change the following information for this person as specified below	ItemsToChange	Keywords (Check Boxes):		Editable	
		Name			
		Department			
		Title			
		Location			
		Phone Number/ Extension			
		Fax Number			
First Name	FirstName	Text		Editable	Default Value Formula: FirstName Input Translation Formula:@ProperCase (FirstName)

TABLE 14.4: *A complete summary of the labels, fields, and field formulas that are included on the Change Request form (continued)*

LABEL NAME	FIELD NAME	DATA TYPE	FORMAT	FIELD TYPE	FORMULA
					Input Validation Formula: @If(FirstName = ""; @Failure ("You must enter a first name before saving this document!");@Success)
Last Name	LastName	Text		Editable	Default Value Formula: LastName
					Input Translation Formula: @ProperCase (LastName)
					Input Validation Formula: @If(LastName = ""; @Failure ("You must enter a last name before saving this document!"); @Success)
Department	Dept	Keywords (Standard): Accounting Executive Sales & Marketing Manufacturing Adminstration Human Resources		Editable	

TABLE 14.4: A complete summary of the labels, fields, and field formulas that are included on the Change Request form (continued)

LABEL NAME	FIELD NAME	DATA TYPE	FORMAT	FIELD TYPE	FORMULA
		Research & Development Engineering			
Title	Title	Text		Editable	Input Translation Formula: @Propercase (Title)
Location	Location	Text		Editable	
Address	Address	Text		Computed for display	@IF(Location !="""; @DbLookup(""", ""; "Locations"; Location; "Address").""")
	City	Text		Computed for display	@If(Location !="""; @DbLookup("", ""; "Locations"; Location; "City");"")
	State	Text		Computed for display	@IF(Location !=""; @DbLookup("", ""; "Locations"; Location; "State");"")
	ZipCode	Text		Computed for display	@If(Location !="""; @DbLookup("", ""; "Locations"; Location; "ZipCode");"")
Main Phone #	MainNum_P	Text		Computed	@If(Location != ""; @DbLookup ("","","Locations"; Location;6);"")

TABLE 14.4: A complete summary of the labels, fields, and field formulas that are included on the Change Request form (continued)

LABEL NAME	FIELD NAME	DATA TYPE	FORMAT	FIELD TYPE	FORMULA
Main Fax #	MainNum_F	Text		Computed	@If(Location !=""; @DbLookup ("";"";"Locations";Location;7);"")
Direct Phone #	AreaCode_P	Text		Editable	Default Value Formula: AreaCode_P Input Translation Formula: @If (AreaCode_P = ""; @DbLookup ("";"";"Locations";Location ;"AreaCode_P"); AreaCode_P)
	Exchange_P	Text		Editable	Default Value Formula: Exchange_P Input Translation Formula: @If (Exchange_P = ""; @DbLookup ("";"";"Locations";Location ;"Exchange_P"); Exchange_P)
	ID_P	Text		Editable	Default Value Formula: ID_P Input Translation Formula: @If (ID_P = ""; @DbLookup ("";"";"Locations"; Location;"ID_P"); ID_P)

TABLE 14.4: *A complete summary of the labels, fields, and field formulas that are included on the Change Request form (continued)*

LABEL NAME	FIELD NAME	DATA TYPE	FORMAT	FIELD TYPE	FORMULA
Extension	Extension	Text		Editable	Default Value Formula: Extension Default Value Formula: AreaCode_F
Direct Fax#	AreaCode_F	Text		Editable	Input Translation Formula: @IF (AreaCode_F ""; @DbLookup (""; ""; "Locations"; Location; "AreadCode_F"); AreaCode_F)
	Exchange_F	Text		Editable	Default Value Formula: Exchange_F Input Translation Formula: @If (Exchange_F = ""; @DbLookup (""; ""; "Locations"; Location; "Exchange_F"); Exchange_F)
	ID_F	Text		Editable	Default Value Formula: ID_F Input translation Formula: @If(ID_F = ""; @DbLookup(""; ""; "Locations";Location; "ID_F"); ID_F)

To test a new form by composing a document, follow these steps by using the Directory Entry form:

1. Make sure the database is selected by clicking on its icon in your Workspace.

2. Choose Compose ➤ Directory Entry. The empty document appears, waiting for your input.

3. Enter data in the fields.

4. Press Ctrl+S to save the document.

5. Press Esc to return to the Workspace.

If you want to continue making changes to the form and then compose new documents to see the effects of the changes, you can switch between the form and document easily without closing either one. Open the form and then leave the window open. Compose a document. You can choose to save it or not, but leave the document window open.

When you pull down the Window menu, the name of the form and the name of the document will appear at the bottom, in addition to the name Workspace. (If you don't give a form a window title name, each document's name will appear in the window bar as **[untitled]**.) To switch between the form and the document, pull down the Window menu and click on the form's name. Notes displays the form window. Make changes to the form and then press Ctrl+S to save the changes. Pull down the Window menu again and then click on the document's name or [untitled]. Notes displays the document window.

Each time you compose a new document based on the form you'll have to test data automatically put into the fields of your document. Simply refresh your document at this point by pressing F9. Notes will update all input translation, input verification, and number formatting.

Refreshing an open document only updates the data; the document won't reflect any changes you've made to the form's design. To update design changes, close the document. Although you haven't created a view, which will list the documents in the database, you can still retrieve the unnamed document. Pull down the View menu and click on the [untitled] view that appears at the bottom of the menu. The unnamed view opens. A number should appear in the leftmost # column, which indicates the number that Notes has given to the unnamed document because you haven't named it. (At this point, you should have saved only one document.) Make sure the numbered document is highlighted and then press F9 to refresh the document. This action updates any design changes you have made to the form since you composed the document.

Of course, this process is for testing purposes only; you'll have to remove the default values before rolling the application out (unless you actually want a default value in a field upon document composition).

▶▶ *What's Next?*

The importance of designing a form by giving a lot of consideration to the ways in which people will use it cannot be overestimated. Users will interact with the forms you create more than any other component of a Notes database. A well-designed form makes life easier for your users. Conversely, a poorly designed form causes confusion and frustration.

Now that you've learned about creating forms for people to enter data in a Notes database, you need to learn about designing views for people to get data out of a database. In the next chapter, we'll show you how to define a view for displaying the documents users will compose in a database. We'll continue to use the three forms that you've created in order to illustrate other Notes features we discuss in later chapters.

CHAPTER 5

Creating a View

▸▸ *F*AST *T*RACK

▶ **To create a view**

select a database in the Workspace. Choose Design ➤
Views. The Design Views dialog box appears. Click on the
New button, which allows you to create a view from
scratch. A blank view window appears in Design mode.

▶ **To define a view's attributes**

open a view in Design mode. Choose Design ➤ View Attributes. The Design View Attributes dialog box appears.
Enter a name in the Name text box. Select either the
Shared View, Private View, or Shared, Private On First Use
option. (Shared View is the default.) Choose either the Default View or No Response Hierarchy option. Either accept the other options or change them to suit your needs.
Click on OK to accept any changes you have made.

▶ **To define a column**

click on the blank column in a view. Choose Design ➤
New Column. The Design Column Definition dialog box
appears. Enter a name in the Title text box. Enter a formula in the Formula box. It refers to the value of a field(s)
in a particular form. Set the width of the column in the
Column Width box. Either accept the other default options or change them. Click on OK to accept your choices.

▶ **To create a category in a view**

click on the leftmost column title to select it. (If a column
has been designated as a Responses Only column, click on
it to select it.) Choose Design ➤ New Column. The Design Column Definition dialog box appears. Leave the Title text box empty. Set the column width to 1. Click on the
Sorting button. The Sorting dialog box appears. Select the

Sort option and then the Category option. (You can't select Category until you've selected Sort.) Choose Ascending or Descending sort order. Click on OK to close the dialog box. Click on OK again to accept the changes. A new column appears to the left of the column title (or Responses Only column).

▶ ***To create a selection formula***   ***419***

display the view in Design mode. Choose Design ➤ Selection Formula. The Design Selection Formula dialog box appears. Enter a formula in the Selection Formula box. Click on OK to accept the formula.

▶ ***To save a view***   ***423***

press Ctrl+S. If you press Esc before you save the changes, a message box will appear, asking you if you want to save your changes. Click on Yes. You'll return to the Workspace or another window that may be open.

▶ ***To edit a view***   ***424***

select the database in the Workspace. Choose Design ➤ Views. The Design Views dialog box will appear. Select the view you want to edit by double-clicking on the view's name. The view window will open. When you want to edit a column, double-click on the column heading. The Design Column Definition dialog box will appear. Make the desired changes and then click on OK to accept the changes. When you return to the view window, press F9 to refresh the view and to see if the changes you made have taken effect. Press Ctrl+S to save the view.

▶ ▶ *T* **hrough** our discussion of creating a form (and the subsequent composing of documents), we've explained how to get information into a Notes database. However, getting data *in* is really only half the battle. Of equal importance is the user's ability to get data *out* of our database in a way that is easy, efficient, and sensible. This is where *views* enter the picture. In this chapter, we take you through the steps of creating a view, in addition to discussing the following topics:

- Defining view attributes
- Using column formulas
- Organizing a view by categories
- Writing a selection formula

▶ ▶ *Getting Information Out of Your Database*

Imagine pouring information into the database, yet later, having no way of accessing that information or a method of access that doesn't allow you to find and retrieve the information you need easily. It would be like a dictionary with no index entries at the top of each page—you could eventually find the word you're looking up, but it would certainly take longer. A Notes database is not meant to be black hole where information goes in, never to be seen again. Therefore, a view serves as a table of contents for a database, displaying a list of stored documents and providing users with the means to read, edit, and/or delete those documents.

A database may have several views, with each one displaying the contents (though not necessarily the entire contents) of the database in a different way. For example, one view might list *all* the documents in the database, while another view lists only a *subset* of documents in the database based on a specific *selection criteria*. These criteria, for instance, could display only those documents that were composed after a certain date.

To gain a better understanding of what we face in getting information out of our database, let's step back a moment and consider a few factors that will play a role in this process:

- We've designed a series of forms for use by our end users so that they can populate our database with documents—the end result is that we have documents of all types in the database.

- The forms are made up of fields (or "containers," as you recall from the previous chapter) that allow us to capture specific types of data, and each field has been assigned a name.

- The overall content of a given document will depend on the form with which it was composed. We can safely say that documents composed with the same form are *generally* alike—even though the specific information may differ, these documents share common fields.

- It's often the case that different documents share common values for specific fields. For instance, with documents that capture address information it's a pretty safe bet that there will be several documents that have the same value for the zip code field. We should be able to use this fact to group those documents together.

- Some documents are designated as responses to other documents—this relationship should somehow be made evident to the end user when viewing the contents of the database.

You should take into account all of the above items when deciding how to show the contents of a Notes database through a view. However, exactly what is meant by "show the contents?" How does a view work?

▶▶ *Understanding View Basics*

A view presents a user with the documents in a database by extracting specific field values from each document and displaying those values in a horizontal format, or *row*, in a view window. Each row refers to a particular document. Technically, the rows of a view are not the documents themselves but rather mini-representations of the documents. By selectively pulling field values from the documents, assembling those field values in row format (again, one row for each document), and presenting the rows in a window known as a "view," users have the means to:

- Identify documents
- Open those documents for subsequent reading and/or editing
- Delete documents from the database

For identification purposes it's important that the field values for each row give users a clue as to what document the row represents. It's essential, therefore, that there be some uniqueness in the field values so users can quickly differentiate one document from another in the view. (The following discussions will deal with this in detail.) Let's use the Directory Entry form from the Corporate Directory database to illustrate this concept. Figure 15.1 shows how the field values in a document correspond with the field values in a row from a view.

How does a view accomplish this feat? First of all, you must understand the core structure of a view. We know that a view has rows and that those rows represent documents. To really get a handle on things, however, we need to break down the structure of a row and understand how it's assembled. Let's examine a single row and the values that appear, as shown in Figure 15.2.

FIGURE 15.1 ▶

The field values in a Directory Entry document correspond to the values that are displayed in the columns of the Corporate Directory view. You'll notice that both the document and the view display the main telephone and fax numbers. (You'll have to scroll down the document to see these numbers.)

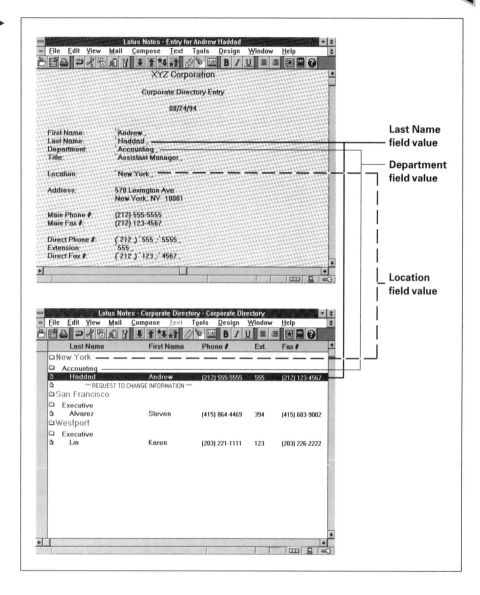

FIGURE 15.2 ▶

A view displays one document in each row.

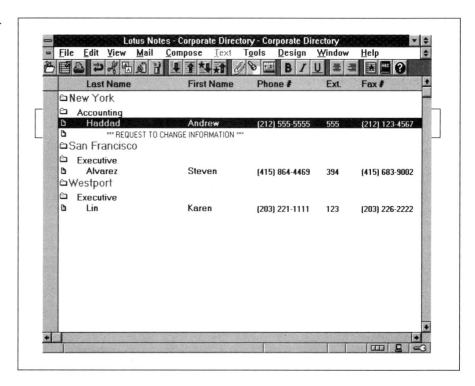

 ▶▶ **NOTE**

While a view looks deceptively like a 1-2-3 for Windows or Excel spreadsheet because of its row/column nature, it definitely is not. There are some vague similarities— column labels with values aligned underneath, some rudimentary totaling capability—but don't look for anything near the power of a full-featured spreadsheet package. In fact, you cannot directly edit any of the data displayed in the view because each data item is not an independent "cell" like a cell that appears in a spreadsheet. To change the information in the view you must open the individual documents and make any changes there or run a macro that directly changes the values.

Although it doesn't appear this way, the row is actually made of a series of independent segments, each segment containing a value. Figure 15.3 shows the parts of a row.

Now extend this idea of identical segmentation to all the rows of the view and the result is a series of vertical partitions, or, *columns*. Figure 15.4 shows the columns in a view.

FIGURE 15.3 ▶

The information that's displayed in a row is actually divided into separate columns. Segment lines appear while the view's in Edit mode. Each column displays a unique value that corresponds to a field value in a document.

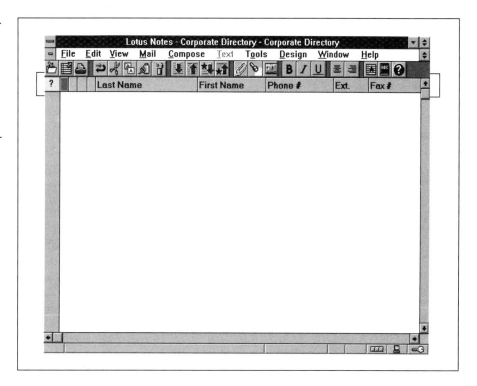

▶▶ *Using Column Formulas*

By creating and "programming" each column of the view, you determine which field values will be presented, where the field values will appear in the row, and how they will be displayed (i.e., what point size, font, etc.). Specifically, it is the *column formula* of a column that dictates what values will appear in that column for each document.

FIGURE 15.4

*If a view displayed
partition lines between
columns, you would
see that the informa-
tion in each row
corresponds to a
particular column.*

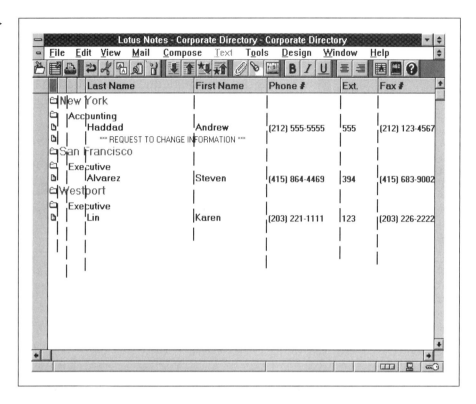

Typically, a column formula makes reference to a field name (or combination of field names), the field being a component of the design of a
form. The value, if any, of the field(s) being referenced will appear in
the view, in that column, *for documents that have a value specified for the
field(s)*. For example, in the case of Directory Entry documents, you, as
the designer, decide to display the value of the FirstName, LastName,
DirectNum_P, Extension, DirectNum_F, and Title fields in a view, as
shown in Figure 15.5.

Hopefully, you're getting the idea at this point. When a user accesses a
view, it simply does what it's been told to do, namely, it goes and re-
trieves the information from each document as specified in the column
formulas. In a sense, a view is a program which executes a series of
commands (the column formulas) and then displays the results, very
much like a stored query in other database environments. Now, let's
look at how you actually create, program, and access a view.

FIGURE 15.5 ▶

There is a direct connection between a field's value in a form to a formula you write for a column. The column formula returns a value that's displayed in a view's column. In this case, the value of the LastName field in the Directory Entry form is returned by the column formula, which, in turn, displays the value in the Last Name column of the Corporate Directory view.

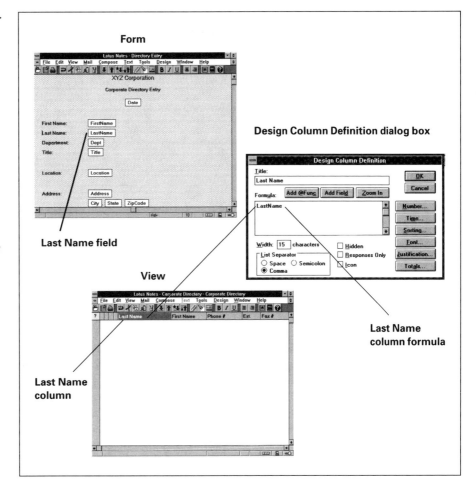

▶▶ *Creating a New View*

Let's create a Corporate Directory view for the Corporate Directory database. The columns in the view correspond to the field values in the Directory Entry form. To create the view, follow these steps:

1. Select the Corporate Directory database in the Workspace.

2. Choose Design ➤ Views. The Design Views dialog box appears, as shown in Figure 15.6.

FIGURE 15.6 ▶

The Design Views dialog box lets you create a new view for a selected database.

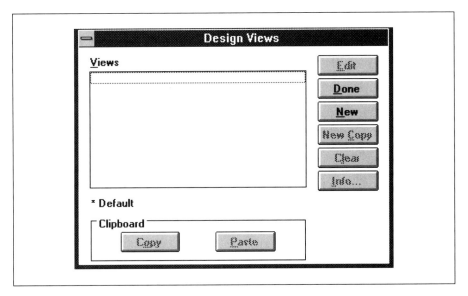

 ▶▶ **T I P**

> You can choose the New Copy and Paste options if a view already exists. The New Copy option allows you to create a view by copying an existing view in the database. Simply highlight the view you wish to copy from the list of views displayed in the dialog box and select New Copy. The Paste option lets you create a view by pasting a view from another database into the current database. You must first open the other database, choose Design ➤ Views, highlight the desired view, and click on Copy. Then choose Design ➤ Views in the target database and click on Paste. The pasted view should now appear in the list of views in the dialog box.

3. Click on the New button, which allows you to create a view from scratch. A blank view window appears in Design mode, as shown in Figure 15.7.

FIGURE 15.7 ▶

A blank view appears in Design mode when you want to define a new view.

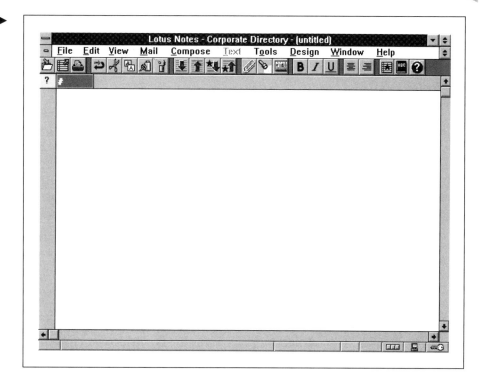

▶ *Defining View Attributes*

You'll notice that the current name of the view is [untitled]. Associated with each view is a set of attributes that assign certain general characteristics to the view. One of the attributes is the view's name. To define view attributes, follow these steps:

1. While in View Design mode, choose Design ➤ View Attributes. The Design View Attributes dialog box appears, as shown in Figure 15.8.

2. Enter **Corporate Directory** in the Name text box.

3. Select the Shared View option if it's not selected. (It's the default.)

4. Choose the Default View option. (Leave the No Response Hierarchy option unchecked.)

5. Click on the Categories button to specify that categories in the view will be fully expanded.

The Design View Attributes dialog box lets you define the attributes for a particular view.

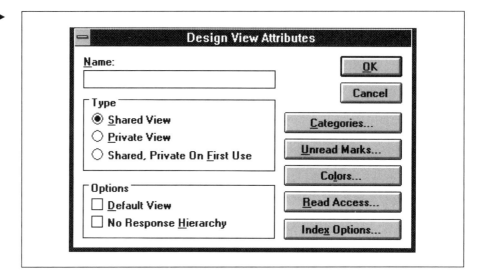

6. Click on the Unread Marks button to activate the option that users will be notified of unread documents. Notes will "flag" or mark either unread response documents and categories that contain unread documents, or only main documents when new ones are added to the database, depending on the option that you choose.

7. Click on the Colors button and select a color for the view's background. (You can choose other color options if you wish.)

8. Click on OK to accept the changes.

We'll leave the Read Access and Index options alone for the moment. You can always come back later and set the options if we need to do so.

Let's look closely at the attributes you can define for a view.

Name

Every view must be assigned a name. This name appears in the View menu and should, therefore, reflect the nature of the view to the user. The length of a view name cannot exceed 32 characters (unless you are using synonyms or cascaded names, to be described later). Make the name as descriptive as possible (so that end users know what they'll see if they elect to display the view) while maintaining a consistent naming convention. For example, we've named the view for the Corporate Directory database "Corporate Directory."

Views can be given more than one name. These additional "aliases," which are called *synonyms*, are typically used to give you, the application developer, a shorthand method of referring to the view in formulas. For this reason, synonyms are usually shorter in length than the formal view name. Like the view name, synonyms cannot exceed 32 characters in length. You are allowed to assign as many synonyms to a view name as will fit in the Name box.

Get into the habit of assigning synonyms to view names. Assuming you keep the length of synonyms down to just a few characters (and you should) you'll find them much easier to work with in @functions that require view names as arguments—you simply substitute the synonym for the full-blown view name. Later, if you decide to change the view name, be sure to maintain the same synonym. That way all formulas that reference the view name *via the synonym* will continue to function correctly. On the other hand, if you use view names themselves in formulas you'll have to manually edit each formula any time you change the view name.

Another feature of the view name is the ability to group several views under a common heading in the View menu. This effect, known as "cascading," keeps the View menu more manageable by creating a two-tiered selection scheme. Rather than directly choosing a view name from the View menu, the user first chooses a heading which, in turn, displays a submenu of actual view names, such as the one shown in Figure 15.9.

You are only allowed a single level of cascading. The heading may be up to 32 characters in length while the unique names under the heading may be up to 30 characters. For all views that you wish to group under a common heading, make sure that the heading portion of the view name is identical.

Type

Each view has an associated type that determines whether a view is available to the general public or to an individual user. A view is typed as either a shared view or a private view. A third type—Shared, Private On First Use—is a hybrid that can be used in special circumstances.

As its name implies, a shared view is designed to allow more than one person access to the view and only makes sense in the context of a server-based database (as opposed to a local database). *The collection of shared*

FIGURE 15.9 ►

A View menu can display a submenu of view names by "cascading" or grouping the names under a common heading.

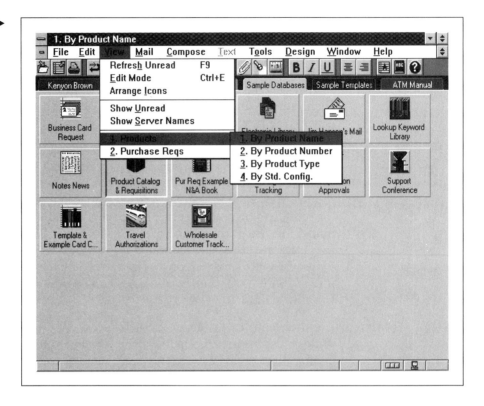

views associated with a database should represent those views that are useful to a majority of the end users. It's important that you gather input from the end users as to what views they want to see before you begin the actual design process. Above all, you want useful, sensible views.

Before you use a private view, you might think to yourself, "When *wouldn't* I want a view to be accessible to multiple users?" Occasionally, a particular user might want a view of the database that isn't offered through the available shared views, or one that only has relevance to *that* user. However, as an application developer, you do not want to get into a situation where you are creating new shared views to satisfy every whim and fancy of your user population. Therefore, users with Reader access to the database can create their own private views of the database. A private view is only accessible to the user who created it and no others.

As a design element, a private view is not stored with the database, but is stored locally in the user's DESKTOP.DSK file. *A private view will not give a user access to documents that he/she does not already have*, so you don't have to worry about your users circumventing any security measures you've put in place. From a visual standpoint, private views appear in the View menu below shared views, separated by a horizontal bar. In the Design Views dialog box, private views are distinguished from shared views by the placement of square brackets around their name.

Perhaps users do not have the necessary expertise to create their own private views or you wish to create a view that will display the contents of the database differently relative to the user accessing the view. The Shared, Private On First Use type lets you create a shared view that becomes private to a user the first time they access it. Prior to first access (and relative to each user), a Shared, Private on First Use view name appears as a standard shared view in the View menu and is actually in a "shared state." After the first access the view name will appear as a private view in the View menu, positioned under the horizontal bar separating shared and private views; the "shared version" of the view will no longer appear in the menu.

Once the shared view becomes private, a user is completely free to modify the view. Again, the name of the (now private) view is surrounded by square brackets in the Design Views dialog box. As the database designer, the obvious question you might ask yourself is "How do I restrict access to a Shared, Private on First Use view to only the user(s) for whom it was designed?" This is accomplished by modifying the Read Access list for the Shared, Private on First Use view (described below) to include only the target user(s).

Default View and No Response Hierarchy Options

The Default View and No Response Hierarchy options can be selected as needed. One view in each database is usually designated as the default view. When the database is first opened this view is automatically displayed, giving the new user their first look at the contents of the database. From then on, the last view a user accessed will be the first view they see next time they open that same database. As a rule of thumb, the view that is accessed most frequently is typically made the default view, although a database is not required to have a default view at all. Only one default view is allowed per database. In the list of views in the Design Views dialog box the default view (if any) is prefaced with an asterisk character (*).

At the outset of this chapter we noted that you can show a response hierarchy, if one exists, in a view. Usually, you express a response hierarchy by indenting response documents, as shown in Figure 15.10.

Notice, for instance, the horizontal alignment of the document "An excellent training facility...." Rather than being perfectly aligned with the "Training Site" column title, it appears offset to the right relative to the document directly above it. This indented format indicates that the document is a response to the document "Marriott Hotel." (We'll explain how indenting is done shortly.) You may, however, choose not to show a response hierarchy (like the one above) in a particular view. By selecting No Response Hierarchy (and with the appropriate column definitions), you can force response documents to appear aligned with their corresponding main documents.

FIGURE 15.10 ▶

Three document types are displayed in this view: a Main document, a Response to Document, and a Response to Response. With the No Response Hierarchy option left blank, the response documents appear indented under the main document to indicate their relationship.

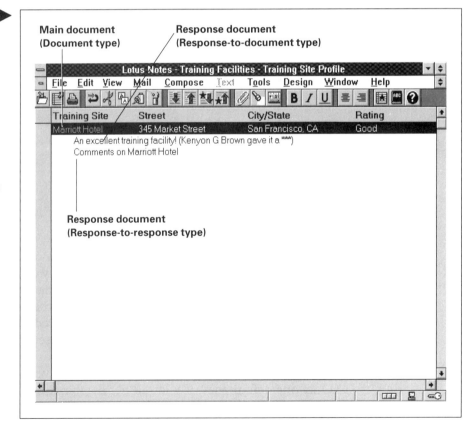

Categories

Choose Categories to specify whether categories in the view will be either fully expanded or fully collapsed when the view is opened. When categories are fully expanded, all documents within each category are displayed in the view. When categories are fully collapsed, only the categories themselves appear in the view and users will have to manually expand the categories by choosing menu selections under the View menu or pressing the + key on the numeric keypad.

Unread Marks

Choose Unread Marks to indicate to users whether they have read particular documents in a database. Each unread document is indicated by an "unread mark" in the markers column at the left of the view; read documents have no such marker. Notes maintains independent unread marks for every user (on the server) so that what shows up as unread to one user does not necessarily show up as unread to another. Once a user opens and closes an unread document the unread mark will be removed for that user.

After you click on the Unread Marks button, you have three different options to choose from:

- **None**: Specifies that no unread marks will be displayed.
- **Unread Documents Only**: Specifies that unread marks be displayed for *main documents only.*
- **Compute and Display at All Levels of View**: Specifies that unread marks be displayed for all documents, main or response, and for collapsed categories that contain unread main or response documents.

It's a good idea to implement Unread Marks for active databases where new documents are frequently being added and timely viewing of new documents is critical.

Colors

You can alter various color attributes of the view through the Colors option. Specifically, you can select the colors for unread documents, column totals, column titles (headings), and the view background. The effective use of color, particularly for the background, can help users differentiate entire views or specific elements in a view.

Read Access

You can choose this option to make sure that documents displayed in a view can only be read by the people named in the read access list. (This is a subset of the people who have access to the database.) In addition, you can create or modify the read access list for a particular document by opening the document in Edit mode and choosing Edit ➤ Security ➤ Read Access. (We also discussed setting read access in Chapter 14. "Designing a Form.")

Index Options

You can use this option to define the rules by which the database index will be updated. (We discuss creating and updating a full-text index in Chapter 20, "Indexing a Notes Database.") Every view has an index that enables Notes to locate documents within a view. Every time documents are added, modified, deleted or recategorized, the index must be updated to reflect the change. (With large databases, indexing can utilize substantial Notes server resources.) You can determine how the index is updated, and how long it is saved.

You can set a view's refresh frequency by choosing one of these options:

- **Automatic:** Updates the view's index every time the view is opened.

- **Manual/Background:** Updates the view whenever the user presses F9 or chooses View ➤ Refresh.

- **Automatic, at most once every [ ] hours**: Lets you specify how frequently the index should be updated. The first time the view is opened, after this selection is made, the index is updated. It is not updated again until the specified interval has passed.

You can also set whether to discard an index by choosing one of these options:

- **Never**: Select this option for heavily used databases, when you do not want to waste time reindexing often.

- **After Each Use**: Select this option when the database is used infrequently, but on a predictable basis. This option deletes the view's index as soon as the database is closed; it is rebuilt the next time the view is opened.

- **On Server After [ ] days of Inactivity:** Select this option when a database is used infrequently, on an unpredictable basis. If you do not know when the view will be used, it's risky to delete the index as soon as the database is closed. Watch database use to see if this option can safely be changed to the After Each Use option. (This option does not affect local databases.)

▶ *Defining the Columns in a View*

The vertical partitions, or *columns*, in a view give the view its structure and meaning. When designing a new view, you'll notice that you're presented with a undefined column at the far left. This is known as the default Document Number column. We are going to delete the column because we don't need to display a number next to each document in the view. However, before we do so, let's look at the column's definitions:

Title: #

Formula: @DocNumber

Width: 5

List Separator: Comma

Number: General (Default)

Time: mm/dd/yy hh:mm:ss (Default Overall Format)

Sorting: not applicable (Default)

Font: Helv, 10, Normal (Default)

Justification: Left (Default)

Totals: None (Default)

As you can see, you can use the default definitions for most of the items. This will save you a lot of time when you have several columns to define.

For the Corporate Directory view, you are going to define columns that correspond to the LastName, FirstName, DirectNum_P, Extension,

DirectNum_F, and Title field values in the Directory Entry form. To define each of the other columns, follow these steps:

1. Click on the # column to select it.

2. Press Del.

►► **T I P**

You don't have to delete the column. You can also change the definitions for the # column in order to use it in another capacity. Click on the # column and choose Design ➤ Column Definitions. Enter new information in the dialog box and then click on OK to accept the changes.

3. Click on Yes to remove the column from the view.

4. Click on the blank column.

5. Choose Design ➤ New Column. The Design Column Definition dialog box appears, as shown in Figure 15.11.

FIGURE 15.11 ►

The Design Column Definition dialog box lets you define a column, which in this case is the Last Name column in the Corporate Directory view.

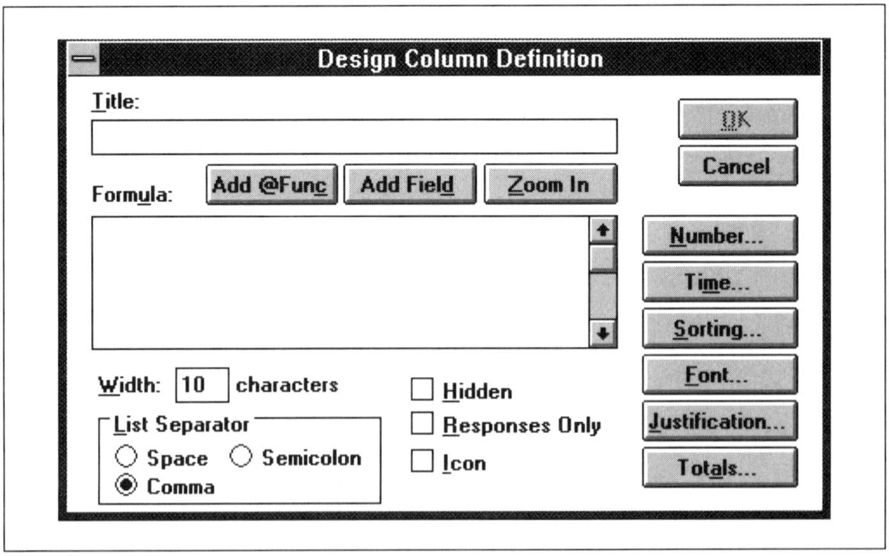

Design Column Definition

Title:

Formula: [Add @Func] [Add Field] [Zoom In]

[OK] [Cancel]

[Number...] [Time...] [Sorting...] [Font...] [Justification...] [Totals...]

Width: 10 characters

List Separator
○ Space ○ Semicolon
● Comma

☐ Hidden
☐ Responses Only
☐ Icon

> **Double-click on a column heading (the box at top of the column) to display the Design Column Definition dialog box.**

6. Enter **Last Name** in the Title text box.

7. Enter **LastName** as the formula in the Formula box. (It refers to the values of the **LastName** fields in the Directory Entry form.)

8. Set the width of the column in the Column Width box to **25**.

9. Choose Comma as the List Separator.

10. Click on the Font button. The Font dialog box appears.

11. Select Helv, 10, Bold.

12. Click on OK to accept your choices.

Using the Last Name column as an example, let's look closely at the meaning of each of the options in the Column Design Definitions dialog box.

Column Title

For each column you can include a title, which is simply a text label that appears at the top of a view column. The column title should indicate what information the column contains. For instance, columns that display the contents of the LastName and FirstName fields of Directory Entry documents have the title "Last Name" and "First Name," respectively. Be sure that the width of the columns (discussed below) is large enough to display the column titles fully.

Column Formula

As we discussed earlier in the "Using Column Formulas" section, the column formula is the key element of the column definition—without it the column will be empty. A column formula usually makes reference to a field name in a form.

▶▶ **N O T E**

All of the rules of writing Notes formulas apply to writing a column formula. (See Chapter 16 for a discussion of writing formulas and macros.)

Column Width

The width of a column, though not a critical element, plays a role in how the column appears to the user. A column should be wide enough to fully display the column title and the values displayed through the column formula. Information will be truncated if it's wider than the column can accommodate, so set the column width accordingly.

List Separator

If a column formula specifies a multivalue field, such as checkbox-style keyword field, you can choose which character—space, semicolon, or comma—will be used to separate the individual values when displayed in the column.

Hidden

Occasionally you may wish to include a column in a view whose values are hidden to the eye. This usually occurs when you want to sort documents in the view based on the value of a field, yet you don't want the value ("sort key") itself to be displayed (or to sort in a specific order, such as "Urgent," "Very Important," "Normal").

Since the column is hidden it does not matter what you set the column title or column width to. You can only see the actual values in the hidden column when you're in View Design mode.

Responses Only

You can read the "Producing a Response Hierarchy" section below for an explanation of this option.

Icon

Notes gives you the option of including icons in a view window, which can give the user more information about the items they're viewing.

There will be times when a title doesn't make this obvious. For example, an attachment is represented by one icon that looks like a paper clip, and a document is represented by another icon that looks like a dog-eared sheet of paper.

There are five defined icons: document, folder, person, group, and attachment. Icons must be displayed in their own column; this column is always the leftmost column in a view. When you define the icon column, you'll need to enter **@DocLevel** in the Formula box. Set the width of the column to 1, and select the Icon option. Click on OK to accept the changes.

  T I P

> **Ignore the formula statement that is found in the Icon section of the "Designing Views" chapter in the** *Application Developer's Reference* **book. It doesn't work—it returns the wrong value and won't display the correct icon. However, the @DocLevel statement works.**

Number

When you click on the Number button, the Design Number Format dialog box appears. You'll use the number format option only when the field uses a number data type, or when the formula returns a numeric value. If you want to display a number in a column, choose an appropriate format.

Time

You click on the Time button to display the Design Time Format dialog box. You'll use the time format option only when a field uses the time data type, or when the formula returns a time-date value. If you want to display a time-date value in a column, choose an appropriate format.

Sorting

When you click on the Sorting button, the Design Column Sort dialog box appears. You can use this option to define the order in which documents in the view will be displayed. These options are available to you:

- **Sort**: Establishes that this column will be sorted; enables the other options.

- **Categorize**: Defines the column as categorized for the grouping of related documents. (See the "Organizing a View by Categories" section later in the chapter.)

- **Ascending** or **Descending**: Determines the order in which the documents will be sorted in this column; these options are dimmed until you select the Sort option.

Font

Clicking on the Font button displays the standard Font dialog box. (We showed you how to change fonts, attributes, and colors in our discussion of formatting text in Chapter 6.) Using different fonts, point sizes, attributes, and colors in a view enhances its appearance and helps a user to differentiate between items.

Justification

You click on the Justification button to display the Design Column Justification dialog box. You can set the column alignment to left, right, and center. Left aligns all values in the column along the left edge of the column. You choose this option when displaying text and time-date values. Right aligns all values in the column along the right edge of the column. Generally, you use this option when you want to display numbers; however, if you use this option, you should use a numeric format that displays a standard number of decimal places, to ensure that the decimal points in the various numbers line up. Center aligns all values at the center of the column. You select this option for displaying small values that you want to stand out.

Totals

You click on the Totals button to display the Design Column Totals dialog box. You can use this option to define the method for calculation and display of numeric totals in a column. You can calculate totals for columns displaying numeric fields, for columns containing formulas that return a numeric result, and for columns that use @Number to successfully convert a textural digit to a number (such as "3" to 3). The following options are available to you:

- **None**: Does no totaling.
- **Total**: Calculates a grand total for all main documents in the view, and displays this total at the bottom of the view.
- **Average per document**: Calculates an overall average for the view. Notes totals the main documents, and then divides that value by the number of documents. For example, if there are four documents in the database and their total is 10, the average per document is 2.5.
- **Average per sub-category**: Calculates an average for each subcategory. Within each subcategory, the documents are summed; that value is divided by the number of documents in that subcategory.
- **Percentage of parent category**: Calculates a total for all main documents in the view; for each category, Notes displays the percentage of the overall view's total represented by that category.
- **Percentage of entire view**: Calculates a total for all main documents in the view; for each document, Notes displays the percentage of the category's total represented by that document. For each category, Notes displays the percentage of the overall view's total represented by that category.
- **Hide Detail Values**: Suppresses the display of subtotals for each category and subcategory.

▶▶ *Producing a Response Hierarchy*

When one document is composed as a response to another, it is helpful to users to be able to see the relationship with just a glance. We can accomplish this by arranging a view so that the correspondence between a response document and responded-to document is obvious. By introducing an indenting scheme in the view, where response documents are positioned directly under their corresponding main documents *and* offset to the right, we can give users the ability to see the response hierarchy quickly and easily. While this may sound easy to implement, it's actually a little tricky.

As you define a column, one of the options that you might select is Responses Only. By activating this option as part of a column definition, you are saying that only response documents will qualify for inclusion in that column in terms of displaying a value. Those rows which represent non-response documents will not display a value for that column, even if they satisfy the column formula. So what we've done through the Responses Only option is to limit the scope of the column to include values only from those documents of type Response or Response to Response. *A view may have one column, and only one column, designated as a Responses Only column.*

The placement of the Responses Only column is the next item of business, and this is where most of the confusion arises. Consider a plain-vanilla view (with no Responses Only columns). The values that are displayed in the view, based on the column definitions, are vertically aligned with the column itself.

For example, in the column at the far left of the view you expect the values for that column to show up there—a typical "what you see is what you get" result. This sounds simplistic and, in fact, it is. With a Responses Only column, however, the rules change so that it is no longer "what you see is what you get." This stems from the fact (and you should keep this in mind throughout this discussion) that we are trying to produce a hierarchical look in the view where response documents appear underneath and offset relative to their corresponding main documents.

Let's look at the Corporate Directory view, which contains a Responses Only column, as shown in Figure 15.12.

You'll notice that the placement of the Responses Only column is to the left of the columns titles in the view, yet the value that's produced by this column appears indented beneath the main document. Several things are going here:

- Notes has automatically matched the response document with its main document.

- The response document has been automatically indented in the view.

Where you place the Responses Only column in the design of the view, either to the left or right of other columns, affects what other values may be displayed for response documents based on other columns. We

FIGURE 15.12

The Responses Only column appears to the left of the Name column. The information in the Responses Only column will appear indented under the document in the Name column.

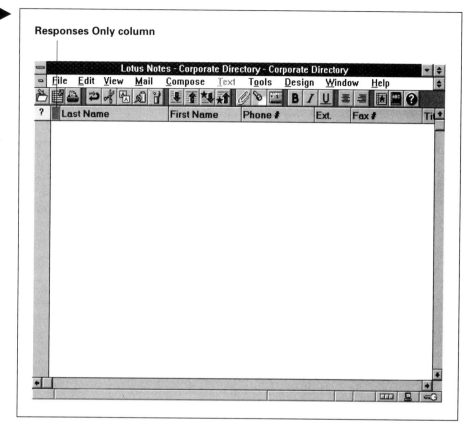

know that the Responses Only column itself will yield a value for response documents, but what about the other columns of the view — will they yield a value for response documents as well?

The answer is, maybe. You might expect that response documents, which satisfy the column formulas of other columns, would produce values for those columns in their respective rows. However, this is not the case. When considering the placement of a Responses Only column, there are two rules that come into play that will affect the outcome:

- Columns to the left of the Responses Only column will yield a value for both main and response documents.

- Columns to the right of the Responses Only column will yield a value for main documents only.

However unintuitive this might seem, it's simply the way Notes views work. You can think of a Responses Only column as a barrier that prevents any column to its right from displaying values for response documents. Figure 15.13 shows an example.

To create the Responses Only column, follow the steps below. Please note that the values returned by this column correspond to the field values of a Change Request form that was created at the conclusion of the last chapter. This form is a Response to Document type. As a Response to Document type, a Change Request document would appear indented under the Directory Entry document that it was responding to. Although this form doesn't, we want to take you through the steps of defining a column for a response-type document:

1. Click on the Last Name column to select it.

FIGURE 15.13 ▶

Columns can appear to the left and right of the Responses Only column, but the other columns cannot display values for response documents.

2. Choose Design ➤ New Column. The Design Column Definition dialog box appears.

3. Don't assign a title to the column; leave the Title text box blank.

4. Enter "✳✳✳ **REQUEST TO CHANGE INFORMATION** ✳✳✳" (including the quotation marks) in the Formula box.

5. Set the width of the column to 1.

 ▶▶ **T I P**

> **Any larger width setting will simply screw up the indenting scheme. Even with a width of 1, the values in the Responses Only column will be fully displayed—yes, another Responses Only anomaly! Also, there is no need to include a column title—given a column width of 1, you would not be able to add a title.**

6. Select the Responses Only option.

7. Click on OK to accept the changes.

The new Responses Only column will appear to the left of the Last Name column.

▶▶ *Organizing a View by Categories*

Categories are a simple yet effective way of giving your views a higher degree of organization and making them easier to read. Essentially, categories allow you to organize documents in a view into logical groupings based on a common field value.

For example, in the Corporate Directory database there might be several documents where the value of the Location field in the Directory Entry documents is San Francisco. We can take advantage of this fact by grouping together all Directory Entry documents with San Francisco in the Location field. The common value, San Francisco, is shared by a subset of Directory Entry documents in the database. This value relates those documents to one another. Therefore, we can express this relationship in the view. In this case, we can identify "Location" as a category that we'll use to organize documents in the view, as shown in Figure 15.14.

To create a Location category in a view, follow these steps:

1. While in View Design mode, click on the Responses Only column to select it.

2. Choose Design ➤ New Column. The Design Column Definition dialog box appears.

3. Don't assign a title to the column; leave the Title text box empty.

4. Enter the field name **Location** in the Column Formula text box.

5. Set the column width to 1.

FIGURE 15.14 ▶

The Location column in the Corporate Directory view is used to identify a category of information. In this case the column returns the value of the Location field in the Directory Entry form. You'll notice that the column appears to the left of the Responses Only column.

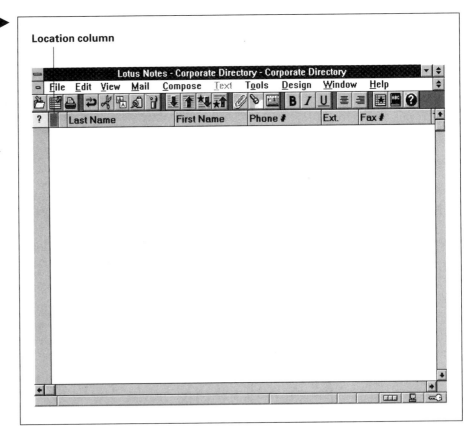

6. Click on the Sorting button. The Design Column Sort dialog box appears, as shown in Figure 15.15.

7. Select the Sort option and then the Category option. (You can't select Category until you've selected Sort.)

8. Choose Ascending sort order.

9. Click on OK to close the dialog box.

10. Click on OK again to accept the changes.

The new Location column appears to the left of the Responses Only column. You might have noticed a couple of peculiar items in the procedure above. First, the column width of 1—yes, the entire value will display in the category column even though the column width would indicate otherwise. Furthermore, since the column width is 1 there is no sense in entering a column title because it won't fit. Second, category columns have to be sorted.

FIGURE 15.15 ▶

The Design Column Sort dialog box lets you sort and categorize the values in a column.

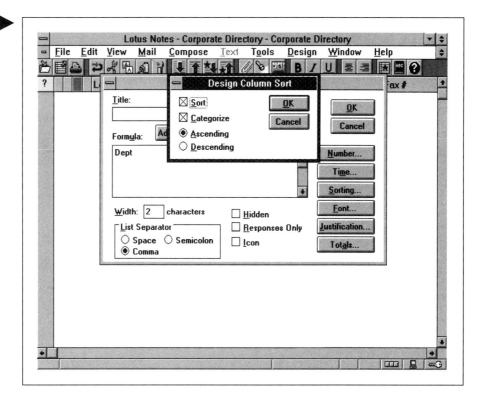

You are not limited to a single category in a view. Multiple categories make sense where documents share additional common field values, such the view that's shown in Figure 15.16. The idea is to produce categories within categories for a more highly organized view. The physical placement of a category column determines whether it's inside or outside another category—a category to the left envelopes categories to its right. As with any good thing, you can overuse categories, so ask yourself "Does the common value represent a useful category and will it enhance the view?" Too many categories can make a view *less* readable and more cumbersome if users are continually having to expand categories to get to the desired document(s) or collapse upper level categories in order to fit the view contents in single window.

In our view we've included an additional category, "Department," in order to group directory entries by location and, within each location, by department. The process of creating this second category is identical to that involved with creating the Location category. The Department category, as a subcategory of location, is placed to the right of the Location category column (and to the left of the Responses Only column).

FIGURE 15.16 ▶

The Corporate Directory view displays the Location and Department column categories that return values for the Location and Department fields in the Directory Entry form. The view also displays the Icon and Responses Only columns.

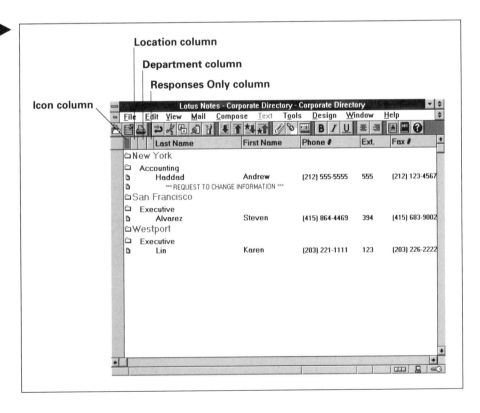

To create a Department category in a view, follow these steps:

1. Click on the Responses Only column first before you define the new column.

2. Choose Design ➤ New Column. The Design Column Definition dialog box appears.

3. Don't assign a title to the column; leave the Title text box empty.

4. Enter the field name **Dept** in the Column Formula text box.

5. Set the column width to 1.

6. Click on the Sorting button. The Design Column Sort dialog box appears.

7. Select the Sort option and then the Category option. (You can't select Category until you've selected Sort.)

8. Choose Ascending sort order.

9. Click on OK to close the dialog box.

10. Click on OK again to accept the changes.

The new Department column appears between the Location column and the Responses Only column. Finally, you can create an icon column to display icons that correspond to the categories and documents that'll appear in the view. The use of icons serves to categorize and identify the different categories and types of documents for the user.

To create an icon category in a view, follow these steps:

1. Click on the Location column first before you define the new column.

2. Choose Design ➤ New Column. The Design Column Definition dialog box appears.

3. Don't assign a title to the column; leave the Title text box empty.

4. Enter @DocLevel in the Column Formula text box.

5. Set the column width to 1.

6. Select the icon option.

7. Click on OK again to accept the changes.

The new icon column appears to the left of the Location column.

So far you've defined five columns in the Corporate Directory view. You'll need to repeat the above steps in order to define each of the remaining columns in the view. The First Name, Phone #, Ext., Fax #, and Title columns appear to the right of the Last Name column. You can assume that the default options apply unless indicated otherwise.

To define the other columns in the Corporate Directory view, follow these steps:

1. For the sixth column, enter the following definitions:

    Title: First Name

    Formula: FirstName

    Width: 10

    List Separator: Comma

    Number: General (Default)

    Sorting: Ascending, Categorized

    Font: Helv, 10, Bold

    Justification: Left (default)

    Totals: None (Default)

2. For the seventh column, enter the following definitions:

    Title: Phone #

    Formula: @If(DirectNum_P != "";DirectNum_P; Main-Num_P)

    Width: 10

    List Separator: Comma

    Number: General (Default)

    Sorting: None

    Font: Helv, 10, Bold

    Justification: Left

    Totals: None (Default)

3. For the eighth column, enter the following definitions:

    Title: Ext.

    Formula: Extension

    Width: 5

    List Separator: Comma

Number: General (Default)

Sorting: Ascending

Font: Helv, 12, Bold

Justification: Left (Default)

Totals: None (Default)

4. For the ninth column, enter the following definitions:

Title: Fax #

Formula: @If(DirectNum_F != "";DirectNum_F; Main-Num_F)

Width: 10

List Separator: Comma

Number: General (Default)

Sorting: None

Font: Helv, 12, Bold

Justification: Left (Default)

Totals: None (Default)

5. For the tenth column, enter the following definitions:

Title: Title

Formula: Title

Width: 15

List Separator: Comma

Number: General (Default)

Sorting: None

Font: Helv, 12, Bold

Justification: Left (Default)

Totals: None (Default)

As you can see, you can use the default definitions for most of the items. This will save you a lot of time when you have a several columns to define.

▶▶ *Writing a Selection Formula*

Which documents in the database should a view include (and, therefore, exclude)? Remember that you can design many views for a database, each presenting the contents of the database differently. Moreover, a given view may only present a subset of documents in the database. This is critical in light of the fact that a typical database will consist of documents composed with a variety of forms, each with unique fields. With such a database, a view that displayed all the documents in the database would look rather messy (for reasons that will be made clear later).

In an earlier discussion, we said that the columns of a view, and the formula associated with each column, dictate which field values will be displayed there for each document. It should be self-evident, then, that there should be consistency between the fields referenced in the column formulas of a view and the fields of a *particular* form (or related forms, such as a main form and its associated response form). If it isn't obvious why this is the case, think about the following scenario.

There exists a database that contains only two documents. Each document was composed using a different form. The design of the forms is such that they do not have any fields in common; that is, the documents consist of unrelated data.

In order to build a view that will display the contents of the database in a meaningful way, and knowing what we do about the structure of a view, the columns would require formulas that reference field names that appear in the design of *different* forms. The result is that a particular column will reference a field that exists in only one of the two documents. (This is acceptable in certain situations but not for this example.)

To ensure that a view will only include documents that meet a specific criteria (and are relevant to the column formulas of the view), we have to make use of a design element known as a *selection formula*. When applied to a view, a selection formula simply narrows the scope of the view to include only a subset of documents in the database, excluding all others. A selection formula expresses the criteria that a document must meet in order to be included in the view. A typical selection formula might be something like the following:

    SELECT Form = "Directory Entry"

With this selection formula, only documents composed with the Directory Entry form will show up in the view. Using the value of the internal Form field is a common practice. It serves to keep like documents together. However, it's frequently the case that we want to make visible, through a view, a document-response hierarchy so that response documents appear with the associated responded-to documents. A slight variation of the selection formula will accommodate this:

SELECT Form = "Directory Entry" | @IsResponseDoc

Now, Directory Entry documents and responses to Directory Entry documents will appear in the view. (@IsResponseDoc is an example of an @function, which are discussed in Chapter 16.) Of course, selection formulas can be more complex, as in the following example:

SELECT (Form = "Directory Entry" & Author = "Jean Luc Picard" & DateCreated > 01/01/94) | @IsResponseDoc

In the above example we are testing the value of three different fields— Form, Author, and DateCreated. For a document to qualify for inclusion in this view requires that *all three* fields exist in the document and that they *all* match the respective specified value (due to the use of the logical operator **&**).

 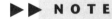 **N O T E**

We include coverage of writing a selection formula in this chapter because it's part of the process of creating a view. However, Chapter 16 provides a thorough discussion of writing formulas and macros.

To create the selection formula for the Corporate Directory view, follow these steps:

1. Display the Corporate Directory view in Design mode.

2. Choose Design ➤ Selection Formula. The Design Selection Formula dialog box appears, as shown in Figure 15.17.

FIGURE 15.17 ▶

The Design Selection Formula dialog box lets you enter a formula that selects the documents you want to display in a particular view.

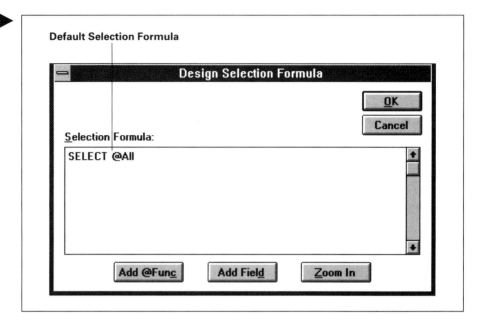

Default Selection Formula

Design Selection Formula

OK

Cancel

Selection Formula:

SELECT @All

Add @Func   Add Field   Zoom In

▶▶ **N O T E**

The default statement SELECT @All would return the selection of *all* documents in a database to appear in a particular view. Such a listing of all the documents wouldn't be practical or useful. If a database used more than one form, and contained hundreds of documents, the view would display all the documents, regardless of their applicability to the view. Users would have to scroll through a seemingly endless listing in order to find the information they wanted. This is why a view's selection formula is useful. You can limit the selection of documents to only those you want displayed in a particular view.

3. Enter the following statement in the Selection Formula box:

SELECT form = "Directory Entry" | form = "Change Request"

4. Click on OK to accept the formula.

The formula selects all the Directory Entry documents and the Change Request documents to appear in the Corporate Directory view. No other documents will appear.

▶ ▶ *Using Form Formulas*

We've characterized a form as a "filter" through which data is entered and displayed. What constitutes a document, in a strict sense, is really an unstructured collection of data (field values) that is maintained separately from the form through which it was created. This is an important point because it makes possible the idea that we can display and edit a document through a form other than the one with which it was originally composed.

When you open a document, what is actually happening? Basically, Notes "plugs in" the field values of the document (currently in an unstructured state) into the fields of a particular form, creating a structured interface to the data which is then displayed on the screen. Notes knows which form to couple with the "raw" field values through the value of either the internal fields FORM or $TITLE (discussed in Chapter 14) or through an alternative method known as *form formulas*.

A form formula is an *optional* component of a view that specifies the form(s) through which documents in the view will be displayed. If no form formula exists for the view, documents are displayed with either the form indicated by their FORM field (usually the form with which they were composed), the form indicated by their $TITLE field (the form stored with the document), or the default form for the database.

▶ *Understanding Form Design*

The key to facilitating this type of "hot-swap" from form to form is in the design of the forms themselves. If the field values of a document are to be filtered through a series of different forms, there must be some consistency in the field definitions across the forms. For example, consider a document composed through Form A. As part of the design of Form A, we've defined several fields, including one named "Last-Name." After composing a document using Form A, we decide to display the document (more accurately, the specific field values in the document) through an alternate form, Form B.

If the value of the LastName field is one of those fields we wish to display, we must define an identical field **LastName** in Form B as well. By no means do you have to define *all* the same fields across the two forms that we're discussing in this example. The power in form formulas lies in the fact that you can selectively "reveal" field values established through one form in another. In the case of Form B, you are also free to add fields to its design that do not appear in Form A.

▶ Creating a Form Formula

As we stated above, form formulas are an optional component of a view and are created as part of the view design. In a typical implementation of form formulas, you first design the "alternate" form (discussed above) and then design a new view that includes a form formula based on the alternate form. An example of a very simple form formula is one that expresses the name of a form in quotation marks, such as the following:

> "Form B"

To create a form formula, follow these steps:

1. Choose Design ➤ Views. The Design Views dialog box appears.

2. Either click on the New button to create a new view, or click on the Edit button to edit an existing view from the list of available views.

3. Once you're in View Design mode, choose Design ➤ Form Formula. The Design Form Formula dialog box appears.

4. Enter a form formula in the text box.

5. Click on OK to accept the formula.

▶ Form Formulas and Selection Formulas

Previously in the chapter, we discussed the use of selection formulas in order to restrict which documents will appear in a view based on some criteria. If the selection formula utilizes the value of the FORM field to determine inclusion in the view, you must account for this when implementing form formulas. For instance, if you've composed a document using Form A and want to display that document in a view whose form formula is "**Form B**", the selection formula for the view would be

SELECT Form = "Form A". This ensures that documents composed with Form A will appear in the view, though they will be *displayed* through Form B.

▶ Some Rules Regarding Form Formulas

There are a few rules regarding usage of form formulas that you should be aware of when implementing them:

- If you modify a form formula, you must "reinitialize" the view after saving it in order for the modification to take affect. This is accomplished by either switching to another view and then switching back, or closing the database and reopening it.

- Documents in which a form is stored are not affected by form formulas—they will always display using the stored form. (You can refer to the section called "Store Form in Documents" in Chapter 14.)

- If you open and *modify* a document from a view with a form formula, the value of the internal FORM field for that document will be set to the form expressed in the form formula. This has implications in views where the selection formula is based on the value of FORM.

▶▶ Saving a View

Although you may have clicked on OK in different dialog boxes to accept changes you made to different elements in a view, you still need to save the view before closing it and returning to the Workspace or another open window. When you want to save the changes you made to a view, press Ctrl+S. If you press Esc before you save the changes, a message box will appear, asking you if you want to save your changes. Click on Yes. You'll return to the Workspace or another window that may be open.

►► *Editing a View*

The next time you want to edit a database's view, select the database's icon in the Workspace. Then choose Design ➤ Views. The Design Views dialog box will appear. Select the view you want to edit by either double-clicking on the view's name or highlighting it and then clicking on the Edit button. The view window will open.

When you want to edit a column, either double-click on the column heading or click on the column heading to select it and then choose Design ➤ Column Definition. The Design Column Definition dialog box will appear. Make the desired changes and then click on OK to accept the changes. When you return to the view window, press F9 to refresh the view and to see if the changes you made have taken affect. Press Ctrl+S to save the view.

►► *Creating Another View in the Same Database*

A Notes database will probably include more than one view, and for good reason: Each view can display documents in a unique way. The needs of the people using the database will vary; therefore, a particular view can list documents in a way that responds to the specific needs of members of a workgroup. In the following sections, you'll need to repeat the above steps in order to define the Locations view in the Corporate Directory database. You can assume that the default options apply unless indicated otherwise.

►► *Defining the Locations View*

The Locations view shows an alphabetical listing of work sites by city. To create the view, follow these steps:

1. Select the Training Facilities database in the Workspace.
2. Choose Design ➤ Views. The Design Views dialog box appears.

    3. Click on the New button, which allows you to create a view from scratch. A blank view window appears in Design mode.

▶ Defining the View's Attributes

To define the view's attributes, follow these steps:

    1. While in View Design mode, choose Design ➤ View Attributes. The Design View Attributes dialog box appears.

    2. Enter **Locations** in the Name text box.

    3. Select the Shared View option if it's not selected. (It's the default.)

    4. Click on the Categories button to specify that categories in the view will be fully expanded.

    5. Click on OK to accept the changes.

▶ Defining the Selection Formula

To ensure that the view will only include documents that meet a specific criteria, you have to make use of a selection formula. When applied to a view, a selection formula simply narrows the scope of the view to include only a subset of documents in the database, excluding all others. A selection formula expresses the criteria that a document must meet in order to be included in the view.

When you choose Design ➤ Selection Formula, the Design Selection Formula dialog box appears. As you can see, the statement **SELECT @All** appears in the Selection Formula box. This is the default selection formula. It returns the selection of *all* documents in a database to appear in a particular view. For the Locations view, enter the statement **SELECT From: "Location Entry"** (including the quotation marks) in the Formula box. This formula displays values that appear only in the Location Entry documents. Click on OK to accept the formula and to close the dialog box.

▶ *Defining the Columns*

For the Locations view, you are going to define seven columns. To define the first column, follow these steps:

1. Double-click on the leftmost column. The Design Column Definition dialog box appears.

  T I P

Double-click on a column heading (the box at top of the column) to display the Design Column Definition dialog box.

2. Enter **Location** in the Title text box blank.

3. Enter the statement **Location** in the Formula box.

4. Enter **10** in the Column Width box.

5. Click on the Sorting button. The Design Column Sort dialog box appears.

6. Select the Ascending option.

7. Click on OK confirm.

8. Click on the Font button. The Font dialog box appears.

9. Select Helv, 10, Bold.

10. Click on OK to accept your choices and the default settings.

To define the other columns in the Locations view, follow these steps:

1. For the second column, enter the following definitions:

> **Title**: Address
> **Formula**: Address
> **Width**: 20
> **List Separator**: Comma
> **Number**: General (Default)
> **Font**: Helv, 10, Bold

Justification: Left

Totals: None (Default)

2. For the third column, enter the following definitions:

Title: City

Formula: City

Width: 10

Number: General

List Separator: Comma

Sorting: None

Font: Helv, 10, Bold

Justification: Left

Totals: None (Default)

3. For the fourth column, enter the following definitions:

Title: State

Formula: State

Width: 4

List Separator: Comma

Number: General (Default)

Sorting: None

Font: Helv, 10, Bold

Justification: Left

Totals: None (Default)

4. For the fifth column, enter the following definitions:

Title: Zip Code

Formula: ZipCode

Width: 10

List Separator: Comma

Number: General

Sorting: None

Font: Helv, 10, Bold

Justification: Left

Totals: None (Default)

5. For the sixth column, enter the following definitions:

Title: Phone #

Formula: @If(AreaCode_P != ""; "(" + AreaCode_P +")" + Exchange_P + "-" + ID_P; "N/A")

Width: 10

List Separator: Comma

Number: General (Default)

Sorting: None

Font: Helv, 10, Bold

Justification: Left

Totals: None (Default)

6. For the seventh column, enter the following definitions:

Title: Fax #

Formula: @If(AreaCode_F != ""; "(" + AreaCode_F +")" + Exchange_F + "-" + ID_F; "N/A")

Width: 10

List Separator: Comma

Number: General

Sorting: None

Font: Helv, 10, Bold

Justification: Left

Totals: None (Default)

7. Press Ctrl+S to save the view.

►► Using Views as "Lookup Tables"

The utility of a view doesn't end at simply being a "table of contents" to the database. A view can also serve another very useful purpose: as a lookup table that can be integrated into the design of a form.

Consider a typical keywords field in a form. The "allowable keywords" are usually a list of text items that you specify in the Design Keyword Format dialog box. However, you can automatically build a list of allowable keywords by specifying a *formula* that returns the contents of a *column* from one of your views.

▶ Modifying the Directory Entry Form

You'll recall that at the end of Chapter 14 you created the Location Entry form that allows a user to enter the locations of the organization's regional offices. Now that you've created the new Locations view that displays the Location Entry documents that users compose, the view can be used as a source of choices contained in the Location field of the Directory Entry form.

Currently, the Location field in the form is simply an Editable field that users will have to fill in manually. By redefining it as a Keywords field, a user can just choose from a list of locations that have been identified as allowable keywords (similar to the Dept field in the Directory Entry form). However, "hard coding" a list of locations forces you, as the database designer, to change the form every time a new office is opened or an existing office is closed. What you (and users) are looking for is a more flexible, dynamic approach to keeping the list of locations in the (now) Keywords field current. This is where using a "lookup" of the contents of a view comes into play.

To redefine the Location field, select the Corporate Directory database and choose Design ▶ Forms. Double-click the Directory Entry form to open it in Edit mode. Then follow these steps:

1. Double-click the Location field. The Field Definition dialog box appears.

2. Change the data type from Text to **Keywords**.

3. Click on the Format button. The Design Keyword Format dialog box appears, as shown in Figure 15.18.

4. Enter the statement **@DbColumn**(""; ""; **"Locations"**; 1) in the Allowable Keywords text box.

5. Select the Formula option.

6. Click on OK to confirm the changes and to close the dialog box.

7. Click on OK again.

8. Press Ctrl+S to save the changes you've made to the form.

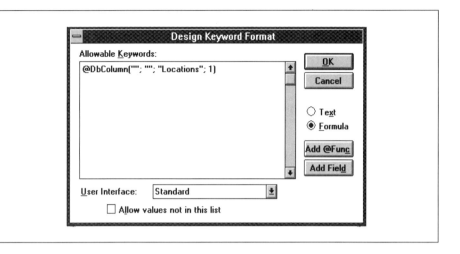

First, notice that the Formula radio button has been selected; this is essential if the allowable keywords will be derived from a formula. By using the @DbColumn function, you instruct Notes to return the contents of column 1 from the Locations view, which is the Location column. Now, any time the Locations view changes—such as when an entry is added or removed—the list of keywords that are displayed through the Location field in a Directory Entry document will automatically reflect the change!

▶▶ *What's Next?*

A view serves as a table of contents for a Notes database, displaying a list of stored documents and providing users with the means to read, edit, and/or delete those documents. A database may have several views, with each one displaying the contents (though not necessarily the entire contents) of the database in a different way. For example, one view might list *all* the documents in the database, while another view lists only a subset of documents in the database based on a specific selection criteria.

To ensure that a view will only include documents that meet a specific criteria, we have to make use of a design element known as a selection formula. When applied to a view, a selection formula simply narrows the scope of the view to include only a subset of documents in a Notes database, excluding all others. In the next chapter, we discuss writing formulas and macros in greater detail. By using formulas and macros in the design of your Notes databases, you can help users to automate tasks and to execute instructions quickly.

► ► **CHAPTER 16**

Writing Formulas and Macros

—

►► *F*AST *T*RACK

▶ **To create a filter macro** 469

choose the database for which to create the macro. Choose Design ➤ Macros. The Design Macros dialog box appears. Click on the New button. The Design New Macro dialog box appears. Fill in the Name text box with the name of the macro. By default, the *Include in 'Tools Run Macros' menu* option is selected. Select one of the *Run* options. Next, select one of *Operation* options. Then select one of the *Run macro on* options. Finally, click on the Formula button and enter the macro formula in the Edit Macro Formula dialog box. When you're finished, click on OK to accept the macro formula. Click on OK again to save the macro definitions.

▶ **To run a filter macro** 472

select a view in the database of your choice. Mark the documents to want the macro to act on. Choose Tools ➤ Run Macros ➤ [*Name of macro*]. At this point, the macro will begin to process all documents in the view, selecting and modifying only those that you marked.

▶ **To create a button** 477

choose Design ➤ Forms and select a form to edit. Once in Form Design mode, position the cursor where you wish to create the button. Choose Edit ➤ Insert ➤ Button. The Insert Button dialog box appears. Enter a label to appear on the button in the Button Text box. Enter the macro formula in the Formula text box. Click on OK to save the button. The button will appear on your form.

Formulas and macros play a significant role in virtually all Notes applications, and are indispensable in bringing functionality, user-friendliness, and automation to your databases. You won't go very far in Notes application development without a good understanding of formulas and macros. In this chapter, we show you how to use formulas in a database. Along the way, we also discuss:

- Defining formulas for different field types
- Using @functions
- Using variables, constants, and operators
- Creating macros

►► *Using Formulas*

To say that formulas are an integral part of a Notes database is an understatement. Certainly in all the major design elements—forms, views, macros—formulas play a significant role. Formulas are the "active ingredient" in Notes; a thorough understanding of them is mandatory if you wish to be a successful Notes application developer.

Let's face it, it's relatively easy to create a simple Notes database—one form, one view, with minimal formulas in each. However, to really bring your application to life, you can add a little bit more pizzazz to it by using formulas. Of course, there are so many possibilities when it comes to creating and using formulas that we can't possibly cover them all. The object of this chapter is to give you a firm foundation in the basics of formulas, including some practical, everyday uses. You should be able to apply the principles you learn here to developing more sophisticated formulas.

Before we go any further let's define "formula." This turns out to be a little tougher than you might think, because there are several aspects to a formula. For the moment we'll propose a definition in terms of what a formula *does*: a formula is something (yet to be described) that performs an action which yields a result. Yes, this definition leaves a lot of room for interpretation, but given the diversity of circumstances where formulas can be applied, it's appropriate. For example, consider the following events that might occur in a Notes application:

- A lowercase word is converted to uppercase.

- A number is multiplied by another to produce a new value.

- A value is checked to see if it is a valid time-date.

In each of the preceding examples, we see an *action*—conversion, multiplication, validity-check—which produces some kind of *result*—an uppercase word, a numeric value, "TRUE" or "FALSE." In Notes, we can implement formulas to handle each of these events. However, formulas do not stand by themselves; they must always be associated with some design element—a field, a column, a button, and so on—and it is only through these design elements that a formula is "activated."

►► *Understanding the Elements of a Formula*

Next, let's describe a formula in terms of what it looks like and how it works. To the eye, a formula is a statement made up of specific component parts. We can classify each component part very precisely. A formula may be very simple or very complex, depending on the needs of the application. Some formulas consist of a single statement, while others consist of multiple statements. In any event, a formula really amounts to a set of instructions to be carried out relative to the design element where the formula is found.

Technically, we say that a formula is *evaluated*, which is a fancy way of saying that each of the instructions in the formula gets executed, and gets executed in a precise order. (How Notes evaluates a formula is itself an important topic that will be covered in detail later in the chapter.)

As an example, we'll start with a very simple formula:

    a + b

The formula's not very exciting, but it will illustrate a few of the possible components of a formula. First, we have the terms *a* and *b*, both of which have an assigned value. Second, there is the operator "+" that expresses a relationship between *a* and *b*, namely that they are to be added together to produce a new value. The evaluation of this formula would simply be "take the value represented by the term *a* and add it to the value represented by the term *b*." The exact values of *a* and *b* are not important—it's the fact that we are adding them together to produce a new value that matters.

► Using Variables

The most common element that you find in Notes formulas is the variable. (The concept of the "variable" is consistent across virtually all programming languages.) A variable is simply a term in a formula that represents a value. The terms *a* and *b* in previous example are variables. As the word *variable* implies, the represented values can change over time. In Notes, fields are an obvious example of variables—a field is representative of a value that may change at any time. For example, let's look at a Directory Entry document from the Corporate Directory database, as shown in Figure 16.1. The value of the *Dept* field may currently be "Accounting" but may be changed to "Executive" in the future.

In Notes formulas, we make reference to the current value of a field by the field's name. Take, for example, the *LastName* field that also appears on the Directory Entry document. The field's input translation formula appears this way:

    @ProperCase(LastName)

We make reference to the current value of the field, whatever it might be, and apply proper-case capitalization to it. Using field names as arguments to @functions, as in the above example, is a very common practice.

In the *a + b* example, we saw that you can use field names in conjunction with an operator to produce a new value. (If this was the formula for a field, the result of the "a + b" operation would be returned in the field where the formula was located.) While you're certainly familiar

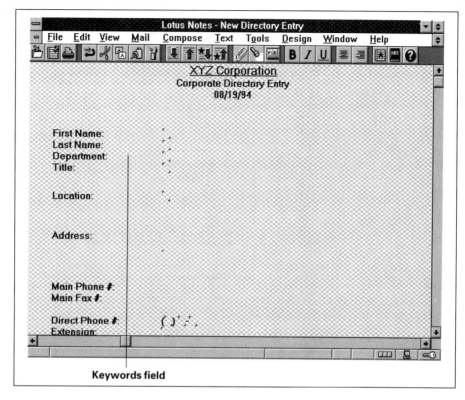

Keywords field

with mathematical operations involving numeric values, there are cases where you may use text values as well. For example, the formula

"(" + AreaCode_P + ") " + Exchange_P + "-" + ID_P

combines a series of text constants (those items in quotation marks) with text values that are represented by field names to produce a formatted phone number. When used in this context, all of the terms must be the same type; that is, they must all be either numeric or text—mixing numeric and text values will produce an error.

In forms which implement inheritance, you often see field formulas which consist of a single field name. For instance, in the Change Request form that's shown in Figure 16.2, the default value formula of the LastName field is itself LastName, indicating that the value of the LastName field in the *parent document* (based on the Directory Entry form) will be inherited by the LastName field in the Change Request document.

FIGURE 16.2 ▶

The default value formula of a field may use the same name, indicating that the value of the field in one document will be inherited by a field of the same name in another document.

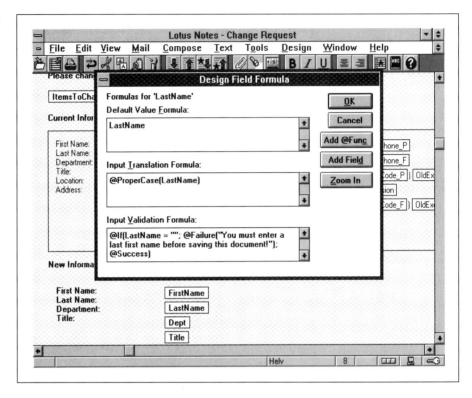

▶ *Using Temporary Fields*

In many cases you will want to declare *temporary fields* in your formulas. Being "temporary," this type of field only exists while the formula is being evaluated, after which it is discarded. (In programming terms, a temporary field is like a local variable in a function; its scope is confined to that function only.) Temporary fields are useful when you want to momentarily store ("buffer") the current value of a form field or if you simply want to make your formulas more readable. Compare the readability of the following formula:

```
@If(@IsNewDoc; "New Directory Entry"; "Entry for " +
FirstName + " " + LastName)
```

with this formula:

```
Name := FirstName + " " + LastName;
@If(@IsNewDoc; "New Directory Entry"; "Entry for " + Name)
```

In the second formula, the temporary field *Name* is assigned a value which is then referenced in the @If statement, making it easier to read. While the difference in readability between the two examples above might not be earth-shattering, you can imagine how effective temporary variables could be in more complex formulas.

 ►► **T I P**

> **If you use temporary variables in your formulas, give the variables names which will be meaningful to someone else reading the formula, while keeping the length of the name as short as possible to avoid typos. (Remember, you're going to be referencing the variable name elsewhere in the formula.) Cryptic names like "x" or "y" will not convey the meaning of the temporary variable.**

► Using Constants

A constant is simply a *hard-coded* value, as opposed to a value, which is *represented* by a variable. A constant is treated as a literal value and is taken exactly as it appears. There are three types of constants available in Notes:

- Text strings
- Numbers
- Time-date values

A *text string* is any set of characters enclosed in quotation marks (""). There are a couple characters, " and \, that require special attention if you wish to display them *as-is* in a text string. In both cases, you must immediately precede these symbols with a backslash (\), which is sometimes referred to as an "escape" character. For example:

    "\"Hello world"\"

produces "Hello world" with the quotation marks included.

    "\\Hello world\\"

produces \Hello world\. You'll recall that the \ symbol is also used in cascaded form names and view names. The selection formula

SELECT Form = "Main Forms\Directory Entry"

will produce an error because Notes will interpret the \ as an escape character and remove it from the text string. To correct this, enter the selection formula as

SELECT Form = "Main Forms\\Directory Entry"

▶▶ **TIP**

Remember to always use the double-slash convention in formulas which involve hierarchical form names, view names, and macro names. Certain formulas may also require the use of DOS-type directory paths, i.e., C:\NOTES\MYDB.NSF. In this case you must use the double-slash convention as well, i.e., C:\\NOTES\\MYDB.NSF, or the path will not be correctly interpreted.

Numbers are any numeric value made of the numerals 0 through 9 and the symbols -, + , E, and e.

Time-date values are any characters that represent a valid time-date and are enclosed in square brackets ([ ]). Depending on how the date separator has been configured for the workstation operating system (Windows 3.1 configures this through the International applet in the Control Panel), the validity of a date value will be determined. If the separator is set to "/", the constant **[11/01/94]** is valid whereas **[11-01-94]** is not.

▶ Using Operators

In broad terms, an operator is a symbol that lets you express an action you want Notes to carry out relative to a single value or multiple values. The result of the action is a new value. If you're not accustomed to using operators beyond the "big four"—+, -, *, /—you might not recognize what action is occurring, but it's there nonetheless.

Notes supports a large number of operators that we will classify into six categories. Table 16.1 list them in *order of precedence*, which dictates the order in which Notes performs an operation when faced with multiple operators in a statement.

While virtually everyone is familiar with some of the operators listed in the table, there might be some that are new to you. Let's examine each category more closely.

▶ **TABLE 16.1:** *Notes supports six categories of operators. They are listed here in order of precedence, which dictates the order in which Notes performs an operation when faced with multiple operators in a statement.*

CATEGORY	OPERATOR	DESCRIPTION
List		
Concatenation	:	
Assignment	:=	assignment
Unary	–	negative
	+	positive
Arithmetic	*	multiplication
	**	permuted multiplication
	/	division
	*/	permuted division
	+	addition, concatenation
	*+	permuted addition
	–	subtraction
	*–	permuted subtraction
Comparison	=	equal
	*=	permuted equal
	<>	not equal
	!=	not equal
	=!	not equal

▶ **TABLE 16.1:** *Notes supports six categories of operators. They are listed here in order of precedence, which dictates the order in which Notes performs an operation when faced with multiple operators in a statement. (continued)*

CATEGORY	OPERATOR	DESCRIPTION
	><	not equal
	*<>	permuted not equal
	<	less than
	*<	permuted less than
	>	greater than
	*>	permuted greater than
	<=	less than or equal
	*<=	permuted less than or equal
	>=	greater than or equal
	*>=	permuted greater than or equal
Logical	!	logical NOT
	&	logical AND
	|	logical OR

List Concatenation

The list concatenation operator : is used to express a list of values. While you might typically work with single values in Notes, there are other operators (described later) and several @functions at your disposal that are expressly designed to handle lists of values. For example,

@Elements("New York" : "Boston" : "San Francisco")

returns the value **3** (the number of values in the list).

▶▶ N O T E

Remember that you can define fields in your forms that are assigned *multiple* values. This is true in fields where you have selected Allow Multi-Values in the Field Definition dialog box, as well as Keywords fields which, by definition, may have multiple values. Any field assigned multiple values is technically a *list* unto itself and can be utilized like any "manually" concatenated list (as in the example above).

Assignment

The assignment operator := is used to assign a value to variable. Don't attempt to use the standard equal sign = for assigning values—it will not work.

Unary

The unary operators + and − are used to indicate or change the sign of a numeric value.

Arithmetic

The standard arithmetic operators *, /, +, and − and their permuted equivalents, **, */, *+, and *−, let you perform calculations involving *discrete values* and *lists of values*. While all of these operators are used in conjunction with numeric values, the + and *+ operators can also be used to concatenate (connect) a series of text values to produce a single "string."

When dealing with lists of values in arithmetic or concatenation operations, we proceed from the assumption that we have two lists, let's say List A and List B, each with a fixed number of elements (values). (For simplicity, we'll also assume that the data type for all the elements is the same.) You have the option of performing either *pair-wise* or *permutation* operations on the two lists. In pair-wise operations, each element in List A is matched with its *parallel* element in List B, and they become the terms of the particular calculation, as shown in the following example:

List A		List B		Resulting List
1 : 2 : 3	+	10 : 20 : 30	=	11;22;33

In a permutation operation every element in List A is matched with *every* element in List B. Using the same example, and substituting *+ for +, we see that this type of operation yields a larger result-set:

List A		List B		Resulting List
1 : 2 : 3	*+	10 : 20 : 30	=	11;21;31;12;22;32;13;23;33

In a case where the *number* of elements in each list is different, the last element in the shorter list will be used repeatedly in order to complete the operation with the remaining elements of the longer list. For example:

List A		List B	Resulting List
"A" : "B"	+	"X" : "Y" : "Z"	"AX";"BY";"BZ"

Comparison

There is a wide variety of comparison operators, both standard and permuted, that allow you to perform comparison operations on discrete values and lists of values. The result of a comparison operation is either TRUE or FALSE (represented by internally as the numbers 1 and 0, respectively)—these are known as *boolean values*. Comparison operators are used in Notes applications to test for certain conditions prior to further action being performed, as in @If and SELECT statements.

Logical

The logical operators ! (NOT), & (AND), and | (OR) let you create complex conditions in Notes formulas, which determine whether some further action will be taken. Since they're used in conjunction with comparison operations, the result of a logical operation is also TRUE or FALSE (boolean).

To illustrate the use of logical operators let's take two variables X and Y and assign X the value 20 and Y the value 40. The individual comparison operations

```
X > 10
Y < 50
```

both yield a TRUE value. If we want to create a complex condition using the individual comparison operations above, we have to introduce a logical operator, as in the following example:

```
X > 10 & Y < 50
"TRUE"   "TRUE"
```

In this expression we're testing for two independent conditions. Since the logical operator in this case is "&" (AND), *both* conditions must be TRUE for the expression to be TRUE. The conditions on either side of the logical operator are evaluated on their own to yield a TRUE or FALSE value, and then those values are combined with the logical operator to yield a TRUE or FALSE value for the expression as a whole. This expression yields a TRUE value because X is greater the 10 (a TRUE value) *and* Y is less than 50 (another TRUE value). However, the statement

```
X > 10 | Y < 30
"TRUE"   "FALSE"
```

also yields a TRUE value because our test condition only requires that *either* X is greater than 10 (a TRUE value) *or* Y is less than 30 (a FALSE value). This is due to the fact that we're using the logical operator "|" (OR).

▶ *Changing the Order of Precedence*

To alter the order of precedence, you have to place parentheses around the operations that you want performed first. Consider the following two statements, one in which "natural" precedence exists and the other in which "forced" precedence exists:

```
X := 1 + 2 * 2 + 1        (X is assigned to 6)

X := (1 + 2) * (2 + 1)    (X is assigned to 9)
```

In the first statement, the multiplication operation, 2 * 2, is performed first, and results in a value of 4. The addition operations are then performed in the order in which they appear. The statement 4 + 2 assigns X the value of 6. In the second statement, each addition operation that appears in parentheses, (1 + 2) and then (2 + 1), is performed first, then followed by the multiplication operation. The statement 3 * 3 assigns X the value of 9.

▸▸ *Using @Functions*

Technically, @functions are prepackaged formulas that exist inside other formulas. Notes includes over 100 @functions that perform a variety of actions integral to most Notes applications. As a formula itself, each @function returns a result of some type.

You will find a comprehensive list of @functions, including required syntax, descriptions, and examples, in your Notes documentation. (You can also choose Help ➤ @Function to display a complete list of functions and their syntax.) However, when you enter any type of formula in a dialog box, you can display a complete list of @functions that are available in Notes. Figure 16.3 shows the Paste Function dialog box, from which you can copy any number of functions in the list and then paste them in a formula. Unfortunately, you can only copy and paste one function at a time; you'll have to repeat the routine for each function you choose.

▶ *Understanding @Functions' Syntax*

@functions come in two basic varieties, ones that require arguments and ones that do not. An *argument* is a parameter or value that the @function requires to perform its action. Very often Notes field names (which represent a value) are used as arguments in @functions. You may also use @functions themselves as arguments. The general syntax of an @function that uses arguments is as follows:

@functionname(argument *1*;argument*2*;...;argument*n*)

The arguments to an @function must be enclosed in parentheses (), and each argument must be separated by a semicolon (;). The number of arguments will vary between @functions—some require only one while others require several. The position of arguments is not arbitrary— every argument has its place—and the value of an argument must be

FIGURE 16.3

The Paste Function dialog box appears when you click on the Add @Func button. It displays a complete list of @functions that you can copy and then paste in a formula.

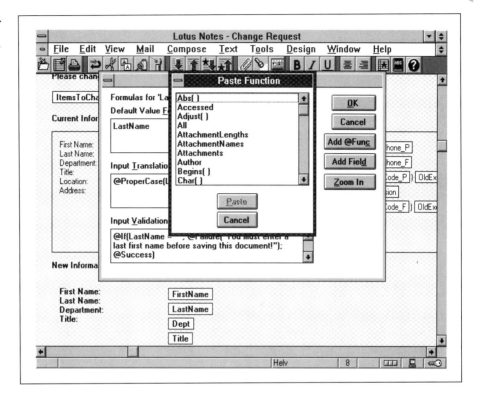

consistent with the explicit syntax of the @function. For example, if an @function specifies that argument*1* must be a text string, supplying any other type of value for that argument (e.g., a number) will result in an error. An @function may be used as an argument to another @function, as long as the "@function-as-argument" yields a result that meets the requirements of the "parent" @function. For @functions that do not require arguments, use the @function name by itself (without parentheses or a semicolon).

▶ *Identifying Types of @Functions*

@functions are broken out into ten different categories, depending on their functionality:

- String
- Mathematical

- Time-Date
- Logical
- View Statistics
- Database and Document Statistics
- List
- Macro
- Lookup
- Miscellaneous

We'll briefly look at the main categories as well as a few other @functions that are used commonly. Many @functions support more than one possible syntax, so refer to your Notes documentation for a complete description.

String @Functions

The string @functions are used in operations related to text strings. The @Text function converts a value to text using the syntax

    @Text(value)

For example, the statement **"Project started on " + @Text(Start-Date)**, where *StartDate* is a time-date value, results in "Project started on 11/1/94."

The @Trim function removes all redundant spaces, including leading and trailing spaces, from a text string using the syntax

    @Trim(string)

For example, the statement **@Trim(" Mastering Lotus   Notes 3.X ")** results in "Mastering Lotus Notes 3.X."

Mathematical @Functions

The mathematical @functions are used in operations related to numeric values. The @Round function rounds a value to the nearest whole number using the syntax

    @Round(number)

For example, the statement **@Round(99.5)** results in 100.

Time-Date @Functions

The time-date @functions are used in operations related to time-date values. The @Created function returns the time-date when a document was created using the syntax

@Created

For example, the statement **@Created** results in 9/1/94 8:45:00. The @Today function returns today's date using the syntax

@Today

For example, the statement **@Today** results in 10/13/94.

Logical @Functions

The logical @functions are used in operations that are related to conditional statements, typically involving the @If function (described below). The @If function is used to test for a particular condition whose TRUE or FALSE value will specifically determine some further action. The function uses the syntax

@If(condition *1*;action *1*;condition*2*;action*2*;...;
condition*99*;action*99*;else_action)

For example, the statement

@If(Revenues < 10000000; "Less than projected"; Revenues >
10000000; "Better than projected"; "Exactly as projected")

results in one of the three text strings (depending on the value of *Revenues*) if this were a formula for a computed text field.

Since @If is such a prominent @function in most Notes applications, let's discuss it in detail. The purpose of any @If statement is to test for a condition and then take action if the condition is met. A condition is said to be "met" if it yields a TRUE value. For this to be the case, the condition must be one of the following:

- A comparison operation
- A logical @function that yields a boolean value (TRUE/FALSE)
- Any of the above, or combination of the above, used in conjunction with the logical operators ! (NOT), & (AND), and | (OR)

You may have up to 99 different conditions/action pairs in an @If statement. In the event that none of the conditions are met, Notes executes the *else_action*, which serves as a "when-all-else-fails" action. If you don't want any specific *else_action* to occur, place "" (NULL) in the *else_action* position. Translating an @If statement into a phrase, we have:

> "If *condition1* is met then perform *action1*, else if *condition2* is met then perform *action2*...else if none of the conditions are met perform *else_action*"

As soon as one of the conditions in the @If statement is met, the corresponding action is performed and no further evaluation of any remaining condition/action pairs occurs; the evaluation of the @If statement ends then and there.

An @If statement may be "nested" in another @If statement as the resulting action of a particular condition. Of course, all the same rules of syntax apply to the nested @If statement. With nested @If statements, you can create very complex (and, if you're not careful, confusing) logic in a formula.

Macro @Functions

The macro @functions, while they may be used in other places, are most often used with macros (discussed later in the chapter) to automate an otherwise manual activity. Unlike most of the other @functions, macro @functions do not yield a result in the traditional sense, but have a "success" or "failure" result associated with them. The @Command function lets you execute Notes menu commands and launch external programs through a formula, using the syntax:

> @Command([command]; parameter; ...)

For example, the statement **@Command([FileOpenDatabase]; "CORPDIR.NSF"; "Corporate Directory")** would result in the opening of the Corporate Directory database in the current Workspace, with the Corporate Directory view displayed. This is equivalent to your manually choosing File ➤ Open Database and selecting Corporate Directory from the list of databases, and then selecting Corporate Directory from the View menu. The Notes *Applications Developers Reference* manual includes a full description of all @Commands available to you.

Lookup @Functions

The Lookup @functions are used to retrieve data from views and documents (either in the current database or another database). You'll recall that in Chapter 15 we introduced the function @DbColumn, which is used to retrieve the contents of a view column as part of a keywords field definition. We redefined the field type of the Location field in the Directory Entry form as *Keywords*, and made use of the @DbColumn function in order to build a list of allowable keywords by retrieving the contents of the first column of the Locations view. Figure 16.4 shows the form.

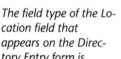

FIGURE 16.4 ▶

The field type of the Location field that appears on the Directory Entry form is Keywords, which uses a @DbColumn function to build a list of allowable keywords.

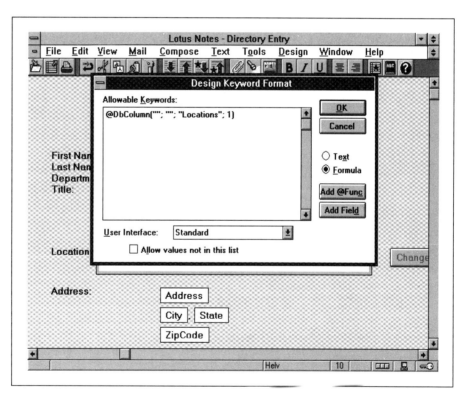

▶ Modifying the Directory Entry Form

Taking this a step further, we will now make use of the value of the Location field as a "key" to the @DbLookup function. Each Location document captures address and telephone/fax number information for that location. We also want to include this same information as part of a Directory Entry document for each employee without having to input it.

As it stands, the field types of the Address, City, State, ZipCode, Main-Num_P and MainNum_F fields on the Directory Entry form are *Editable*. A user has to enter information into them manually. However, since this information is captured elsewhere, this is unnecessary and redundant. If we redefine these fields as *Computed* and use the @DbLookup function in the field formulas (with the value of Location field as the key), we can automatically fill in the values of these fields. For example, the formula of the (now Computed) Address field becomes:

```
@If(Location != ""; @DbLookup(""; ""; "Locations"; Location;
"Address"); "")
```

as shown in Figure 16.5. This formula instructs Notes to search the *Locations view* in the current database, find all documents containing the value of the key field (Location) in the first sorted column of the view (there should only be one), and return the value of the Address field from those documents to our Address field in the Directory Entry document. You can apply this same formula to the remaining fields mentioned above, substituting the respective field names for "Address."

▶▶ Types of Formulas

Think about the design elements you've encountered throughout the book. It should occur to you that in almost every case you find the presence of formulas. You'll recall that at the outset of this chapter we stated that formulas cannot stand by themselves—they are associated with a particular design element. Therefore, when we consider the different types of formulas that Notes supports we classify them in terms of this association.

FIGURE 16.5

The formula for the Address field on the Directory Entry form uses a @DbLookup function to furnish the data for the field. The formulas for the other Computed fields are similar (except for the particular field's name).

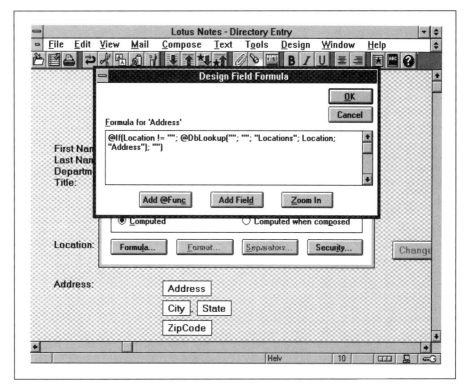

► *Using Field Formulas*

As a general classification, field formulas represent those formulas included in the definition of the fields in your forms. Depending on the type of field in question, either Editable or Computed, both the *number* of formulas and the *behavior* of the formulas associated with the field will vary.

► *Defining Editable Fields*

In the case of an Editable field, there are actually *three* different formulas available to you and you may choose to implement any combination of them (or none of them). Figure 16.6 shows the Design Field Formula dialog box where you enter the formulas.

FIGURE 16.6 ►

The Design Field Formula dialog box lets you enter a Default Value Formula, Input Translation Formula, and Input Validation Formula for a field.

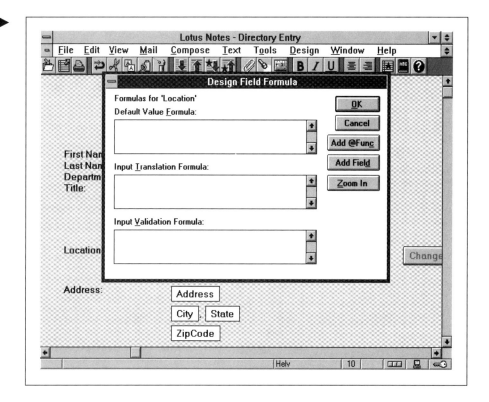

Default Value Formula

The Default Value formula specifies the *initial* value to automatically appear in the field when the form is used to compose a new document. You may override a default value by entering a new value. Default formulas let you provide the user with "likely" field values at the outset of document creation.

Input Translation Formula

The Input Translation formula specifies how the present value of a field will be transformed when the document is refreshed (by either choosing View ► Refresh Fields or pressing F9), or saved by pressing Ctrl+S. For instance, a user may input lowercase text into a field, which is then automatically converted to uppercase by the Input Translation formula.

Input translation is particularly important when you want a uniform format for your fields across documents. It's a good idea to establish standards for input translation *before* you start defining forms and fields. (Applying input translation afterwards can be very time-consuming.) As an example, you might decide upon the following standards:

- All proper names will have proper case capitalization.

- All two-letter state codes will be converted to uppercase.

- All phone numbers will be automatically punctuated ("-", "(", ")").

Once you work out the logic for a particular kind of input translation you can apply it to all similar fields.

Input Validation Formula

The Input Validation formula specifies a "validity-check" that will be applied to the field when the document is refreshed (again by choosing View ➤ Refresh Fields or pressing F9) or saved by pressing Ctrl+S. This can ensure that a value will be accepted or rejected depending on whether or not it meets a specific criterion. In the latter case the value must be corrected before Notes will allow the document to be saved. If an Input Translation formula exists for the field the translation will occur *before* validation, that is, the result of the translation process is "handed to" the validation process.

In the absence of an Input Validation formula, Notes will perform some validation automatically on Editable fields. Specifically, Notes will check that the value supplied in the field corresponds to the data type of the field. For instance, if a field has a data type of Number but a user inputs **ABC**, Notes will display the message that's shown in Figure 16.7 when the document is refreshed or saved.

In the case where an invalid value is supplied in a field with a data type of Time you might see the message that's shown in Figure 16.8.

If you see an error message that is not the result of *your* input validation, it's Notes doing its own validation.

FIGURE 16.7 ►

The error message "Cannot convert text to number" appears when text is entered into a field that has a data type of Number.

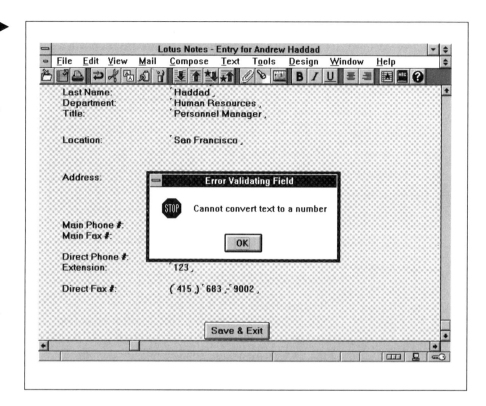

► Defining Computed Fields

Computed, Computed When Composed, and Computed For Display fields have a single formula associated with them. Figure 16.9 shows the Design Field Formula dialog box where you enter a formula for a *Computed*-type field. Unlike the situation with Editable fields, however, the formula is not optional—you must supply a formula as part of the field definition before Notes will let you save the form.

 ►► **N O T E**

You can refer to Chapter 14 for a description of each type of computed field.

FIGURE 16.8 ▶

The "Unable to interpret..." error message appears when an invalid value is entered into a field with a data type of Time.

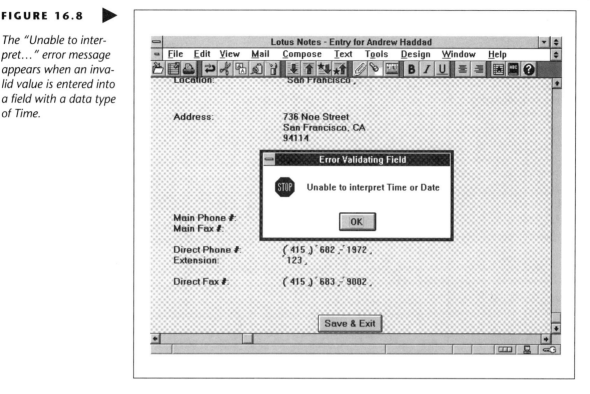

The only difference between the three types of computed fields, as it relates to formulas, is *when* the formula is evaluated:

- Computed field formulas are evaluated when a document is opened, refreshed, saved.

- Computed When Composed field formulas are evaluated when a document is opened only.

- Computed For Display field formulas are evaluated when a document is opened and refreshed (but no value is stored in the document).

▶▶ *Using Keywords Formulas*

With a Keywords field you have the option of building a list of allowable keywords through a formula rather than hard-coding the list. This

FIGURE 16.9 ▶

The Design Field Formula dialog box is where you enter a formula for a Computed-type field.

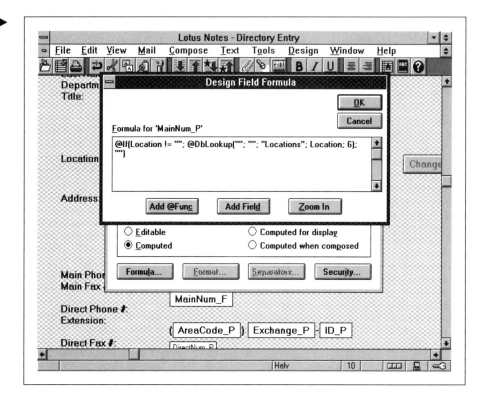

usually involves using the @DbColumn or @DbLookup functions. (You can refer to Chapter 15 for a discussion of using Keywords formulas.)

▶▶ *Understanding Formula Syntax*

A syntax of a formula in Notes is generally described as:

    Statement1;
    Statement2;
    Statement3;

and so on. In a multistatement formula, each statement is separated by a semicolon. (Don't confuse this with the separation of arguments inside an @function, which also involves semicolons.) You may include as many statements as necessary in your formulas, although longer formulas will take more time to evaluate.

For most formulas, Notes demands that the formula contain a "main expression," which is an expression in the formula that will generate some kind of resulting value: text, numeric, boolean, success/failure. For instance, if the field formula for a field named "ABC" is simply:

```
Temp1 := 7
```

which assigns a value of 7 to a temporary field Temp1, Notes will display the formula error message "No main or selection expression in formula" because this formula, as it stands, does nothing to produce a meaningful result.

▶ *Understanding How Notes Evaluates a Formula*

It's important to understand the order in which Notes executes the instructions that make up a formula. Oftentimes, it is this "order-of-execution" issue that causes a formula you've written to behave in unexpected (and undesired) ways.

As a rule, Notes evaluates a formula in top-down fashion—each statement is evaluated in the order in which it is encountered (with all the rules of precedence applied within each statement), from the beginning of the formula to the end.

The @Command "Syndrome"

To every rule there is an exception, and in terms of the top-down evaluation rule, the @Command is it. Regardless of where an @Command statement is encountered in a formula, Notes will always evaluate it last. If there are multiple @Command statements in the formula, Notes will evaluate them last in the order in which they appear.

To clarify this point, let's look at some sample formulas that include @Command statements:

```
@Command([EditDocument]; "1");
@Prompt(...)
```

Here the @Command statement stands by itself as part of a formula and is executed *after* the @Prompt statement.

```
@If(@Prompt(...); @Do(@Command([FileSave]); @Trim(...)); "");
@Prompt(...)
```

Now the @Command statement appears as the first expression in an @Do statement but is executed *after* the second expression @Trim, and *after* the @Prompt statement. The use of the @Command in any place other than as the last action in a formula can result in very unpredictable behavior. Later in the chapter, we'll discuss a technique involving macros whereby you can "fake" Notes into executing @Commands *before* other statements in a formula.

▶▶ *Using Macros*

Macros are self-contained mini-programs that you can implement and use in a variety of ways. The power of macros lies in their ability to automate a series of operations that, if done manually, would take much longer. If there are routine tasks that need to be performed on a database, a smart applications developer will "macro-tize" those tasks.

Macros come in many shapes and sizes. A macro can come in the form of an option in the Tools menu, a button on a form, or a custom SmartIcon. Other types of macros can be *automatically triggered* at specific times or as the result of particular events.

 ▶▶ **N O T E**

You can see how a macro is used to update a 1994 Calendar database in Chapter 23. The macro automatically updates the calendar to 1995.

The types of operations that a macro can perform are endless and depend on the context in which the macro is found:

- At the view level, a macro can perform a "batch" update of several documents in a database based on a specific selection criteria.

- At the document level, a macro (in the form of a button) can make the process of data entry more user-friendly by automating certain tasks.

- As a custom SmartIcon, a macro can perform a series of tasks associated with a particular database or the Workspace as a whole (as we discussed way back in Chapter 3).

- As a background task, a macro can perform a routine operation on a database based on a specific time-schedule.

As you can see, the utility of macros is fairly extensive.

► Types of Macros

Notes supports a variety of macros, each with its own unique characteristics and method of operation:

- Filter macros
- Search macros
- Execute-once macros
- Buttons
- SmartIcons

Filter Macros

As you can imagine, there will be times when you will want to modify the contents of several documents rather than just a single document. For example, you might wish to change the value of the *same* field across a large number of documents. In the case of a single document, you could simply open the document and make the necessary changes. Manually opening and editing a large number of documents, however, is time-consuming and prone to error.

Therefore, a *filter macro* allows you to update any number of documents in a database without the hassle of opening, editing, and saving each one individually—in a sense, a filter macro does this for you. It executes an update operation on a selected range of documents, where the update operation and the range of documents are components of the macro definition. The particular update is applied to each individual document, one after another, until the "cycle" is completed. This behavior is referred to as "iterative operation."

Three different types of filter macros are available in Notes; their differences affect *how* and *when* they are actually executed.

Direct What we're calling a *direct* macro you will see referred to as an "update" or "selection" macro in the Notes documentation. By "direct" we mean that this type of macro can be invoked on demand through the Tools ➤ Run Macros command, as shown in Figure 16.10. The actual action performed by the macro can be an update operation or simply a selection operation.

For example, Figure 16.11 shows several documents have been marked in a view, after which you might perform some further action on them such as a mass deletion. Figure 16.12 shows the same marked documents after the Delete key has been pressed. A trash can icon appears in the markers column to the left of the documents. If a refresh is performed by pressing F9, a message will appear confirming that you indeed want to remove the selected documents from the database. (You

FIGURE 16.10 ►

By choosing the Run Macros command from the Tools menu, a user can invoke a macro.

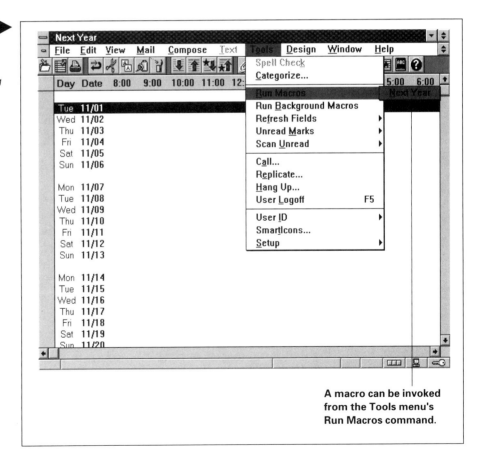

A macro can be invoked
from the Tools menu's
Run Macros command.

FIGURE 16.11

Before a user can invoke a macro to perform some action on several documents at a time, the documents must be selected in a view.

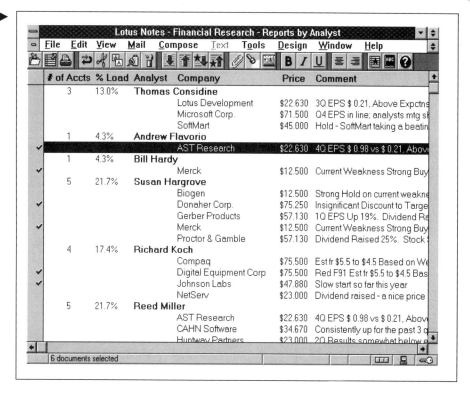

could use an @Command function as part of the macro to automate this step, but only after you're sure your macro works properly!) After the refresh is completed, the documents are permanently removed from the database, and the view looks like Figure 16.13. This type of macro is appropriate for ad hoc operations that need to occur at random times.

Background A background macro performs an unattended update operation on a database by running automatically according to a schedule. Based on that schedule, the macro is activated at specific time intervals without any user intervention required. This type of macro is appropriate for operations that need to be performed on a strict, routine basis on either local or server-based databases.

Mail/Paste A mail/paste macro updates documents as they are either mailed or pasted to a database. In the strict sense of the word, a mail/paste macro is truly a "filter" through which incoming documents are

FIGURE 16.12 ▶

A trash can icon appears in the markers column to the left of the same marked documents after the Delete key has been pressed.

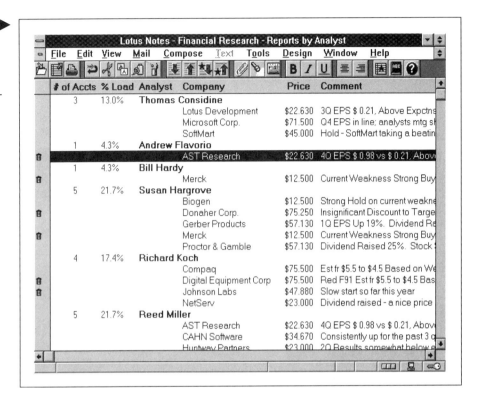

processed. You often find mail/paste macros used in Notes applications involving workflow automation where information is moving from database to database and needs to be transformed in some way as it progresses through the workflow cycle.

Search Macros

Search macros combine Notes' full text search capabilities with a macro formula, resulting in a macro that performs an update operation on documents returned as the result of a search query. Search macros are only applicable for databases that have had a full text index created for them and are created through the Search Bar.

Search macros are a very powerful facility in Notes. For instance, you could create a search macro that looks for specific documents in a large reference or news database and then forwards them to particular users using Notes mail.

FIGURE 16.13 ▶

After the refresh is completed by pressing F9, the documents are permanently removed from the view (and the database).

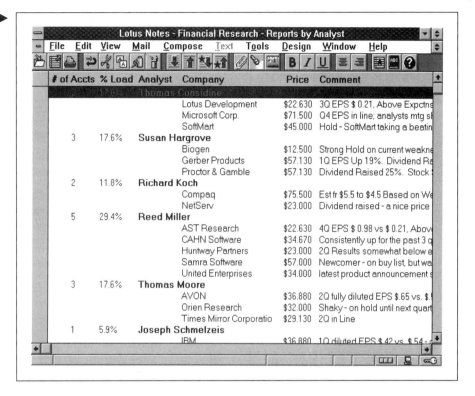

Execute-Once Macros

An execute-once macro performs a sequence of Notes operations on a set of selected documents in a view. While this sounds identical to a filter macro, unlike a filter macro, which repeatedly performs an *update* operation on *each* selected document, an execute-once macro is designed to perform a single task on *all* of the selected documents once.

It's a subtle point, but it's basically a matter of "seeing the forest for the trees"—an execute-once macro sees the selected documents as a single entity and has no iteration capabilities whereby it traverses through the set of documents one at a time, performing the macro operation on each. For this reason, an execute-once macro cannot be used as a means to *update* documents—it's designed to perform non-update related tasks such as batch printing or deleting of documents.

Creating an execute-once macro is similar to creating a filter macro (discussed below) except that you should choose *Execute once* in the Run options drop-down box. At this point, both the Operation and

Run macro on drop-down boxes disappear from the Design New Macro dialog box because neither of these choices are relevant in an execute-once macro; this type of macro cannot update documents or select documents on which to run.

  TIP

> An effective use of execute-once macros is in SmartIcon formulas where you break up a lengthy formula into a sequence of separate execute-once macros, basically creating a number of subroutines. To invoke the execute-once macros use @Command([ToolsRunMacro]; *"macro-name"*) where *"macro-name"* is the name of the macro enclosed in quotation marks.

Buttons

A button is a special kind of macro that is created as part of the design of a form. Also, users themselves can add buttons to rich text fields in documents. Usually buttons perform tasks that are related to the current document and are very effective in adding a degree of user-friendliness to your forms. For instance, an Exit button could be added to the design of a form which, when clicked on, automatically saves and closes the current document. The same operation performed manually would require that the user press the Esc key and then select Yes when prompted to save the document.

SmartIcons

You can program and add your own SmartIcons to a Notes SmartIcon set. Since SmartIcons exist outside the scope of any particular database, they can perform tasks related to the Workspace as well as to a database. Besides the 100+ predefined SmartIcons that come with Notes, there are a number of programmable SmartIcons which you can modify and use for your own purposes. You also have the option of creating SmartIcons from scratch.

▶▶ **N O T E**

We discussed using and customizing SmartIcons in Chapter 3. You can refer to "Creating or Editing Formulas for SmartIcons" for more information on formulas. Creating a SmartIcon from scratch is more involved—you have to create the graphical image that appears on the SmartIcon as well as the formula. In the Windows environment, the graphical image is referred to as a "bitmap" and can be created using the Paintbrush accessory. The easiest way to accomplish this is to use one of .BMP files in \WIN subdirectory of your Notes application directory as a template, making sure to save your image under a new name (File ➤ Save As) so that the original .BMP file remains intact. Be sure to save the new bitmap to the \WIN subdirectory. When you reenter Notes, the SmartIcon you've created should appear in the Tools ➤ SmartIcons dialog box, and it can manipulated just like any other programmable SmartIcon.

▶▶ *Creating a Filter Macro*

The process of creating any of the three types of filter macros is essentially the same, with some slight differences between each type. In the case of a background macro, there might be some additional steps you'll need to take beyond defining the macro. In general, however, just follow these steps:

1. Choose the database for which to create the macro.

2. Choose Design ➤ Macros. The Design Macros dialog box appears, as shown in Figure 16.14.

3. Click on the New button. The Design New Macro dialog box appears, as shown in Figure 16.15.

FIGURE 16.14 ▶

The Design Macros dialog box lets you create a meacro. You can also copy an existing macro from one database and paste it in another database.

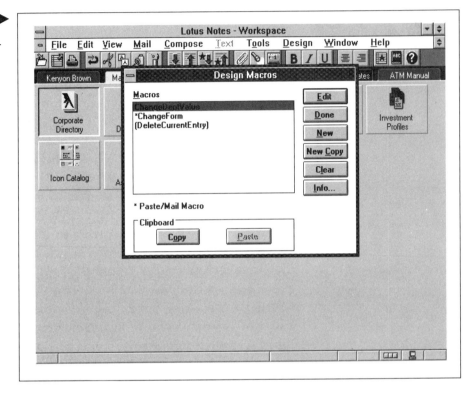

4. Fill in the Name text box with the name of the macro. (You can refer to Chapter 14 for a discussion of naming conventions for synonyms and cascading names.)

5. By default, the *Include in 'Tools Run Macros' menu* option is selected, indicating that the macro will appear when the user chooses Tools ▶ Run Macros. If you don't want the macro to appear here, deselect this option. This is appropriate with macros that will be called by other macros rather than run directly by the user. When you deselect this option, the macro name will appear in the list of macros enclosed in parentheses (which is the standard Notes convention for hidden design elements). If this macro will be called by another macro you must include the parentheses in the macro name. See "Calling a Macro from a Macro," which appears later in the chapter.

FIGURE 16.15

FIGURE 16.15

The Design New Macro dialog box lets you define the new macro, including its name and how it will be run.

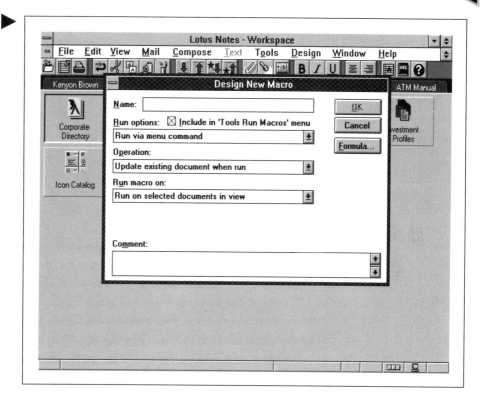

▶▶ TIP

You can choose the New Copy and Paste options if a macro already exists. The New Copy option allows you to create a macro by copying an existing macro in the database. Simply highlight the macro you wish to copy from the list of macros displayed in the dialog box and select New Copy. The Paste option lets you create a macro by pasting a macro from another database into the current database. You must first open the other database, choose Design ➤ Macros, highlight the desired macro in the Design Macros dialog box, and click on Copy. Then choose Design ➤ Macros in the target database and click on Paste. The pasted macro should now appear in the list of macros in the dialog box.

At this point, you need to select one of the *Run* options:

- **Run via menu command**: Select this option if you will run the macro directly from the Tools ➤ Run Macros menu or will call the macro from another macro.

- **Run periodically in background**: Select this option if the macro will run as a background task. You'll notice that additional drop-down boxes are added to the Design New Macro dialog box which allow you to indicate where to run the macro (Server/workstation on which to run) and when to run the macro (Frequency).

 ▸▸ **T I P**

For background macros running on a Notes server, there are no other steps necessary for successful background operation. However, if there are databases stored locally on a workstation, which include background macros, the macros will have to execute on the workstation. Therefore, additional setup is necessary. In the case of Windows workstations, you must load the DOS terminate-and-stay-resident program SHARE.EXE prior to loading Windows and launching Lotus Notes. Once in Notes, choose Tools ➤ Setup ➤ User and select Background Program as a startup option.

- **Run when documents pasted/mailed into database**: Selecting this option results in a mail/paste macro which only runs when documents are either pasted or mailed into the database. The macro operates on pasted/mailed documents only and no others.

- **Execute Once**: Selecting this option is not appropriate for a filter macro. Refer to the discussion above concerning execute-once macros.

Next, you need to select one of the following *Operation* options:

- **Update existing document when run**: This is the standard Operation option associated with filter macros and it indicates that the macro has permission to modify the contents of a document as dictated by the macro formula.

- **Select document when run**: This option is useful for testing the selection formula portion of the macro without actually modifying any documents. With this option selected, the macro will place a check mark next to each document that satisfies the selection criteria but will not modify the contents of the documents in any way. Once you're satisfied that the correct documents are being chosen, you can change the Operation option to "Update existing document when run" or "Create new document when run" so that the macro's update operations are executed.

- **Create new document when run**: This is used for testing and as a means of producing an audit trail of changes to documents. This option makes a copy of each document to be changed and applies the modifications to the *copy*, leaving the original document intact.

Next, select one of the following *Run macro on* options:

- **Run on all documents in database**: The macro will traverse the entire database and process every document each time it is invoked, even those that were previously processed by the macro. Actually, the *Run macro on* option is a bit of a misnomer. What you're really indicating with this option is that a document should be *considered* as a candidate for the macro operation but not necessarily modified. Only those documents that satisfy the selection criteria of the macro formula, specified with a **SELECT** statement (see below), will actually have the macro operation performed on them.

- **Run on documents not yet processed by macro**: This option lets you implement an incremental processing scheme, where only those documents that are new since the last time the macro was invoked qualify to have the macro operation performed on them. For background or mail/paste macros, this is the only option available.

- **Run on documents not yet marked read by you**: This option instructs the macro to run only on unread documents. Since unread documents are always relative to a particular user, the documents selected by the macro will differ across users.

- **Run on all documents in view**: This option is similar to "Run on all documents in database" except that the range of potential documents on which the macro operation will be performed is limited to only those documents in the current view. Needless to say, it's important that you switch to the current view before you run a macro of this type.

- **Run on selected documents in view**: Only selected documents in the current view will be considered for the macro operation. A document is considered "selected" if it is the currently highlighted document in the view or has check mark next to it in the markers column of the view. (You can check a document by highlighting it and then pressing the spacebar or by clicking the markers column next to the document.)

Finally, click on the Formula button and enter the macro formula in the box, as shown in Figure 16.16. When you're finished, click on OK to accept the macro formula and to close the dialog box. Click on OK again to save the macro definitions.

FIGURE 16.16 ►

The Edit Macro Formula dialog box lets you enter a formula for a macro.

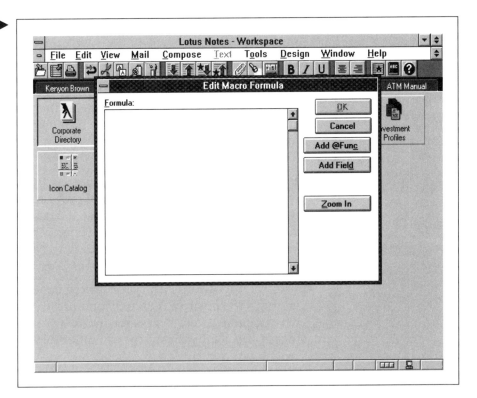

Never run a filter macro on a production database without testing it first! Once you execute a filter macro, the changes that the macro has applied to the selected documents *cannot be undone*. If the macro doesn't execute properly and winds up "damaging" your database (figuratively speaking), your only recourse is to do one of the following:

- Write another macro that attempts to correct what the original macro did. (There's no guarantee that this will work.)

- Delete the database and restore if from a replica or backup copy (if one exists). (Any changes made to the database since the last time it was replicated or backed up will be lost.)

Therefore, make a copy of the database, or at least cut and paste a subset of the documents along with the macro to a "dummy" database, and test the macro there. Only after you're satisfied that the macro is working properly should you use it in the production database.

▶ Writing a Filter Macro for the Corporate Directory Database

Suppose the XYZ Corporation decides to rename the Accounting department to "Accounting and Finance." After changing the design of the Dept field in the Directory Entry form so that "Accounting and Finance" appears in the list of allowable keywords, we're still faced with the fact that there are hundreds of preexisting Directory Entry documents with the old value "Accounting" in the Dept field.

To automate the process of changing "Accounting" to "Accounting and Finance" in each of these documents, we'll create a filter macro with the following parameters:

Name: ChangeDeptValue

Include in 'Tools Run Macros' menu: Selected

Run Options: Run via menu command

Operation: Update existing document when run

Run macro on: Run on all documents in view

Formula:

```
SELECT Dept = "Accounting";
FIELD Dept := "Accounting and Finance"
```

To run this macro, you would switch to the Corporate Directory view and choose Tools ➤ Run Macros ➤ ChangeDeptValue. At this point, the macro would begin to process all documents in the view, selecting

TRICKING NOTES INTO EXECUTING @COMMAND STATEMENTS FIRST

Earlier in the chapter the evaluation of @Commands was discussed, namely, that Notes always evaluates them last regardless of where they appear in a formula. However, if you absolutely need to have an @Command execute before other statements, you'll have to break up the formula into one or more "subroutine macros" *and then invoke the macro(s) through an @Command as well.* In this way, you can essentially "fake" Notes into executing the @Command in question before other statements. For example, if we take the formula:

```
@Command([commandname]; ...);
Next Statement;
Next Statement;
Next Statement;
and so on
```

we know that the @Command statement will be evaluated last. However, we could take the statments following the @Command and put them into a subroutine macro, then rework the formula as follows:

```
@Command([commandname]; ...);
@Command([ToolsRunMacro]; "subroutine macro name")
```

Now, our target @Command is executed first followed by the @Command below (which, in turn, executes the statements therein).

and modifying only those with the value "Accounting" in the Dept field. If another department were renamed in the future, you could simply modify the macro formula to reflect the old department name and the new department name.

▶ *Including the SELECT Statement in Filter Macros*

A SELECT statement that sets forth the criteria that a document must meet in order for the update operation to be performed on it must appear in the formula of a filter macro. While the *Run macro on* option specifies "candidacy" for the operation, the SELECT statement of the macro formula is the ultimate authority as to whether the operation actually will be performed. For instance, the *Run macro on* option of a filter macro might be set to "Run on all documents in view", however, the selection formula

    SELECT ZipCode = "12345"

refines the macro execution to include only those documents with the value "12345" in the ZipCode field. By default, the selection formula for a macro is the all-inclusive SELECT @All, which says that all eligible documents are to have the macro operation performed on them.

▶▶ *Creating a Button*

All in all, including a button in the design of a form is a simple process. Of course, the most important aspect of a button is its *action,* which is a result of the macro formula associated with the button. The aesthetic characteristics of a button also need to be considered—placement, size, color, and so on.

To create a button, perform the following steps:

1. Choose Design ➤ Forms and select a form to edit.
2. Once in Form Design mode, position the cursor where you wish to create the button.
3. Choose Edit ➤ Insert ➤ Button. The Insert Button dialog box appears, as shown in Figure 16.17.

FIGURE 16.17 ▶

The Insert Button dialog box lets you define a button on a form.

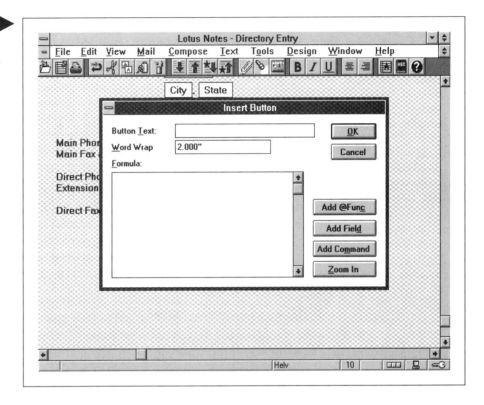

4. Enter a label to appear on the button in the Button Text box. The label should indicate what the button does. Notes will automatically size the button to fit the label.

5. Enter the macro formula in the Formula text box.

6. Click on OK to save the button.

The button will now appear on your form. Once the form is saved, the button will be visible in new and preexisting documents composed with the form.

▶ Adding a Button to the Directory Entry Form

We'll add a very simple button to the Directory Entry form, which will automate the process of saving and closing a Directory Entry document. Select the Corporate Directory database and then follow these steps:

1. Choose Design ➤ Forms and select the Directory Entry form to edit.

2. Move the insertion point to the bottom of the form and press the ↵ key a couple of times to add a few lines.

3. Click on the Text Align Center SmartIcon or choose Text ➤ Alignment ➤ Center to position the cursor in the center of the form.

4. Choose Edit ➤ Insert ➤ Button. The Insert Button dialog box appears.

5. Fill in the Insert Button dialog box as follows:

    Button Text: Save & Exit

    Word Wrap: 2.000

    Formula: @Command([FileSave]); @Command([FileCloseWindow])

6. Click OK to save the button.

7. Press Ctrl+S to save the form.

The new button appears at the bottom of the form, as shown in Figure 16.18.

▶▶ *Creating a Search Macro*

A search macro is similar to a filter macro in terms of functionality, but because it employs the Notes full text search query syntax as a means of selecting documents for the macro operation (as opposed to the SELECT statement in filter macros), a search macro can be enormously more powerful in its scope. Rather than confining the selection criteria to the contents of a particular field, as in a typical filter macro, a search macro gives you this same capability *plus* the added dimension of keyword searching.

FIGURE 16.18 ▶

The new Save & Exit button appears at the bottom of the Directory Entry form. The button automates the process of saving and closing a Directory Entry document.

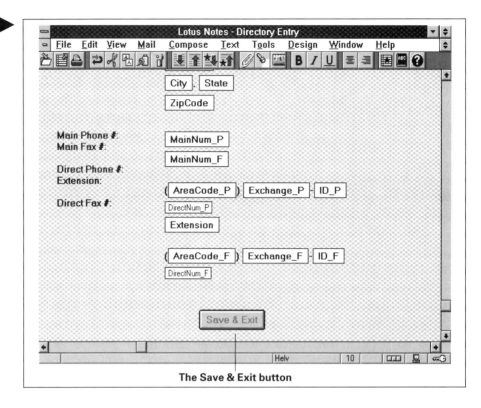

The Save & Exit button

All of the methods and rules related to full text search queries are discussed in Chapter 20. To "attach" a macro operation to a search query, do the following:

1. After building the search query (using any of methods at your disposal), expand the Search Bar by clicking the ▼ symbol.

2. At the left of the expanded Search Bar you'll see the Define Action area, which includes the buttons labeled "Form," "Function," and "Execute." The Form and Function buttons are used to describe the action that will be performed on the set of documents returned by the search query.

3. Click on Form to create an "action by form," whereby you select a form from your database and enter values into the form fields that will replace the current values for those same fields in the returned set of documents. Only forms which have the form attribute "Include in Query by Form" selected will appear in the list of available forms. Click on Done after entering the appropriate values.

A FEW WORDS ON BUTTON LABELS AND WORD WRAP

You may choose not to place a label *on* a button but rather *next to* the button—this is similar to placing a static text label next to a field. A button with no label appears quite small and this turns out to be useful if you need to fit a number of buttons in a small space on your form. Create the button as you normally would, but leave the Button Text box empty. After saving the button, open up a space to the right of the button and type a static text label that indicates what the button does. By controlling the point size of the button and the static text, you'll be able to squeeze several buttons horizontally and vertically into a space smaller than if you had placed labels on the buttons.

Unfortunately, you cannot precisely control the size of labeled button. For instance, if a button label is "OK," Notes will automatically size the button to fit the label. But if you want the OK button to have the same dimensions as a button labeled "Cancel" there is no way to stretch the OK button so that it's the same size as the Cancel button. With the Word Wrap parameter, you can control how a button with a lengthy label gets broken up so that part of the label wraps around to a second line.

4. Click on Function to create an action formula. The Action Formula dialog box appears and you may enter a standard Notes formula. This formula is similar to a filter macro formula, but without a SELECT statement. Click on OK to accept the formula.

5. Click on Execute to activate the search macro.

Just as with filter macros, be sure to test your search macros on a copy of the database before executing them in a production database!

▶▶ *Calling a Macro from a Macro*

When you open a document in Read or Edit mode, you'll notice that the menu option Tools ➤ Run Macros has been grayed out, making the option unavailable. The means that you cannot invoke a macro from the Notes menu while a document is displayed; in effect, macros that are normally available from the menu, when you're at the view level, are disabled when you're at the document level.

A more noteworthy implication is that in this same context (at the document level) a *button formula* cannot invoke a macro either, and for the same reason. For instance, if the formula for a button you've created includes the statement

    @Command([ToolsRunMacro]; "MyMacro")

Notes will not be able execute "MyMacro" when a user clicks on the button because the macro is disabled. However, there is an exception to this rule. You can include other statements in the button formula that force Notes to get around this limitation. In effect, the formula would execute the following actions when the a user clicks the button:

1. Close the document window (storing the button formula in the system's cache).

2. Open the view.

3. Invoke the macro and process the selected documents.

4. Close the view window.

5. Open the document again.

The formula will work. As a rule, however, we suggest that you don't attempt to invoke a macro from a button.

▶▶ *What's Next?*

As you have seen, using formulas can automate many tasks in a Notes database. Formulas play a significant role in the designs of forms, views, and macros. They are the "active ingredient" in Notes and help to bring the applications you create to life. Therefore, as a database designer, you need to give careful consideration to what you want formulas to accomplish.

In the next chapter, we put the finishing touches on the Corporate Directory database that you've created over the course of the previous three chapters. We also discuss the rationale for integrating workflow into a Notes application.

Up to now, we've shied away from providing you with a formal model of the workflow process because we first wanted to take you through the steps of creating a database. Although we've talked a lot about workflow automation throughout the book by defining what workflow is and providing examples of how different organizations have used Notes databases to automate workflow, our discussions have been anecdotal.

You might think that this discussion of workflow comes late in the development process that we've taken you through. You're right. However, the design and functionality of a database will evolve over time as the needs of an organization and the people using the application change.

Now that you've created the Corporate Directory database, we want to look closely at some of the application's components in order to illustrate how workflow can be integrated into its design. In this way, we hope to stress that the database development process is ongoing.

► ► **CHAPTER 17**

Applying Workflow
to a Database

——

▶▶ FAST TRACK

▶ **Notes comes equipped with workflow automation features**   **489**

that are expressly designed to literally replace paper documents with electronic documents; Notes is not a word processor with which you'll wind up producing paper anyway. To fully replace a paper document with an electronic version requires not only the means to create the document but to *move* the document, electronically, through a business environment in the same way a paper document would. This is what Notes workflow automation is all about. By recreating and improving on the "circuit" a document travels, workflow automation brings all of us closer to a paperless environment.

▶ **Notes supports two models of workflow**   **489**

officially known as the *send model* and the *share model*.

▶ **The send model actively routes documents**   **489**

to a one or more recipients (a user and/or a database) using Notes mail. Notifications can be sent to the originator and to those involved in forwarding the document, informing them that the document has reached the next recipient. At any point along the workflow path, other documents may be automatically "triggered" and routed to additional recipients, creating a very sophisticated network of "branch" paths in the workflow.

▶ **The share model relies on the recipient**   **490**

to routinely check for the existence of a document that is intended for their viewing in a shared database. This model is common in applications that involve a response-to scheme, where a user composes a main document, posts the document in the database, and awaits a response (in the form of response document) from the recipient.

▶ *To modify the access control list*   498

of the Corporate Directory database, select the Corporate Directory database in the Workspace. Choose File ➤ Database ➤ Access Control. The Database Access Control List dialog box now appears. Highlight the -Default- entry in the People, Servers, Groups box. Click on Author in the Access Level box. Click on Update. Highlight the current entry in the text box just below the People, Servers, Groups box and press Delete to remove it. Enter **Directory Administrators** in the text box. Select Editor in the Access level box. Click on the Add button. Click on OK to save the access control list.

▶ *To modify the Compose Access list*   509

select the Corporate Directory database in the Workspace. Choose Design ➤ Forms. The Design Forms dialog box appears. Double-click on the Directory Entry form to open it. Once in form design mode, choose Design ➤ Form Attributes. The Design Form Attributes dialog box appears. Click on the Compose Access button. The Compose Access Control List dialog box appears. Click on "Only the following users:" in the "Form may be used by" portion of the dialog box. The Add button and drop-down list below it should now become active. Click on the down-arrow below the Add button. Select Directory Administrators and click on the Add button. The group name should appear in the top portion of the dialog box. Click on OK to save the Compose Access list and to close the dialog box. Click OK to save the form attributes. Press Ctrl+S to save the Directory Entry form.

▶▶ *T*here's a saying in the Notes developers' community: A database is never finished; it evolves…slowly. The design and functionality of a database will evolve over time as the needs of the organization and the people using the application change. The database development process is ongoing. Part of the process involves evaluating the workflow components of the application.

The concept of workflow automation has been discussed sporadically throughout this book. Notes comes with several features that are expressly designed for workflow automation. In this chapter, you'll incorporate workflow automation features into the structure of the Corporate Directory database, modifying its access control, and changing the design of the Change Request form. You'll learn about applying workflow to a Notes application, including:

- Establishing a mail-in database document
- Changing a form's access control
- Adding routing buttons to the Change Request form
- Creating macros in the Corporate Directory database

Towards the end of the chapter we'll apply a few finishing touches to the Corporate Directory application. We'll show you how to add a little sparkle to the final product.

▶▶ *Understanding Workflow Fundamentals*

Everybody has, at some time or another, probably been a participant in the ever-popular game of "paper chase"—filling out forms, sending documents (and then trying to find if they got to where they're supposed to), receiving and forwarding documents, filing documents (and then throwing them away when it comes time to clean up your files).

Notes endeavors, first and foremost, to *literally* replace paper documents with electronic documents; Notes is not a word processor with which you'll wind up producing paper anyway. To fully replace a paper document with an electronic version requires not only the means to create the document but to *move* the document, electronically, through a business environment in the same way a paper document would. This is what Notes workflow automation is all about. By recreating and (hopefully) improving on the circuit a document travels, workflow automation brings all of us closer to a paperless environment. To this end, however, you must first understand the current processes of your business environment (as they relate to workflow automation) and what amount of "re-engineering" will be necessary. Before you put the first field on the first form of your first workflow application, you should have a clear understanding of the interaction between workers, the documents you plan to "electronic-size," security (in regard to sensitive information), and any other issues relevant to workflow. We stressed in an earlier chapter the need to have a blueprint of your application before you start coding. This holds doubly true for workflow applications.

▶ *Working with a Workflow Model*

At this point, you should have a clear understanding of how to create a document in Notes. The next question is "How do I move a document?" To answer that, you have to understand that moving a document is a relative concept—either the document can be "delivered" to a recipient or a recipient can "pick up" the document. Think of it like the postal service: Sometimes a package is delivered to your doorstep; other times you have to go down to the post office and pick it up yourself.

Notes supports both methods or "models" of workflow described above, officially known as the *send model* and the *share model* (which we discussed in Chapter 9, "Communicating with Notes Mail"). In the *send model*, documents are actively routed to a one or more recipients (a user and/or a database) using Notes Mail. Notifications can be sent to the originator and to those involved in forwarding the document, informing them that the document has reached the next recipient.

At any point along the workflow path, other documents may be automatically "triggered" and routed to additional recipients, creating a very sophisticated network of branch paths in the workflow. Applications that are based on the send model are ideal for situations where workflow is initiated on an ad hoc, inconsistent basis, and participants cannot know with certainty when and if thier involvement is needed. This model is also better in situations where time constraints demand that a document be immediately attended to or wherever there is an element of urgency to the workflow.

The *share model* relies on the recipient to routinely check for the existence of a document that is intended for their viewing in a shared database. This model is common in applications that involve a response-to scheme, where a user composes a main document, posts the document in the database, and awaits a response (in the form of response document) from the recipient. The success of an application that is based on the share model depends on the workflow participants faithfully checking the database for new documents. For this reason, it is best suited for applications where workflow is continuous and consistent.

Of course, workflow applications are not restricted to one model of another, and may combine the two into a *hybrid model* using elements of each. Some of the workflow-related features that are found in Notes include:

- Notes e-mail engine, which is the basis for moving information through the workflow process (discussed in Chapters 1 and 9)

- @functions and @commands, which are used specifically in workflow applications (discussed in Chapter 16)

- Form attributes and reserved fields, which you can incorporate into the designs of your forms to make them "mail-enabled" (discussed in Chapters 11 and 14)

▶▶ *Putting Workflow to Work*

When you last left the Corporate Directory database, you had an application that was "response oriented." When a user wishes to notify an administrator that a change to a Directory Entry needs to occur, he or she composes a Change Request document, which appears as a response document—"REQUEST TO CHANGE INFORMATION"—underneath the Directory Entry in question in the Corporate Directory view, as shown in Figure 17.1. An administrator scanning the Corporate Directory sees this response document and performs the following steps:

1. Opens the Change Request document and examines the proposed changes.

2. Closes the Change Request document.

3. Edits the Directory Entry document and applies the changes.

4. Saves and closes the Directory Entry document.

5. Deletes the Change Request document.

This procedure is acceptable if the number of employees is small and the number of change requests is relatively low. However, imagine an organization with thousands of employees where changes in employee status are common. The task of auditing the Corporate Directory on a

FIGURE 17.1 ▶

The Corporate Directory view displays a Change Request document, which appears as a response-type document "REQUEST TO CHANGE INFORMATION" under the Directory Entry document.

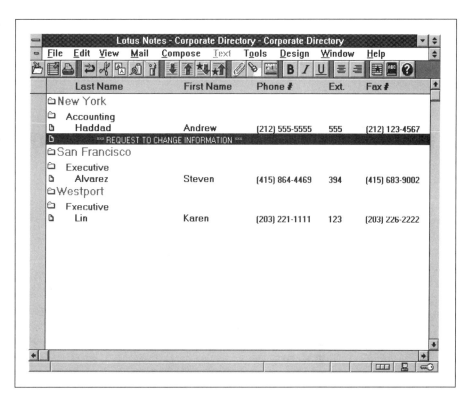

routine basis and picking out change requests would become burdensome. In this context, the method of tracking change requests by visual scan is a weakness in the application. In order to improve the interaction between user and administrator, and to make the application more efficient and easier to use, we will move away from the current response-to scheme and put Notes' workflow automation capabilities to work.

We can characterize the old method of user/administrator interaction as "passive" because the administrator is not notified (in a traditional sense) that a change request is pending, but must discover this by paging through the Corporate Directory view. With the new method, which implements workflow, we are going to make user/administrator interaction "active" by introducing the following elements:

- Change Request documents will now be *routed* to the administrator using Notes Mail.

- The administrator will be able to apply the proposed changes automatically by sending the Change Request document back to the Corporate Directory database, where it will update the original Directory Entry document.

Don't worry if this sounds confusing at the moment—the remainder of the chapter will clearly spell out how this is accomplished.

▸▸ *Redesigning the Change Request Form for Workflow*

The first order of business is to redesign the Change Request form. The form is used as a means to keep the data in the Corporate Directory database current. It provides the workflow component of the application. Inevitably, employees will get promoted; change job titles, departments, or locations; or leave the company entirely. It's important that the database keep pace with these changes and not become outdated. The theory behind the database is that only the database administrator(s) should be allowed to update the directory—if anyone could update the directory at any time, it would very likely lead to gross inaccuracies.

Placing the burden of maintaining the directory solely on the database administrator, however, assumes that the person will always be aware of changes in employee status. While this is feasible in a small company, it's virtually impossible in a large company. Therefore, to assist the database administrator in this effort, we'll make all other users of the directory active participants in its maintenance through the Change Request form.

Any person in the organization can compose a Change Request document and forward it to the person who is responsible for managing the database. A Change Request notifies the database administrator that an entry in the Corporate Directory needs to be updated and indicates exactly what should be changed. However, the database administrator decides whether to approve or deny the request. If a specific request is approved, the information in the corresponding Directory Entry document is updated automatically.

▶ Mail-Enabling the Form

The first and most important step in the redesign process is to mail-enable the Change Request form and the application as a whole. The central theme of the workflow process we wish to implement is *to bring the change request to the administrator rather than forcing the administrator to go and find the change request.* Thus, in order to accomplish this we must give the user the ability to send a Change Request document to an administrator by using the e-mail capabilities of Notes.

The Change Request document will arrive in the mail database of the administrator, where he or she can access it just like any other mail memo. By itself, this type of functionality is an improvement over the old-style response-document method. Now, an administrator does not have to seek out pending change requests documents, but is directly notified of their existence.

To begin, we will make use of certain form attributes that are related to workflow automation:

1. Select the Corporate Directory database in the Workspace.

2. Choose Design ➤ Forms and select the Change Request form to edit.

3. Choose Design ➤ Form Attributes. The Design Form Attributes dialog box appears, as shown in Figure 17.2.

4. Change the form type from Response to Document.

5. Select the following options:

- Store form in documents
- Mail documents when saving

6. Click on OK.

Since we are abandoning the response-to strategy in our application, a form type of document is now appropriate. The Store form in documents option is necessary because we are mailing Change Request documents to another database (the administrator's mail database) where the Change Request form does not exist. If we were to send the document without storing the form within it, the document would not display correctly. (An alternative to storing the form in the document is

FIGURE 17.2 ▶

The Design Form Attributes dialog box lets you choose workflow automation options for a form.

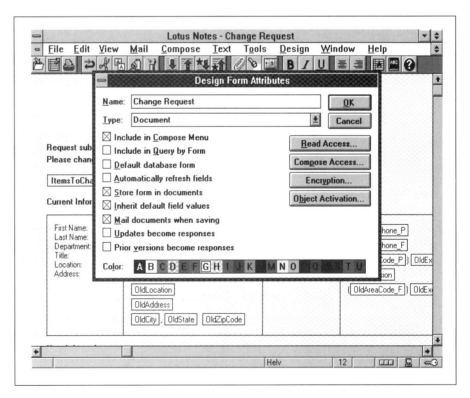

to copy and paste the Change Request form to each administrator's mail database. However, if there several administrators, or if the "administrator role" tends to change hands frequently, this alternative could require too much maintenance to be effective.)

By storing the Change Request form in the document we ensure that the administrator will be able to correctly display the document. The Mail documents when saving option instructs Notes to send the document to a recipient (this will be a directory administrator) when the document is saved. You can refer to Chapter 14 for a detailed discussion on form attributes.

▶ *Establishing a Mail-In Database Document*

The "workflow circuit" that a Change Request document will travel can be divided into two parts:

- **User-to-administrator:** A user originates a Change Request document and sends it to an administrator.

- **Administrator-to-database:** An administrator "posts" the Change Request document to the Corporate Directory database, replacing the original Directory Entry document.

For the first part, the recipient is a *user*; for the second part, the recipient is a *database*. Technically, there is very little difference between the two because a "user" in this context is really a user's mail database. For identification purposes, we know we can make reference to a user's mail database by the person's Notes ID (such as John Smith/XYZ), but how do you refer to an application database as the recipient of a document?

To enable this functionality, you must create a Mail-In Database document in the Public Name & Address Book. The content of the document establishes a "mail-in" name that can be referenced in a routing application (like the Corporate Directory database) and makes an application database "addressable" in the same fashion as a user's mail database, as shown in Figure 17.3.

With a Mail-In Database document in place, you identify the database as a recipient by its mail-in name. At this point, you should consult your Notes Administrator to have a Mail-In Database document created.

FIGURE 17.3 ▶

The content of a Mail-In Database document in the Public Name & Address Book establishes a "mail-in" name that can be referenced in a routing application (like the Corporate Directory database).

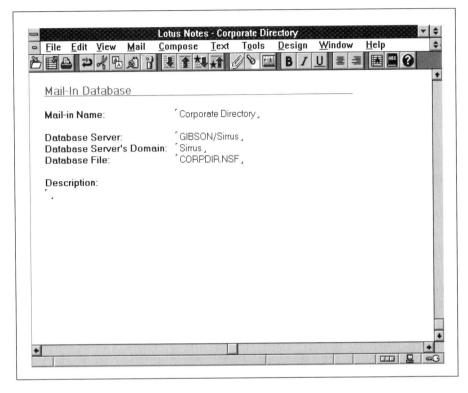

▶▶ *Changing a Database's Access Control*

While a discussion of access control (and database security in general) might seem a bit out of place at this point, the fact is that it does play a role (either directly or indirectly) in workflow. Managing the access control of a database involves identifying the people who will use the database and what tasks they can perform with the database. Earlier, when we mentioned the workflow circuit that a Change Request document will travel, we identified two kinds of recipients of the document: a user (which in this context is really a user's mail database), and the application database itself, which is the Corporate Directory.

When considering how to apply access control and other security measures to the Corporate Directory database, you should first identify the kinds of activities that will occur within the database, and the people who will be performing those activities:

Activities	Person
Adding, modifying, and deleting directory entries	Administrator
Adding, modifying, and deleting location entries	Administrator
Creating change requests	User
Reading directory entries	Everyone
Reading location entries	Everyone

Based on this assessment, the first thing to note is that two distinct groups emerge, each engaging in different activities:

- Administrators
- Everyone else

This fact lends itself to the creation of a new group in the Public Name & Address Book which we will call "Directory Administrators." As the name implies, this group will be made up of Notes users assigned the task of managing the Corporate Directory database. As for "everyone else," we will use the -Default- entry in the access control list of the database.

 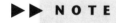 **NOTE**

> **You'll need to see your Notes Administrator to get the Directory Administrators group created.**

Secondly, the different activities that will occur in the database revolve around particular *types* of documents rather than the database as a whole. For instance, both administrators and users need the ability to compose new documents, but the types of documents that you will allow a user to compose is different from those that an administrator will compose.

If you were to assign Author access to everyone and leave it at that, this would allow for document composition. However, by itself, this does nothing to limit "regular" users to a particular type of document, specifically the Change Request document. Moreover, Author access would constrain the administrators to modifying and deleting only those Directory Entry documents and Location Entry documents that they themselves composed. In reality, we want each administrator to be able to manage the entire database, which makes Author access inappropriate for this group.

For now (and with the understanding that some refinement will be necessary), you'll set the access control list for the database as follows:

-Default-	Author
Directory Administrators	Editor

Follow the steps below to modify the access control list of the Corporate Directory database:

1. Select the Corporate Directory database.

2. Choose File ➤ Database ➤ Access Control. The Database Access Control List dialog box now appears, as shown in Figure 17.4.

3. Highlight the -Default- entry in the People, Servers, Groups box .

4. Click on Author in the Access Level box.

5. Click on Update.

6. Highlight the current entry in the text box just below the People, Servers, Groups box and press Delete to remove it.

7. Enter **Directory Administrators** in the text box.

8. Select Editor in the Access level box.

9. Click on the Add button.

10. Click on OK to save the access control list.

FIGURE 17.4

The Database Access Control List dialog box lets you set access control for a database.

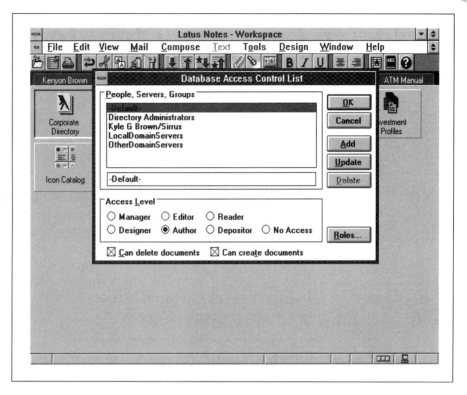

▶▶ NOTE

As a rule, you should assign Manager access to yourself and one other user in the organization (as a safety precaution in case your Notes ID is lost). Also, if the database will be replicated you need to assign the servers involved in the replication cycle appropriate access to the database. You should consult your Notes Administrator.

▶▶ *Adding Routing Buttons to the Change Request Form*

To make the routing of a document as seamless as possible is an important aspect in any workflow application. For our purposes, we need a mechanism to get a Change Request document from the user to the administrator, and from the administrator to the Corporate Directory database.

You've already begun the process of mail-enabling the Change Request form through the selection of specific form attributes. Now you'll complete the process by adding two buttons to the design of the form—one button will be used for routing the change request from the user to the administrator, and the other button from the administrator to database. You could handle both tasks with a single button, but this would make the button formula extremely complex. To keep things simple, you'll create a separate button for each task.

▶ *Creating the Send Change Request Button*

You'll position the buttons at the bottom of the Change Request form, as shown in Figure 17.5. To begin, let's focus on the button that will move the document to the mail database of a chosen administrator.

 ▶▶ **N O T E**

> You can refer to Chapter 16 for more information on using buttons in a database.

To create the Send Change Request button, follow these steps:

1. Select the Corporate Directory database.

2. Choose Design ➤ Forms. The Design Forms dialog box appears.

3. Double-click on the Change Entry form to open it in Design mode.

4. Place the insertion point at the bottom of the form below the last field (refer to Figure 17.5 if you need a guide).

FIGURE 17.5 ▶

You can insert buttons on the Change Request form by editing it in Design mode.

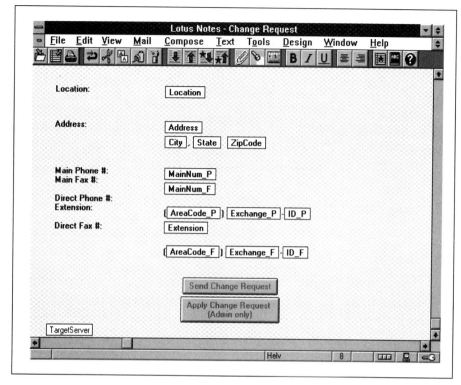

5. Click on the Text Align Center SmartIcon or choose Text ➤ Alignment ➤ Center to position the insertion point in the center of the form.

6. Choose Edit ➤ Insert ➤ Button. The Insert Button dialog box appears.

7. Fill in the following definitions for the button:

> **Button Text:** Send Change Request
>
> **Word Wrap:** 1.6 (although this value can be changed)

In the Formula box, enter the following statements:

```
AdminList := @DbLookup(""; TargetServer : "NAMES.NSF";
"Groups"; "Directory Administrators"; "Members");
Admin := @Prompt([OKCANCELLIST]; "Directory Administrator";
"Please select the name of your Corporate Directory administrator
from the list below."; ""; Adminlist);
FIELD SendTo := Admin;
```

```
FIELD SaveOptions := "0";
FIELD MailOptions := "1";
FIELD Subject := "REQUEST TO CHANGE CORPORATE DIREC-
TORY";
@Command([FileCloseWindow])
```

Click on OK to accept the definitions. The button appears on the form. Press Ctrl+S to save the form.

Let's break down the formula and see how it works. First, the reserved field **SendTo** must have a value assigned to it in order to identify the recipient of the change request. Notes always looks to the value of the SendTo field when a document is to be routed. The SendTo field establishes the "addressees" (there can be more than one) of the document and routing cannot occur without it. Since we're assuming that there is more than one directory administrator in the organization, we want to present the user who's composing the Change Request document with a list of administrators from which they can select the appropriate one. Similarly, the other reserved, mail-related fields **SaveOptions**, **MailOptions,** and **Subject** will have a value assigned to them. This turns out to be quite easy if we "button-drive" the process.

The list of administrators to which a Change Request document may be sent needs to be drawn from some source. For this purpose, we will make use of the same Directory Administrators group in the Public Name & Address Book (NAMES.NSF) that was created for the purpose of access control to the Corporate Directory database. By using @DbLookup, we can retrieve the contents of the multivalue **Members** field (in the Directory Administrators group document) and incorporate it into a list from which users will choose an administrator.

Using @DbLookup, the temporary field **AdminList** is assigned the value of the Members field in our Directory Administrators group document in the Public Name & Address Book. Another temporary field **Admin** is assigned the result of a prompt which displays the value of **AdminList** in an OK-CANCEL list-style prompt box. (See the description of @Prompt in the Notes *Application Developers Reference* manual). Next, the reserved, mail-related fields **SendTo, SaveOptions, MailOptions,** and **Subject** are assigned values.

You'll notice that these fields do not appear in the design of the Change Request form. Rather, they are *internal* fields *in the document* that are created and assigned a value on the fly using the formula keyword FIELD. Understand that these fields are every bit as real as fields "physically instantiated" on the form. In fact, we could have created editable fields on our Change Request form with these names if it was our intention to allow users to specify the values themselves. Since this is not the case (except for the SendTo field), we set their values through the button formula instead. Once created, they remain with the document and maintain their values until they're changed. Fields introduced in this manner in no way affect or change the design of the form.

SendTo is assigned the value of the temporary field **Admin** and identifies the recipient of the change request. The SaveOptions and MailOptions fields can take on a value of either 0 or 1. Setting SaveOptions to 0 instructs Notes not to save the change request in the current database (whereas 1 would force it to be saved) even if a user selects Save in the Document Save dialog box (since it's being routed to user's mail database, this isn't necessary). Setting MailOptions to 1 will ensure that the document is mailed even if the user deselects Mail in the dialog box (whereas 0 would guarantee that the document would not be mailed). The idea in both cases is to override any alternate choice a user might select in the Document Save dialog box.

  N O T E

> The Document Save dialog box is the same dialog box that appears when using, composing, and saving a standard Notes mail memo. You can refer to Chapter 9 for details.

Subject is assigned a text string that appears in the Subject column of the All by... views of a user's mail database. This will flag the administrator that a change request is pending when they scan for new mail. Finally, **@Command([FileCloseWindow])** triggers the routing process by initiating a save of the document—the **Mail document when saving** attribute will kick in and display the Document Save dialog box, after which the document is mailed to the user identified in the SendTo field.

► Creating the Apply Change Request (Admin Only) Button

The Change Request document, having been sent to an administrator, now resides as a document in his or her mail database. From any of the All by... views of the database, the administrator will see the document subject as "REQUEST TO CHANGE CORPORATE DIRECTORY." It's now the job of the administrator to open the document, review the requested changes, and apply the changes.

Actually, rather than updating the original directory entry, the change request will *replace* the original. If you're scratching your head at this point, remember that the Change Request form has all the same fields as a Directory Entry form, and by manipulating the internal FORM field of what was originally a change request document, we can make a change request appear as a directory entry. We'll expand upon how this is accomplished shortly. Refer to Chapter 14 for a discussion of the FORM field.

A second button, positioned below the other, will handle this task. (The logic of the button formula will be nearly identical to that of the first button.) To create the button, repeat the same steps you followed above. Fill in the Insert Button dialog box using these definitions:

Button Text: Apply Change Request (Admin Only)

Word Wrap: 1.6 (although this value can be changed)

In the Formula box, enter the following statements:

```
AdminList := @DbLookup(""; TargetServer : "NAMES.NSF";
"Groups"; "Directory Administrators"; "Members");
@If(!@Member(@Name([Canonicalize]; @UserName); AdminList);
@Do(@Prompt([OK]; "Error Message"; "You are not authorized to
make changes to the Corporate Directory"); @Return("")); "");
FIELD SendTo := "Corporate Directory";
FIELD SaveOptions := "";
FIELD MailOptions := "";
ENVIRONMENT OldFName := OldFName;
ENVIRONMENT OldLName := OldLName;
@Command([FileOpenDatabase]; TargetServer : "CORPDIR.NSF";
"Corporate Directory");
@Command([ToolsRunMacro]; "(DeleteCurrentEntry)");
```

```
@Command([ViewRefreshFields]);
@Command([FileCloseWindow]);
@Command([FileCloseWindow])
```

Click on OK to accept the definitions. The button appears on the form. Press Ctrl+S to save the form. Press Esc to close the form window and to return to the Workspace.

Since this is an "Admin Only" task, the formula first checks to make sure that the user clicking the button is an authorized directory administrator. Using @Member, the formula determines if the current user (returned with @UserName) is listed in the Member field of the Directory Administrators group document. If not, the formula displays an error message and terminates. Otherwise, the formula continues on to assign the mail-in database name "Corporate Directory" to the **SendTo** field, and null values to **SaveOptions** and **MailOptions,** which gives the administrator complete control over saving and mailing the document when it's closed.

The next sequence of commands allows us to delete the existing directory entry in the Corporate Database in order to make room for a new entry. Using the formula keyword ENVIRONMENT, two environment variables, which identify the directory entry to be deleted, are written to the NOTES.INI file (this is a local file on the administrator's workstation), which identify the directory entry to be deleted. These variables will be referenced by a filter macro in the Corporate Directory database named "(DeleteCurrentEntry)." (We'll create this macro in the next section.)

To invoke the macro, we need to open the database to the Corporate Directory view with **@Command([FileOpenDatabase];...)**, call the macro with **@Command([ToolsRunMacro];...)**, and then refresh and close the view with **@Command([ViewRefreshFields])** and **@Command([FileCloseWindow])**. The last two statements return the focus back to the Change Request document; the final statement, **@Command([FileCloseWindow])**, triggers the routing of the document to the Corporate Directory database.

TIP

> Notes has no direct means of passing values between macros. The NOTES.INI file, however, can serve as an intermediary for communicating values between macros. Using the ENVIRONMENT keyword or the @SetEnvironment function in the formula of a macro, you can write values to this file which are then read by the formula of another macro using the @Environment function. Just remember that any value you write to the NOTES.INI file must be text; if you need to write any other type of value you must convert it to text first (see the @Text function in your *Application Developer's Reference*).

▶▶ Creating Macros in the Corporate Directory Database

To finish the development of the Corporate Directory application, you need to define two macros. The first is a filter macro named "DeleteCurrentEntry." This macro is invoked from the Apply Change Request button formula.

▶ Creating the DeleteCurrentEntry Macro

This macro will delete the original Directory Entry document for which the Change Request document was composed. To create the DeleteCurrentEntry macro, follow these steps:

1. Select the Corporate Directory database.
2. Choose Design ➤ Macros. The Design Macros dialog box appears.
3. Click on the New button. The Design New Macro dialog box appears.
4. Enter **DeleteCurrentEntry** in the Name text box.
5. Deselect the "Include in 'Tools Run Macros' menu" option.

6. Choose the Run via menu command option from the Run options drop-down list.

7. Choose the Update existing document when run option from the Operation drop-down list.

8. Choose the Run on all documents in view option from the Run macro on drop-down list.

9. Click on the Formula button.

10. In the Formula box, enter the following statements:

SELECT FirstName = @Environment("OldFName") & LastName = @Environment("OldLName");
@DeleteDocument

11. Click on OK to save the formula and to close the dialog box.

12. Click on OK to save the macro definitions.

After you've saved the macro, you'll notice that the macro name appears in the Design Macros dialog box as "(DeleteCurrentEntry)." The appearance of the parentheses in the name is due to the fact that the Include in 'Tools Run Macros' menu option was deselected, rendering the macro *hidden*. When referencing the macro name in formulas, you must include the parentheses (as we did in the last section).

When this macro is executed at the Corporate Directory view level, it will select all documents where the field **FirstName** is equal to the environment variable **OldFName**, and the field **LastName** is equal to the environment variable **OldLName**. You'll recall that we wrote the variables to the NOTES.INI file. We use the @Environment function here to retrieve them.

When a document is found that matches the selection criteria, it's marked for deletion (not actually deleted), using the **@DeleteDocument** function. The **@Command([ViewRefreshFields])** statement in the button formula will complete the deletion process by prompting the user to delete the document permanently.

▶ Creating the Mail/Paste Macro

You'll recall that we need to manipulate the FORM field of a Change Request document when it's sent to the Corporate Directory database by an administrator. The reason for doing this is to have it appear as a

Directory Entry document. This is accomplished with a mail/paste macro that we discussed in Chapter 16.

Just follow the steps below to create the mail/paste macro:

1. In the Corporate Directory database, choose Design ➤ Macros. The Design Macros dialog box appears.

2. Click on the New button. The Design New Macro dialog box appears.

3. Enter **ChangeForm** in the Name text box.

4. Choose the Run when documents pasted/mailed into database option from the Run Options drop-down list.

5. Choose the Update existing document when run option from the Operation drop-down list.

6. Click on the Formula button.

7. In the Formula box, enter the following statements:

   SELECT $TITLE = "Change Request";
   FIELD Form := "Directory Entry"

8. Click on OK to save the formula.

9. Click on OK to save the macro definition.

Whenever a Change Request document is mailed to the database, the mail/paste macro will change the value of the field FORM from "Change Request" to "Directory Entry." When the document is subsequently opened, it will appear as a Directory Entry document.

▸▸ *Refining Database Security*

Earlier we said that some refinement in database security would be necessary, and so we'll address this issue now. Assigning Author access to -Default- (all Notes users) leaves open the possibility that a regular user will be able to compose Directory Entry and Location Entry documents, which is a right that is reserved for administrators only. To limit their rights so that they can only compose Change Request documents, we have to modify the Compose Access list of both the Directory Entry and the Location Entry forms. (You can refer to Chapter 14 for details on Compose Access.)

Just follow the steps below to modify the Compose Access list:

1. Select the Corporate Directory database.

2. Choose Design ➤ Forms. The Design Forms dialog box appears.

3. Double-click on the Directory Entry form to open it.

4. Once in Form Design mode, choose Design ➤ Form Attributes. The Design Form Attributes dialog box appears.

5. Click on the Compose Access button. The Compose Access Control List dialog box appears, as shown in Figure 17.6.

6. Click on "Only the following users:" in the "Form may be used by" portion of the dialog box. The Add button and drop-down list below it should now become active.

7. Click on the down-arrow below the Add button.

FIGURE 17.6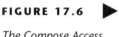

The Compose Access Control List dialog box lets you identify who can compose documents with a form.

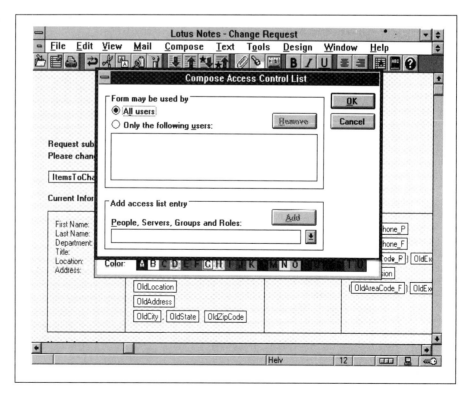

8. Select Directory Administrators and click on the Add button. The group name should appear in the top portion of the dialog box.

9. Click on OK to save the Compose Access Control list and to close the dialog box.

10. Click OK to save the form attributes.

11. Press Ctrl+S to save the Directory Entry form.

Press Esc to close the form and return to the Workspace. You'll need to repeat the above process to change the compose access for the Location Entry form.

With the Compose Access list for these two forms limited to the Directory Administrators group only, the form names won't appear in the Compose menu for regular users, even though the Include in Compose Menu option is selected for these forms in the Design Form Attributes dialog box. The only form name that a regular user will see displayed on the Compose menu is Change Request. Of course, administrators will see all three form names on the menu.

The entries in a Compose Access list, if any, must have at least Author access at the database level (through the ACL) in order for the assignment to have any meaning. *A Compose Access list can only serve to refine rights assigned at the database level, not grant rights that don't exist at the database level first.* For instance, if a particular user only has Reader access at the database level, adding that user to the Compose Access list of a form in the database has no effect; the user doesn't have sufficient rights (Author or above) at the database level to compose a document and the Compose Access list cannot bestow that right. Since we've granted Editor access to the Directory Administrators group, the minimum ACL requirements have been satisfied.

▶▶ *Inserting a Table*

The redesigned Change Request form will now include a table that displays the current information on a person as well as a section that displays the new information. By displaying the current data on the Change Request form, the administrator doesn't have to open the corresponding Directory Entry form to find the information.

You insert a table on a form just as you would objects and buttons. A table allows you to organize a series of fields in cells in a particular way. A *cell* is the intersection of a row and a column, and looks like a cell that you'd find in a spreadsheet. Each cell can contain one or more fields. As you'll recall, the Change Request form currently displays information as shown in Figure 17.7. At this point, you can start redesigning the form, which will look like Figure 17.8. You can use the figure as a reference.

▶ Adding Section Labels

Before you add the table to the form, you should add labels that will identify two distinct sections on the form: Current Information and New Information. (Don't confuse using labels in this way with the *Section* data type, which is a special type of field that defines an area on a form.) To add the fields, follow these steps:

1. Select the Corporate Directory database in the Workspace.

2. Choose Design ➤ Forms. The Design Forms dialog box opens.

3. Double-click on the Change Request form to open it.

4. Once in Design mode, place the insertion point below the ItemsToChange field. (You may need to press ↵ one or two times to add space between the field and the next blank line.)

5. Type the label **Current Information:** and then highlight the text to select it.

6. Press Ctrl+B (or choose Text ➤ Bold) to apply the Bold formatting attribute. (Press Ctrl+B after the colon to make sure the attribute has been turned off.)

7. Press ↵ two times to insert two blank lines.

8. Repeat steps 5 and 6 to add the label **New Information:**.

▶ Creating the Table

To create the table, follow these steps:

1. Position the insertion point between the two labels.

FIGURE 17.7 ▶

The current Change Request form allows you to enter new information, but it doesn't display current information on a person. An administrator would have to open a Directory Entry document to find the information.

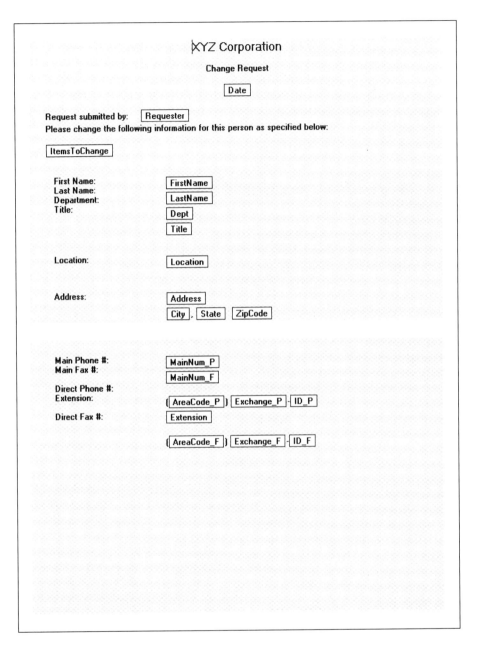

FIGURE 17.8 ▶

The redesigned Change Request form includes a table that will display the current information that's taken from the corresponding Directory Entry form.

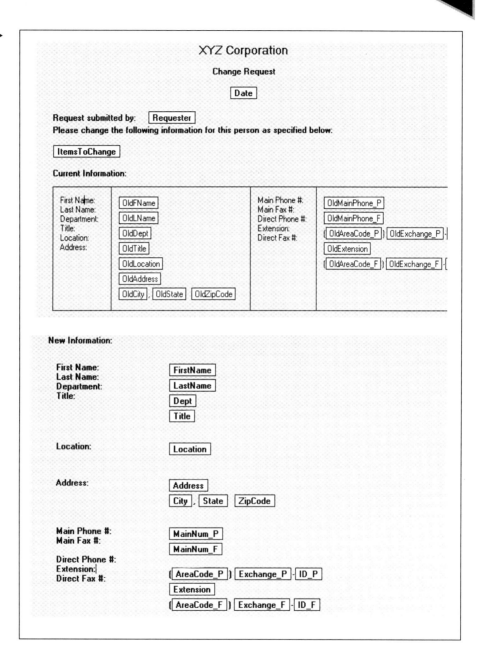

2. Choose Edit ➤ Insert ➤ Table. The Insert Table dialog box appears, as shown in Figure 17.9.

3. Enter **1** in the Number of rows box and **4** in the Number of columns box.

4. In the Cell Borders area, select Single for the Left, Right, Top, and Bottom borders.

5. Click on OK to accept the other default parameters, including Fit to window. The table will appear. It will automatically fit the width of your monitor screen.

As you can see, all of the cells in the table are the same height and width. Unfortunately, Notes doesn't provide you with much in the way of formatting tools. So you'll have to manually tweak the cells in order to change their size.

FIGURE 17.9 ▶

The Insert Table dialog box lets you choose the number of rows and columns you want to appear in a table that you've inserted in a form.

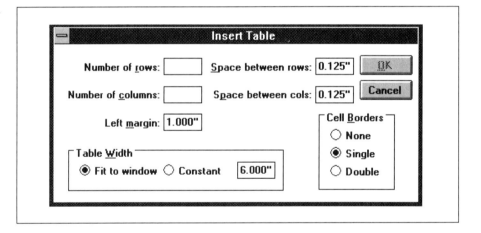

▶ Increasing the Height and Width of Cells in a Table

The only way to increase the height of cells in a table is by pressing ↵ to insert carriage returns. (Every time you press ↵, the cell gets longer.) To make the height of the cells in the row larger, follow these steps:

1. Position the insertion point in the first column.

2. Press ↵ one time to increase the cell's height. All the other cells in the row will change also.

▶ *Formatting the Table*

As you enter labels and insert fields, you will increase the height of the cells more. At this point, you can format the table to suit your purposes. You may want to change the width of the columns, justify the column alignment of the text that appears in the cells, add or delete a row or column, etc.

One way to accomplish these changes is by accessing the Table command that now appears under the Insert command on the Edit menu. First, make sure the cursor is positioned in the column location where you want to make the change(s); if the cursor is positioned outside the table, the Actions command will appear dimmed under the Insert command instead.

To increase the width of each column, follow these steps:

1. With the insertion point in the first column, choose Edit ➤ Table ➤ Format. The Edit Table Format dialog box appears, as shown in Figure 17.10.

FIGURE 17.10 ▶

The Edit Table Format dialog box lets you set the width of each column in a table.

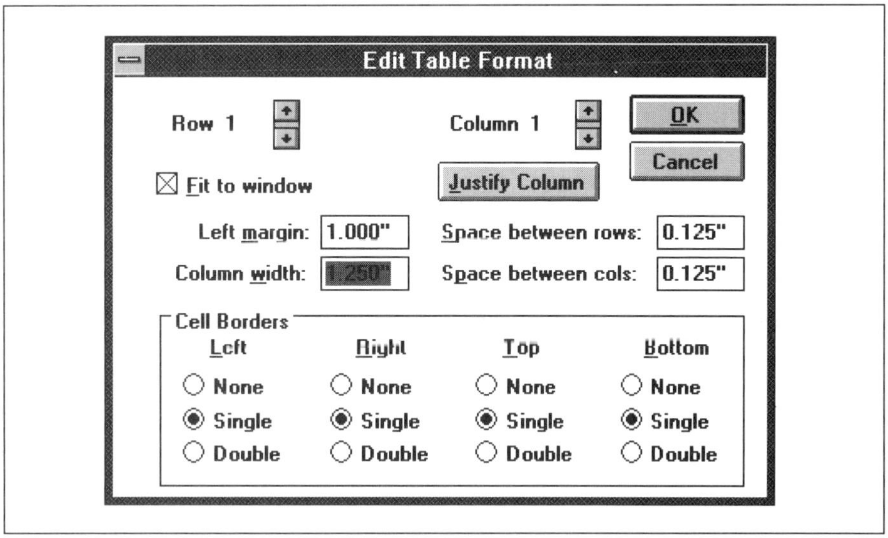

2. Enter **1″** in the Column width box.

3. Deselect the Fit to window option (if the checkbox is selected).

4. Repeat the steps for the other columns, entering the following column widths:

> **Column 2:** 2″
>
> **Column 3:** 1″
>
> **Column 4:** 2.6″

5. Click on OK to accept the changes.

▶ Adding Field Labels

Now you can enter labels in columns 1 and 3 to properly identify the fields. Unfortunately, entering and formatting text in a table can become an arduous task. You can either input all the text at the same time and then format it later, or you can add a label in a column and then format the text immediately.

To add the labels, follow these steps:

1. Position the insertion point in the upper left corner of column 1 and type **First Name:** for the name of the first field. Don't worry about the format or placement of the static text for now.

2. Press ↵ to move the insertion point to the next line.

3. Type **Last Name:** and press ↵ to move to the next line.

4. Repeat the steps to enter the other labels in column 1, using Figure 17.8 as a reference.

5. Move the insertion point to column 3 and repeat the steps to add the remaining labels.

▶ Formatting the Labels

The methods you use to format text on a form are similar to those for formatting text in most other Windows applications. However, as we mentioned earlier, Notes text formatting tools don't offer you the variety or sophistication of features that you'll find in other applications, especially word processors or desktop publishers. In fact, Notes text formatting features are downright crude in comparison. This is ironic since most of your development time will be spent on designing database interfaces that include a lot of formatted text that users will read.

To format the labels in the columns, follow these steps:

1. Highlight First Name and then choose Text ➤ Font (or press Ctrl+K). The Font dialog box appears. As you can see, the default Font Name is Helv (for Helvetica) and the size is 10 point.

2. If you want to change the font, highlight the selection in the Font Name & Size box. If you want to change the point size of the font to another size, enter the size in the drop-down list box or click on the arrow and choose a size.

3. Select the Bold option.

  TIP

If you only need to apply a single formatting attribute to selected text, such as boldface or italics, you can do this faster by highlighting the text and then selecting the specific attribute from the Text menu. Open the menu and then click on the command you want in order to change the format. You can apply an attribute even faster by using keystroke combinations. Highlight the text and then press the appropriate keystroke(s) to make the format change, such as Ctrl+B for bold or Ctrl+I for italic.

4. If you want the text to appear in a color other than black (which is the default), click on a selection in the Color Bar at the bottom of the dialog box.

5. Click on OK to apply the changes.

▶▶ **N O T E**

> **You can automatically align anything that appears in a column of cells by accessing the Edit Table Format dialog box. However, I don't consider this a shortcut because you might need to position text and field items in different locations within the same cell. Therefore, you might as well highlight each item separately in the cell and then change its alignment. If you want the alignment of all the items in a column of cells to appear the same, use the following method. Position the cursor in the desired cell and then choose Edit ➤ Table ➤ Format. In the dialog box, click on the Justify Column button to display the Justify Table Column dialog box. Choose the desired alignment by clicking one of the radio buttons and then clicking on OK to close the dialog box. Click on OK again to apply the changes.**

▶ *Defining the Fields*

Now that you've entered and formatted all the static text, for the labels, you can create and position the fields in the table. As you can see in Figure 17.8, the name of each new field in the table corresponds to a current field name that appears below the table. The values of the new fields on the Change Request form are inherited from the values of the fields that are contained in the Directory Entry form. The fields below the table (under the New Information label) will allow a user to enter new information. The administrator subsequently evaluates the change request.

To add the fields in the table, follow the steps below:

1. Place the insertion point at the top of column 2.

2. Choose Design ➤ New Field. The Design New Field dialog box appears.

3. Click on OK to accept the default option. The Field Definition dialog box appears.

4. Enter the following information (unless already indicated):

> **Name**: OldFName
>
> **Help Definition (optional)**: Enter the current first name of the person.
>
> **Data Type**: Text
>
> **Field Type**: Computed when composed
>
> **Formula**: FirstName

5. Click OK to accept the changes. The field will appear.

If you want to format the field, follow these steps:

1. Highlight the field to select it.

2. Choose Text ➤. The Font dialog box appears.

3. If you want to change the font, highlight the selection in the Font Name & Size box. If you want to change the point size of the font, enter the size in the drop-down list box or click on the arrow and choose a size.

4. Select the Bold option.

5. If you want to change the color of the text that'll appear in the field, select a color from the Color Bar at the bottom of the dialog box.

6. Click on OK to confirm the change. The field's text color changes from black to red.

You'll need to repeat the above steps to create and format the other fields. You can refer to Table 17.1 and Table 17.2 for additional information. Table 17.1 includes a summary of all the field definitions, and Table 17.2 provides a summary of all the field formulas.

▶ Defining the TargetServer Field

The last field you need to add to the redesigned form is the TargetServer field that appears at the bottom (as shown in Figure 17.3). The field identifies the *target server* from where the user will open the Corporate Directory database. The specific server where a database can be located is relative in Notes because a user can open the database from any server where it is stored. Instead of specifying a target server, we've

▶ **TABLE 17.1:** *A summary of labels and field definitions for the Change Request form*

LABEL NAME	FIELD NAME	DATA TYPE	FIELD TYPE
	Date	Time	Computed for display
Request submitted by	Requester	Text	Computed
Please change the following information for this person as specified below	ItemsToChange	Keywords (Check Boxes):	Editable
		Name	
		Department	
		Title	
		Location	
		Phone Number/Extension	
		Fax Number	
Current Information			
First Name	OldFName	Text	Computed when composed
Last Name	OldLName	Text	Computed when composed
Department	OldDept	Keywords (Standard):	Computed when composed
		Accounting	
		Administration	
		Engineering	
		Executive	
		Human Resources	
		Manufacturing	
		Research & Development	
		Sales & Marketing	

TABLE 17.1: *A summary of labels and field definitions for the Change Request form (continued)*

LABEL NAME	FIELD NAME	DATA TYPE	FIELD TYPE
Title	OldTitle	Text	Computed when composed
Location	OldLocation	Text	Computed when composed
Address	OldAddress	Text	Computed when composed
	OldCity	Text	Computed when composed
	OldState	Text	Computed when composed
	OldZipCode	Text	Computed when composed
Main Phone #	OldMainPhone_P	Text	Computed when composed
Main Fax #	OldMainPhone_F	Text	Computed when composed
Direct Phone #	OldAreaCode_P	Text	Computed when composed
	OldExchange_P	Text	Computed when composed
	OldID_P	Text	Computed when composed
Extension	OldExtension	Text	Computed when composed
Direct Fax #	OldAreaCode_F	Text	Computed when composed
	OldExchange_F	Text	Computed when composed
	OldID_F	Text	Computed when composed

▶ **TABLE 17.1:** *A summary of labels and field definitions for the Change Request form (continued)*

LABEL NAME	FIELD NAME	DATA TYPE	FIELD TYPE
New Information			
First Name	FirstName	Text	Editable
Last Name	LastName	Text	Editable
Department	Dept	Keywords (Standard):	Editable
		Accounting	
		Administration	
		Engineering	
		Executive	
		Human Resources	
		Manufacturing	
		Research & Development	
		Sales & Marketing	
Title	Title	Text	Editable
Location	Location	Keywords (Standard):	Editable
Address	Address	Text	Computed
	City	Text	Computed
	State	Text	Computed
	ZipCode	Text	Computed
Main Phone #	MainNum_P	Text	Computed
Main Fax #	MainNum_F	Text	Computed
Direct Phone #	AreaCode_P	Text	Editable
	Exchange_P	Text	Editable
	ID_P	Text	Editable

► **TABLE 17.1:** *A summary of labels and field definitions for the Change Request form (continued)*

LABEL NAME	FIELD NAME	DATA TYPE	FIELD TYPE
Extension	Extension	Text	Editable
Direct Fax #	AreaCode_F	Text	Editable
	Exchange_F	Text	Editable
	ID_F	Text	Editable
	TargetServer	Text	Computed when composed

► **TABLE 17.2:** *A summary of field formulas for the Change Request form*

LABEL NAME	FIELD NAME	FORMULA
	Date	@Created
	Requester	@Name([CN];@UserName)
First Name	OldFName	FirstName
Last Name	OldLName	LastName
Department	OldDept	Dept
Title	OldTitle	Title
Location	OldLocation	Location
Address	OldAddress	Address
	OldCity	City
	OldState	State
	OldZipCodc	ZipCode
Main Phone #	OldMainPhone_P	MainNum_P
Main Fax #	OldMainPhone_F	MainNum_F
Direct Phone #	OldAreaCode_P	AreaCode_P
	OldExchange_P	Exchange_P
	OldID_P	ID_P

▶ **TABLE 17.2:** *A summary of field formulas for the Change Request form (continued)*

LABEL NAME	FIELD NAME	FORMULA
Extension	OldExtension	Extension
Direct Fax #	OldAreaCode_F	AreaCode_F
	OldExchange_F	Exchange_F
	OldID_F	ID_F
First Name	FirstName	Input Translation Formula: @ProperCase(FirstName)
		Input Validation Formula: @If(FirstName = ""; @Failure ("You must enter a first name before saving this document!"); @Success)
Last Name	LastName	Input Translation Formula: @ProperCase(LastName)
		Input Validation Formula: @If(LastName = ""; @Failure ("You must enter a last name before saving this document!"); @Success)
Department	Dept	Default Value Formula: Dept
Title	Title	Input Translation Formula: @ProperCase(Title)
Location	Location	Allowable Keywords Formula: @DbColumn (""; TargetServer: "CONSULT.NSF"; "Training Site Locations"; 1)
Address	Address	@If(Location != ""; @DbLookup (""; TargetServer: "CONSULT.NSF"; "Training Site Locations"; Location; "Address"); "")

TABLE 17.2: *A summary of field formulas for the Change Request form (continued)*

LABEL NAME	FIELD NAME	FORMULA
	City	@If(Location != ""; @DbLookup (""; TargetServer: "CONSULT.NSF"; "Training Site Locations"; Location; "City"); "")
	State	@If(Location != ""; @DbLookup (""; TargetServer: "CONSULT.NSF"; "Training Site Locations"; Location; "State"); "")
	ZipCode	@If(Location != ""; @DbLookup (""; TargetServer: "CONSULT.NSF"; "Training Site Locations"; Location; "ZipCode"); "")
Main Phone #	MainNum_P	@If(Location != ""; @DbLookup (""; TargetServer: "CONSULT.NSF"; "Training Site Locations"; Location; 6); "")
Main Fax #	MainNum_F	@If(Location != ""; @DbLookup (""; TargetServer: "CONSULT.NSF"; "Training Site Locations"; Location; 7); "")
Direct Phone #	AreaCode_P	Default Value Formula: AreaCode_P Input Translation Formula: @If(AreaCode_P = ""; @DbLookup (""; TargetServer: "CONSULT.NSF"; "Training Site Locations"; Location; "AreaCode_P"); AreaCode_P)
	Exchange_P	Default Value Formula: Exchange_P

▶ **TABLE 17.2:** *A summary of field formulas for the Change Request form (continued)*

LABEL NAME	FIELD NAME	FORMULA
		Input Translation Formula: @If(Exchange_P = ""; @DbLookup (""; TargetServer: "CONSULT.NSF"; "Training Site Locations"; Location; "Exchange_P"); Exchange_P)
	ID_P	Default Value Formula: ID_P
		Input Translation Formula: @If(ID_P = ""; @DbLookup (""; TargetServer: "CONSULT.NSF"; "Training Site Locations"; Location; "ID_P"); ID_P)
Extension	Extension	Default Value Formula: Extension
Direct Fax #	AreaCode_F	Deafult Value Formula: AreaCode_F
		Input Translation Formula: @If(AreaCode_F = ""; @DbLookup (""; TargetServer: "CONSULT.NSF"; "Training Site Locations"; Location; "AreaCode_F"); AreaCode_F)
	Exchange_F	Default Value Formula: Exchange_F
		Input Translation Formula: @If(Exchange_F = ""; @DbLookup (""; TargetServer: "CONSULT.NSF"; "Training Site Locations"; Location; "Exchange_F"); Exchange_F)
	ID_F	Default Value Formula: ID_F

▶ **TABLE 17.2:** *A summary of field formulas for the Change Request form (continued)*

LABEL NAME	FIELD NAME	FORMULA
		Input Translation Formula: @If(ID_F = ""; @DbLookup (""; TargetServer: "CONSULT.NSF"; "Training Site Locations"; Location; "ID_F"); ID_F)
	TargetServer	@Name([CN]; @Subset(@DbName; 1))

increased the application's flexibility by enabling Notes to identify the server from which the database is opened as the target server. In other words, the server where the database is stored *becomes* the target server when the user opens the database.

It isn't necessary that this field be displayed when a user composes a Change Request document so you should make use of the Hide-When feature in the Text Paragraph dialog box. When the user selects a main Directory Entry document in the Corporate Directory view and chooses Compose ➤ Change Request, Notes assigns the name of the target server as the value of the field. To create the field, follow these steps:

1. Position the insertion point at the bottom of the form. (You might have to press ↵ one or two times to insert blank lines between the existing fields and the new field.)

2. Choose Design ➤ New Field. The Design New Field dialog box appears.

3. Click on OK to accept the default option. The Field Definition dialog box appears.

4. Enter the following information (unless already indicated):

    Name: TargetServer

    Help Definition (optional): Assigns the name of the target server from where the user opens the database.

    Data Type: Text

Field Type: Computed when composed
Formula: @Name([CN];@Subset(@DbName;1))

5. Click OK to accept the changes. The field will appear.

To hide the field, follow these steps:

1. Position the cursor on the same line as the TargetServer field.

2. Choose Text ➤ Paragraph. The Text Paragraph dialog box appears.

3. In the Hide when portion of the dialog box, select Reading and Editing. Notice that Printing is automatically selected when you select Reading.

4. Click OK to accept the changes.

► ► *Using Notes' Graphics Capabilities*

Up to now, we haven't discussed using graphics in a database. Graphics certainly enhance the appearance of documents, and they can effectively help to communicate their intent. You'll notice that all database icons in the Workspace display graphics that strive to capture their purpose. These graphics have been created in Notes. As a database designer, you'll need to learn to create graphics for icons, in addition to creating and inserting graphics in forms.

► *Creating the Database's Icon*

As we mentioned above, each database icon in your Workspace will display a graphic that identifies it. Therefore, the graphic that appears on a database's icon should reflect the application's purpose. The name of the database should also communicate its function.

After you create the new Corporate Directory database, only the title you gave the database appears on the icon. The area above the title is empty. You can design the icon's graphic by using Notes' Design Icon dialog box. Although the design icon tools aren't very sophisticated, they allow you to create simple bitmap graphics. You paint individual pixels, just as you would in any other drawing program that enables you to create bitmap graphics. (Each one of the squares on the grid in the dialog box represents a pixel, which stands for "picture element.")

To create the graphic, follow these steps:

1. Choose Design ➤ Icon. The Design Icon dialog box appears, as shown in Figure 17.11.

2. Select the Draw drawing mode (the icon with the highlighted pencil tip).

3. Select the Paintbrush tool, which enables you to fill one pixel at a time. (This tool gives you more flexibility than the other tools for adding detail to the graphic.)

4. Point on the pixel you want to change and then click on the mouse button to add color, which you select at the bottom of the dialog box.

5. Select the Erase tool (the one with the highlighted eraser) and click on a pixel to restore it to the original background color.

6. Use the Roller, Spray, and Snap-to-Line tools to fill large areas of the grid. You'll need to experiment with each one in order to discover which one suits your need. (Remember: If you make a mistake, you can always click on the Undo button to undo your last action.)

FIGURE 17.11 ▶

The Design Icon dialog box lets you create the bitmap graphic that will appear on the database's icon.

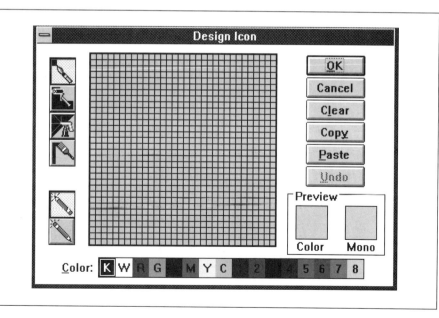

7. When you're satisfied with the design and size of the graphic, click on OK to save it and to close the dialog box. The graphic will appear on the database's icon in the Workspace.

As you can see in Figure 17.12, we created a "walking fingers" graphic for the Corporate Directory database icon. The graphic's not very complex, but it does get its message across.

FIGURE 17.12 ▶

We created a "walking fingers" graphic for the Corporate Directory database icon.

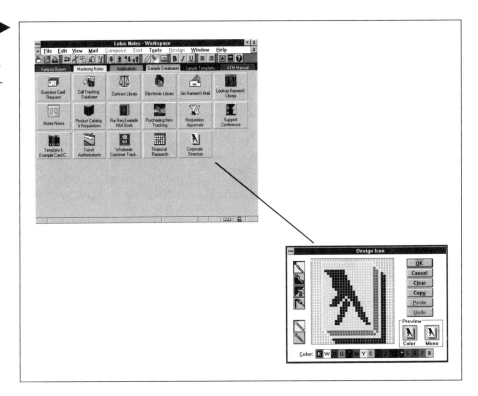

▶ Inserting a Graphic on a Form

You can also insert the same graphic on a form so it appears on all the documents that users compose with the form. Inserting a graphic in this way is an easy and convenient method of adding graphics to forms without a lot of fuss. To insert a graphic on a form, follow these steps:

1. Click on the Corporate Directory database icon to select it.

2. Choose Design ➤ Icon. The Design Icon dialog box appears, displaying the graphic you created for the icon.

3. Click on the Copy button to copy the graphic to the Clipboard. (If you press Ctrl+C, Notes will beep, letting you know that you can't use this keyboard shortcut.)

4. Click on the Cancel button to close the dialog box.

5. Open the Directory Entry form (or another form).

6. Place the Insertion Point to the left of the XYZ Corporation label.

7. Press ↵ two times to move the label down.

8. Place the insertion point at the top of the form. (Make sure that it's centered.)

9. Press Ctrl+V to paste the graphic on the form. The graphic will appear.

10. Press Ctrl+S to save the form.

11. Press Esc to close the form window.

The graphic that appears at the top of the form is similar to the table because it's an object that's been inserted in the form. In this case, the graphic appears above the label. (As we discussed previously, you can insert graphic objects anywhere on a form because a form is actually a large rich text field that can contain text and graphics.)

When you click on the graphic to select it, a marquee will appear around it with a resizing handle in the lower right corner. The graphic might or might not also appear darkened (highlighted). If you hold the mouse button down while you point on the handle, you can drag the handle to increase or decrease the size of the graphic. This action is similar to the way you might modify the appearance of a graphic you've created in another application. If you've never used a drawing application to create a graphic, all you're doing is changing its size to fit the form. It's no big deal.

If the graphic appears marqueed but isn't highlighted, and you open the Edit menu, you'll notice that the Cut and Copy commands aren't available (they appear dimmed). However, the Paste command is available. You might think this is odd since the graphic appears selected with the marquee. What's going on? You must make sure the graphic is highlighted in order to cut or copy it. Otherwise, you won't be able to perform those actions.

▶▶ **T I P**

This probably sounds obvious, but after you select a graphic, open the Edit menu and see if the Cut and Copy commands are available. If they appear dimmed, the graphic hasn't been selected correctly. You need to make sure a marquee surrounds the graphic and it appears darkened.

With the graphic still selected, open the Edit menu. You'll see a Resize Picture command under the Insert command. When you choose the command, the current width and height of the graphic will appear at the bottom of your screen. This information is handy to know when you resize the graphic. As you drag the handle, the new width and height will change accordingly.

▶▶ **T I P**

For you graphics purists who like to create your own original artwork for forms, you can take advantage of the Notes Icon command to design *bitmap graphics*. If you don't use or have access to another Windows drawing program, the Notes Icon command works in a pinch (although it does have limitations). Unfortunately, you can only use this method for a database that doesn't display a graphic on its icon. The secret is to create the graphic(s) *before* you create the bitmap you want displayed on the database icon.

▶▶ *Creating the About Database and Using Database Documents*

As the designer of a database, you have the option of including two help documents with the application. One is called the "About the…Database" document, and the other is called the "Using the…Database" document. Together, these documents describe a database and explain how to use it. Although you don't have to create these documents, every database should include them.

When a user is unfamiliar with a database, he or she can read the documents to learn more about it. In many situations, these documents become the only assistance users will receive. Therefore, as the database's designer, you have a responsibility to explain the functionality of a database as thoroughly as you can. If users don't understand your database, they won't use it. If they don't use the database, it serves no purpose.

▶ Writing the About Database Document

When a user opens a database for the first time, the About Database document appears. Since this document is a user's introduction to the database, it should include a thorough description of the database's purpose and features, in addition to any other pertinent information that a user might find helpful. A user can subsequently display the About Database document by choosing Help ➤ About [database name].

The About Database document is also useful for displaying information about a database when a user browses through the list of databases in the Open Database dialog box (File ➤ Open Database). A user can highlight a database in the list box and click on the About button to open the document. The user can read about the database first in order to determine whether to open it. To create the About Database document, follow these steps:

1. Click on the database's icon to select it.

2. Choose Design ➤ Help Document ➤ About Database. The About Database window opens.

3. Write a description of the database.

4. Press Ctrl+S to save the document.

5. Press Esc to close the window and to return to the Workspace.

▶ Writing the Using Database Document

The Using Database document should explain how to use the database, describing its forms and views. It should also include explanations of macros. For example, the Using Database document for the

Corporate Directory database explains how the application automates workflow. The document describes the process of composing Directory Entry documents, composing Change Request documents, and sending the change requests to an administrator.

A user can display the Using Database document by choosing Help ➤ Using [database name]. To create the Using Database document, follow these steps:

1. Click on the database's icon to select it.

2. Choose Design ➤ Help Document ➤ Using Database. The Using Database window opens.

3. Write a description of the database.

4. Press Ctrl+S to save the document.

5. Press Esc to close the window and to return to the Workspace.

▶▶ *What's Next?*

Part of the ongoing process of designing a Notes database involves evaluating the workflow components of the application. Notes comes with several features that are expressly designed for workflow automation, such as its e-mail engine, which is the basis for moving information through the workflow process, @functions and @commands that are used specifically in workflow applications, and form attributes and reserved fields that you can incorporate into the designs of your forms to make them "mail-enabled."

Applying access control to a database is also part of managing the workflow of a Notes application. The roles of users in any organization change over time as well as the kinds of tasks they perform. In the next chapter, we discuss setting a database's access control privileges, in addition to using other data security features that Notes provides. Data security is a major issue nowadays. Telecommunications has helped to make information easily accessible through e-mail, online services, and the Internet. However, many people are accessing the information with little monitoring. We show you how you can build security into your Notes databases.

CHAPTER 18

Building Security into Notes Databases

▶▶ FAST TRACK

▶ **To assign access levels and access roles**   **540**

in the access control list (ACL), choose File ➤ Database ➤ Access Control. Each Notes database contains an ACL that details who can open the database, and what they can do to its information. Access levels and access roles are set by you, the database designer, or the database manager. If a user has been assigned the appropriate access level, she or he can access the particular database. If not, access is denied.

▶ **To change a user name**   **543**

choose Mail ➤ Send User ID ➤ Request New Name. If Notes prompts you for a password, enter it. Enter the new name in the Change User Name dialog box. Click on OK. The Mail New Name Request dialog box appears. You use this dialog box to mail the name change request to your certifier. When you receive the ID back, choose Tools ➤ User ID ➤ Merge Copy to merge new certificates into your ID file.

▶ **To set your password**   **548**

choose Tools ➤ User ID ➤ Password ➤ Set. If your ID file is already password-protected, you'll see the Enter Password dialog box. Enter the current password. If you're setting a new password, the Set Password dialog box appears. Enter a new password. Click OK. Notes asks you to confirm the password by typing it again; type it exactly as you did the first time. Click OK again.

▶ **To select the encryption key**   **557**

choose Edit ➤ Security ➤ Encryption Keys while a *docu-ment* is open. (You can also choose Design ➤ Form Attrib-utes while a *form* is open, then click on the Encryption button in the Design Form Attributes dialog box.) In either case, the Encryption Keys dialog box appears. To ap-ply a new key, select it from the Encryption Keys Available list and then select Add. Conversely, to delete an existing key, select it from the Document Encryption Keys list and then click on Remove. Click on OK to accept your changes.

▶ **To select an encryption key to apply to a view**   **559**

select the view or documents in the view. Choose Edit ➤ Security ➤ Encryption Keys while a view is open. Select Show All. Select an individual key from Document's En-cryption Keys. Select Add or Remove to either apply the key to all the documents or remove that key from all the documents. Click on OK.

▶ **To specify a password for an exported encryption key**   **561**

choose Tools ➤ User ID ➤ Encryption Keys. Enter your password in the Enter Password dialog box. The User ID Encryption Key dialog box appears. Highlight an encryp-tion key in the list. Click on the Export button. The User ID Encryption Key Export dialog box appears. Enter a password into the Password box. Enter the same password into the Confirmation box. Click on OK. The Specify File for the Exported Key dialog box appears. Enter the file name and the directory where you want to export the file to. Click on OK again to perform the export.

►► **D**ata security is a major issue nowadays. Telecommunications has helped to make information easily accessible through e-mail, online services, and the Internet. However, many people are accessing the information with little monitoring. In this chapter, we show you how you can build security into your Notes databases, and discuss the following topics:

- Changing your User ID
- Setting a password
- Logging off
- Using encryption keys

►► *Protecting Access to Databases*

As we've discussed previously, you can set user access privileges for using databases (see Chapter 4, "Accessing Notes Databases"). Each Notes database contains an access control list (ACL) that appears in the Database Access Control List dialog box, which is shown Figure 18.1. The ACL details who can open the database and what they can do to its information. If a user has the appropriate access level, she or he can access the particular database. If not, access is denied. Both of the ACL's elements, access levels and access roles, are set by you, the database designer, or the database manager. (The database manager usually creates and maintains the access control list.) To assign access levels and access roles in the access control list (ACL), choose File ➤ Database ➤ Access Control.

FIGURE 18.1 ▶

The Database Access Control List dialog box details who can open the database and what they can do to its information.

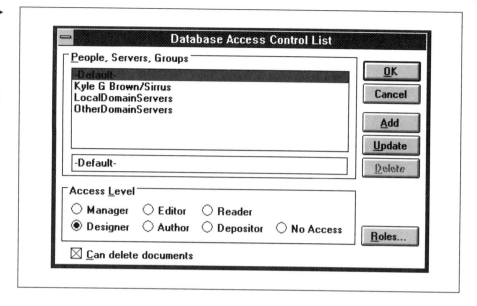

In addition to designating access levels, however, Notes protects your work and the work of other users on shared databases in a variety of other ways:

- User IDs can be protected with passwords.
- Users are granted or denied access to Notes servers through the *certificates* stored in their User IDs.
- Information can be encrypted so that only specific users can decrypt it.
- If you're using Notes with a modem, you can use a secure modem channel by selecting Encrypt Network Data in the Port Setup dialog box.

▶▶ *Using IDs*

A User ID is a file that identifies a Notes user. Every Notes user—person or server—has a unique User ID. The terms User ID, ID, and ID file are used interchangeably in Notes. The contents of a User ID are either assigned by a certifier when the ID is created, or added later.

The following information is assigned:

- The name of the ID owner (which can be changed later by the owner or certifier)
- The Notes license number
- A certificate (which allows access to servers that trust the certifier)
- A public key (which is used to encrypt documents sent to the owner)
- A private key (which is used to decrypt documents sent to the owner)
- A password can be added to prevent unauthorized access to Notes servers using the ID (added by the owner)
- Additional certificates to allow access to additional servers (added by certifiers)

▶ Why You Need a User ID

When you try to open a database on a server, the server looks at your ID to see if you have any certificates in common. If you do, access is allowed; if you don't, access is denied. This checking process is called *authentication*, and it's the reason why it sometimes takes a few moments to access a server that you haven't used recently.

You also need a ID to sign Notes mail memos. When you sign a Notes mail memo and send it, all of your certificate(s) are attached to the memo. The recipient's workstation checks these against its own certificates.

If you receive a signed memo and you don't have a certificate in common with the sender, Notes displays a message saying that the authenticity of the memo cannot be assured. If you know that you and the sender have a certificate in common, the memo may have been tampered with en route.

To get information about your User ID, choose Tools ➤ User ID ➤ Information. You'll see the following information about your ID:

- File name and location
- Number

- Type of license (North American or International)
- Name (your user name)

You can also change your user name, copy your public key to the Clipboard (if you have a distinguished name, you can copy your certified public key), and find out the name of the certifier who created your User ID.

 ►► **N O T E**

> **North American and International versions of the Notes software use different encryption algorithms and have different licenses. U.S. export restrictions require the North American version to be more difficult to decrypt. This has virtually no effect on Notes users—wherever you are, you can communicate with Notes users with either North American or International licenses.**

► *Changing Your User Name*

You can change the user name associated with your User ID file. You might change your user name for any number of reasons: maybe you just got married and changed your last name, or maybe you'd rather use your nickname.

The process of changing your user name involves a couple of other people and so may take a few hours or even a few days. Don't worry, you can continue to use your original ID, switching to the new one once the changeover process is complete. Using the new ID, you can read any signed or encrypted mail that was created with the original name.

 ►► **W A R N I N G**

> **If you're not a Notes Mail user, changing the user name removes *all* the certificates from the ID, so after you change the name you'll need to acquire new certificates before you can use any shared databases.**

Depending on whether you use Notes Mail, you can change your user name in two different ways:

- If you use Notes Mail, choose Mail ➤ Send User ID ➤ Request New Name, and if Notes prompts you for a password, as shown in Figure 18.2, enter it.

- If you don't use Notes Mail, after backing up your ID and switching to the backup copy, choose Tools ➤ User ID ➤ Information, then select Change User Name.

If you use Notes Mail, you change your user name in this manner:

1. Enter the new name in the Change User Name dialog box that appears in Figure 18.3.

FIGURE 18.2 ▶

The Enter Password dialog box prompts you to enter your password when you want to change your user name and make other modifications to your User ID.

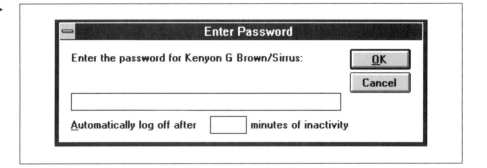

FIGURE 18.3 ▶

Enter your new name in the Change User Name dialog box.

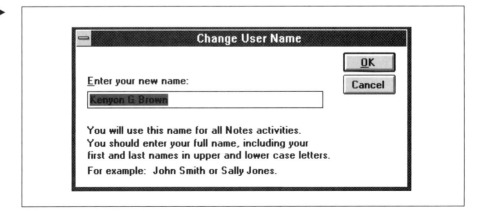

2. Click on OK. The Mail New Name Request dialog box appears, as shown in Figure 18.4. You use this dialog box to mail the name change request to your certifier.

3. When you receive the ID back, choose Tools ➤ User ID ➤ Merge Copy to merge new certificates into your ID file.

FIGURE 18.4 ▶

Use the Mail New Name Request dialog box to mail the name change request to your certifier.

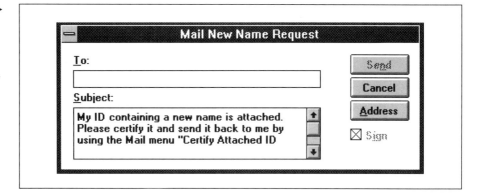

If you don't use Notes Mail and you want to change your user name, follow these steps:

1. Enter your new user name in the Change Name dialog box.

2. Click on OK. Using this method causes you to lose any certificates that you have in the newly named ID file until you get it back.

3. Choose Tools ➤ User ID ➤ Create Safe Copy to save a copy of the newly named ID onto a floppy disk, then deliver the disk to a certifier to be stamped with certificate(s).

4. You have the option of choosing Tools ➤ User ID ➤ Switch To to use your old ID until you get the new one.

5. When you receive the ID back, switch to this ID again and choose Tools ➤ User ID ➤ Merge Copy to merge new certificates into this ID file.

▶▶ N O T E

Your Notes Administrator will update your Person document and Group documents in the public Name & Address Book to reflect your name change.

You, your Notes Administrator, and various database managers may need to change the access control list for any databases you use that have your name listed individually. This includes changing your Notes Mail database. If you or the Administrator don't have the necessary access to change the ACL, contact the database managers.

▶ Switching to a Different User ID

You can share a workstation with another Notes user (who has a different User ID) by using the Tools ➤ User ID ➤ Switch To command to tell Notes that one of you is leaving and the other is beginning Notes. You can both keep your IDs on floppy disks or on the workstation's hard disk. Be sure to password-protect your IDs. After you use the command to select the ID you want to use, Notes prompts you for a password if that ID file is password-protected.

▶▶ N O T E

When two or more people use Notes on the same PC or Macintosh workstation, each installs Notes separately, storing the Notes *program* files in the same directory, but storing *data* files in his or her own data directory. This provides each user with his or her own copy of the DESKTOP.DSK file, which lets each user see a different set of database icons in the Notes Workspace. In Windows, each user must also have his or her own copy of the NOTES.INI file; other copies, such as the one usually stored in the Windows directory, must be removed.

Each user, after switching to his or her ID, uses the User Setup dialog box to change to his or her personal data directory.

▶ *Keeping Your User ID Secure*

Keeping your User ID electronically secure means:

- Keeping your ID physically secure
- Password-protecting it
- Logging off servers when you leave your office

You can keep your User ID on a floppy disk, your hard disk, or a file server. The most secure option is to keep it on a floppy disk that you store in a safe place when you aren't using it (perhaps in a locked drawer). Just make a backup copy of your ID file on a floppy disk using your operating system's file copy procedure. Store the backup in a secure place.

If you change your mind about where to keep your ID, you can tell Notes where your ID is located during setup (right after installation). You can change your mind later, though. If you originally told Notes that your ID is stored on the hard disk, you can later copy it to a floppy disk and delete the file from the hard disk (use Windows to copy and delete the file). When Notes asks for the location of your ID file the next time you access a Notes server, type in its new location, as in **a:\kbrown.id**.

When you keep your User ID on a floppy disk, you must insert the disk whenever you access a server, sign mail, or read encrypted mail. Most people just leave it in their floppy drive while they use Notes. If you remove the floppy from the drive, *you cannot access Notes servers.*

You should log off your password when you leave your workstation to prevent an unauthorized person from accessing your organization's databases using your User ID (posing as you). This is especially important if you work in a cubicle or you don't lock your office when you step out. In the Enter Password dialog box, you can set automatic logoff to occur after any number of minutes that you specify. Otherwise, you can press F5 to log off, thus clearing your password and forcing the next person (which might be you or someone else) to enter a password in order to access the server.

► Setting Your Password

As we mentioned above, you can protect your User ID by setting a password that controls access from your Workspace to databases on Notes servers. You can also change your existing password. However, this password *doesn't* protect databases stored locally (on your hard disk), which includes all replicas you may have made. Once you set a password, you must enter it when you access a Notes server for the first time after launching Notes. However, you can change your password after it's been set unless your Notes Administrator specified that you cannot change it when you were registered as a new Notes user.

To set your password, follow these steps:

1. Choose Tools ➤ User ID ➤ Password ➤ Set. If your ID file is already password-protected, you'll see the Enter Password dialog box.

2. Enter the current password.

3. If you are setting a new password, the Set Password dialog box appears, as shown in Figure 18.5.

4. Enter a new password.

5. Click OK.

6. Notes asks you to confirm the password by typing it again; type it exactly as you did the first time.

7. Click OK again.

FIGURE 18.5 ►

Enter a new password for your User ID in the Set Password dialog box.

Set Password

Passwords are case sensitive.

The minimum number of characters required for a password for this ID is 8

Enter the new password:

[OK]

[Cancel]

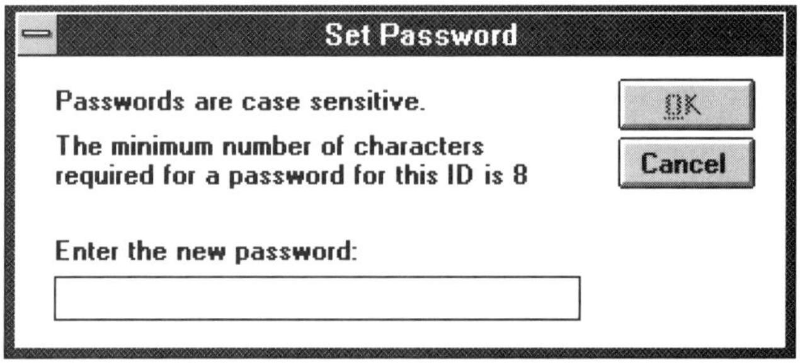

For security reasons, the entry isn't displayed on your screen. It's safest to use at least eight characters; the maximum number of characters you can use is 31. However, your Notes Administrator may have set a minimum password length when your ID was created.

Notes passwords are case-sensitive. For example, Notes considers *MysteryTour* and *mysterytour* to be different passwords. Notes won't accept a password unless it matches the original exactly.

▶ Entering Your Password

As we've said, you set password protection to force you to enter your current password each time you want to access databases from your Workspace to databases on Notes servers. Passwords are case-sensitive; for example, *Mango* is not the same as *mango*.

During the password entry procedure, you can also have Notes automatically log off (prevent access to servers from your workspace) after a number of minutes of inactivity that you specify. This is a useful security precaution if you tend to forget to log off when you leave your desk.

To enter your password, follow these steps:

1. Enter your password in the Enter Password dialog box.

2. If you want Notes to log off automatically after a certain number of minutes of inactivity, specify that number.

3. Click on OK.

▶ Clearing and Changing Your Password

You can change the password that controls access from your Workspace to databases on Notes servers. Choose Tools ➤ User ID ➤ Password ➤ Clear. First, the Enter Password dialog box appears. Enter the current password and then click on OK.

 ▶▶ **N O T E**

> **If your Notes Administrator required a password to be used when your ID was created, you won't be able to clear it.**

The Clear Password dialog box appears. If you want to *temporarily* log off Notes servers so that your password must be reentered to access them again, choose Tools ➤ User Logoff instead.

To clear your password, enter your password into the text box. Click on OK. Your password is cleared. To specify another password, choose Tools ➤ User ID ➤ Password ➤ Set and follow the same steps as above.

▶▶ *Examining Your User ID Certificates*

A *certificate* is an electronic "stamp" attached to your User ID by a Notes certifier. (The certifier is usually the Notes Administrator.) Certificates allow you access to specific Notes servers.

When you were registered as a Notes user, your User ID should have included the certificate(s) required to access the servers you need for your job. As you make wider use of Notes, your job changes, or your organization adds servers, you may need access to other servers. If you're denied access to them because you're not certified, ask the proper certifier for the certificate you need.

You can see information about the certificates that are attached to your User ID. The information provided about your certificates includes:

- The names of each certificate on your ID
- The date and time each one was created, and the date and time they expire
- The ID number and name of the certifier

To review the certificates that you already have, choose Tools ➤ User ID ➤ Certificates. If your ID file is password-protected, you must enter your password in the Enter Password dialog box. The Currently Held Certificates dialog box appears, as shown in Figure 18.6, which lists your current certificates. Select the certificate you want information on. You can delete a certificate by selecting it and clicking on Delete. Your Notes Administrator may also ask you to check your ID for hierarchical name information.

FIGURE 18.6 ▶

The Currently Held Certificates dialog box lists the name(s) of the certificate on your ID. In this case, only one certificate is available.

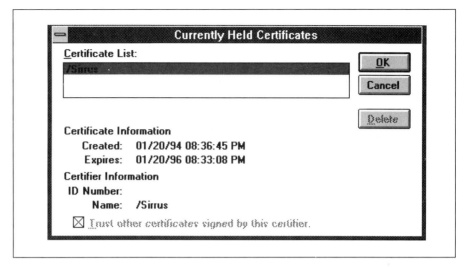

▶ *Sending and Receiving Certificates*

You may send your ID file to a certifier and receive it back for several reasons. Generally, you send an ID file to get certificates you didn't already have. But you may also send an ID file to request cross certificates, to request a new user name, or to get a new public key. To get more certificates when you and your certifier both use Notes Mail, follow these steps:

1. Get the name of the certifier from your Notes Administrator (if it's not the same person).

 ▶▶ **N O T E**

> **The certifier's name might be a person or an organizational unit, like Administration.**

2. Choose Mail ➤ Send User ID ➤ Request Certificate.

3. Enter your password in the Enter Password dialog box. The Mail Certificate Request dialog box appears, as shown in Figure 18.7, where you create and send a "safe" copy of your ID file—minus the private key and current certificates. The certifier then certifies your safe copy and sends it back to you. You'll get the new certificate as a Notes mail memo.

FIGURE 18.7 ▶

The Mail Certificate Request dialog box enables you to create and send a "safe" copy of your User ID file to the certifier.

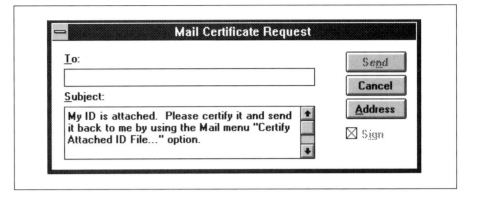

4. Open the memo and choose Mail ➤ Accept Certificate.

5. Click on Merge. The certificate is added to your ID file.

If you or your certifier don't use Notes Mail (or if neither of you is authorized to access each other's server), follow these steps:

1. Get the name of the certifier from your Notes Administrator.

2. Choose Tools ➤ User ID ➤ Create Safe Copy. The Enter Safe Copy ID File Name dialog box appears, as shown in Figure 18.8, where you create a safe copy of your ID file on a floppy disk.

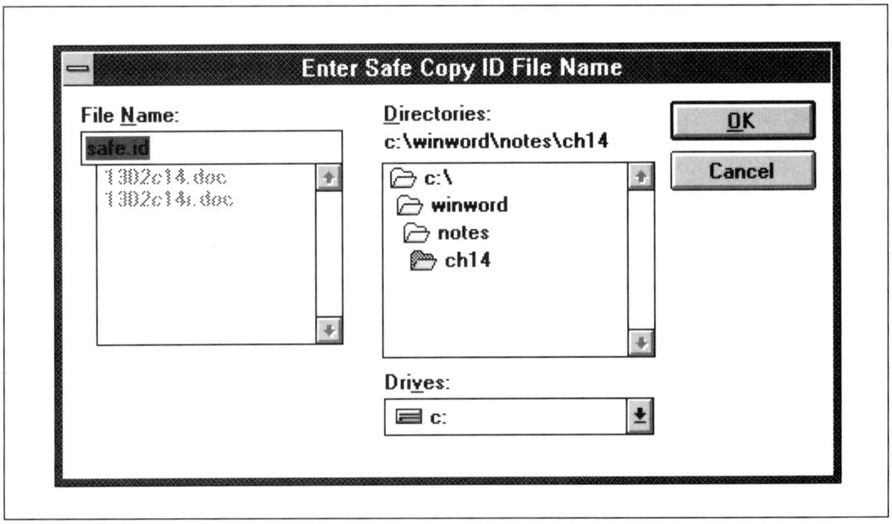

FIGURE 18.8 ▶

The Enter Safe Copy ID File Name dialog box allows you to create and save the safe copy of the ID to a floppy disk.

Enter Safe Copy ID File Name

File **N**ame:
safe.id
1302c14.doc
1302c14r.doc

Directories:
c:\winword\notes\ch14

📂 c:\
📂 winword
📂 notes
📂 ch14

OK

Cancel

Dri**v**es:
🖳 c:

3. Physically take (or mail) the disk to the certifier, who adds a new certificate to your ID file. (You have to physically obtain a safe copy that's been certified by the Administrator.)

4. Insert the certified ID file into your floppy disk drive.

5. Choose Tools ➤ User ID ➤ Merge Copy. The Choose User ID to Merge into Current ID dialog box appears, as shown in Figure 18.9. Enter the path and file name of the safe copy of the ID.

6. Click on OK. The Merge Certificates dialog box appears.

7. Click on OK again in order to merge the new certificate into your User ID, or select Cancel if you change your mind.

FIGURE 18.9 ▶

You enter the path and file name of the safe copy of the ID in the Choose User ID to Merge into Current ID dialog box.

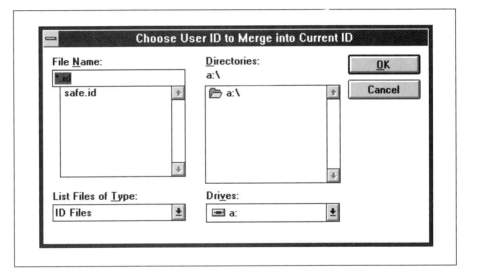

▶▶ *Logging Off*

User Logoff protects your organization from unauthorized entry into databases stored on Notes servers. If you leave your office and workstation unlocked, however, anyone can use your local databases.

> **▶▶ TIP**
>
> **Password-protect your User ID, and use Tools ➤ User Logoff when you leave your workstation.**

If you have a password for your User ID, you must type it into the Password dialog box the first time you open a database on a Notes server. When you leave your workstation unattended, choose Tools ➤ User Logoff (or press F5). When you return to Notes and try to access a Notes server, you must type your password again. In the Enter Password dialog box, you can set up automatic logoff after any number of minutes that you specify.

If your User ID isn't password-protected and if your User ID is on your hard disk, user logoff has no real effect. Although it seems to log you out, as soon as anyone attempts to access a shared database, Notes looks for the User ID, finds it on your hard disk, sees that no password is set, and permits database access.

If your User ID is on a floppy disk and someone enters your office and can find your ID floppy, they can insert it into your floppy drive and access shared databases.

▶▶ *Encrypting Documents*

Notes provides document security by letting you encrypt fields in documents. Encryption means encoding or "scrambling" data so that only those who have the secret encryption key(s) can read your documents. There are some differences between encrypting document fields and encrypting Notes mail memos (which we discussed in Chapter 9, "Communicating with Notes Mail").

Encrypting a document means applying a secret encryption key to one or more fields and then sending the key to users of your choice. Users who don't have this key can still read any unencrypted fields in an encrypted document.

A document cannot be encrypted unless its form has one or more fields defined as encryptable by you, the database designer. If you have a color monitor, and you're composing a document, you can recognize encryptable fields by their red field brackets. To encrypt an encryptable field, use an existing encryption key of your own, or create a new encryption key.

All encryptable fields in a document will be encrypted using the key(s) you select; you cannot select a different key for each encryptable field in a single document.

Any user who has *any* key or keys to a document can read *all* the encrypted fields in that document. Be careful not to give out a key to one field and forget that you're providing access to some other field you want to keep secret.

As the database designer, you may want to encrypt all documents created with a specific form. There are two ways to do this: by adding encryption keys to the form, or by adding keywords that refer to encryption keys. Add encryption keys when you, as the database designer, want to decide which key(s) will be used with this form. Add keywords that *refer to* encryption keys when you want users to choose the key(s) they want from a set of keys that you provide. However, you must send the appropriate encryption key(s) to any user whom you want to read encrypted documents. Just follow these steps:

1. Chose Mail ➤ Send User ID ➤ Encryption Key.

2. Enter your password, if one has been set, in the Enter Password dialog box.

3. Select one or more encryption keys from the list, if they exist.

4. Click on Mail. The Mail Address Encryption Key dialog box appears, as shown in Figure 18.10. Enter the names of users to whom you want to send the key(s). Notes will ask you whether you want to let the recipients send the key to other users. If you select Yes, the recipients can distribute the key; otherwise they can only use it themselves. Your decision depends on the nature of the documents encrypted with this key, and on your relationship with the recipients.

▶ *Encrypting Incoming Mail*

You can prevent any unauthorized access to your mail when it reaches your mail server, either by administrative access to your mail database

FIGURE 18.10 ▶

You enter the names of users to whom you want to send the encryption key(s) in the Mail Address Encryption Key dialog box.

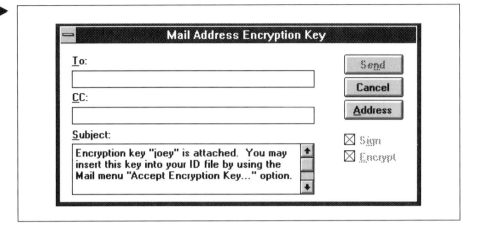

or by unauthorized access to the server. Only you can read your encrypted incoming mail. Either the Administrator sets a default for all incoming mail to be encrypted by using **MailEncryptIncoming=1** in the NOTES.INI file that's located on the server, or each user can elect to encrypt their incoming mail by setting the option in the person entry on the server's N&A Book.

▶ *Encrypting Outgoing Mail*

As we discussed way back in Chapter 9, you can also encrypt outgoing mail to ensure that nobody except your recipients can read your memos while in transit, when stored in intermediate mail boxes, and on arrival in the recipient's mail file. When you encrypt a document, Notes scrambles the information using the recipient's public key so that it can be decoded only by the recipient. You set this option by selecting Encrypt in the Send dialog box. Choose Mail ➤ Send (or click on the Send button when it's displayed in the mail document you're composing) and click the Encrypt checkbox. Then click on the Send button to send the mail message.

▶ *Encrypting Saved Mail*

You can ensure that your saved copies of mail memos are always encrypted whether or not you send them to others encrypted. Encrypting saved mail effectively prevents anyone from reading your mail on the server, even the server administrator or others with access to the server.

In order to encrypt mail, Notes creates a unique public and private key for each user. If someone sends you encrypted mail (by selecting Encrypt in the Mail Send dialog box), Notes uses your public key to encrypt the message, making it unreadable to any user except you. When it delivers the message, Notes uses your private key to decrypt (decode) the message for you.

▶▶ **N O T E**

> **We discuss the use of your private key and your public key in Chapter 9, "Communicating with Notes Mail."**

Since your public key must be available to anyone wanting to send you encrypted mail, the Notes Administrator must put your public key in the public Name & Address Book when you're registered as a Notes user. However, to maintain security, your *private* key is stored in your User ID, where only you can access it. This means that any user who has access to your public key can *send* you encrypted mail, but *only you* can decrypt that mail. If your public key is ever lost from or corrupted in the Name & Address Book, you must send a new copy to your Notes Administrator. To do so, use the Mail Public Key dialog box. Choose Mail ➤ Send User ID ➤ Public Key. Fill in the To, CC, and Subject text boxes. (You must enter a recipient in the To text box; entering information in the other text boxes is optional.) Select the Sign and Encrypt options if you desire. Then click on the Send button to mail your Public key to the designated recipient.

▶ *Selecting an Encryption Key*

You can select encryption keys to apply to an open document or a form. You also must select an encryption key to remove it from a document. If you add an encryption key to a form, all documents composed with that form are automatically encrypted with the selected key. To select the encryption key, follow these steps:

1. Choose Edit ➤ Security ➤ Encryption Keys while a document is open, or choose Design ➤ Form Attributes while a form is open in order to click on the Encryption button in the Design Form Attributes dialog box. In either case, the Encryption Keys dialog box

appcars, as shown in Figure 18.11. It displays the following settings and options:

- **Encryption Keys Available:** Shows the keys in your User ID. These are keys you created using Tools ➤ User ID ➤ Encryption Keys, New or keys that other Notes users have given you.
- **Document Encryption Keys:** Shows the keys that have been applied to the current document.
- **Add:** Adds the key selected under Encryption Keys Available to the list of keys used to encrypt the document.
- **Remove:** Deletes the key selected under Document Encryption Keys from the document.
- **Remove All:** Deletes all encryption keys from the document.

2. To apply a new key, select it from the Encryption Keys Available list and then select Add. Conversely, to delete an existing key, select it from the Document Encryption Keys list and then click on Remove.

3. Click on OK to accept your changes.

FIGURE 18.11 ▸

The Encryption Keys dialog box enables you to manage the keys in your User ID and the keys applied to the current document.

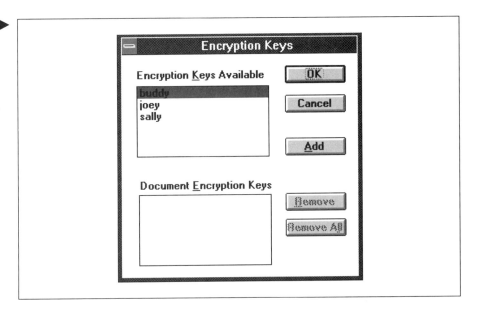

You can also select encryption keys to apply to documents in a view, or remove a current encryption key from a document.

 ►► **N O T E**

> **An encryption key can provide extra security for draft documents you're working on in Notes Mail. For example, some users share a mail file with a coworker or assistant. If you do this, your associate has the public key to your mail file, but you can still apply an encryption key to a draft in process to prevent your associate from having access to it.**

To select encryption keys to apply to documents in a view, follow these steps:

1. Select the view or documents in the view.

2. Choose Edit ➤ Security ➤ Encryption Keys while a view is open. The following options and settings are displayed:

- **Document's Encryption Keys:** Shows the keys that have been applied to the current or selected document(s). Since each document may use different keys, the Document's Encryption Keys list is empty.

- **Your Encryption Keys:** Shows the keys in your User ID. These are keys you created using Tools ➤ User ID ➤ Encryption Keys, New or keys that other Notes users have given you.

- **Remove:** Deletes the key selected under Document's Encryption Keys from the document.

- **Remove All:** Deletes all encryption keys from the document.

- **Add:** Adds the key selected under Your Encryption Keys to the list of keys used to encrypt a particular document.

- **Show All:** Shows all the encryption keys used in all the selected documents.

▶▶ **W A R N I N G**

If you have multiple documents selected and select OK at this point, without selecting Show All first, then *all encryption keys for all selected documents will be deleted* (Notes displays a message asking you to confirm this before actually deleting the keys).

3. Select Show All.

4. Select an individual key from Document's Encryption Keys.

5. Select Add or Remove to either apply the key to all the documents or remove that key from all the documents.

6. Repeat steps 4 and 5 as needed.

7. Click on OK.

▶▶ **N O T E**

If you select Show All and OK without using Add or Remove to select specific keys, then all the documents are encrypted with the keys found by Show All.

You can review, add, or delete encryption keys from your User ID file or export an encryption key for Notes users who don't use Notes Mail. Just follow these steps:

1. Choose Tools ➤ User ID ➤ Encryption Keys. If your user ID is password-protected, Notes asks you to enter the password. The User ID Encryption Keys dialog box appears, as shown in Figure 18.12.

2. Click on New to create a new key. The Add Encryption Key dialog box appears. This is where you create the key.

3. To delete an existing key, select it in the Encryption Key List, then click on Delete.

4. To get information about an existing key, select from in the Encryption Key List. Then read the Comment and note the creation date and restrictions at the bottom of the dialog box.

FIGURE 18.12

You can add or delete encryption keys from your User ID, as well as export keys to share with other Notes users, in the User ID Encryption Keys dialog box.

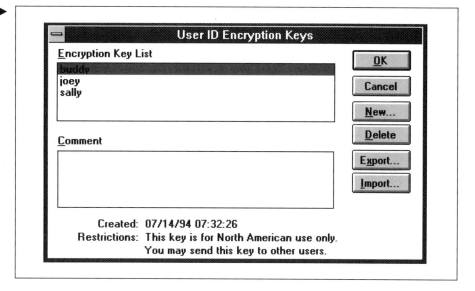

5. To import a key, click on Import. The standard Choose File dialog box appears, where you can select the encryption key file you want.

6. To export a key, click on Export. Notes opens the User ID Encryption Key Export dialog box, where you enter a password for the encryption key. Then you see a standard Save File dialog box, where you specify where to store the encryption key so that the intended users can find it. Be sure to tell them the password so they can use the key!

7. When you're done, click on OK.

Since you'll be sharing valuable documents with other people in your workgroup, you'll need to give them the encryption keys you've used. They must have the keys stored on their workstations or they won't be able to access the documents.

As a precaution, you can specify a password for an encryption key when you export it. Although you can export an encryption key without password-protecting it, doing so undermines the security obtained by using an encryption key and sharing it with a limited number of users. Follow these steps:

1. Choose Tools ➤ User ID ➤ Encryption Keys.

2. Enter your password in the Enter Password dialog box. The User ID Encryption Key dialog box appears.

3. Highlight an encryption key in the list.

4. Click on the Export button. The User ID Encryption Key Export dialog box appears, as shown in Figure 18.13.

5. Enter a password into the Password box.

6. Enter the same password into the Confirmation box.

7. Click on OK. The Specify File for the Exported Key dialog box appears, as shown in Figure 18.14.

FIGURE 18.13 ▶

The User ID Encryption Key Export dialog box lets you set a password for an encryption key when you export it.

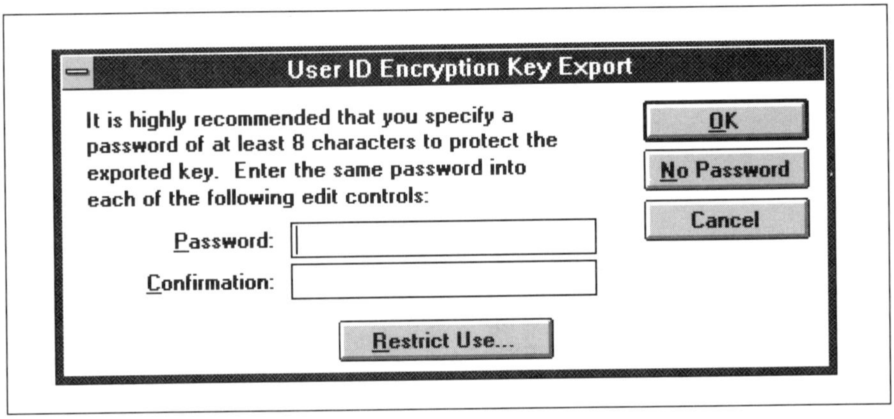

FIGURE 18.14 ▶

The Specify File for the Exported Key dialog box lets you specify the name of the file and the directory where you want to export the file to.

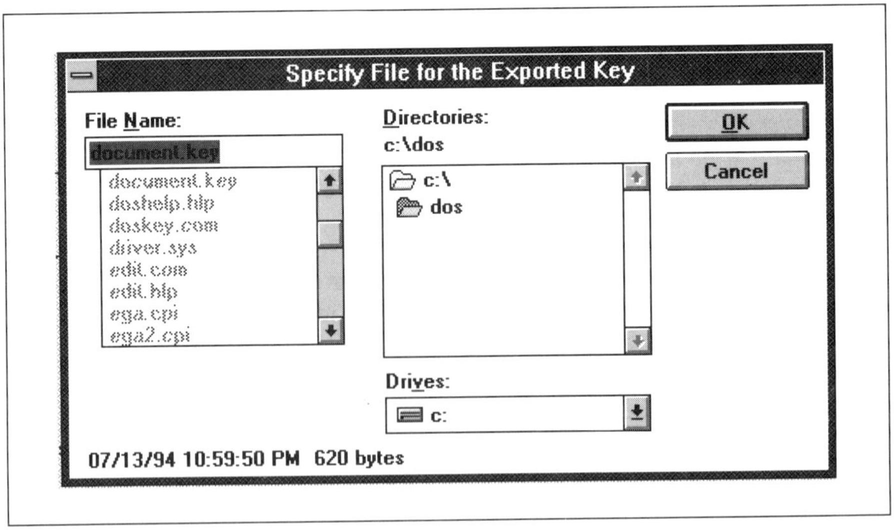

8. Enter the file name and the directory where you want to export the file to.

9. Click on OK again to perform the export.

The Status Bar at the bottom of the Notes window will display the message that the key encryption [*name of key*] has been successfully exported. From now on, people in your workgroup can access the information contained in the documents.

▶▶ *What's Next?*

In the next chapter, we discuss replicating databases and the issues involved in database exchange. Notes' power lies in its ability to distribute and manage data in multiple copies of the same database. These copies can reside on servers, networked computers, or remote computers in other locations. For those of you who work at home or spend a lot of time outside your office, updating the information you're using is particularly important. However, regardless of where a copy of a database is stored, Notes provides you and other members of a workgroup an efficient way to keep your work up-to-date.

CHAPTER 19

Replicating Databases

▶ ▶ *F*AST *T*RACK

▶ **Database replication is a procedure**   **569**

that updates and distributes copies of the same Notes database, known as *replicas*, which are stored on different servers. Replication makes all copies of a database essentially
identical *over time*, which means they don't become exact
copies instantly.

▶ **To create a new replica of a database**   **572**

choose File ➤ New Replica. The New Replica dialog box
appears. Choose the server where the database you want
to copy is stored. Notes fills this box in for you if you selected the database on your Workspace before you began
the replication process. Enter a name in the Filename text
box, if Notes hasn't filled it in for you. Choose the server
where your new replica will be stored in the New Replica,
Server text box. Choose Local to store it on your hard disk
or a floppy disk. Type a name in the Filename text box (for
the new replica. You can choose to copy the Replicate Access Control List (ACL), or to select the Only replicate
documents saved in the last [ ] days option. Select one of
the options under Initialize and Copy. Click on New to
continue.

▶ **To update a replica**   **573**

click on the database's icon in your Workspace to select it,
or you can open it. Choose Tools ➤ Replicate. Enter your
password, if one has been created. The Tools Replicate dialog box appears. Enter or select the server if necessary. Select the desired Replicate options from the list. Click on
OK to begin replication.

▶ *There are two methods of selective replication*   **575**

local selective replication and *global* selective replication. The local method is useful for a database that is locally administered at each site and would be appropriate for smaller sites, individual departments, and dial-up users. For centralized database management, where an organization supports more than one site, global selective replication is a more useful method.

▶ *To review the replication history of a database*   **581**

click on the database's icon to select it. Choose File ➤ Database ➤ Information. Click on the Replication button. Click on the View History button. The Replication History dialog box appears. The replication history reflects the date and time of the last replication, the server with which the database replicated, and whether documents were sent or received, or both. Click on the By Date or By Server button to display information in either of these ways. Click on Cancel to close the dialog box.

▶ *Your Notes Log database contains*   **583**

additional replication information. Select the database and choose the Replication Events view from the View menu. The view appears. When you double-click one of the replication events in the view, a Replication Log Entry document appears. The document reveals how many documents in a particular database were added, deleted, and updated on both sides of the replication. The Events field displays additional information or problems that have occurred.

►► **O**ne of the most impressive features in Lotus Notes is a process known as *database replication*. Basically, replication is a procedure that updates and distributes copies of the same Notes database, known as *replicas*, which are stored on different servers. In this chapter, we discuss replication by explaining how to:

- Create a new database replica
- Update a replica
- Perform selective replications
- Track replication events
- Handle replication conflicts

Suppose there are two copies of an insurance policy database, one on a claims adjuster's notebook computer and the other back at the company's headquarters, which is used by her assistant. Yesterday the copies were identical, but today the claims adjuster investigated a house that was damaged by fire and an office building with burst water pipes. She subsequently wrote her reports and added them to the copy of the database on her notebook computer. Back at company headquarters, her assistant responded to telephone calls from the distraught policy holders and recorded the status of the calls in the copy of the database on her workstation.

The two copies of the database are now out of synch with each other because changes have been made to them separately. Both copies must now be resynchronized and made identical again through replication. Notes can handle this task automatically when the claims adjuster returns to her office. She replicates the copy of the database on her notebook computer with the insurance company's database.

Replication is a powerful tool because the process enables copies of the same database on different networks, located in different locations, or even different time zones, to reflect changes and become identical over time. The servers connect to each other at scheduled intervals, and the databases replicate changes to documents, access control lists, and the design elements in forms and views.

▶▶ *How Does Replication Work?*

Replication makes all copies of a database essentially identical *over time*, which means they don't become exact copies instantly. The process is an ongoing one. If a user makes changes in one copy of a database, replication ensures that those changes are added to all copies, as long as the replication options are set up to do so. However, since many people can be using copies of the same database and updating the individual copies daily, making all of them identical at the same time is unlikely.

▶ *Managing Replication*

Replication takes time and requires specific Notes server resources. If you are developing a database for a multiserver environment, and you want to have the database replicated, work with the Notes Administrator to determine the replication schedule that makes the most sense for the system topology.

You can set up replication between servers, or between a workstation and a server for Dial-up users, which we discussed in Chapter 10. Both methods are similar.

 ▶▶ **N O T E**

> **Defining replication settings for a database requires Manager access; however, you only need Designer access to define the selective replication formula.**

▶ *Handling Frequent Document Updates*

There are two types of replication you can consider for handling periodic document updates: *server-to-server replication* and *dial-up (workstation-to-server replication)*. Server-to-server replication occurs during scheduled server replication, or when the Notes Administrator manually forces replication. Replication for a local database on a workstation occurs when you perform a data exchange using the Tools ➤ Replicate command.

Dial-up (workstation-to-server) replication is handy if you use Notes on a LAN workstation as well as remotely. You can create a complete or partial database replica on your computer before leaving your office, save it to a floppy disk, and then copy it to your laptop or remote workstation once you are off-site or on the road.

▶ Scheduling Regular Replication

Replication is typically scheduled every few hours of a work day for Notes databases with time-sensitive information. This can be crucial for organizations whose databases are accessed and modified by many people. For databases that aren't modified as often or where the information isn't critical, replication can be conducted once a day. When a database is replicated over telephone lines between distant sites, replication might be scheduled once or twice a week and during the evening hours when long distance rates are lower.

 ▶▶ **N O T E**

> **Your organization's Notes Administrator is the person responsible for setting up and scheduling replication of databases. If you work off-site or on the road and you use Dial-up Notes, you should find out from the Notes Administrator when the best time is to replicate.**

▶ Monitoring Database Replication

If you're a Dial-up Notes user who is using Notes off-site, replication keeps your workstation copy of a database current with the database on the server. However, the process isn't fool-proof and isn't without its problems, especially when you're using telephone lines. You should always monitor the process once databases begin replicating to make sure they continue to replicate as you want them to. The message area on the Status Bar at the bottom of your Workspace displays all activity during the replication process. If a problem or conflict should occur, such as the sudden interruption of a telephone call that results in stopping replication, Notes will notify you.

►► **NOTE**

When you work off-site, it's useful to schedule server calls shortly before you begin working. This way you'll see the latest information in your local database replicas when you begin working—and again after you're done—so you can upload information to shared databases and use it when you send Notes mail. (Remember from Chapter 10 that the process of replication can run in the background, allowing you to continue working on other tasks on your remote machine.)

►► *Creating a Replica of a Database to a Workstation*

A replica is a copy of a shared database that you store either on a server or on your workstation. It can be displayed in your Notes Workspace just like the source database. Before you can use the database exchange feature of Dial-up Notes, you must first create local replicas of the shared databases you want to use. Creating local database replicas lets you use databases without being connected to a Notes server using a LAN (local area network) or telephone lines.

You can create a partial or full replica of any shared database. A partial replica contains a subset of the documents in the source database, based on selection criteria you specify in the Selective Replication dialog box. A full replica contains all the documents that exist in the source database at the time the replica is made.

►► **N O T E**

You must know the name of the server and the file name of the database you want to replicate before you attempt replication.

To update a database replica with information from the source database (and to update the shared database with information that you create locally), you perform replication, also known as *database exchange*. To do this, you can use a Remote Connection document or call the server directly using the Call Server dialog box. To create a new replica of a database, follow these steps:

1. Choose File ➤ New Replica. The New Replica dialog box appears, as shown in Figure 19.1.

2. Choose the server where the database you want to copy is stored. Notes fills this box in for you if you selected the database on your Workspace before you chose File ➤ New Replica.

3. Enter a name in the Filename text box, if Notes hasn't filled it in for you.

FIGURE 19.1 ►

The New Replica Dialog Box lets you create a new replica of a selected database.

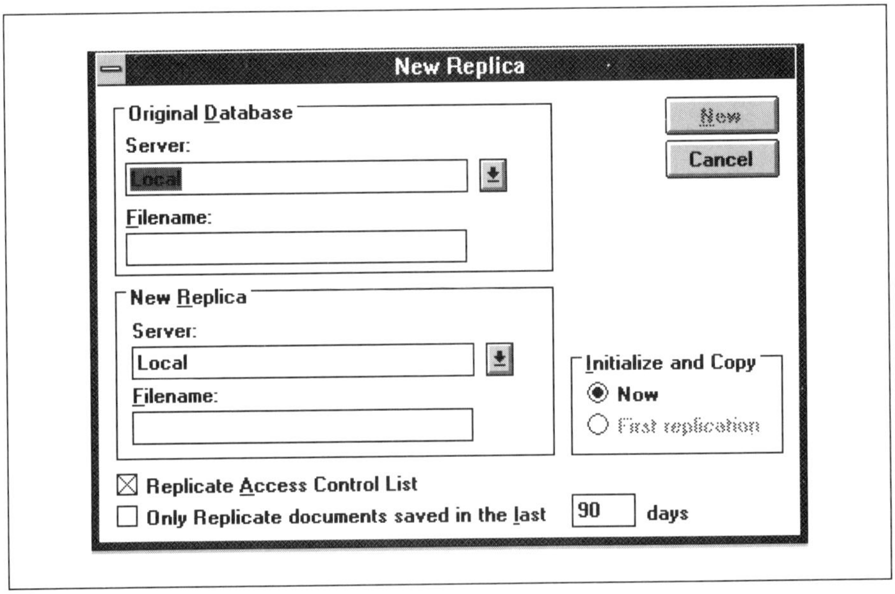

New Replica

┌─ Original **D**atabase ─────────────┐
Server:
`Local`   ▼
Filename:

┌─ New **R**eplica ───────────────────┐
Server:
`Local`   ▼
Filename:

┌ **I**nitialize and Copy ┐
◉ **N**ow
○ First replication

[New]
[Cancel]

☒ Replicate **A**ccess Control List
☐ Only Replicate documents saved in the **l**ast `90` days

4. Choose the server where your new replica will be stored in the New Replica, Server text box. Choose Local to store it on your hard disk or a floppy disk.

5. Type a name in the Filename text box (up to eight characters) for the new replica. Notes adds the .NSF extension for you.

6. You have the option to copy the Replicate Access Control List (ACL). This is selected by default. You can also select the Only replicate documents saved in the last 90 days option, which fills the new replica with those documents created in the 90 day time period. This is the default time period. Or you can specify a different time period. This option is especially useful for Dial-up Notes users who create smaller versions of shared databases to use on a laptop workstation.

7. Select one of the options under Initialize and Copy. The Now option fills the replica with documents as soon as you select New. The First replication fills the replica with documents at the first scheduled or forced replication. Until that time, the replica is called a "replica stub" because it consists only of a blank database icon and the Notes ID you were assigned. (There is no design or any documents.) If you're making a replica copy on a floppy disk to bring home, use this option because it guarantees that the replica will fit on the disk.

8. Click on New to create the new replica.

▶ *Updating a Replica*

Now that you've created a replica of a database on your workstation, you can update it at regular intervals, providing that you have access to the server and to the database. To update the replica, follow these steps:

1. Click on the database's icon in your Workspace to select it, or you can open it.

2. Choose Tools ➤ Replicate.

3. Enter your password, if one has been created. The Tools Replicate dialog box appears, as shown in Figure 19.2.

4. Enter or select the server if necessary (any server that contains a replica of the database will do).

FIGURE 19.2 ►

The Tools Replicate dialog box lets you set replication options for replicating a selected database.

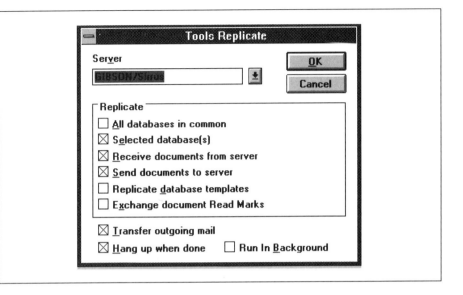

5. Select the desired Replicate options from the list. Typically, you would choose the Selected database(s), Receive documents from server, and Send documents to server options.

6. Select the Transfer outgoing mail and Hang up when done options. The first option sends mail but doesn't replicate your entire mail database, and the second option ends the telephone connection when replication is complete. The Run In Background options allows you to continue to work while replication is proceeding in the background.

7. Click on OK to begin replication.

 ►► **T I P**

The length of time for replicating a database depends of the number of changes that have been made. Sometimes the procedure can take quite a while. So a word to the wise: If you need to replicate long distance, do it in the evening when telephone rates are lower. (Also, read on to find out how you can restrict the number of changes that are replicated.)

▶ *Replicating Selective Information*

There are two approaches for handling selective replication: *local* selective replication and *global* selective replication. The local approach is useful for a database that is locally administered at each site and would be appropriate for smaller sites, individual departments, and dial-up users. For example, if space on your workstation or laptop is limited and you want your replica to receive only certain types of information from the source database, this approach would be suitable. By replicating only part of the source database, you can also save the time and expense of long remote replication times. However, you must have Designer or Manager access to create formulas for selective replication of a database.

T I P

> **Selection formulas for replication are the same as selection formulas for views, which we discussed in Chapter 15.**

To specify what documents a replica will receive when replicating a particular database directly, follow the steps below. You define a replication formula only for the current database that's been selected; this formula affects what gets copied into the current database whenever its server is the destination server during replication:

1. Click on the database's icon to select it.

2. Choose File ➤ Database ➤ Information. The Database Information dialog box appears.

3. Click on the Replication button. The Replication Settings dialog box appears.

4. Click on the Selective button. The Selective Replication dialog box appears, as shown in Figure 19.3.

5. In the Copy Documents selected by text box, write a formula to select which documents will replicate from the source to the destination. The default formula **SELECT @All** selects all documents from the source. Notes adds the word SELECT to all selection

FIGURE 19.3 ▶

The Selective Replication dialog box enables you to replicate only certain types of information from the source database.

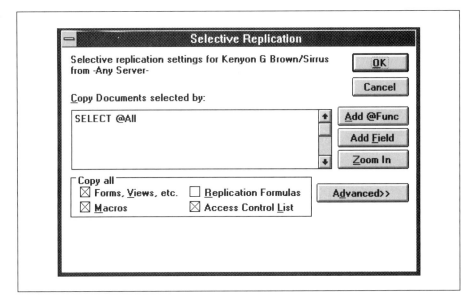

formulas when they are saved, so you don't have to type it. You can choose these options:

- Click the Add @Func button to display a list of available @functions that you can paste into the formula.
- Click the Add Field button to display a list of all the fields from all the forms in the database that you can use in the formula.
- Click on the Zoom In button to enlarge the editing area when you're writing a formula.

6. Select any of the following options:

- Forms, Views, etc. to copy the high-level design elements, i.e., all forms, views, and shared fields.
- Macros to copy all macros.
- Replication Formulas to copy any replication formulas created at the source database. This is useful for a centrally administered database where a database manager sets up replication formulas for all other servers.
- Access Control List to copy the ACL.

7. Click on OK to save the replication criteria. This information will be saved with the database and will not appear in other replicas of the database unless the managers have chosen to replicate replication formulas.

 ▶▶ **WARNING**

The @IsResponseDoc function will replicate *all* response documents, even those whose main (parent) documents are not selected by the formula. These orphaned response documents will not show up in any hierarchi-cal views.

For centralized database management, where an organization supports more than one site, global selective replication is a more useful approach. The current database is managed and maintained at a central location. You define the replication formula for the current database, in addition to one or more replicas at the different sites. In this way, you can control how they replicate even when they're not replicating directly with the current database.

A database manager sets up selective replication on a master database that replicates to other servers. Replicas receive those documents that the database manager determines are suitable to each individual site. The main advantage to this approach is that the database manager knows what each site is receiving and can control and predict the costs for dial-up connections to remote sites. Selective replication also saves disk space at each site, since they don't need to store the entire database.

To set up selective replication for all replicas of a particular database, you would follow the same steps as above. When the Selective Replication dialog box appears, click on the Advanced button. The Selective Replication dialog box now displays a list of Destination and Source servers at the bottom, as shown in Figure 19.4. You can define a replication formula for each combination of servers that replicate the current database. Follow these steps:

1. Create a formula that selects which documents will replicate.

2. Choose to copy forms, views, etc., macros, replication formulas, or the access control list from the source database. (If you want all

FIGURE 19.4 ▶

The Selective Replication dialog box displays a list of Destination and Source servers when you click on the Advanced button.

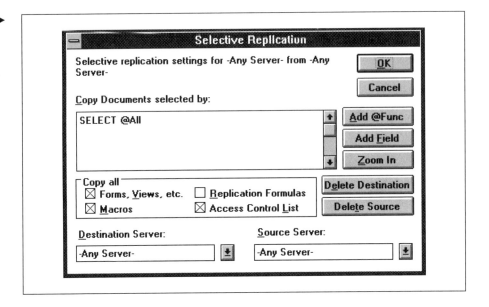

the replicas to use the same replication formulas, select Replication Formulas.)

3. Enter the specific server's name, or accept the default of -Any Server- from the Destination Server list box. This identifies the server that will receive the updates. The new name will stay as a choice in the list box, unless you remove it by selecting Delete Destination.

4. Enter the new name or accept the default name -Any Server- from the Source Server list box. The default name means that the criteria you specify will hold when replicating from any server. The new name you enter will identify what server the database originates from. This name will stay as a choice in the From box, unless you remove it by selecting Delete Source.

5. Change the criteria for different servers by changing the formula for each Destination Server and Source Server combination.

6. Click on OK to save the replication criteria.

The information will be saved in other replicas of the database unless the managers have chosen to replicate the replication formula.

▶▶ *Handling Replication Conflicts*

Database replicas aren't identical at all times. As we have mentioned, servers connect to other servers to update the replicas on a scheduled basis. Sometimes two users might edit the same document between data exchanges, resulting in simultaneous updates. The replicas contain different information until the next time the servers replicate. You might open multiple copies of a document yourself, edit one or more of them, and then close and save each version of the document. In any case, there would be different replicas of the database.

Notes handles the situation by maintaining a revision history of each document. During replication, Notes updates the revision history and detects the concurrent updates. At this point, Notes designates the update with the most changes as the main (original) document, or the "winner." The other revised documents are considered response documents, or "losers." (In case of a tie, the most recent update wins.) A view marks each response document with a diamond-shaped symbol in the left column and displays each one on a separate line, indented below the main document. The losers are considered "conflicting" documents and are labeled with [**Replication or Save Conflict**]. Users can see immediately that a conflict has occurred and must be resolved.

If a document is edited in one replica and deleted in another, the deletion takes precedence. The database designer can exclude conflicting documents from a view by adding the following to the view's selection formula (see Chapter 15 for more information):

```
& !@IsAvailable($Conflict)
```

You might wonder what you can do about simultaneous updates when you want to delete the losers but save their information. You can compare all versions of the document to see if the responses (losers) contain any information that you want to add to the winning document. If they do, copy the information and paste it into the winning document. Then delete the losers.

What if you want to delete the winner and make a loser the saved document or new winner? You would open the loser you want to use, switch to Edit mode, then save the document. This would remove the document's conflict status, remove the black diamond, and promote it to main document status. You would then select the response documents, if any, and choose Edit ➤ Cut or press Ctrl+X. You would place the pointer anywhere on the new winner (the document you chose to keep) and choose Edit ➤ Paste or press Ctrl+V. This makes the documents you cut previously into response documents to the new winner. Finally, you would delete the old winning document.

▶ *Preventing Replication Conflicts*

As the designer of a database, you can use two methods to reduce the potential for replication conflicts: You can assign users Author access so they can edit only the documents they compose, or you can take advantage of release 3's version control feature, which saves edited copies as *different* documents. This way, Notes will save the original document as the main one and the revisions as responses. Notes can also save the most recent update as the main document, with the previous ones as responses.

To use Notes' version control, you have to go back and edit the form that was used to compose the document. Follow these steps:

1. Click on the database's icon to select it or open the database.

2. Choose Design ➤ Forms. The Design Forms dialog box appears.

3. Highlight the form you want to edit from the list and click on the Edit button. (You can also double-click on the form's name.) This displays the form in Design mode.

4. Choose Design ➤ Form Attributes. The Design Form Attributes dialog box appears, as shown in Figure 19.5.

5. Select either the Updates become responses or the Prior versions become responses option, depending on your preference.

6. Click on OK to confirm the change.

7. Press Ctrl+S to save the form.

8. Press Esc to close the form.

FIGURE 19.5

The Design Form Attributes dialog box lets you choose either the Updates become responses option or the Prior versions become responses option to prevent replication conflicts.

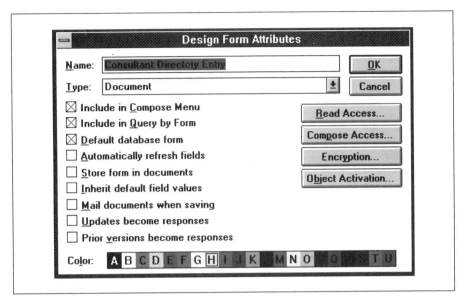

▶ *Keeping Track of Previous Replications*

One of the most useful features of replication is how Notes tracks each replication event for each database. By tracking the events, Notes creates a replication history of a database. Notes determines which documents to replicate the next time it does so with the same server on the basis of the dates it records. This information can be useful for reviewing replication events and troubleshooting problems. To review the replication history of a database, follow these steps:

1. Click on the database's icon to select it.

2. Choose File ➤ Database ➤ Information. The Database Information dialog box appears.

3. Click on the Replication button. The Replication Settings dialog box appears.

4. Click on the View History button. The Replication History dialog box appears, as shown in Figure 19.6. The replication history reflects the date and time of the last replication, the server with which the database replicated, and whether documents were sent or received, or both.

FIGURE 19.6 ▶

The Replication History dialog box displays the date and time of the last replication, the server with which the database replicated, and whether documents were sent or received, or both.

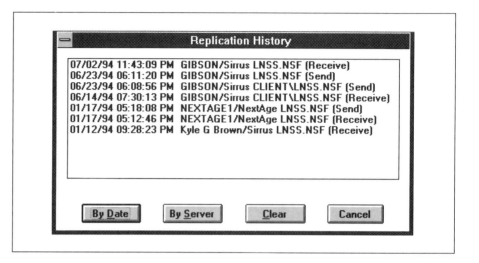

Replication History
07/02/94 11:43:09 PM GIBSON/Sirrus LNSS.NSF (Receive)
06/23/94 06:11:20 PM GIBSON/Sirrus LNSS.NSF (Send)
06/23/94 06:08:56 PM GIBSON/Sirrus CLIENT\LNSS.NSF (Send)
06/14/94 07:30:13 PM GIBSON/Sirrus CLIENT\LNSS.NSF (Receive)
01/17/94 05:18:08 PM NEXTAGE1/NextAge LNSS.NSF (Send)
01/17/94 05:12:46 PM NEXTAGE1/NextAge LNSS.NSF (Receive)
01/12/94 09:28:23 PM Kyle G Brown/Sirrus LNSS.NSF (Receive)

[By **D**ate] [By **S**erver] [**C**lear] [Cancel]

 ▶▶ **T I P**

When you experience replication problems (and you probably will), you can manually clear a database's history and start over with a clean slate. Just click on the Clear button in the Replication History dialog box. This forces Notes to replicate all the documents that have changed since the database was created, not just those documents that have been modified since the last replication.

5. Click on the By date or By Server button to display information in either of these ways.

6. Click on Cancel to close the dialog box.

Notes will update the replication history of a database only if the replication has been successful. If the replication fails, no history will be recorded. Notes will try to replicate the same changes during the next replication.

As we discussed earlier, Notes compares the date of the last replication with the date when each document was last modified. In this way, Notes includes or excludes a document from the next replication. If a document contains changes that occurred since the last replication, the document will be included in the next replication. If the document hasn't been modified since the last replication, Notes will exclude it from the next replication. Thus, Notes doesn't take any more time than it needs to complete replication. With large databases that contain hundreds of documents, a lot of time can be saved. Otherwise, replicating would be an inefficient process.

To see a document's last modification date, follow these steps:

1. Select a database.

2. Open a view.

3. Select or open a document.

4. Choose Design ➤ Document Info. The Design Document Info dialog box appears, as shown in Figure 19.7. It displays the date of the last modification, in addition to other pertinent information.

5. Click on OK to close the dialog box.

You can also view your Notes Log database that's located in your Workspace to see additional replication information. Select the database and choose the Replication Events view from the View menu. The view is shown in Figure 19.8. When you double-click one of the replication events in the view, a Replication Log Entry document appears, as

FIGURE 19.7 ▶

The Design Document Info dialog box displays the date of the last modification, in addition to other pertinent field and database information.

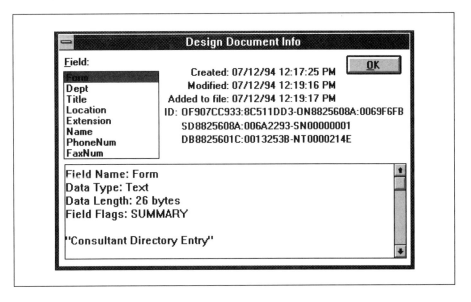

shown in Figure 19.9. The document reveals how many documents in a particular database were added, deleted, and updated on both sides of the replication. The Events field displays additional information or problems that have occurred.

Like any database, the documents and views in the Notes Log database occupy disk space. Therefore, you can choose *not* to collect such data about a database on your workstation. Just follow these steps:

1. Click on the database's icon to select it.

2. Choose File ➤ Database ➤ Information. The Database Information dialog box appears.

3. Click on the User Activity button. The User Activity dialog box appears, as shown in Figure 19.10.

4. Deselect the Record Activity option.

5. Click on OK to save the change.

FIGURE 19.8 ▶

The Replication Events view lets you choose a server and see the number of database replications that have taken place on the server.

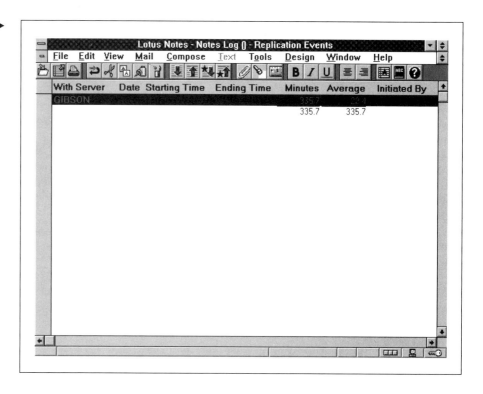

FIGURE 19.9 ▶

The Replication Log Entry reveals how many documents in a particular database were added, deleted, and updated on both sides of the replication. The Events field displays additional information or problems that have occurred.

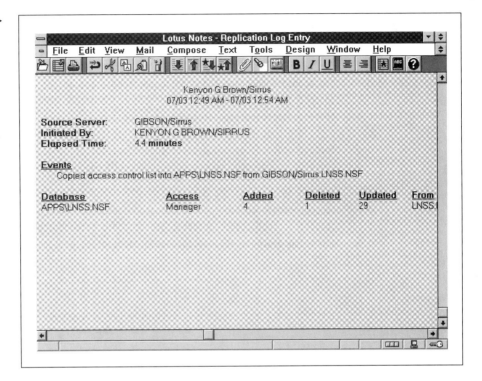

FIGURE 19.10 ▶

The User Activity dialog box lets you choose to record the amount of replication activity that a particular database has undergone.

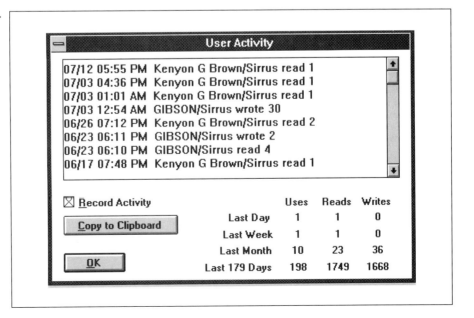

▶▶ *What's Next?*

Replication is a powerful tool because the process enables copies of the same database on different networks, located in different locations, or even different time zones, to reflect changes and become identical over time, which means they don't become exact copies instantly. The process is an ongoing one. If a user makes changes in one copy of a database, replication ensures that those changes are added to all copies, as long as the replication options are set up to do so.

In the next chapter, we discuss indexing a database and performing searches for words and phrases. You can create a full text index for a database to help users search for specific information. This can be an invaluable feature of any Notes database.

CHAPTER 20

Indexing a
Notes Database

▸▸ *F*AST *T*RACK

▶ ***To perform a simple query on multiple databases*** **607**

click on one database icon to select it. Hold down the
Shift key and click on as many other database icons as you
want. Choose Edit ➤ Find. A list of the selected databases
appears in the view window. To open them, double-click
the database titles, or click the arrows in the left margin,
or select a database using the arrow keys and then press ↵.
Type your query into the search box as usual, and press
the Search button or press ↵.

▶ ***The Query Builder helps*** **612**

you automatically build queries using *and, or,* or *not* logical
operators that allow you to search for more than one word
or to exclude specific words. You can also refine your
search. To create complex full text queries, open a database and choose Edit ➤ Find. Type one or more words
(separated by commas) into the field options. Click on Options. Specify how you want the search results displayed.
Click on Search to perform the search and show the
search results.

▶ ***You use Query by Form to search*** **613**

for text in specific fields in a form. To use Query by Form,
open a view in a full text indexed database. Click and hold
down the right mouse button on the Form button in the
Search Bar. Notes displays the list of forms available for
Query by Form in this database. Choose a form Notes displays the form without any text in the fields, just as it looks
before you compose a document. Enter your query into
the field you want to search, just as you'd type text into
any document. Click on Search.

►► **O****ne of** Notes' greatest strengths is its indexing capabilities. You can create a full text index for a database to help users search for specific information. This can be an invaluable feature of any Notes database. By searching for a particular word or phrase, users can locate the information quickly (if it exists). Otherwise, imagine the amount of time they would spend reading documents and scrolling through views in order find a piece of information they needed.

A full text index is made up of a special index files of the particular database's text that allow Notes to process queries within seconds. These separate index files enable Notes to conduct a complex search of a specific database. When Notes creates the index files, it "catalogs" all the data in the documents in a selected database on the basis of options you have set. (We describe the options below in "Creating a Full text Index.") The structure of the index files provides users with a sophisticated way of locating documents in a database.

Over time, a Notes database can become very large. Inevitably, you're not going to remember all the documents you've composed, edited, or read. You may or may not be able to recall the document where you can find an important piece of information that you know exists but you don't know where the document is in which the information is located. By creating a full text index for a database that you've designed, you give users the means to conduct a full text search of the database.

Notes provides two methods for finding text in databases: *plain text search* and *full text search*. In this chapter, we explain the differences between using the two methods and cover these topics:

- Creating a full text index
- Reindexing
- Using the Search Bar
- Using Find and Replace

Release 3 must be running on a workstation or server in order to create or perform a full text index on any database. However, you can perform a plain text search on a database that resides on a server or workstation running earlier versions of Notes (versions 1.X and 2.X), or on a database that has not been indexed for full text search.

▶▶ *Using Plain Text and Full Text Searches*

A plain text search doesn't provide the full functionality of full text search, and it's slower because the database isn't indexed in advance. However, a plain text search does allow you to replace text that matches your criteria with other text that you specify (using find and replace). However, you can only search for a particular word or phrase in the documents in the database's current view. You should use a plain text search when you or the Notes Administrator don't want to use disk space for a full text index, which can be quite large.

Performing a full text search lets you search for words, phrases, numbers, and data, as well as perform queries using wildcards, logical operators, proximity, and other advanced features. A query is a single set of search criteria. It can be a single word or phrase, or it can include the wildcards *and* and *or*, and other special operators. The results of a full text search can also rank documents by "relevance," which simply means that Notes will display the document(s) that most closely matches the search criteria you have set.

 ▶▶ **N O T E**

> **Object Linking or Embedding (OLE) information that is embedded in Rich Text or Text format is indexed along with the rest of the text in a document. However, the data must be rendered as text in the Notes document— you can't search OLE data that is represented by its server application's icon or as a bitmap.**

Notes provides you with a convenient way to conduct searches: the *Search Bar*. You can use the Search Bar to enter simple or complex queries. However, if you haven't created a full text index for a database and you try to perform a query or display the Search Bar, Notes will display the message that's shown in Figure 20.1.

FIGURE 20.1

This message appears when you try to perform a query or display the Search Bar before you've created a full text index for a database.

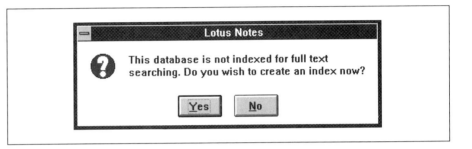

We're jumping the gun by discussing the Search Bar before you've created an index, but we wanted to tell you about this handy feature. Figure 20.2 shows the Search Bar.

FIGURE 20.2

You use the Search Bar for building a query.

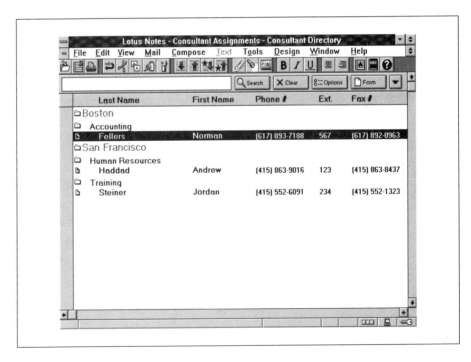

In databases that are indexed for full text searching, you can expand the Search Bar to use advanced search features. You can find out what the full text Search Bar buttons do without activating them. Just click and hold the right mouse button and check the active window's title bar.

Like the ruler, the Search Bar can stay at the top of the screen while you perform multiple searches or while you do other unrelated tasks. When you're done searching, you can close the Search Bar, but there's no need to.

▶▶ *Creating a New Full Text Index*

As we mentioned above, before you can perform a full text search, the database you want to search must have a full text index. For shared databases (those on a server), indexes can be created by anyone with Designer access to the databases. For local databases (those on workstations), users can create the indexes themselves, which is very handy because they don't have to rely on you to create the index for them.

The size of a full text index can be significant and take up a lot of room on a computer. Therefore, before you index every database at your site (or those on your workstation), determine the need for full text searching for each database. Sometimes enhancing or adding views can assist users in locating their documents quickly without the need for a full text index.

To create a new full text index, click on the database's icon in the Workspace to select it for indexing. Then follow these steps:

1. Choose File ➤ Full Text Search ➤ Create Index. The Full Text Create Index dialog box appears, as shown in Figure 20.3.

2. Select any of the following options:

   • **Case Sensitive Index:** Users must use the "exactcase" operator to search for exact cases they specify. Using a case-sensitive index increases the size of the index by about 5–10%.

   • **Exclude words in Stop Word File:** Identifies a list of words that you don't want Notes to index. These are usually words such as: *the*, *a*, *an*, *were*, and so on. Excluding words in a Stop

FIGURE 20.3 ►

The Full Text Create In-dex dialog box lets you select specific settings when creating the full text index.

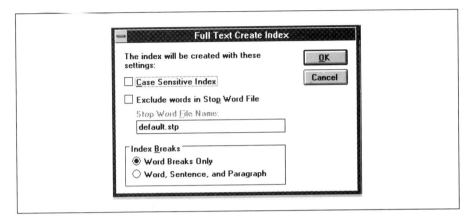

Word file decreases the size of the index about 15–20% for a typical file, but it also prevents users from searching for the listed words in a query. If a Stop Word file includes the word *of*, you can't search for *cost of living* (but you could search for *lost* OR *living*). The default Stop Word file's file name is DE-FAULT.STP. It's located in your Notes program directory. Although it can be edited using any ASCII editor, it's best to copy the file under a new name and edit the copy, so you can revert to the default Stop Word file at any time.

 ►► **TIP**

The line [0-9]+ in DEFAULT.STP tells Notes not to index numbers. You may want to create a Stop Word file with only this line in it (call it something like NONUMBER.STP) and use it with databases where users won't need to search for numbers.

3. Select one of the options under Index Breaks (these options only affect proximity searching):

- **Word Breaks Only:** Doesn't allow users to restrict searches to words within the same sentence or paragraph. This is the default option.
- **Word, Sentence, and Paragraph:** Allows users to search for words within the same sentence or paragraph. Selecting

this option increases the size of the index. Also note that individual bullet items are each separate paragraphs (a paragraph is defined as the text between two hard returns). Most users search more successfully using the proximity operator NEAR than using Word, Sentence, and Paragraph.

4. Click on OK. If the database is located on a workstation, Notes displays the message telling you that the index must be indexed manually.

5. Click on OK to continue. Notes displays a message when indexing is complete, as shown in Figure 20.4. The message box displays the number of documents that have been added, updated, deleted, and the size indexed. (Since you're creating a new index, only the number of documents that have been added to the index will be displayed.)

6. Click on OK again.

The index files are subsequently stored in a directory that takes its name from the indexed database itself, in the form *DATABASEFILE-NAME.FT*, which is created by Notes when you first create the index.

FIGURE 20.4 ▶

Notes displays a message when indexing is complete, showing the number of documents that have been added, updated, deleted, and the size indexed.

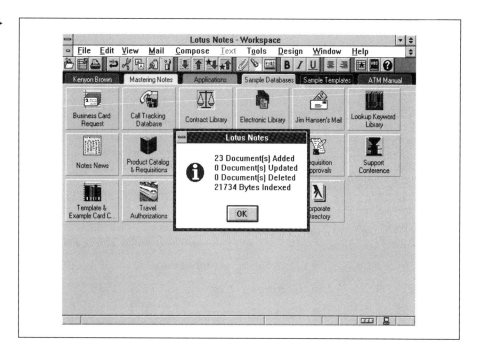

For example, if the database is SCHEDULE.NSF, the full text index subdirectory is SCHEDULE.FT. This directory is stored by Notes in the same directory as the database to which it belongs—normally, that's your Notes data directory.

The size of a full text index depends on three factors:

- Database size
- Percentage of the database that is text
- Whether the Word Breaks Only or the Word, Sentence and Paragraph option was selected in the Full Text Create Index dialog box (see above)

The percentage of a database that is text ranges from about 25% to about 75%. The text portion is the contents of text and rich text fields, and number and date-time fields. The nontext portion includes bitmaps, attachments, buttons, macros, database design information (authors, keywords, views), audio notes, and other nontext features. The size of an index that includes Word Breaks only accounts for approximately 50% of the text component of the database. The size of an index that includes Word, Sentence, and Paragraph Breaks accounts for almost 75% of the text component of the database.

These percentages are important to keep in mind because indexes can become huge and occupy an immense amount of space on a computer. For a server, this might not be an issue. However, for a workstation with limited hard disk space, the size of an index should be monitored. You may decide not to create a full text index and be satisfied performing a plain text search instead.

▶ *Full Text Search Limitations*

After a full text index is created, all of the text in all the documents in the database is indexed, with the following exceptions:

- Text within encrypted fields
- Text within attachments
- Computed text
- Keyword synonyms

- Words you exclude when you use a Stop Word file

- Text that is new or has been modified since the database was last indexed

- Text that appears in a view but isn't located in any document (such as column headings)

Because all text is indexed (with the above exceptions), you can successfully search for text in fields that aren't displayed in the current form, and in paragraphs that are hidden using the Hide When options in the Text Paragraph dialog box.

▶▶ **T I P**

A full text search finds all instances of query expressions in all documents located in the current view. If this view doesn't display all the documents in the database, you may need to query more than one view (just choose another view and click the Search button—the query remains in the Search Bar until you change it). To find all instances of a query expression in all documents in a database, create and display a view that contains all the documents in the database.

Document Size Limitations

The default document size limitation for creating an index is approximately 100,000 words for Windows. You can increase the limit by changing the following variable in NOTES.INI:

    ft_max_instances=<max # of words>

For example, the expression **ft_max_instances=200000** would increase the document size to 200,000 words. The full text index uses an amount of memory equal to about ten times the setting of ft_max_instances. So, in Windows, changing the setting to 200,000 uses about 2MB of memory to index documents. If your workstation or server runs low on memory as a result of specifying too high a setting, performance will be slowed down significantly.

Using Characters

You might wonder what constitutes a "word" in a document that is indexed. Any text you enter is a word. Also, the following characters may be part of words:

:	colon
\	backslash
.	period
&	ampersand

This feature allows you to search documents for expressions such as *cc:Mail*, *5.95*, and *AT&T*. Also, the @ (at sign) can be used as a prefix or be embedded within words. If it's embedded within a word, the word is treated as two separate words. For example, the expression **first@last** is interpreted during the search as the words *first* and *last*.

Matching Numbers

When your query finds a match in a field of type numeric or date-time, the match will not be highlighted. However, the document will be returned in the search results. You can only search for dates using the numeric operators < , = , > when the dates are in a field with the time-date data type. You cannot search for dates that include a year earlier than 1932.

▶▶ **N O T E**

You can't query date/time or numeric fields that are added to a form after the database is full text indexed. To do so, the full text index must first be deleted and then recreated.

Finding Hidden Text

When a full text search finds nondisplayed text (hidden text), the document containing that text is selected by the search, but no text is highlighted. You'll receive the message "Some highlights are not visible with this form."

Revising Documents

Documents in a database are sometimes revised between index updates. After a document is revised but before it is reindexed, queries may select this document and return it erroneously in search results. Also if a revised document is appropriately selected, Notes can't always highlight the search terms correctly and you'll receive the message "Some highlights are not visible."

Using Computed Fields

Using computed fields in forms can produce unexpected search results. What you see on your computer screen in fields that are computed for display isn't actually stored in the Notes document; therefore computed data can't be indexed or queried. This may result in unexpected behavior, because you may not know which fields are computed for display and which fields are actually stored in the document.

Using Keyword Fields

Using keyword synonyms prevents indexing of the keyword. However in the specific case of Query by Form, this restriction doesn't apply. This is because Notes allows keyword synonyms for display, but an alternate value is actually stored in the document. For example, the database designer can specify a keyword such as **Sunday|1**, where the user can select the synonym 1 but the actual keyword is Sunday.

Using Encrypted Text

Encrypted fields in documents aren't indexed and cannot be queried. This is because Notes servers generally don't have the encryption keys necessary to decrypt documents while they're being indexed. In addition, indexing confidential information could result in a breach of security: Queries that select documents with encrypted fields allow users to guess at the contents of the documents, even if they can't read them.

▶▶ **N O T E**

File attachments aren't indexed in Notes Release 3, and cannot be queried.

Performing Multiple Database Searches

You can create queries that span multiple databases. However, note the following limitations:

- You can't execute saved queries and macros for multiple database views.

- To use Query by Form, the selected field name must be used in a form in all of the selected databases.

- You can't print, cut, or copy documents from multiple databases. You must do these operations from one database at a time. For example, to print documents from all the databases in the view, expand the view for each database—one at a time -- and select and print the documents.

▶ Reindexing a Database

Since most databases change over time (documents are added, deleted, and modified), reindexing should take place periodically. Server-based databases can be set up to reindex automatically. However, you need to update the index of local databases (those on workstations) yourself using File ➤ Full Text Search ➤ Update Index.

If the server or workstation runs out of disk space during index creation, the index is unusable. When this happens, use File ➤ Full Text Search ➤ Delete Index to remove the unusable index. Retrieve or add disk space (if you can) and then recreate the index using File ➤ Full Text Search ➤ Create Index. Errors that occur during index creation or updating are indicated in the server's log.

▶ *Deleting the Index*

It is not safe to delete individual index files from the index directories in which they're stored. If you delete the *DATABASEFILENAME.FT* directory using DOS, the index will no longer function. If this happens (either by mistake or to reclaim server disk space), you can recreate the index any time using File ➤ Full Text Search ➤ Create Index. If the index is set to update automatically, you don't need to take any action because the index will be recreated at the next scheduled update time.

▶▶ *Searching for Words and Phrases*

If a database hasn't had a full text index created, you can still find words or phrases. Notes will search for a word or phrase in either selected documents in the active view or in only the titles of documents in the view. To search multiple views, you must search each view separately.

▶▶ **T I P**

If you know a particular view shows all documents in the database, search that view.

When Notes finds a word or phrase in documents in a view, it check-marks those documents that contain the word or phrase. If you want to use more sophisticated search features such as wildcard searching, and have Notes visually flag occurrences in the text of documents, the database *must* have an index for full text searching.

To search for a word or phrase, follow these steps:

1. Open the database you want to search.

2. Choose Edit ➤ Find. The Find dialog box appears, as shown in Figure 20.5. (To search only selected documents, select those documents in the view before you choose the Find command.)

3. Enter the word or phrase you want to find in the Find box.

4. Select any of the following:

   - **Case Sensitive:** Searches for occurrences of a word or phrase that have the capitalization you typed.
   - **Accent Sensitive:** Searches for occurrences of the word or phrase that have the accents you typed.
   - **Whole Word:** Searches only for occurrences of a word with spaces around it. For example, Notes ignores *Corp* if it occurs within *Corporation*.
   - **Backwards:** Searches backwards to the beginning of the document instead of forward to the end.

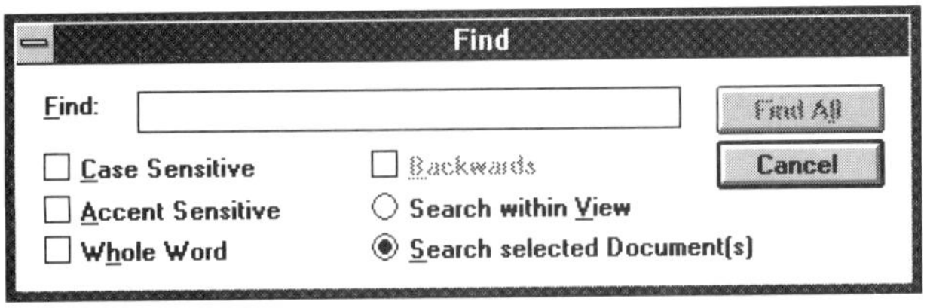

FIGURE 20.5 ▶

The Find dialog box lets you search for a particular word or phrase.

Find
Find: [_____]   Find All
☐ Case Sensitive   ☐ Backwards   Cancel
☐ Accent Sensitive   ○ Search within View
☐ Whole Word   ◉ Search selected Document(s)

5. Select one of the following:

- **Search within View:** Searches all document titles in the view, without searching contents of documents.
- **Search Selected Document(s):** Searches both titles and contents of selected (checkmarked) documents.

6. Select Find All or Find Next.

7. Click on Cancel when you're finished.

▶▶ *Using Find & Replace*

With Find & Replace, you can find words or phrases in a single document and replace them with other words or phrases. Notes will find and replace a word or phrase only in the active document. You can decide whether to replace each occurrence of the word or phrase as you find it, or replace all occurrences at once. If you want to find and replace a word or phrase in all the documents in a database, you *must* create an index for full text searching. To use Find & Replace, follow these steps:

1. Open the document you want to search in Edit mode and choose Edit ➤ Find & Replace. (If you open the document in Read mode, many of the Find & Replace options will be unavailable.) The Find & Replace dialog box appears, as shown in Figure 20.6.

2. Enter the word or phrase you want to find in the Find box.

3. Enter the word or phrase you want to replace it with in the Replace With box.

FIGURE 20.6

The Find & Replace dialog box lets you search for and replace words and phrases in a document.

Find and Replace
Find:
Replace With:
☐ Case Sensitive ☐ Backwards
☐ Accent Sensitive ☐ Whole Word
Replace
Cancel
Find Next
Replace Then Find
Replace All

4. Select any of the following:

- **Case Sensitive:** Searches for occurrences of a word or phrase that have the capitalization you typed.
- **Accent Sensitive:** Searches for occurrences of the word or phrase that have the accents you typed.
- **Whole Word:** Searches only for occurrences of a word with spaces around it. For example, Notes ignores *Jan* if it occurs within *Janice*.
- **Backwards:** Searches backwards to the beginning of the document instead of forward to the end.

5. Select any of the following:

- **Replace:** Replaces the next or selected occurrence of the word or phrase.
- **Cancel:** Stops searching and closes the dialog box.
- **Find Next:** Skips the current occurrence of the word or phrase and finds the next one. When Notes has just found an occurrence you don't want to replace, select Find Next. (If there are no occurrences, you see a message saying that your word or phrase was not found. Click on OK.)
- **Replace Then Find:** Replaces the current occurrence of the word or phrase and finds the next one. Selecting this option is the same as selecting Replace and then selecting Find Next.
- **Replace All:** Replaces all occurrences of the word or phrase in the document. When you select this option, Notes warns you that it cannot be undone. Click on OK to replace all occurrences, or click on Cancel to return to the Find & Replace dialog box. All occurrences are replaced. When Notes can't find any occurrences in the document, you'll see a message saying that your word or phrase was not found. Click on OK.

6. When you finish searching, select Cancel.

▶▶ *Performing Simple Full Text Queries*

Performing a simple full text query means searching for a single word in one or more databases. Notes selects a view for documents that satisfy your query and highlights the matching words within the documents. Before you can use full text search, the database you want to search must have a full text index in order to process queries within seconds.

 ▶▶ **N O T E**

> **A search is always performed in the current view unless multiple databases are selected. To search another view, choose it from the View menu, then repeat the search.**

To perform a simple query on a single database, follow these steps:

1. Open a database, then choose Edit ➤ Find if the Search Bar isn't already displayed. The Find dialog box appears.

2. Type a single word (the simplest form of query).

3. Click on Search or press ↵.

You can view the results in the following ways:

- To display search results sorted by relevance to your query, choose View ➤ Show Only Search Results or select Sorted by Relevance in the Search Options dialog box. A gray-scaled bar at the left side of the view indicates relevance; darker (more intense) gray next to a document means it's more relevant.

- To display search results as checkmarked documents in a normal view, choose View ➤ Show Only Search Results to deselect it or select Selected in View in the Search Options dialog box.

INTERPRETING THE RESULTS OF A FULL TEXT SEARCH

When a user completes a full text search of a particular database, Notes displays a new view of the database. This view contains only the documents that meet the search criteria. These documents are listed in the order of their relevance to the corresponding search criteria that's been set.

The first documents listed in the view are the ones Notes has found that contain the most occurrences of the search criteria. These documents are probably going to be the most useful to you. In this case "relevance" is based on the number of times your search criteria occurs in each document. The further down the view's list you go, the less likely documents are to be relevant to you because they contain the least number of occurrences of the search criteria.

  TIP

> You find the selected (checkmarked) documents just as you would any other time, by clicking the icon for Next Selected Document, scrolling, or pressing F3 (Shift+F3 goes to the *previous* selected document).

- To show search results in another view, choose the view from the View menu, then click Search again.

- To perform another query on the current search results, click the down arrow to expand the Search Bar, as shown in Figure 20.7, then click Refine; or press Shift while you click Search. (To collapse the bar, click the up arrow.)

- To clear the search results and display the original view, click Clear.

FIGURE 20.7

The Search Bar looks like this after it's been expanded.

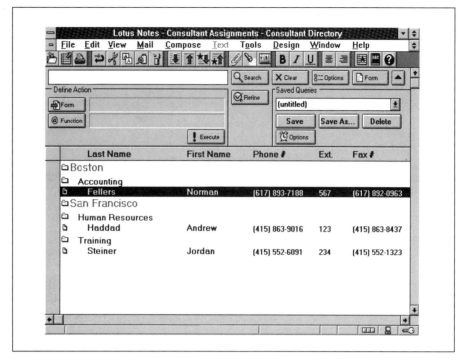

- To find the words that match your query, open any search result document.

Each word that matched your query is enclosed in a red rectangle (on a color monitor). To move from one instance of your search word to the next, Press Ctrl++. To move to the previous instance, press Ctrl+−. As you select each search word, its outline turns from red to blue (these colors may vary, depending on the document's background color). When you're done searching, you can hide the Search Bar by choosing View ➤ Show Search Bar again. But it's not necessary, as all other Notes functions work with or without the Search Bar.

▶▶ **N O T E**

Notes displays the Search Bar at the top of the view. The Search Bar is a toggle—it stays at the top of the view until you remove it by choosing View ➤ Show Search Bar.

To perform a simple query on multiple databases, follow these steps:

1. On your Workspace, click on one database icon to select it. Hold down the Shift key and click on as many other database icons as you want.

2. Choose Edit ➤ Find. A list of the selected databases appears in the view window, as shown in Figure 20.8.

3. To open them, double-click the database titles, or click the arrows in the left margin, or select a database using the arrow keys and then press ↵. The view displayed for each database is either the last view you used or its default view if you haven't opened the database before.

4. Type your query into the search box as usual, and press the search button or press ↵.

The view shows all the documents from all the selected databases that fit the search criteria. This view is sorted by database (in the order you selected them), and then by the relevance rank of its documents.

FIGURE 20.8

A list of databases that you want to query appears in a view window.

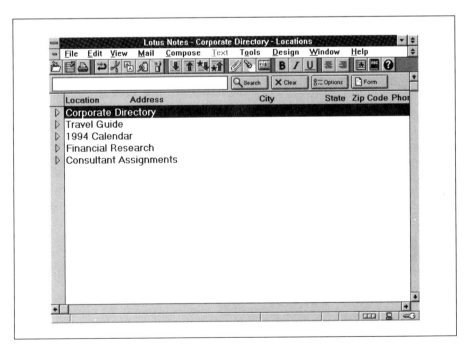

▶▶ T I P

**If a database has been indexed for full text search, and
you want to search only the document *titles* in a view,
press Shift while you choose Edit ➤ Find to open the
Find dialog box. Select Search within View.**

▶▶ *Building a Query*

You can build a query using the Search Bar and the Query Builder,
or with the Query by Form option that you access from the bar. The
Query Builder is a dialog box that helps you automatically build queries using *and, or,* or *not* logical operators that allow you to search for
more than one word using *or* to exclude specific words. You can also refine your search by using the following options:

Wildcards	Let you search for words using unspecified as well as specified letters.
Relevance ranking	Sorts the documents that satisfy your query by how well they match the query. Documents with multiple occurrences of query expressions are ranked higher than those with a single occurrence. Also, the ranking depends on the length of the document; a short document with one occurrence may rank higher than a longer document with two occurrences.
Hyphenated words	Lets you find words that may or may not have been hyphenated. For example, *full-text*, *full text*, and *fulltext* all satisfy the query **full-text**, while only *full text* satis-fies the query **full text**.

▶ *Using the Query Builder*

You can create complex full text queries in the following manner:

1. Open a database and choose Edit ➤ Find. The Query Builder dialog box appears, as shown in Figure 20.9.

2. Type one or more words (separated by commas) into the following fields:

   - **ALL of these words:** Performs the *and* operation between all words in this field. Selected documents must contain every word you type in this field. Select Anywhere in document or Near each other. Near each other performs a proximity search.

   - **One or more of these words:** Performs the *or* operation between all words in this field. Selected documents must contain at least one of the words you type here.

   - **Exclude documents with these words:** Performs the *not* operation on all words in this field. Selected documents must not contain any of the words you type here.

3. If you want to search only in documents created or modified before or after a specific date, select Find documents stored After or Before.

FIGURE 20.9 ▶

The Query Builder dialog box lets you create complex full text queries.

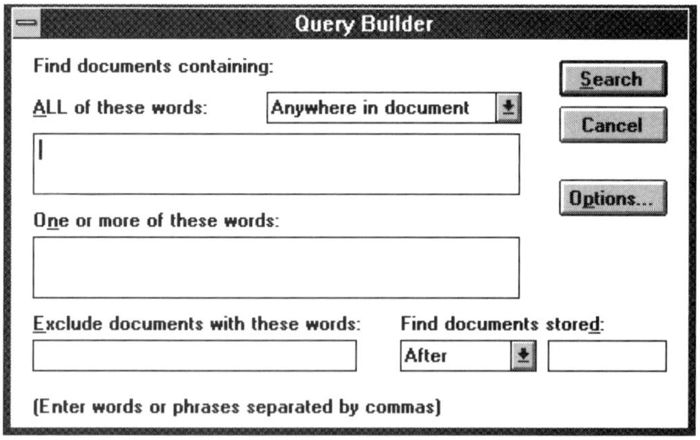

4. Select Options to open the Search Options dialog box, where you specify how you want the search results displayed. If you skip this step, the search results will be sorted by relevance, the default option.

5. Select Search to perform the search and show the search results.

▶ *Using Query by Form*

You can use Query by Form to search for text in specific fields in a form. Query by Form is available only when t the database is full text indexed, and the database designer has made at least one form available for Query by Form (this is done by keeping the default in the Design Form Attributes dialog box). First, however, you must display the Search Bar. Choose View ➤ Show Search Bar. The bar appears. To use Query by Form, follow these steps:

1. Open a view in a full text indexed database. The view must be able to display the form you're using for your query. Not all forms are available in all views.

2. Click and hold down the right mouse button on the Form button in the Search Bar. Notes displays the list of forms available for Query by Form in this database.

3. Choose a form. Notes displays the form without any text in the fields, just as it looks before you compose a document. For example, Figure 20.10 displays the Consultant Directory form from the Consultant Assignment database. You'll notice that the Search Bar has changed in order to perform the query.

4. Enter your query into the field you want to search, just as you'd type text into any document. The query can include the following elements:

- Any number of words—put phrases in quotes.
- Multiple items (words or phrases) separated by commas.
- Advanced query features (Boolean operators, wildcards, exactcase, and so on).
- Numbers, letters, spaces, and special characters. Examples of valid queries would be: "**full text search,**" **mail, Notes mail,** and **cc:Mail**.

FIGURE 20.10 ▶

The Search Bar has changed in order to perform a query on a document, which in this case is the Consult-ant Directory form from the Consultant Assignments database.

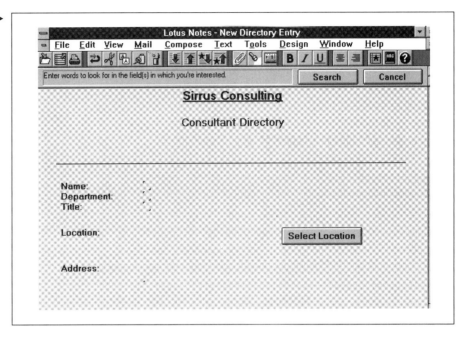

5. Click on Search.

Notes displays your search results just as if you'd performed a search using the Search Bar itself, or the Query Builder. To use Query by form again, repeat steps 2 through 5.

▶▶ *Choosing Search Options*

You can specify how to sort the search results, and whether to include variants of the word specified in your search. Open a database and then follow these steps:

1. Choose View ➤ Show Search bar.

2. Click the Options button in the bar (or select Options from the Query Builder dialog box). The Search Options dialog box appears, as shown in Figure 20.11.

FIGURE 20.11

The Search Options dialog box lets you specify how to sort the search results, and whether to include variants of the word specified in your search.

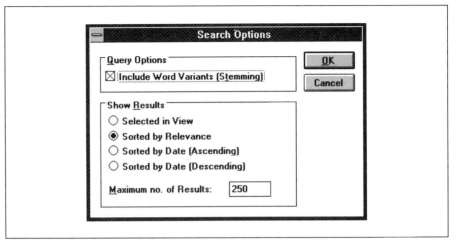

3. If you want to search for variants of the query word, select Include Word Variants (Stemming). This is the default. For example, if the query word is *print*, documents that contain the words *print*, *prints*, *printed*, and *printing* are selected. To search for the exact word only, deselect Include Word Variants (Stemming).

4. Select one of the following search result options:

   - **Selected in View:** Displays search results as checkmarked documents in the current view.
   - **Sorted by Relevance:** Displays only documents in the current view that were selected by the query. Relevance is indicated by the gray-scaled bar to the left of the documents, with darkest gray indicating the most relevant. For example, a document in which the search word appears twice has a higher relevance than a document in which it appears only once. Also, a short document with a single occurrence of the search word is ranked higher than a longer document with a single occurrence.
   - **Sorted by Date (Ascending):** Displays only documents in the current view that were selected by the query, sorted by date of last modification, oldest first.
   - **Sorted by Date (Descending):** Displays only documents in the current view that were selected by the query, sorted by date of last modification, newest first.

5. Specify the maximum number of search results you want to display. When your query is relatively imprecise, you're likely to find many documents. This can take a while and usually necessitates performing a more targeted search afterwards. By restricting the number of search results, you discover that you need a more targeted query without wasting a lot of time.

6. Click on OK.

►► *What's Next?*

Creating a full text index for a database can help users search for specific information. This can be an invaluable feature of any Notes database. By searching for a particular word, phrase, or numerical data, users can locate the information quickly (if it exists).

In the next chapter, we discuss linking and embedding objects in Notes databases, either at the time you create a form or when users compose documents. (Remember that a rich text field in a document can contain a DDE or OLE object.) By inserting objects that have been created in other Windows applications, users can create "compound" documents that draw on several outside sources for supplying important data.

► ► **CHAPTER 21**

Linking and Embedding Objects in Notes

———

▶ ▶ *F*AST *T*RACK

a pointer to the data in the original source file. Since the link points to the original data, any changes made to the linked file are reflected in the Notes document automatically. You use linking when you want a central place to store certain information that you and others can link to. This means the source file can *not* be moved or deleted (or the link will have to be recreated).

the object in the Notes document contains a copy of the source data. Embedding allows you to insert information from a source file into a Notes document so that you create a true "compound" document made up of data from several different sources. Once an object is embedded, you can access the application it was created in by clicking on the object. You use embedding when you may not have access to the original source file; for example, when it's not possible to store it on a file server where everyone can access it, or when it may be moved or deleted.

Open the non-Notes file and then select the data you want to link. Highlight any data range, such as paragraphs from a document or a range from a spreadsheet. Copy the selection to the Clipboard (most applications use Edit ➤ Copy or Ctrl+C to copy a selection to the Clipboard). If you're creating a new file in the server application, be sure to save the file before you try to create the link—without a file name, Notes won't know where to link. If you want to change the scope of your selection after you've created the link, delete the old link and create a new one. You can't change the data selection in a link after it's been created. Open the Notes document and then press Ctrl+E to edit the document or compose a new document to hold the object. Place the insertion point where you want the link to appear (it must be in a rich text field). Choose Edit ➤ Paste Special. Click on the Link button, or Cancel if you change your mind. The object appears on the document, with the data outlined to indicate that it's linked information.

▶ *To embed data into a document*   638

Select the data you want to embed, such as a spreadsheet chart or some text from a word processor, and copy it to the Clipboard using Edit ➤ Copy. Open the Notes document and place the insertion point in a rich text field where you want the pasted information to appear. Choose Edit ➤ Paste Special. The Paste Special dialog box appears. Select a data format from the Display As list. The listed formats vary, depending on what's on the Clipboard, and are determined by the creating application. Click on the Embed button, which inserts a copy of the source data that can be edited later using the server application. This option is dimmed when the source application doesn't support DDE or OLE. Press Ctrl+S to save the pasted information in the Notes document.

►► **B**y *taking* advantage of two Windows features—Dynamic Data Exchange (DDE) and Object Linking and Embedding (OLE)—you can give your database applications the additional power of using information created with other Windows software. DDE and OLE allow you to insert *objects* that have been created in other Windows applications—files, parts of files, or links to files—into Notes documents. A linked or embedded object is displayed in a Notes document like any other element, but with this difference: The object maintains certain connections with the original document or application it was created in. In this chapter, we'll discuss several topics related to linking and embedding objects, including:

- The differences between linking and embedding
- Inserting objects in documents
- Editing embedded or linked objects

►► *Linking and Embedding Objects*

An object is data that's presented in graphical terms to a user; that is, it uses a picture such as an icon to communicate its message or intent (although text can be part of an object). As far as Notes is concerned, an object is a piece of data that's been created by a Windows application other than Notes itself. An object can represent text, graphics, media, charts, or a file that contains information. You can either link or embed an object. If it's linked, the object contains a pointer to the data in the original source file. If it's embedded, the object contains a copy of the source data.

USING LOTUS MULTIMEDIA TOOLS IN NOTES

The Windows version of Notes includes the Lotus Multimedia Tools, which are OLE utilities for linking or embedding media into documents. Contact your Notes Administrator if you are interested in taking advantage of these tools. They include the following:

➤ Lotus Sound

➤ Lotus Media Player

➤ Lotus Annotator

Lotus Sound is an OLE server application. It lets a user record, play, link, or embed sound objects in a Notes document. The user can place a sound object in a document by choosing Edit ➤ Insert ➤ Object and then selecting Sound from the list of available OLE servers. To create sounds, you need a sound card or a sound parallel device that's supported in Windows 3.1. To play sounds using a PC speaker, you can use SPEAKER.DRV, which is shareware available on a variety of online bulletin board services such as CompuServe.

Lotus Media Manager is also an OLE server application. It is a player device that allows a user to view any media type that's compatible with any Windows 3.1 Media Control Interface (MCI) driver. Lotus Media Manager enables a user to view, link, or embed sound, MIDI, and many formats of movie files. Media Manager supports any type of MCI-compatible file format, including the following:

➤ AVI (Video for Windows)

➤ LSM (Lotus SmartMovies)

➤ FLI (AutoDesk Animator)

▶ To use movies that have sound, you need a sound card or equivalent. If you don't have a sound card, the movies will play without sound on any VGA screen. LSM movies work without sound under Windows 3.0. If you want to use sound, you need Windows 3.1. Annotator and Media Manager also work in Windows 3.0, but if you want sound, you need Windows 3.1.

Lotus Annotator is an OLE client/server application. It provides basic text editing capabilities, and supports all types of media. You can enter a message and embed movies, sounds, and clip art into one annotation.

To Install Lotus Multimedia Tools, follow the steps below. Your Notes Administrator should have the necessary installation disk and may have stored the files on a file server for your access:

1. Start Windows to display the Program Manager.

2. Insert the disk labeled "Lotus Multimedia Tools" into drive A.

3. Choose File ➤ Run.

4. Enter a:\install.

5. Click on OK to perform the install.

The Lotus Multimedia Tools also come with WinHelp files. Once the tools are installed, you should read Multimedia Tools Help for additional operating information.

If you're a fan of Windows applications, you're familiar with the copy and paste commands that the applications provide. The Windows version of Notes uses the same commands. You can select data (such as a view, document, field contents, etc.) from one Notes database or data from another Windows application, copy the data to the Windows Clipboard, and paste it elsewhere in the same database or in another database. The Clipboard provides you with the means to share data between applications as a one-time transfer. If you need to update the data often, you'll have to use the copy-and-paste routine repeatedly.

By using simple Clipboard cut-and-paste techniques, you can transfer data from one application to another application with a one-time technique. But no awareness or connection exits between the two applications sharing the data in this way. Microsoft Corporation, the creator of Windows, recognized that this wasn't an efficient way to update data on a regular basis, and so it addressed the task of performing manual updates by creating technologies that automate the process in several different ways. These technologies are known as Dynamic Data Exchange (DDE) and Object Linking and Embedding (OLE).

The following two sections describe the differences between linking and embedding in greater detail. In addition, for basic object linking and embedding terminology, see Table 21.1.

▶ **TABLE 21.1:** *Basic DDE and OLE terminology*

DDE AND OLE TERMINOLOGY	DEFINITION
DDE or OLE Server	Also called the server application, or simply the application. An application that provides data that can be linked to or embedded within a client. Notes cannot act as a DDE or OLE server.
DDE Client	An application that asks for, receives, and displays DDE server data. Notes can act as a client of these DDE servers.
OLE Client	An application that receives, stores, and displays an OLE object. Notes can act as a client of these OLE servers .
Link (noun and verb)	A data conversation for sharing information be-tween a DDE or OLE client and a DDE or OLE server. Linking inserts a visual representation of the item into a Notes document. When the data changes in the server applica-tion, the changes appear in Notes (the client) in one of two ways: automatic update and manual update.

▶ **TABLE 21.1:** *Basic DDE and OLE terminology (continued)*

DDE AND OLE TERMINOLOGY	DEFINITION
Automatic Update	A link in which the server automatically sends new data to the client as soon as the data changes.
Manual Update	A link in which the server sends new data only on request of the client. (You choose Edit ➤ Links ➤ Update or View ➤ Refresh Fields to perform a manual update.) In addition to the data itself, the following information is passed between server and client when a link is established or activated: Application (the name of the server application), Topic, and Item. This information can be viewed or changed for a specific document in Edit mode using Edit ➤ Links ➤ Change Link.
Topic	The complete path to the source file containing linked or embedded data, including the file name. The topic cannot be redefined while the link is active.
Item	The data within a topic that is of interest to the client. An item is of a specific data type, such as text, spreadsheet range, chart, picture, or voice.
Object	A copy of the OLE server data for embedding into a Notes document, or a pointer to the server data for linking.

▶ *What Is Linking?*

As we mentioned above, when you choose the Edit ➤ Paste command (Ctrl+V) in Notes, the data that you've copied to (and which is subsequently stored by) the Windows Clipboard is inserted in the database where you want it to appear. You can continue pasting the same data until you copy new data to the Clipboard; the old data that was stored on the Clipboard is subsequently replaced by the new data. Furthermore, if you exit Windows entirely, the data is lost forever; it isn't saved for future Windows sessions.

USING SHARED FIELDS

As we discussed in Chapter 15, "Creating a View," by using *shared* fields in the same database, you can reuse a field in any number of forms within the particular database. This is analogous to linking, although a shared field can only be used once on each form. When you create a new field, you have the option of choosing the "Create shared field that can be used in other Forms" option in the Design New Field dialog box. Every time you update the contents of one occurrence of the shared field, all other occurrences in the other forms are automatically updated also, because they share the same field definition. To reuse a shared field within the same database, open the new form where you want the shared field to appear, position the insertion point where you want to place the field, and choose Design ➤ Use Shared Field. Select the shared field you want to use from the list in the Use Shared field Definition dialog box. Click on OK to confirm the selection.

Notes provides you with the Paste Special command on the Edit menu (Edit ➤ Paste Special) when you want to use the data *dynamically*. Instead of treating the data *statically*, that is, pasting it in a database and then updating it manually if need be, you have the option of updating it automatically without having to fuss with it each time you want to change it. The command appears dimmed and unavailable unless you put data from an application that supports DDE and OLE in the Clipboard.

When the command is available, Notes is providing you with a means to *link* the data back to some other Windows application—the server application—whenever you want the data in a database—the client application—updated. Creating this link establishes a long-term relationship between the server application's data and the database.

Let's say you want a particular field in a document to contain data that's been created in another Windows application. You want the data to be updated automatically, so you create a link. When the data in the server application changes, Notes displays the change in the field's contents the next time you open the document.

When you create a link in a Notes document, you are inserting a pointer to information in an external file. Since the link points to the original data, any changes made to the linked file are reflected in the Notes document automatically. You can think of a link as a pipeline between the Notes document and the source file, which can be anything from a word processing document to a graphic. For example, suppose you want to include the latest sales figures from a Lotus 1-2-3 for Windows spreadsheet in a financial research document in a Notes database. Instead of frequently pasting, importing, or retyping the sales figures to keep them up-to-date, you can create a link to the 1-2-3 file in your Executive Summary in Notes, and every time a change is made to the 1-2-3 file, that change will show up in the Notes database.

What this all means is that you use linking in Notes when you want a central place to store specific data that you and other members in a workgroup can link to as long as everyone has proper access. When people need to edit a document that contains a field whose contents are linked to a server application, they must be able to locate the application. This means the source file can *not* be moved or deleted (or the link will have to be recreated). Subsequently, all users who need to edit the information will have access to the server application and the source file on a file server; all users must use the same directory mapping (e.g., m:\netware\sales\public\results.wk3) in order to activate or update the linked data in Notes. Users who only need to read the information do not need access to the original file or to the server application (to be readable, the link must not be represented as an icon in the Notes document).

► What Is Embedding?

Embedding allows you to insert information from a server application file into a Notes document so that you create a true "compound" database made up of data from several different sources. A compound Notes database, by definition, means that the documents in a database utilize data from different sources, which may come from another database or another Windows application.

▶▶ **N O T E**

Embedded objects are much more robust than links and are typically more useful in a networking environment such as Notes where workflow automation applications are implemented. Notes databases, particularly in large organizations, are more often than not designed as compound applications so they can utilize other Windows application to furnish data in documents. These Windows applications must be stored on a central file server that the Notes server can access. In this way, embedded data can be shared more easily with Notes users in other locations. (Remember that an organization might support more than one worksite and maintain several Notes servers.) However, keep in mind that an embedded object uses more memory and storage space in the Notes database than a linked object. The size of an embedded object, such as graphic, can be large.

You might think this sounds exactly like using the copy and paste commands or creating a link to update data in a Notes database. However, embedding lets you access the server application directly by clicking on the object. In this way, you can make changes to the object in the application where it was created originally.

Let's say you, as a database's designer, paste a graphic that you created in Visio 2.0 from Shapeware into a form, but you later want to modify the graphic. You're going to have to exit Notes, open Visio, edit the graphic, copy it in the Clipboard, exit Visio, launch Notes again, select the database, open the document, delete the old version of the graphic, and paste the new version. What a bother! Unfortunately, the only physical change you can make to an object that you insert in a form (and documents for that matter) in this way is sizing it. You're limited to selecting the object and then dragging the object's handles in order to increase or decrease its size.

However, if you embed the object in a document, you simply click on the object to launch the server application where you created it. You don't exit Notes. With the server application open, you can edit the object, save the changes, then return to Notes and the document that contains the object. The object will reflect the changes you made to it in the server application. Although the data is physically attached to the document, Notes relinquishes control over that part of the document to the OLE server application. Once the object is embedded in the Notes document, it's no longer associated with the original file; any changes made to one are *not* reflected in the other automatically as it would if it were linked to the original file.

You use embedding when you may not have access to the original source file; for example, when it's not possible to store it on a file server where everyone can access it, or when it may be moved or deleted.

▶▶ *Using Dynamic Data Exchange (DDE)*

Just as you would use the Clipboard to copy and paste data, Dynamic Data Exchange (DDE) lets you perform a similar action by displaying data that's been created with other Windows applications within Notes documents. However, DDE improves on this way of transferring data by enabling a client application to establish a link to the source of the shared information (the server application). Changing the data in the server application can modify the data in the client application automatically. DDE extends the capabilities of the Clipboard by making links that can be reactivated and updated. Creating a DDE link is like building a bridge between a Notes document and a file that's been created with another Windows application. If the data is changed, it will be updated in Notes. However, both applications must be running before you can create or activate a link.

 ▶▶ **T I P**

> **Running two applications simultaneously uses a lot of memory. You'll see a marked slowdown in your workstation's performance. Therefore, try not to open too many applications at the same time.**

DDE is a Windows protocol—a set of programming-level commands that Windows supports in order to allow a program to query another program for data without the need for user action. DDE is good because it's a fairly universal way to get data from one Windows program such as Notes to another. However, DDE can be troublesome because every program uses DDE slightly differently, and because DDE links suffer from some annoying inflexibilities. Under DDE, one application (the "server") provides data to another application (the "client") over a linkage called a "conversation."

There are times when you shouldn't use DDE. When the link is from one Notes document to another document, you should create a doclink. (For more information on doclinks, see Chapter 6, "Creating a Document.") Another reason not to use DDE to link a Notes document with another document is that Notes cannot act as a DDE server, which means that updating data in a Notes document won't update the data in a Windows client application that you attempt to link to it. A good rule of thumb to follow is if the contents a Notes database doesn't depend on whether the original data changes, you should use copy and paste commands to transfer data through the Clipboard. You don't need to mess with DDE. If users with reader access will need to edit the data and you can't guarantee that a server application will be available to them, you should utilize the Notes Import command (File ➤ Import) or the Clipboard. When the server application doesn't support DDE, you should utilize file attachments, the Import command, or the Clipboard.

➤ Creating DDE Links

You create a DDE object by copying the data that comprises it to the Clipboard and then pasting it into Notes. The DDE server application renders the data in one or more formats and you select the one you want to use. Then you paste the data as a linked or embedded object.

If you select Link, a DDE link is established between the Notes document and the source file. If you select Embed, a copy of the source file is attached to the Notes document and embedded using Document Inset Protocol (DIP), a proprietary protocol that allows embedding of files whose source applications don't support OLE. To create a DDE link, follow these steps:

1. Open the non-Notes file and select the data you want to link. Highlight any data range, such as paragraphs from a document or a range from a spreadsheet.

2. Copy the selection to the Clipboard (most applications use Edit ➤ Copy or Ctrl+C to copy a selection to the Clipboard). If you're creating a new file in the server application, be sure to save the file before you try to create the link—without a file name, Notes won't know where to link. If you want to change the scope of your selection after you've created the link, delete the old link and create a new one. You can't change the data selection in a link after it's been created.

3. Open the Notes document and then press Ctrl+E to edit the document or compose a new document to hold the object.

4. Place the insertion point where you want to link to appear (it must be in a rich text field).

5. Choose Edit ➤ Paste Special. Notes displays the Paste Special dialog box, as shown in Figure 21.1, where you can change the data format and paste your data as a plain Clipboard paste, an OLE embedded object, or a DDE or OLE link.

6. Click on the Link button, or click Cancel if you change your mind.

The object appears on the document, with the data outlined to indicate that it's linked information.

With Notes, you can link data from a server, such as Lotus Freelance Graphics for Windows 1.0 or Lotus 1-2-3 for Windows 1.0, to the client, Notes. Both client and server must have built-in support for DDE. With one exception, Notes functions only as a DDE client, not as a

FIGURE 21.1 ▶

The Paste Special dialog box lets you change the data format of an object and paste your data as a plain Clipboard paste, an OLE embedded object, or a DDE or OLE link.

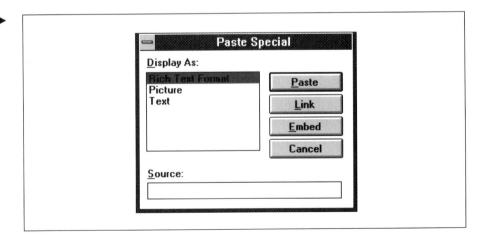

server. This exception is the Lotus Mail Connection, which lets you send documents created with other Windows applications that support DDE, such as Lotus 1-2-3 for Windows, as Notes mail memos. The Lotus Mail Connection uses Notes as a DDE server. This means that Notes documents can receive linked data, but can't provide it via DDE to other applications. To provide Notes data to other applications, you can copy and paste using the Clipboard, or you can export Notes documents and views.

▶ *The Limitations of DDE*

There are several limitations to using DDE when you want to link information between a Notes document and a non-Notes application. As we mentioned earlier, you must save the source file *before* you create a DDE link. The Clipboard requires a named file to paste a link. You must also launch the server application *before* you activate a DDE link. The DDE server must already be running and the linked file must already be open before you can activate a DDE link in Notes.

You can change only the linked part of a file. Even though you linked only *part* of a file, when the link is activated the *whole* file is displayed in the server application. Although you can modify the nonlinked part of the file, when the link is updated, only changes to the linked part will appear in the Notes document.

You can link a read-only file with DDE or OLE, but embed it with OLE only. This means you can create a DDE link to a read-only file (a file that you do not have privileges to edit). However, you can create *embedded* objects only to those read-only files created by applications that support OLE.

▶▶ *Using Object Linking and Embedding*

Object Linking and Embedding (OLE) is the next step beyond DDE in sharing data between Notes databases and other Windows applications and in creating compound documents. OLE is a superset of DDE functionality that includes improved linking as well as object embedding.

▶▶

Lotus Notes release 3.1.5 includes *Notes/FX* (Notes Field Exchange), a new feature that uses OLE embedding to enable you to exchange data between fields in a Notes document and fields in files created in other Windows applications that support field exchange. For example, you can maintain data in an Improv 2.1 worksheet and access and update it in Notes. You can also use Notes to provide document descriptions and keywords for Ami Pro R3.01 word processing documents.

OLE works in Notes like this: Two copies of the data are maintained in a Notes document (the client application). One copy appears in a graphical format that is used only to visually represent the embedded object. When a user selects this object in the document, Notes launches the server application and transfers to it the second copy of the data, which appears in the original server format. The user can then utilize the server application to modify the data in its original form. When the user is finished, the updated data is immediately available as an updated object in the Notes document.

You can embed existing files or parts of files, or you can create a new OLE object while your Notes document is open. Once an object has been embedded, changes to the original file or to the embedded object have no effect on each other because the object is a copy of the original and is no longer associated with it. Activating an object launches the application that was used to create it, so you or other Notes users can edit the data.

If you want the users of a database you're designing to see a document from an OLE server application when they enter or read information, you can design a database form as an OLE "seamless" object. When users enter or read information in such a form, they see a document from the OLE server application instead of a Notes document. For example, in an Expense Report database, you might want users to compose a Lotus 1-2-3 for Windows spreadsheet instead of a Notes text-based document.

You shouldn't use OLE when you want to include a link in one Notes document to another. As we mentioned earlier in the chapter, you should create a doclink to allow readers to jump directly to the document, or use the Clipboard for copying and pasting data. If readers need to *edit* the data and don't have the server application, they should use Import or the Clipboard. When the server application doesn't support OLE, you should use file attachments, the Import command, or the Clipboard.

▶ Embedding Objects in a Form

The main difference between graphics and tables is that graphics can be created in another application and then *embedded* in the forms, while tables cannot. You can't create a table in, say, a Windows word processor and then embed it as a table; you can only embed it as word processing document.

When you embed any OLE object in a form, you can choose when to activate the embedded object and how changes to the object will be presented to users. You'll recall that the purpose of embedding an object in a form, whether the object is a Windows spreadsheet, chart, or drawing, is to reflect changes in the object and then to display those changes in the documents that users compose, edit, or read.

In the case of the Corporate Directory database, however, users only edit the forms; they never compose any new documents with the forms. Therefore, the graphics that appear at the top of the forms are never activated. They never change. They're only used to beautify and to add visual interest to the forms.

If you want to create a graphic in a drawing program that supports OLE and then embed it in a form, follow these steps using your favorite application. I use Visio 2.0 from Shapeware:

1. Position the cursor in the desired location.

2. Choose Edit ➤ Insert ➤ Object. The Insert Object dialog box appears, as shown in Figure 21.2.

3. Select the Object Type you want to use from the list box. (I selected Visio 2.0 Drawing from the list. Visio is a great business drawing program for the artistically challenged person like myself.)

FIGURE 21.2 ►

The Insert Object dialog box lets you select the Object Type of the object you want to insert on a form.

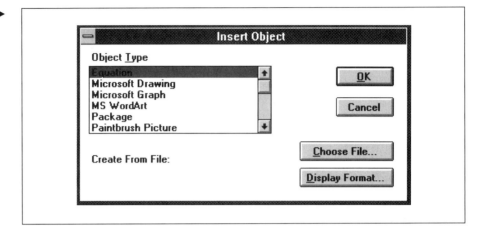

4. Click on OK. An object container appears on the form, including the name of the object type. (In my case, "New VISIO 2.0 Drawing Object" appears.) Subsequently, the drawing program in which you want to create the object opens.

5. Create the graphic.

6. Save the file *only* if you want to create a link to the drawing rather than embed a copy of it. Otherwise, you can skip this step.

7. Make sure the drawing is selected and then copy it to the Clipboard.

8. *Don't* exit the program. To embed the drawing, Notes needs certain information from the program which is more quickly obtained if the program is still running.

9. Press Alt+Tab to return to the form.

At this point, you have several options open to you in deciding how you want to embed the drawing, or more importantly, how you want to handle the drawing from now on. If you know that you're not going to make further changes to the drawing, you can simply embed it by using Notes' Paste command. However, this action will stop you from modifying the drawing in the program in which it was created. You'll only be able to resize the drawing in Notes. Most of the time you'll probably want to treat the drawing in this way once people begin to use the database. You won't want other users modifying it.

If you want the option—and flexibility—of changing the drawing later on as you develop the database, you're better off using the Paste Special command to embed the drawing. You always use this command when you want to *link* an object, which allows you to make changes to an object in the source program and then show those changes dynamically in a Notes database. (A link consists of a reference from the container application, Notes, to the original source application.) However, this command also provides you with the option of embedding an object, which will allow you to edit it if you choose to do so.

Just remember that the drawing program must exist on either your system (or the server) if you want to continue editing the object. Otherwise, you'll get a "Lotus Notes OLE Error Report" telling you that the link failed because Notes can't find the source application.

To embed the drawing in the form, follow these steps:

1. Choose Edit ➤ Paste Special. The Paste Special dialog box appears, as shown in Figure 21.3. As you can see, you have a choice of selecting the Paste, Link, and Embed commands.

2. Click on the Embed button. The drawing appears on the form.

3. To resize the drawing, point the mouse on the handle in the lower right corner of the object's container. Hold the mouse button down and drag the handle to increase or decrease the size of the drawing.

FIGURE 21.3 ▶

The Paste Object dialog box gives you the choice of pasting, linking, or embedding an object when you want to place it on a form.

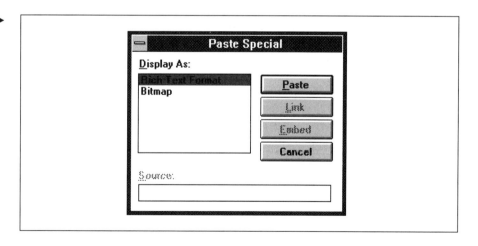

To edit the drawing, simply double-click on it. The drawing program opens, allowing you to modify the object. Make the changes you want and then exit the program. You don't have to save the drawing unless you want to link to it. (In fact, you must save the file before you can link to it.) Changes to the embedded drawing will be saved when you save the form in Notes. When you return to the form, the drawing will display the new changes.

Alternatively, you can edit the drawing by following these steps:

1. Choose Edit ➤ *Actions*, where you'll see the name of the drawing program displayed below the Insert command. The name replaces *Actions* on the menu. (In my case, the menu displays "Object: VISIO 2.0 Drawing Program.")

2. Click on the object's name and choose Edit (or Open command to open another file) from the submenu. The drawing program opens.

3. Make the desired changes.

4. Exit and program to return to the form.

The drawing will reflect the changes you made to it.

▶ *Embedding Data*

If you're creating a new file using an OLE server and you want to create a *link* to it in Notes, you must save the file when exiting the server application. If you want to *embed* the object in Notes, it's not necessary to save the file in the OLE server application. To embed data into a document, follow these steps:

1. Select the data you want to embed, such as a spreadsheet chart or some text from a word processor, and copy it to the Clipboard using Edit ➤ Copy.

2. Open the Notes document and place the insertion point in a rich text field where you want the pasted information to appear.

3. Choose Edit ➤ Paste Special. The Paste Special dialog box appears.

4. Select a data format from the Display As list. The listed formats vary, depending on what's on the Clipboard, and are determined by the creating application.

▶▶ **N O T E**

Most DDE and OLE server applications support the standard Notes data formats: Rich Text, Picture, Bitmap, and Text. Some servers support fewer formats, for example, Freelance Graphics supports only Picture format for linking or embedding. The source file's path is displayed in the Source text box. You cannot edit it if the source file is from an OLE server. You *can* edit it if it's from a DDE server.

5. Click on the Embed button, which inserts a copy of the source data that can be edited later using the server application. This option is dimmed when the source application doesn't support DDE or OLE.

6. Press Ctrl+S to save the pasted information in the Notes document.

▶▶ **N O T E**

Even when you only select part of a file to embed, some OLE servers, such as Word for Windows 2.0 and AmiPro 2.0, display the entire file when you activate the object. The actual embedded data is correct, however. You can see this by looking at the data representation in the Notes document (unless an icon is displayed instead of the data).

You can also paste data with special formats into Notes documents, such as objects you want to link or embed using DDE or OLE, or perform a simple paste of data in a format other than the default format. Before you begin, however, first launch the server application and open a file where the data is located. If you're creating a *new* file using a DDE server application, be sure to save the file before you copy the data to the Clipboard. Without a file name, the DDE server won't put the DDE link information on the Clipboard for Notes, and the Embed and Link options in the Paste Special dialog box will be dimmed (unavailable).

▶▶ **T I P**

To perform a simple paste using the default format, it's easier to use the Edit ➤ Paste command.

If you have trouble with an embedded or linked object, (such as receiving "Error Activating Object" messages), first check the following:

- Make sure the server application is available. It must be installed on your hard disk or be available to you on a networked file server. The server application may be unavailable if, for instance, it is busy printing.

- Make sure the path of the server application hasn't changed.

▶ Creating an Object from Scratch

You can create a new OLE object from scratch or create an object from an existing file and embed it into a Notes document. Before you begin, however, open the Notes document and place the insertion point in a rich text field where you want the object to appear. Then follow the steps below to create a new OLE object from scratch:

1. Choose Edit ➤ Insert ➤ Object. The Insert Object dialog box appears, as shown in Figure 21.4.

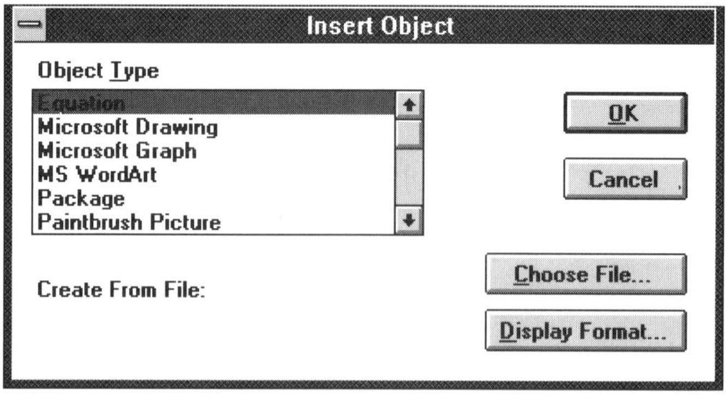

FIGURE 21.4 ▶

The Insert Object dialog box lets you select an object type. All the OLE server applications registered in your database are listed in the Object Type box.

Insert Object dialog box

Object Type
Equation
Microsoft Drawing
Microsoft Graph
MS WordArt
Package
Paintbrush Picture

OK
Cancel

Create From File:

Choose File...
Display Format...

2. Select an Object Type. All the OLE server applications registered in your database are listed in the Object Type box. Notes launches the application you selected, which creates a blank work document that becomes your active window.

3. Create your object data in the OLE server application. You can even insert other objects into this object if the OLE server application can also act as an OLE client.

4. Choose File ➤ Update in the server application.

5. Exit the server application.

The OLE object is now embedded in your Notes document, in the default format, Picture. To create a new OLE object from an existing file, follow these steps:

1. Choose Edit ➤ Insert ➤ Object. The Insert Object dialog box appears.

2. Select an Object Type.

3. Select Choose File. The Choose File dialog box appears, as shown in Figure 21.5.

4. Select the file you want to use as an OLE object.

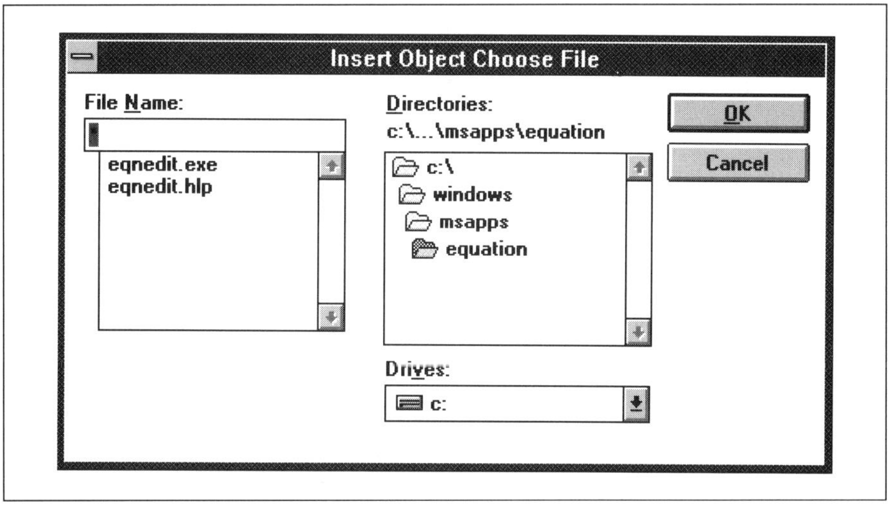

FIGURE 21.5 ▶

The Choose File dialog box lets you select the file you want to use as an OLE object.

5. Click on OK. The name of the file you select appears under Create From File in the Insert Object dialog box.

6. Click on OK, or Cancel if you change your mind.

► Selecting the Data Format for an Object

The OLE object is now embedded in your Notes document, in the default format, Picture. To select a nondefault display format, follow these steps:

1. Select an object type, as you did in Step 2 above.

2. Select Display Format. Notes opens the Display Format dialog box, as shown in Figure 21.6.

3. Specify a data type for the object.

4. Click on OK.

FIGURE 21.6 ►

The Display Format dialog box lets you specify a data type for the object.

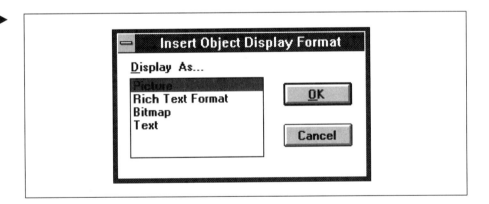

►► Displaying Linked or Embedded Data in Notes

Some server applications display the actual data in the Notes document, such as the spreadsheet cells or the text of a word processing document. But if the object contains multiple data formats, or if the object's native format is something other than rich text, text, picture, or bitmap (for example, a sound or movie object), many applications display the program icon. For example, when Picture or Bitmap format is selected for a Lotus AmiPro object, the AmiPro icon appears in the Notes document.

To see the data in that case, double-click the icon, or select the icon and then choose Edit ➤ <type of object>. The server application is launched (if it is available) and the object is opened for reading and editing. Saving your changes to the object requires Editor access to the Notes document.

▶▶ *Editing an Embedded or Linked Object in Notes*

When you edit an embedded object, choose the File ➤ Update command in the server application to update the Notes document, or choose View ➤ Refresh Fields from the Notes document (it must be in Edit mode). When you edit a linked object, it is automatically updated if Automatic Update is selected in the Edit Links dialog box. Or, if Manual Update is selected, choose View ➤ Refresh Fields, or select Update from the Edit ➤ Links dialog box, or press F9. Otherwise it will be updated the next time the link is activated.

▶▶ *Activating DDE or OLE Links*

You can activate DDE or OLE links in order to update or edit the data, switch between automatic and manual updating, change the link parameters, or delete (unlink) a link. To edit a link in a document, follow these steps:

1. Choose Edit ➤ Links. The Edit Links dialog box appears, as shown in Figure 21.7.

2. Select the link(s) you want to use. You can activate only one link at a time; if you select more than one link, the Change Link, Activate, and Deactivate options remain unavailable. If you select a link that's already active, the Activate button remains dimmed.

FIGURE 21.7 ▶

The Edit Links dialog box lets you select the link(s) you want to use. You can activate only one link at a time.

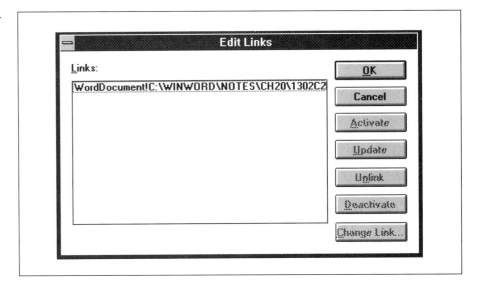

3. Select any of the following options:

- **Activate**: If it's an OLE link, this launches the OLE server application (if it's not already running) and opens the source file. If it's a DDE link, the file must already be open in the server application. If the link has Automatic Update specified, the data is updated immediately in the Notes document. If the link has Manual Update specified, select Update, or choose View ▶ Refresh, or press F9 to update the link.

- **Update**: Updates an active Manual Update link or an inactive link. If the data has been edited since the last time this link was updated, you'll see those changes now. If multiple links are selected, Update refreshes the data for all of them.

- **Unlink**: Permanently removes one or more links from the Notes document. If you change your mind before leaving the dialog box, select Unlink again, or select Cancel. Otherwise, to restore the link, you'll have to recreate it from scratch. Any data that is displayed remains in the Notes document as static data, as if it had been inserted into the Notes document using Edit ▶ Paste.

- **Deactivate**: Terminates the selected active link (ends this editing session). If it's an OLE link, this closes the OLE file and

the server application, unless the application was running before the link was activated.

- **Change Link**: Opens the Change Link dialog box, where
you can edit the properties of the selected link (this button is
dimmed when more than one link is selected). You must deactivate the link—using the Deactivate option—before you
can use the Change Link option.

4. Click on OK, or Cancel if you change your mind. However, if
you've changed a link's properties, it's too late to cancel those
changes.

▶▶ *Changing the Definition of a Link*

You can change the definition of a DDE or OLE link, or switch it to
automatic or manual update. To change a link in a document, follow
these steps:

1. Choose Edit ➤ Links.

2. Select and deactivate the link.

3. Select Change Link. The Change Link dialog box appears, as
shown in Figure 21.8. The name of the DDE or OLE server application that was used to create the linked data is displayed. Don't
change the application name.

4. Change the topic if you desire. You can specify a different file
name of the linked data or path.

FIGURE 21.8 ▶

*The Change Link dia-
log box displays the
name of the DDE or
OLE server application
that was used to cre-
ate the linked data is
displayed. Don't
change the appli-
cation name.*

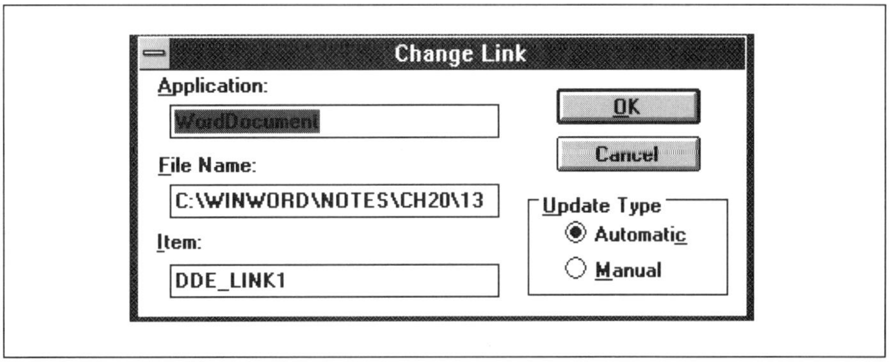

5. You can modify the linked selection if you desire.

6. Select Automatic if you want the link to be automatically updated whenever it is activated by yourself or other users, or select Manual if you want the link to be updated by yourself and other users as needed.

 ▶▶ **N O T E**

Manual updating is particularly useful for large bitmaps, so users who are editing the bitmap can decide when to repaint the it rather than wait for it to repaint with every change. To manually update, choose View ➤ Refresh Fields or press F9.

▶▶ *Performing a Full Text Search of DDE and OLE Information*

Notes can index and search for text within linked or embedded information if two conditions are met:

- The data type is in either Text or Rich Text format.

- The information itself is represented in the Notes document (full text search doesn't work when an icon is displayed instead of the data).

▶▶ *What's Next?*

There are many reasons for deciding when to use the Clipboard's Copy, Cut, and Paste commands; DDE; and OLE. Using the Clipboard to copy (or cut) and paste data is best for a one-time transfer of data. When you don't need to update data that often, use this method.

DDE offers a more dynamic method of updating data on a regular basis. As a database designer, you can establish a one-way dynamic link between the contents of a field in a Notes document and another Windows application. Changes made to the link-to application are reflected automatically in the document. OLE goes farther by providing a two-way dynamic link. By embedding a graphical object in a document (as part of a database's design), a user can click on the object to launch the Windows application in which the object was created. This link-to application activates the object, enabling the user to make changes to it without having to exit Notes.

In the next chapter, we discuss managing databases and performing routine maintenance tasks. As the designer of a database, you might find yourself in the role of database manager. You might also have to maintain many other databases at one time. Therefore, you'll need to know the different ways in which you can organize databases so they can be accessed efficiently by users.

► ► CHAPTER **22**

Managing Databases

▶▶ *F*AST *T*RACK

▶ **To display information about a database**   **653**

    select a database in the Workspace. Choose File ➤ Database ➤ Information. The Database Information dialog box appears. Enter a different name in the Title text box when you want display a new name on the database icon. Enter the particular categories in the Categories text box that you want this database listed under in the server's database catalog. Separate multiple categories with commas. Click on the Design Template button. The Design Template Options dialog box appears. Select the Database is a Design Template option if this database is to be used as a design template. Enter the name for this design template in the Template Name text box. Alternatively, select the Inherit Design from Template if this database is to inherit its design elements from a design template. Enter the name of the source template in the Based on Template text box. Click on OK to accept your selection, or click on Cancel.

▶ **To view user activity**   **657**

    click on the User Activity button. The User Activity dialog box appears. Click on the Record Activity button to record user activity. Then click on OK. To stop recording user activity, deselect Record Activity and then click on OK. A table at the lower right of the dialog box summarizes the total uses, reads, and writes for the past day, week, and month. Click on Copy to Clipboard to copy the user information to another application, such as a spreadsheet. You can then paste the information into the other application. Click on OK.

▶ **To display database usage**   **660**

click the Show Usage button to display a figure indicating how much of the database's allocated space is actually in use. The figure appears as a percentage, and is displayed next to the database size.

▶ **To read or print a synopsis of all the design elements**   **660**

within a selected database, select a database. Choose Design ➤ Synopsis. The Design Synopsis dialog box appears. Select the elements you want to summarize. Choose from the available options. Click on OK to accept your choices. The list of elements you've selected, along with their definitions, are displayed in a view window.

▶ **To summarize the field contents of a database**   **662**

select a document in a view or open a document. Choose Design ➤ Document Info. The Design Document Info dialog box appears. Document statistics and field data are displayed. Select a field from the list displayed in the upper left corner of the dialog box. The field's contents are displayed in the box below the list. Select another field to see its contents. Click on OK to close the dialog box.

▶ **To compact a database**   **664**

select a database by clicking on its icon in the Workspace. Choose File ➤ Database ➤ Compact. The Compacting Database message box appears, displaying the percentage of compaction as it progresses.

► ► **M**_anaging_ a database means monitoring its activity and making sure that it is functioning properly at all times. A database manager is the person who is assigned to maintaining a database, overseeing its usage, security, and so on. Sometimes the database manager is you, the person who created the database. At other times, somebody else is assigned the role of the manager.

As a database ages and grows in size, some of its documents can become outdated. Other documents may not be accessed frequently. Therefore, the database manager should perform routine maintenance on the database. In this chapter, we discuss the tasks involved in managing a database, including:

- Getting information about databases and documents
- Displaying user activity
- Summarizing the field contents of a database
- Compacting a database

Database management often overlaps with Notes server administration. Therefore, before performing the tasks described in this chapter, you should check whether the Notes Administrator is already performing them. You don't want to step on anyone's toes!

▶ ▶ *Performing Database Management Tasks*

Some tasks that are generally performed by the database manager include:

- Maintaining the database's access control list (ACL), which we discussed in Chapters 4 and 18

- Creating database replicas and defining replication settings, which we discussed in Chapter 19

- Compacting the database to remove unused space, thus saving disk space

▶ ▶ *Getting Information about Databases and Documents*

There are three ways to get quick summary information about documents and databases and their use:

- **Database Information** provides information about the database's size and number of documents, as well as design template settings, replication settings, and user activity.

- **Database Design Synopsis** provides a printable, detailed summary of all the design elements within a selected database.

- **Design Document Info** provides information about the database's size and number of documents, as well as design template settings, replication settings, and user activity.

▶ *The Database Information Dialog Box*

To display information about a database, go to the Database Information dialog box. Just follow these steps:

1. Select a database in the Workspace.

2. Choose File ➤ Database ➤ Information. The Database Information dialog box appears, as shown in Figure 22.1.

From this dialog, you can change a database's settings or access several other dialog boxes. For example, to display a new name on the database icon, enter a different name in the Title text box. (The title is originally created when the database itself is created; however, you can change it at any time.) To change the particular categories that you want this database listed under in the server's database catalog, enter new categories in the Categories text box. Separate multiple categories with commas. You can also access the Design Template Options, Replication Settings, User Activity, and Database Settings dialogs, each of which is discussed in the following sections, by clicking on the buttons in the lower right corner of the Database Information dialog.

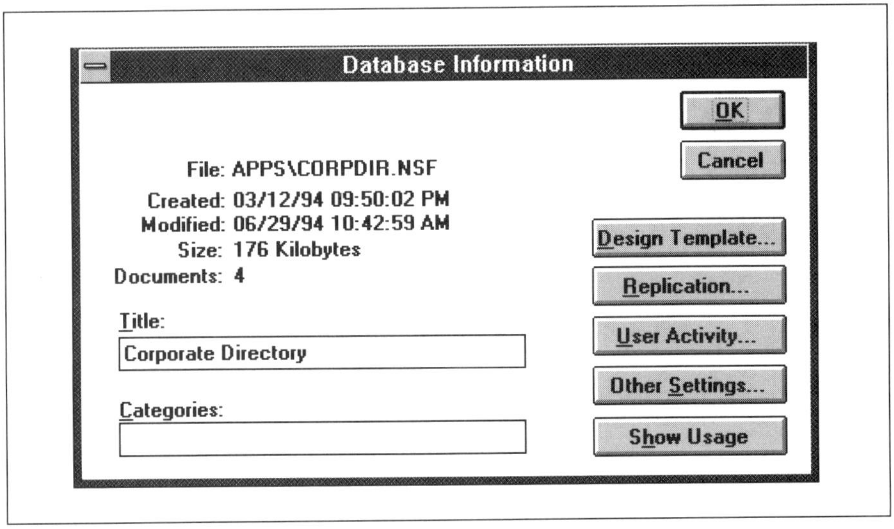

FIGURE 22.1 ▶

The Database Information dialog box provides information about the current database and allows you to modify the settings for that database.

Designating Design Templates

To check whether a particular database is a design template or to change its designation, go to the Design Template Options dialog box. Just follow these steps:

1. Click on the Design Template button. The Design Template Options dialog box appears, as shown in Figure 22.2.

FIGURE 22.2

The Design Template Options dialog box lets you designate the database as a design template, or designate when you want the database to inherit its design from a template.

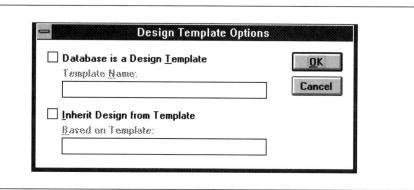

2. Select the Database is a Design Template option if this database is to be used as a design template. Enter the name for this design template in the Template Name text box. Alternatively, select the Inherit Design from Template option if this database is to inherit its design elements from a design template. Enter the name of the source template in the Based on Template text box.

3. Click on OK to accept your selection, or click on Cancel.

 ▶▶ **N O T E**

We discuss designating databases as design templates and inheriting designs from design templates in Chapter 12, "Basing a Database on a Design Template."

Selecting Replication Settings

You can also check or change a database's replication settings from the Database Information dialog. Click on the Replication button. The Replication Settings dialog box opens, as shown in Figure 22.3. From here, you can choose a number of replication settings.

 ▶▶ **N O T E**

We discuss selective replication and choosing other replication settings in Chapter 19, "Replicating Databases."

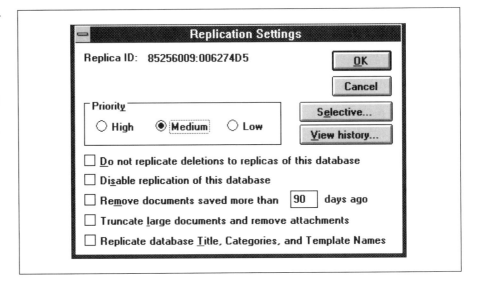

If you are going to change replication settings, start by selecting a priority level. The priority level is used for scheduling database replication. The default is Medium. Select any of the options that are displayed:

- **Do not replicate deletions to replicas of this database**: Prevents deletions to local replicas from being propagated to other replicas of this database. This option is selected by default.

- **Disable replication of this database**: Prevents replication of this database during any replications you perform, even if it is included in the databases selected for the replication.

- **Remove documents saved more than <number> days ago**: Removes documents saved longer than the number of days specified. You will be prompted each time you open the database until you answer Yes to delete the documents, change the number of days specified, or turn this option off.

- **Truncate large documents and remove attachments**: Removes bitmaps and other large objects and all attachments from documents being received over a dial-up connection. Select this option to avoid long connect times when it isn't practical to receive large files over a dial-up connection. A truncated file appears with the word *Truncated* as part of document name.

- **Replicate database Title, Categories, and Template Names**: Gives this database the same title, categories, and template names as the original database.

If you click on the Selective button, the Selective Replication dialog box appears. The options in this dialog box allow you to replicate only certain types of information from the source database. When you click on the View history button, the Replication History dialog box appears. The information you see in this dialog box lets you check when and with which server this database last replicated.

Click on OK to close either dialog box. You'll return to the Replication Settings dialog box. Click on OK again to return to the Database Information dialog box.

Displaying User Activity

User activity is recorded by default for all databases on servers unless it has been disabled by the Notes Administrator, or has been disabled for an individual database in the User Activity dialog box. To get to this dialog, click on the User Activity button. The User Activity dialog box appears, as shown in Figure 22.4.

FIGURE 22.4 ▶

The User Activity dialog box lets you record and display data about the usage levels for a database.

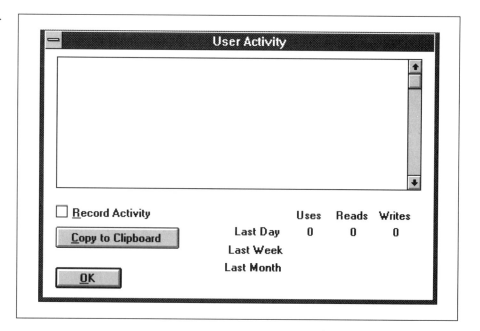

	Uses	Reads	Writes
Last Day	0	0	0
Last Week			
Last Month			

You might want to record user activity to check whether a database is really being used or is just wasting disk space. Also, since this feature shows who is using the database and in what way, the data can be used for billing purposes. Only someone with Manager access to the database can turn this feature on or off, but anyone with at least Reader access can view the information when the feature is on.

To record user activity, select Record Activity and then click on OK. To stop recording user activity, deselect Record Activity and then click on OK.

 ▶▶ **N O T E**

The recording remains active even if you click on Cancel in the File Database Information dialog box after closing this dialog box. You have to deselect Record Activity in order to stop it.

When you read the user activity information, the text box shows read and write information for each user. A read occurs when the user opens a document. A write occurs when the user saves a new or modified document or deletes a document.

The table at the lower right of the dialog box summarizes the total uses, reads, and writes for the past day, week, and month. A use occurs each time a user opens the database and performs at least one read or write.

To copy the user information to another application, such as a spreadsheet, click on Copy to Clipboard. You can then paste the information into the other application. When you're finished, click on OK to close the User Activity dialog box. You'll return to the Database Information dialog box.

Choosing Additional Settings

To select additional settings for a database, you can use the Database Settings dialog box that appears in Figure 22.5. To get to the Database Settings dialog, click on the Other Settings button in the Database

Information dialog box. You can choose from the following options:

- **Do not list in Database Catalog**: Suppresses the database name from the server's database catalog.

- **Do not list in 'Open Database' dialog**: Suppresses the database name from the Open Database dialog box. Users can still open and add this database, but must do so by entering the name manually in the dialog box.

FIGURE 22.5

The Database Settings dialog box lets you establish additional settings for a database.

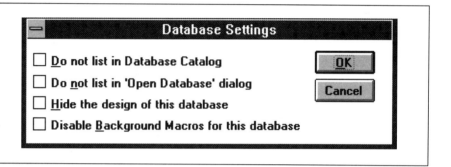

WARNING

Once you select this option, it cannot be canceled. All copies and replicas of this database will inherit its design, and will inherit this setting.

- **Hide the design of this database**: Disables design functionality for this database, effectively removing access to the Design menu. This prevents *all* users from seeing or changing the database's design settings.

- **Disable Background Macros for this database**: Disables automatic activation of all background macros stored in the current database. You can run them manually by choosing Tools ➤ Run Background Macros.

Click on OK to accept the changes or click on Cancel. You'll return to the Database Information dialog box.

To display database usage, click the Show Usage button to display a figure indicating how much of the database's allocated space is actually in use. The figure appears as a percentage, and is displayed next to the database size, as shown in Figure 22.6.

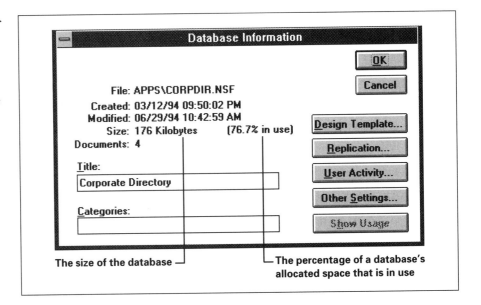

The size of the database — The percentage of a database's allocated space that is in use

▶ *The Database Design Synopsis Dialog Box*

The Database Design Synopsis dialog box provides a printable, detailed summary of all the design elements within a selected database. To display this information, follow these steps:

1. Select a database.

2. Choose Design ➤ Synopsis. The Design Synopsis dialog box appears, as shown in Figure 22.7.

3. Select the elements you want to summarize. You can choose the following options:

   • **Synopsis Header**: Displays a one-line title that includes the date and time of the synopsis.

FIGURE 22.7

The Design Synopsis dialog box lets you check off a list of database design elements whose definitions you want to see and/or print.

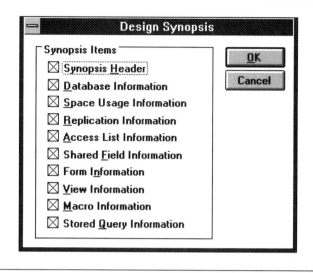

- **Database Information**: Displays the information recorded in the Database Information dialog box: title, location, categories, and so on.
- **Space Usage Information**: Displays the file size, number of documents, and space used by the database.
- **Replication Information**: Displays the current information from the database's replication settings.
- **Access List Information**: Displays a name-by-name listing of ACL entries and any privileges assigned to them.
- **Shared Field Information**: Displays a list of all shared fields, their types, and their definitions.
- **Form Information**: Displays the information stored as attributes in each form. The information includes a list of all fields that belong only to that form and their definition data.
- **View Information**: Displays the information stored as view attributes in each view. The information that's stored as part of the column definition for each column in the view is included, in addition to the information that's stored as part of the Design Macro dialog box, including the macro formula and run options for each macro.

- **Stored Query Information**: Displays the formula and selected options for each full text search query currently stored in the database.

4. Click on OK to accept your choices. The list of elements you've selected, along with their definitions, are displayed in a view window, as shown in Figure 22.8.

FIGURE 22.8 ▶

A view window displays a summary of the design elements that are selected in the Design Synopsis dialog box. This summary is for the Corporate Directory database.

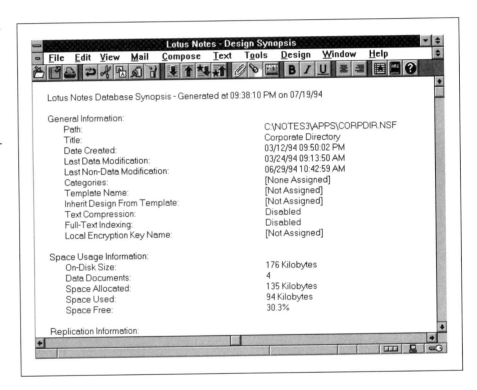

▶ *Summarizing the Field Contents of a Database*

The Design Document Info dialog box provides an online summary of the field contents of a selected document. You can use this dialog box to determine when a particular document was created and last modified, and to examine the contents of its hidden fields. For example, you can determine the name of the form with which a document was created by using the Document Info dialog box to examine the Form field.

SAVING THE DESIGN SYNOPSIS

Notes displays the design synopsis of a database in a window, the way a Notes document is displayed. The synopsis is not stored—when you close the window, the information will be lost. To preserve the design synopsis, you can print it by choosing File ➤ Print and then selecting the appropriate print settings.

Another way to save the synopsis is to paste it into a Notes document by choosing Edit ➤ Select All and then Edit ➤ Copy. Then compose a new document in a database and choose Edit ➤ Paste to paste the synopsis. You can also paste it into another application, say a word processor, by choosing Edit ➤ Select All and then Edit ➤ Copy. Then open the file in another application and choose Edit ➤ Paste to paste the synopsis.

Finally, if you want to export the synopsis to another application, choose File ➤ Export. Enter a name in the File Name text box, and select the directory and drive where you want to export the synopsis. If possible, select Microsoft Word RTF (Rich Text Format) from the Save File as Type list box. Using this file type will enable the synopsis to retain its formatting attributes. Otherwise, if you use ASCII Text, the default file type, all the formatting attributes will be stripped out, and the end of each line will include a "hard-carriage" return, or paragraph character. Text won't word-wrap automatically. You'll then have to read through the synopsis and delete the paragraph characters you don't want.

To get this information, follow these steps:

1. Select a document in a view or open a document.

2. Choose Design ➤ Document Info. Figure 22.9 shows the Design Document Info dialog box, in which document statistics and field data are displayed.

FIGURE 22.9 ▶

The Design Document Info dialog box displays document statistics and field data information.

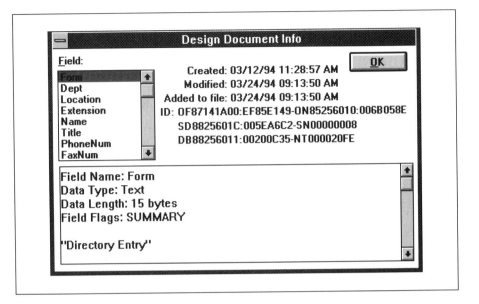

> ▶▶ **N O T E**
>
> **Some internal fields that are displayed in this dialog box are not readable because of the manner in which the information is stored. In addition, if a field has been encrypted and you do not have the appropriate encryption key, you will not be able to see the field's contents in the Design Document Info dialog box.**

3. Select a field from the list displayed in the upper left corner of the dialog box. The field's contents are displayed in the box below the list.

4. Select another field to see its contents.

5. Click on OK to close the dialog box.

▶▶ *Compacting a Database*

Compacting a database means removing the unused space—known as "white space"—that is left by deleted documents. Removing the unused space frees up hard disk space and improves a computer's performance. When a user accesses a database that contains a lot of unused space, Notes searches the space in order to locate views and documents. The more unused space there is, the longer Notes takes to access a view or document. There is a direct correlation between unused space in a database and the time Notes takes to open a database.

To find out how much unused space is available within a database, follow these steps:

1. Select or open a database.

2. Choose File ➤ Database ➤ Information. The Database Information dialog box appears.

3. Click on the Show Usage button. The percentage of space in use is displayed next to the size of the database.

4. Click on OK.

In general, it isn't necessary to compact a database unless it has at least 10–15% unused space and the database is rather large (e.g., over 5MB). Your Notes Administrator can advise you on your organization's standards.

▶ Using the Compact Command

The Compact command in Notes works by making a temporary copy of the active or selected database, and copying it *over* the original file, preserving the original Read/Unread markers and removing unused space. Users who try to open the database during the copying process see the message "Database is in use by you or another user."

If there isn't enough disk space to store the temporary copy, the Compact operation cannot be completed and the message "Insufficient Disk Space" is displayed. If the database to be compacted has a full text index, Notes deletes the full text index before compacting, because the index will be invalidated. Once compaction is complete, you can create a new full text index. (See Chapter 20, "Indexing a Notes Database," for more information.)

▶▶

Compacting is a new feature in version 3.X. When compacting is performed on a database that was created with Notes Release 2.1 or earlier, the File ➤ Database ➤ Compact command converts the database to the version 3.X structure.

To compact a database, follow these steps:

1. Select a database by clicking on its icon in the Workspace.

2. Choose File ➤ Database ➤ Compact. (Notes Administrators can perform the Compact command globally on all databases on a Notes Release 3 server.) The Compacting Database message box appears, displaying the percentage of compaction as it progresses.

 ▶▶ N O T E

Compacting a large database can take a while, causing delays for other users. You should check with your Notes Administrator before compacting a shared database—perhaps you can arrange to do it after normal work hours.

▶▶ *Organizing Your Notes Data Directory*

In order to properly manage Notes databases files that are stored on your workstation, you can locate them in the same data directory. By organizing files in this way, you gain easier access to them, and you'll always know where they're located. Otherwise, you might find the files in the main Notes directory with other program files. This is an inefficient way to store the database files. You'll have a difficult time locating a file you need to move or copy. You might also accidentally select a program file by mistake.

Later on when you want to archive databases that you no longer use, you'll have to scroll through the list of files in order to find and select them. This will take time. Therefore, creating a separate Notes data subdirectory makes sense; you can organize database files in one convenient location. (You can also create a separate directory for your stored databases and another one for templates.) A Notes data subdirectory could contain:

- Your locally stored databases (.NSF and .NS2 files)
- Your locally stored templates (.NTF files)
- Your DESKTOP.DSK file (your personal Notes Workspace setup)
- .CLS files (Character and Language Sequence files) that you installed

Notes creates the DESKTOP.DSK file for you and keeps track of changes you make to your Workspace, such as the arrangement of your database icons. Your NOTES.INI file is automatically added to your Windows directory when you install Notes. It contains operating instructions for running Notes on your workstation.

To move your Notes data files to a new Notes data subdirectory, follow these steps:

  TIP

> **If you want to select more than one database icon at a time, click on any icon, hold the Shift key down, and click on the other icons you want to select.**

1. In the Workspace, select the icon(s) that represent a *local* database (a database that is stored on your hard disk or floppy disk rather than on a server).

2. Press Delete to remove the icons from your Workspace. You'll have to do this separately for each tabbed page that contains local database icons.

▶▶ **N O T E**

This action *does not* delete the databases from your hard disk; it only removes the icons from your Workspace. (To *delete* a database, choose File ➤ Database ➤ Delete. However, make sure you want to do this. It's irreversible!)

3. Press Alt+Tab to display the Program Manager window. (There's no need to exit Notes.)

4. Double-click on the File Manager icon. The File Manager window appears.

5. Choose File ➤ Create Directory to create a new Notes data subdirectory in the main Notes directory. The Create Directory dialog box appears.

6. Enter a name in the Name text box. For example, KEN_DATA.

7. Click on OK. Windows creates the subdirectory.

▶▶ **T I P**

Since the files share the same extension, you could also move to the old data subdirectory and then choose File ➤ Select Files. The Select Files dialog box appears. Enter the extension in the text box. (Make sure you include the asterisk in the name, as in *.NSF.) Click on Select and then click on Close. The selected files appear highlighted.

Now locate the old Notes data subdirectory. Select the data files you want to move by holding down the Shift key and clicking on each file name separately. Then follow the steps below:

1. Choose File ➤ Move (or Copy).

2. Enter the path name of the new Notes Data subdirectory in the To text box.

3. Click on OK. Windows will move (or copy) the files to the new subdirectory.

4. Choose File ➤ Exit to close File Manager window.

5. Press Alt+Tab to display the Notes Workspace.

At this point, you'll need to add the databases to your Workspace again. First, however, you have to indicate to Notes the new path to the directory. Choose Tools ➤ Setup ➤ User. Enter the new path of the data directory into the Data Directory text box in this format:

drive:\directory\data_directory_name

For example, c:\NOTES\KEN_DATA would be the name of the path to the KEN_DATA Notes data directory.

 ▶▶ **T I P**

Make sure that all the local databases have been removed from their original subdirectory location so you aren't making copies and wasting hard disk space.

After you enter the path name, you can add the databases to the Workspace and place their icons on the pages of your choice. Choose File ➤ Open Database. Select the databases you want to add to your Workspace from the list box. Then click on the Add Icon button. The databases will appear on the Workspace.

▶▶ *What's Next?*

The value of monitoring database activity and making sure that a database is functioning properly at all times cannot be underestimated. As the designer of a database, you might find yourself in the role of database manager. You might also have to manage many other databases at one time. Therefore, you'll need to organize databases so they can be accessed efficiently by users. You can perform routine maintenance on databases by overseeing their usage, security, and so on. As databases grow in size and mature, documents can become outdated. Other documents may not be accessed frequently. These are the kinds of issues you might need to address.

Over the course of the chapters in Part Three, we show you how the sample databases on the Companion Disk were created. We reveal some of the secrets and shortcuts that database designers have up their sleeves when they set about creating databases. The sample databases also provide good examples of workflow automation.

PART THREE

▶ ▶ **P**art Three shows you how four databases have been created by providing step-by-step walkthroughs. These same databases are included on the Companion Disk that accompanies the book. The templates are provided for you to customize to suit your own needs.

Chapter 23, "Group Scheduling," shows you how to create a unique 1994 calendar and appointment schedule application, which you can easily modify for 1995 or a later year. You use this calendar to keep the daily schedule of any person, place, or thing.

Chapter 24, "Investment Profiles," shows you how to create an Investment Profiles database. It assists people in a workgroup to gather background information on companies to use as a basis for making investment decisions. This chapter takes you through the steps of designing the forms and views for the Investment Profiles database, defining each form's attributes, adding fields, formatting the forms, creating the views, and writing the selection formulas.

Chapter 25, "Training Facilities," shows you how to create a Training Facilities database. This database is useful for evaluating multiple work sites. This chapter takes you through the steps of designing the forms and views for the Training Facilities database, defining each form's attributes, adding fields, formatting the forms, creating the views, and writing the selection formulas.

Chapter 26, "Consultant Assignments," shows you how to create a Consultant Assignments database. It helps an organization to track employees' work and assign them to projects. This chapter takes you through the steps of designing the forms and views for the Consultant Assignments database, defining each form's attributes, adding fields, formatting the forms, creating the views, and writing the selection formulas.

The glossary defines all the important Notes terms that you'll need to understand and use frequently as a database designer. The appendix describes important third-party products and services that you might find beneficial in using Notes.

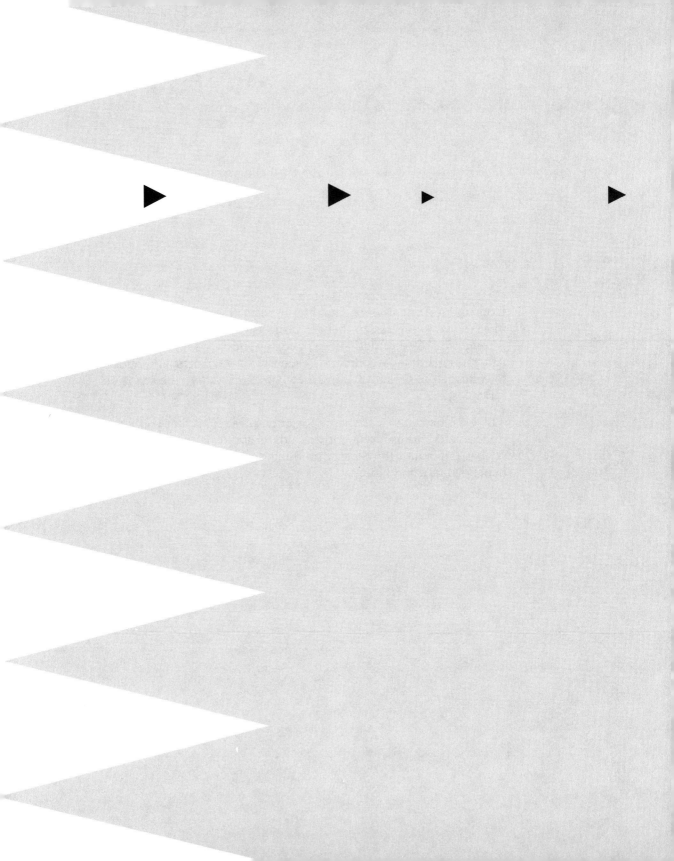

► ► CHAPTER **23**

Group Scheduling

▶ ▶ *F*AST *T*RACK

▶ **To view the detail schedule for a day** *683*

use the appropriate monthly view and highlight the desired day. There is a blank line in the view that separates the weeks. (If you can't see all the weeks, check to see that the view is fully expanded.)

▶ **To edit the detail schedule for a day** *683*

select the day from the appropriate monthly view and open the document in Edit mode by pressing Ctrl+E. Use the space bar or type a first letter to select any activity in the Event column for a specific time slot. (The activity you choose here will appear at the view level.) You can also type an optional description. Press Ctrl+S to save your changes.

Patrick Joyce created this unique 1994 calendar and appointment schedule application, which you can easily modify to suit your own needs. The database contains 14 views and 377 documents! However, unlike other databases in which you compose documents, you don't compose a single one in the 1994 Calendar database. The developer has created separate forms that you edit as if they were documents.

The database is similar to a calendar application that Lotus provides in its Application Library on CompuServe, although Patrick says his application is the only one with a "calendar look and feel." For example, Figure 23.1 shows the view for the month of September 1994 and Figure 23.2 displays the view for the entire year.

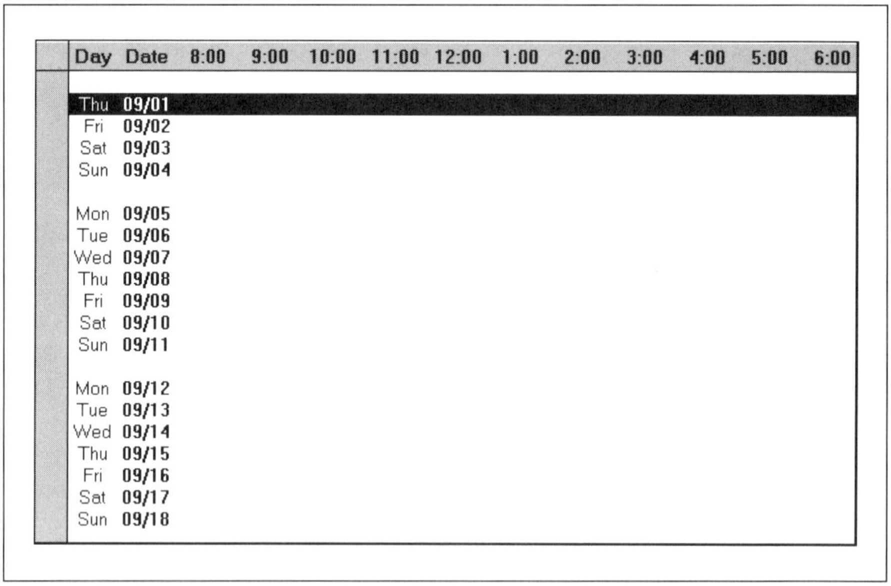

FIGURE 23.1 ▶

This view provides an easy way to display the daily schedule of events for a given month, which in this case is September.

Day	Date	8:00	9:00	10:00	11:00	12:00	1:00	2:00	3:00	4:00	5:00	6:00
Thu	09/01											
Fri	09/02											
Sat	09/03											
Sun	09/04											
Mon	09/05											
Tue	09/06											
Wed	09/07											
Thu	09/08											
Fri	09/09											
Sat	09/10											
Sun	09/11											
Mon	09/12											
Tue	09/13											
Wed	09/14											
Thu	09/15											
Fri	09/16											
Sat	09/17											
Sun	09/18											

FIGURE 23.2

This view displays each month of the year.

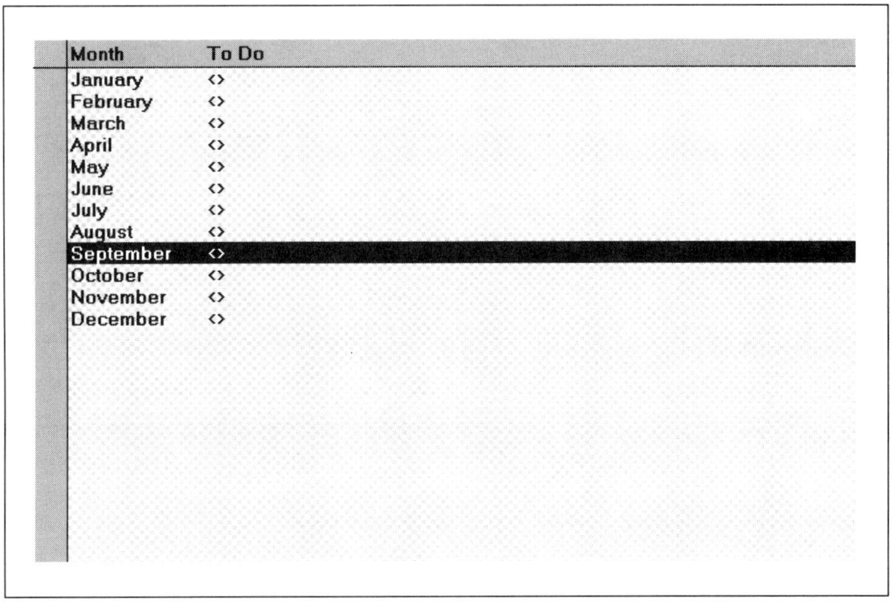

Month	To Do
January	<>
February	<>
March	<>
April	<>
May	<>
June	<>
July	<>
August	<>
September	<>
October	<>
November	<>
December	<>

▶▶ *What Does the Calendar Database Do?*

You can use this calendar to keep the daily schedule of any person, place, or thing. For example, a manager can keep his or her schedule in the calendar. Then other users with Reader access can check the schedule at any time, while those with Editor access (such as an assistant) can make changes. You can do the same for scheduling the use of conference rooms, equipment, and so on.

You can look at a full month at a time or individual days. Figure 23.3 displays a calendar for a particular month. Figure 23.4 displays the schedule for a specific day. When looking at the month, you'll see that each day in the calendar displays a doclink button. If you click on this doclink, you'll see the full schedule for the specific day in the month. You can also edit both of these forms directly in order to schedule appointments and display events.

FIGURE 23.3 ▶

This calendar form provides an easy way to display a schedule of events for a particular month.

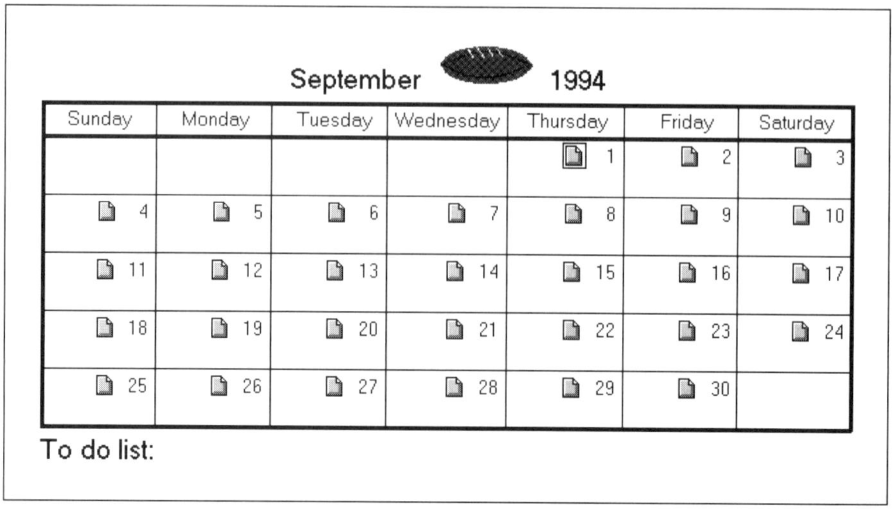

September 1994

Sunday	Monday	Tuesday	Wednesday	Thursday	Friday	Saturday
				1	2	3
4	5	6	7	8	9	10
11	12	13	14	15	16	17
18	19	20	21	22	23	24
25	26	27	28	29	30	

To do list:

FIGURE 23.4 ▶

This daily schedule form displays a schedule for a specific day in a month.

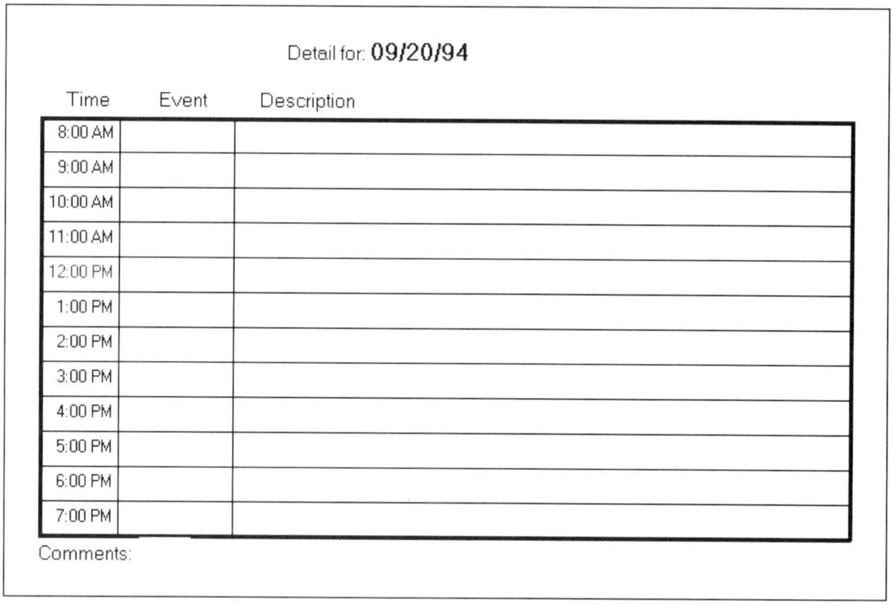

Detail for: **09/20/94**

Time	Event	Description
8:00 AM		
9:00 AM		
10:00 AM		
11:00 AM		
12:00 PM		
1:00 PM		
2:00 PM		
3:00 PM		
4:00 PM		
5:00 PM		
6:00 PM		
7:00 PM		

Comments:

▶ Important Features of the Calendar Database

We must emphasize that this Calendar database is a little different from most databases in that you never compose any documents. All monthly and daily schedule documents have already been created. All you need to do is edit the documents to fill in your activities.

The Calendar database includes the following important features:

- Tables for both the monthly and daily forms
- Doclinks from the month to the individual day schedules
- To Do items for the month display at the view level
- A keyworded Event column for the daily schedule that is designed to fit in view columns

Two forms are used in the 1994 Calendar database: a monthly calendar form and a daily schedule form. There are 12 monthly calendar forms, one for each month of the year, and a daily schedule form for each day in a month.

One of the interesting aspects of the database is how each monthly calendar form uses the Notes *doclink* feature to link each day in a given month with a daily schedule form; in other words, you can access a daily schedule form from a monthly calendar form in order to schedule appointments from 8:00 a.m. to 7:00 p.m.

There's a view for each month of the year that lists all the days for that month. From there you can select a specific day. You can then go into Edit mode to add, change, or delete hourly entries. Each hour has two fields, a keyword field and a text field.

The keyword field designates the type of activity. You may want to customize the keywords for these fields. Make sure each keyword is short enough to fit in the hourly columns in the view. The text fields are for details, and will expand to any size as you type.

There is also a yearly view that lists the twelve monthly documents. These documents are displayed with a specialized form that looks like a standard calendar. There is a text field for each day, as well as a doclink. The doclinks point to the individual daily documents mentioned above. Each month also has a To Do list. To Do entries show up in the view.

▶▶ **N O T E**

Entries you make in the hourly slots for a given day have no relationship to entries you make on the monthly calendar for that day.

▶ *Who Should Use the Calendar Database?*

This application is useful for anyone who wants to set or view the schedule for an individual, a conference room or other facility, a department's travel commitments, or the reservations for a piece of equipment. The default access is Reader, but anyone who will be allowed to make changes to the calendar will need to have Editor access also.

▶ *Why Use the Calendar Database?*

This group scheduling database has an authentic calendar look and feel. One reason for using the application is to maintain one central calendar of the schedule for any person, place, or thing. You can also replicate the database to remote sites, or dial in to access it remotely when you are on the road.

▶▶ *Using the Calendar Database*

The most important thing to remember when working with the Calendar database is this: You don't compose anything. A document has been created for each day and month of 1994. To make entries, you don't use the Compose menu. Instead, you select the appropriate document from the appropriate view and then edit that document.

▶▶ **W A R N I N G**

Do not delete any of the documents in the Calendar database. A document has been prepared for each day and month of 1994. If you delete any of them, it is extremely difficult to recreate those documents.

To try out the Calendar database, you need to copy the file to your hard disk and then add the database to your Workspace. Click on its icon to select it and follow these steps:

1. To edit one of the months, choose Other from the View menu and then select the Year - 1994 view.

2. Highlight a month and then press Ctrl+E to bring it up in Edit mode. The text fields in each daily cell of the table appear.

3. Fill in an entry for any day you choose. Also, enter information in the To Do list field at the bottom of the screen. Each entry is automatically placed on a separate line when you save the document.

4. Press Ctrl+S to save the document.

5. Press Esc to return to the view. The new To Do list item appears.

6. To change the schedule for a day, display the same month again.

7. Double-click on the doclink button for any day. This brings you to the Daily Schedule document for that day.

8. Press Ctrl+E to go into Edit mode and select an event in the second column by pressing the spacebar to automatically scroll through the list of predefined choices. You can also type your own entry.

9. Enter an optional description in the third column if you desire.

10. Save the document and then press Esc. You return to the month calendar. Press Esc again to return to the Year - 1994 view.

11. To see the event you selected for the date in that month, switch to the month's view by selecting the particular month from the View menu. The Event items appear in the hourly columns of the view. You'll also notice that blank lines separate the weeks of the month.

▶▶ *Customizing and Updating the Calendar Database*

From this point on, we're going to take you through the steps of duplicating the Calendar database by creating it from scratch. You might ask yourself, "Can't I just install the database and use it as is?" The answer is yes. (We don't want you to feel as if we're forcing you to reinvent the wheel.) All you have to do after decompressing the Calendar database file is to follow the steps in Chapter 4 for adding the database to your Workspace.

Our main reason for helping you to duplicate the Calendar database is to reveal how it was designed. You could consider the process a variation of "backwards engineering." By recreating the database from scratch, you'll be able to analyze its design and look closely at its components. You'll experience firsthand the development process the designer was in engaged in as he created the application. Along the way, we'll point out interesting design tips and shortcuts that you can use when you create your own databases. You can always apply what you've learned about duplicating one database to a new database.

 ▶▶ **W A R N I N G**

> **We've said it once but we'll say it again: Don't work with your only existing copy of the database. Make a backup copy of the database file and store it in a safe place before you add it to your Workspace. As you modify the Calendar database, you could remove one of the forms or views accidentally, or delete a doclink unintentionally. Remember that you don't compose any documents in this database; all the documents have been created for you. The database won't work correctly if an item is missing. If you damage the database, you can remove it from your system and reinstall your backup copy.**

Another reason for analyzing the Calendar database is to discover ways for customizing the application to suit your own needs. For example, you might decide that you don't like the layout of the forms. Perhaps you want to include more fields, or change the graphics that are used. The developer has given his permission to customize the database if you desire. However, the database's unique structure is tightly integrated. If you start customizing the design, you might discover that it doesn't work correctly.

Finally, you should know that you can update the Calendar database to display a new year. The application includes a macro that you can apply to all the documents in the database. Be sure to read "Updating the Calendar with a Macro" at the end of the chapter.

▶▶ *Duplicating the Forms*

The 1994 Calendar database utilizes two forms: a Month form and a Daily Schedule form. The developer has included 12 Month forms (one for each month of the year) and 365 Daily Schedule forms (one for each day of the year), for a total of 377 forms. The forms are ready for members of a workgroup to fill in their daily and monthly schedules. Each person's schedule can be posted and displayed in order to track his or her appointments, vacations, meetings, and so on. Some people may like the accountability that's built into the database, others may not.

Since a user doesn't actually compose any documents in this database, the forms are used as documents. Unlike other databases, forms are not available from the Compose menu. The forms are treated as documents that have been composed already. Therefore, a user only edits the documents. All the documents are "data-ready;" that is, a user can input data in a specific document by choosing a view and then selecting and opening a particular document in Edit mode.

▶ *Recreating the Month Form*

If you want to recreate or modify a monthly calendar form, you first need to go behind the scenes in order to see how it was put together. You'll discover design and programming techniques that you can apply to your own databases. You can also learn shortcuts that can save you time during the development process. (By tearing apart the design of an existing database, you'll learn how the various elements were used and gain an appreciation of the developer's method in the process.) As you can see in Figure 23.5, the monthly calendar form is made up of a series of formatted cells. Actually, it's a table. Since the form for each month is structured in the same way, let's step through the process of building one.

FIGURE 23.5 ►

The structure of the monthly calendar form.

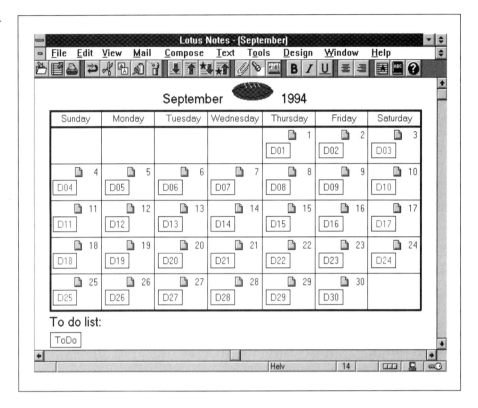

Creating a New Database

You always have the option of creating a new database or using a copy of an existing database. As we discussed in Chapter 12, creating a new database from scratch might be easier than using an existing database and then modifying it to fit your own needs. A database may contain only a few elements that you find useful. Therefore, the time involved in removing all the elements that you don't want could be considerable. That's why we suggest you use a database first before making modifications to it. Follow the steps in "Using the Calendar Database" that appear earlier in the chapter. Then after using the database, you can decide how you want to proceed.

If you want to get a jump-start on creating the calendar for 1995, you can create a new database by following these steps:

1. Choose File ➤ New Database. The New Database dialog box appears.

2. Make sure that -Blank- is highlighted in the Template list box.

3. Highlight the appropriate server name in the Server list box.

4. Enter **1995CAL** or another appropriate name in the Filename text box. There's no need to include an extension because Notes appends .NSF to the file name automatically. (You can also include the path in the file name in order to make sure the database is stored in the appropriate directory.)

5. Enter **1995 Calendar** or another appropriate name in the Title text box. Just make sure the name is descriptive.

6. Click on OK. By default, a blank view appears.

7. Press Esc to close the view. You'll return to the Notes Workspace, which displays the new 1995 Calendar database icon as shown in Figure 23.6.

FIGURE 23.6 ▶

The Notes Workspace displays the icon for the new 1995 Calendar database.

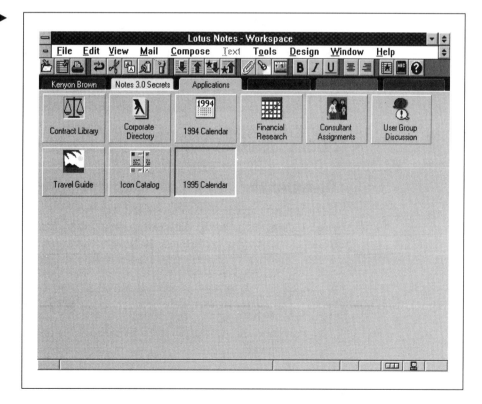

An icon always appears in the Workspace, with the title you gave the database. *Before* you start creating any forms or views, you need to make sure the icon is selected by clicking on it. Otherwise, you'll either save the forms or views to a database that you unknowingly selected or you won't be able to create the forms or views because you haven't selected a database.

 ▶▶ **N O T E**

> **If a specific database isn't selected in the Notes Workspace, the Design menu will appear dimmed. Subsequently, you won't be able to access the Views or Forms commands.**

You could also modify the existing 1994 Calendar database by making a copy of it and then adjusting the dates that appear on all the forms and views. (For 1995, you would move each date forward by one day. For example, since January 1 fell on Saturday this year, it will fall on Sunday next year, and so on.) This would be the quickest and easiest way to reuse the calendar.

For the purpose of this discussion, however, it's good practice recreating existing forms and views. In that way, you'll learn how they were built. You can just as easily create new forms and views for the 1995 Calendar database by using the 1994 Calendar database as a model.

Opening the 1994 Calendar Database

Let's create the monthly calendar form for January 1995. First, however, let's add the 1994 Calendar database to the Workspace in order to access its forms and views. Follow these steps:

1. Choose File ➤ Open Database. The Open Database dialog box appears, as shown in Figure 23.7.

2. Select the name of the appropriate server or double-click on Local, then click on the Open button. (You can also double-click on the server's name to open it.) A list of directories and files should appear.

FIGURE 23.7

The Open Database dialog box lets you select a database to add to your Workspace.

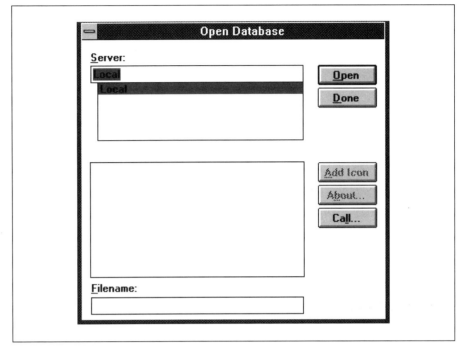

3. Double-click on the name of the directory where the databases are stored (the directory where you copied the sample databases from the Companion Disk that accompanies the book).

4. Select 1994 Calendar and click on the Done button (or double-click on the database name).

 ▶▶ **N O T E**

> **If you haven't already copied the sample databases from the Companion Disk to your hard disk, see "Using the Companion Disk Databases" in Chapter 4.**

The 1994 Calendar icon now appears in the Workspace. However, as we mentioned above, after you create 1995 Calendar database, make sure it is selected as you create the new forms and views for it. Otherwise, they will become part of the 1994 Calendar database (or another database that you unknowingly selected).

We need to display both databases in the Workspace because we need to access both of them at the same time. As you create the forms and views for the new 1995 calendar, you'll go back and forth between both databases frequently in order to learn how the 1994 Calendar was constructed.

Opening Multiple Windows at the Same Time

To simplify going from one database to another, let's open both files at the same time. You can open multiple databases in Notes so that you can easily perform operations across forms and documents, just as you can open multiple documents in other Windows applications. The Notes Window menu displays all the windows that are open at a given time. Remember that each time you display a view, form, or document you open an active window. Notes allows you to open as many as nine windows at a time.

 ▶▶ **N O T E**

> **If you try to open more than nine windows at a time, Notes will tell you to close a window before you open another one. Each open window uses additional memory from your computer. You'll discover that your system begins to run sluggishly as you open more windows, especially if you are running Notes on a minimum or near minimum recommended hardware configuration.**

To open windows and add their titles to the Window menu, follow these steps:

1. Click on the 1994 Calendar icon to select it.

2. Choose Design ➤ Forms. The Design Forms dialog box appears.

3. Highlight (January) and click on Edit. The January 1994 form appears.

4. Open the Window menu. You'll see that (January) appears with a checkmark next to it below the Workspace title.

5. Click on Workspace to return to the Workspace. Both the 1994 and 1995 Calendar icons are displayed.

6. Now click on the 1995 Calendar icon to select it.

7. Choose Design ➤ Forms. The Design Forms dialog box appears, as shown in Figure 23.8.

8. Click on the New button. A blank form appears, displaying (untitled) in the title bar. The form is actually a large rich text field.

9. Pull down the Window menu. You'll see the (untitled) title at the bottom of the menu. This is the default name for the new form, which you'll change shortly.

10. Click on the (January) title to display the January 1994 form, pull down the Window menu, and click on the (untitled) title to display the new form.

11. Repeat the previous action to go back and forth between the two forms or any other open window.

FIGURE 23.8 ▶

The Design Forms dialog box gives you the choice of creating a new form or editing an existing form.

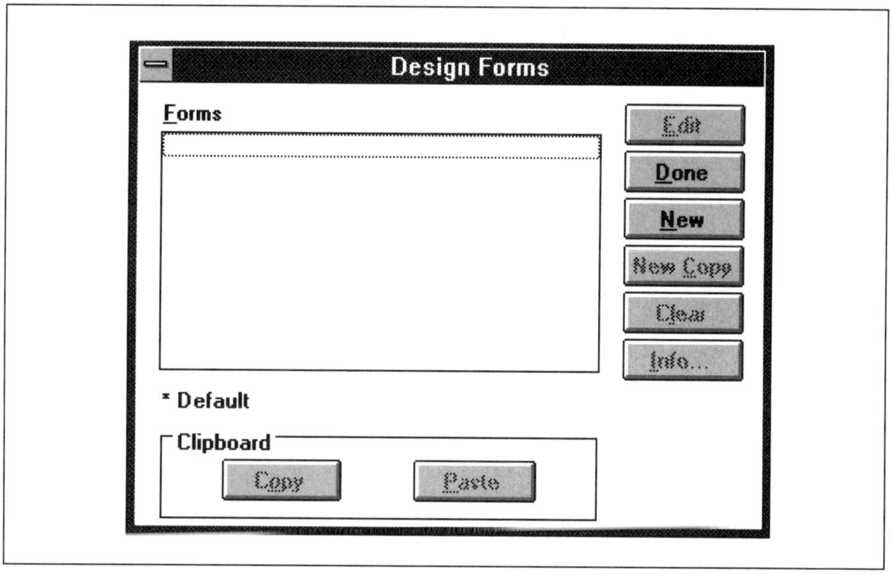

A much faster way to display any database view, form, or document that's open is to press Ctrl+F6. Use this keystroke combination to cycle forward through the open windows in Notes. To close any open window in Notes, you can use the Esc key. Display the active window you want to close and then press Esc.

The instructions above illustrate how to open more than one window at a time in Notes. By opening multiple windows and adding their names to the Window menu, you can save yourself a lot of time going back and forth between databases, forms, and views. Now that you've created the 1995 database and created a new form, let's continue. Just make sure that the 1995 Calendar database is selected.

Defining a Form's Attributes

Before we begin, let's get some design preliminaries out of the way by defining various form attributes. When you create a new form, you should get in the habit of defining its attributes first, especially its name and the *type* you want associated with it. (We discussed types of forms in Part Two.)

When you switch to the (January) form in the 1994 Calendar database, you might ask why parentheses enclose the name. Although the developer chose to include parentheses around all the form names, in order to hide them from users by not displaying them on the Compose menu, you don't need to do the same. This is an old method that was used in earlier versions of Notes. Release 3 supports this method, but now lets you hide a form by deselecting the Include in Compose Menu default option in the Form Attributes dialog box.

▶▶ **W A R N I N G**

Be wary when you use an application that was created in an earlier version of Notes. Most of the time you shouldn't have any problem. However, a method that was used in an earlier release might conflict with a new feature in Release 3. Although the conflict probably won't be fatal, it could cause confusion. For example, older versions of the Calendar database have been created in earlier releases of Notes. The developer has been updating the database for each subsequent year, but continues to use a few old methods in Release 3. He hides forms from users by using parentheses in the forms' names. If you use this method in Release 3, it will override the Include in Compose Menu default option in the Form Attributes dialog box. You will get the same results, but you should use this new option instead because it's available to everyone else using Release 3. Hence, you won't confuse the users of the database.

To define the new form's attributes, follow these steps:

1. Choose Design ➤ Form Attributes. The Design Form Attributes dialog box appears, as shown in Figure 23.9.

2. Enter **January 1995** in the Name text box. (Remember: Don't include the parentheses as part of the name.)

3. Click on Include in Compose Menu to *deselect* it. This action will hide the form by not displaying it on the Compose menu.

4. Make sure that Document appears in the Type box and Include in Query by Form is checked (nothing else should be checked).

5. Click OK to accept the changes.

FIGURE 23.9 ▶

The Design Form Attributes dialog box lets you define many of the form's attributes, including its name and type.

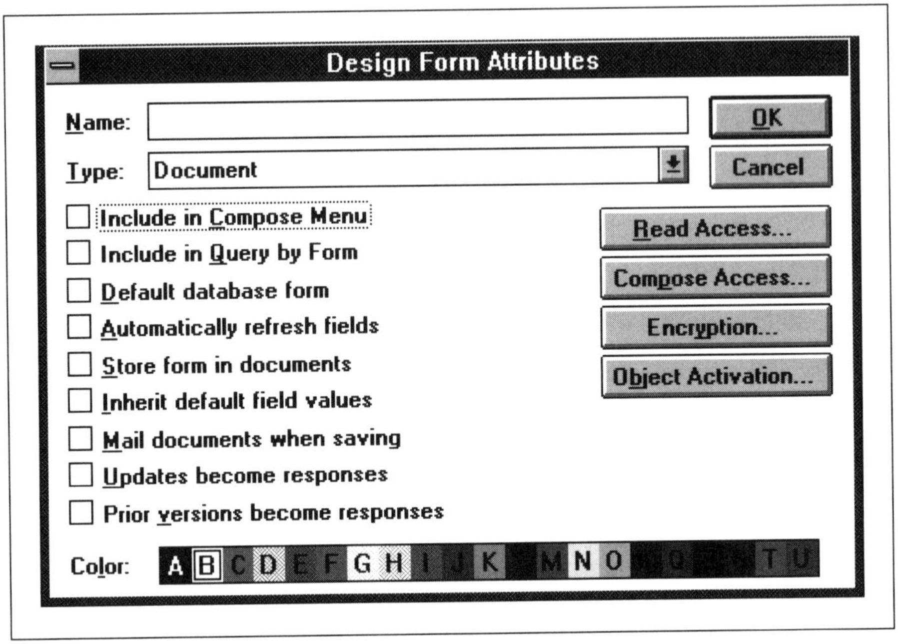

Design Form Attributes

Name: [   ]   **OK**

Type: [Document   ▼]   **Cancel**

☐ Include in Compose Menu
☐ Include in Query by Form   **Read Access...**
☐ Default database form
☐ Automatically refresh fields   **Compose Access...**
☐ Store form in documents   **Encryption...**
☐ Inherit default field values
☐ Mail documents when saving   **Object Activation...**
☐ Updates become responses
☐ Prior versions become responses

Color: A B C D E F G H I J K L M N O P Q R S T U

▶▶ T I P

Sometimes you'll want to create a form that is going to be used one time or for a single purpose; you won't want users to compose multiple documents that are based on the form. In the case of the 1994 Calendar database, all the documents are created already. You don't compose documents with it. The only way to prevent users from composing documents is by not displaying the form's name on the Compose menu. For example, display any monthly calendar form in the 1994 Calendar database and then choose Compose. The words (None Available) will appear dimmed. If you don't want a form's name to appear in the Compose menu, always deselect the Include in Compose Menu default option in the Form Attributes dialog box. This action will prevent a user from composing a document with a form, forcing the user to *edit* the form instead.

Displaying a Form's Title in the Window Bar

To change the title that's displayed in the window's title bar, follow these steps:

1. Choose Design ➤ Window Title. The Design Window Title dialog box appears, as shown in Figure 23.10.

2. Enter @**Now** in the Window Title Formula box. This statement returns your system's *current* date and time, which is displayed in the window's title bar. The current date appears regardless of the monthly calendar form that's displayed.

3. Click OK to confirm.

▶▶ **TIP**

> Sometimes a formula will include more than one function. You can certainly type all the functions, but this becomes especially tiresome because of the @ sign. Furthermore, you may not remember the correct spelling of a function or even that a particular function exists. If don't have a copy of the Notes reference documentation at your disposal or the System Administrator didn't install the Help files (which include a complete listing and explanation of the functions) on your system or the server, you're sunk. However, don't fret. Another way to enter functions in the Window Title Formula box is to click on the Add @Func button that appears at the bottom of the Design Window Title dialog box. A list of functions appears. You can double-click on the selected function to paste it in the formula box automatically.

FIGURE 23.10 ▶

The Design Window Title dialog box lets you identify information that you want to display in the window's title bar.

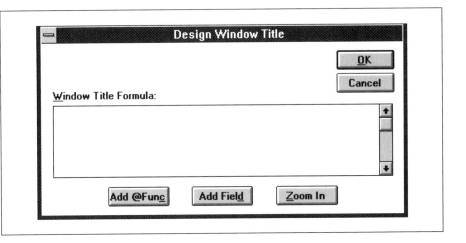

Inserting a Table

At this point, you can start laying out the form. Use Figure 23.5 as a model if you need a reference. To insert the table, follow these steps:

1. With the insertion bar in the upper left corner of the screen, press ↵ to move down to the next line. You can add more space between the top of the form and the table if you want.

2. Choose Edit ➤ Insert ➤ Table. The Insert Table dialog box appears, as shown in Figure 23.11.

FIGURE 23.11 ▶

The Insert Table dialog box lets you format the cells of a table that you've inserted in a form.

3. Enter 7 in the Number of rows box and 7 in the Number of columns box.

4. Click on OK to accept the other default parameters, including Fit to window. The table will appear. It will automatically fit the width of your monitor screen.

As you can see, all of the cells in the table are the same height and width. Unfortunately, Notes doesn't provide you with much in the way of formatting tools. So you'll have to manually tweak the cells in order to change their size.

Increasing the Height of Cells in a Table

Unlike other table formatting options available to you, the only way to increase the height of cells in a table is by pressing ↵ to insert carriage returns. To make the height of the cells in rows 2 through 7 larger, follow these steps:

1. Position the cursor in the first column, second row.

2. Press ↵ two times to increase the cell's height. All the other cells in the row will change also.

3. Press the ↓ to move down to the next row.

4. Press ↵ two times.

5. Repeat the steps to increase the height of the cells in rows 4 through 7.

Adding Labels

Let's enter static text in the cells to properly identify the days on the calendar. Unfortunately, entering and formatting text in a table can become an arduous task. You can either input all of the text at the same time and then format it later, or you can enter text in each cell and then format the text one cell at a time.

It's a toss-up which method is more time-consuming. Notes doesn't provide those convenient word processing features for formatting tables that we've all come to know and love, such as drag-and-drop/copy-and-drop, selecting and formatting text in cells at the same time, etc. Oh well, maybe these features will appear in the next version…

To add the name of the month, position the insertion bar in the upper left corner of the form and type **January 1995**. (You'll recall our discussion of using static text as labels in Part Two.) Don't worry about the format or placement of the static text for now.

To add the names of the days of the week and the dates, follow these steps:

1. Position the cursor in the cell in the first row, first column, and type **Sunday**.

2. Press the → or the Tab key to move the cursor to the next cell and type **Monday**.

3. Repeat the steps, entering the names of the other days of the week.

4. Position the cursor in the cell in the second row, first column under the word *Sunday* and type **1**.

5. Press the Tab key to move the cursor to the next cell and type **2**. (If you press →, the cursor will move down to the next line in the cell because you increased the height of the cell by pressing ↵.)

6. Repeat the steps until you've entered all the remaining numbers from 3 to 31.

Formatting a Table

At this point, you can format the table to suit your purposes. You may want to change the width of the columns, justify the column alignment of the text that appears in the cells, or add or delete a row or column. One way to accomplish these changes is by accessing the Table command that now appears under the Insert command on the Edit menu. First, make sure the cursor is positioned in the column/row location where you want to make the change(s); if the cursor is positioned outside the table, the Actions command will appear dimmed under the Insert command instead.

You'll notice in Figure 23.5 that the outside border of the table appears thicker than the inside border of each cell. You can change the appearance of cell line widths by accessing the Format command. Unfortunately, you can only change the borders one cell at a time.

To change the border widths of the cells, follow the steps on the next page (or you can display the cells with single-width borders).

1. Place the cursor in the cell in the first row, first column (which displays "Sunday").

2. Choose Edit ➤ Table ➤ Format. The Edit Table Format dialog box appears, as shown in Figure 23.12.

3. In the Cells Border area, click on the following radio buttons:
   - **Left:** Double
   - **Right:** Single
   - **Top:** Double
   - **Bottom:** Double

4. Refer to Figure 23.5 to see the border widths of the other cells.

Formatting Labels

The methods you use to format text on a form are similar to those for formatting text in most other Windows applications. However, as I mentioned earlier, Notes text formatting tools don't offer you the variety—or sophistication, for that matter—of features that you'll find in other applications, especially word processors or desktop publishers. In fact, Notes text formatting features are downright crude in comparison. This is ironic since most of your development time will be spent on designing database interfaces that include a lot of formatted text that users will read.

To format the text at the top of the monthly calendar form, follow these steps:

1. Highlight January 1995 and then choose Text ➤ Font (or press Ctrl+K). The Font dialog box appears. As you can see, the default Font Name is Helv (for Helvetica) and the size is 10 point.

2. Change the size of the font to 14 point and select Bold.

3. If you want the text to appear in a color other than black (which is the default), click on a selection in the Color Bar at the bottom of the dialog box.

4. Click on OK to apply the changes.

5. Choose Text ➤ Alignment.

6. Click on Center.

FIGURE 23.12 ►

The Edit Table Format dialog box lets you modify a table after you've inserted it in a form.

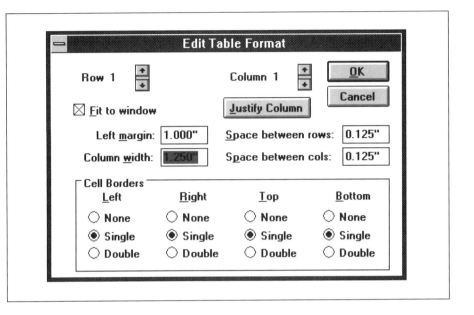

▶▶ **N O T E**

You can automatically align anything that appears in a column of cells by accessing the Edit Table Format dialog box. However, I don't consider this a shortcut because you might need to position text and field items in different locations within the same cell. Therefore, you might as well highlight each item separately in the cell and then change its alignment. If you want the alignment of all the items in a column of cells to appear the same, use the following method. Position the cursor in the desired cell and then choose Edit ➤ Table ➤ Format. In the dialog box, click on the Justify Column button to display the Justify Table Column dialog box. Choose the desired alignment by clicking one of the radio buttons and then clicking on OK to close the dialog box. Click on OK again to apply the changes.

To format the names of the week, follow these steps (or you can choose to display the text by using the default font, point size, color, and normal attribute):

1. Highlight **Sunday** and press Ctrl+K to display the Font dialog box.

2. Select the desired formatting attributes.

3. Click on OK to apply the changes.

4. Choose Text ➤ Alignment and click on Center.

5. Repeat the steps to format the other names.

▶▶ **T I P**

If you only need to apply a single formatting attribute to selected text, such as boldface or italics, you can do this faster by highlighting the text and then selecting the specific attribute from the Text menu. Open the menu and then click on the command you want in order to change the format. You can apply an attribute even faster by using keystroke combinations. Highlight the text and then press the appropriate keystroke(s) to make the format change, such as Ctrl+B for bold or Ctrl+I for italic.

Inserting a Graphic in a Form

Before we go on, let's discuss the graphic that appears at the top of the January 1994 form that we're using as our model. This graphic is similar to the table because it's an object that's been inserted in the form. In this case, the graphic appears between the text. (As we discussed in Part Two, you can insert graphic objects anywhere on a form because a form is actually a large rich text field that can contain text and graphics.)

When you click on the graphic to select it, a marquee will appear around it with a resizing handle in the lower right corner. The graphic might or might not also appear darkened (highlighted). If you hold the mouse button down while you point on the handle, you can drag the handle to increase or decrease the size of the graphic. This action is similar to the way you might modify the appearance of a graphic you've created in another application. If you've never used a drawing application to create a graphic, all you're doing is changing its size to fit the form. It's no big deal.

If the graphic appears marqueed but isn't highlighted, and you open the Edit menu, you'll notice that the Cut and Copy commands aren't available (they appear dimmed). However, the Paste command is available. You might think this is odd since the graphic appears selected with the marquee. What's going on? You must make sure the graphic is highlighted in order to cut or copy it. Otherwise, you won't be able to perform those actions.

  TIP

This probably sounds obvious, but after you select a graphic, open the Edit menu and see if the Cut and Copy commands are available. If they appear dimmed, the graphic hasn't been selected correctly. You need to make sure a marquee surrounds the graphic and it appears darkened.

I mention this because you might as well take advantage of copying the graphics that were created for the monthly calendar forms in the 1994 Calendar database. It's certainly easier than creating twelve individual graphics yourself. We realize we stated earlier that for the purpose of this discussion we wanted you to recreate the 1995 Calendar database from scratch. However, our purpose is not to teach you how to create graphics—and certainly not to teach you to draw.

Just highlight the Party Hat graphic in the January 1994 form, copy it to the Clipboard, return to the January 1995 form, place the cursor between the word and the year, and paste it. With the graphic still selected, open the Edit menu. You'll see a Resize Picture command under the Insert command. When you choose the command, the current width and height of the graphic will appear at the bottom of your screen. This information is handy to know when you resize the graphic. As you drag the handle, the new width and height will change accordingly.

▶▶ T I P

> **If you click the Clear button in the Design Icon dialog box and then have second thoughts, you can always click the Undo or Cancel buttons to restore a graphic. However, it will appear on the database icon after you click on OK and close the dialog box.**

Creating Bitmap Graphics with Notes

For you graphics purists who like to create your own original artwork for forms, you can take advantage of the Notes Icon command to design *bitmap graphic*s. If you don't use or have access to another Windows drawing program, the Notes Icon command works in a pinch (although it does have limitations). Unfortunately, you can only use this method for a database that doesn't display a graphic on its icon. The secret is to create the graphic(s) *before* you create the bitmap you want displayed on the database icon.

As we discussed in Part Two, when you create a new database or open an existing database Notes adds the icon to the Workspace. Subsequently, selecting the icon enables you to access the database quickly. After you open an existing database, such as the 1994 Calendar database, the icon that appears in the Workspace displays a bitmap graphic. When you created the new 1995 Calendar database, however, only the title you gave the database appeared on the icon. The area above the title is empty. Our advice is not to create the bitmap graphic you want to appear on the icon yet. Create the graphics you want to include on the monthly calendar forms first.

What happens if you don't? To illustrate the problems that you'll encounter, select the 1994 Calendar database by clicking on the icon in the Workspace and then follow these steps:

1. Choose Design ➤ Icon. The Design Icon dialog box appears, as shown in Figure 23.13. As you can see, the bitmap graphic that appears on the icon is displayed.

2. Click on the Copy button to copy the graphic to the Clipboard. (Warning: Make sure you've made a copy of the graphic before you go on to the next step!)

FIGURE 23.13 ▶

The Design Icon dialog box will display the bit-mapped graphic that appears on the se-lected database's icon.

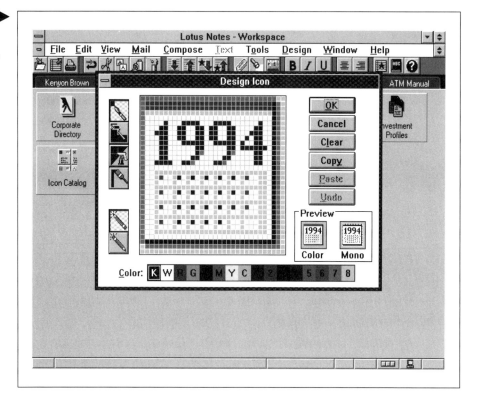

3. Click on the Clear button. The graphic disappears from the dialog box. If you click on the Undo button, the graphic reappears.

4. If you selected the Undo button in the previous step, choose the Clear button again to clear the dialog box.

5. With the dialog box cleared, click OK to accept the change. The dialog box closes, revealing that the icon's graphic has been erased. Don't panic! You copied the graphic to the Clipboard.

6. With the icon still selected, choose Design ➤ Icon again.

7. In the Design Icon dialog box, select Paste. The graphic will reappear.

8. Click OK to confirm. Once again, the database icon displays the 1994 Calendar graphic.

You should always create an icon's graphic *after* you've created the other graphics you want to use in a database. Otherwise, you'll delete the graphic from the icon and you won't be able to store a permanent copy of it on the Clipboard. Any other graphic you create and then copy to the Clipboard will *replace* the graphic you stored previously on the Clipboard. Don't expect to create a graphic, copy it to the Clipboard, paste it in forms, return to the Design Icon dialog box, and then retrieve the graphic for the database icon. It will be long gone!

You design an icon in Notes by painting individual pixels, just as you would in any other drawing program that enables you to create bitmap graphics. (Each one of the squares on the grid in the dialog box represents a pixel, which stands for "picture element.")

To create a new graphic that you want to use in a form, follow these steps:

1. Open the Design Icon dialog box.

2. Select the Draw drawing mode (the icon with the highlighted pencil tip).

3. Select the Paintbrush tool, which enables you to fill one pixel at a time. (This tool gives you more flexibility than the other tools for adding detail to the graphic.)

4. Point to the pixel you want to change and then click on the mouse button to add color, which you select at the bottom of the dialog box.

5. Select the Erase tool (the one with the highlighted eraser) and click on a pixel to restore it to the original background color.

6. Use the Roller, Spray, and Snap-to-Line tools to fill large areas of the grid. You'll need to experiment with each one in order to discover which one suits your need. (Remember: If you make a mistake, you can always click on the Undo button to undo your last action.)

7. When you're satisfied with the design and size of the graphic, click on Copy to store it on the Clipboard. (Warning: Do this *before* performing the next step.)

8. Click on the Clear button to erase the graphic, or it will appear on the database icon. (If you change your mind, click the Undo or Cancel buttons.)

9. Click on OK to confirm and to close the dialog box.

10. Open the form where you want to use the graphic, position it in the desired location, and select Paste from the Edit menu (or press Ctrl+V). The graphic will appear.

Later, if you want to modify the graphic, select it and then choose Copy from the Edit menu (or press Ctrl+C). Open the Design Icon dialog box. Click on Paste. The graphic will appear. Make the desired changes and then copy it to the Clipboard. Return to the form and paste the graphic. (If the old graphic hasn't been removed, select and delete it first.)

Embedding Objects in a Form

The main difference between the graphics and the tables that are used in the monthly calendar forms is that the graphics can be created in another application and then *embedded* in the forms, while the tables cannot. You can't create a table in, say, a Windows word processor and then embed it as a table; you can only embed it as word processing document.

As we discussed in Chapter 21, when you embed any OLE object in a form, you can choose when to activate the embedded object and how changes to the object will be presented to users. You'll recall that the purpose of embedding an object in a form, whether the object is, for example, a Windows spreadsheet, chart, or drawing, is to reflect changes in the object and then to display those changes in the documents that users compose, edit, or read.

In the case of the 1994 Calendar database, however, users only edit the forms; they never compose any new documents with the forms. Therefore, the graphics that appear at the top of the forms are never activated. They never change. They're only used to beautify and to add visual interest to the forms.

If you want to create a graphic in a drawing program that supports OLE and then embed it in a monthly calendar form, follow these steps using your favorite program. I use Visio 2.0 from Shapeware:

1. Position the cursor in the desired location.

2. Choose Edit ➤ Insert ➤ Object. The Insert Object dialog box appears, as shown in Figure 23.14.

FIGURE 23.14

*The Insert Object
dialog box*

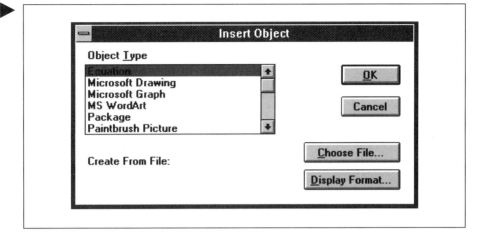

3. Select the Object Type you want to use from the list box. (I selected Visio 2.0 Drawing from the list. Visio is a great business drawing program for the artistically challenged person like myself.)

4. Click on OK. An object container appears on the form, including the name of the object type. (In my case, "New VISIO 2.0 Drawing Object" appears.) Subsequently, the drawing program in which you want to create the object opens.

5. Create the graphic.

6. Save the file *only* if you want to create a link to the drawing rather than embed a copy of it. Otherwise, you can skip this step.

7. Make sure the drawing is selected and then copy it to the Clipboard.

8. *Don't* exit the program. To embed the drawing, Notes needs certain information from the program which is more quickly obtained if the program is still running.

9. Press Alt+Tab to return to the January 1995 form.

At this point, you have several options open to you in deciding how you want to embed the drawing, or more importantly, how you want to handle the drawing from now on. If you know that you're not going to make further changes to the drawing, you can simply embed it by using Notes' Paste command. However, this action will stop you from modifying the drawing in the program in which it was created. You'll only be able to resize the drawing in Notes. Most of the time you'll probably want to treat the drawing in this way once people begin to use the database. You won't want other users modifying it.

If you want the option and flexibility of changing the drawing later on as you develop the database, you're better off using the Paste Special command to embed the drawing. You always use this command when you want to *link* an object, which allows you to make changes to an object in the source program and then show those changes dynamically in a Notes database. (A link consists of a reference from the container application, Notes, to the original source application.) However, this command also provides you with the option of embedding an object, which will allow you to edit it if you choose to do so.

Just remember that the drawing program must exist on either your system (or the server) if you want to continue editing the object. Otherwise, you'll get a "Lotus Notes OLE Error Report" telling you that the link failed because Notes can't find the source application.

To embed the drawing in the form, follow these steps:

1. Choose Edit ➤ Paste Special. The Paste Special dialog box appears, as shown in Figure 23.15. As you can see, you have a choice of selecting the Paste, Link, and Embed commands.

2. Click on the Embed button. The drawing appears on the form.

3. To resize the drawing, point the mouse on the handle in the lower right corner of the object's container. Hold the mouse button down and drag the handle to increase or decrease the size of the drawing.

FIGURE 23.15 ▶

The Paste Special dialog box gives you the choice of pasting, linking, or embedding objects.

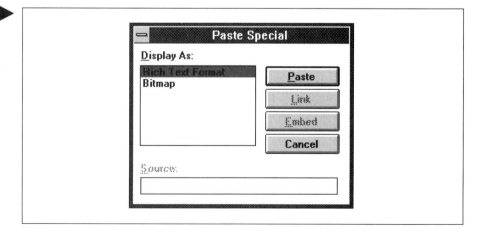

To edit the drawing, simply double-click on it. The drawing program opens, allowing you to modify the object. Make the changes you want and then exit the program. You don't have to save the drawing unless you want to link to it. (In fact, you must save the file before you can link to it.) Changes to the embedded drawing will be saved when you save the form in Notes. When you return to the form, the drawing will display the new changes.

Alternatively, you can also edit the drawing by following these steps:

1. Choose Edit ➤ *Actions*, where you'll see the name of the drawing program displayed below the Insert command. The name replaces *Actions* on the menu. (In my case, the menu displays "Object: VISIO 2.0 Drawing Program.")

2. Click on the object's name and choose Edit (or Open to open another file) from the submenu. The drawing program opens.

3. Make the desired changes.

4. Exit and program to return to the form.

The drawing will reflect the changes you made to it.

Defining the Fields

Now that we've entered and formatted all the static text, and inserted a graphic we want to appear on the monthly calendar form, let's create and position the fields. As you can see in Figure 23.5, each day of the month displays a field that is numbered consecutively from 1 to 31, depending on the number of days in the given month. These fields will contain text and provide you with the option of entering and recording important upcoming events.

You'll also notice that another icon appears in each cell of the table. It's called a *doclink* icon. This icon establishes a link between the monthly calendar form and the daily schedule form, which we haven't created yet. When you click on the icon for a particular day, you're transferred automatically to the daily schedule form for that day. We'll reserve discussing the creation of doclinks until we build the daily schedule form later in this chapter.

To add the first field to the January 1995 form, follow these steps. You can create the remaining fields on your own:

1. Place the cursor in the January 1 cell. (Use Figure 23.5 as a guide.)

2. Choose Design ➤ New Field. The Design New Field dialog box appears.

3. Click on OK to accept the default option. The Field Definition dialog box appears.

4. Enter the following information (unless already indicated):

   - **Name**: D01
   - **Help Definition**: Enter the major event(s) for the day.
   - **Date Type**: Text
   - **Allow Multi-Values**: Check (to select)
   - **Field Type**: Editable

5. Click OK to accept the changes. The field will appear.

6. If you want to change the color of the text that will appear in the field (weekends appear in red; weekdays in blue), highlight the field and then choose Text ➤ Font. The Font dialog box appears.

7. Select red in the Color Bar at the bottom of the dialog box.

8. Click on OK to confirm the change. The field's text color changes from black to red.

Repeat the steps to create the other fields. Remember to include a consecutive number in each field's name, such as D02, D03, etc.

You'll notice that you selected the Allow Multi-Values option in the Field Definition dialog box. This enables a user to type multiple entries in the field. For example, if the person uses a comma to separate a series of events that occur on a given day, such as *Mom and Dad's 40th anniversary, Mail Tax Return, Dinner with Mr. Manzi*, each comma will change automatically to a semicolon when the form is saved. The semicolon is the default multivalue separator, and it is always displayed in a field unless you change it.

The last items you need to add to the form are a "To do list" label and a field. The information you enter in the field will also appear on a view that you'll create later in the chapter. Using Figure 23.5 as a guide, position and format the label below the table.

To create the field, follow these steps:

1. Position the cursor under the label and select the New Field command from the Design menu.

2. Click OK in the dialog box to accept the option.

3. Enter the following text and options in the Field Definition dialog box:

   Name: ToDo

   Help Definition: Enter the major event(s) for the month.

   Date Type: Text

   Allow Multi-Values: Check (to select)

   Field Type: Editable

4. Click the Separators button. The Design Field Separators dialog box appears.

5. In the Multi-Value Separators area, select the following options:

Input	Display
Comma	(Don't select)
Semicolon	(Default)
New Line	Select (which deselects the Semicolon option)

6. Click OK to accept the changes.

7. Click OK to close the dialog box. The field will appear.

This time we've selected the New Line option as the multivalue separator that we want displayed in the field. If a person types a series of entries in the field and separates each entry with either a comma or semicolon, or hits ↵ after each entry, only a line break will appear after each entry when the form is saved. All the commas and semicolons will disappear, resulting in the display of each entry on a separate line.

▶ *Recreating the Daily Schedule Form*

The design of the daily schedule form is so similar to the monthly calendar form that we won't take you through the steps of building it. We want to focus on the individual fields in the daily schedule form instead, because their inclusion illustrates several interesting uses of the form. Figure 23.16 reveals the structure of the daily schedule form.

As we mentioned in the previous section on recreating the monthly calendar form, you'll need to create a link between the two forms. By using Notes *doclink* feature, you'll enable a user to go from a specific date on the calendar to the individual day's schedule. Furthermore, you'll need to show the specific appointments you entered in the day's schedule on a view that you'll create later in this chapter.

▶▶ **N O T E**

You can't make links between forms as you create the forms; you can only create links between documents when you edit them. We'll discuss this in "Duplicating the Views" below.

FIGURE 23.16 ▶

The structure of the daily schedule form reveals that it is a formatted table. Many of the table's cells contain fields.

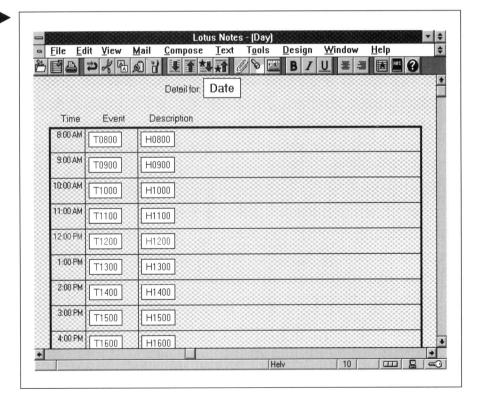

First, click on the 1994 Calendar database icon to select it, choose Design ➤ Forms, and double-click on (Day) in order to edit it. While leaving the form open, return to the Workspace and select the 1995 Calendar database. Open a new form. From now on, use the Window menu to go back and forth between the forms.

▶ Defining the Form's Attributes

With the new form displayed, choose Design ➤ Form Attributes. In the dialog box, enter **Day** in the name text box. *Don't* include parentheses around the name. It's not necessary. Click on Include in Compose Menu to deselect the default option. The form will not be displayed on the Compose menu.

Click on the Default database form option to designate the form as the *default* database form. From now on, the form will appear with an asterisk (*) next to its name in the Forms list when you open the Design Forms dialog box. Finally, make sure the form's type is Document (the default type). Click on OK to accept the changes.

▶▶ **W A R N I N G**

> The reason you designate a form as the *default* is to ensure that even if the form is renamed, or is deleted from the database, users can still view documents created with the obsolete form by displaying them with the default form. In the case of the 1994 Calendar database, however, users don't create documents; they edit the existing forms. Unfortunately, if you change the name of the form and then save it, the database won't work correctly.

Defining the Window Title

To change the title in the window's title bar, choose Design ➤ Window Title. In the Design Window Title dialog box, the following statement should appear in the Window Title Formula text box:

```
"Current Date and Time: " + @Text(@Now)
```

Click on OK to accept. The statement returns the string (the text between the quotation marks) and the current date and time. The @Text function converts the number value returned by the @Now function to text. (The @Now function returns your system's *current* date and time.) All this means is that you won't be able to use the number for arithmetic calculations. Subsequently, when you later edit the form, the window's title bar displays **Current Date and Time:** *mm/dd/yy hh:mm:ss AM or PM*.

Designing the Form

Let's begin laying out the new form. With the blank form displayed, insert the table and format it. Add the labels by entering the static text and formatting it. You can even add a drawing to the form if you desire.

Now let's insert the fields. As you can see in Figure 23.16, the four kinds of fields that appear on the form display the date, event, description, and user's comments.

The field next to the *Detail for* label that appears at the top of the form is named "Date." This field displays the date for each day in a given month. (Don't confuse this date with the *current* system date that appears in the window's title bar.)

Defining the Fields

To recreate how the field was defined, follow the steps below. You can also switch to the existing Day form in the 1994 Calendar database and read along to learn how the field was defined:

1. Choose Design ➤ Field Definition. The Field Definition dialog box appears. As you can see, the field's data type is Time and field type is Computed.

2. Click on the Formula button. The Design Field Formula dialog box appears. The Formula text box displays the statement **Date**. This statement is referenced in each of the month views.

3. Click on OK to close the dialog box.

4. Now click on the Format button. The Design Time Format dialog box appears, displaying the selected options.

5. Click OK to close.

6. Click OK.

The columns below the Event and Description labels display 12 fields each. The numbers (T0800, H0800, etc.) coincide with the times of day that appear in the column below the Time label, although the numbering scheme reflects military time.

All the Event field names are referenced in each month view. This means that when you open a view for a given month, specific events you entered on a particular day will appear below their scheduled times. We'll cover this in detail when we discuss the database's views.

We only need to examine one of the Event fields because they're all defined in a similar way. Select the field that's named "T0800." When you open the Field Definition dialog box, you'll see that the data type is Keywords, which allows you to create a list of specific words (or phrases) that a user can only enter in the field. Other words won't be accepted. When a user tries to enter unspecified words, Notes beeps.

Using Keywords

Click on the Format button to display the Design Keyword Format dialog box, as shown in Figure 23.17. At this point, you enter the desired keywords in the Allowable Keywords text box, pressing ↵ after each one. The keywords are:

Brkfst

Dinner

Flight

Hlday

Lunch

Mtg

MISC

Offsite

Revw

Trip

Vactn

Make sure that the User Interface type is Standard (the default) and that the "Allow values not in this list" option is selected. Click on OK to accept the other default options. When you return to the dialog box, click on OK to confirm.

You'll have to repeat the above steps as you create each of the remaining Event fields. Obviously, you'll need to give each field a unique name. Use Figure 23.16 as a reference. To save yourself the time and hassle of entering the same list of keywords, copy the list to the Clipboard and then paste the list in each of the Allowable Keywords text boxes. You'll have to use the keyboard combinations Ctrl+C to copy the selected text and Ctrl+V to paste the text because the Edit menu's Copy and Paste commands aren't accessible when the Design Keyword Format dialog box is open.

FIGURE 23.17 ▶

The Design Keyword Format dialog box lets you identify the list of keywords in the Allowable Keywords text box.

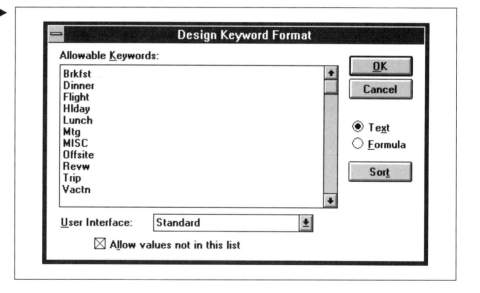

►► **TIP**

Don't be deceived into thinking that the Windows Cut, Copy, and Paste commands aren't available to you just because they aren't accessible from the Notes Edit menu. When a dialog box doesn't provide you with copy-and-paste options to enter information in a text box, you can always use Ctrl+X to cut selected text and then store it on the Clipboard, Ctrl+C to copy selected text to the Clipboard, and Ctrl+V to paste the text wherever the cursor is positioned in the text box. Using these commands will save you a lot of time.

Later, when you want to enter information in the field, you have the choice of entering an event of your choice or pressing the spacebar to display and cycle through the list of keywords. You can also type the first letter of the desired keyword, or press ⏎ to display the Select Keywords dialog box, as shown in Figure 23.18. As you can see, all the event keywords you created now appear in a list box. Double-click on the desired event in order to display it in the field automatically, or highlight the event and then click on OK to accept your choice.

FIGURE 23.18 ►

The Select Keywords dialog box displays the event keywords in a list that you created when you defined the field.

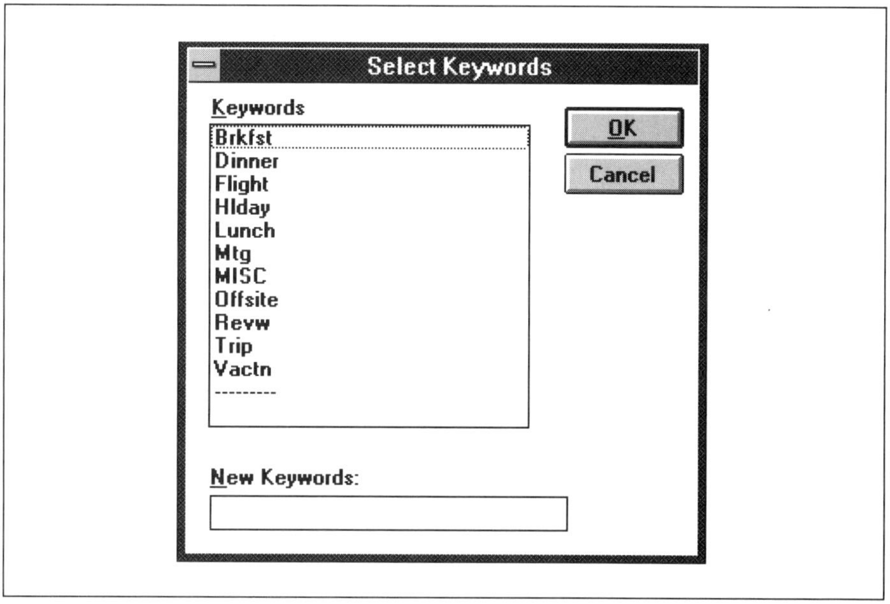

Select Keywords

Keywords

Brkfst
Dinner
Flight
Hlday
Lunch
Mtg
MISC
Offsite
Revw
Trip
Vactn

New Keywords:

OK
Cancel

▶▶ **N O T E**

Although the "Allow values not in this list" option allows a user to enter other words or phrases in the Event fields that are not displayed in the Select Keywords dialog box, these items aren't added to the list for future use. The only way to add new words to the list is by opening the Design Keyword Format dialog box, entering them, and clicking OK to accept the changes.

Using Rich Text Fields

Just as we only had to examine only one of the Event field because all of them are defined similarly, we only need to look at one Description fields. Select the field that's named "H0800." Open the Field Definitions dialog box. As you can see, the field's data type is Rich Text. This data type gives users the flexibility to enter text, enhanced text, or graphics. Enhanced text includes text that's been formatted with attributes such as bold, italics, underlining, or color. Graphics include pictures, graphs, popups, buttons, and embedded OLE objects.

The option of embedding objects is handy. Let's say that a user wants to enter detailed information in these fields regarding scheduled appointments. Rather than entering text in the fields, the user can embed OLE objects, such as word processing documents that would allow the person to write long descriptions. The use of embedded objects also gives the user more privacy if the person doesn't want the information displayed prominently. However, the information in these fields only appears on this form; it's not referenced anywhere else.

Finishing the Form

The remaining field on the form is the Comments field, "DayComments." Select it and then open the Field Definition dialog box. You'll notice that its data type is also Rich Text. Like the information in the Description fields, the information in this field only appears on the daily schedule form. The field isn't referenced anywhere else.

▶▶ *Duplicating the Views*

After users select a database from the Workspace, they open the View menu to see a list of all the views, from which they subsequently select documents to read or edit. However, as a developer, you create the views last, after you've created the forms in the database.

The 1994 Calendar database includes three kinds of views that you can duplicate for the 1995 Calendar database: a year view, a month view, and a date view that is hidden. There are 14 views in all—1 year view, 12 month views, and 1 date view. The year and month views give you access to the forms you recreated in the previous section. The hidden date view is referenced by the month view. This section will take you through the steps of recreating the three views, analyzing the developer's methods.

As you saw earlier in Figure 23.2, the year view displays the entire year, from January to December. From the year view you can open the monthly calendar forms.

The month view displays each day in the month, from which you can access a specific daily schedule form. The database utilizes the month view 12 times, one for each month of the year. For example, Figure 23.1 displayed the view for September 1994.

Before we begin, select the 1994 Calendar database and then choose Design ➤ Views. From the views list in the Design Views dialog box, choose Year - 1994 in order to edit it. You can either double-click on the view or select the view and click on the Edit button. While displaying this view, switch to the 1995 Calendar database. Choose Design ➤ Views. Click on the New button. A blank view will appear, displaying **(untitled)** in the window title bar. From now on, use the Window menu to go back and forth between views.

▶ *Defining the Year View*

Switch to the 1994 Calendar database's year view again. When the year view appears in Edit mode, it displays all the columns that have been defined for the view, as shown in Figure 23.19. (You can also refer to Figure 23.2.)

FIGURE 23.19 ▶

The year view for the 1994 Calendar database reveals its structure.

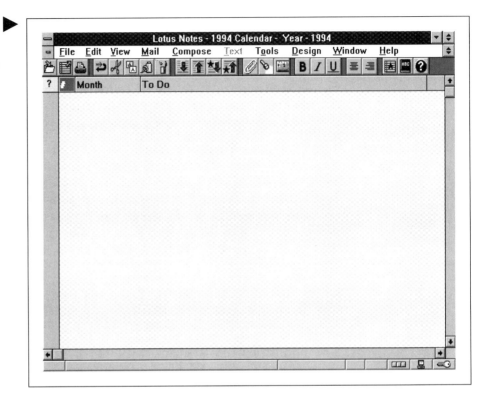

Defining the View Attributes

Choose Design ➤ View Attributes to open the Design View Attributes dialog box, as shown in Figure 23.20. This dialog box displays the view's name and identifies its type as "Shared View," which is the default type. The Default View option is also selected. Click OK to close the dialog box.

Switch to the (untitled) view in the 1995 Calendar database. Open the View Attributes dialog box and enter the following information:

> **Name:** Year - 1995
>
> **Type:** Shared
>
> **Options:** Default View (select)

Click on OK to accept the changes. The name, **1995 Calendar - Year - 1995**, appears in the window's title bar. You can't define a window title

FIGURE 23.20 ▶

The Design View Attributes dialog box displays the attributes for the 1994 Calendar database.

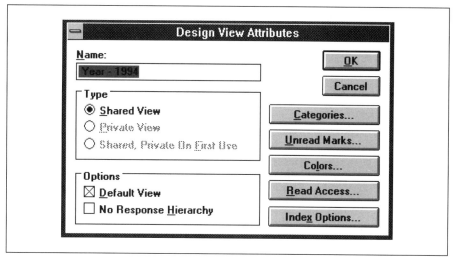

for a view the way you do for a form. A view's window title bar always displays the name of the database and the name you give the view, in addition to the name of the program, Lotus Notes.

  ▶▶ **TIP**

You can display a lot of information in a window's title bar—sometimes too much information—causing the title bar to look crowded. However, it's good to display the names of the database and the particular view (or form), so that users can see right away what they're using. Our advice is to keep the names of your databases, forms, and views short, descriptive, and to the point.

You probably noticed the asterisk (*) that appeared next to the Year - 1994 view's name when you selected it in the Design View dialog box. The asterisk indicates that this is the default view for the 1994 Calendar database. As we discussed in Chapter 14, every database should have a default view. Remember the first time you opened the 1995 Calendar database after you created it? The database displayed a blank default view. From now on, however, after you create all the views, the database will display the last view used.

 **NOTE**

Typically, the default view contains all documents in a database, sorted by category, by date, or by author. In the case of the 1994 Calendar, however, you don't compose documents. When you select the Year - 1994 view from the View menu, the database displays each month of the year from which you edit a specific month form; when you select a specific month view, the database displays each day of the month from which you edit the corresponding daily schedule form.

Defining the Selection Formula

Switch to the Year - 1994 view (if you haven't already). Let's examine the view's *selection formula*. As we discussed in Chapters 14 (views) and 16 (formulas), the selection formula determines which documents appear in the view. You'll recall that every view must have a selection formula.

Choose Design ➤ Selection Formula. The Design Selection Formula dialog box appears, as shown in Figure 23.21.

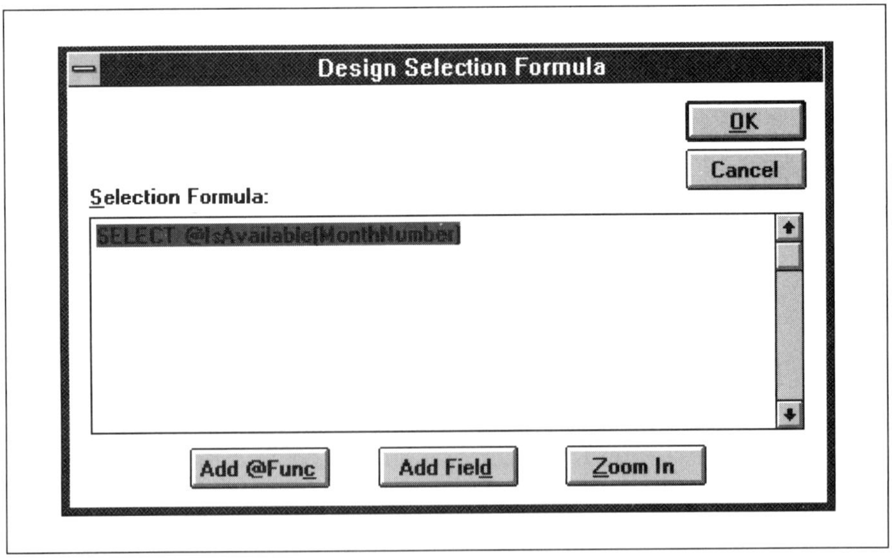

FIGURE 23.21 ▶

The Design Selection Formula dialog box lets you include a formula that identifies the documents you want displayed in a particular view.

> **Design Selection Formula**
>
> [OK]
> [Cancel]
>
> Selection Formula:
>
> SELECT @IsAvailable(MonthNumber)
>
> [Add @Func] [Add Field] [Zoom In]

The statement

SELECT @IsAvailable(MonthNumber)

appears in the Selection Formula text box. If you don't define a specific formula, Notes uses the default formula **Select@All,** which selects every document in the database and displays them in the view. However, the 1994 Calendar database doesn't include documents that users compose; users edit the forms instead. This particular selection formula checks the forms for the existence of the field name **Month-Number**. The function **@IsAvailable** returns 1 (for TRUE) if the field is contained in at least one of the forms or 0 (for FALSE). In other words, the view displays the contents of the field if it's found.

What about in this case, where you can't find a field named Month-Number, but it's referenced in a formula? You click on the Add Field button and see the field listed in the Paste Field dialog box. You explore all the forms, but you don't see where the field was used. Where is it? The developer decided to add and set this field (and three others) in forms by using macros that aren't included with the database. Since he revises the database each year, he might have decided to update it by using macros that he doesn't want to include. The database was designed in an earlier version of Notes and has changed with each subsequent new release. Maybe the way the macros set and add fields has changed in Release 3…. Whatever the reason, the field is set—you can't change it.

▶▶ **T I P**

> When you open a view and select a document, choose Design ➤ Document Info to open the Design Document Info dialog box. As you can see, the dialog box contains a lot of important information, such as when a document was created, when it was last modified, etc. A list box in the upper left corner displays all the fields contained in the database. The text box below it summaries the attributes for a given field and displays its value at the bottom.

The MonthNumber field is treated as an internal field. It's referenced just like any other field, but it's used temporarily. The field is used only for formula processing. It has no attributes, such as the ones you defined for the Date and ToDo fields, other than the ones assigned to it within the formula. What information is the formula returning and subsequently displaying in the view? The months of the year in ascending order.

To create the same selection formula for the Year - 1995 view, switch to the view and choose Design ➤ Selection Formula to open the Design Selection Formula dialog box. Enter the formula that appears above. (You can also switch to the Year -1994 view, open the Design Selection Formula dialog box, highlight the formula, press Ctrl+C to copy it to the Clipboard, return to the Year - 1995 view, open the dialog box, and press Ctrl+V to paste the formula.)

Defining the Columns

Now let's examine the view's structure. As you can see, the view displays three columns: #, Month, and To Do. (Remember that the ? column is used to refresh the view after changes are made.) When you click on a column to select it, you can see how it was defined.

To see the definition for the # column, choose Design ➤ Column Definition. The Design Column Definition dialog box appears, as shown in Figure 23.22.

FIGURE 23.22

The Design Column Definition dialog box displays the attributes for the # column.

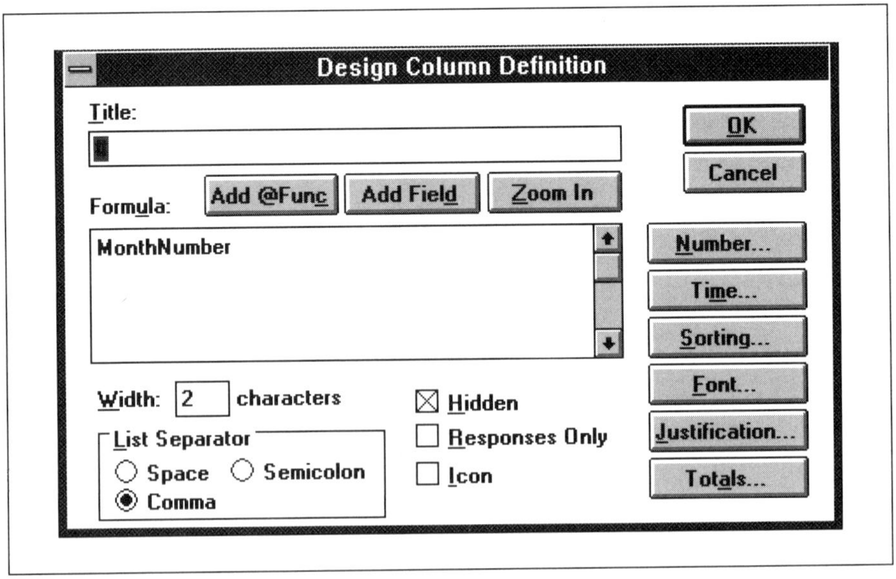

The column's most significant attribute is that it is *hidden*. This means that the column will not appear in the year view. The column is used only for sorting purposes; it doesn't display any useful information. The **MonthNumber** statement in the Formula text box returns the correct number of each month in ascending order but doesn't display the numbers. The temporary field, MonthNumber, is referenced in the selection formula that we discussed above.

To define a similar column in the Year - 1995 view, switch to the view and follow these steps:

1. Choose Design ➤ New Column. The Design Column Definition dialog box appears.

2. Enter the following information:

   Title: #

   Formula: MonthNumber

   Width: 2

   Hidden: Select

3. Click on the Sorting button. The Design Column Sort dialog box appears, as shown in 23.23.

4. Click the Sort check box. This action selects the Ascending option (the default) automatically.

5. Click OK to confirm and to close the dialog box.

6. Click on OK to accept all the changes.

The title appears at the top of the column. To define the other columns in the Year - 1995 view, you can switch to the Year - 1994 view to see how the columns were defined. Return to the Year - 1995 view. Choose Design ➤ New Column. Enter the following information for the Month and To Do columns, respectively, in the Design Column Definition dialog box:

   Title: Month

   Formula: @Right(@Left(Form; ")"); "(")

   Width: 10

FIGURE 23.23 ▶

The Design Column Sort dialog box lets you sort documents in a view in ascending or descending order.

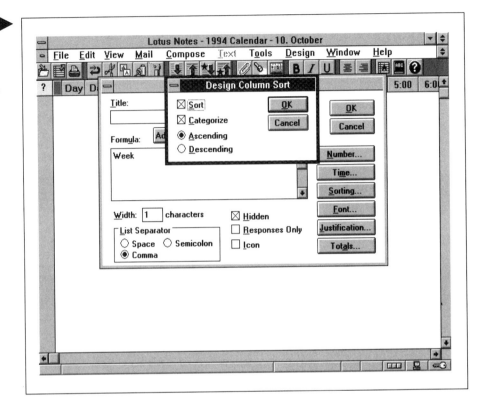

Title: To Do

Formula: "<" + ToDo + ">"

Width: 40

List Separator: Space

The new columns appear in the view. As we discussed above, if you want to format the column titles, select the particular column, choose Design ▶ Column Definition to open the Design Column Definition dialog box, and click on the Font button.

▶▶ **T I P**

> **While you're defining a *new* column, you can format the title that appears at the top of the column by clicking on the Font button in the Design Column Definition dialog box. If you want to format the title later on, select the column, choose Design ➤ Column Definition to open the Design Column Definition dialog box, and click on the Font button. In both cases, the Font dialog box opens, displaying the same options that are available when you select the Font command from the Text menu. You can change the font and point size, apply attributes such as bold and italics, and choose a different color in which to display the text. Select the desired options and click on OK to accept your choices.**

The Month Column Formula

The formula

    @Right(@Left(Form; ")"); "(")

references the field named "Form." As we discussed earlier, this is one of those fields that you didn't define purposely in the forms. However, this field hasn't been added and set with a macro. The Form field is created automatically by Notes for each document. It's stored internally.

The field contains the value of the name of the form, which is this case is "(Name of Month)." As you'll recall, parentheses enclose the names of the months when you named them in the Form Attributes dialog box. The statement returns the string in the field, which in this case is January, the name of the month, and displays it in the view without the parentheses.

The To Do Column Formula

The formula

    "<" + ToDo + ">"

returns the value of the ToDo field that you defined on the month form. You might recall that you enter information in the field as a series of items in a To Do list. When you save the document, the database automatically places each item on a separate line if the items are separated by either a comma or semicolon. The statement places each item between the < and > symbols, and the view displays the series of items on one line.

▶ Defining the Month View

The 1994 Calendar database includes 12 month views, one for each month of the year. The developer decided to create 12 separate views rather than one view that would display the dates for a given month. The rationale for creating separate views is easy to understand since the number of days changes from month to month and the dates fall on different days of the week. For example, Figure 23.1 showed you the view for September.

Figure 23.24 reveals the structure of the month view; this same structure is used 12 times. Therefore, we only need to look at one month view to learn how it was defined. As you can see, the columns correspond directly to the field definitions we discussed above in "Recreating the Daily Schedule Form."

Defining the View Attributes

Switch to the 1994 Calendar database and choose Design ▶ Views. Double-click on 1. January to open the view in Edit mode. Choose Design ▶ View Attributes to open the Design View Attributes dialog box. The dialog box displays the view's name and identifies its type as Shared View, which is the default type. Click OK to close the dialog box.

Now switch to the 1995 Calendar database and click on the New button in the Design Views dialog box to create a new view. Remember our discussion of designating a default view? The month view you're about to recreate is not designated as the default view because the year view has already been designated as the default. A database can include only one default view, which typically contains all the documents in the database.

FIGURE 23.24

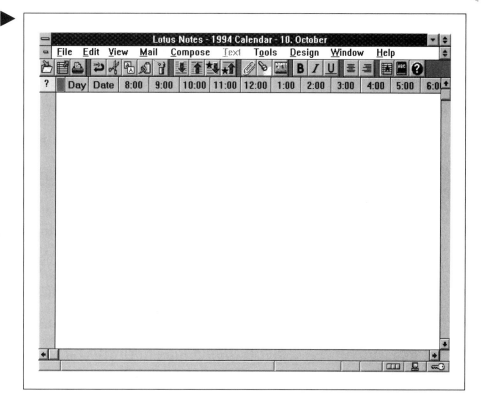

Open the View Attributes dialog box and enter the following information:

Name: 1. January

Type: Shared

Click on OK to accept the changes. The name "1995 Calendar - 1. January" appears in the window's title bar.

Defining the Selection Formula

Switch back to the Year - 1994 view to examine the view's selection formula. Choose Design ➤ Selection Formula. The Design Selection Formula dialog box appears.

The statement

```
SELECT "a" = MonthKey
```

appears in the Selection Formula text box.

The **MonthKey** field is another internal field that the developer has added and set in the documents with a macro. You might think it's strange that the statement *selects* only the text string, **a,** and makes it the equivalent of the MonthKey field, and not the other way around. Usually a statement would select only that field and make it equal to the text string. Remember that SELECT identifies documents with a specific value in a field. (The expression that follows a SELECT statement carries out an action on the documents selected.)

The statement is saying "find a document that contains the field MonthKey and give the field the value of the text string, **a,**" in other words, make it equal to (or the equivalent of) **a**. Although the statement doesn't reflect standard syntax, you get the same results. The statement associates a given month with a corresponding letter of the alphabet, such as *a* for January, *b* for February, etc.

To create the same selection formula for the Year - 1995 view, switch to the view and choose Design ➤ Selection Formula to open the Design Selection Formula dialog box. Enter the formula that appears above. (You can also switch to the Year -1994 view, open the Design Selection Formula dialog box, highlight the formula, press Ctrl+C to copy it to the Clipboard, return to the Year - 1995 view, open the dialog box, and press Ctrl+V to paste the formula.)

Defining the Columns

The view displays 15 columns. The first column is hidden, which is why it isn't given a title.

The other columns correspond to the fields you created in the daily schedule form:

> (no title)
>
> Day
>
> Date
>
> 8:00
>
> 9:00
>
> 10:00
>
> 11:00
>
> 12:00

1:00

2:00

3:00

4:00

5:00

6:00

7:00

To see the definition for the first column, choose Design ➤ Column Definition. The Design Column Definition dialog box appears.

As we mentioned above, the column's most significant attribute is that it is *hidden*. This means that the column will not appear in the month view. The column is used only for sorting purposes; it doesn't display any useful information. The statement in the Formula text box includes only the field, Week. As we discussed earlier, Week is another one of those fields that the developer added and set in the forms with a macro. The formula returns the numbers of the weeks in a given month in ascending order but doesn't display the numbers.

To define a similar column in the Year - 1995 view, switch to the view and follow these steps:

1. Choose Design ➤ New Column. The Design Column Definition dialog box appears.

2. Enter the following information:

   Title: (blank)

   Formula: Week

   Width: 1

   Hidden: Select

3. Click on the Sorting button. The Design Column Sort dialog box appears.

4. Click the Sort and Categorize check boxes. This action selects the Ascending option (the default) automatically.

5. Click OK to confirm and to close the dialog box.

6. Click on OK to accept all the changes.

▶▶ **N O T E**

You select the Categorize option in the Design Column Sort dialog box when you want to group related documents in categories. For example, the month view in the 1994 Calendar database groups the days in a given month by *week* in ascending order because the Sort by Ascending order option was also selected. In this way, the view enables users to easily locate specific dates.

The title appears at the top of the column. To define the other columns in the Year - 1995 view, you can switch to the Year - 1994 view to see how the columns were defined. Return to the Year - 1995 view. Choose Design ▶ New Column. Enter the following information for the Day, Date, and 8:00 AM - 7:00 PM time columns, respectively, in the Design Column Definition dialog box:

Title: Day

Formula: DNum := @Weekday(Date);

@Middle("SunMonTueWedThuFriSat"; 3 * (DNum - 1); 3)

Width: 3

Justification: Center

Title: Date

Formula: Date

Width: 4

Sorting: Sort; Ascending

Justification: Center

Title: 8:00

Formula: T0800

Width: 4

Justification: Center

Repeat the steps for defining the remaining time columns for 9:00 AM to 7:00 PM. Remember to change the formula for each column to reflect the corresponding field name, such as T0900, T1000, T1100, etc.

The new columns appear in the view. As we discussed above, if you want to format the column titles, select the particular column, choose Design ➤ Column Definition to open the Design Column Definition dialog box, and click on the Font button.

The Day Column Formula

The formula

```
DNum := @Weekday(Date);@Middle("SunMonTueWedThuFriSat";
3 * (DNum - 1); 3)
```

creates the temporary field, DNum. As we discussed in the Chapter 16, a temporary field exists only within a formula. It's used only for formula processing. It has no attributes other than the ones assigned to it within the formula.

In this case, the statement creates the temporary field, DNum, which consists of the contents of the field "Date," computes the day of the week, and returns a number that identifies the day. @Weekday numbers are 1 through 7, with Sunday = 1, Monday = 2, and so on. Then how does the formula assign a number and the corresponding name of the day of the week to DNum? The statement includes the @Middle function to return such a value.

The part of the expression that uses the @Middle function searches the text string from left to right, beginning at the point of the *offset*, which is the number of characters returned by the value of 3 * (DNum -1) (the string offset starts at 0 for the first character), and returns *numberchars*, the number of characters, which is 3. Subsequently, the view displays the *abbreviated* name of the corresponding day of the week.

The Date Column Formula

The date column formula references the Date field that you defined on the daily schedule form. The formula returns the value of the Date field. The view displays the date of a given day of the week.

The Specific Time Columns Formula

The specific time column formulas reference the fields you defined in the Event column (T0800, T0900, etc.) on the daily schedule form. The formulas return the values of the fields. The view displays the events you entered on the form for a given day.

▶ *Defining the By Date View*

The By Date view is hidden, which means that users can't select it from the View menu. Parentheses enclose the name, which hides it from users by not displaying it on the menu. However, the view is important because it displays the dates that appear at the top of the daily schedule forms.

Defining the View Attributes

Switch to the 1994 Calendar database and choose Design ▶ Views. Double-click on (By Date) to open the view in Edit mode. (It appears at the bottom of the list, so you might overlook it.) The view appears, as shown in Figure 23.25.

Choose Design ▶ View Attributes to open the Design View Attributes dialog box. The dialog box displays the view's name and identifies its type as Shared View, which is the default type. Click OK to close the dialog box.

Now switch to the 1995 Calendar database and click on the New button in the Design Views dialog box to create a new view. Open the View Attributes dialog box and enter the following information:

> **Name:** (By Date)
>
> **Type:** Shared

Click on OK to accept the changes. The name, 1995 Calendar - (By Date), appears in the window's title bar.

Defining the Selection Formula

Switch back to the Year - 1994 view to examine the view's selection formula. Choose Design ▶ Selection Formula. The Design Selection Formula dialog box appears.

FIGURE 23.25

At first glance, the By Date view doesn't reveal anything unusual.

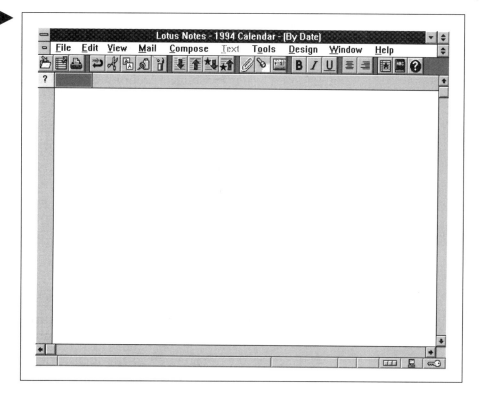

The formula

SELECT @All

appears in the Selection Formula text box.

The statement **SELECT @All** selects all documents for an operation, which is in this case are all the daily schedule documents in the database.

To create the same selection formula for the Year - 1995 view, switch to the view and choose Design ➤ Selection Formula to open the Design Selection Formula dialog box. Enter the formula that appears above. (You can also switch to the Year -1994 view, open the Design Selection Formula dialog box, highlight the formula, press Ctrl+C to copy it to the Clipboard, return to the Year - 1995 view, open the dialog box, and press Ctrl+V to paste the formula.)

Defining the Column

Now let's examine the view's structure. As you can see, the view displays one column with no title. After you click on the column to select it, choose Design ➤ Column Definition. The Design Column Definition dialog box appears, displaying the column's attributes.

To define a similar column in the Year - 1995 view, switch to the view and follow these steps:

1. Choose Design ➤ New Column. The Design Column Definition dialog box appears.

2. Enter the following information:

   Title: (blank)

   Formula: Date

   Width: 5

3. Click on the Time button. In the Design Time Format dialog box, choose the last option in the Date Format selection area, and choose the first option in the Overall Format selection area.

4. Click on the Sorting button and then click the Sort check box. This action selects the Ascending option (the default) automatically.

5. Click on the Justification button and select Left.

6. Click on OK to accept all the changes.

The Column's Formula

The Date field is referenced in the column's formula. The formula returns the date for a given day. You'll recall that the field Date was defined on the daily schedule form. The value of the field is computed automatically; the formula returns the value and displays it in the view.

►► *Creating the Links between the Documents*

After you create the views, you can add links between documents by using the Notes *doclink* feature. A *doclink* creates a link from one document to another, thus providing direct access to the documents. Figure 23.26 shows a detail from the January 1994 month form, revealing a doclink icon that connects a day on the month form to a corresponding daily schedule form.

Only the month forms displays the icon. When you click on the icon for a specific day, you open the corresponding daily schedule form. When you press Esc, you return to the same day on the month form. Although the information on the month form doesn't depend directly on information that may change in the daily schedule form, you're able to see right away if you have any appointment or schedule conflicts.

FIGURE 23.26 ►

A detail from the January 1994 month form shows a doclink icon.

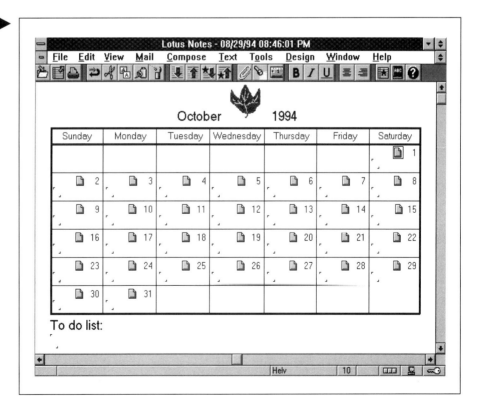

What's great about this feature is that the two documents that share a link don't have to reside in the same view, the same database or even on the same Notes server. However, to use a doclink to open a document in another database, you must have the proper access privileges and the database must be on a Notes server in your network.

To use a doclink, follow these steps:

1. Switch to the 1994 Calendar database and select the Year - 1994 view from the View menu.

2. Highlight January and press Ctrl+E to edit the document. (You can also press ↵.) The January 1994 document appears. This is the link-from document.

3. Double-click on the doclink icon that appears in the cell for January 1. The corresponding daily schedule document appears. This is the link-to document.

4. Press Esc to close the document and to return to the January 1994 document.

▶▶ **T I P**

> **You can display the name of the target (link-to) document's database and view in a *popup* by pressing and holding the mouse button while over the doclink icon. Just remember that you can't display the popup while you're in Design Edit mode.**

▶ *Adding Doclinks to Documents*

You can't add a doclink to a month form as you're creating it. You can only add links between documents as you're editing them. To create a doclink, follow these steps:

1. Switch to the 1995 Calendar database and select the 1. January view from the View menu. The view opens.

2. Highlight the Sun 01/01 document in the view and press Ctrl+E to edit the document. The daily schedule form appears. This is the document where you want the link to go to. It's called the *link-to* document.

3. Choose Edit ➤ Make Doclink. This command puts the doclink on the Clipboard.

4. Press Esc to exit the document.

5. Select the Year - 1995 view and highlight January.

6. Press Ctrl+E to edit the document. The documents opens.

  TIP

> **You don't have to open a document from a view in order to create a doclink. Simply highlight the document in the view and choose Edit ➤ Make Doclink. This action places the doclink on the Clipboard.**

If you try to paste the doclink in the January 1995 month form now, you won't succeed. Go ahead and try—nothing will happen because the Paste command on the Edit menu is dimmed. This isn't the usual way for doclinks to behave. In fact, this is atypical of how you correctly add doclinks. The reason for the strange behavior is that you don't compose documents in this particular database. The developer made the decision to create all the documents for you. All you have to do is edit the forms, which in this database are considered the documents. How do you create a doclink in this case? *You must open the form in Design Edit mode* and then paste the doclink where you want the icon to appear.

To paste the doclink, follow these steps:

1. With the January 1995 document displayed, choose Design ➤ Forms.

2. Double-click on (January) to open the document in design edit mode. The form appears. This is the link-from document.

3. Position the insertion point in the cell for January 1, which contains the field D01. Place the cursor to the left of the number.

4. Choose Edit ➤ Paste. The doclink icon appears in the cell.

5. Repeat the steps. Remember to select the specific daily schedule form (the link-to document) first *before* opening the desired month form (the link-from document) and pasting the Doclink.

▶▶ *Updating the Calendar with a Macro*

As we mentioned in the "Customizing and Updating the Calendar Database" section early in the chapter, you don't need to create the database from scratch or modify it to display a new year. The database includes a macro that enables the user to update the documents to display the next year. The macro is handy to use because it automates the task of updating automatically. However, using it can be a little tricky, so read the following sections carefully.

The database includes a macro named "Next Year" that updates the daily schedule documents in the month views automatically. The macro adjusts the dates of the daily schedule documents forward by one year. You have to run this macro to correctly update the dates on the documents to 1995.

You highlight *all* the documents in a given month at the same time and then run the macro to adjust the dates. You shouldn't run the macro on individual documents. Otherwise you'll get strange results!

▶

BE CAREFUL WHEN USING A MACRO

Be careful when you run any macro. The purpose of creating a macro is to automate a task. By having the macro perform a series of actions, you (hopefully) achieve a desired result. However, the result can sometimes be less than perfect.

With some macros, you may experience problems. Sometimes developers don't provide instructions for using the macro, or some macros may be designed for use with a version of the software different from yours. Don't just experiment blindly with a macro, or you may get disastrous results.

The lesson here? Don't make changes to the only copy of a database you're using! We've said it before but we'll say it again: Always work with *copies* of databases. You might be sorry if you don't.

Switch to the 1994 Calendar database and choose Design ➤ Macros.
The Design Macros dialog box opens, as shown in Figure 23.27. Double-
click on Next Year to edit the macro. The Edit Existing Macro dialog
box opens. You'll notice that the Include in Tools Run Macros menu option is selected. This option displays the macro's name when you
choose the Tools ➤ Run Macros menu.

Click on the Formula button. The Edit Macro Formula dialog box
opens, displaying the macro's formula:

FIELD Date := @Adjust(Date; 1; 0; 0; 0; 0; 0); SELECT @All

Click on the Cancel button in each dialog box to return to a view or
the Workspace.

The macro is called a *filter macro* because you can run it manually from
the Tools ➤ Run Macros menu. As we mentioned in Chapter 16, a filter macro lets you update a series of documents in batch mode, so you
don't have to manually edit, update, and save each document. The macro
operates on a range of selected documents; the actions performed on
those documents are determined by the macro's formula. In the 1994
Calendar database, you run the macro on all the documents in a given
month view.

FIGURE 23.27 ▶

*The Design Macros
dialog box displays the
list of macros in a
database.*

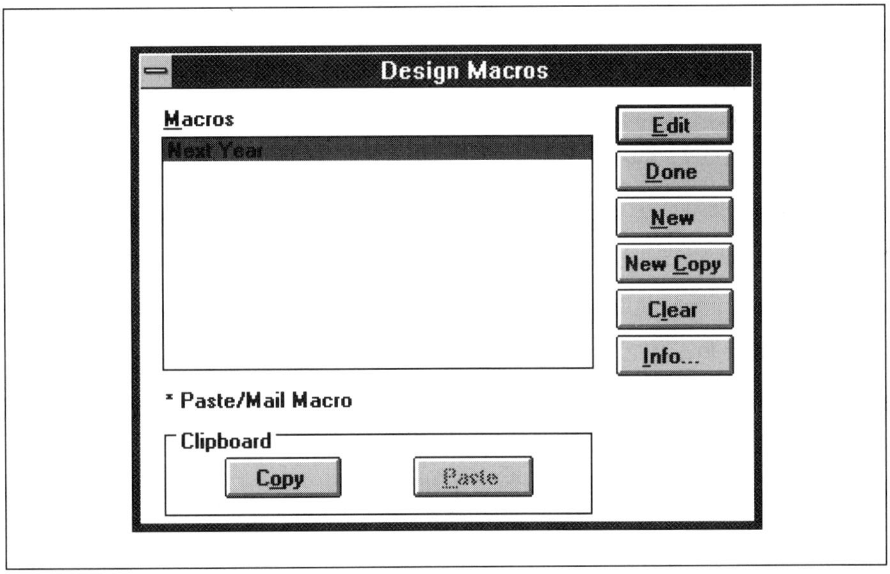

▶▶ **T I P**

A filter macro can only operate on the database in which it's stored.

The formula creates a new field called "Date" and assigns to that field the *adjusted* value of the existing Date field you defined in the daily schedule form. In this case, the @Adjust function adjusts the value of the Date field by the amount in each succeeding argument in increments of the argument. The amount of the adjustment is positive, although it can also be negative.

The arguments 1, 0, 0, 0, 0, 0 represent the order of the value that changes most slowly (year) to the value that changes most quickly (second); that is, the arguments represent year, month, week, day, hour, second, respectively. The @Adjust function acts on the arguments from the one that changes most quickly to the one that changes most slowly. The argument 1 adjusts the current year forward by one year. In other words, the formula returns the date one year from the date in the existing Date field and assigns that value to the new Date field.

▶ *Writing the Macro*

The macro is easy to write. Switch to the 1995 Calendar Database and choose Design ▶ Macros. The Design Macros dialog box opens.

▶▶ **T I P**

You don't have to actually open a view in order to write a macro. Simply click on the database icon to select the database and then choose the Design ▶ Macros menu.

Click on the New button to open the Design New Macro dialog box. Enter **New Year** in the Name text box. Click on the Formula button to open the Edit Macro Formula dialog box. Enter a formula in the text box. You can enter the same formula that appears above or copy the formula from the 1994 Calendar database and paste it in the text box.

Click on OK to confirm and to close the dialog box. Click on OK again to accept the changes.

▶▶ **W A R N I N G**

If you click on OK in the Design New Macro dialog box after you name a macro but before you enter a formula, Notes beeps and displays a message that you must enter a formula for your macro. We suggest that you do what Notes says.

▶ *Running the Macro*

After you write a macro, you should test it in order to make sure that it works. First, you select a group of documents, which *must* be all the documents in a given month. Choose Highlight a document and press the spacebar. A checkmark appears to the left of the document. Press ↓ to move down to the next document and press the spacebar to select. Repeat this action for all the documents you want to select.

▶▶ **T I P**

To select all the documents in a view, choose Edit ➤ Select All. A checkmark will appear to the left of all the document names, including the spaces between the weeks.

Choose Tools ➤ Run Macros ➤ Next Year to run the macro. When the macro finishes, all the dates in the month view should be adjusted forward by one year.

▶▶ *Testing the Database*

As we discussed at the end of Chapter 14, you should get in the habit of testing the functionality of a new database once you're finished creating the forms and views. All you need to do is compose a few documents based on each form in order to check if you can enter data correctly without getting any error messages.

Next, you should open each of the views to see if the documents are displayed correctly. If a view doesn't display any documents, open the view in Edit mode and check its selection formula. The reason why a view usually doesn't display documents is because the selection formula is wrong. If the selection formula is correct, you should check the formula for each column's definition in order to make sure that the column is referencing the correct field. If a column isn't referencing the correct field, the view won't return (and display) the value for that field.

Many errors occur in Design mode when you're creating forms and fields, and defining their contents. In fact, most errors are the result of typos that you introduce when you include the names of fields and forms in formulas. Sometimes an error message will give you a clue that Notes can't find a specific name of a form or a field. You'll have to open a form and check the spelling of the field names.

▶▶ *What's Next?*

In the next chapter, we show you how to duplicate an Investment Profiles database we modified from an existing application that was posted in the LotusComm forum on CompuServe. The database enables members of a workgroup to collect detailed financial data on specific companies, which can be used to help clients make investment decisions.

▶ ▶ CHAPTER **24**

Investment Profiles

▶▶ *F*AST *T*RACK

▶ **The database includes five "Profiles by..." views** **784**

which select, sort, and categorize Input Company Profile documents, and a Financial History view, which provides financial background information documents on the companies. Using these forms, a user can locate company profile research and analysis quickly and easily.

▶ **The Profiles by Buy/Sell/Hold view** **784**

displays the trading stock status of a company.

▶ **The Profiles by Company view** **792**

shows an alphabetical listing of current Input Company Profile documents by company.

▶ **The Profiles by Date Posted view** **796**

displays the date the Input Company Profile documents were written. The view sorts the documents in descending order.

▶ **The Profiles by Researcher view** **798**

shows account responsibilities for each researcher. The view shows the researcher's account load by number as well as a percentage of the entire account load.

▶ **The Profiles by Ticker view** **802**

displays ticker symbol of each company.

▶ **The Financial History view** **805**

shows an alphabetical listing of Financial Background Information documents by company.

▶ ▶ ***T****he* Investment Profiles database is based on a reference database that we located in the Application Library of the Lotus Communications forum on CompuServe. We modified it extensively in order to help people in a workgroup to gather background information on companies to use as a basis for making investment decisions. This chapter takes you through the steps of designing the forms and views for the Investment Profiles database. It assumes you have been given either Designer or Manager access designation, so you can create the database. The chapter covers:

- Defining each form's attributes
- Adding fields
- Formatting the forms
- Creating the views
- Writing the selection formulas

The database you'll create in this chapter is a good example of an application that can aid users in organizing research information in Notes and then using the information to track the results of decisions that have been made based on the information, which in this case will be investment decisions. This database combines the best features of a reference-tracking-discussion application.

The Investment Profiles database gives members of a workgroup the means to gather research and background information on companies and then to analyze the statistics. Like any good discussion database, this database presents information in a way that can engage people in meaningful and substantive discourse. Each researcher can compose an input company profile document or a financial background information

▶ # TRACKING INVESTMENTS ONLINE

The Investment Profiles database enables a user to take on the dual roles of a researcher and a trader. Many people who invest in the stock market or in mutual funds manage their own investment portfolios. The need for consulting a broker or financial planner is diminishing because of the abundance of investment information that is available through online services such as CompuServe, or through discount brokerage companies such as Charles Schwab. However, this application is suited to the needs of a brokerage firm or financial planner.

We're not recommending one online investment service or brokerage firm over another; each one has its strengths and weaknesses. A word to the wise, however: do your homework. You need to spend a lot time studying the information on different stocks, bonds, money market funds, and mutual funds before you take the plunge and start investing.

Online information can be presented "unfiltered," which means that no investment recommendation is being made; you interpret the statistics and then make a decision based on your own analyses. However, "biased" information on particular investment products can come directly from a broker or a company, which means they want you to believe their statistics and invest in the products they're recommending. The information might be accurate or it might not. Unfortunately, investment scams exist; some have been discovered on several online services. You need to be careful.

document to add to the database. The following two figures show views listing each of these types of document. Figure 24.1 shows the view for profiles on companies (by researcher) and Figure 24.2 displays the view for financial background information on companies.

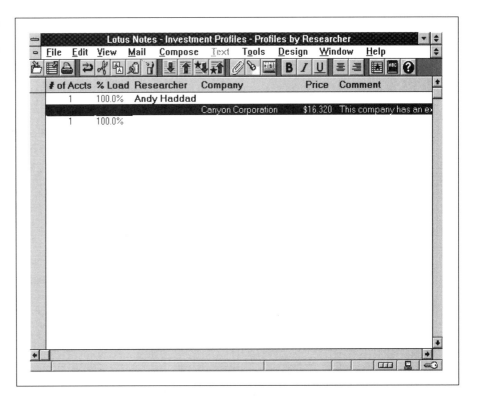

▶▶ *What Does the Investment Profiles Database Do?*

You can use the Investment Profiles database as a repository for research on and analyses of companies. Researchers can post this information to the database and then traders can refer to it. This database is a good example of a Notes reference application that can facilitate quick and effective information exchange within a company.

Researchers create two main types of documents for this database: profile documents for particular companies, as shown in Figure 24.3, and financial background information documents for the same companies, as shown in Figure 24.4. You can edit both of these forms to update information, which changes daily to reflect domestic and worldwide financial markets.

FIGURE 24.2

This view displays a listing of the financial background information documents on specific companies.

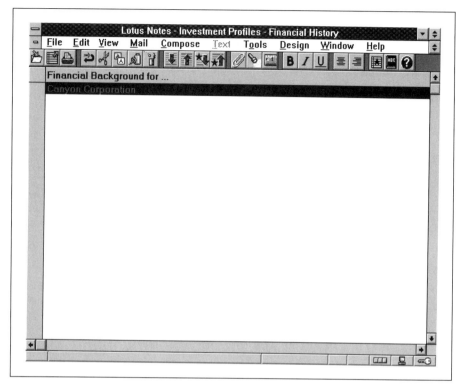

The database provides the means to streamline workflow through a group. Researchers develop financial profiles on companies and can categorize profiles by selecting the five "Profiles by..." views. (Each view sorts and categorizes researchers' profiles differently.) Traders use these profiles in making decisions on stock purchases and in handling customer questions.

The structure of a researcher's profile is the same for each company. Therefore, information can be accessed quickly and easily. A user simply selects one of the five "Profiles by..." views, opens a document, and reads it. A document contains complete financial data on a company, and can include a doclink to a Financial Background Information document (if one exists) and a graph from a spreadsheet. The range of data that a researcher can track on a company can vary, depending on the amount of information that is available.

A user can easily distinguish between the reading/printing and the editing sections of an Input Company Profile document. The researcher

FIGURE 24.3 ▶

An Input Company Profile document provides an easy way to enter financial data on a particular company.

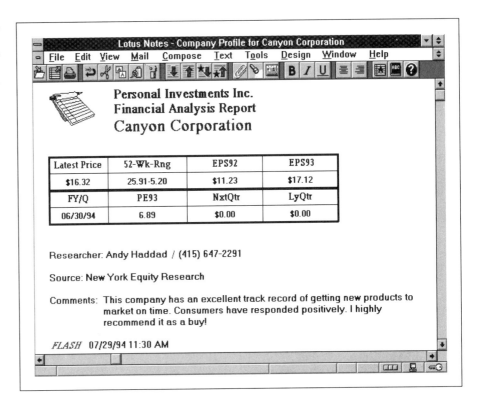

selects and then enters data in clearly defined sections of the document. The trader subsequently reads specific sections of the document. The researchers see what they need to see when entering information on a document and the traders see what they need to see for reference.

Doclinks are used to link the two forms. While editing or reading an Input Company Profile document, the user would click on the doclink to the Financial Background Information document on the particular company. The financial history can be very long, so putting it in a separate document and doclinking to it tightens up the display of the main document.

Information can be added easily to the Investment Profiles database. You can add information by:

- Entering data in an Input Company Profile document
- Importing rows of data from a spreadsheet

FIGURE 24.4 ▶

A Financial Background Information document can display a lengthy description of a company's financial history.

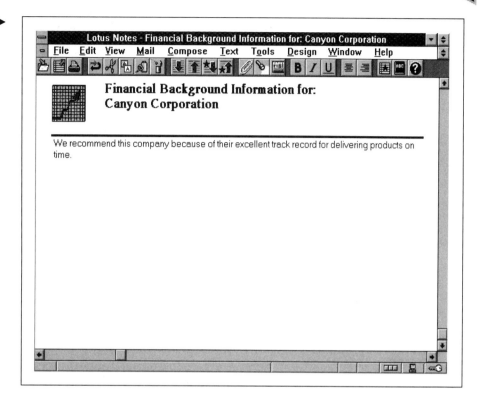

- Importing newswire data into a Financial Background Information document

Similarly, a lengthy financial history on a company can be imported into a Financial Background Information document, separate from the main Input Company Profile for the company. This information might come from a newswire or other industry news source.

To read about a particular company, you can select one of the five database "Profiles by..." views, which select, sort, and categorize Input Company Profile documents, and the Financial History view, which provides financial background information documents on the companies. In this way, you can refer to company profile research and analysis easily:

- **Profiles by Buy/Sell/Hold**: Shows the trading stock status.

- **Profiles by Company**: Shows an alphabetical listing of current Input Company Profile documents by company.

- **Profiles by Date Posted**: Shows the date the Input Company Profile documents were written. The view sorts the documents in descending order.

- **Profiles by Researcher**: Shows account responsibilities for each researcher. The view shows the researcher's account load by number as well as a percentage of the entire account load.

- **Profiles by Ticker**: Shows ticker symbols of each company.

- **Financial History**: Shows an alphabetical listing of Financial Background Information documents by company.

► Important Features of the Investment Profiles Database

The Investment Profiles database includes the following important features:

- Allows importing of financial analysis data from a spreadsheet

- Displays column totals and percentages in a view

- Displays information section and data entry section on a form

- Uses doclinks to link the Input Company Profile form to Financial Background Information form

A researcher can import financial analysis from a spreadsheet to the Investment Profiles database. By using a spreadsheet, a user can compile financial data on companies and perform calculations before importing the information into the Investment Profiles database. When he or she has finished, he or she can then post that information in the database for the other members of the workgroup (or the rest of the company) to use.

Column totals and percentages can be displayed in a view. The columns that display numerical values can be totaled at the category and entire view levels. The % of Accts column in the Profiles by Researcher view is an example. Columns can also show percentages or average values at the category and entire view levels. Column totals, averages, and percentages make views that display numerical data more meaningful.

Separate information sections and data entry sections can be displayed on the Input Company Profile form. It is sometimes useful to design forms with one section where information is displayed when reading or printing a document and another section where information is displayed when editing a document. The Hide-When feature on the Style menu allows a form designer to specify when a section on the form is displayed.

A doclink is used on the Input Company Profile form to link to a detailed financial history of a company, if one is available. Because these financial histories are very long, it is a good design idea to put them in a separate document and link to them from the main Input Company Profile form through a doclink. This keeps the information in the main display succinct and uncluttered.

▶ Who Should Use the Investment Profiles Database?

A researcher can use the database when she or he has completed a new profile on a company and is ready to post it for the traders. This can be on any schedule required (weekly, monthly, quarterly…). A trader can use the database daily, to help determine what stocks to act on or to answer clients' questions on a specific company.

▶ Why Use the Investment Profiles Database?

Researchers will use this database as a vehicle to share their research on and analysis of companies and their stocks. Traders will use this database to review the analysis as they work with their customers. A researcher can be in the next room or halfway around the world. By using Notes, a researcher can distribute his or her analysis and stock evaluations on companies to the entire company, thereby avoiding meetings, phone calls, express packages, or e-mails.

Notes also allows the researcher to use a spreadsheet to compile figures and do calculations. When ready, the researcher can then post those figures to the Notes database using File ➤ Import. For the trader, Notes' user interface makes it easy to scan the profiles put together by all the researchers: by buy/sell/hold recommendation, by company, by date the analysis was posted, by researcher, or by the company's ticker symbol.

▶▶ *Using the Investment Profiles Database*

To try out the Investment Profiles database, you need to copy the file to your hard disk and add the database to your Workspace. Click on its icon to select it and follow these steps:

1. To compose an Input Company Profile document, choose Compose ➤ Input Company Profile. The blank document appears.

2. Fill in the profile on any company you choose.

3. Press Ctrl+S to save the document.

4. Press Esc to return to the Workspace.

5. Choose View ➤ Profiles by Company. The Profiles by Company view appears. The document you just composed will be displayed.

6. Press Esc to close the view and to return to the Workspace.

To compose a Financial Background Information document, make sure the database is selected. Choose Compose ➤ Financial Background Information and then follow these steps:

1. Complete the document.

2. Press Ctrl+S to save the document.

3. Press Esc to close the document window.

4. Choose View ➤ Financial History. The Financial History view opens, displaying the document that you just composed.

5. Press Esc to close the window.

To see how the doclink works between the Input Company Profile document and the Financial Background Information document, choose one of the Profiles by... views and open the document either by pressing ↵ to display it in Read mode or Ctrl+E to display it in Edit mode. When the document appears, click on the doclink icon. The Financial Background Information document appears.

▶ *Importing Information into the Database*

By composing new Input Company Profile and Financial Background Information documents, researchers add more company profiles to the database. Thus, the importance (and relevance) of the database increases because it reflects extensive research information; by posting their research and analysis of companies, researchers increase the comprehensiveness and usefulness of the information.

Researchers can also import information from other sources. For example, by importing data from a companion spreadsheet, other relevant financial information can be added to the database. To import data from a spreadsheet, you would do the following: Select one of the "Profiles by..." views and choose Files ➤ Import. Select the spreadsheet you are importing. Click on the Import button. In the dialog box that appears, you would specify the following:

- Input Company Profile as the form you are using for importing.
- If you are importing data kept in a named range in the spreadsheet, enter the name of the range.
- Select COL file as the import type.
- Enter the name of the COL file.

Click on OK to begin the import. Press Ctrl+S to save the document.

You can also import data on a company that comes from a newswire service or another industry source and include the data in a Financial Background Information document. Simply compose a Financial Background Information document and either paste in the history from the Clipboard (if the information can be copied to the Clipboard) or import the information directly.

To import the information, choose File ➤ Import, enter the name of the imported document and its type. Click on Import to begin importing the information. Press Ctrl+S to save the Financial Background Information document.

▶ Creating Doclinks between the Two Different Documents

Once you have created a Financial Background Information document, you can create a doclink to link this document to the corresponding main Input Company Profile document. Open the Financial Background Information document or highlight it from the Financial History view. Then choose File ➤ Links ➤ Make DocLink. Open and edit the particular Input Company Profile document that will contain the doclink.

Next, go to the Most Recent Financial History field (at the bottom of the document) and choose Edit ➤ Paste (or press Ctrl+V). The doclink icon appears. Press Ctrl+S to save the Input Company Profile document.

▶▶ Creating the Investment Profiles Database

If you "test drove" the database by following the instructions above for composing documents and opening views, you saw firsthand how the application works. From this point on, we're going to take you through the steps of duplicating the Investment Profiles database by creating it from scratch. You might ask yourself, "Can't I just install the database and use it as is?" The answer is yes. (We don't want you to feel as if we're forcing you to reinvent the wheel.) All you have to do after decompressing the Investment Profiles database file is to follow the steps in Chapter 4 for adding the database to your Workspace.

Our main reason for helping you to duplicate the Investment Profiles database is to reveal how it was designed. You could consider the process a variation of "backwards engineering." By recreating the database from scratch, you'll be able to analyze its design and look closely at its components. You'll experience firsthand the development process the designer was engaged in as he created the application. Along the way, we'll point out interesting design tips and shortcuts that you can use when you create your own databases. You can always apply what you've learned about duplicating one database to a new database.

►► W A R N I N G

We've said it once but we'll say it again: Don't work with your only existing copy of the database. Make a backup copy of the database file and store it a safe place before you add it to your Workspace. As you modify the Investment Profiles database, you could remove one of the forms or views accidentally, or delete a doclink unintentionally. The database won't work correctly if an item is missing. Fortunately, you can remove it from your system and reinstall your backup copy if you damage the database.

Another reason for analyzing the Investment Profiles database is to discover ways for customizing the application to suit your own needs. For example, you might decide that you don't like the layout of the forms. Perhaps you want to include more fields, or change the graphics that are used. You can customize the database if you desire. However, the database's unique structure is tightly integrated. If you start customizing the design, you might discover that it doesn't work correctly.

You're going to create a new database and name it "Online Investment Reports" to distinguish it from "Investment Profiles" so you don't confuse the two files. The database functions as a repository of financial background information on companies. As a workflow-automation application, it provides the means for a researcher to gather financial data on companies and a trader to use the information in order to aid clients in making investment decisions. To create the Investment Profiles database, follow these steps:

1. Choose File ➤ New Database. The New Database dialog box appears, as shown in Figure 24.5.

2. Make sure that -Blank- is highlighted in the Template list box.

3. Highlight the appropriate server name in the Server list box or choose Local to store the database on your workstation.

FIGURE 24.5 ►

The New Database dialog box lets you name a new database and indicate where the database should be stored, on a server or on your workstation.

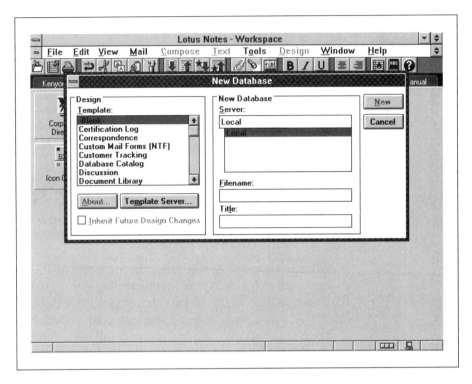

►► **W A R N I N G**

You should use a different file name when you recreate the database or Notes will respond by asking you if you want to replace the existing file. You don't! You should also give the database a new title so you don't confuse it with the existing title.

4. Enter **INVEST2**, or another appropriate name, in the Filename text box. There's no need to include an extension because Notes appends .NSF to the file name automatically. (You can also include the path in the file name to ensure the database is stored in the appropriate directory.)

5. Enter **Online Investment Reports**, or another appropriate name, in the Title text box. Just make sure the name is descriptive.

6. Click on OK. By default, a blank view appears.

7. Press Esc to close the view. You'll return to the Notes Workspace, which displays the new Investment Profiles title on database's icon, as shown in Figure 24.6.

FIGURE 24.6 ▶

The Notes Workspace displays the title on the new Online Investment Reports database icon. You'll notice that the Investment Profiles database icon also appears.

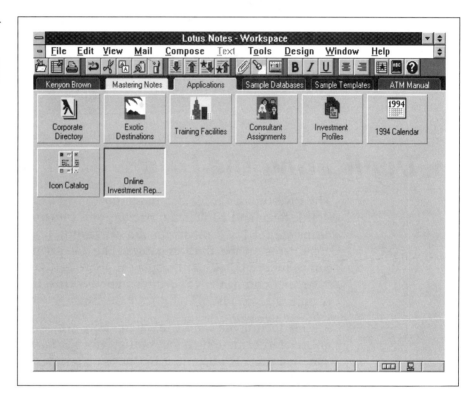

▸▸ N O T E

> An icon always appears in the Workspace with the title
> you give the database; the "icon" is actually just a blank
> square until you create a graphic for it. You need to make
> sure the icon is always selected by clicking on it *before*
> you start creating any forms or views. Otherwise, you'll
> either save the forms or views to a database that you
> unknowingly selected or you won't be able to create the
> forms or views because you haven't selected a database.
> If a specific database isn't selected, the Design menu will
> appear dimmed. Subsequently, you won't be able to
> access the Views or Forms commands.

▸▸ Duplicating the Forms

The Investment Profile database utilizes two forms: an Input Company Profile form and a Financial Background Information form. These forms are ready for members of a workgroup to use for composing documents on specific companies. The documents that each Evaluator composes are posted and displayed in order to track financial data on particular companies. This information is used to help clients make investment decisions.

All the documents can be updated easily, which is important since the financial information changes on a daily basis. An Evaluator can revise data in a specific document by choosing a view and then selecting and opening a particular document in Edit mode. Once the information is updated, the document can again be posted so other people in the workgroup can use it. In this way, everyone has access to the most current financial information on a specific company.

▸ Recreating the Input Company Profile Form

The Input Company Profile form enables Evaluators to input, organize, and store financial data on a company. The form displays the most current information that's available on a company and tracks financial data over the previous two-year period. The form is divided into three sections: the top section displays financial data, the middle section displays a financial report, and the bottom section displays hidden field information. To create the Input Company Profile form, follow these steps:

1. Return to the Notes Workspace (if you aren't there already) and click on the Investment Profiles database (or the new name you gave the database) icon to select it.

2. Choose Design ➤ Forms. The Design Forms dialog box appears, as shown in Figure 24.7.

3. Click the New button. A blank form appears, as shown in Figure 24.8.

You are now in Form Design mode, or just Design mode. The form is entirely blank because it is actually a large rich text field. You'll recall that a rich text field can contain graphics and objects as well as the formats you apply to text.

FIGURE 24.7 ▶

You begin designing a new form by opening the Design Forms dialog box.

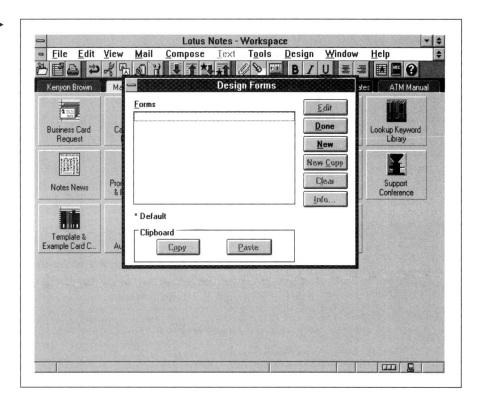

FIGURE 24.8 ▶

When you click the New button, a blank form appears.

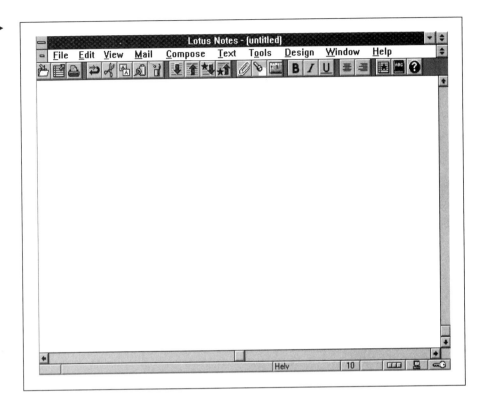

Defining the Form's Attributes

A form may have a number of characteristics, or *attributes*, associated with it that give the form identity and establish important overall qualities of the form. An attribute can be as simple as the form's name, or it can be more sophisticated. For example, an attribute can specify whether or not information may be passed from another document to a document based on this form.

Certain attributes are mandatory. For these attributes you must provide a value or, sometimes, Notes provides a default value for you. Other attributes can be ignored entirely since they are used only in more obscure implementations. To define the Input Company Profile form's attributes, follow these steps:

1. Choose Design ➤ Form Attributes. The Design Form Attributes dialog box appears, as shown in Figure 24.9.

FIGURE 24.9 ▶

The Design Form Attributes dialog box lets you specify a form's name, type, and other attributes.

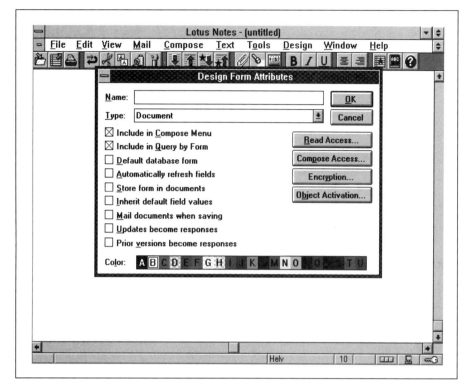

2. Enter **Input Company Profile** in the Name text box.

3. Make sure that Document appears in the Type box.

4. Select the following options (nothing else should be checked):

- Include in Compose Menu
- Include in Query by Form
- Default Database Form

5. Click OK to accept the changes.

Creating a Title for a Form's Window Bar

You'll want to display a title in a form's window bar because it helps users to identify the form as they compose new documents. The title can also display useful information, such as the date and time, or a name or subject that is significant to the database. To create a title that will appear in the window's title bar, follow these steps:

1. Choose Design ➤ Window Title. The Design Window Title dialog box appears, as shown in Figure 24.10.

2. Enter the following statement in the Window Title Formula box. (This statement returns and displays in the window's title bar the name of the form and the name of the person that is entered in the Name field.)

   @If(@IsNewDoc; "New Company Profile"; "Company Profile for " + Company)

3. Click OK to confirm.

FIGURE 24.10 ▶

The Design Window Title dialog box lets you include a formula that returns a title that is displayed in the form's window bar.

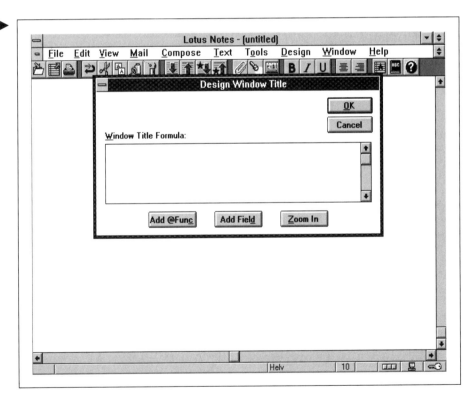

Each time a user composes a document using the Input Company Profile form, the title "New Company Profile" will appear in the window bar (without the quotation marks). When the user opens a view and selects a document to read or edit later on, the window bar will display the title "Company Profile for [*name of company entered in the form's Name field*]." The formula helps the user to quickly identify the subject of the document, which in this case is a person.

Inserting the Table

At this point, you can start laying out the Input Company Profile form. Use Figure 24.11 as a model (or select the Investment Profiles database and open the form to view it on screen) if you need a reference. As you can see, the form includes a table of 16 cells that displays specific information a user enters in the corresponding fields below it (you can't enter data into the table directly).

We won't take you through the steps of inserting the table since we discussed creating one in the previous chapter. However, remember Notes doesn't provide you with much in the way of formatting tools. You'll have to manually tweak the cells in order to change their size.

Adding Labels to the Form

After you've created the table, you can add labels to the cells and the rest of the form in order to properly identify the fields. Unfortunately, entering and formatting static text can become arduous. You can either input all of the text at the same time and then insert and define the fields later, or you can add one label at a time and then define its corresponding field. It's a toss-up which method is more time-consuming.

To begin, position the insertion point at the top of the form. You might have to press ↵ several times to move the table down until you position it where you want it on the form. With the insertion point at the top of the form, select Center alignment. Enter **Personal Investments Inc.** Press ↵ to move the insertion point to the next line. Enter **Financial Analysis Report** below the previous line (making sure that it's also center aligned). Continue adding the other labels, using Figure 24.11 as a reference.

FIGURE 24.11 ▶

Editing the Input Company Profile form in Design mode reveals the placement of fields, labels, and the graphic.

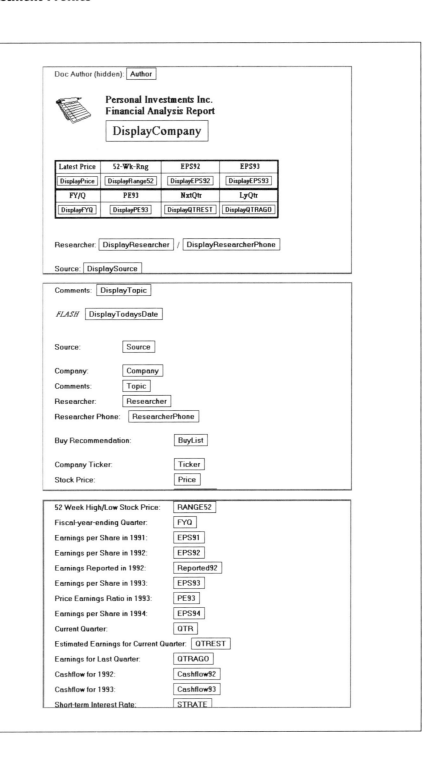

FIGURE 24.11 ▶

Editing the Input Company Profile form in Design mode reveals the placement of fields, labels, and the graphic. (continued)

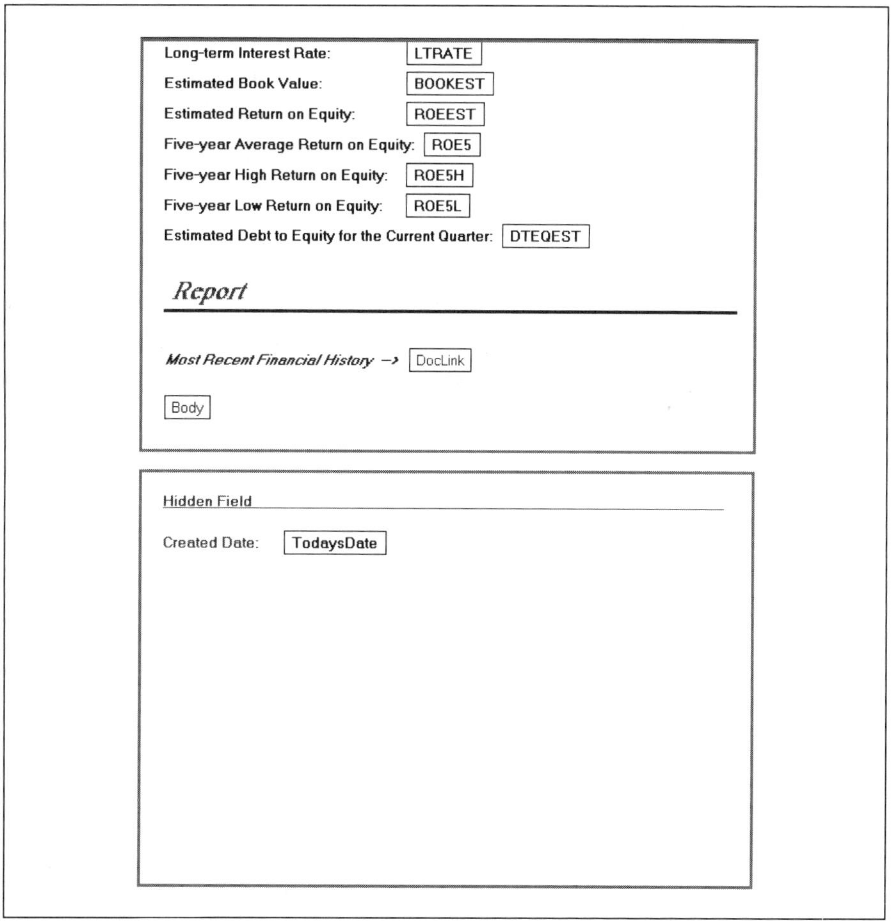

Long-term Interest Rate:	LTRATE
Estimated Book Value:	BOOKEST
Estimated Return on Equity:	ROEEST
Five-year Average Return on Equity:	ROE5
Five-year High Return on Equity:	ROE5H
Five-year Low Return on Equity:	ROE5L
Estimated Debt to Equity for the Current Quarter:	DTEQEST

Report

Most Recent Financial History → DocLink

Body

Hidden Field

Created Date: TodaysDate

Formatting the Labels

The methods you use to format text on a form are similar to those for formatting text in most other Windows applications. However, as we mentioned in the previous chapter, Notes text formatting tools don't offer you the variety—or sophistication, for that matter—of features that you'll find in other applications, especially word processors or desktop publishers.

▶▶ TIP

If you only need to apply a single formatting attribute to selected text, such as boldface or italics, you can do this faster by highlighting the text and then selecting the specific attribute from the Text menu. Open the menu and then click on the command you want in order to change the format. You can apply an attribute even faster by using keystroke combinations. Highlight the text and then press the appropriate keystroke(s) to make the format change, such as Ctrl+B for Bold or Ctrl+I for Italic.

Inserting a Graphic in a Form

A graphic appears at the top of the Input Company Profile form. Like the table, the graphic is an object that's been inserted in the form. As we discussed in the previous chapter, you can insert graphic objects anywhere on a form because a form is actually a large rich text field that can contain text and graphics.

When you click on the graphic to select it, a marquee will appear around it with a resizing handle in the lower right corner. The graphic might or might not also appear darkened (highlighted). If you hold the mouse button down while you point on the handle, you can drag the handle to increase or decrease the size of the graphic. This action is similar to the way you might modify the appearance of a graphic you've created in another application.

Insert the graphic the way we described in "Inserting a Graphic in a Form" in Chapter 23. You can either create your own graphic or copy the graphic from the existing form. Select the database and open the form. Select the graphic and then press Ctrl+C to copy it to the Clipboard. Position the insertion point in the new form and then press Ctrl+V to paste it. Change the size of the graphic by dragging the handle.

Defining the Fields

Now that we've entered all the static text and inserted a table and graphic on the Input Company Profile form, let's create and position the fields. To add the first field for the Input Company Profile form, follow the steps below. You can add the remaining fields on your own:

1. Place the insertion point at the top of the form. (Use Figure 24.11 as a guide.)

2. Choose Design ➤ New Field. The Design New Field dialog box appears.

3. Click on OK to accept the default option. The Field Definition dialog box appears.

4. Enter the following information (unless already indicated):

   Name: Author
   Help Definition (optional): Original author of the document
   Data Type: Text
   Field Type: Computed when composed
   Formula: @UserName

5. Click OK to accept the changes. The field will appear.

6. If you want to change the color of the text that will appear in the field, highlight the field and choose Text ➤ Font. The Font dialog box appears.

7. Select a color from the Color Bar at the bottom of the dialog box.

8. Click on OK to confirm the change. The field's text color changes from black (the default) to the new color you selected.

Repeat the above steps to create the other fields. You can refer to Tables 24.1 and 24.2 to create the other fields. Table 24.1 summarizes all the field definitions, and Table 24.2 summarizes all the field formulas.

Saving a Form

When you're finished creating a form (and after modifying a form), press Ctrl+S to save it. If you press Esc or Ctrl+W to close the window *before* saving the form, Notes will ask you if you want to save your changes. Click on Yes. You'll return to the Workspace.

▶ **TABLE 24.1:** *A summary of field definitions for the Input Company Profile form*

LABEL NAME	FIELD NAME	DATA TYPE	FIELD TYPE
Doc Author	Author	Text	Computed when composed
Financial Analysis Report	DisplayCompany	Text	Computed for display
Latest Price	DisplayPrice	Number (Number Format: Currency: 2 Decimal Places)	Computed
52-Wk-Rng	DisplayRange52	Text	Computed
EPS92	DisplayEPS92	Number (Number Format: Currency: 2 Decimal Places)	Computed
EPS93	DisplayEPS93	Number (Number Format: Currency: 2 Decimal Places)	Computed
FY/Q	DisplayFYQ	Time (Time Format: 07/28/94 10:23:04 AM)	Computed
PE93	DisplayPE93	Text	Computed
NxtQtr	DisplayQTREST	Number (Number Format: Currency: 2 Decimal Places)	Computed
LtQtr	DisplayQTRAGO	Number (Number Format: Currency: 2 Decimal Places)	Computed
Researcher	DisplayResearcher	Text	Computed
	DisplayResearcher-Phone	Text	Computed
Source	DisplaySource	Text	Computed
Comments	DisplayTopic	Text	Computed
FLASH	DisplayTodaysDate	Time (Time Format: 07/28/94 10:23 AM)	Computed

TABLE 24.1: *A summary of field definitions for the Input Company Profile form (continued)*

LABEL NAME	FIELD NAME	DATA TYPE	FIELD TYPE
Source	Source	Keywords: New York Equity Research UK Equity Research Tokyo Equity Research	Editable
Company	Company	Text	Editable
Comments	Topic	Text	Editable
Researcher	Researcher	Text	Editable
Researcher's Phone	ResearcherPhone	Text	Editable
Buy Recommendation	BuyList	Keywords: Yes No Hold	Editable
Company Ticker	Ticker	Text	Editable
Stock Price	Price	Number (Number Format: Currency: 2 Decimal Places)	Editable
%2 Week High?low Stock Price	RANGE52	Text	Editable
Fiscal-year-ending Quarter	FYQ	Time (Time Format: 07/94)	Editable
Earnings per Share in 1991	EPS91	Number (Number Format: Currency: 2 Decimal Places)	Editable
Earnings per share in 1992	EPS92	Number (Number Format: Currency: 2 Decimal Places)	Editable

► **TABLE 24.1:** *A summary of field definitions for the Input Company Profile form (continued)*

LABEL NAME	FIELD NAME	DATA TYPE	FIELD TYPE
Earnings Reported in 1992	Reported92	Number (Number Format: Currency: 2 Decimal Places)	Editable
Earnings per share in 1993	EPS93	Number (Number Format: Currency: 2 Decimal Places)	Editable
Price Earnings Ratio in 1993	PE93	Number (Number Format: Currency: 2 Decimal Places)	Editable
Earnings per Share in 1994	EPS94	Number (Number Format: Currency: 2 Decimal Places)	Editable
Current Quarter	QTR	Number (Number Format: Currency: 2 Decimal Places)	Editable
Estimated Earnings for Current Quarter	QTREST	Number (Number Format: Currency: 2 Decimal Places)	Editable
Earnings for Last Quarter	QTRAGO	Number (Number Format: Currency: 2 Decimal Places)	Editable
Cashflow for 1992	Cashflow92	Number (Number Format: Currency: 2 Decimal Places)	Editable
Cashflow for 1993	Cashflow93	Number (Number Format: Currency: 2 Decimal Places)	Editable
Short-term Interest Rate	STRATE	Number (Number Format: Currency: 2 Decimal Places)	Editable
Long-term Interest Rate	LTRATE	Number (Number Format: Currency: 2 Decimal Places)	Editable

▶ **TABLE 24.1:** *A summary of field definitions for the Input Company Profile form (continued)*

LABEL NAME	FIELD NAME	DATA TYPE	FIELD TYPE
Estimated Book Value	BOOKEST	Number (Number Format: Currency: 2 Decimal Places)	Editable
Estimated Return on Equity	ROEEST	Number (Number Format: Currency: 2 Decimal Places)	Editable
Five-Year Average Return on Equity	ROE5	Number (Number Format: Currency: 2 Decimal Places)	Editable
Five-year High Return on Equity	ROE5H	Number (Number Format: Currency: 2 Decimal Places)	Editable
Five-year Low Return on Equity	ROE5L	Number (Number Format: Currency: 2 Decimal Places)	Editable
Estimated Debt to Equity for the Current Quarter	DTEQEST	Number (Number Format: General)	Editable
Most Recent Financial Histiry	DocLink	Rich Text	Editable
	Body	Rich Text	Editable
Form Name	Form	Text	Editable
Created Date	TodaysDate	Time (Time Format: 07/28/94)	Editable

We've already taken you through the steps of naming a form by entering its name in the Form Attributes dialog box. (You'll recall that a name is one of many attributes you can set for a form.) This name will appear on the Compose menu when users start composing documents with the form. However, while you're creating a form, you can place labels and fields and then save your work *before* you identify other specific attributes in the Form Attributes dialog box. (You can do this at a later time. However, until you specify the attributes you want, you'll have to be satisfied with using the default options.)

▶ **TABLE 24.2:** *A summary of field formulas for the Input Company Profile form*

Label Name	Field Name	Formula
Doc Author	Author	@UserName
Financial Analysis Report	DisplayCompany	Company
Latest Price	DisplayPrice	Price
52-Wk-Rng	DisplayRange52	Range52
EPS92	DisplayEPS92	eps92
EPS93	DisplayEPS93	EPS93
FY/Q	DisplayFYQ	FYQ
PE93	DisplayPE93	pe93
NxtQtr	DisplayQTREST	qtrest
LtQtr	DisplayQTRAGO	qtrago
Researcher	DisplayResearcher	Researcher
	DisplayResearcherPhone	ResearcherPhone
Source	DisplaySource	Source
Comments	DisplayTopic	Topic
FLASH	DisplayTodaysDate	TodaysDate
Form Name	Form	DisplayReport
Created Date	TodaysDate	@Created

If you want to save a form without going through the steps of opening the Form Attributes dialog box and setting attributes (specifically, the form's name), press Ctrl+S. The Save Form dialog box appears. Enter a name in the Name text box and then click on OK. The name will appear on the Compose menu and in the Form Attributes dialog box. Just remember, however, that all you've done is saved the form under a specific name. You haven't set any other form attributes.

The change will take effect immediately. With the form window still open (you don't have to close it), you can pull down the Compose menu and click on the form's name. A blank document will open in which you can enter data in the fields. When you're finished composing the document, press Ctrl+S to save the information. To close the document's window, press Esc. Press Esc again to close the form's window and to return to the Workspace.

Formatting a Form

You format a form in order to change and enhance its appearance. Formatting allows your creative side to come out. By applying different formatting attributes, you help users to distinguish one form from another in the same database, and to give each form a distinctive look and feel. You can format a form after you've created it, or you can apply formats to a form while you're designing it. Some designers like to place the labels and fields and then format the form; others prefer to format a form as they go along.

Notes provides a set of formatting tools that is similar to those found in other Windows applications. For instance, you can change the background color of a form as well as format the labels and the text that users will enter in fields. The choices you make will be purely subjective, so keep in mind that a person will be using the form for data input. You don't want to overwhelm the user with a form that appears too busy.

You shouldn't clutter a form with too many different fonts and point sizes. You should keep the number of colors you use to a few and consider if they complement each other. If you decide to add a background color to the form (instead of white, the default), make sure the color of the labels and the field text contrast with it. You don't want the text to appear too light against the background.

The following instructions assume that you have created the Input Company Profile form and want to format it. We also assume that you placed all the labels and fields that we described earlier in the chapter. To change the form's background color, follow these steps:

1. If the form isn't open, click on the Investment Profiles database icon to select it.

2. Choose Design ➤ Forms. The Design Forms dialog box appears.

3. Double-click on Input Company Profile (or highlight the form and click on the Edit button). The form window opens in Edit mode.

4. Choose Design ➤ Form Attributes. The Design Form Attributes dialog box appears.

5. To change the background color of the form from the default color, white, select another color from the bar at the bottom of the dialog box.

6. Click on OK to accept the change. The form's background color will reflect your choice.

7. Press Ctrl+S to save the form.

 ▸▸ **TIP**

When you highlight a label (any static text) on a form in order to apply formatting attributes, you can pull down the Text menu and choose one of several attributes directly from the menu. Just click on the command. You can also use the available keystroke combinations to execute the same commands.

To format the labels, follow the steps below. (You can format all the labels at one time without affecting the format of the fields because the fields are *plain text* fields; they won't accept any formatting):

1. Choose Edit ➤ Select All to highlight all the labels (and the text fields) at the same time.

2. Choose Text ➤ Font. The Font dialog box appears.

3. Change the font and point size if you wish.

4. Select one or more of the attribute options on the right, such as Bold.

5. Select a color for the text from the color bar at the bottom.

6. Click on OK to accept the changes. The labels will reflect your choices.

7. Press Ctrl+S to save the form.

As we mentioned above, the fields you placed on the form are text fields. In order to be able to change the formatting of the text in the fields, you would need to change them to *rich text fields*. Then when users entered text in the fields, the text would reflect the attributes you applied to the fields.

► Recreating the Financial Background Information Form

The Financial Background Information form is designed to display a lengthy financial history of a company (if the Researcher wants to elaborate). The structure of the Input Company Profile form doesn't give a researcher the room to interpret the data except for the Report section at the bottom of the form. Therefore, the Financial Background Information document can be very useful to a trader when making investment recommendations to clients. To recreate the Financial Background Information form, follow these steps:

1. Select the Investment Profiles database.

2. Choose Design ➤ Forms.

3. Click on the New button. A blank form appears.

4. Press Ctrl+S to save the form.

5. Either press Esc to return to the Workspace, or follow the steps in the next section.

Defining the Form's Attributes

To define the form's attributes, follow these steps:

1. Choose Design ➤ Form Attributes.

2. Enter **Financial Background Information** in the text box.

3. Select Document as the type.

4. Select the Include in Compose Menu and Include In Query by Form options. Don't check any other options.

5. Click on OK to save the new attributes.

6. Press Ctrl+S to save the form.

7. Press Esc to return to the Workspace, or follow the steps below.

Defining the Window Title

To create a title that will appear in the window's title bar, follow these steps:

1. Choose Design ➤ Window Title. The Design Window Title dialog box appears.

2. Enter the following statement in the Window Title Formula box. (This statement returns and displays in the window's title bar the name of the form and the name of the person that is entered in the Name field.)

@If(@IsNewDoc; "New Financial Background Information"; "Financial Background Information for: " + Company)

3. Click OK to confirm.

Defining the Fields

To add the labels and fields to the form, follow these steps:

1. Select the Investment Profiles database if it isn't selected.

2. Choose Design ➤ Forms.

3. Double-click on Financial Background Information to edit the form. A blank form appears.

4. Create and position the labels. (Use Figure 24.12 as a reference.)

5. Add the graphic by copying it from the Input Company Profile form and then pasting it in the desired location in this form.

6. Choose Design ➤ New Field to define each of the fields below:

> **Name**: Author
> **Help Definition** (optional): Original author of the document
> **Data Type**: Text
> **Field Type**: Computed when composed
> **Formula**: @UserName
>
> **Name**: Company
> **Help Definition** (optional): Enter company name

> **Data Type**: Text
>
> **Field Type**: Editable
>
> **Name**: Financials
>
> **Help Definition** (optional): Enter, paste, or import full text of company financials
>
> **Data Type**: Rich Text
>
> **Field Type**: Editable

7. Click on OK to save each field's definition.

8. Press Ctrl+S to save the form.

9. Press Esc to return to the Workspace.

FIGURE 24.12 ▶

When you edit the Financial Background Information form in Design mode, the placement of fields, labels, and the graphic is revealed.

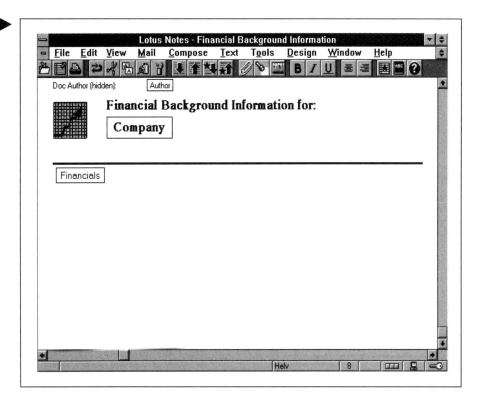

▶▶ *Duplicating the Views*

The Investment Profiles database uses five "Profiles by..." views, which select, sort, and categorize Input Company Profile documents, and a Financial History view, which provides financial background information documents on the companies:

- **Profiles by Buy/Sell/Hold**: Shows the trading stock status.

- **Profiles by Company**: Shows an alphabetical listing of current Input Company Profile documents by company.

- **Profiles by Date Posted**: Shows the date the Input Company Profile documents were written. The view sorts the documents in descending order.

- **Profiles by Researcher**: Shows account responsibilities for each researcher. The view shows the researcher's account load by number as well as a percentage of the entire account load.

- **Profiles by Ticker**: Shows ticker symbols of each company.

- **Financial History**: Shows an alphabetical listing of Financial Background Information documents by company.

These views allow you to refer to company profile research and analysis easily.

▶ *Defining the Profiles by Buy/Sell/Hold View*

Let's create the Profiles by Buy/Sell/Hold view for the Investment Profiles database. This view shows the trading stock status of a company. The columns in the view correspond to the field values in the Input Company Profile form. To create the view, follow these steps:

1. Select the Investment Profiles database in the Workspace.

2. Choose Design ➤ Views. The Design Views dialog box appears, as shown in Figure 24.13.

3. Click on the New button, which allows you to create a view from scratch. A blank view window appears in Design mode, as shown in Figure 24.14.

FIGURE 24.13 ▶

*The Design Views dia-
log box lets you create
new view for a selected
database.*

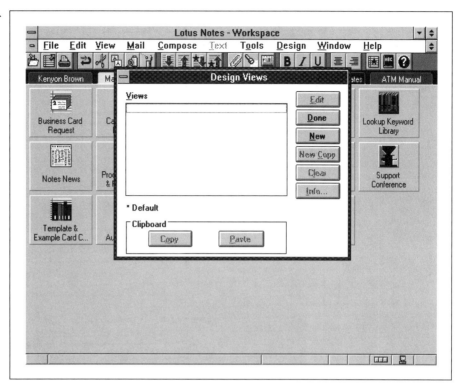

▶▶ **TIP**

**You can choose the New Copy and Paste options if a
view already exists. The New Copy option allows you to
create a view by copying an existing view in the
database. Simply highlight the view you wish to copy
from the list of views displayed in the dialog box and
select New Copy. The Paste option lets you create a
view by pasting a view from another database into the
current database. You must first open the other
database, choose Design ➤ Views, highlight the desired
view, and click on Copy. Then choose Design ➤ Views in
the target database and click on Paste. The pasted
view should now appear in the list of views in the
dialog box.**

FIGURE 24.14

A blank view appears in Design mode when you want to define a new view.

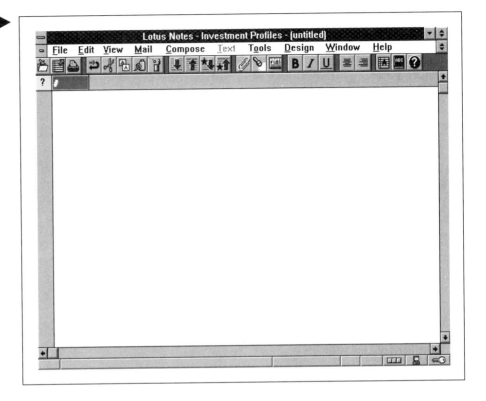

Defining the View's Attributes

You'll notice that the current name of the view is [untitled]. Associated with each view is a set of attributes which assign certain general characteristics to the view. One of the attributes is the view's name. To define view attributes, follow these steps:

1. While in View Design mode, choose Design ➤ View Attributes. The Design View Attributes dialog box appears, as shown in Figure 24.15.

FIGURE 24.15

The Design View Attributes dialog box lets you define the attributes for a particular view.

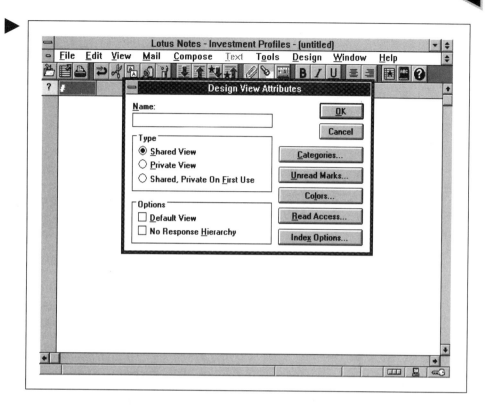

▶▶ **TIP**

You can create an *accelerator key* for a view name by placing an underscore to the left of a letter in the name. An accelerator key allows the user to open a menu and then press the specific key in order to execute a command, which in this case is opening a particular view. When a database has several views, using accelerator keys is a convenient way to open the views quickly.

2. Enter **Profiles by _Buy/Sell/Hold** in the Name text box.

3. Select the Shared View option if it's not selected. (It's the default.)

4. Click on the Categories button to specify that categories in the view will be fully expanded.

5. Click on OK to accept the changes.

Defining the Selection Formula

To ensure that a view will only include documents that meet a specific criteria, we have to make use of a selection formula. When applied to a view, a selection formula simply narrows the scope of the view to include only a subset of documents in the database, excluding all others. A selection formula expresses the criteria that a document must meet in order to be included in the view. To create the selection formula for the Profiles by Buy/Hold/Sell view, follow these steps:

1. Display the view in Design mode.

2. Choose Design ➤ Selection Formula. The Design Selection Formula dialog box appears, as shown in Figure 24.16.

FIGURE 24.16 ▶

The Design Selection Formula dialog box lets you enter a formula that selects the documents you want to display in a particular view.

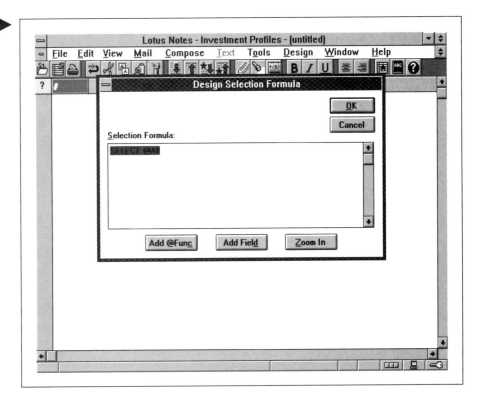

3. Enter the following statement in the Selection Formula box:

SELECT form = "Input Company Profile"

4. Click on OK to accept the formula.

The formula selects all the Input Company Profile documents to appear in the view. No other documents will appear.

▶▶ **N O T E**

> The default statement **SELECT @All** would return the selection of *all* documents in a database to appear in a particular view. Such a listing of all the documents wouldn't be practical or useful. If a database used more than one form, and contained hundreds of documents, the view would display all the documents, regardless of their applicability to the view. Users would have to scroll through a seemingly endless listing in order to find the information they wanted. This is why a view's selection formula is useful. You can limit the selection of documents to only those you want displayed in a particular view.

Defining the Columns

For the Profiles by Buy/Sell/Hold view, you are going to define three columns. To define each of the other columns, follow these steps:

1. Double-click on the leftmost column. The Design Column Definition dialog box appears, as shown in Figure 24.17.

▶▶ **T I P**

> Double-click on a column heading (the box at top of the column) to display the Design Column Definition dialog box.

FIGURE 24.17 ▶

*The Design Column
Definition dialog box
lets you define a col-
umn, which in this
case is the Name col-
umn in the Corporate
Directory view.*

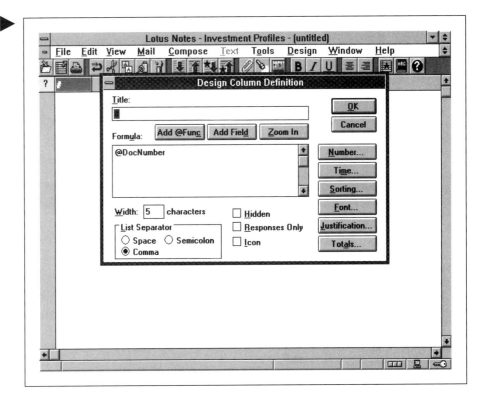

2. Leave the Title text box blank.

3. Enter the following statement in the Formula box. (It refers to the value of the BuyList field in the Input Company Profile form.)

@If(BuyList = "Yes"; "Buy"; BuyList = "No";"Sell";"Hold")

4. Set the width of the column in the Column Width box to 3.

5. Click on the Font button. The Font dialog box appears.

6. Select Helv, 10, Bold.

7. Click on the Sorting button. The Design Column Sort dialog box appears.

8. Select Ascending, Categorized.

9. Click on OK to accept your choices.

Defining the Other Columns in the View

To define the other columns in the Profiles by Buy, Sell, Hold view, follow these steps:

1. For the second column, enter the following definitions:

Title: Company/Researcher

Formula: Company + "(" + Researcher + "-" + ResearcherPhone + ")"

Width: 34

List Separator: Comma

Number: General (Default)

Sorting: Ascending

Font: Helv, 10, Bold

Justification: Left (default)

Totals: None (Default)

2. For the third column, enter the following definitions:

Title: Price

Formula: Price

Width: 6

List Separator: Comma

Number: Currency (2 Decimal Places)

Sorting: None

Font: Helv, 10, Bold

Justification: Center

Totals: None (Default)

As you can see, you can use the default definitions for most of the items. This will save you a lot of time when you have several columns to define.

Saving a View

Although you may have clicked on OK in different dialog boxes to accept changes you made to different elements in a view, you still need to save the view before closing it and returning to the Workspace or another open window. When you want to save the changes you made to a view, press Ctrl+S. If you press Esc before you save the changes, a message box will appear, asking you if you want to save your changes. Click on Yes. You'll return to the Workspace or another window that may be open.

► Duplicating the Other Views

You'll need to repeat the above steps in order to define each of the four other "Profiles by…" views and the Financial History view. You can assume that the default options apply unless indicated otherwise.

► Defining the Profiles by Company View

The Profiles by Company view shows an alphabetical listing of current Input Company Profile documents by company. To create the view, follow these steps:

1. Select the Investment Profiles database in the Workspace.

2. Choose Design ► Views. The Design Views dialog box appears.

3. Click on the New button, which allows you to create a view from scratch. A blank view window appears in Design mode.

Defining the View's Attributes

To define the view's attributes, follow these steps:

1. While in View Design mode, choose Design ► View Attributes. The Design View Attributes dialog box appears.

2. Enter **Profiles by _Company** in the Name text box.

3. Select the Shared View option if it's not selected. (It's the default.)

4. Click on the Categories button to specify that categories in the view will be fully expanded.

5. Click on OK to accept the changes.

Defining the Selection Formula

The selection formula expresses the criteria that a document must meet in order to be included in the view. To create the selection formula for the Profiles by Company view, follow these steps:

1. Display the view in Design mode.

2. Choose Design ➤ Selection Formula. The Design Selection Formula dialog box appears.

3. Enter the following statement in the Selection Formula box:

   SELECT form = "Input Company Profile"

4. Click on OK to accept the formula.

The formula selects all the Input Company Profile documents to appear in the view. No other documents will appear.

Defining the Columns

For the Profiles by Company view, you are going to define seven columns. To define the first column, follow these steps:

1. Double-click on the leftmost column. The Design Column Definition dialog box appears.

2. Enter **Company/Researcher** in the Title text box.

3. Enter the following statement in the Formula box. (It refers to the value of the BuyList field in the Input Company Profile form.)

   Company + "(" + Researcher + ")"

4. Enter **14** in the Column Width box.

5. Click on the Font button. The Font dialog box appears.

6. Select Helv, 12, Bold.

7. Click on the Sorting button. The Design Column Sort dialog box appears.

8. Select Ascending, Categorized.

9. Click on OK to accept your choices and the default settings.

To define the other columns in the Profiles by Company view, follow these steps:

1. For the second column, enter the following definitions:

> **Title**: Price
> **Formula**: Price
> **Width**: 5
> **List Separator**: Comma
> **Number**: Currency (3 Decimal Places)
> **Parentheses on Negative Numbers**: Yes
> **Punctuated at Thousands**: Yes
> **Sorting**: None
> **Font**: Helv, 10, Bold
> **Justification**: Center
> **Totals**: None (Default)

2. For the third column, enter the following definitions:

> **Title**: 52-Wk-Rng
> **Formula**: RANGE52
> **Width**: 9
> **List Separator**: Comma
> **Number**: General
> **Sorting**: Descending
> **Font**: Helv, 10, Bold
> **Justification**: Center
> **Totals**: None (Default)

3. For the fourth column, enter the following definitions:

> **Title**: PE93
> **Formula**: PE93
> **Width**: 4
> **List Separator**: Comma
> **Number**: General
> **Sorting**: None (Default)
> **Font**: Helv, 10, Bold

Justification: Center

Totals: None (Default)

4. For the fifth column, enter the following definitions:

      Title: FY/Q

      Formula: FY/Q

      Width: 5

      List Separator: Comma

      Number: General

      Sorting: None (Default)

      Font: Helv, 10, Bold

      Justification: Center

      Totals: None (Default)

5. For the sixth column, enter the following definitions:

      Title: EPS92

      Formula: EPS92

      Width: 6

      List Separator: Comma

      Number: Currency (2 Decimal Places)

      Sorting: None (Default)

      Font: Helv, 10, Bold

      Justification: Center

      Totals: None (Default)

6. For the seventh column, enter the following definitions:

      Title: EPS93

      Formula: EPS93

      Width: 6

      List Separator: Comma

      Number: Currency (2 Decimal Places)

      Sorting: None (Default)

      Font: Helv, 10, Bold

      Justification: Center

      Totals: None (Default)

As you can see, you can use the default definitions for most of the items. This will save you a lot of time when you have several columns to define.

▶ Defining the Profiles by Date Posted View

The Profiles by Date Posted shows the date the Input Company Profile documents were written. The view sorts the documents in descending order. To create the view, follow these steps:

1. Select the Investment Profiles database in the Workspace.

2. Choose Design ➤ Views. The Design Views dialog box appears.

3. Click on the New button, which allows you to create a view from scratch. A blank view window appears in Design mode.

Defining the View's Attributes

To define the view's attributes, follow these steps:

1. While in View Design mode, choose Design ➤ View Attributes. The Design View Attributes dialog box appears.

2. Enter **Profiles by _Date Posted** in the Name text box.

3. Select the Shared View option if it's not selected. (It's the default.)

4. Click on the Categories button to specify that categories in the view will be fully expanded.

5. Click on OK to accept the changes.

Defining the Selection Formula

The selection formula expresses the criteria that a document must meet in order to be included in the view. To create the selection formula for the Profiles by Company view, follow these steps:

1. Display the view in Design mode.

2. Choose Design ➤ Selection Formula. The Design Selection Formula dialog box appears.

3. Enter the following statement in the Selection Formula box:

   SELECT form = "Input Company Profile"

4. Click on OK to accept the formula.

The formula selects all the Input Company Profile documents to appear in the view. No other documents will appear.

Defining the Columns

For the Profiles by Company view, you are going to define seven columns. To define the first column, follow these steps:

1. Double-click on the leftmost column. The Design Column Definition dialog box appears.

2. Enter **Posted** in the Title text box.

3. Enter the following statement in the Formula box. (It refers to the value of the BuyList field in the Input Company Profile form.)

   @Left@Text(TodaysDate);5)

4. Enter 5 in the Column Width box.

5. Click on the Font button. The Font dialog box appears.

6. Select Helv, 10, Bold.

7. Click on the Sorting button. The Design Column Sort dialog box appears.

8. Select Descending, Categorized.

9. Click on OK to accept your choices and the default options.

To define the other columns in the Profiles by Date Posted view, follow these steps:

1. For the second column, enter the following definitions:

   Title: Company

   Formula: @If(BuyList = "Yes"; Company + "(Buy)";
   BuyList = "No"; Company + "(Sell)"; Company +
   "(Hold)")

   Width: 20

   List Separator: None

Number: General (Default)

Sorting: Ascending

Font: Helv, 10, Bold

Justification: Left (Default)

Totals: None (Default)

2. For the third column, enter the following definitions:

Title: Comment

Formula: Topic

Width: 33

List Separator: Comma

Number: General

Sorting: None

Font: Helv, 10, Bold

Justification: Left

Totals: None (Default)

3. For the fourth column, enter the following definitions:

Title: Ticker

Formula: Ticker

Width: 4

List Separator: None

Number: General

Sorting: None (Default)

Font: Helv, 10, Bold

Justification: Left

Totals: None (Default)

As you can see, you can use the default definitions for most of the items. This will save you a lot of time when you have several columns to define.

▶ *Defining the Profiles by Researcher View*

The Profiles by Researcher view shows account responsibilities for each researcher. The view shows the researcher's account load by number as well as a percentage of the entire account load. To create the view, follow these steps:

1. Select the Investment Profiles database in the Workspace.

2. Choose Design ➤ Views. The Design Views dialog box appears.

3. Click on the New button, which allows you to create a view from scratch. A blank view window appears in Design mode.

Defining the View's Attributes

To define the view's attributes, follow these steps:

1. While in View Design mode, choose Design ➤ View Attributes. The Design View Attributes dialog box appears.

2. Enter **Profiles by _Researcher** in the Name text box.

3. Select the Shared View option if it's not selected. (It's the default.)

4. Click on the Categories button to specify that categories in the view will be fully expanded.

5. Click on OK to accept the changes.

Defining the Selection Formula

The selection formula expresses the criteria that a document must meet in order to be included in the view. To create the selection formula for the Profiles by Company view, follow these steps:

1. Display the view in Design mode.

2. Choose Design ➤ Selection Formula. The Design Selection Formula dialog box appears.

3. Enter the following statement in the Selection Formula box:

   SELECT form = "Input Company Profile"

4. Click on OK to accept the formula.

The formula selects all the Input Company Profile documents to appear in the view. No other documents will appear.

Defining the Columns

For the Profiles by Researcher view, you are going to define seven columns. To define the first column, follow these steps:

1. Double-click on the leftmost column. The Design Column Definition dialog box appears.

2. Enter **# of Accts** in the Title text box.

3. Enter **1** in the Formula statement box.

4. Enter **6** in the Column Width box.

5. Click on the Font button. The Font dialog box appears.

6. Select Helv, 10, Bold.

7. Click on the Justification button.

8. Select the Center alignment option.

9. Click on the Totals button.

10. Select Total.

11. Select the Hide Detail Values option.

12. Click on OK to accept your choices.

To define the other columns in the Profiles by Researcher view, follow these steps:

1. For the second column, enter the following definitions:

> **Title**: % Load
> **Formula**: 1
> **Width**: 5
> **List Separator**: Comma
> **Number**: Fixed (1 Decimal Places)
> **Percentage (value ★ 100)%**: Yes
> **Sorting**: None
> **Font**: Helv, 10, Bold
> **Justification**: Left (default)
> **Totals**: Percentage of Entire View
> **Hide Detail Values**: Yes

2. For the third column, enter the following definitions:

> **Title**: Researcher
> **Formula**: @RightBack(Researcher;"")
> **Width**: 1
> **List Separator**: None
> **Number**: General
> **Sorting**: Ascending
> **Font**: Helv, 10, Bold
> **Justification**: Left
> **Totals**: None (Default)

3. For the fourth column, enter the following definitions:

> **Title**: Researcher
> **Formula**: Researcher
> **Width**: 9
> **List Separator**: None
> **Number**: General
> **Sorting**: Descending, Ascending
> **Font**: Helv, 10, Bold
> **Justification**: Left
> **Totals**: None (Default)

4. For the fifth column, enter the following definitions:

> **Title**: Company
> **Formula**: Company
> **Width**: 13
> **List Separator**: None
> **Number**: General
> **Sorting**: Ascending
> **Font**: Helv, 10, Bold
> **Justification**: Left
> **Totals**: None (Default)

5. For the sixth column, enter the following definitions:

> **Title**: Price
>
> **Formula**: Price
>
> **Width**: 5
>
> **List Separator**: Comma
>
> **Number**: Currency (3 Decimal Places)
>
> **Parentheses on Negative Numbers**: Yes
>
> **Punctuated at Thousands**: Yes
>
> **Sorting**: Descending
>
> **Font**: Helv, 10, Bold
>
> **Justification**: Center
>
> **Totals**: None (Default)

6. For the seventh column, enter the following definitions:

> **Title**: Comment
>
> **Formula**: Topic
>
> **Width**: 35
>
> **List Separator**: None
>
> **Number**: General
>
> **Sorting**: None
>
> **Font**: Helv, 10, Bold
>
> **Justification**: Left
>
> **Totals**: None (Default)

As you can see, you can use the default definitions for most of the items. This will save you a lot of time when you have several columns to define.

▶ Defining the Profiles by Ticker View

The Profiles by Ticker view shows ticker symbols of each company. To create the view, follow these steps:

1. Select the Investment Profiles database in the Workspace.

2. Choose Design ➤ Views. The Design Views dialog box appears.

3. Click on the New button, which allows you to create a view from scratch. A blank view window appears in Design mode.

Defining the View's Attributes

To define the view's attributes, follow these steps:

1. While in View Design mode, choose Design ➤ View Attributes. The Design View Attributes dialog box appears.

2. Enter **Profiles by _Ticker** in the Name text box.

3. Select the Shared View option if it's not selected. (It's the default.)

4. Click on the Categories button to specify that categories in the view will be fully expanded.

5. Click on OK to accept the changes.

Defining the Selection Formula

The selection formula expresses the criteria that a document must meet in order to be included in the view. To create the selection formula for the Profiles by Ticker view, follow these steps:

1. Display the view in Design mode.

2. Choose Design ➤ Selection Formula. The Design Selection Formula dialog box appears.

3. Enter the following statement in the Selection Formula box:

SELECT form = "Input Company Profile"

4. Click on OK to accept the formula.

The formula selects all the Input Company Profile documents to appear in the view. No other documents will appear.

Defining the Columns

For the Profiles by Ticker view, you are going to define seven columns. To define the first column, follow these steps:

1. Double-click on the leftmost column. The Design Column Definition dialog box appears.

2. Enter **Ticker** in the Title text box.

3. Enter the following statement in the Formula box:

Ticker + "(" + Company + ")"

4. Enter **8** in the Column Width box.

5. Click on the Font button. The Font dialog box appears.

6. Select Helv, 10, Bold.

7. Click on the Sorting button. The Design Column Sort dialog box appears.

8. Select Ascending, Categorized.

9. Click on OK to accept your choices.

To define the other columns in the Profiles by Ticker view, follow these steps:

1. For the second column, enter the following definitions:

Title: Price
Formula: Price
Width: 6
List Separator: Comma
Number: Currency (3 Decimal Places)
Parentheses on Negative Numbers: Yes
Punctuated at Thousands: Yes
Sorting: None
Font: Helv, 10, Bold
Justification: Center
Totals: None (Default)

2. For the third column, enter the following definitions:

Title: Comment
Formula: Topic
Width: 34
List Separator: Comma
Number: General
Sorting: None

> **Font**: Helv, 10, Bold
> **Justification**: Left
> **Totals**: None (Default)

As you can see, you can use the default definitions for most of the items. This will save you a lot of time when you have several columns to define.

▶ Defining the Financial History View

The Financial History view shows an alphabetical listing of Financial Background Information documents by company. To create the view, follow these steps:

1. Select the Investment Profiles database in the Workspace.

2. Choose Design ➤ Views. The Design Views dialog box appears.

3. Click on the New button, which allows you to create a view from scratch. A blank view window appears in Design mode.

Defining the View's Attributes

To define the view's attributes, follow these steps:

1. While in View Design mode, choose Design ➤ View Attributes. The Design View Attributes dialog box appears.

2. Enter **_Financial History** in the Name text box.

3. Select the Shared View option if it's not selected. (It's the default.)

4. Click on the Categories button to specify that categories in the view will be fully expanded.

5. Click on OK to accept the changes.

Defining the Selection Formula

The selection formula expresses the criteria that a document must meet in order to be included in the view. To create the selection formula for the Financial History view, follow these steps:

1. Display the view in Design mode.

2. Choose Design ➤ Selection Formula. The Design Selection Formula dialog box appears.

3. Enter the following statement in the Selection Formula box:

   SELECT form = "Financial Background Information"

4. Click on OK to accept the formula.

The formula selects all the Financial Background Information documents to appear in the view. No other documents will appear.

Defining the Columns

For the Financial History view, you are going to define seven columns. To define the only column in the view, follow these steps:

1. Double-click on the leftmost column. The Design Column Definition dialog box appears.

2. Enter **Financial Background for**... in the Title text box.

3. Enter **Company** in the Formula statement box.

4. Enter **36** in the Column Width box.

5. Click on the Font button. The Font dialog box appears.

6. Select Helv, 10, Bold.

7. Click on the Sorting button. The Design Column Sort dialog box appears.

8. Select Ascending.

9. Click on OK to accept your choices.

As you can see, you can use the default definitions for most of the items. This will save you a lot of time when you have several columns to define.

▶▶ Testing the Database

As we discussed at the end of Chapter 14, you should get in the habit of testing the functionality of a new database once you're finished creating the forms and views. All you need to do is compose a few documents based on each form in order to check if you can enter data correctly without getting any error messages.

Next, you should open each of the views to see if the documents are displayed correctly. If a view doesn't display any documents, open the view in Edit mode and check its selection formula. The reason why a view usually doesn't display documents is because the selection formula is wrong. If the selection formula is correct, you should check the formula for each column's definition in order to make sure that the column is referencing the correct field. If a column isn't referencing the correct field, the view won't return (and display) the value for that field.

Many errors occur in Design mode when you're creating forms and fields, and defining their contents. In fact, most errors are the result of typos that you introduce when you include the names of fields and forms in formulas. Sometimes an error message will give you a clue that Notes can't find a specific name of a form or a field. You'll have to open a form and check the spelling of the field names.

▶▶ *What's Next?*

The Investment Profiles database is a good example of an application that can aid users in organizing research information in Notes and then using the information to track the results of decisions that have been made based on the information. This database gives members of a workgroup the means to gather research and background information on companies and then to analyze the statistics, and it presents information in a way that can engage people in meaningful and substantive discussion.

In the next chapter, we take you through the steps of creating a Training Facilities database. Managers and administrators use this application to evaluate and track the resources of multiple work sites around the country. This particular database critiques conference, hotel, and other facilities that are rented as locations for training seminars. The evaluations are used by a company to plan and schedule training that it conducts in many major cities. The information helps the company to identify possible sites that it must reserve far in advance for upcoming seminars.

► ► CHAPTER **25**

Training Facilities

►► **F**AST **T**RACK

▶ **The response-type forms inherit default field values** **820**

from main document form type. When you define the attributes for the two response-type forms, you select the Inherit default field values option in the Form Attributes dialog box. This option allows field values to be passed from one document to another.

▶ **The Training Site Profile form** **827**

gives a company the means to organize and display the most current background data that's available on a site. An Evaluator assesses its facilities and equipment, as well as gives it an overall rating. The form can identify trainers who have worked at the site and who can be contacted for more information later on. The form also includes a field for entering comments, where an Evaluator can elaborate on the strengths and shortcomings of a site.

▶ **The Site Evaluation form** **842**

is designed to display a lengthy description of a particular site (if the Evaluator wants to elaborate). The structure of the Training Site Profile form doesn't give an Evaluator the room to add a descriptive evaluation of a site except for the Evaluator's Comments section at the bottom of the form.

▶ **The Evaluator's Comments form** **846**

is designed to display a lengthy written evaluation of a particular site, including the Evaluator's personal comments (if the Evaluator wants to elaborate). The structure of the other two forms don't give an Evaluator the room to add a descriptive evaluation of a site except for the Evaluator's Comments section at the bottom of each of the forms.

►► *he* Training Facilities database is based on an evaluation tracking database that we located in the Application Library of the
Lotus Communications forum on CompuServe. We modified
the application in order to make it useful for evaluating multiple work
sites, which in this case are training facilities located around the country. This chapter takes you through the steps of designing the forms
and views for the Training Facilities database. It assumes you have been
given either Designer or Manager access designation, so you can create
the database for your organization. The chapter covers:

- Defining each form's attributes
- Adding fields
- Formatting the forms
- Creating the views
- Writing the selection formulas

This database combines the best features of a typical tracking-discus-
sion application to help users who work in, say, a training or consultants firm, to write and maintain site evaluations. The information can
be used to plan future training seminars, which are conducted in different cities. The database enables a person, such as a Training Manager
or Administrator, to evaluate potential sites for hosting future training
courses and seminars.

The Training Facilities database gives members of a workgroup—called
Evaluators—the means to write detailed evaluations of training sites.
An Evaluator can compose a training site profile, site evaluation, or
Evaluator's comments document to add to the database. Feedback
from trainers and attendees can also be added to the documents easily.
Once the documents are part of the database, other members of the
workgroup, such as an administrator, can open the views and read the
Evaluators' comments, which are displayed below the name of the

THE LOGISTICS OF CONDUCTING PROFESSIONAL TRAINING

Professional training and executive education courses represent a huge—and lucrative—market today. People in almost every type of business often need continuing education in their particular area of work in order to learn new skills (or maintain the skills they have).

Continuing education has traditionally been provided by colleges and universities, which deliver short, intensive courses through local extension programs. However, enrollment and the number of course offerings are often limited.

The main advantage that a training company has over an extension program is that the training company can bring the classroom to the student, wherever the person lives. However, the logistics of planning nation-wide training seminars are complex and depend on accurate appraisals of facilities and the resources they can offer. Conducting seminars in cities around the country entails finding sites that offer convenient locations in close proximity to hotel accommodations, as well as adequate facilities and equipment that are suited for hands-on training and demonstrations.

facility. The database displays the comments in the views in this way to enable an administrator to get a quick assessment of a particular site.

The following figures show examples of the views available in the Training Facilities database. Figure 25.1 displays the Training Site Profile view, which shows an alphabetical listing of all the profiles in the database. Figure 25.2 shows the By Region view, which displays an alphabetical and categorized listing of training site profiles by region. Figure 25.3 displays the By City/Trainer view, which shows a listing of training sites, categorized by city, and the names of the trainer(s) who have worked at the sites.

FIGURE 25.1 ▶

The Training Site Pro-
file view displays an
alphabetical listing of
all the training site profiles in the Training
Facilities database.

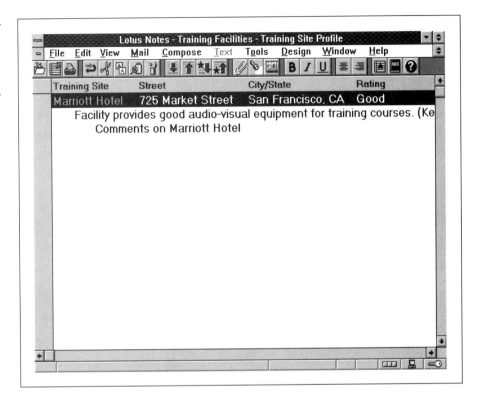

▶▶ *What Does the Training Facilities Database Do?*

You can use the Training Facilities database to collect evaluations of sites for future training seminars. An Evaluator can post this information to the database and then an administrator can refer to it. The database shows how a Notes tracking application can facilitate quick and effective information exchange within a firm, thus supporting the workflow process. Figure 25.4 displays a Training Site Profile document for a particular site. Figure 25.5 shows the Site Evaluation document for the same site. Figure 25.6 displays an Evaluator's Comments document about the site. Anyone can revise information in these forms to reflect the status of a particular training site. The Evaluator can update the database periodically by notifying the workgroup that a particular site is undergoing renovations, expanding its facilities, unavailable on a specific date, and so on.

FIGURE 25.2 ▶

The By Region view shows an alphabetical (and categorized) listing of training site profiles by region.

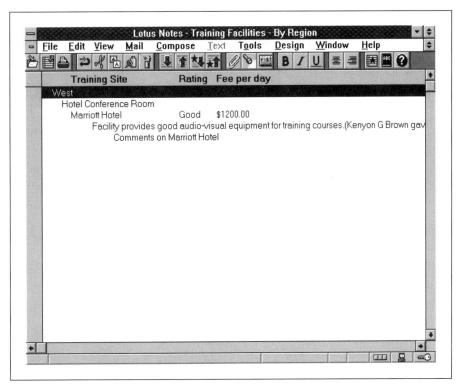

As we mentioned above, the database provides the means to streamline workflow through a group. Evaluators write profiles on training sites and then can categorize the profiles in two of the views. (However, each view sorts and categorizes researchers' profiles differently.) An administrator uses these profiles to select particular sites for planning training seminars. Scheduling seminars and reserving facilities must often be planned up to two years in advance. Competition among training companies for large room rentals (especially in hotels) is fierce because of limited facilities. Training companies must also compete for space with other organizations and individuals who plan activities, such as trade shows, conferences, banquets, and receptions. Therefore, an administrator depends on the evaluations for providing accurate information that can be used in making long-term plans.

FIGURE 25.3 ▶

The By City/Trainer view displays a listing of training sites, which are categorized by city, and the names of the trainer(s) who have worked at the sites.

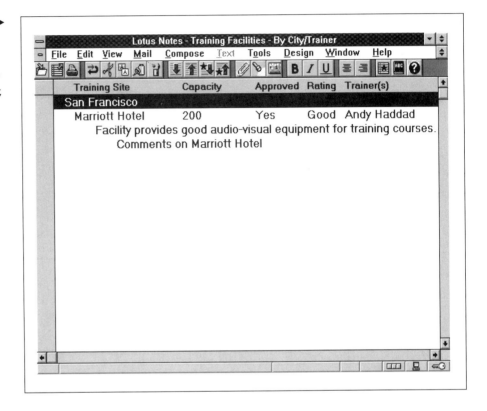

To access profiles, you can choose one of the three views, which display, sort, and/or categorize the three kinds of documents:

- **By City/Trainer**: Displays an alphabetical and categorized listing of training site profiles by the city where the facility is located, and by the trainer(s) who have conducted training seminars at the facility.

- **By Region**: Displays an alphabetical and categorized listing of training site profile documents by geographical region.

- **Training Site Profile**: Displays an alphabetical listing of training site profile documents by the name of the facility.

A Training Site Profile document contains complete background information on a facility; the structure of a profile is the same for each facility. Therefore, information can be accessed quickly and easily. Simply select one of the three views, open a document, and read it.

FIGURE 25.4 ▶

A Training Site Profile document provides an easy way to enter background data on a particular site.

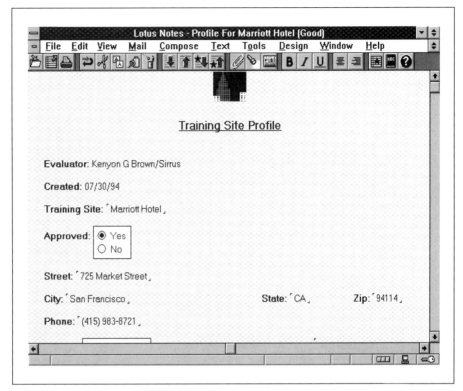

Information can be added easily to documents in the database. Users can add information by:

- Entering data in a document
- Importing data from a word processor

By composing new documents, Evaluators add more training site profiles to the database. Thus, the importance (and relevance) of the database increases because the evaluations reflect extensive firsthand knowledge of particular sites. They can include anecdotes from trainers in the field and feedback from attendees. Decisions to use particular sites are subsequently based on this information.

Evaluators can also import information from other sources in two ways, either as a new Notes document or as data in a specific field. (You can also attach a word processing file to a document.) Each of the forms contains one or more Comments fields that are rich text fields.

FIGURE 25.5 ▶

A Site Evaluation document can display a lengthy description of what a possible training site can offer.

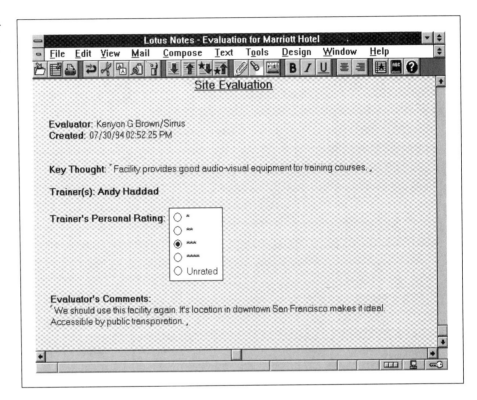

You'll recall that you can attach files, link, and import data into a rich text field. By importing a companion word-processed document that's been written by, say, a trainer, you're adding other relevant background information to a particular document.

▶ Important Features of the Training Facilities Database

The Training Facilities database includes the following important features:

- All three form types are used to identify and display a hierarchy of documents in the views.

- Form names appear in numerical order on the Compose menu to identify the order in which a person would use them.

- Each form name includes a synonym that is referenced in formulas.

FIGURE 25.6 ▶

The Evaluator's Comments document shows an Evaluator's comments on a particular site.

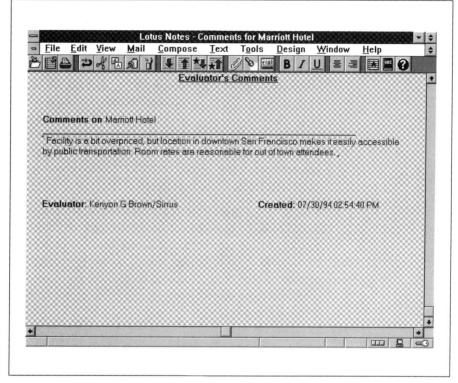

- The Site Evaluation and Evaluator's Comments forms inherit several default field values from the Training Site Profile form.

All three form types are used to identify and display a hierarchy of documents in the views. The Training Site Profile form is the main Document form type. The Site Evaluation form is a Response to Document form type. The Evaluator's Comments form is a Response to Response form type. By using all three form types, the hierarchy of the documents can be displayed in the views. When a person opens one of the views, the relationship between the documents can be seen immediately.

Form names appear in numerical order on the Compose menu to identify the order in which a person would use them. By preceding each form name with a number that you enter in the Name text box in the Form Attributes dialog box, you create a particular sequence that's displayed on the Compose menu. This sequence can correspond to the form types of the documents. For example, a main Document form type could appear as 1 on the menu, a Response to Document form type could appear as 2, and a Response to Response form type could appear as 3. This numbering scheme can help guide a user to compose documents in a specific order.

Each form name includes a synonym or "alias" that is referenced in formulas. When you define a form's attributes, you can include a synonym as part of the form's "proper" name. Using a synonym instead of the proper name (which can be long) makes it easier and more convenient to write selection formulas and other formulas that reference the form. From then on, if you make modifications to the form, including its proper name, the form can still be referenced in views as long as the synonym hasn't been changed.

The Site Evaluation and Evaluator's Comments forms inherit several default field values from the Training Site Profile form. When you define the attributes for the two response-type forms, you select the Inherit default field values option in the Form Attributes dialog box. This option allows field values to be passed from one document to another, which in turn allows for a consistent thread to be maintained across related documents.

▶ Who Should Use the Training Facilities Database?

An Evaluator can use the database when he or she has completed a new profile on a training site and is ready to post it for others to read. This can be done at any time (weekly, monthly, quarterly). Other members of a workgroup can use the database daily, to help determine what training sites should be reserved for upcoming seminars.

▶ Why Use the Training Facilities Database?

Evaluators will use this database as a vehicle to share their evaluations on training sites. Others will use this database to review the evaluations as they plan and schedule upcoming seminars. An Evaluator can be in the next room or in another city. By using Notes, an Evaluator can distribute his or her evaluations on training facilities to the entire company, thereby avoiding meetings, phone calls, express packages, or e-mail messages.

▶▶ *Using the Training Facilities Database*

To try out the Training Facilities database, you need to copy the file to your hard disk and then add the database to your Workspace. (You should read the directions on the inside back cover of the book for installing the sample databases on the Companion Disk to your system.) Click on the Training Facilities icon to select it. To compose a Training Site Profile document, follow these steps:

1. Choose Compose ➤ Training Site Profile. The blank document appears.

2. Fill in the profile on any facility you choose.

3. Press Ctrl+S to save the document.

4. Press Esc to return to the Workspace.

5. Choose View ➤ Training Site Profile. The Training Site Profile view appears. The document you just composed will be displayed.

6. Press Esc to close the view and to return to the Workspace.

To compose a Site Evaluation document, make sure the database is selected. Choose Compose ➤ Site Evaluation and then follow these steps:

1. Complete the document.

2. Press Ctrl+S to save the document.

3. Press Esc to close the document window.

4. Choose View ➤ By City/Trainer. The By City/Trainer view opens, displaying the document that you just composed. You'll notice that it appears indented below the Training Site Profile document you composed earlier.

5. Press Esc to close the window.

To compose an Evaluator's Comments document, make sure the database is selected. Choose Compose ➤ Evaluator's Comments and then follow these steps:

1. Complete the document.

2. Press Ctrl+S to save the document.

3. Press Esc to close the document window.

4. Choose View ➤ By Region. The By Region view opens, displaying "Comments..." to identify the document that you just composed. You'll notice it also appears indented below the Training Site Profile and Site Evaluation documents you composed earlier.

5. Press Esc to close the window.

▶ Importing a Word Processing File as a Notes Document

To import a word processing file and save it as a document in the database, follow these steps:

1. Select the database.

2. Choose a view.

3. Highlight a document to select it. (You don't need to open the document.)

4. Choose File ➤ Import. The Import dialog box appears.

5. Select the file you want to import in the File Name list box.

6. Select the File Type. (It will usually be Structured Text.)

7. Click on the Import button. If you chose the Structured Text file type, the Structured Text Import dialog box appears.

8. Select one of the existing form names from the Use Form list. The word processing file will become the form you choose.

9. Choose the form type from the Import As list, either as a main document or response document.

10. Click on OK. The Import as... message box appears, indicating the progress of the import.

▶ *Importing a Word Processing File into a Rich Text Field*

To import a word processing file into a specific rich text field, follow these steps:

1. Select the database.

2. Choose a view.

3. Open a document in Edit mode.

4. Place the insertion point in either the Comments from Trainer(s) field or the Evaluator's Comments field.

5. Choose File ➤ Import. The Import dialog box appears.

6. Select the file you want to import in the File Name list box.

7. Select the File Type. You should select Rich Text Format to retain the formatting attributes, margin settings, and page breaks.

8. Click on the Import button to begin the import.

When the import is complete, the data in the word processed document will appear in the field. Press Ctrl+S to save the document.

▶▶ *Creating the Training Facilities Database*

If you "test drove" the database by following the instructions above for composing documents and opening views, you saw firsthand how the application works. From this point on, we're going to take you through the steps of duplicating the Training Facilities database by creating it from scratch. You might ask yourself, "Can't I just install the database and use it as is?" The answer is yes. (We don't want you to feel as if we're forcing you to reinvent the wheel.) All you have to do after decompressing the Training Facilities database file is to follow the steps in Chapter 4 for adding the database to your Workspace.

Our main reason for helping you to duplicate the Training Facilities database is to reveal how it was designed. You could consider the process a variation of "backwards engineering." By recreating the database from scratch, you'll be able to analyze its design and look closely at its components. You'll experience firsthand the development process the designer was in engaged in as he created the application. Along the way, we'll point out interesting design tips and shortcuts that you can use when you create your own databases. You can always apply what you've learned about duplicating one database to a new database.

 ▶▶ **WARNING**

We've said it before but we'll say it again: Don't work with your only existing copy of the database. Make a backup copy of the database file and store it in a safe place before you add it to your Workspace. As you modify the Training Facilities database, you could remove one of the forms or views accidentally, or delete a doclink unintentionally. The database won't work correctly if an item is missing. Fortunately, you can remove it from your system and reinstall your backup copy if you damage the database.

Another reason for analyzing the Training Facilities database is to discover ways for customizing the application to suit your own needs. For example, you might decide that you don't like the layout of the forms. Perhaps you want to include more fields, or change the graphics that are used. You can customize the database if you desire. However, the database's unique structure is tightly integrated. If you start customizing the design, you might discover that it doesn't work correctly.

You're going start by creating a new database and naming it "Training Sites" (instead of "Training Facilities"). The database functions as a repository of background information on training sites. As a workflow-automation application, it provides the means for an Evaluator to assess a facility and write an evaluation on it. An administrator can then use the information to plan future training seminars at the sites. To create the database, follow these steps:

1. Choose File ➤ New Database. The New Database dialog box appears, as shown in Figure 25.7.

FIGURE 25.7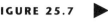

The New Database dialog box lets you name a new database and indicate where the database should be stored, on a server or on your workstation.

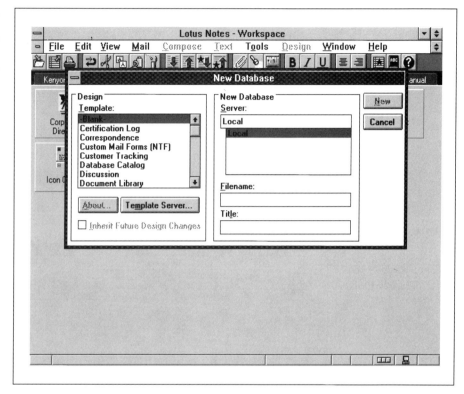

2. Make sure that -Blank- is highlighted in the Template list box.

3. Highlight the appropriate server name in the Server list box or choose Local to store the database on your workstation.

▶▶ **WARNING**

You should use a different file name when you recreate the database or Notes will respond by asking you if you want to replace the existing file. You don't! You should also give the database a new title so you don't confuse it with the existing title.

4. Enter **SITE2**, or another appropriate name, in the Filename text box. There's no need to include an extension because Notes appends .NSF to the file name automatically.

5. Enter **Training Sites,** or another appropriate name, in the Title text box. Just make sure the name is descriptive.

6. Click on OK. By default, a blank view appears.

7. Press Esc to close the view. You'll return to the Notes Workspace, which displays the new Training Sites title on the database's icon, as shown in Figure 25.8.

FIGURE 25.8 ▶

The Notes Workspace displays both the Training Facilities and the new Training Sites database icons.

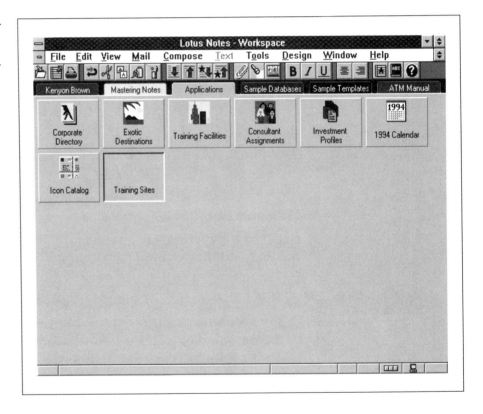

▶▶ **N O T E**

> An icon always appears in the Workspace, with the title
> you give the database; the "icon" is actually just a blank
> square until you create a graphic for it. You need to
> make sure the icon is always selected by clicking on it
> *before* you start creating any forms or views. Otherwise,
> you'll either save the forms or views to a database that
> you unknowingly selected or you won't be able to create
> the forms or views because you haven't selected a data-
> base. If a specific database isn't selected, the Design
> menu will appear dimmed. Subsequently, you won't be
> able to access the Views or Forms commands.

▶▶ *Duplicating the Forms*

The Training Facilities database uses three forms. The Training Site
Profile form is the main Document form type. The Site Evaluation
form is a Response to Document form type. The Evaluator's Comments form is a Response to Response form type. This use of all three
form types allows the response-type documents to inherit field values
from the Training Site Profile form, which enables a consistent thread
to be maintained across related documents, and it allows the hierarchy
of the documents to be displayed in the views.

▶ *Recreating the Training Site Profile Form*

The Training Site Profile form gives a company the means to organize
and display the most current background data that's available on a site.
An Evaluator assesses its facilities and equipment, and gives it an overall rating. The form can identify trainers who have worked at the site,
who can be contacted for more candid information. (Feedback and anecdotes from trainers can often provide insights that aren't reflected in
a document.) The form also includes a field for entering comments,
where an Evaluator can elaborate on the strengths and shortcomings of

a site. To create the Training Site Profile form, follow these steps:

1. Return to the Notes Workspace (if you aren't there already) and click on the database's icon to select it.

2. Choose Design ➤ Forms. The Design Forms dialog box appears, as shown in Figure 25.9.

3. Click the New button. A blank form appears, as shown in Figure 25.10.

You are now in Form Design mode, or just Design mode. The form is entirely blank because it is actually a large rich text field. You'll recall that a rich text field can contain graphics and objects as well as the formats you apply to text.

FIGURE 25.9 ▶

You begin designing a new form by opening the Design Forms dialog box.

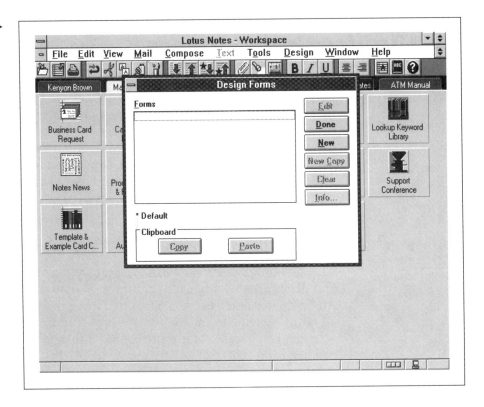

FIGURE 25.10 ▶

When you click the New button, a blank form appears.

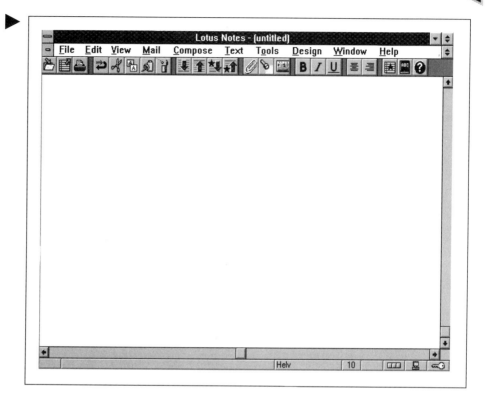

Defining the Training Site Profile Form's Attributes

A form may have a number of characteristics or *attributes* associated with it that give the form identity and establish important overall qualities of the form. An attribute can be as simple as the form's name, or it can be more sophisticated. For example, an attribute can specify whether or not information may be passed from another document to a document based on this form.

Certain attributes are mandatory. For these attributes you must provide a value or, sometimes, Notes provides a default value for you. Other attributes can be ignored entirely since they are used only in more obscure implementations. To define the Training Site Profile

FIGURE 25.11 ▶

The Design Form Attributes dialog box lets you specify a form's name, type, and other attributes.

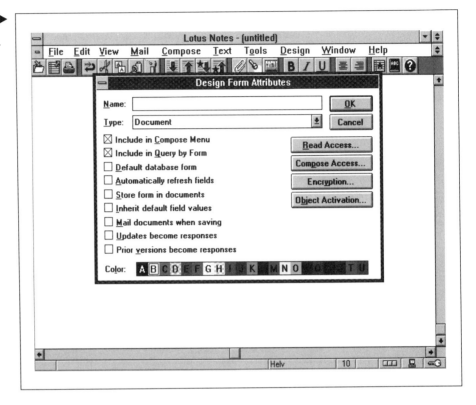

form's attributes, follow these steps:

1. Choose Design ➤ Form Attributes. The Design Form Attributes dialog box appears, as shown in Figure 25.11.

2. Enter **1. Training Site Profile | Profile** in the Name text box.

3. Make sure that the word *Document* appears in the Type box.

4. Select the following options (nothing else should be checked):

   - Include in Compose Menu
   - Include in Query by Form
   - Default Database Form

5. Click OK to accept the changes.

▶▶ **N O T E**

> **As we've discussed previously, by placing a number to the left of a form's name in the Design Form Attributes dialog box, you can force the Compose menu to display the forms in numerical order. Otherwise, the forms will appear in alphabetical order. If you design more than one form for a database and you want to display an informal hierarchy of forms to indicate the order in which a user would compose documents, including a number in the form's name is a good idea Also, by placing a synonym to the right of a form's name, you can reference the synonym in formulas. Otherwise, you'll have to enter the entire name of the form, which could be long, including a number if you've used one. Remember that you must precede the synonym with the | symbol.**

Creating a Title for a Form's Window Bar

You'll want to display a title in a form's window bar because it helps users to identify the form's name as they compose new documents. The title can also display useful information, such as the date and time, or a name or subject that is significant to the database. To create a title that will appear in the window's title bar, follow these steps:

1. Choose Design ➤ Window Title. The Design Window Title dialog box appears, as shown in Figure 25.12.

2. Enter the following statement in the Window Title Formula box. (This statement returns and displays in the window's title bar the name of the form and the name of the site that is entered in the Establishment field.)

@If(@IsNewDoc; "New Profile"; "Profile For " + Establishment + " (" + Rating + ")")

3. Click OK to confirm.

Each time a user composes a document using the Input Company Profile form, the title "New Profile" will appear in the window bar

FIGURE 25.12 ▶

The Design Window title dialog box lets you include a formula that returns a title that is displayed in the form's window bar.

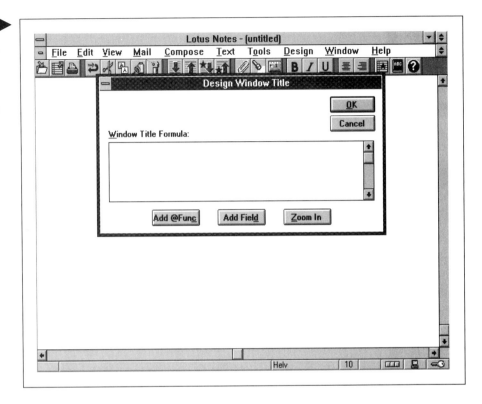

(without the quotation marks). When the user opens a view and selects a document to read or edit later on, the window bar will display the title "Profile for [*name of company entered in the form's Establishment field*]." The formula helps the user to quickly identify the subject of the document, which in this case is an establishment.

Inserting a Graphic in a Form

A graphic appears at the top of the Training Site Profile form. Like the table, the graphic is an object that's been inserted in the form. As we discussed in the previous chapter, you can insert graphic objects anywhere on a form because a form is actually a large, rich text field that can contain text and graphics.

When you click on the graphic to select it, a marquee will appear around it with a resizing handle in the lower right corner. The graphic might or might not also appear darkened (highlighted). If you hold the mouse button down while you point on the handle, you can drag the handle to increase or decrease the size of the graphic. This action is similar to the way you might modify the appearance of a graphic you've created in another application.

Insert the graphic using the method we described in previous chapters. You can either create your own graphic or copy the graphic from the existing form. Select the database and open the form. Select the graphic and then press Ctrl+C to copy it to the Clipboard. Position the insertion point in the new form and then press Ctrl+V to paste it. Change the size of the graphic by dragging the handle.

Adding Labels to the Form

Now you can add labels to the Training Site Profiles form in order to properly identify the fields. Use Figure 25.13 as a reference (or select the Training Facilities database and open the form to view it on screen). Unfortunately, entering and formatting static text can become arduous. You can either input all of the text at the same time and then

FIGURE 25.13 ▶

The Training Site Profile form reveals the labels and fields that are used to store background information on a particular facility.

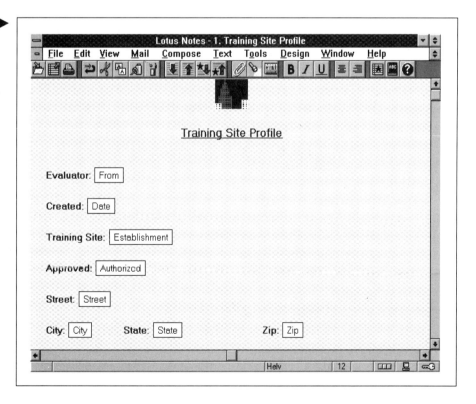

FIGURE 25.13 ►

The Training Site Pro-file form reveals the labels and fields that are used to store back-ground information on a particular facility (continued).

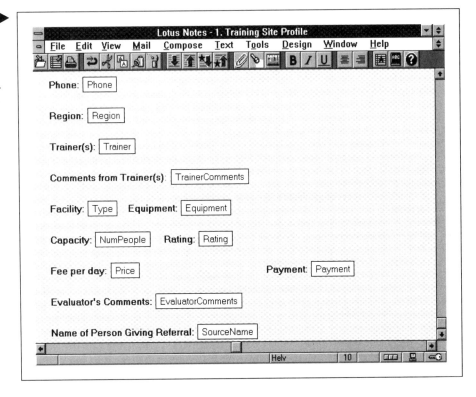

insert and define the fields later, or you can add one label at a time and then define its corresponding field. It's a toss-up which method is more time-consuming.

To begin, position the insertion point at the top of the form. You might have to press ↵ several times to move the table down until you position it where you want it on the form. (You might want to add a graphic at the top of the form, as we described above.) With the insertion point at the top of the form, select Center alignment. Enter **Training Site Pro-file**. Press ↵ to move the insertion point to the next line. At this point, you should change the alignment to Left. Continue adding the other la-bels, using Figure 25.13 as a reference.

Formatting the Labels

The methods you use to format text on a form are similar to methods of formatting text in most other Windows applications. However, as we mentioned in the previous chapter, Notes text formatting tools don't offer you the variety or sophistication of features that you'll find in other applications, especially word processors or desktop publishers.

> **TIP**
>
> **If you only need to apply a single formatting attribute to selected text, such as boldface or italics, you can do this faster by highlighting the text and then selecting the specific attribute from the Text menu. Open the menu and then click on the command you want in order to change the format. You can apply an attribute even faster by using keystroke combinations. Highlight the text and then press the appropriate keystroke(s) to make the format change, such as Ctrl+B for Bold or Ctrl+I for Italic.**

Defining the Fields

Now that we've entered all the static text and inserted a table and graphic on the Input Company Profile form, let's create and position the fields. To add the fields for the Input Company Profile form, follow the steps below to create the first one. You can add the remaining fields on your own:

1. Place the insertion point at the top of the form. (Use Figure 25.13 as a guide.)

2. Choose Design ➤ New Field. The Design New Field dialog box appears.

3. Click on OK to accept the default option. The Field Definition dialog box appears.

4. Enter the following information and options for "Evaluator" (unless already selected):

    Field Name: From

    Help Definition (optional): Original author of the document

    Data Type: Author Names

Field Type: Computed when composed

Formula: @Author

5. Click OK to accept the choices. The field will appear.

6. If you want to change the color of the text that will appear in the field, highlight the field and then choose Text ➤ Font. The Font dialog box appears.

7. Select a color from the Color Bar at the bottom of the dialog box.

8. Click on OK to confirm the change. The field's text color changes from black (the default) to the new color you selected.

Repeat the above steps to create the other fields. You can refer to Tables 25.1 and 25.2 to create the other fields. Table 25.1 summarizes all the field definitions, and Table 25.2 summarizes all the field formulas.

▶ **TABLE 25.1:** *A summary of field definitions for the Training Site Profile form*

LABEL NAME	FIELD NAME	DATA TYPE	FIELD TYPE
Evaluator	From	Author Names	Computed when composed
Created	Date	Time	Computed for display
Training Site	Establishment	Text	Editable
Approved	Authorized	Keywords (Radio Buttons): Yes No	Editable
Street	Street	Text	Editable
City	City	Text	Editable
State	State	Text	Editable
Zip	Zip	Text	Editable
Phone	Phone	Text	Editable
Region	Region	Keywords (Radio Buttons): East West	Editable

TABLE 25.1: *A summary of field definitions for the Training Site Profile form (continued)*

LABEL NAME	FIELD NAME	DATA TYPE	FIELD TYPE
		South	
		North	
Trainer(s)	Trainer	Text	Editable
Comments from Trainer(s)	TrainerComments	Rich Text	Editable
Facility	Type	Keywords (Check Boxes):	Editable
		Authorized Training Center	
		Hotel Conference Room	
		College/University Lab	
		Other	
Equipment	Equipment	Keywords (Check Boxes):	Editable
		Computer Workstations	
		Audio/Visual	
		Video	
		Laser Disc	
		Overhead Display	
		Other	
Rating	Rating	Keywords (Radio Buttons):	Editable
		Excellent	
		Good	
		Satisfactory	
		Poor	
Fee per Day	Price	Currency (2 Decimal Places)	Editable
Payment	Payment	Keywords (Check Boxes):	Editable
		Cash	
		Check	

▶ **TABLE 25.1:** *A summary of field definitions for the Training Site Profile form (continued)*

LABEL NAME	FIELD NAME	DATA TYPE	FIELD TYPE
		MC/Visa	
		American Express	
Evaluator's Comments	EvaluatorComments	Rich Text	Editable
Capacity	NumPeople	Number	Editable
Name of Person Giving Referral	SourceName	Text	Editable

▶ **TABLE 25.2:** *A summary of field formulas for the Training Site Profile form*

LABEL NAME	FIELD NAME	FORMULA
Evaluator	From	@Author
Created	Date	@Created
Training Site	Establishment	Input Translation Formula: @Trim(Establishment)
		Input Validation Formula: @If(Establishment = ""; @Failure ("You must enter an establishment name"); @Success
State	State	Input Translation Formula: @Trim(@UpperCase(State))
		Input Validation Formula: @If (@Length(State) !=2; @Failure ("You must enter a 2-character state code"); @Success)
Zip	Zip	Input Validation Formula: @If(@Length(Zip) = 5; @Success; @Length(Zip) = 10; @Success; @Failure("You must enter either five characters or the ten character extended zip code."))

▶ **TABLE 25.3:** *A summary of field formulas for the Training Site Profile form*

LABEL NAME	FIELD NAME	FORMULA
Trainer(s)	Trainer	Input Translation Formula: @Trim (@ProperCase (Trainer))
		Input Validation Formula: @If (Trainer = ""; @Failure ("You must enter a name of trainer");@Success)
Equipment	Equipment	Input Validation Formula: @If (Type = "College/University Lab" & Equipment = ""; @Failure ("You must enter equipment for all college/university labs."); @Success)
Rating	Rating	Default Value Formula: "Unrated"

Saving a Form

When you're finished creating a form (and after modifying a form), press Ctrl+S to save it. If you press Esc or Ctrl+W to close the window *before* saving the form, Notes will ask you if you want to save your changes. Click on Yes. You'll return to the Workspace.

We've already taken you through the steps of naming a form by entering its name in the Form Attributes dialog box. (You'll recall that a name is one of many attributes you can set for a form.) This name will appear on the Compose menu when users start composing documents with the form. However, while you're creating a form, you can place labels and fields and then save your work *before* you identify other specific attributes in the Form Attributes dialog box. (You can do this at a later time. However, until you specify the attributes you want, you'll have to be satisfied with using the default options.)

If you want to save a form without going through the steps of opening the Form Attributes dialog box and setting attributes (specifically, the form's name), press Ctrl+S. The Save Form dialog box appears. Enter a name in the Name text box and then click on OK. The name will appear on the Compose menu and in the Form Attributes dialog box. Just remember, however, that all you've done is saved the form under a specific name. You haven't set any other form attributes.

The change will take effect immediately. With the form window still open (you don't have to close it), you can pull down the Compose menu and click on the form's name. A blank document will open in which you can enter data in the fields. When you're finished composing the document, press Ctrl+S to save the information. To close the document's window, press Esc. Press Esc again to close the form's window and to return to the Workspace.

Formatting a Form

You format a form in order to change and enhance its appearance. Formatting allows your creative side to come out. By applying different formatting attributes, you help users to distinguish one form from another in the same database, and you give each form a distinctive look and feel. You can format a form after you've created it, or you can apply formats to a form while you're designing it. Some designers like to place the labels and fields and then format the form; others prefer to format a form as they go along.

Notes provides a set of formatting tools that is similar to those found in other Windows applications. For instance, you can change the background color of a form as well as format the labels and the text that users will enter in fields. The choices you make will be purely subjective, so keep in mind that a person will be using the form for data input. You don't want to overwhelm the user with a form that appears too busy.

You shouldn't clutter a form with too many different fonts and point sizes. You should keep the number of colors you use to a few and consider if they complement each other. If you decide to add a background color to the form (instead of white, the default), make sure the color of the labels and the field text contrast with it. You don't want the text to appear too light against the background.

The following instructions assume that you have created the Training Site Profile form and want to format it. We also assume that you placed all the labels and fields that we described earlier in the chapter. To change the form's background color, follow these steps:

1. If the form isn't open, click on the Training Facilities database icon to select it.

2. Choose Design ➤ Forms. The Design Forms dialog box appears.

3. Double-click on Training Site Profile (or highlight the form and click on the Edit button). The form window opens in Edit mode.

4. Choose Design ➤ Form Attributes. The Design Form Attributes dialog box appears.

5. To change the background color of the form from the default color, white, select another color from the bar at the bottom of the dialog box.

6. Click on OK to accept the change. The form's background color will reflect your choice.

7. Press Ctrl+S to save the form.

 ▶▶ **TIP**

When you highlight a label (any static text) on a form in order to apply formatting attributes, you can pull down the Text menu and choose one of several attributes directly from the menu. Just click on the command. You can also use the available keystroke combinations to execute the same commands.

To format the labels, follow the steps below. (You can format all the labels at one time without affecting the format of the fields because the fields are *plain text* fields; they will accept any formatting, although the data they contain will be stored internally in plain text format.)

1. Choose Edit ➤ Select All to highlight all the labels (and the text fields) at the same time.

2. Choose Text ➤ Font. The Font dialog box appears.

3. Change the font and point size if you wish.

4. Select one or more of the attribute options on the right, such as Bold.

5. Select a color for the text from the Color Bar at the bottom.

6. Click on OK to accept the changes. The labels will reflect your choices.

7. Press Ctrl+S to save the form.

▶ Recreating the Site Evaluation Form

The Site Evaluation form is designed to display a lengthy description of a particular site (if the Evaluator wants to elaborate). Figure 25.14 reveals the structure of the Site Evaluation form. The structure of the Training Site Profile form doesn't give an Evaluator the room to add a descriptive evaluation of a site except for the Evaluator's Comments section at the bottom of the form. Therefore, the Site Evaluation form

FIGURE 25.14 ▶

The Site Evaluation form reveals the labels and fields that are used to help an Evaluator add a lengthy description of a particular facility.

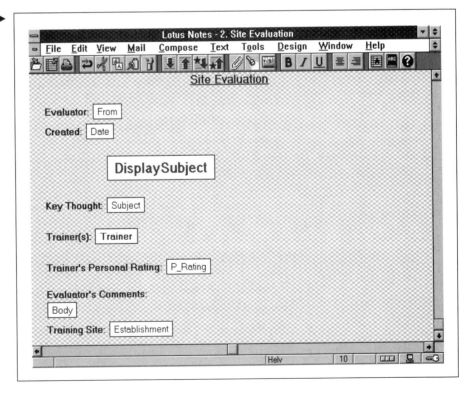

can be very useful to an Evaluator when making recommendations to the company.

To recreate the Site Evaluation form, follow these steps:

1. Select the Training Facilities database.
2. Choose Design ➤ Forms.
3. Click on the New button. A blank form appears.
4. Press Ctrl+S to save the form.
5. Either press Esc to return to the Workspace, or follow the steps in the next section.

Defining the Form's Attributes

To define the form's attributes, follow these steps:

1. Choose Design ➤ Form Attributes.
2. Enter **2. Site Evaluation | Evaluation** in the text box. (Make sure you precede the synonym with the | symbol.)
3. Select Response to Document as the type.
4. Select the Include in Compose Menu and Include In Query by Form options. (Don't check any other options.)
5. Click on OK to save the new attributes.
6. Press Ctrl+S to save the form.
7. Press Esc to return to the Workspace, or follow the steps below.

Defining the Window Title

To create a title that will appear in the window's title bar, follow these steps:

1. Choose Design ➤ Window Title. The Design Window Title dialog box appears.
2. Enter the following statement in the Window Title Formula box. (This statement returns and displays in the window's title bar the name of the form and the name of the site that is entered in the Establishment field.)

@If(@IsNewDoc; "Site Evaluation"; "Evaluation for " +
Establishment)

3. Click OK to confirm.

Defining the Fields

To add the labels and fields to the form, follow these steps:

1. Select the Training Facilities database if it isn't selected.

2. Choose Design ➤ Forms.

3. Double-click on Site Evaluation to edit the form. A blank form
appears.

4. Create and position the labels. (Use Figure 25.14 as a reference.)
You'll notice that "Site Evaluation" appears as a title at the top of
the form.

5. If you want to add a graphic, copy it from the Training Site Profile
form and then paste it in the desired location in this form.

6. Choose Design ➤ New Field to define each of the fields below:

> **Label**: Evaluator
>
> **Field Name**: From
>
> **Help Definition** (optional): Displays the document
> author
>
> **Data Type**: Author Names
>
> **Field Type**: Computed when composed
>
> **Formula**: @Author
>
>
> **Label**: Created
>
> **Field Name**: Date
>
> **Help Definition** (optional): Displays the creation date of
> the document
>
> **Data Type**: Time
>
> **Time Format**: mm/dd/yy hh:mm:ss
>
> **Field Type**: Computed for display
>
> **Formula**: @Created

Field Name: DisplaySubject

Help Definition (optional): Displays the subject value centered in the heading

Data Type: Text

Field Type: Computed for display

Formula: Subject

Label: Key Thought

Field Name: Subject

Help Definition (optional): Enter a brief description of your comments

Data Type: Text

Field Type: Editable

Label: Trainer(s)

Field Name: Trainer

Help Definition (optional): Inherits the value of the Rating field on the Training Site Profile form

Data Type: Names

Field Type: Computed when composed

Formula: Trainer

Label: Trainer's Personal Rating

Field Name: P_Rating

Help Definition (optional): Rate the site

Data Type: Keywords

Keyword User Interface: Radio Buttons

Allowable Keywords: *, **, ***, ****, Unrated

Field Type: Editable

Default Value Formula: "Unrated"

Label: Evaluator's Comments

Field Name: Body

Help Definition (optional): Enter your comments

Data Type: Rich Text

Field Type: Editable

Label: Training Site

Field Name: Establishment

Help Definition (optional): Inherits the value of the Establishment field on the Training Site Profile form

Data Type: Text

Field Type: Computed when composed

Formula: Establishment

7. Click on OK to save each field's definition.

8. Press Ctrl+S to save the form.

9. Press Esc to return to the Workspace.

▶ Recreating the Evaluator's Comments Form

The Evaluator's Comments form is designed to display a lengthy written evaluation of a particular site, including the Evaluator's personal comments (if the Evaluator wants to elaborate). Figure 25.15 displays the structure of the Evaluator's Comments form. The structure of the other two forms don't give an Evaluator the room to add a descriptive evaluation of a site except for the Evaluator's Comments section at the bottom of each of the forms. Therefore, the Evaluator's Comments form can be very useful to a company when choosing possible sites.

To recreate the Evaluator's Comments form, follow these steps:

1. Select the Training Facilities database.

2. Choose Design ➤ Forms.

3. Click on the New button. A blank form appears.

4. Press Ctrl+S to save the form.

5. Either press Esc to return to the Workspace, or follow the steps in the next section.

FIGURE 25.15

The Evaluator's Comments form reveals the labels and fields that are used to help an Evaluator add his or her personal comments on a particular facility.

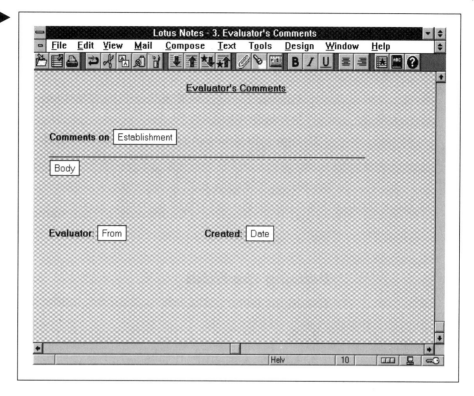

Defining the Form's Attributes

To define the form's attributes, follow these steps:

1. Choose Design ➤ Form Attributes.

2. Enter **3. Evaluator's Comments | Comments** in the text box. (Make sure you precede the synonym with the | symbol.)

3. Select Response to Response as the type.

4. Select the Include in Compose Menu and Include In Query by Form options. (Don't check any other options.)

5. Click on OK to save the new attributes.

6. Press Ctrl+S to save the form.

7. Press Esc to return to the Workspace, or follow the steps below.

Defining the Window Title

To create a title that will appear in the window's title bar, follow these steps:

1. Choose Design ➤ Window Title. The Design Window Title dialog box appears.

2. Enter the following statement in the Window Title Formula box. (This statement returns and displays in the window's title bar the name of the form and the name of the site that is entered in the Establishment field.)

   @If(@IsNewDoc; "Comments"; "Comments for " + Establishment)

3. Click OK to confirm.

Defining the Fields

To add the labels and fields to the form, follow these steps:

1. Select the Training Facilities database if it isn't selected.

2. Choose Design ➤ Forms.

3. Double-click on Evaluator's Comments to edit the form. A blank form appears.

4. Create and position the labels. (Use Figure 25.15 as a reference.) You'll notice that "Evaluator's Comments" appears as a title at the top of the form.

5. If you want to add a graphic, copy it from the Training Site Profile form and then paste it in the desired location in this form.

6. Choose Design ➤ New Field to define each of the fields below:

   Label: Comments on

   Field Name: Establishment

   Help Definition (optional): Inherits the value from the Establishment field on either the Training Site Profile form or the Site Evaluation form

   Data Type: Text

   Field Type: Computed when composed

   Formula: Establishment

Field Name: Body
Help Definition (optional): Enter your comments
Data Type: Text
Field Type: Editable

Label: Evaluator
Field Name: From
Help Definition (optional): Displays the author's name
Data Type: Author Names
Field Type: Computed when composed
Formula: @Author

Label: Created
Field Name: Date
Help Definition (optional): Displays the creation date of the document
Data Type: Time
Time Format: mm/dd/yy hh:mm:ss
Field Type: Computed for display
Formula: @Created

7. Click on OK to save each field's definition.
8. Press Ctrl+S to save the form.
9. Press Esc to return to the Workspace.

▶▶ *Duplicating the Views*

The Training Facilities database includes three views:

- **By City/Trainer** displays an alphabetical listing of sites by city and the trainer(s) who have conducted training at the site.
- **By Region** displays an alphabetical listing of sites by region.

- **Training Site Profile** displays an alphabetical listing of sites by name, in ascending order.

These views allow you to find information on particular sites quickly and easily.

► *Defining the By City/Trainer View*

Let's create the By City/Trainer view for the Training Facilities database. This view displays an alphabetical listing of sites by city and the trainer(s) who have conducted training at each particular site. The columns in the view correspond to the field values in the Training Site Profile form. To create the view, follow these steps:

1. Select the Training Facilities database in the Workspace.

2. Choose Design ➤ Views. The Design Views dialog box appears, as shown in Figure 25.16.

FIGURE 25.16 ►

The Design Views dialog box lets you create a new view for a selected database.

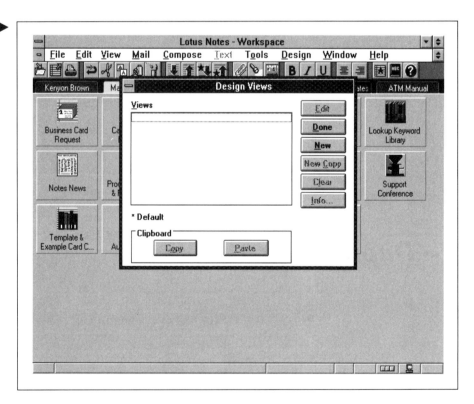

TIP

> You can choose the New Copy and Paste options to create a view if another view already exists. The New Copy option allows you to create a view by copying an existing view in the database. Simply highlight the view you wish to copy from the list of views displayed in the dialog box and select New Copy. The Paste option lets you create a view by pasting a view from another database into the current database. You must first open the other database, choose Design ➤ Views, highlight the desired view, and click on Copy. Then choose Design ➤ Views in the target database and click on Paste. The pasted view should now appear in the list of views in the dialog box.

3. Click on the New button, which allows you to create a view from scratch. A blank view window appears in Design mode, as shown in Figure 25.17.

Defining the View's Attributes

You'll notice that the current name of the view is [untitled]. Associated with each view is a set of attributes that assign certain general characteristics to the view. One of the attributes is the view's name. To define view attributes, follow these steps:

1. While in View Design mode, choose Design ➤ View Attributes. The Design View Attributes dialog box appears, as shown in Figure 25.18.

2. Enter **By City/Trainer** in the Name text box.

FIGURE 25.17 ►

A blank view appears in Design mode when you want to define a new view.

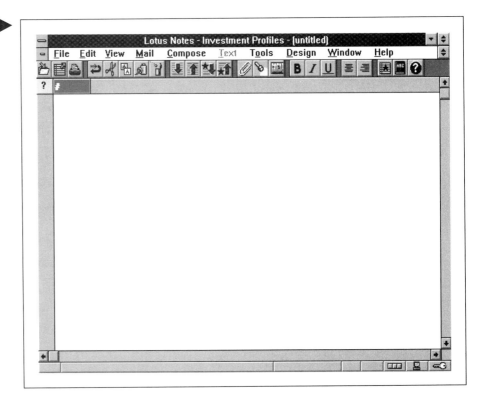

► ► TIP

You can create an *accelerator key* for a view name by placing an underscore to the left of a letter in the name. An accelerator key allows the user to open a menu and then press the specific key in order to execute a command, which in this case is opening a particular view. When a database has several views, using accelerator keys are a convenient way to open the views quickly.

3. Select the Shared View option if it's not selected. (It's the default.)

4. Click on the Categories button to specify that categories in the view will be fully expanded.

5. Click on OK to accept the changes.

FIGURE 25.18

The Design View Attributes dialog box lets you define the attributes for a particular view.

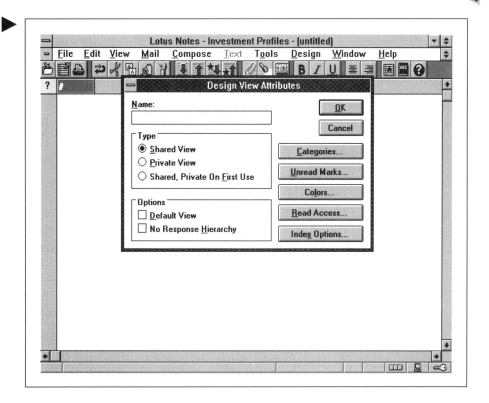

Defining the Selection Formula

To ensure that a view will include only documents that meet a specific criteria, we have to make use of a selection formula. When applied to a view, a selection formula simply narrows the scope of the view to include only a subset of documents in the database, excluding all others. A selection formula expresses the criteria that a document must meet in order to be included in the view.

When you choose Design ➤ Selection Formula, the Design Selection Formula dialog box appears, as shown in Figure 25.19. As you can see, the statement **SELECT @All** appears in the Selection Formula box. This is the default selection formula. It returns the selection of *all* documents in a database to appear in a particular view, which in this case is the By City/Trainer view. There's no need to modify the formula. Press Esc to close the dialog box.

FIGURE 25.19 ▶

The Design Selection Formula dialog box lets you enter a formula that selects the documents you want to display in a particular view. The default statement SELECT @All appears in the Selection Formula box.

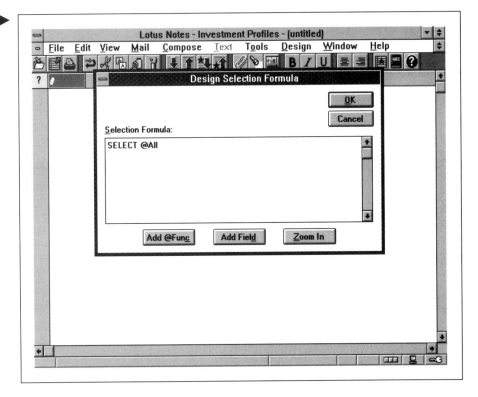

Defining the Columns

For the By City/Trainer view, you are going to define eight columns. To define each of other columns, follow these steps:

> *1.* Double-click on the leftmost column. The Design Column Definition dialog box appears, as shown in Figure 25.20.

  TIP

Double-click on a column heading (the box at top of the column) to display the Design Column Definition dialog box.

FIGURE 25.20

The Design Column Definition dialog box lets you define a column, which in this case uses the @IsExpandable ("+";"") formula to indicate that the current level of documents can be expanded in the view.

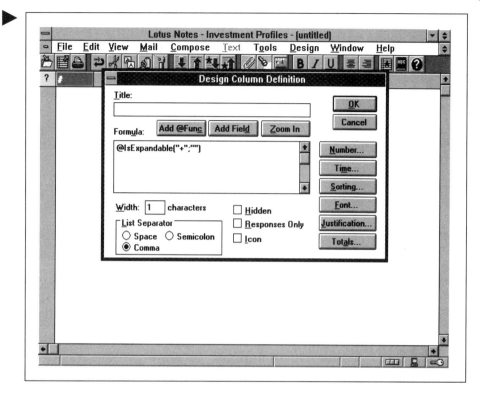

2. Leave the Title text box blank; don't assign a title to the column.

3. Enter the statement **@IsExpandable("+";"")** in the Formula box. (It indicates that the current level of documents can be expanded.)

4. Set the width of the column in the Column Width box to 1.

5. Click on the Font button. The Font dialog box appears.

6. Select Helv, 10, Bold.

7. Click on OK to accept your choices.

Defining the Other Columns in the View

To define the other columns in the By City/Trainer view, follow these steps:

1. For the second column, enter the following definitions:

Title: not assigned

Formula: City

Width: 1

List Separator: Comma

Number: General (Default)

Sorting: Ascending, Categorized

Font: Helv, 10, Bold

Justification: Left (default)

Totals: None (Default)

2. For the third column, enter the following definitions:

Title: not assigned

Formula: @If(Form = "Evaluation";Subject + "("
+@Name([CN]; From) + "gave it a " +P_Rating + ")";
"Comments on " + Establishment)

Width: 1

List Separator: Comma

Number: General (Default)

Sorting: None

Font: Helv, 10, Bold

Justification: Left

Totals: None (Default)

3. For the fourth column, enter the following definitions:

Title: Training Site

Formula: Establishment

Width: 15

List Separator: Comma

Number: General (Default)

Sorting: Ascending

> **Font**: Helv, 10, Bold
> **Justification**: Left (default)
> **Totals**: None (Default)

4. For the fifth column, enter the following definitions:

> **Title**: Capacity
> **Formula**: NumPeople
> **Width**: 10
> **List Separator**: Comma
> **Number**: General (Default)
> **Sorting**: None
> **Font**: Helv, 10, Bold
> **Justification**: Left (default)
> **Totals**: None (Default)

5. For the sixth column, enter the following definitions:

> **Title**: Approved
> **Formula**: Authorized
> **Width**: 7
> **List Separator**: Comma
> **Number**: General (Default)
> **Sorting**: None
> **Font**: Helv, 10, Bold
> **Justification**: Left (default)
> **Totals**: None (Default)

6. For the seventh column, enter the following definitions:

> **Title**: Rating
> **Formula**: Rating
> **Width**: 5
> **List Separator**: Comma
> **Number**: General (Default)
> **Sorting**: None

> **Font**: Helv, 10, Bold
>
> **Justification**: Left (default)
>
> **Totals**: None (Default)

7. For the eighth column, enter the following definitions:

> **Title**: Trainer(s)
>
> **Formula**: Trainer
>
> **Width**: 20
>
> **List Separator**: Comma
>
> **Number**: General (Default)
>
> **Sorting**: None
>
> **Font**: Helv, 10, Bold
>
> **Justification**: Left (default)
>
> **Totals**: None (Default)

As you can see, you can use the default definitions for most of the items. This will save you a lot of time when you have a several columns to define.

Saving the View

Although you may have clicked on OK in different dialog boxes to accept changes you made to different elements in a view, you still need to save the view before closing it and returning to the Workspace or another open window. When you want to save the changes you made to a view, press Ctrl+S. If you press Esc before you save the changes, a message box will appear, asking you if you want to save your changes. Click on Yes. You'll return to the Workspace or another window that may be open.

▶ Duplicating the Other Views

You'll need to repeat the above steps in order to define the other views. You can assume that the default options apply unless indicated otherwise.

▶ Defining the By Region View

The By Region view shows an alphabetical listing of training sites by region. To create the view, follow these steps:

1. Select the Training Facilities database in the Workspace.

2. Choose Design ➤ Views. The Design Views dialog box appears.

3. Click on the New button, which allows you to create a view from scratch. A blank view window appears in Design mode.

Defining the View's Attributes

To define the view's attributes, follow these steps:

1. While in View Design mode, choose Design ➤ View Attributes. The Design View Attributes dialog box appears.

2. Enter **By Region** in the Name text box.

3. Select the Shared View option if it's not selected. (It's the default.)

4. Click on the Categories button to specify that categories in the view will be fully expanded.

5. Click on OK to accept the changes.

Defining the Selection Formula

As before, when you choose Design ➤ Selection Formula, the Design Selection Formula dialog box appears. The statement **SELECT @All** will work for this view as well; there's no need to modify the formula. Press Esc to close the dialog box.

Defining the Columns

For the By Region view, you are going to define seven columns. To define the first column, follow these steps:

1. Double-click on the leftmost column. The Design Column Definition dialog box appears.

2. Leave the Title text box blank; don't assign a title to the column.

3. Enter the statement **@IsExpandable("+";"")** in the Formula box.

4. Enter **1** in the Column Width box.

5. Click on the Font button. The Font dialog box appears.

6. Select Helv, 10, Bold.

7. Click on OK to accept your choices and the default settings.

To define the other columns in the By Region view, follow these steps:

1. For the second column, enter the following definitions:

> **Title**: not assigned
> **Formula**: Region
> **Width**: 1
> **Number**: General (Default)
> **Sorting**: Ascending, Categorized
> **Font**: Helv, 10, Bold
> **Justification**: Left
> **Totals**: None (Default)

2. For the third column, enter the following definitions:

> **Title**: not assigned
> **Formula**: Type
> **Width**: 1
> **Number**: General
> **Sorting**: Ascending, Categorized
> **Font**: Helv, 10, Bold
> **Justification**: Left
> **Totals**: None (Default)

3. For the fourth column, enter the following definitions:

> **Title**: not assigned
> **Formula**: @If (Form = "Evaluation"; Subject + "(" +
> @Name ([CN]; From) + "gave it a" + P_Rating + ")";
> "Comments on" + Establishment)
> **Width**: 1
> **Responses Only**: Yes
> **Number**: General (Default)

Sorting: None
Font: Helv, 10, Bold
Justification: Left
Totals: None (Default)

4. For the fifth column, enter the following definitions:

Title: Training Site
Formula: Establishment
Width: 15
Number: General
Sorting: Ascending
Font: Helv, 10, Bold
Justification: Left
Totals: None (Default)

5. For the sixth column, enter the following definitions:

Title: Rating
Formula: Rating
Width: 6
Number: General (Default)
Sorting: None (Default)
Font: Helv, 10, Bold
Justification: Left
Totals: None (Default)

6. For the seventh column, enter the following definitions:

Title: Fee per day
Formula: Price
Width: 8
List Separator: Comma
Number: Currency (2 Decimal Places)
Sorting: None (Default)
Font: Helv, 10, Bold
Justification: Left
Totals: None (Default)

7. Press Ctrl+S to save the view.

As you can see, you can use the default definitions for most of the items. This will save you a lot of time when you have several columns to define.

▶ Defining the Training Site Profile View

The Training Site Profile view displays an alphabetical listing of all training sites in the database. The view sorts the documents in ascending order. To create the view, follow these steps:

1. Select the Training Facilities database in the Workspace.

2. Choose Design ➤ Views. The Design Views dialog box appears.

3. Click on the New button, which allows you to create a view from scratch. A blank view window appears in Design mode.

Defining the View's Attributes

To define the view's attributes, follow these steps:

1. While in View Design mode, choose Design ➤ View Attributes. The Design View Attributes dialog box appears.

2. Enter **Training Site Profile** in the Name text box.

3. Select the Shared View option if it's not selected.

4. Select Default Database View option.

5. Click on the Categories button to specify that categories in the view will be fully expanded.

6. Click on OK to accept the changes.

▶ Defining the Selection Formula

To define the selection formula for the Training Site view, simply leave the **SELECT @All** statement in the Selection Formula box. This formula returns the selection of *all* documents in the database. Press Esc to close the dialog box.

Defining the Columns

For the Training Site Profile view, you are going to define five columns. To define the first column, follow these steps:

1. Double-click on the leftmost column. The Design Column Definition dialog box appears.

2. Leave the Title text box blank; don't assign a title to the column.

3. Enter the following statement in the Formula box. (It returns the name of the Evaluator and the rating the person gave the training site on the Site Evaluation form.)

   @If (Form = "Evaluation"; Subject + "(" + @Name ([CN]; From) + "gave it a" + P_Rating + ")"; "Comments on " + Establishment)

4. Enter 1 in the Column Width box.

5. Click on the Font button. The Font dialog box appears.

6. Select Helv, 10, Bold.

7. Click on OK to accept your choices and the default options.

To define the other columns in the Training Site Profile view, follow these steps:

1. For the second column, enter the following definitions:

   Title: Training Site
   Formula: Establishment
   Width: 12
   List Separator: Comma
   Number: General (Default)
   Sorting: Ascending
   Font: Helv, 10, Bold
   Justification: Left (Default)
   Totals: None (Default)

2. For the third column, enter the following definitions:

   Title: Street
   Formula: Street
   Width: 15

List Separator: Comma
Number: General (Default)
Sorting: None
Font: Helv, 10, Bold
Justification: Left (Default)
Totals: None (Default)

3. For the fourth column, enter the following definitions:

Title: City/State
Formula: City + "," State
Width: 15
List Separator: Comma
Number: General (Default)
Sorting: Ascending
Font: Helv, 10, Bold
Justification: Left (Default)
Totals: None (Default)

4. For the fifth column, enter the following definitions:

Title: Rating
Formula: Rating
Width: 6
List Separator: Comma
Number: General (Default)
Sorting: Ascending
Font: Helv, 10, Bold
Justification: Left (Default)
Totals: None (Default)

5. Press Ctrl+S to save the view.

6. Press Esc to close the view window and return to the Workspace.

▶▶ *Testing the Database*

As we discussed at the end of Chapter 14, you should get in the habit of testing the functionality of a new database once you're finished creating the forms and views. All you need to do is compose a few documents based on each form in order to check if you can enter data correctly without getting any error messages.

Next, you should open each of the views to see if the documents are displayed correctly. If a view doesn't display any documents, open the view in Edit mode and check its selection formula. Usually, a view doesn't display documents because the selection formula is wrong. If the selection formula is correct, you should check the formula for each column's definition in order to make sure that the column is referencing the correct field. If a column isn't referencing the correct field, the view won't return (and display) the value for that field.

Many errors occur in Design mode when you're creating forms and fields, and defining their contents. In fact, most errors are the result of typos that you introduce when you include the names of fields and forms in formulas. Sometimes an error message will give you a clue that Notes can't find a specific name of a form or a field. You'll have to open a form and check the spelling of the field names.

▶▶ *What's Next?*

The Training Facilities database is a good example of an application that can aid users in writing and tracking evaluations in Notes. Decisions are made on the basis of the evaluations, which in this case are taken from planning and coordinating training seminars in various cities around the country. The database gives employees of a training company the means to assess the evaluations and to choose the appropriate sites for conducting seminars. It presents information in a way that can involve people in an ongoing evaluation process.

In the next chapter, we take you through the steps of creating the Consultant Assignments database that we mentioned frequently in Part One. It works effectively as a companion application to the Training

Facilities database because documents can be doclinked. The Consultant Assignments database allows an organization to maintain a directory of consultants around the country and to assign them to training seminars near where they live.

CHAPTER 26

Consultant Assignments

► ► *F*AST *T*RACK

uses buttons to automate tasks, and enables the Training Facilities database to doclink to Consultant Directory Entry documents in order to access additional background data of consultants.

▶ ***To compose an Consultant Directory Entry document***   **881**

choose Compose ➤ 1. Consultant Directory Entry. The blank document appears. Fill in the entry on any person you choose. Press Ctrl+S to save the document. Press Esc to return to the Workspace. Choose View ➤ Consultant Directory. The view appears. The document you just composed will be displayed. Press Esc to close the view and to return to the Workspace.

▶ ***To compose a Site Location Entry document***   **882**

make sure the database is selected. Choose Compose ➤ 2. Site Location Entry. Complete the document. Press Ctrl+S to save the document. Press Esc to close the document window. Choose View ➤ Training Site Location. The view opens, displaying the document that you just composed. Press Esc to close the window.

▶ ***To see how the Input Change Request form works***   **882**

select the Consultant Assignments database. Open the Consultant Directory view and select a document. (You don't need to open the document.) Choose Compose ➤ 3. Input Change Request. A document appears, displaying the current information on a person. Complete the document. Click on the Send Change Request button. The Document Save dialog box appears. Choose the options you want. Click on the Yes button. The document is sent to the administrator.

►► ***T**he* Consultant Assignments database is a *server-based* personnel directory application that we located in the Application Library of the Lotus Communications forum on CompuServe. We've modified it extensively in order to help an organization to track independent contractors (known as "consultants") and retain them to provide certain services, such as designing training seminars, writing technical documentation, or conducting usability testing at various sites around the country. This chapter takes you through the steps of designing the forms and views for the Consultant Assignments database. It assumes you have been given either Designer or Administrator access designation, so you can create databases. The chapter covers:

- Defining each form's attributes
- Adding fields
- Formatting the forms
- Creating the views
- Writing the selection formulas

Unlike the other databases that we've discussed so far, this database must be stored on a server because it references people whose names are included in an organization's public Name & Address Book. The database can be also be referenced by the Training Facilities database that you created in the previous chapter. One of the forms in that database can access the information in one of the forms in the Consultant Assignments database by using doclinks.

The database you'll create in this chapter is a good example of an application that can aid users in maintaining personnel information in Notes. An administrator can use the information to track the whereabouts and availability of consultants to take on new assignments. This database is also a good starting point for developing an application that can track team members working on projects in different locations, such as field technicians, sales specialists, visiting home care nurse practitioners, and so on. It his combines the best features of an evaluation-tracking-discussion application.

The Consultant Assignments database enables an organization to gather and maintain personnel data on in-house staff as well as consultants who live in different cities. The background information on consultants is used to hire them for assignments near where they live. The database functions as a directory of all employees in an organization. As a workflow-automation application, it provides the means for an administrator to track and update information on each employee, such as address changes, promotions, terminations, and so on.

Since the organization transfers employees to its other regional offices around the country, changes in an employee's status, such as title and address, can be forwarded to the administrator for input. In this way, a current personnel file on every employee can be maintained easily.

The Consultant Assignments database also gives the administrator the means to gather data on employees and then to use the data to make assignments. Like any good discussion database, this database presents information in a way that can engage people in meaningful and substantive discourse. The administrator can compose an Consultant Directory Entry document or a Site Location Entry document to add to the database. The following two figures show views listing these two kinds of documents. Figure 26.1 shows the Consultant Directory view and Figure 26.2 displays the Training Site Locations view. Figure 26.3 shows the Availability view, which lists consultants and their current availability.

►► *What Does the Consultant Assignments Database Do?*

Anyone can use the Consultant Assignments database as a repository of background data on employees. An administrator can post information to the database and then other staff members can refer to it.

An administrator can create two main types of documents for this database: Consultant Directory Entry documents for all consultants, as shown in Figure 26.4, and Site Location Entry documents for all

FIGURE 26.1 ▶

The Consultant Directory view shows a listing of the employees of a company.

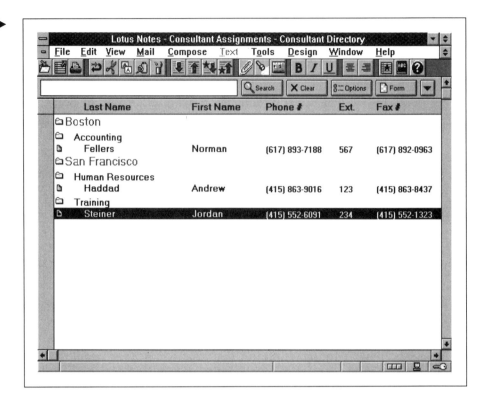

training sites, as shown in Figure 26.5. In order to update the information on a Consultant Directory Entry document, any member of the workgroup can compose an Input Change Request and send it to an administrator, as shown in Figure 26.6.

The database provides the means to streamline workflow through a group. An administrator enters background data on an employee and can categorize the data in the Consultant Directory view. The administrator subsequently uses the information to make training assignments.

The structure of a Consultant Directory Entry is the same for each person. Therefore, information can be accessed quickly and easily. A user simply selects the Consultant Directory view, opens a document, and reads it. A document contains complete background data on a person, which can be accessed by the Training Facilities database. (The Training Site Profile form includes an Additional Information field. When a person composes a document, he or she may include a doclink in the

FIGURE 26.2 ▶

The Training Site Locations view displays a listing of training sites by city.

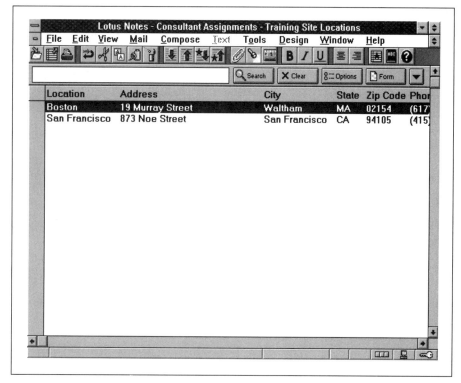

rich text field, which accesses the information in the Consultant Directory Entry document.)

To obtain information about a person, the user selects the Consultant Directory view, which selects, sorts, and categorizes Consultant Directory Entry documents, and the Training Site Locations view, which lists the location of each training site. The user can also select the Availability view to check the current availability of employees.

▶ Important Features of the Consultant Assignments Database

The Consultant Assignments database includes the following important features:

- Allows importing of information from a word processor to the Consultant Directory Entry document

FIGURE 26.3 ▶

The Availability view shows a listing of employees and their current availability.

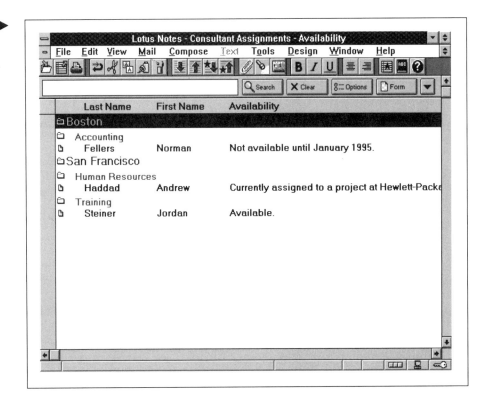

- Uses @DbLookups of documents in the Training Site Locations view to furnish data to the Location field in the Consultant Directory Entry form

- Displays current data on the Input Change Request document to make it easier for a person to compose the document and send to the administrator

- Uses buttons to automate tasks

- Enables the Training Facilities database to doclink to Consultant Directory Entry documents in order to access additional background data of consultants

Importing Information from a Word Processor

A administrator can import information from a word processed document to a Consultant Directory Entry document. By using a word processor, an administrator can collect additional background data on

FIGURE 26.4 ▶

A Consultant Directory Entry document provides an easy way to enter background data on a particular contractor

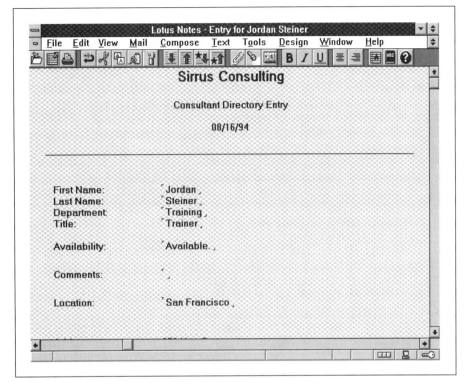

an individual before importing the information into the Consultant Assignments database. He or she can then post that information in the database for the other members of the workgroup (or the rest of the company) to use.

Using the DbLookup Function

By using @DbLookups of columns in the Training Site Locations view to furnish data to the Location field in a Consultant Directory Entry document, users can automate the task of updating the contents of the field. The utility of a view doesn't end at simply being a "table of contents" to the database. A view can also serve another very useful purpose: as a lookup table of data, which can be integrated into the design of a form.

Consider a typical keywords field in a form. The "allowable keywords" are usually a list of text items that you specify in the Design Keyword Format dialog box. However, you can build a list of allowable keywords

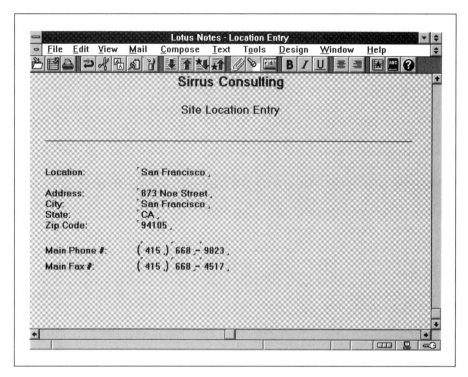

automatically by specifying a *formula* that returns the contents of a *column* from one of your views (in the same database or even an entirely separate one).

The Consultant Directory Entry form includes a field named "Location," whose data type is Keywords. Since the Training Site Locations view displays the Site Location Entry documents that users compose, the view can be used as a source of choices contained in the Location field.

When the insertion point is moved to the Keywords field, a user can just choose from a list of locations that have been identified as allowable keywords; the list of locations changes every time a person adds a new Site Location Entry document to the database (or removes a document). Such a dynamic approach keeps the list of locations in the Keywords field current. This is where using a "lookup" of the contents of a view comes into play.

FIGURE 26.6 ▶

An Input Change Request document enables a person to identify changes in an employee's background data and then send the request to the Personnel Administrator.

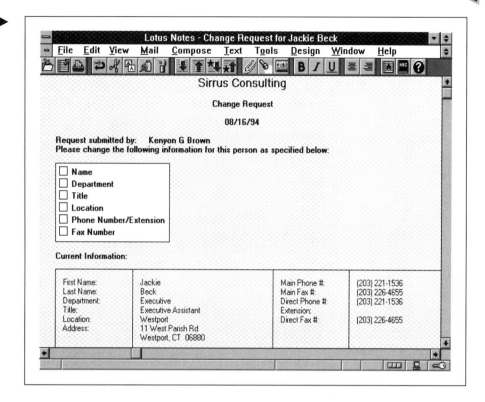

By using the @DbColumn function in the Location field's keyword formula, you instruct Notes to return the contents of a particular column from the Training Site Locations view, which in this case is the Location column. Now, any time the Locations view changes—such as when an entry is added or removed—the list of keywords that are displayed through the Location field in a Directory Entry document will automatically reflect the change!

Using the Input Change Request Form

When a person wants to update a Consultant Directory Entry document on an individual, he or she must first select the document in the Consultant Directory view. Next, the person chooses the Input Change Request form from the Compose menu. The Input Change Request document subsequently displays the current background data on a person, which makes it easier for the requester to compose the document and send to the Personnel Administrator.

Using Buttons to Automate Tasks

The Consultant Directory Entry form includes a Save & Exit Button that displays the address, main telephone number, and main fax number of a location *after* a site has been entered in the Location field. (If you press Ctrl+S to save the form instead of clicking on the button, the information will appear automatically.) As we discussed above, the data in the Location field is furnished automatically by the Training Site Locations view.

The Input Change Request form includes two buttons: Send Change Request and Apply Change Request. A user clicks on the Send Change Request button after he or she has composed the document. The request is sent via a Notes Mail memo to a designated administrator or administrator. Once the person has received the request, he or she approves or denies it. If the request is approved, the person clicks on the Apply Change Request button to update the specific information in the Consultant Directory Entry document.

Doclinking Forms in Different Databases

The information in a Consultant Directory Entry document can be accessed by a Training Site Profile document in the Training Facilities database. The Training Site Profile document contains an Additional Information field. Since the field's data type is Rich Text, a person can include a doclink in the field that links to the data contained in a Consultant Directory Entry document. Because both of these documents serve different purposes, it is a good design idea to keep the data in separate documents and use a doclink. This keeps the information in the documents succinct and uncluttered.

▶ Who Should Use the Consultant Assignments Database?

An administrator can use the database when she or he has completed a new entry on an individual and is ready to post it. This can be on any schedule required (weekly, monthly, quarterly…). Anyone else can use the database daily to help determine the availability of contractors for specific assignments.

▶ *Why Use the Consultant Assignments Database?*

Administrators will use this database as a vehicle to track the availability of independent contractors and trainers. Others will use this database to review the background data on individuals. A administrator can be in the next room or halfway around the world. By using Notes, an administrator can distribute staff background data to the entire company, thereby avoiding meetings, phone calls, express packages, or e-mails.

Notes also allows the administrator to use a word processor to write additional information. When ready, the administrator can then import the information to the Notes database using File ➤ Import. For anyone using the database, Notes' user interface makes it easy to scan the information put together by the administrator.

▶▶ *Using the Consultant Assignments Database*

To try out the Consultant Assignments database, you need to copy the file to your hard disk and add the database to your Workspace. Click on its icon to select it and follow these steps:

1. To compose an Consultant Directory Entry document, choose Compose ➤ 1. Consultant Directory Entry. The blank document appears.

2. Fill in the entry on any person you choose.

3. Press Ctrl+S to save the document.

4. Press Esc to return to the Workspace.

5. Choose View ➤ Consultant Directory. The view appears. The document you just composed will be displayed.

6. Press Esc to close the view and to return to the Workspace.

To compose a Site Location Entry document, make sure the database is selected. Choose Compose ➤ 2. Site Location Entry and then follow these steps:

1. Complete the document.

2. Press Ctrl+S to save the document.

3. Press Esc to close the document window.

4. Choose View ➤ Training Site Location. The view opens, displaying the document that you just composed.

5. Press Esc to close the window.

To see how the Input Change Request form works, select the Consultant Assignments database and follow these steps:

1. Open the Consultant Directory view and select a document. (You don't need to open the document.)

2. Choose Compose ➤ 3. Input Change Request. A document appears, displaying the current information on a person.

3. Complete the document.

4. Click on the Send Change Request button. The Document Save dialog box appears.

5. Choose the options you want.

6. Click on the Yes button. The document is sent to the administrator.(This assumes that Notes Mail is set up properly and there is an mail address for the "administrator.")

You can press Esc to close the window and return to the Workspace.

▶▶ *Creating the Consultant Assignments Database*

If you "test drove" the database by following the instructions above for composing documents and opening views, you saw firsthand how the application works. From this point on, we're going to take you through the steps of duplicating the Consultant Assignments database by creating it from scratch. You might ask yourself, "Can't I just install the database and use it as is?" The answer is yes. (We don't want you to feel as if we're forcing you to reinvent the wheel.) All you have to do after decompressing the Consultant Assignments database file is to follow the steps in Chapter 4 for adding the database to your Workspace.

Our main reason for helping you to duplicate the Consultant Assignments database is to reveal how it was designed. You could consider the process a variation of "backwards engineering." By recreating the database from scratch, you'll be able to analyze its design and look closely at its components. You'll experience firsthand the development process the designer was in engaged in as he created the application. Along the way, we'll point out interesting design tips and shortcuts that you can use when you create your own databases. You can always apply what you've learned about duplicating one database to a new database.

  WARNING

We've said it once but we'll say it again: Don't work with your only existing copy of the database. Make a backup copy of the database file and store it in a safe place before you add it to your Workspace. As you modify the Consultant Assignments database, you could remove one of the forms or views accidentally, or delete a doclink unintentionally. The database won't work correctly if an item is missing. Fortunately, you can remove it from your system and reinstall your backup copy if you damage the database.

Another reason for analyzing the Consultant Assignments database is to discover ways for customizing the application to suit your own needs. For example, you might decide that you don't like the layout of the forms. Perhaps you want to include more fields, or change the graphics that are used. You can customize the database if you desire. However, the database's unique structure is tightly integrated. If you start customizing the design, you might discover that it doesn't work correctly.

You're going to create a new database and name it "Training Assignments" to distinguish it from "Consultant Assignments" so you don't confuse the two files. The database functions as a repository of background information on staff members. As a workflow-automation application, it provides the means for an administrator to gather personnel data on employees and anyone else to use the information in order to make work assignments. To create the Consultant Assignments database, follow these steps:

1. Choose File ► New Database. The New Database dialog box appears, as shown in Figure 26.7.

2. Make sure that -Blank- is highlighted in the Template list box.

3. Highlight the appropriate server name in the Server list box or choose Local to store the database on your workstation.

FIGURE 26.7 ►

The New Database dialog box lets you name a new database and indicate where the database should be stored, on a server or on your workstation.

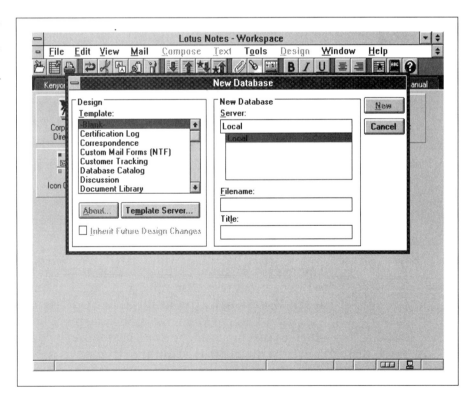

►► WARNING

> You should use a different file name when you recreate the database or Notes will respond by asking you if you want to replace the existing file. You don't! You should also give the database a new title so you don't confuse it with the existing title.

4. Enter **CONSULT2**, or another appropriate name, in the File-name text box. There's no need to include an extension because Notes appends .NSF to the file name automatically.

5. Enter **Training Assignments**, or another appropriate name, in the Title text box. Just make sure the name is descriptive.

6. Click on OK. By default, a blank view appears.

7. Press Esc to close the view. You'll return to the Notes Workspace, which displays the new Training Assignments title on database's icon, as shown in Figure 26.8.

►► NOTE

> An icon always appears in the Workspace with the title you give the database; the "icon" is actually just a blank square until you create a graphic for it. You need to make sure the icon is always selected by clicking on it *before* you start creating any forms or views. Otherwise, you'll either save the forms or views to a database that you unknowingly selected or you won't be able to create the forms or views because you haven't selected a database. If a specific database isn't selected, the Design menu will appear dimmed. Subsequently, you won't be able to access the Views or Forms commands.

FIGURE 26.8 ▶

The Notes Workspace displays the title on the new Training Assignments database icon. You'll notice that the Consultant Assignments database icon also appears.

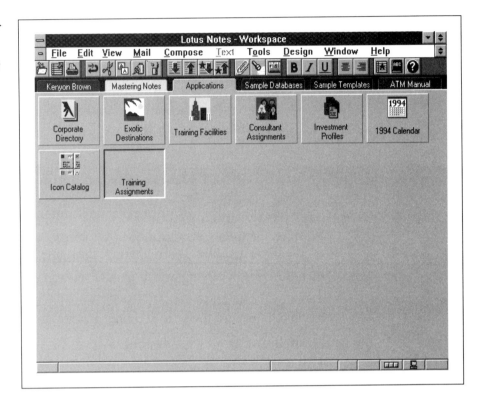

▶▶ *Duplicating the Forms*

The Consultant Assignments database utilizes three forms: a Consultant Directory Entry form, a Site Location Entry form, and an Input Change Request form. These forms are ready for members of a workgroup to use for composing documents on specific individuals and training sites.

All the documents can be updated easily, which is important since the data can change often. A administrator can revise data in a specific document by choosing a view and then selecting and opening a particular document in Edit mode. Once the information is updated, the document can again be posted so other people in the workgroup can use it. In this way, everyone has access to the most current background information on a specific person.

▶ Recreating the Consultant Directory Entry Form

The Consultant Directory Entry form enables a administrator to input, organize, and store background data on a individual. The form displays the most current information on a person and tracks the person's availability. To create the form, follow these steps:

1. Return to the Notes Workspace (if you aren't there already) and click on the Consultant Assignments database (or the new name you gave the database) icon to select it.

2. Choose Design ➤ Forms. The Design Forms dialog box appears, as shown in Figure 26.9.

3. Click the New button. A blank form appears, as shown in Figure 26.10.

FIGURE 26.9 ▶

You begin designing the Consultant Directory Entry form by opening the Design Forms dialog box.

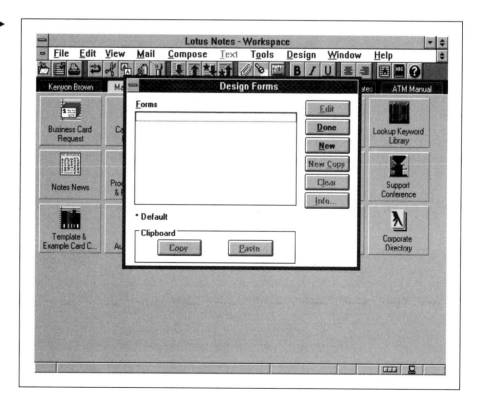

FIGURE 26.10

When you click the New button, a blank form appears.

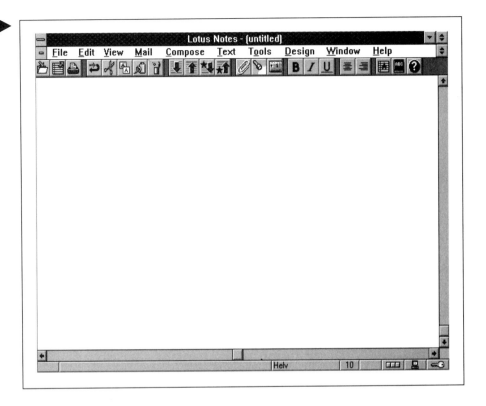

Defining the Form's Attributes

A form may have a number of characteristics, or *attributes*, associated with it that give the form identity and establish important overall quali-ties of the form. An attribute can be as simple as the form's name, or it can be more sophisticated. For example, an attribute can specify whether or not information may be passed from another document to a docu-ment based on this form.

Certain attributes are mandatory. For these attributes you must pro-vide a value or, sometimes, Notes provides a default value for you. Other attributes can be ignored entirely since they are used only in more obscure implementations. To define the Consultant Directory Entry form's attributes, follow these steps:

1. Choose Design ➤ Form Attributes. The Design Form Attributes dialog box appears, as shown in Figure 26.11.

2. Enter **1. Consultant Directory Entry** in the Name text box.

FIGURE 26.11

The Design Form Attributes dialog box lets you specify a form's name, type, and other attributes.

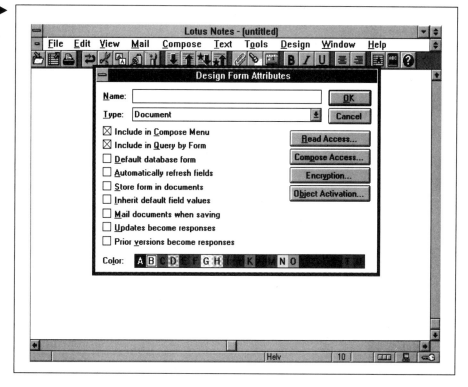

3. Make sure that Document appears in the Type box.

4. Select the following options (nothing else should be checked):

- Include in Compose Menu
- Include in Query by Form
- Default Database Form

5. Click OK to accept the changes.

Creating a Title for the Form's Window Bar

You'll want to display a title in a form's window bar because it helps users to identify the form as they compose new documents. The title can also display useful information, such as the date and time, or a name or subject that is significant to the database. To create a title that will appear in the window's title bar, follow these steps:

1. Choose Design ➤ Window Title. The Design Window Title dialog box appears, as shown in Figure 26.12.

2. Enter the following statement in the Window Title Formula box. (This statement returns and displays in the window's title bar the name of the form and the name of the person that is entered in the Name field.)

   @If(@IsNewDoc; "New Directory Entry"; "Entry for " + FirstName + " " + LastName)

3. Click OK to confirm.

FIGURE 26.12 ▶

The Design Window Title dialog box lets you include a formula that returns a title that is displayed in the Consultant Directory Entry form's window bar.

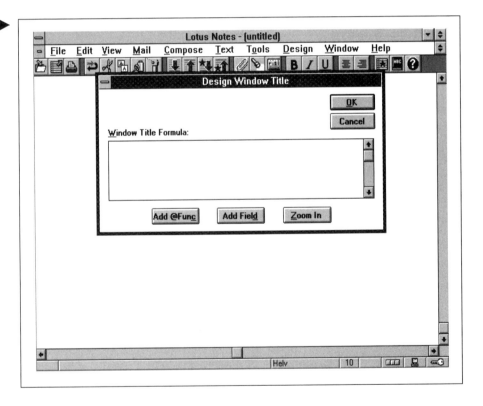

Each time a user composes a document using the Consultant Directory Entry form, the title "New Directory Entry" will appear in the window bar (without the quotation marks). When the user opens a view and selects a document to read or edit later on, the window bar will display the title "Entry for [*name of person*]," returning the values of the form's FirstName and LastName fields. The formula helps the user to quickly identify the subject of the document, which in this case is a person.

Adding Labels to the Form

Now you can add labels to the form in order to properly identify the fields. Unfortunately, entering and formatting static text can become arduous. You can either input all of the text at the same time and then insert and define the fields later, or you can add one label at a time and then define its corresponding field. It's a toss-up which method is more time-consuming.

To begin, position the insertion point at the top of the form. You might have to press ↵ several times to move the table down until you position it where you want it on the form. With the insertion point at the top of the form, select Center alignment. Enter **Sirrus Consulting** (or another name). Press ↵ to move the insertion point to the next line. Enter **Consultant Directory Entry** (making sure that it's also center aligned). Then continue adding the other labels, using Figure 26.13 as a reference.

Formatting the Labels

The methods you use to format text on a form are similar to those for formatting text in most other Windows applications. However, as we mentioned in the previous chapter, Notes text formatting tools don't offer you the variety or sophistication of features that you'll find in other applications, especially word processors or desktop publishers.

FIGURE 26.13 ▶

The structure of the Consultant Directory Entry form reveals the placement of labels and fields.

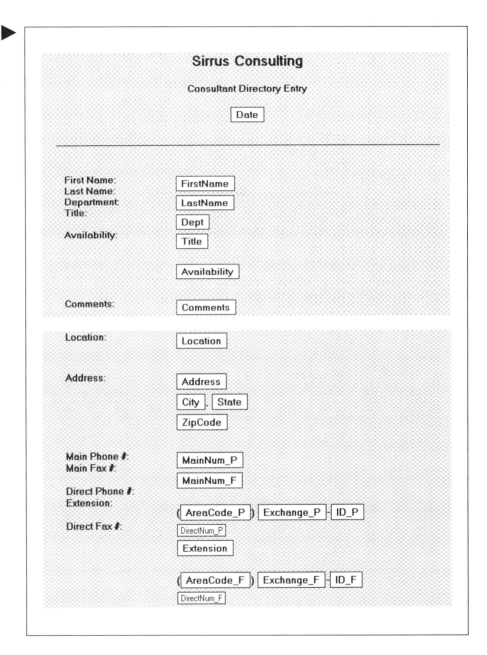

▶▶ **TIP**

If you only need to apply a single formatting attribute to selected text, such as boldface or italics, you can do this faster by highlighting the text and then selecting the specific attribute from the Text menu. Open the menu and then click on the command you want in order to change the format. You can apply an attribute even faster by using keystroke combinations. Highlight the text and then press the appropriate keystroke(s) to make the format change, such as Ctrl+B for Bold or Ctrl+I for Italic.

Defining the Fields

Now that you've entered all the static text on the Consultant Directory Entry form, you can create and position the fields. To add the first field on the form, follow the steps below. You can add the remaining fields on your own:

1. Place the insertion point at the top of the form. (Use Figure 26.13 as a guide.)

2. Choose Design ➤ New Field. The Design New Field dialog box appears.

3. Click on OK to accept the default option. The Field Definition dialog box appears.

4. Enter the following information (unless already indicated):

   Name: Date

   Help Definition (optional): Today's date

   Data Type: Time

   Time Format: mm/dd/yy

   Field Type: Computed for display

   Formula: @Today

5. Click OK to accept the changes. The field will appear.

6. If you want to change the color of the text that will appear in the field, highlight the field and choose Text ➤ Font. The Font dialog box appears.

7. Select a color from the Color Bar at the bottom of the dialog box.

8. Click on OK to confirm the change. The field's text color changes from black (the default) to the new color you selected.

Repeat the above steps to create the other fields, using Figure 26.13 as a reference. You can refer to Tables 26.1 and 26.2 to define the other fields. Table 26.1 summarizes all the form's field definitions, and Table 26.2 summarizes all the field formulas.

▶ **TABLE 26.1:** *A summary of field definitions for the Consultant Directory Entry form*

LABEL NAME	FIELD NAME	DATA TYPE	FIELD TYPE
	Date	Time	Computed for display
First Name	FirstName	Text	Editable
Last Name	LastName	Text	Editable
Department	Dept	Keywords (Standard):	Editable
		Accounting	
		Administration	
		Engineering	
		Executive	
		Human Resources	
		Manufacturing	
		Research & Development	
		Sales & Marketing	
		Training	
Title	Title	Text	Editable
Availability	Availability	Text	Editable
Comments	Comments	Rich Text	Editable
Location	Location	Keywords	Editable

TABLE 26.1: *A summary of field definitions for the Consultant Directory Entry form (continued)*

LABEL NAME	FIELD NAME	DATA TYPE	FIELD TYPE
Address	Address	Text	Computed
	City	Text	Computed
	State	Text	Computed
	ZipCode	Text	Computed
Main Phone #	MainNum_P	Text	Computed
Main Fax #	MainNum_F	Text	Computed
Direct Phone #	AreaCode_P	Text	Editable
	Exchange_P	Text	Editable
	ID_P	Text	Editable
	DirectNum_P	Text	Computed
Extension	Extension	Text	Editable
Direct Fax #	AreaCode_F	Text	Editable
	Exchange_F	Text	Editable
	ID_F	Text	Editable
	DirectNum_F	Text	Computed

TABLE 26.2: *A summary of field formulas for the Consultant Directory Entry form*

Label Name	Field Name	Formula
First Name	FirstName	Input Translation Formula: @ProperCase(FirstName)
		Input Validation Formula: @If(FirstName = ""; @Failure ("You must enter a first name before saving this document!"); @Success)
Last Name	LastName	Input Translation Formula: @ProperCase(LastName)
		Input Validation Formula: @If(LastName = ""; @Failure ("You must enter a last name before saving this document!"); @Success)
Title	Title	Input Translation Formula: @ProperCase(Title)

▶ **TABLE 26.2:** *A summary of field formulas for the Consultant Directory Entry form (continued)*

Label Name	Field Name	Formula
Location	Location	Allowable Keywords Formula: @DbColumn (""; ""; "Training Site Locations"; 1)
Address	Address	@If(Location != ""; @DbLookup (""; ""; "Training Site Locations"; Location; "Address"); "")
	City	@If(Location != ""; @DbLookup (""; ""; "Training Site Locations"; Location; "City"); "")
	State	@If(Location != ""; @DbLookup (""; ""; "Training Site Locations"; Location; "State"); "")
	ZipCode	@If(Location != ""; @DbLookup (""; ""; "Training Site Locations"; Location; "ZipCode"); "")
Main Phone #	MainNum_P	@If(Location != ""; @DbLookup (""; ""; "Training Site Locations"; Location; 6); "")
Main Fax #	MainNum_F	@If(Location != ""; @DbLookup (""; ""; "Training Site Locations"; Location; 7); "")
Direct Phone #	AreaCode_P	Input Translation Formula: @If(AreaCode_P = ""; @DbLookup (""; ""; "Training Site Locations"; Location; "AreaCode_P"); AreaCode_P)
	Exchange_P	Input Translation Formula: @If(Exchange_P = ""; @DbLookup (""; ""; "Training Site Locations"; Location; "Exchange_P"); Exchange_P)
	ID_P	Input Translation Formula: @If(ID_P = ""; @DbLookup (""; ""; "Training Site Locations"; Location; "ID_P"); ID_P)
	DirectNum_P	"(" + AreaCode_P + ")" + Exchange_P + "-" + ID_P
Direct Fax #	AreaCode_F	Input Translation Formula: @If(AreaCode_F = ""; @DbLookup (""; ""; "Training Site Locations"; Location; "AreaCode_F"); AreaCode_F)
	Exchange_F	Input Translation Formula: @If(Exchange_F = ""; @DbLookup (""; ""; "Training Site Locations"; Location; "Exchange_F"); Exchange_F)
	ID_F	Input Translation Formula: @If(ID_F = ""; @DbLookup (""; ""; "Training Site Locations"; Location; "ID_F"); ID_F)
	DirectNum_F	"(" + AreaCode_F + ")" + Exchange_F + "-" + ID_F

Adding the Save & Exit Button

The Consultant Directory Entry form includes a Save & Exit button. When a user places the insertion point in a document's Location field and presses the spacebar (or presses ⏎) to display the choices in the Allowable Keywords dialog box, the location's address and main telephone and fax numbers don't appear immediately. However, when the user clicks on the Save & Exit button (or presses Ctrl+S to save the document), Notes fills in the Address, City, State, Zip Code, Main Phone #, and Main Fax # fields.

You'll recall that these fields are *Computed fields*, and the information in these fields is furnished by the Training Site Locations view by using a @DbLookup of the Location column. When the user clicks on the button, Notes fills in the "missing" information automatically, and closes the document window. To create the button, follow these steps:

1. Place the insertion point at the bottom of the form.

2. Click on the Text Align Center SmartIcon, or choose Text ➤ Alignment ➤ Center, to center the button.

3. Choose Edit ➤ Insert ➤ Button. The Insert Button dialog box appears, as shown in Figure 26.14.

4. Enter **Save & Exit** in the Button Text box.

5. Enter the following statement in the Formula box:

   @Command([FileSave]); @Command([FileCloseWindow])

6. Click on OK to accept the choices.

The button appears on the form, as shown in Figure 26.15. As you can see, it displays the name that you gave it.

▶ Saving the Form

When you're finished creating a form (and after modifying a form), press Ctrl+S to save it. If you press Esc or Ctrl+W to close the window *before* saving the form, Notes will ask you if you want to save your changes. Click on Yes. You'll return to the Workspace.

FIGURE 26.14 ▶

The Insert Button dialog box lets you define a button that you insert on a form.

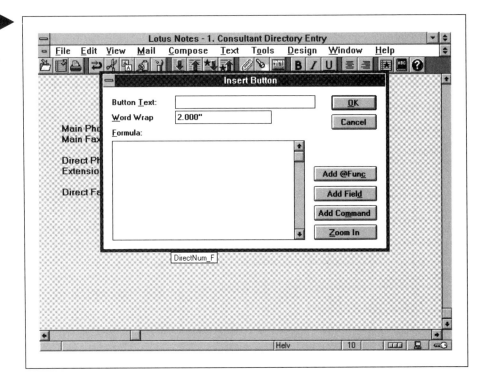

We've already taken you through the steps of naming a form by entering its name in the Form Attributes dialog box. (You'll recall that a name is one of many attributes you can set for a form.) This name will appear on the Compose menu when users start composing documents with the form. However, while you're creating a form, you can place labels and fields and then save your work *before* you identify other specific attributes in the Form Attributes dialog box. (You can do this at a later time. However, until you specify the attributes you want, you'll have to be satisfied with using the default options.)

If you want to save a form without going through the steps of opening the Form Attributes dialog box and setting attributes (specifically, the form's name), press Ctrl+S. The Save Form dialog box appears. Enter a name in the Name text box and then click on OK. The name will appear on the Compose menu and in the Form Attributes dialog box. Just remember, however, that all you've done is saved the form under a specific name. You haven't set any other form attributes.

FIGURE 26.15 ▶

The Save & Exit button appears at the bottom of the Consultant Directory Entry form. When a user clicks on the button to save the data, Notes computes the Address, City, State, Zip Code, Main Phone #, and Main Fax # fields automatically because their field types are Computed.

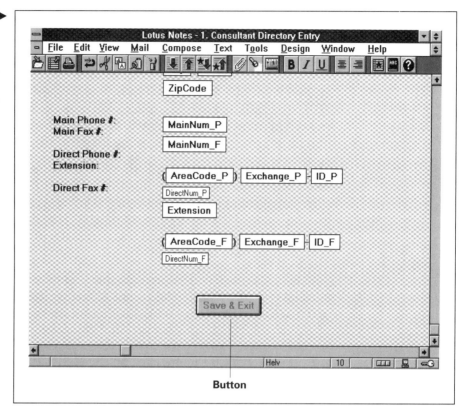

Button

The change will take effect immediately. With the form window still open (you don't have to close it), you can pull down the Compose menu and click on the form's name. A blank document will open in which you can enter data in the fields. When you're finished composing the document, press Ctrl+S to save the information. To close the document's window, press Esc. Press Esc again to close the form's window and to return to the Workspace.

▶ Formatting the Form

You format a form in order to change and enhance its appearance. Formatting allows your creative side to come out. By applying different formatting attributes, you help users to distinguish one form from another in the same database, and you give each form a distinctive look and feel. You can format a form after you've created it, or you can apply formats to a form while you're designing it. Some designers like to place the labels and fields and then format the form; others prefer to format a form as they go along.

Notes provides a set of formatting tools that is similar to those found in other Windows applications. For instance, you can change the background color of a form as well as format the labels and the text that users will enter in fields. The choices you make will be purely subjective, so keep in mind that a person will be using the form for data input. You don't want to overwhelm the user with a form that appears too busy.

You shouldn't clutter a form with too many different fonts and point sizes. You should keep the number of colors you use to a few and consider if they complement each other. If you decide to add a background color to the form (instead of white, the default), make sure the color of the labels and the field text contrast with it. You don't want the text to appear too light against the background.

The following instructions assume that you have created the Consultant Directory Entry form and want to format it. We also assume that you placed all the labels and fields that we described earlier in the chapter. To change the form's background color, follow these steps:

1. If the form isn't open, click on the Consultant Assignments database icon to select it.

2. Choose Design ➤ Forms. The Design Forms dialog box appears.

3. Double-click on Consultant Directory Entry (or highlight the form and click on the Edit button). The form window opens in Edit mode.

4. Choose Design ➤ Form Attributes. The Design Form Attributes dialog box appears.

5. To change the background color of the form from the default color, white, select another color from the bar at the bottom of the dialog box.

6. Click on OK to accept the change. The form's background color will reflect your choice.

7. Press Ctrl+S to save the form.

►► **T I P**

When you highlight a label (any static text) on a form in order to apply formatting attributes, you can pull down the Text menu and choose one of several attributes directly from the menu. Just click on the command. You can also use the available keystroke combinations to execute the same commands.

To format the labels, follow the steps below:

1. Choose Edit ➤ Select All to highlight all the labels (and the text fields) at the same time.

2. Choose Text ➤ Font. The Font dialog box appears.

3. Change the font and point size if you wish.

4. Select one or more of the attribute options on the right, such as Bold.

5. Select a color for the text from the Color Bar at the bottom.

6. Click on OK to accept the changes. The labels will reflect your choices.

7. Press Ctrl+S to save the form.

As we mentioned above, the fields you placed on the form are text fields. In order to be able to change the formatting of the text in the fields, you would need to change them to *rich text fields*. Then when users entered text in the fields, the text would reflect the attributes you applied to the fields.

► *Recreating the Site Location Entry Form*

The Site Location Entry form is another document-type form, which will be used to create a lookup table of training site locations in the Consultant Assignments database. We'll tie this lookup table back to the Consultant Directory Entry form so that the Address, City, State, Zip Code, Main Phone #, and Main Fax # fields can be automatically filled in by selecting a location.

Defining the Form's Attributes

To create the Site Location Entry form, follow these steps:

1. Select the Consultant Assignments database.

2. Choose Design ➤ Forms.

3. Click on the New button. A blank form appears.

4. Choose Design ➤ Form Attributes.

5. Enter **2. Site Location Entry** in the text box (including the number).

6. Select Document as the type.

7. Select the Include in Compose Menu and Include In Query by Form options. (Don't check any other options.)

8. Click on OK to save the new attributes.

9. Press Ctrl+S to save the form.

10. Press Esc to return to the Workspace.

Defining the Window Title

To create a title that will appear in the form window's title bar, follow these steps:

1. Choose Design ➤ Window Title. The Design Window Title dialog box appears.

2. Enter the following statement in the Window Title Formula box. (This statement returns and displays in the window's title bar the name of the form and the name of the location that is entered in the City field.)

   "Site Location Entry"

3. Click OK to confirm.

Defining the Fields

To add the labels and fields to the form, follow these steps:

1. Select the Consultant Assignments database if it isn't selected.

2. Choose Design ➤ Forms.

3. Double-click on Site Location Entry to edit the form. A blank form appears.

4. Create and position the labels. (Use Figure 26.16 as a reference.)

5. Choose Design ➤ New Field to define each of the fields. (You can refer to Tables 26.3 and 26.4.)

6. Press Ctrl+S to save the form.

7. Press Esc to return to the Workspace.

Table 26.3 includes a summary of all the field definitions, and Table 26.4 includes a summary of all the formulas. The completed Site Location Entry form is shown in Figure 26.16.

FIGURE 26.16

The Site Location Entry form allows the user to enter the locations of an organization's regional offices, which is reflected in the Consultant Directory Entry form.

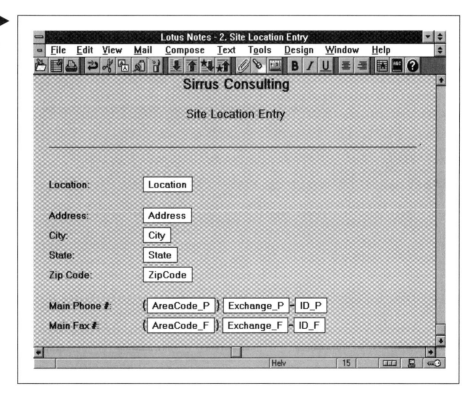

▶ **TABLE 26.3:** *A summary of field definitions for the Site Location Entry form*

LABEL NAME	FIELD NAME	DATA TYPE	FIELD TYPE
Location	Location	Text	Editable
Address	Address	Text	Editable
City	City	Text	Editable
State	State	Text	Editable
Zip Code	ZipCode	Text	Editable
Main Phone #	AreaCode_P	Text	Editable
	Exchange_P	Text	Editable
	ID_P	Text	Editable
Main Fax #	AreaCode_F	Text	Editable
	Exchange_F	Text	Editable
	ID_F	Text	Editable

▶ **TABLE 26.4:** *A summary of field formulas for the Site Location Entry form*

LABEL NAME	FIELD NAME	FORMULA
Main Phone #	AreaCode_P	Input Validation Formula: @If(AreaCode_P = "" & (Exchange_P != "" | ID_P != ""); @Failure ("You must supply the Area Code portion of the phone number"); @Success)
	Exchange_P	Input Validation Formula: @If(Exchange_P = "" & (AreaCode_P != "" | ID_P != ""); @Failure ("You must supply the Exchange portion of the phone number"); @Success)
	ID_P	Input Validation Formula: @If(ID_P = "" & (AreaCode_P != "" | Exchange_P != ""); @Failure ("You must supply the ID portion of the phone number"); @Success)

► **TABLE 26.4:** *A summary of field formulas for the Site Location Entry form (continued)*

LABEL NAME	FIELD NAME	FORMULA
Main Fax #	AreaCode_F	Input Validation Formula: @If(AreaCode_F = "" & (Exchange_F != "" | ID_F != ""); @Failure ("You must supply the Area Code portion of the fax number"); @Success)
	Exchange_F	Input Validation Formula: @If(Exchange_F = "" & (AreaCode_F != "" | ID_F != ""); @Failure ("You must supply the Exchange portion of the fax number"); @Success)
	ID_F	Input Validation Formula: @If(ID_F = "" & (AreaCode_F != "" | Exchange_F != ""); @Failure ("You must supply the ID portion of the fax number"); @Success)

► *Recreating the Input Change Request Form*

The Input Change Request form is used as a means to keep the data in the Consultant Assignments database current. It provides the workflow component of the application. Inevitably, employees will get promoted, change job titles, departments, locations, or they leave the company entirely. It's important that the Consultant Assignments database keep pace with these changes and not become outdated. The theory behind the database is that only the database administrator(s) should be allowed to update the Directory—if anyone could update the Directory at any time, that would very likely lead to gross inaccuracies.

Placing the burden of maintaining the Directory solely on the database administrator, however, assumes that the person will always be aware of changes in employee status. While this is feasible in a small company it's virtually impossible in a large company. Therefore, to assist the database administrator in this effort we'll make all other users of the Directory active participants in its maintenance through the Change Request form.

Any person in the organization can compose a Change Request document and forward it to the person who is responsible for managing the database. A Change Request notifies the database administrator that an entry in the Consultant Assignments needs to be updated and indicates exactly what should be changed. However, the database administrator decides whether to approve or deny the request. If a specific request is approved, the information in the corresponding Directory Entry document is updated automatically.

Defining the Form's Attributes

To create the Input Change Request form, follow these steps:

1. Select the Consultant Assignments database if it isn't selected.
2. Choose Design ➤ Forms.
3. Click on the New button. A blank form appears.
4. Choose Design ➤ Form Attributes.
5. Enter **3. Input Change Request** in the text box. (Include the number.)
6. Select Document as the type.
7. Select the Include in Compose Menu option (don't check any other options).
8. Click on OK to save the new attributes.
9. Press Ctrl+S to save the form.
10. Press Esc to return to the Workspace.

Defining the Window Title

To create a title that will appear in the form window's title bar, follow these steps:

1. Choose Design ➤ Window Title. The Design Window Title dialog box appears.
2. Enter the following statement in the Window Title Formula box. (This statement returns and displays in the window's title bar the name of the form and the name of the person that is entered in the Name field.)

   "Change Request for " + FirstName + "" + LastName

3. Click OK to confirm.

Defining the Fields

To add the labels and fields to the form, follow these steps:

1. Select the Consultant Assignments database if it isn't selected.

2. Choose Design ➤ Forms.

3. Double-click on Input Change Request to edit the form. A blank form appears.

4. Create and position the labels. (Use Figure 24.17 as a reference.)

5. Insert and format the table.

6. Choose Design ➤ New Field to define each of the fields. (You can refer to Table 26.5 and Table 26.6.)

7. Press Ctrl+S to save the form when you're finished.

8. Press Esc to return to the Workspace.

Table 26.5 includes a summary of all the field definitions. Table 26.6 includes a summary of all the formulas. The finished Input Change Request form is shown in Figure 26. 17.

Adding the Send Change Request and Apply Change Request Buttons

As you can see in Figure 26.17, the Input Change Request form includes two buttons: "Send Change Request" and "Apply Change Request." The former is for the user, the latter is for an administrator. After a "requester" composes a document, he or she clicks on the Send Change Request button in order to send the document to an administrator. The Document Save dialog box appears, as shown in Figure 26.18, which gives the user the option of only saving the document or saving and mailing the document.

If the user chooses the Mail option and clicks on the Yes button, the document becomes attached to a Notes Mail memo automatically. After the user fills in the To field (at least one recipient must be identified) and clicks on the memo's Send button, the memo is sent to the recipient, the administrator. When the administrator receives the change request, he or she approves or denies the change. If a request is approved, the administrator clicks on the Apply Change Request button. The change is automatically made to the document by updating the specific field(s).

FIGURE 26.17 ▶

The Input Change Request form allows the user to request that specific changes be made to the Consultant Directory Entry form. The document is forwarded to an administrator who approves or denies the request.

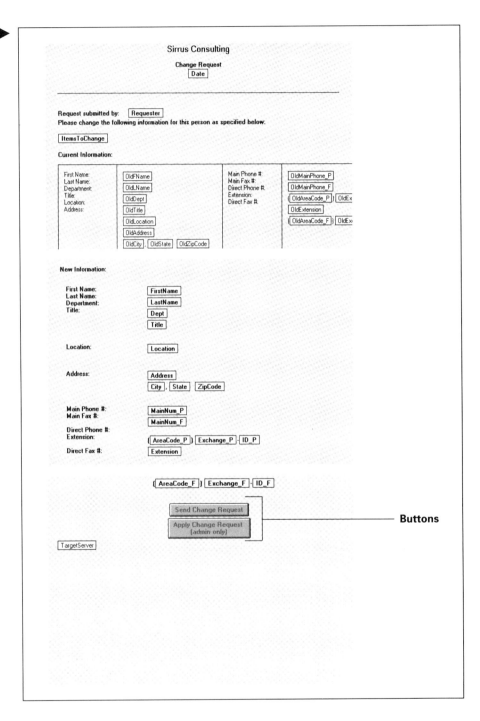

▶ **TABLE 26.5:** *A summary of labels and field definitions for the Input Change Request form*

LABEL NAME	FIELD NAME	DATA TYPE	FIELD TYPE
	Date	Time	Computed for display
Request submitted by	Requester	Text	Computed
Please change the following information for this person as specified below	ItemsToChange	Keywords (Check Boxes):	Editable
		Name	
		Department	
		Title	
		Location	
		Phone Number/ Extension	
		Fax Number	
Current Information			
First Name	OldFName	Text	Computed when composed
Last Name	OldLName	Text	Computed when composed
Department	OldDept	Keywords (Standard):	Computed when composed
		Accounting	
		Administration	
		Engineering	
		Executive	
		Human Resources	
		Manufacturing	
		Research & Development	
		Sales & Marketing	

▶ **TABLE 26.5:** *A summary of labels and field definitions for the Input Change Request form (continued)*

LABEL NAME	FIELD NAME	DATA TYPE	FIELD TYPE
Title	OldTitle	Text	Computed when composed
Location	OldLocation	Text	Computed when composed
Address	OldAddress	Text	Computed when composed
	OldCity	Text	Computed when composed
	OldState	Text	Computed when composed
	OldZipCode	Text	Computed when composed
Main Phone #	OldMainPhone_P	Text	Computed when composed
Main Fax #	OldMainPhone_F	Text	Computed when composed
Direct Phone #	OldAreaCode_P	Text	Computed when composed
	OldExchange_P	Text	Computed when composed
	OldID_P	Text	Computed when composed
Extension	OldExtension	Text	Computed when composed
Direct Fax #	OldAreaCode_F	Text	Computed when composed
	OldExchange_F	Text	Computed when composed
	OldID_F	Text	Computed when composed

TABLE 26.5: *A summary of labels and field definitions for the Input Change Request form (continued)*

LABEL NAME	FIELD NAME	DATA TYPE	FIELD TYPE
New Information			
First Name	FirstName	Text	Editable
Last Name	LastName	Text	Editable
Department	Dept	Keywords (Standard):	Editable
		Accounting	
		Administration	
		Engineering	
		Executive	
		Human Resources	
		Manufacturing	
		Research & Development	
		Sales & Marketing	
Title	Title	Text	Editable
Location	Location	Keywords (Standard)	Editable
Address	Address	Text	Computed
	City	Text	Computed
	State	Text	Computed
	ZipCode	Text	Computed
Main Phone #	MainNum_P	Text	Computed
Main Fax #	MainNum_F	Text	Computed
Direct Phone #	AreaCode_P	Text	Editable
	Exchange_P	Text	Editable
	ID_P	Text	Editable

▶ **TABLE 26.5:** *A summary of labels and field definitions for the Input Change Request form (continued)*

LABEL NAME	FIELD NAME	DATA TYPE	FIELD TYPE
Extension	Extension	Text	Editable
Direct Fax #	AreaCode_F	Text	Editable
	Exchange_F	Text	Editable
	ID_F	Text	Editable
	TargetServer	Text	Computed when composed

▶ **TABLE 26.6:** *A summary of field formulas for the Input Change Request form*

LABEL NAME	FIELD NAME	FORMULA
	Date	@Created
	Requester	@Name([CN];@UserName)
First Name	OldFName	FirstName
Last Name	OldLName	LastName
Department	OldDept	Dept
Title	OldTitle	Title
Location	OldLocation	Location
Address	OldAddress	Address
	OldCity	City
	OldState	State
	OldZipCode	ZipCode
Main Phone #	OldMainPhone_P	MainNum_P
Main Fax #	OldMainPhone_F	MainNum_F
Direct Phone #	OldAreaCode_P	AreaCode_P
	OldExchange_P	Exchange_P
	OldID_P	ID_P

► **TABLE 26.6:** *A summary of field formulas for the Input Change Request form (continued)*

LABEL NAME	FIELD NAME	FORMULA
Extension	OldExtension	Extension
Direct Fax #	OldAreaCode_F	AreaCode_F
	OldExchange_F	Exchange_F
	OldID_F	ID_F
First Name	FirstName	Input Translation Formula: @ProperCase(FirstName)
		Input Validation Formula: @If(FirstName = ""; @Failure ("You must enter a first name before saving this document!"); @Success)
Last Name	LastName	Input Translation Formula: @ProperCase(LastName)
		Input Validation Formula: @If(LastName = ""; @Failure ("You must enter a last name before saving this document!"); @Success)
Department	Dept	Default Value Formula: Dept
Title	Title	Input Translation Formula: @ProperCase(Title)
Location	Location	Allowable Keywords Formula: @DbColumn (""; TargetServer: "CONSULT.NSF"; "Training Site Locations"; 1)
Address	Address	@If(Location != ""; @DbLookup (""; TargetServer: "CONSULT.NSF"; "Training Site Locations"; Location; "Address"); "")
	City	@If(Location != ""; @DbLookup (""; TargetServer: "CONSULT.NSF"; "Training Site Locations"; Location; "City"); "")
	State	@If(Location != ""; @DbLookup (""; TargetServer: "CONSULT.NSF"; "Training Site Locations"; Location; "State"); "")
	ZipCode	@If(Location != ""; @DbLookup (""; TargetServer: "CONSULT.NSF"; "Training Site Locations"; Location; "ZipCode"); "")
Main Phone #	MainNum_P	@If(Location != ""; @DbLookup (""; TargetServer: "CON-SULT.NSF"; "Training Site Locations"; Location; 6); "")

▶ **TABLE 26.6:** *A summary of field formulas for the Input Change Request form (continued)*

LABEL NAME	FIELD NAME	FORMULA
Main Fax #	MainNum_F	@If(Location != ""; @DbLookup (""; TargetServer: "CONSULT.NSF"; "Training Site Locations"; Location; 7); "")
Direct Phone #	AreaCode_P	Default Value Formula: AreaCode_P
		Input Translation Formula: @If(AreaCode_P = ""; @DbLookup (""; TargetServer: "CONSULT.NSF"; "Training Site Locations"; Location; "AreaCode_P"); AreaCode_P)
	Exchange_P	Default Value Formula: Exchange_P
		Input Translation Formula: @If(Exchange_P = ""; @DbLookup (""; TargetServer: "CONSULT.NSF"; "Training Site Locations"; Location; "Exchange_P"); Exchange_P)
	ID_P	Default Value Formula: ID_P
		Input Translation Formula: @If(ID_P = ""; @DbLookup (""; TargetServer: "CONSULT.NSF"; "Training Site Locations"; Location; "ID_P"); ID_P)
Extension	Extension	Default Value Formula: Extension
Direct Fax #	AreaCode_F	Default Value Formula: AreaCode_F
		Input Translation Formula: @If(AreaCode_F = ""; @DbLookup (""; TargetServer: "CONSULT.NSF"; "Training Site Locations"; Location; "AreaCode_F"); AreaCode_F)
	Exchange_F	Default Value Formula: Exchange_F
		Input Translation Formula: @If(Exchange_F = ""; @DbLookup (""; TargetServer: "CONSULT.NSF"; "Training Site Locations"; Location; "Exchange_F"); Exchange_F)
	ID_F	Default Value Formula: ID_F
		Input Translation Formula: @If(ID_F = ""; @DbLookup (""; TargetServer: "CONSULT.NSF"; "Training Site Locations"; Location; "ID_F"); ID_F)
	TargetServer	@Name([CN]; @Subset(@DbName; 1))

FIGURE 26.18

The Document Save dialog box gives the user the option of only saving the Input Change Request document or saving and mailing the document to an administrator who evaluates the request.

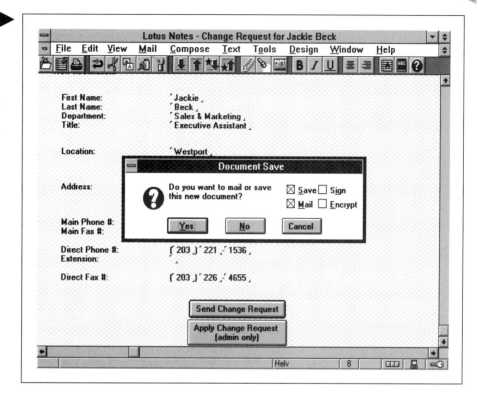

To create the Send Change Request button, follow these steps:

1. Place the insertion point at the bottom of the form (using Figure 26.17 as a guide).

2. Click on the Text Align Center SmartIcon, or choose Text ➤ Alignment ➤ Center, to center the button.

3. Choose Edit ➤ Insert ➤ Button. The Insert Button dialog box appears.

4. Enter **Send Change Request** in the Button Text box.

5. Enter the following statement in the Formula box:

   FIELD SaveOptions := "0"; FIELD MailOptions := "1";
   FIELD Subject := "REQUEST TO CHANGE CONSULTANT DIRECTORY";
   FIELD SendTo := @Name([Canonicalize]; @Prompt([OKCANCELLIST]; "Directory Administrator"; "Please select the name of your Corporate Directory administrator from the list below."; "";

@Name([CN]; @DbLookup(""; TargetServer : "PUBLIC.NSF";
"Groups"; "Directory Administrators"; "Members"))));
@Command([FileCloseWindow])

6. Click on OK to accept the choices.

To create the Apply Change Request button, follow these steps:

1. Place the Insertion Point at the bottom of the form (using Figure 26.17 as a guide).

2. Click on the Text Align Center SmartIcon, or choose Text ▶ Alignment ▶ Center, to center the button.

3. Choose Edit ▶ Insert ▶ Button. The Insert Button dialog box appears.

4. Enter **Apply Change Request (Admin Only)** in the Button Text box.

5. Enter the following statement in the Formula box:

FIELD SaveOptions := ""; FIELD MailOptions := "";
FIELD SendTo := "Consultant Directory";
ENVIRONMENT OldFName := OldFName;
ENVIRONMENT OldLName := OldLName;
@Command([FileOpenDatabase]; TargetServer : "CON-SULT2.NSF"; "Consultant Assignments");
@Command([ToolsRunMacro]; "(DeleteCurrentEntry)"); @Command([FileCloseWindow]);
@Command([FileCloseWindow])

6. Click on OK to accept the choices.

The buttons appear on the form, displaying the names that you gave them.

▶▶ *Duplicating the Views*

The Consultant Assignments database includes three views:

- The **Availability** view displays an alphabetical and categorized listing of staff and their current availability.

- The **Consultant Directory** view displays an alphabetical and categorized listing of staff by city and department.

- The **Training Site Locations** view displays an alphabetical listing of training sites by city.

These views allow you to find information on particular staff members and sites easily.

▶ *Defining the Consultant Directory View*

Let's create the Consultant Directory view first. This view displays an alphabetical and categorized listing of staff by city and department. The columns in the view correspond to the field values in the Consultant Directory Entry form. To create the view, follow these steps:

1. Select the Training Facilities database in the Workspace.

2. Choose Design ➤ Views. The Design Views dialog box appears, as shown in Figure 26.19.

 ▶▶ **TIP**

> You can choose the New Copy and Paste options if a view already exists. The New copy option allows you to create a view by copying an existing view in the database. Simply highlight the view you wish to copy from the list of views displayed in the dialog box and select New Copy. The Paste option lets you create a view by pasting a view from another database into the current database. You must first open the other database, choose Design ➤ Views, highlight the desired view, and click on Copy. Then choose Design ➤ Views in the target database and click on Paste. The pasted view should now appear in the list of views in the dialog box.

3. Click on the New button, which allows you to create a view from scratch. A blank view window appears in Design mode, as shown in Figure 26.20.

FIGURE 26.19 ▶

The Design Views dialog box lets you create a new view for a selected database.

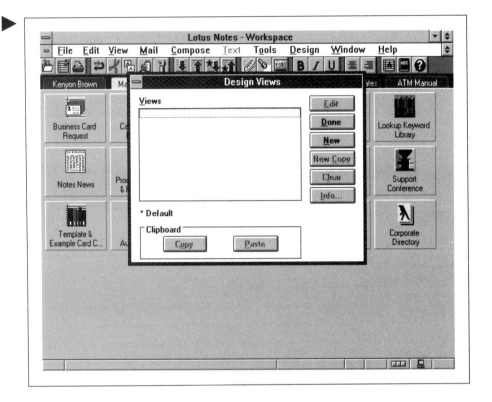

Defining the View's Attributes

You'll notice that the current name of the view is [untitled]. Associated with each view is a set of attributes which assign certain general characteristics to the view. One of the attributes is the view's name. To define view attributes, follow these steps:

1. While in View Design mode, choose Design ▶ View Attributes. The Design View Attributes dialog box appears, as shown in Figure 26.21.

FIGURE 26.20

*A blank view appears
in Design mode when
you want to define a
new view.*

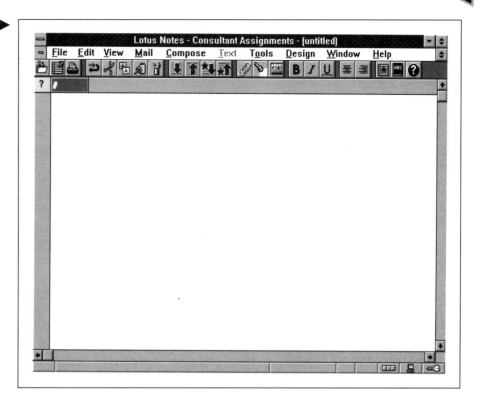

TIP

**You can create an *accelerator key* for a view name by
placing an underscore to the left of a letter in the
name. An accelerator key allows the user to open a
menu and then press the specific key in order to
execute a command, which in this case is opening a
particular view. When a database has several views,
using accelerator keys are a convenient way to open
the views quickly.**

2. Enter **Consultant Directory** in the Name text box.

3. Select the Shared View option if it's not selected. (It's the default.)

FIGURE 26.21 ►

The Design View Attributes dialog box lets you define the attributes for a particular view.

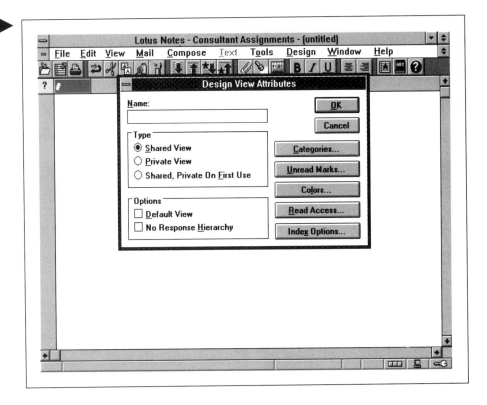

4. Click on the Categories button to specify that categories in the view will be fully expanded.

5. Click on OK to accept the changes.

Defining the Selection Formula

To ensure that a view will only include documents that meet a specific criteria, we have to make use of a selection formula. When applied to a view, a selection formula simply narrows the scope of the view to include only a subset of documents in the database, excluding all others. A selection formula expresses the criteria that a document must meet in order to be included in the view.

When you choose Design ➤ Selection Formula, the Design Selection Formula dialog box appears, as shown in Figure 26.22. As you can see, the statement **SELECT @All** appears in the Selection Formula box. (This is the default selection formula. It returns the selection of *all*

FIGURE 26.22

The Design Selection Formula dialog box lets you enter a formula that selects the documents you want to display in a particular view. The default statement SELECT @All appears in the Selection Formula box.

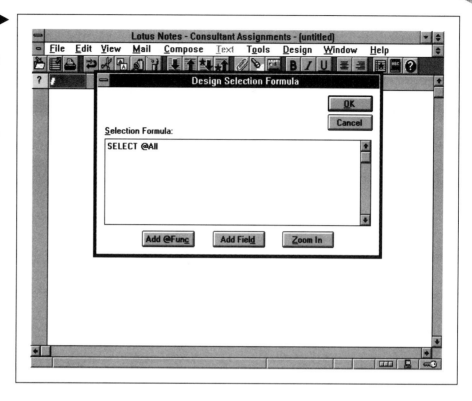

documents in a database to appear in a particular view, which in this case is the Consultant Directory view.)

Enter the statement **SELECT Form = "1. Consultant Directory Entry"** (including the quotation marks) in the Selection Formula box. This statement selects and returns the values of the contents of the fields in the Consultant Directory Entry form.

Defining a Column

For the Consultant Directory view, you are going to define nine columns. To define the first column, follow these steps:

1. Double-click on the leftmost # column. The Design Column Definition dialog box appears, as shown in Figure 26.23.

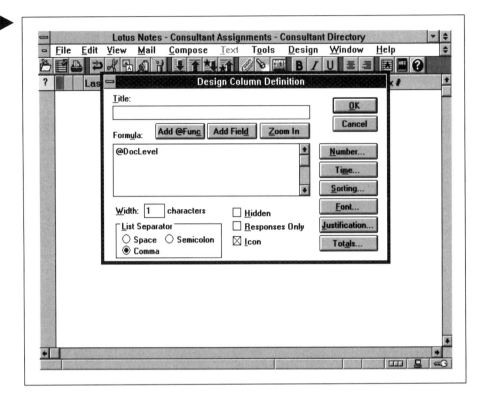

 ▶▶ **T I P**

Double-click on a column heading (the box at top of the column) to display the Design Column Definition dialog box.

2. Delete the # and leave the Title text box blank; don't assign a title to the column.

3. Enter the statement **@DocLevel** in the Formula box. This formula display an icon in the leftmost column that corresponds to each type of category in the view.

4. Set the width of the column in the Column Width box to 1.

5. Select the "Icon" check box.

6. Click on OK to accept your choices.

Defining the Other Columns in the View

To define the other eight columns in the Consultant Directory view, follow these steps:

1. For the second column, enter the following definitions:

> **Title**: not assigned
> **Formula**: Location
> **Width**: 1
> **List Separator**: Comma
> **Number**: General (Default)
> **Sorting**: Ascending, Categorized
> **Font**: Helv, 10, Bold
> **Justification**: Left (default)
> **Totals**: None (Default)

2. For the third column, enter the following definitions:

> **Title**: not assigned
> **Formula**: Dept
> **Width**: 1
> **List Separator**: Comma
> **Number**: General (Default)
> **Sorting**: Ascending, Categorized
> **Font**: Helv, 12, Bold
> **Justification**: Left
> **Totals**: None (Default)

3. For the fourth column, enter the following definitions:

> **Title**: Last Name
> **Formula**: LastName
> **Width**: 15
> **List Separator**: Comma
> **Number**: General (Default)
> **Sorting**: Ascending
> **Font**: Helv, 10, Bold

Justification: Left (default)

Totals: None (Default)

4. For the fifth column, enter the following definitions:

Title: First Name

Formula: FirstName

Width: 10

List Separator: Comma

Number: General (Default)

Sorting: None

Font: Helv, 10, Bold

Justification: Left (default)

Totals: None (Default)

5. For the sixth column, enter the following definitions:

Title: Phone #

Formula: @If (DirectNum_P != ""; DirectNum_P; MainNum_P)

Width: 10

List Separator: Comma

Number: General (Default)

Sorting: None

Font: Helv, 10, Bold

Justification: Left (default)

Totals: None (Default)

6. For the seventh column, enter the following definitions:

Title: Ext.

Formula: Extension

Width: 5

List Separator: Comma

Number: General (Default)

Sorting: None

Font: Helv, 12, Bold

Justification: Left (default)

Totals: None (Default)

7. For the eighth column, enter the following definitions:

Title: Fax #

Formula: @If (DirectNum_F != ""; DirectNum_F; MainNum_F)

Width: 10

List Separator: Comma

Number: General (Default)

Sorting: None

Font: Helv, 10, Bold

Justification: Left (default)

Totals: None (Default)

8. For the ninth column, enter the following definitions:

Title: Title

Formula: Title

Width: 15

List Separator: Comma

Number: General (Default)

Sorting: None

Font: Helv, 10, Bold

Justification: Left (default)

Totals: None (Default)

As you can see, you can use the default definitions for most of the items. This will save you a lot of time when you have a several columns to define.

Saving a View

Although you may have clicked on OK in different dialog boxes to accept changes you made to different elements in a view, you still need to save the view before closing it and returning to the Workspace or another open window. When you want to save the changes you made to a view, press Ctrl+S. If you press Esc before you save the changes, a message box will appear, asking you if you want to save your changes. Click on Yes. You'll return to the Workspace or another window that may be open.

Editing a View

The next time you want to edit a database's view, select the database's icon in the Workspace. Then choose Design ➤ Views. The Design Views dialog box will appear. Select the view you want to edit by either double-clicking on the view's name or highlighting it and then clicking on the Edit button. The view window will open.

When you want to edit a column, either double-click on the column heading or click on the column heading to select it and then choose Design ➤ Column Definition. The Design Column Definition dialog box will appear. Make the desired changes and then click on OK to accept the changes. When you return to the view window, press F9 to refresh the view and to see if the changes you made have taken affect. Press Ctrl+S to save the view.

▶ Duplicating the Other Views

You'll need to repeat the above steps in order to define the other two views. You can assume that the default options apply unless indicated otherwise.

▶ Defining the Training Site Locations View

The Training Site Locations view shows an alphabetical listing of cities where training seminars are conducted. To create the view, follow these steps:

1. Select the Training Facilities database in the Workspace.

2. Choose Design ➤ Views. The Design Views dialog box appears.

3. Click on the New button, which allows you to create a view from scratch. A blank view window appears in Design mode.

Defining the View's Attributes

To define the view's attributes, follow these steps:

1. While in View Design mode, choose Design ➤ View Attributes. The Design View Attributes dialog box appears.

2. Enter **Training Site Locations** in the Name text box.

3. Select the Shared View option if it's not selected. (It's the default.)

4. Click on the Categories button to specify that categories in the view will be fully expanded.

5. Click on OK to accept the changes.

Defining the Selection Formula

To ensure that a view will only include documents that meet a specific criteria, we have to make use of a selection formula. When applied to a view, a selection formula simply narrows the scope of the view to include only a subset of documents in the database, excluding all others. A selection formula expresses the criteria that a document must meet in order to be included in the view.

When you choose Design ➤ Selection Formula, the Design Selection Formula dialog box appears. As you can see, the statement **SELECT @All** appears in the Selection Formula box. This is the default selection formula. It returns the selection of *all* documents in a database to appear in a particular view, which in this case is the Training Site Locations.

Enter the statement **SELECT Form = "2. Site Location Entry"** (including the quotation marks) in the Selection Formula box. This statement selects and returns the values of the contents of the fields that are contained in the form.

Defining a Column

For the Training Site Locations view, you are going to define seven columns. To define the first column, follow these steps:

1. Double-click on the leftmost column. The Design Column Definition dialog box appears.

2. Enter **Location** in the Title text box.

3. Enter the statement **Location** in the Formula box. (The statement returns the value of the Location field in the Site Location Entry form.)

4. Enter **10** in the Column Width box.

5. Click on the Font button. The Font dialog box appears.

6. Select Helv, 10, Bold.

7. Click on the Sorting button. The Design Column Sort dialog box appears.

8. Choose the Ascending option.

9. Click on OK to accept your choices and the default settings.

To define the other six columns in the Training Site Locations view, follow these steps:

1. For the second column, enter the following definitions:

   Title: Address
   Formula: Address
   Width: 20
   List Separator: Comma
   Number: General (Default)
   Sorting: None
   Font: Helv, 10, Bold
   Justification: Left
   Totals: None (Default)

2. For the third column, enter the following definitions:

   Title: City
   Formula: City
   Width: 10
   List Separator: Comma
   Number: General
   Sorting: None
   Font: Helv, 10, Bold

Justification: Left

Totals: None (Default)

3. For the fourth column, enter the following definitions:

Title: State

Formula: State

Width: 4

List Separator: Comma

Number: General (Default)

Sorting: None

Font: Helv, 10, Bold

Justification: Left

Totals: None (Default)

4. For the fifth column, enter the following definitions:

Title: Zip Code

Formula: ZipCode

Width: 10

List Separator: Comma

Number: General

Sorting: None

Font: Helv, 10, Bold

Justification: Left

Totals: None (Default)

5. For the sixth column, enter the following definitions:

Title: Phone #

Formula: @If (AreaCode_P != ""; "(" + AreaCode_P + ")" + Exchange_P + "-" + ID_P; "N/A")

Width: 10

List Separator: Comma

Number: General (Default)

Sorting: None (Default)

Font: Helv, 10, Bold

Justification: Left

Totals: None (Default)

6. For the seventh column, enter the following definitions:

Title: Fax #

Formula: @If (AreaCode_F != ""; "(" + AreaCode_F + ")" + Exchange_F + "-" + ID_F; "N/A")

Width: 10

List Separator: Comma

Number: General

Sorting: None (Default)

Font: Helv, 10, Bold

Justification: Left

Totals: None (Default)

7. Press Ctrl+S to save the view.

As you can see, you can use the default definitions for most of the items. This will save you a lot of time when you have several columns to define.

► *Defining the Availability View*

The Availability view shows an alphabetical and categorized listing of staff and their current availability. To create the view, follow these steps:

1. Select the Training Facilities database in the Workspace.

2. Choose Design ➤ Views. The Design Views dialog box appears.

3. Click on the New button, which allows you to create a view from scratch. A blank view window appears in design mode.

Defining the View's Attributes

To define the view's attributes, follow these steps:

1. While in View Design mode, choose Design ➤ View Attributes. The Design View Attributes dialog box appears.

2. Enter **Availability** in the Name text box.

3. Select the Shared View option if it's not selected. (It's the default.)

4. Click on the Categories button to specify that categories in the view will be fully expanded.

5. Click on OK to accept the changes.

Defining the Selection Formula

To ensure that a view will only include documents that meet a specific criteria, we have to make use of a selection formula. When applied to a view, a selection formula simply narrows the scope of the view to include only a subset of documents in the database, excluding all others. A selection formula expresses the criteria that a document must meet in order to be included in the view.

When you choose Design ➤ Selection Formula, the Design Selection Formula dialog box appears. As you can see, the statement **SELECT @All** appears in the Selection Formula box. This is the default selection formula. It returns the selection of *all* documents in a database to appear in a particular view, which in this case is the Training Site Locations.

Enter the statement **SELECT Form = "1. Consultant Directory Entry"** (including the quotation marks) in the Selection Formula box. This statement selects and returns the values of the contents of the fields that are contained in the form.

Defining a Column

For the Availability view, you are going to define six columns. To define the first column, follow these steps:

1. Double-click on the leftmost # column. The Design Column Definition dialog box appears.

2. Delete the # and leave the Title text box blank; don't assign a title to the column.

3. Enter the statement **@DocLevel** in the Formula box. (The statement returns and displays an icon that corresponds to the category of document.)

4. Enter **1** in the Column Width box.

5. Click on OK to accept your choices and the default settings.

To define the other six columns in the Availability view, follow these steps:

1. For the second column, enter the following definitions:

   Title: Not Assigned

   Formula: Location

   Width: 1

   List Separator: Comma

   Number: General (Default)

   Sorting: Ascending, Categorized

   Font: Helv, 10, Bold

   Justification: Left

   Totals: None (Default)

2. For the third column, enter the following definitions:

   Title: Not Assigned

   Formula: Dept

   Width: 1

   List Separator: Comma

   Number: General

   Sorting: Ascending, Categorized

   Font: Helv, 10, Bold

   Justification: Left

   Totals: None (Default)

3. For the fourth column, enter the following definitions:

   Title: Last Name

   Formula: LastName

   Width: 10

   List Separator: Comma

   Number: General (Default)

   Sorting: Ascending

   Font: Helv, 10, Bold

   Justification: Left

   Totals: None (Default)

4. For the fifth column, enter the following definitions:

> **Title**: First Name
> **Formula**: FirstName
> **Width**: 10
> **List Separator**: Comma
> **Number**: General
> **Sorting**: None
> **Font**: Helv, 10, Bold
> **Justification**: Left
> **Totals**: None (Default)

5. For the sixth column, enter the following definitions:

> **Title**: Availability
> **Formula**: Availability
> **Width**: 50
> **List Separator**: Comma
> **Number**: General (Default)
> **Sorting**: None (Default)
> **Font**: Helv, 10, Bold
> **Justification**: Left
> **Totals**: None (Default)

6. Press Ctrl+S to save the view.

As you can see, you can use the default definitions for most of the items. This will save you a lot of time when you have a several columns to define.

▶▶ *Testing the Database*

As we discussed at the end of Chapter 14, you should get in the habit of testing the functionality of a new database once you're finished creating the forms and views. All you need to do is compose a few documents based on each form in order to check if you can enter data correctly without getting any error messages.

Next, you should open each of the views to see if the documents are displayed correctly. If a view doesn't display any documents, open the view in edit mode and check its selection formula. The reason why a view usually doesn't display documents is because the selection formula is wrong. If the selection formula is correct, you should check the formula for each column's definition in order to make sure that the column is referencing the correct field. If a column isn't referencing the correct field, the view won't return (and display) the value for that field.

Many errors occur in Design mode when you're creating forms and fields, and defining their contents. In fact, most errors are the result of typos that you introduce when you include the names of fields and forms in formulas. Sometimes an error message will give you a clue that Notes can't find a specific name of a form or a field. You'll have to open a form and check the spelling of the field names.

▶▶ *What's Next?*

The Consultant Assignments database is a good example of an Notes application that can aid users in tracking the availability of personnel. The database functions as a directory of all employees in an organization. The database enables an organization to gather and maintain personnel data on in-house staff as well as consultants who live in different cities. The background information on consultants is used to hire them for assignments near where they live.

Since the organization depends heavily on the availability of independent contractors, changes in their current status, such can be forwarded to the administrator for input. In this way, a current personnel file on every employee can be maintained easily. As a workflow-automation application, it provides the means for an administrator to track and update information on each employee, such as address changes, promotions, terminations, and so on.

► ► **APPENDIX**

Third-Party Products and Services

***T**here* are many add-ins, third-party applications, and services that can help you get more out of Notes. The following list of products and services represents only a sample of what's currently available. It's by no means exhaustive.

►► *Products*

Many products enhance Notes' workflow capabilities by helping to identify the workflow automation process during the development of a database. These products often employ intricate, rules-based logic to systematize and speed up a business's workflow, showing the developer how to move and coordinate data within a workgroup. Many workflow products can manage structured and text-based data that are contained in forms or in formatted, editable documents; and some can manage images as well. The following products are listed in alphabetical order.

► *Forms 1.0 for Windows*

Forms is an electronic forms package from Lotus. Forms is tightly integrated with Notes and cc:Mail, which enables users to connect to databases smoothly. By using the included Open Database Connectivity (ODBC) drivers, Forms makes linking to databases and updating fields within the database easy; no complicated steps are involved. Forms' e-mail routing and tracking features are extensive. The workflow functions allow an organization to route forms among different mail systems, which is important when sending mail through Notes.

Lotus Development Corporation, (800) 346-1305.

► *Lotus Notes Companion Products*

The Lotus Notes companion products encompass a large sector of media, from fax to video, and are supported quite differently from Notes itself. A brief description of each product currently in the Companion Product category follows below.

Lotus Development Corporation, (800) 437-6391.

Lotus Notes Document Imaging (LNDI)

Lotus Notes Document Imaging provides users with the power of image processing on their electronic desktops. LNDI (pronounced "Lindy") allows users to bring paper-based files into any Lotus Notes database in the form of image documents. Users can electronically share contracts, technical diagrams, newspaper clippings, photographs, handwritten comments, and any other type of information. LNDI is made up of two components: client software that lets users add image documents to Notes databases (via embedding or linking), fax images, and OCR images; and server software that lets users store image documents outside of a Notes database in a specially designed storage system called the Mass Storage System. The LNDI services can be used with INFAX and OCR.

Lotus Notes Incoming Fax Gateway (INFAX)

Lotus Notes Incoming Fax Gateway is a set of programs that accepts faxes from a fax machine or computer board capable of sending faxes and a phone line, processes the faxes, and routes them to the appropriate Notes mail address. This is a Notes server add-in program. Notes Incoming Fax Gateway can be configured for optional services such as the Lotus Notes Optical Character Recognition (OCR) Service and Lotus Notes Document Imaging (LNDI). Using the OCR service, Notes users can receive faxes in text format, instead of bitmap images. By using LNDI, Notes users can receive faxes as Document Imaging documents.

Lotus Notes Optical Character Recognition (OCR)

Lotus Notes Optical Character Recognition Service consists of a Notes server add-in program and Notes databases that accept images as attachments through Notes mail, extract the image attachments, convert the image to OCR text format, and send the text to the appropriate Notes mail destination. The OCR service can be used with INFAX and Lotus Notes Document Imaging (LNDI).

Lotus Notes Outgoing Fax Gateway (OUTFAX)

The Lotus Notes Outgoing Fax Gateway routes Notes mail to any fax machine worldwide. It is an extension of the Lotus Notes Mail Router. Lotus Notes communicates with the target fax machine through an internal fax board and a phone line.

Lotus Notes Phone Notes (PhoneNotes)

This is a screen-oriented development environment, based on Notes forms, that makes it possible for end users to create their own applications, bringing the Notes ease of application building to a new market. The connection of these applications to Notes databases allows the phone system to be a front end to Notes and workflow and document management. This product broadens the range of applications for Notes.

PhoneNotes, which is designed to make the telephone a limited remote client for Notes, allows users to dial into a Notes database and perform a variety of functions, such as creating documents and databases, and playing back data via text-to-voice-conversion technology. It also enables users to embed voice messages in Notes databases and gives them the ability to access Notes functionality from a telephone's touch-tone keypad.

Lotus Notes Video Notes (VideoNotes)

VideoNotes integrates full-motion video into Notes. Full-motion video is a very demanding data type. Sound must be synchronized with images. Digital video files can be huge. VideoNotes solves the problem of large-object storage and provides enterprise-wide distribution and management of video. It will support the full Notes model, especially the routing and replication features that give Notes its dominant position in workgroup computing. With VideoNotes, Lotus will offer developers and end users effective tools for leveraging this data type. For information providers and others looking to Notes as a publishing platform,

VideoNotes supplies both a conduit for the delivery of multimedia content to customers and a ready-made distribution system at the customer's site.

▶ VB/Link for Lotus Notes

VB/Link is a Visual Basic custom control that enables developers to create customized Windows applications to read, update, and display information stored in Lotus Notes databases. Do you want to write a Visual Basic routine that imports data from your favorite database or application and puts it into a Notes database? No problem. Would you like to create a viewer program so that you can quickly and easily scan local Notes databases without loading Notes? Again, no problem.

Brainstorm Technologies, (617) 492-3399, FAX: (617) 492-9126.

▶ ViP

ViP is Lotus's Windows-based visual programming environment for Notes. It's aimed at corporate developers building custom applications that use information in Notes databases. The ViP toolkit contains an interface builder, reporting tools, and Open Database Connectivity (ODBC) and Datalens drivers. ViP uses LotusScript, a Visual Basic-like macro language. Although LotusScript will work with Visual Basic macros, it does not support Visual Basic objects, which are used to create custom controls and interfaces.

Lotus Development Corporation, (800) 346-1305.

▶▶ *Services*

There's a wide array of services available to Notes users and developers. The following services provide technical information, sample databases, training, online documentation, and discussions of Notes issues. They are listed in alphabetical order.

▶ *CompuServe Lotus Notes Information Service (CLNIS)*

CLNIS is an information hub that provides Lotus Notes with global connectivity. Using Notes and connecting with a Lotus Notes server on the CompuServe Network, members can exchange mail via Lotus Notes Mail, and the same mail services accessible on the CompuServe Mail Hub, as well as a Private Service, which allows restricted access to Notes information. CLNIS allows connectivity without requiring the user to manage local network services or make extensive equipment purchases. It frees associations and other organizations from the need to run their own server computer.

CompuServe, (800) 233-2247. Ask for the CompuServe Lotus Notes Information Service Representative.

▶ *INFOCITE*

Delivers self-selected bibliographies, abstracts, and excerpts into individual Lotus Notes mailboxes. These may also be stored in a Notes database for future retrieval. The finely tuned INFOCITE products are drawn from thousands of business, trade, legal, and industry journals and newsletters.

Information Broadcasting Company, Inc., (800) 388-0086; Fax, (703) 276-8603.

▶ *Lotus Communication Forum*

This is a CompuServe forum that can be accessed through **GO LO-TUSCOMM**. This forum offers support for all versions of Lotus Notes, and includes information on servers, workstations, and platforms. Its libraries contain technical notes, third-party product overviews, help and utility files, bug fixes, sample Notes databases, and more.

In addition to the database templates and example databases that are included with Notes (see Chapter 13, "Using Notes Templates and Databases," for a complete description), Lotus provides more sample databases in its Notes Apps library. All you have to do is download the databases. The sample databases are described below.

CompuServe, (800) 233-2247.

AGENDA.ZIP

This database is a personal information manager, similar to Lotus Agenda. You create tasks, assign them priorities, and track their progress. It can be used by an individual or by a group.

APPLIB.ZIP

The Application Library Card Catalog is a compilation of the 50 Notes applications also listed separately in this forum—but without any data (just the views and forms). Applications are classified by the Notes technical features they use, by the business areas they serve, and by the categories of Notes application design they represent (discussion, tracking, etc.).

APTRK.ZIP

This is the tracking database used by the Notes Application Marketing team to manage the Application Library project. The project objective is to compile a library of 50 Notes applications. These applications can be used by Notes sales people and advocates to demonstrate a range of Notes' application capabilities. They can also be used by Notes application developers as a source of working applications to copy and use and to review for technical reference.

BOOKRV.ZIP

This is a discussion database for readers. Users can compose a book review or comment on the reviews submitted by other contributors. Database views sort book reviews by genre (mystery, romance, history), format (novel, play), fiction/non-fiction, reviewer's rating, etc.

BOSTON.ZIP

This is a listing of hotels, restaurants, attractions, night spots, sporting events, etc. for the Boston area. You can read other people's recommendations (good and bad) about many attractions to help you plan your activities. You can also offer your own comments or rebuttals on the reviews given by others.

BPLAN.ZIP

This database provides an example of how you might import spreadsheet data and then use Notes views to analyze the numbers in different ways. A .WK1 file and a .COL file are included.

CHEFS.ZIP

This database is an electronic chef's conference. It is based on a core of recipes submitted by its users. You can browse through the recipes by date submitted, author, and food category. In addition to this reference book of recipes, the interactive nature of Notes allows readers to participate in an active discussion on recipes and cooking.

CLLCTR.ZIP

This application combines three databases that comprise a subset of many tracking files you can set up to route and handle problem calls from the computer users in your company. The people answering the telephones in the dispatch center use the Call Dispatch database to compose request documents, which are then routed by type to the customized databases that each support person uses to track requests. Tech Services Call Tracking and Support Center Call Tracking are the two companion databases included.

CLPART.ZIP

This is a compilation of Notes database icons that people have submitted for general use. You can add your own creations, or copy someone else's.

CNTRCT.ZIP

This database is used by a corporate legal department as a central place to consolidate and organize master copies of legal agreements. The text of the agreements is linked into Notes documents via OLE. The agreements are then tracked by attorney responsible, file name, revision number and other relevant criteria.

CORRSP.ZIP

This a populated version of the Correspondence template, including Quick Letters, faxes, and a mail merge form.

DEMORM.ZIP

You can reserve time in two demo rooms. Views are by the month—you select the day you want and then edit that document, which uses a table to create time slots. The views tell you which hours are available.

DOCTOR.ZIP

This database is used to collect sign-off on a patient's treatment by the physicians that were involved in that treatment.

ECO.ZIP

This application provides a process where engineers can make requests for Engineering Change Orders (ECOs). The requests can include Attachment response documents with scanned images of engineering drawings related to the changes. The managers (who have the appropriate privileges) will then assign the change a completion date. All changes are then tracked in the various views.

EMPREC.ZIP

This is a database of employee records, which are structured hierarchically into an organization chart.

EVENTS.ZIP

This an event-driven calendar that serves as a contrast to the visual calendar. The database provides multiple views (by date, by person, etc.), but neither the forms nor views have a calendar look.

EXCBRF.ZIP

This database defines and organizes an executive briefing. It combines all aspects of setting up and holding a briefing: letters of invitation and welcoming, briefing agendas, room and other facilities scheduling, background company, and speaker profiles.

EXP.ZIP

This database lets you enter all your expense items, and then print from the view level. You get an expense report that can be signed and submitted as is. You can also use the various views to analyze your expenses for the year.

FIN.ZIP

This Notes database is a repository for research on and analysis of companies. Stock analysts post this information to the database and then traders refer to it. This database shows how a Notes reference application can facilitate quick and effective information exchange within a company.

FRMCAT.ZIP

This is a collection of Notes formulas that people have contributed for general use. You can add formulas and copy formulas to your databases to make application development easier.

FRMRTE.ZIP

The two databases in this application provide a full routing application. The Forms Routing database contains the forms you should put in everyone's Notes mail file. They can then compose an approval request at any time, or respond to a request sent to them. The Routing Tracking database receives a copy of every approval document as it moves through the process. This is where you can go to check on the progress of a document.

INTEVT.ZIP

This database lists general events and presentations at Lotus. Events are entered into the database before they happen. They are then kept for historical views after they have been held.

INVENT.ZIP

This database inventories and tracks all computer system equipment in a department. It is a group-maintained database, requiring each member of the group to be responsible for his or her own equipment. The collective database gives quick and easy access to an entire group's or department's inventory of computer equipment.

JNKML.ZIP

The two databases in this application (SHOTCOMM.NSF, SHOTRED.NSF) are used by the Lotus Corporate Communications department to send out shotgun e-mail messages. Shotgun e-mails are messages for wide distribution within the company. Examples of such messages are organizational announcements or notification of employee benefits information.

JOBCAN.ZIP

This database tracks job candidates and matches them with the agencies that originally submitted them.

JOBPST.ZIP

This database tracks employment opportunities and hiring for the general employee population. Hiring Managers can post new openings to the database for approval by Human Resources. When approved, the opening will appear in all the public views. Employees can inquire about a job by composing an Inquiry document, which is automatically mailed to the appropriate Human Resources Administrator.

LIBRY.ZIP

This database lists all the materials in your company or departmental library. Users can browse the listings by Author, Title, or Subject. Librarians can check out materials. Also, there is a view called Guided Tours that lists suggested reading lists for various training purposes. Users can track their progress through a Guided Tour with a form designed for that purpose.

LITIGT.ZIP

This database provides a simple way to consolidate frequently changing information regarding numerous litigation activities occurring simultaneously. There may be a wide number of activities happening in different countries around the world. The corporate legal department needs to keep tabs on all active litigation, to allocate resources, to determine exposure and to report progress.

MEETMN.ZIP

This database tracks agendas, meeting minutes, and action items.

MYGOAL.ZIP

This database helps you record your personal values and goals and then organize intermediate tasks to achieve them. It follows the Franklin time-management style and makes interesting use of main documents and response documents to establish a hierarchy between short-range and long-range goals. It includes advanced selection criteria in views. However, it's meant for personal use, not group use.

NEWS.ZIP

This database is used to distribute news about Lotus and the Microcomputer Industry to Lotus employees. Lotus employees use this information to keep informed about goings-on in the industry, competitors, customers—the things that affect the success of the company. Information is fed into this database from three different sources: industry-specific articles collected from various electronic newswires; thousands of business, trade, legal, and industry journals and newsletters; and news items from selected newspapers, such as the *New York Times* and the *Washington Post*.

NOTEBK.ZIP

This is a structured document-building database. You create the sections of the Notebook in advance. Then, as the project progresses, team members fill in the details. Attachment documents can contain meeting reports, spreadsheets, graphics, etc.

PEOPLE.ZIP

This database can give you a listing of employees with their phone and office numbers (scanned photos are also supported). You also get a map of the headquarters area, and floor plans for each floor.

PERFIN.ZIP

This database is used to share monthly financial data, using graphs.

PHONE.ZIP

This database is a company phone book, with employees, offices, and frequently called numbers. You also get a view that lists scanned images from the quick reference card on the telephone's advanced features. Also, there's a mail-in form to notify the database manager about corrections to the employee listings.

RACE.ZIP

This database provides a quick way to enter and view race results. The format here is for a cross-country ski race, but you could easily modify it to suit any other type of race. You can enter names and addresses for entrants in several cross-country races. Then as they cross the finish line, you enter the finish times and Notes calculates the results. There are multiple ways to view the entrants and the race results.

REALST.ZIP

The database contains profiles of all corporate properties, the rent and other payments made on those properties, and options on leased properties. The application allows Informational Users to browse this information and Real Estate Managers to update it.

RELOC.ZIP

This database routes forms for reimbursement of employee-relocation expenses. Each designated approver receives the form via e-mail. If the expense is approved, the document is sent to the next approver. If the expense is rejected, routing ceases. A copy of each approval (or a rejection) of the reimbursement request is automatically mailed to the database. This allows the employee-relocation specialist to track the approval status.

SALES.ZIP

This database tracks customers, prospects, and sales leads. It contains profiles of all customer accounts by individual site. Sales reps can summarize their customer calls or visits in the Activity Report form. There are three different Activity views, which show account history at a glance or allow for detailed review of each report. Leads can be tracked using the Lead Report form and viewed by status (open/closed). Using the contact information captured in the account profile, letters can be generated and automatically addressed to the customer.

SALES2.ZIP

This database distributes sales activity data from corporate head-quarters to its field offices.

SCHED.ZIP

This is a unique calendar application in which you never compose or edit the time/date documents. Instead you use filters to reserve or un-reserve time slots. Optionally, you can also enter a description for your event. The key is that, although everyone has Editor access, they cannot change reservations made by other users. The filters take care of that.

SEYBLD.ZIP

This database is a forum for electronically distributing the industry newsletter "Patricia Seybold's Notes on Information Technology." This database also provides means for readers and authors to correspond with each other on the issues discussed in the articles. Many articles are submitted to the database at the draft stage giving readers access to the latest industry news and author.

SUGGST.ZIP

This is a suggestion box application intended for use by participants at conference. They can make suggestions for changes in the conference, or in the product line. Response documents can only be created by privileged users—either the conference organizers or the product managers. This means that all responses are "official."

TELMKT.ZIP

This database demonstrates using a Notes form as a call script. It is a reference database of interested parties, internal and external. It includes views for mailing lists, mail-enabled forms, filters for mass-updates for flags like "Got this mailing". It is a working database, not a yacht but a fishing boat.

TKCONF.ZIP

This database shows schedule and multiple views. It uses graphics on forms to enhance the display of the information.

TKTIPS.ZIP

This database provides two different forms, one for posting simple technical tips, and one for providing more detailed technical information (technotes).

USRGRP.ZIP

This is a typical Notes discussion database, offering a forum for disseminating information and sharing comments and opinions among the members of a group. Even though all of the names and companies in the database are fictitious, the discussion contents are real. Many members of the Users Group use this database to participate in an ongoing discussion about the product and issues surrounding its implementation within their organizations.

▶ Lotus Professional Developer's Program

This program is for professional developers interested in creating products around Lotus Notes, cc:Mail, or Lotus Desktop products, either for commercial sale or for internal corporate use. The Lotus Professional Developer's Program provides access to a wide range of Lotus technologies and services to assist commercial and corporate developers in the conceptualization and development of new products.

To help developers define business and marketing opportunities, Lotus offers a variety of information and consulting services. These services include product and program information, developer orientation days, developer forums and access to professional developer consultants.

Lotus offers a wide range of products and services to equip developers. Through the Lotus Professional Developer's Program, developers have access to low-cost software, toolkits, full technical support and developer training. In addition, the Program offers access to a range of discussion, technical and marketing forums.

Lotus provides a selection of marketing programs to members of the Lotus Professional Developer's Program. Members can use Lotus Professional Developer logos, list products and services in Lotus partner catalogs, use quotes from Lotus executives in press releases and send mailings to the Lotus customer base (Lotus communications products only). In addition, members of the Lotus Professional Developer's Program can use Lotus marketing presentations and product literature. More extended marketing services are available through the Lotus Business Partner Program.

Lotus Development Corporation, Developer Relations, (800) DEV-RELS.

▶ NewsEDGE for Lotus Notes

Delivers real-time news stories from multiple newswires into Notes databases according to interest profiles set by individual users or profiles designed for group access. NewsEDGE can also deliver all news items from selected sources, such as the *Wall Street Journal*, into dedicated, source-specific Notes databases for archiving and full-text searching.

Desktop Data, Inc., (617) 890-0042; fax, (617) 890-1565.

▶ The Virtual College

An online teleprogram offered at New York University, which trains managers and professionals to design and work with electronic environments that connect people as well as computers. Participants receive instruction, interview clients, conduct analyses, resolve problems, and build Lotus Notes applications—at work, at home, and even while traveling. The program uses Notes to provide a rich, multimedia instructional environment.

New York University, (212) 998-7190; fax, (212) 995-4131.

▶ *WorldCom*

WorldCom is the international network exclusively for Lotus Notes and cc:Mail users. Companies can exchange messages, send files, and replicate databases easily and efficiently. Both flat and hierarchical systems can connect to WorldCom via toll-free lines in 50 countries around the world or the Internet.

WorldCom also provides gateways to the Internet and, via X.400, to more than 100 public e-mail systems worldwide. WorldCom can even register an independent Internet domain for your company, so your Internet address is as simple as name@domain.com.

WorldCom public databases include Usenet News Groups and the LNotes-L mailing list from the Internet and a Lotus Notes forum. Companies can store private or commercial Lotus Notes databases on WorldCom for their clients, trading partners, branch offices or remote users. It provides services in five main areas:

- **E-mail:** Connectivity with more than 100 systems worldwide
- **Internet navigation:** Conversion of mailing lists, including LNotes-L, conversion of the UserNet News Groups, FTP service, customized FTP document retrieval databases
- **News Services:** AP Online, Carthage Today, First! by Individual, The Notes Report, The Burton Group Information Services, Track-IT, and an ever-growing number of others
- **Public Discussion Forums:** Focusing on Lotus Notes, Networking, and other subjects
- **Private Database Storage:** Free storage of private databases on WorldCom's servers

WorldCom, (800) 774-2220.

▶ *Worldwide Association of Lotus Notes Users and Technologists (WALNUT)*

WALNUT is an independent user group. Provides a discussion database on Notes issues, documentation, and additional databases. Members can ask questions, post ideas, and look for help on Notes topics.

WALNUT provides a variety of electronic membership plans for Notes users.

One related service is the CompuServe Lotus Notes Information Service, which requires a CompuServe User ID number that is certified specifically for use with Notes. The service is set up as a client/server interaction; CompuServe computers access the local Notes server and replicate databases on a predetermined schedule.

Contact David Dimmick, WALNUT Executive Director;
Dave Dimmick@DOK@CSERVE, or 72662,2356.

▶▶ *Glossary*

@ A character that must appear before a predefined Notes function. (See *function*.)

About Database document (or Policy document) An optional document written by the designer or manager of a database to describe the purpose of the database. If a database has an About Database document, it's automatically displayed the first time you open the database. To see it again, choose Help ➤ About <database>.

access control A security feature that specifies the tasks that can be performed by each user of a Notes database. Some users may have access to all activities, while others may be limited to specific operations.

access control list (ACL) A list of database users (individual users, Notes servers, and groups of users and/or servers) created and updated by the database's manager. The ACL specifies which users can access the database and what activities they can perform. To see the ACL for a selected or open database, choose File ➤ Database ➤ Access Control.

access levels Database usage controls assigned to users in a database's ACL. The levels are Manager, Designer, Editor, Author, Reader, Depositor, and No Access. In addition to access levels, a database designer can define more specific access roles.

access role A level of database access assigned to a user or group that specifies their ability to use specific forms, views, or documents in the database.

active window The window in which you are working; the front-most window; the window with the insertion point. Up to nine windows can be open at once, but you can work in only one at a time.

attach Store a file with a Notes document. You can attach virtually any type of file, even an entire Notes database. The attached file, or *attachment*, is copied and stored in the Notes database, and remains with the document until the document or the attachment is deleted. If you mail the document, the file is mailed with it. (See also *embedding.*)

attachment A file attached to a Notes document using either the Edit ➤ Insert File Attachment or the File ➤ Attach command. An attachment remains with the Notes document until either the attachment or the Notes document is deleted. Deleting an attachment requires at least Editor access to the document, or Author access if you wrote the document yourself.

authentication An automatic security check. During authentication, Notes checks that the user or Notes server trying to gain access to a particular Notes server has a trusted certificate in common with it.

background macro A macro that's executed on a regularly scheduled basis, often used in workflow applications. For example, a background macro could look in a Course Enrollment database daily and forward new enrollment applications to the Course Administrator.

button A button is used in a form to invoke a macro. It executes instructions that you write, which in turn perform specific actions. A button can be used to help users navigate through the application or to automate certain tasks within the application. A button is handy to use because it performs the actions automatically, thus saving a person time when editing or reading a document.

categorize To assign a document to a category in a view. To do this, the database designer must have specified that the view's first column sorts by the field called "Categories." The database may let you create new categories, or it may restrict you to predefined categories. (Many views are sorted chronologically or by discussion topic and therefore don't use categories.)

category A name (word, phrase, number) used to group documents in a view. Categories are used to group and sort documents in a view. For example, documents related to purchase orders might be grouped under the category "Purchasing."

certificate A unique electronic stamp stored in a User ID file. Certificates permit you to access specific Notes servers. Your User ID may have many certificates.

certifier A person, often the administrator of one or more Notes servers, who uses a special Certifier ID to certify User IDs.

CLS files Character and Language Services files (or CLS files) let you convert characters like foreign currency symbols and accented letters to other characters when importing or exporting files. CLS files also control collation (the order in which characters are sorted). You select a CLS file by choosing Tools ➤ Setup ➤ User Setup, International.

database A group of documents and their forms and views, stored under one name and opened through a database icon on your workspace. A database is always one and only one file, with the .NSF extension. A database can be as small and simple as a workgroup telephone book containing a few documents and a single view, or as large and complex as a customer service system.

database catalog A special Notes system database containing information about databases stored on a single Notes server, a group of servers, or all the servers in a domain.

database exchange The process of making the main database that's stored on a server and a copy—a replica—that's stored on a workstation identical over time. Changes that have been made to the replica are passed back to the main database; likewise, any changes made to the main database are passed back to the replica. (See *replication.*)

data type A field is categorized by the type of data it can contain. The data type also determines how a user can enter data in a field.

DDE (dynamic data exchange) A method for displaying data created with other Windows applications, such as graphics or spreadsheet ranges, within Notes documents. DDE objects can be reactivated and updated to reflect the current state of changing data. (Compare with *OLE.*)

default setting An initial setting that Notes uses until you specify another setting.

default view The view displayed the first time you open a database. The default view is specified by the database designer in the Design View Attributes dialog box. Notes remembers the view displayed when you close a database, so the next time you open it, that view is displayed rather than the default view.

design template A feature that lets database designers share field definitions among forms within a database, share high-level design elements (fields, forms, views, macros) among many databases, and optionally store all database design elements with a template, so that when the template is changed, the change will be reflected automatically in all databases created with that template. (Compare with *template.*)

detach Make a local copy of a file attached to a Notes document. The file remains attached to the document until the attachment icon is deleted (which requires Editor access to the document).

dial-up Notes A Notes feature that allows you to access databases by calling Notes servers using a modem instead of using Notes on a local area network. It includes special functionality to reduce the amount of data transferred and stored on the local workstation.

distinguished names A method of ensuring that each Notes user is assigned a unique name that can never be confused with any other name in the system, no matter how large the Notes installation grows. When a hierarchical certifier registers a user, the name on the User ID inherits the distinguished name of the certifier. For example, if the certifier's name is Sales\Acme\US and he certifies Lisa Smith, her fully distinguished name is Lisa Smith\Sales\Acme\US. (See release 3.1.5 specifications for more information.)

doclink An icon representing direct access from one Notes document to another. The documents don't have to be in the same view or even in the same database. Double-click a doclink to go to its target document, or move to the doclink (in Read-only mode) using the keyboard arrow keys and then press spacebar. Notes opens the target document without closing the document you branched from. A doclink is similar to a "hypertext" link.

document A document is the default form type that's assigned to a form unless it's designated as a response-type form. A document is created by using a form on the Compose menu. A document can range from a short answer to a coworker's question to a multipage market analysis. Documents consist of fields containing text, numbers, graphics, scanned images, or even voice messages. (See also *form.*)

document type There are three types of documents types: Document, Response to Document, and Response to Response.

domain A group of Notes servers with the same public Name & Address Book. Domains are used to define the scope of a Notes mail environment.

Edit mode Edit mode lets you modify a document. A document is automatically in Edit mode when you first compose it. To put a document in Edit mode later, you must have Editor access (or better) to the database or you must be the document's author. Open the document and then choose Edit ➤ Edit Document or View ➤ Edit Mode. Or, highlight the document in a view and press Ctrl+E. (See also *Read-only mode.*)

encrypt Encode a field in a document so that only users who have the secret encryption key can read it. When a user with the key opens an encrypted document, the encrypted information is displayed. When a user without the key opens an encrypted document, the encrypted information is not displayed. Encryption is also used to protect transmission between a Notes client and its server on any port (modem or network).

export The process of saving a Notes document or view in a non-Notes format by using the File ➤ Export command. You can export data to other applications, such as word processors, spreadsheets, and graphics programs.

field A named area on a form for entering a single type of information. A field is the smallest entity in Notes. Fields may contain formulas or data or both. Fields are also used to define view columns.

file server A computer that stores and provides user access to shared files. (Compare with *Notes server.*)

form Forms control how you enter information into Notes and how that information is displayed and printed. To create a document, you fill in a form from the Compose menu in a database. Database designers can create any number of forms for a database. Forms contain fields and static objects. A document needs a form to be created or displayed. Forms can be used to query information using the full-text engine.

form type Each form in a database has a type associated with it. The type dictates how users use a particular form. There are three form types: Document, Response to Document, and Response to Response.

formula An expression used to select documents from a database, calculate values for display, validate and translate new entries, etc. Formulas are used most often by database designers, but also may be used by anyone to write macros or create custom SmartIcons or buttons. Formulas are the "proprietary" language of Notes, and used for data transformations. Formulas combine Notes @functions and Notes fields.

full text search A Notes feature that lets you search a database for words and phrases, as well as perform more complex searches using wildcards and logical operators. To perform a full text search, the database you want to search must have a full text index—a special file that lets Notes process searches within seconds. You can create and use a full text index only with Notes Release 3 software.

function A predefined Notes formula that performs a specific type of calculation. @functions are used in designing Notes applications and writing macros. Performs a specific manipulation, including string, date/time, or numerical.

group Also called a user group or mailing list, a group is a named set of Notes users defined with the Group form in a Name & Address Book. Putting users in a group makes it easier to send mass mail or to assign everyone the same access level in a database's access control list.

home server The server on which your Notes mail file is stored. If you don't use Notes Mail, your Notes Administrator assigns you a home server.

icon A graphical element that represents an object, command, or option on your computer screen. The word *icon* can refer to several different items in Notes. The most important is the icon on your Workspace that represents a database. One piece of information that can appear on a database icon is its picture icon. This icon is created by the database designer to provide a visual identity for a database. *Icon* also refers to buttons or other active places on the screen that display small pictures, such as SmartIcons and the buttons in the Search Bar.

import The process of bringing data and files into a Notes database from other applications by using the File ➤ Import command. You can import word processing, spreadsheet, graphics, ASCII, and Rich Text format files.

keyword One of the predefined choices in a keyword field. A keyword can be one or more words. Keywords can be predefined by the database designer or added by the authors of the documents. Keywords are useful in creating views with meaningful categories. (See also *categories* and *views*.)

local area network (LAN) A group of computers that can share devices such as printers and file servers, and possibly communicate with each other. Since the connections are made over cable or dedicated lines, a local area network is often confined to one building. Notes uses the communication protocols of the LAN, but doesn't necessarily need the other devices (such as a printer or file server). (Compare to *wide area network*.)

local database A Notes database stored on your computer's hard disk or on a floppy disk.

macro A formula that defines an action or set of actions. Notes supports a variety of macros for SmartIcons, buttons, and for filtering documents.

mail gateway Software that lets you send mail to and receive mail from users of other electronic mail systems. The Lotus Mail Exchange facility, which connects Notes Mail and cc:Mail users, is an example of a mail gateway. (See Chapter 9 for additional information on gateways to other products.)

Name & Address Book The Name & Address Book is a special Notes system database. The Name & Address Book is the central facility to schedule replication between servers and manage security. The public Name & Address Book is a database containing the name and domain address of every Notes user, user group, and server in a domain. If you perform Notes Setup while you're connected to a local area network, Notes adds this database to your Workspace. The personal Name & Address Book is a database containing the names and computer addresses of users and user groups. Unlike the public Name & Address Book, this one only contains information that you enter yourself. Notes adds this database to your workspace during Setup.

Notes database See *database*.

Notes server A computer that stores Notes databases and allows users to share them. It communicates either through the network or by accepting incoming phone calls from workstations.

Notes workstation A personal computer—PC or Macintosh, desktop or portable—running the Notes workstation software. The workstation contains the entire user interface for Notes. It can replicate, send mail, perform a full-text index, and so on.

Notes mail database (or Notes mail file) A Notes database where you send and receive mail. Although your mail database is stored on a server, only you can open it. You can keep a local copy of your mail database also, perhaps on a laptop or home computer, and use dial-up Notes features to exchange the local and server replicas to make them identical and to send your outgoing mail. (See also *database exchange*.)

OLE (object linking and embedding) A method for linking and embedding data created with other Windows, Program Manager, and Macintosh applications in Notes documents and forms to create "compound documents." You can link to and embed existing files or parts of files, or you can create new OLE objects that don't exist outside the Notes document. Activating an OLE object launches the application used to create it so that you or other Notes users can read or edit the data. (Compare with *DDE*.)

outgoing mail database A local repository for the mail you want to send when you use Notes with a modem rather than over a local area network. When you select Workstation-based mail in the Location Setup dialog box, your outgoing mail is held in a file called MAIL.BOX until you replicate with your mail file on your mail server.

plain text field A plain text field can't contain objects that include formatted data. (See also *rich text field*.)

popup A Notes feature that lets you attach a block of text or a formula to a specific place in a document or form. The presence of a popup may be indicated by a green rectangle (on a color monitor).

private view A view that you design and save for your own use with a database. No one else sees a private view and its name appears only on your own View menu. You can create a private view for any database for which you have at least Reader access. Choose Design ➤ Views to begin designing a private view.

Read-only mode Read-only mode lets you read but not modify a document. To modify a document, you must have Editor access (or better) to the database or you must be the document's author. (See also *Edit mode*.)

refresh You refresh a view or document to reflect changes that have been made to it after editing or making deletions. Refreshing also recalculates computations in fields. To refresh, press F9.

remote server A Notes server that you access using a modem and telephone lines rather than a local area network (LAN). A server is a local server if you're using it on a LAN; the same server is a remote server if you use a modem to connect to it (usually from off-site).

replica A copy of a database that is updated by exchanging information with the original database, either on a regular schedule or at will. Notes servers can connect to other Notes servers and periodically update all replicas of a database so that they become identical.

replication The process of updating replicas of a database to make them identical.

response document A document created using a Response form, a typical component of a discussion database. In a view, response documents are usually indented underneath the document to which they respond. Response documents typically "inherit" information from the parent document, which is the document highlighted when the Compose Response was invoked. (See also *form type.*)

rich text field A type of field a database designer can put on a form. You can format the text in a rich text field using options in the Text Font dialog box, such as bold and color, and you can include pictures, tables, popups, DDE and OLE objects, edition files and other special data created in Notes, imported from other applications, or pasted from the Clipboard. Plain text, another data type, cannot accommodate styled text or special objects. Data validation and many other formula facilities won't work in a rich text field. (See also *plain text field.*)

role See *access role.*

routing applications See *workflow automation.*

server See *Notes server, file server.*

shared database A Notes database that resides on a Notes server.

sign When you select the sign option, Notes attaches a unique electronic "signature" to a document or field when a document is mailed. The signature is derived from the sender's User ID. This security measure assures the recipient that the same user who wrote the document also sent it.

SmartIcons Customizable buttons that choose one or more Notes commands or execute a Notes formula. SmartIcons are available in the latest releases of most Lotus products for Windows. To find out what SmartIcons do, click and hold them with the right mouse button and check the active window's title bar.

Status Bar The bar across the bottom of your screen that includes indicators and controls for disk and network access, messages, current typeface and point size, new mail delivery, workstation- or server-based mail, SmartIcons toggle, and your access level to the active database.

stub (or replica stub) A new database replica that has not yet been filled with documents. A stub is created when you choose File ➤ New Replica and then select Initialize and Copy at First Replication, or File ➤ Database ➤ Copy and then select Forms and Views only. The database is no longer a stub once the first replication takes place.

static text Text that remains constant on every document created with a particular form, as opposed to fields in which you type information or Notes calculates information.

template A Notes database design that you can use as a starting point for a new database.

user group See *group.*

User ID A file assigned to each user that uniquely identifies that user to Notes. All Notes users (and servers) must have a User ID. It is the "private" section of the public/private key Notes security system. ID files must be kept in a secure location and should preferably also include a password to protect them from unauthorized use. (See also *distinguished names.*)

Using Database document or Help document An optional document written by the designer of a database that explains how to use the database. If a database has a Using Database document, it's available when you choose Help ➤ Using <database name>.

view A view is a list of documents in a database that are usually sorted or categorized to make finding documents easier. A database can have any number of views. To change views, choose another view from the view menu. Most views are created by the database designer, but you can create private views that only you can see. (A view can also look different to different users, or be altogether absent for some users, depending on their access roles.)

wide area network (WAN) A group of computers that can communicate and share devices such as file servers. Unlike local area networks, wide area networks use telephone lines. Notes servers communicate using telephone lines.

workflow automation A method for supporting workgroup applications. Notes supports two basic workflow models: shared applications and routing applications. Shared applications are generally discussion databases where different people contribute at different points and you can check on the status of something at any time. Routing applications are mail-based, where information is passed from one person to another, with each person modifying it in some way.

Workspace The Notes "desktop," which includes Notes windows, menus, and SmartIcons, and the six tabbed pages where you display database icons. You can organize your Workspace by naming the tabbed pages; by adding, moving, and removing icons; and by customizing your SmartIcons palettes.

►► *I*ndex

Note to the Reader:

Page numbers in boldface refer to primary discussions of topics. Page numbers in italics refer to illustrations.

Z

[1302] Mastering Lotus Notes

GET A FREE CATALOG JUST FOR EXPRESSING YOUR OPINION.

Help us improve our books and get a *FREE* full-color catalog in the bargain. Please complete this form, pull out this page and send it in today. The address is on the reverse side.

Name _____   Company _____

Address _____   City _____ State ____ Zip _____

Phone (___) _____

1. How would you rate the overall quality of this book?

- ❏ Excellent
- ❏ Very Good
- ❏ Good
- ❏ Fair
- ❏ Below Average
- ❏ Poor

2. What were the things you liked most about the book? (Check all that apply)

- ❏ Pace
- ❏ Format
- ❏ Writing Style
- ❏ Examples
- ❏ Table of Contents
- ❏ Index
- ❏ Price
- ❏ Illustrations
- ❏ Type Style
- ❏ Cover
- ❏ Depth of Coverage
- ❏ Fast Track Notes

3. What were the things you liked *least* about the book? (Check all that apply)

- ❏ Pace
- ❏ Format
- ❏ Writing Style
- ❏ Examples
- ❏ Table of Contents
- ❏ Index
- ❏ Price
- ❏ Illustrations
- ❏ Type Style
- ❏ Cover
- ❏ Depth of Coverage
- ❏ Fast Track Notes

4. Where did you buy this book?

- ❏ Bookstore chain
- ❏ Small independent bookstore
- ❏ Computer store
- ❏ Wholesale club
- ❏ College bookstore
- ❏ Technical bookstore
- ❏ Other _____

5. How did you decide to buy this particular book?

- ❏ Recommended by friend
- ❏ Recommended by store personnel
- ❏ Author's reputation
- ❏ Sybex's reputation
- ❏ Read book review in _____
- ❏ Other _____

6. How did you pay for this book?

- ❏ Used own funds
- ❏ Reimbursed by company
- ❏ Received book as a gift

7. What is your level of experience with the subject covered in this book?

- ❏ Beginner
- ❏ Intermediate
- ❏ Advanced

8. How long have you been using a computer?

years _____

months _____

9. Where do you most often use your computer?

- ❏ Home
- ❏ Work

- ❏ Both
- ❏ Other _____

10. What kind of computer equipment do you have? (Check all that apply)

- ❏ PC Compatible Desktop Computer
- ❏ PC Compatible Laptop Computer
- ❏ Apple/Mac Computer
- ❏ Apple/Mac Laptop Computer
- ❏ CD ROM
- ❏ Fax Modem
- ❏ Data Modem
- ❏ Scanner
- ❏ Sound Card
- ❏ Other _____

11. What other kinds of software packages do you ordinarily use?

- ❏ Accounting
- ❏ Databases
- ❏ Networks
- ❏ Apple/Mac
- ❏ Desktop Publishing
- ❏ Spreadsheets
- ❏ CAD
- ❏ Games
- ❏ Word Processing
- ❏ Communications
- ❏ Money Management
- ❏ Other _____

12. What operating systems do you ordinarily use?

- ❏ DOS
- ❏ OS/2
- ❏ Windows
- ❏ Apple/Mac
- ❏ Windows NT
- ❏ Other _____

13. On what computer-related subject(s) would you like to see more books?

_____

_____

_____

_____

14. Do you have any other comments about this book? (Please feel free to use a separate piece of paper if you need more room)

_____

_____

_____

_____

PLEASE FOLD, SEAL, AND MAIL TO SYBEX

SYBEX INC.
Department M
2021 Challenger Drive
Alameda, CA
94501

Installation Instructions

Before you begin using any of the sample databases, you need to copy them to your hard disk and then add the files to your Workspace. First, however, open the Windows File Manager and do a little maintenance work:

1. Put the disk in your computer's disk drive.

2. Open Windows File Manager. Select the appropriate drive icon in order to display the files on the diskette.

3. Choose File ➤ Select.

4. Click on the Select button and then the Close button. All the files will appear highlighted.

5. Choose File ➤ Copy to copy the files to the desired Notes subdirectory. (You should create a new subdirectory in the Notes directory first. Call it, say, Samples. You can also copy the files to the Notes Examples directory that was created when you installed the client version of Notes.)

6. Enter the name of the directory to which you want the files copied.

7. Click on OK to start the copying process.

Each one of the files has been compressed with LHA, a shareware file compression program. You don't need to have a copy of the program present on your hard disk since we provide the files as self-extracting archives.

As you can see in the File Manager, each file appears with a .EXE extension because the LHA program saves self-extracting archives as executable files. You simply double-click on a file icon in order to expand the desired file you want to access in Notes later on. Remember that expanding the files will take up room on your hard disk. So you may want to open only a few in order to save space. These files are big!